Hidden Casualties

Environmental, Health and Political Consequences of the Persian Gulf War

Hidden Casualties

Environmental, Health and Political Consequences of the Persian Gulf War

Edited by
Saul Bloom, John M. Miller,
James Warner and Philippa Winkler

ARC/Arms Control Research Center
North Atlantic Books

This book is the second in the *Hidden Casualties* series. *Hidden Casualties, Volume I: The Environmental Consequences of the Persian Gulf Conflict* was published by ARC/Arms Control Research Center in January 1991, before war broke out.

❦

Published by

North Atlantic Books, P.O. Box 12327, Berkeley, California, 94701

and ARC/Arms Control Research Center, 833 Market Street, Suite 1107, San Francisco, CA 94103.

Copyright © ARC/Arms Control Research Center, 1994

ISBN 1-55643-163-5

❦

Library of Congress Cataloging-in-Publication Data

Bloom, Saul
    Hidden Casualties: the environmental, health and political consequences of the Persian Gulf War/edited by Saul Bloom . . . [et al.]
    p.   cm.
    Includes bibliographical references and index.
        1. Persian Gulf War, 1991—Environmental aspects. 2. Persian Gulf War, 1991—Health aspects. 3. Iraq—Armed Forces—Weapons systems. 4. Oil Spills—Environmental aspects—Persian Gulf Region. 5. Oil wells—Kuwait—Fires and fire prevention. 6. Oil wells—Fires and fire prevention—Environmental aspects—Persian Gulf Region.   I. Bloom, Saul
DS79.744.E58H53 1993   93-5473
956.704'421 dc20   CIP

❦

Mark Kaswan, Production Manager. Design and typography by Rob Lowe. Cover by Vicki Rinehart. Illustrations by Carol Melnick.

❦

Table of Contents

ABOUT ARC/ARMS CONTROL RESEARCH CENTER

ACKNOWLEDGEMENTS

FOREWORD
Representative Nancy Pelosi, United States Congress

INTRODUCTION
Saul Bloom, Executive Director, ARC/Arms Control Research Center

1 The Physical and Political Environment of the Gulf

INTRODUCTION 2

VALUE OF THE GULF MARINE ENVIRONMENT...3
Boyce Thorne-Miller, Friends of the Earth

TERRESTRIAL AND FRESHWATER ECOLOGY OF THE GULF REGION...........................8
World Conservation Monitoring Centre

ARAB STATES, ARAB NATIONALISM AND THE GULF WAR 20
Interview with Professor Clovis Maksoud, The American University

OPERATION DESERT STORM...40
Background Information

2 The Oil Spills

INTRODUCTION 46

A PREWAR ENVIRONMENTAL ASSESSMENT 49
Sandia National Laboratories

POSSIBLE IMPACTS OF THE MINA AL AHMADI SPILL 51
Boyce Thorne-Miller, Friends of the Earth

GENERAL OBSERVATIONS 53
Interview with Burr Heneman, Center for Marine Conservation

IMPACTS ON BIRD POPULATIONS 63
Interview with Mike Evans, International Council for Bird Preservation

SEA TURTLES 68
Interview with James Perran Ross, Ph.D., Florida Museum of Natural History

THE VOYAGE OF THE *MOUNT MITCHELL* 70
Interview with Sylvia A. Earle, Ph.D., National Oceanic and Atmospheric Administration

3 The Oil Fires

INTRODUCTION 82

PREWAR ENVIRONMENTAL AND HEALTH ASSESSMENTS 85
Pacific-Sierra Research Corporation—Sandia National Laboratories

OIL FIRES, AIR POLLUTION AND REGIONAL HEALTH EFFECTS..............86
Interview with Halûk Özkaynak, Ph.D., Harvard University School of Public Health

TESTIMONY OF THE U.S. INTERAGENCY STUDY GROUP ON THE KUWAIT OIL FIRES.....90
Professor Peter V. Hobbs, University of Washington

PROBLEMS ASSESSING HEALTH RISKS 91
John S. Evans, Sc.D., C.I.H., Harvard University School of Public Health

CHRONOLOGY OF A COVERUP 92
Background Information

THE GAG ORDER: DID THE U.S. GOVERNMENT HIDE FACTS ABOUT THE FIRES? ..95
Interview with Lara Hilder, Sierra Club Committee on Military Impacts on the Environment

INTERNATIONAL RESPONSE 103
Interview with Abdullah Toukan, Ph.D., High Council for Science and Technology, Jordan

THE DOWNWIND IMPACTS OF THE OIL FIRES....................................105
Thomas J. Sullivan, Ph.D., Lawrence Livermore National Laboratory

CRITIQUING THE OFFICIAL U.S. ANALYSIS 109
Interview with Adam Trombly, Aspen Institute for Advanced Studies

THE GLOBAL IMPACTS OF THE OIL FIRES: SIX QUESTIONS 113
Richard D. Small, Ph.D., Pacific-Sierra Research Corporation; Hugh Church, Sandia National Laboratories;
Farn Parungo, Ph.D., National Oceanic and Atmospheric Administration; Thomas J. Sullivan, Ph.D.,
Lawrence Livermore National Laboratory; Adam Trombly, Aspen Institute for Advanced Studies;
John Cox, Ph.D., Campaign for Nuclear Disarmament

4 Desert Impacts

INTRODUCTION 128

DESERT ECOLOGY 129
Interview with Tony Burgess, Ph.D., University of Arizona

DEPLETED URANIUM—RADIOACTIVE RESIDUE IN THE DESERT AND THE U.S. 134
Background Information

UNEXPLODED ORDNANCE (UXO)..137
Background Information

DESERT UPDATE 139
Interview with Sylvia A. Earle, Ph.D., National Oceanic and Atmospheric Administration

5 Human Ecology

INTRODUCTION 144

DEFENSE DEPARTMENT CRITICAL OF BOMBING 145
United Press International

BOMBING CIVILIAN FACILITIES..146
Background Information

ON THE ROAD IN IRAQ—THE FIRST FIELD TRIP 149
Ross Mirkarimi with Saul Bloom, ARC/Arms Control Research Center

WATERBORNE DISEASES AND AGRICULTURAL CONSEQUENCES...........156
International Study Team—ARC/Arms Control Research Center

ENVIRONMENTAL ASSESSMENTS OF BOMBED SITES, AND FIELD NOTES 163
International Study Team—ARC/Arms Control Research Center

ON THE ROAD IN IRAQ—THE SECOND FIELD TRIP 172
Ross Mirkarimi, ARC/Arms Control Research Center

THE CONTINUING IMPACTS 174
Background Information

6 Human Casualties

INTRODUCTION 180

CENSORSHIP AT THE U.S. CENSUS BUREAU 182
Interview with Beth Osborne Daponte, M.A., Carnegie Mellon University

IRAQI WAR DEATHS 189
U.S. Census Bureau

CHILD MORTALITY, NUTRITION AND HEALTH CARE 193
International Study Team

PSYCHOLOGICAL IMPACTS OF THE WAR ON IRAQI CHILDREN 198
International Study Team

THE EXPERIENCE OF CHILDREN IN KUWAIT: OCCUPATION, WAR AND LIBERATION 203
James Garbarino, Ph.D., Erikson Institute of Advanced Study in Child Development

PALESTINIAN YOUTH IN KUWAIT 206
Mohamad Marzoued, *Children at Risk*

UNHEARD VOICES: IRAQI WOMEN ON WAR AND SANCTIONS 207
Bela Bhatia, M.A., M.S.; Mary Kawar, M.Sc, Women Studies Center, Jordan; Mariam Shahin, *Jordan Times*

THE IRAQI KURDS 225
Cyrus Salam, Kurdish National Congress

SCUD ATTACKS DRIVE 4,000 FROM ISRAELI HOMES 228
Hugh Orgel, Jewish Telegraph Agency

AFTERMATH OF THE GULF CRISIS: REFUGEES, STATELESS PEOPLE AND RETURNED MIGRANTS 230
British Refugee Council

THE INTERNATIONAL RESPONSE TO THE REFUGEE CRISIS 235
Background Information

THE "GULF WAR SYNDROME" 237
Background Information

7 Destroying Iraq's Nuclear, Biological and Chemical Arsenal: Implications for Arms Control

INTRODUCTION 246

WHAT UNSCOM FOUND IN IRAQ—PART ONE..............................248
Interview with Jay C. Davis, Ph.D., Lawrence Livermore National Laboratory and
United Nations Special Commission

IRAQ'S QUEST FOR THE NUCLEAR GRAIL: WHAT CAN WE LEARN?......................254
David Albright and Mark Hibbs, *Arms Control Today*

BOMBING NUCLEAR REACTORS: WARFARE TAKES AN OMINOUS TURN..............264
Interview with Bennett Ramburg, Ph.D., University of California

CHEMICAL AND BIOLOGICAL WEAPONS..267
Background Information

SADDAM HUSSEIN'S CHEMICAL ARSENAL..271
Interview with Matthew Meselson, Ph.D., Ph.B., Harvard University

WHAT UNSCOM FOUND IN IRAQ—PART TWO..............................276
Interview with Bryan Barrass, United Nations Special Commission

INCINERATION: THE WISEST CHOICE?..285
Background Information

NERVE GAS LINKED TO VETERANS' ILLNESSES.....................................286
Background Information

8 Arms Trade Policy And Legal Issues

INTRODUCTION 292

THE ARMS TRADE..294
Interview with Lora Lumpe, Federation of American Scientists

INTERNATIONAL LEGAL ISSUES—PART ONE.......................................298
Interview with Professor Francis Boyle, University of Illinois

INTERNATIONAL LEGAL ISSUES—PART TWO.......................................303
Interview with Karen Parker, Attorney-At-Law and Nongovernmental Representative,
United Nations Human Rights Commission

LAWS OF WAR AND THE ENVIRONMENT: A DEBATE IN THE UN 306
UN Representatives Abdullah Salah, Jordan; Hans Winkler, Austria; Nazihah Mohammed Rus, Malaysia; James Crawford, Australia; Safa S. Ahmed, Iraq; Hans Correll, Sweden; and Philippe de Korodi, International Committee of the Red Cross

UPDATE ON SANCTIONS 309
Background Information

RESISTING THE WAR: CONSCIENTIOUS OBJECTORS AND THE "STOP/LOSS" ORDER 311
Interview with Sam Diener, CCCO

IN THE BRIG 315
Interview with Tahan Jones, ex-Marine

9 Iraqgate Chronicles

INTRODUCTION 322

DOING BUSINESS: THE ARMING OF IRAQ, 1974–1993 324
Chronology compiled by Daniel Robicheau and Saul Bloom

THE ASIAN CONNECTION 361
Background Information

Recommendations

APPENDIX 1: INTERNATIONAL LAW 367

UNITED NATIONS GENERAL ASSEMBLY RESOLUTION 44/224

EXCERPTS FROM INTERNATIONAL AGREEMENTS ON WAR AND THE ENVIRONMENT

A NEW GENEVA CONVENTION?

UNITED NATIONS SECURITY COUNCIL RESOLUTIONS

APPENDIX 2: ADDITIONAL RESOURCES 393

APPENDIX 3: FURTHER READING 397

APPENDIX 4: BIOGRAPHIES 407

APPENDIX 5: ABBREVIATIONS AND GLOSSARY 415

INDEX 427

About ARC/Arms Control Research Center

ARC is a nonprofit, public interest organization concerned with the effects of military policies and activities on international security, environmental quality, human health and economic vitality. Headquartered in San Francisco, ARC's major projects are the Arms Control Research Center and, cosponsored by the Foreign Bases Project in New York City, the International Clearinghouse on the Military and the Environment.

THE ARMS CONTROL RESEARCH CENTER

The Arms Control Research Center is the research and analytical arm of ARC. Since 1983, it has provided the public, policymakers and government agencies with accurate, credible research on a wide variety of topics dealing with the effects of the military on the environment, the economy and society, as well as nuclear and conventional disarmament.

ARC/Arms Control Research Center maintains three ongoing programs:

The **Military Base Closures** program addresses the impacts of the closing of military bases on communities in California. This program monitors the investigation and remediation of toxic contamination of closing military facilities and provides technical assistance to grassroots community-based organizations, policymakers, elected officials and the media.

The **Defense Conversion** program works with policymakers, elected officials and nationally-based organizations to craft an effective national defense reduction program that will be socially and environmentally responsible.

ARC's **international program** focuses on documenting the environmental, human and geo-strategic impacts of military policies, activities and wars. Our goals are to promote nonmilitary solutions for international conflict resolution, to promote greater public and policymaker awareness of the broad impacts of militarism and military activities, to make a case for control of conventional and unconventional weapons proliferation and to develop international accords promoting greater protection for the environment and civilian populations in times of war.

THE INTERNATIONAL CLEARINGHOUSE ON THE MILITARY AND THE ENVIRONMENT

The International Clearinghouse on the Military and the Environment, based in New York, focuses on the environmental impacts of military facilities in other countries, including foreign U.S. bases. The Clearinghouse, in conjunction with the Research Center, is also active in issues relating to the United Nations.

Acknowledgements

The Hidden Casualties staff would like to thank our colleagues at ARC/Arms Control Research Center for their assistance and support. *Hidden Casualties, Volume II* was one of many projects at ARC—the flexibility and patience of our colleagues helped this project enormously. We are especially grateful to Mark Kaswan, ARC's Treasurer and the Production Manager for *Hidden Casualties, Volume II*, for his unstinting efforts and fine eye for detail which have been invaluable. A sincere "thank-you" also goes to Barbara Hodgkinson, our chief copy editor, for her invaluable help.

We also wish to thank Elizabeth MacDowell and Ruth Schein for copy editing assistance, our proofreaders Charles Goff III, Ruth Kaswan, B. J. Ivey and Katherine Karsh, and our expert readers T. M. Hawley (sections of Chapters Two and Three) and Lydia Gans (Chapters Five and Six).

Of the many people who helped ARC obtain data, we wish to especially thank Sarah Zaidi of the International Study Team; Sarah Graham-Brown of the Gulf Information Project, British Refugee Council; Tim Trevan, UN Special Commission; Ian Lee Doucet, Medical Educational Trust, London; Mariam Hapte, UNICEF; Virginia N. Sherry, Middle East Watch, New York; Eduardo Cohen, *The Other Americas Radio Journal Project*, KPFA-FM; Marshall Windmiller, Department of International Relations, San Francisco State University; Dr. David Levinson; Barry Preestler, University of California at Berkeley; Shamira Virgei; Nuremberg Actions Vigil; and ARC's interns, Adam Ballochey, Lynn Heinisch and Saul Tolton.

We also thank our friends at the following organizations for their assistance with the book with reprint rights, interviews and their insights: *The Bulletin of Atomic Scientists*, Citizens Alert, CCCO (formerly the Central Committee for Conscientious Objectors), Earth Island Institute, the Federation of American Scientists, Friends of the Earth, Greenpeace, the International Union for the Conservation of Nature and Natural Resources, the Military Families Network and the Rural Alliance for Military Accountability.

We thank Vicki Rinehart of Creative Technologies for the original design of the book's cover, Carol Melnick for the illustrations in Chapters One and Two and the cartoon in Chapter Nine, Louise Cainkar who provided photographs from her tour in Iraq immediately following the war, and the United Nations for other photographs. Thanks also go to Rob Lowe for providing critical help in making photographs and other graphics usable.

We would also like to thank the financial backers of the project. *Hidden Casualties, Volume II*, could not have been produced without our funders: the Tides Foundation, Funding Exchange, Carol and W.H. Ferry, Vanguard Foundation, Mark and Francis Lilenthal, Claudia Chester, Ethel Sanjines, the New York Friends Group and Bob Gould at Physicians for Social Responsibility. We are grateful to our co-publishers at North Atlantic Books and Earthscan for their interest, cooperation and support.

Foreword: Representative Nancy Pelosi

U.S. Congressmember Nancy Pelosi argued on the floor of Congress for a negotiated solution to the Iraqi-Kuwait conflict, in the official debate that took place three days prior to the outbreak of war, January 12, 1991.

At the Earth Summit in Rio, I asked Jacques Cousteau about the need for new international laws regarding ecoterrorism as a weapon of war. He responded that war should be abolished. I agree but until we do abolish war, we must consider its environmental costs.

As Congress considered the use of force in the Persian Gulf, debate centered on the potential human costs of such a conflict. Many believed, as I did, that the advocates of intervention had failed to demonstrate a compelling "American interest," and that truth was indeed the first casualty of this war. Opposing arguments were abundant, but unsuccessful in preventing the military actions launched in January 1991. On January 12, I raised the issue of the long-term environmental consequences that could severely compound the immediate risks to human life.

The outcome of the Persian Gulf War has now illustrated the failure of the world community to create and enforce mechanisms capable of preventing the use of the environment as a tool of war. Information made available by organizations such as ARC/Arms Control Research Center to the member governments of the United Nations Coalition regarding the environmental consequences of the Gulf War was largely ignored in the passion to subdue Saddam Hussein.

Sadly, much of what was warned against came to pass. Oil fires burned for months, spewing tons of pollutants into the atmosphere, and an oil spill 30 times greater than the Exxon *Valdez* spill blackened the beaches and wildlife habitats of the Gulf coast, devastating marine populations and the economic health of the region. Saddam Hussein's ecoterrorism was predicted, and yet no preventive action was taken.

The Persian Gulf War may be ranked by some as a minor incident in the history of conflict between nations. However, it stands as a major, historic point in the changing nature of war, as it raised the specter of large-scale environmental devastation, not only as a casualty, but also as a strategy of warfare. As governments begin to accept the irrelevance of national borders in any understanding of a global environment, it is essential to implement effective multilateral mechanisms to prevent the use of the environment as a tool of war.

The legacy of the Persian Gulf War highlights the lack of attention given by the international community to the issues of ecological warfare and the need for heightened awareness of this threat. Military strikes on chemical, nuclear and industrial facilities can wreak global environmental havoc, and should be outlawed by international treaty.

Our efforts to achieve peaceful solutions to conflicts are motivated by a concern for human life. This sense of humanity should also guide us to protect the foundation of human life—the natural environment. It is my hope that the issues raised in this book will contribute to a better understanding of the importance of environmental protection in the context of international conflict and will inspire much-needed action.

Introduction

Saul Bloom

THE GULF WAR CONTINUES

More than two years ago, after 45 days of aerial bombardment and an intense eight-day ground war, Iraq signed a cease-fire to end the Persian Gulf War.[1] But the war continues.

To date, Iraq refuses to comply with many of the terms of the cease-fire. Instead, President Saddam Hussein throws the weight of his military (which, according to a recent report,[2] has regained 80 percent of its former strength) against the rebellious Kurds in the North and the Shiites and Marsh Arabs in the South. In addition, Iraq alternately bars, then acquiesces to inspection by the United Nations Special Commission charged with searching out and destroying Iraq's missiles and unconventional (nuclear, biological and chemical) arsenal.

On the other hand, having created a Kurdish enclave above the 36th parallel and a "no-fly zone" below the 32nd parallel, Britain, France and the United States enforce a de facto partitioning of Iraq. UN lawyers have said that no language in existing resolutions gives the U.S., Britain and France authority to enforce the no-fly zones.[3] Nevertheless, members of the UN-sanctioned Gulf Coalition, particularly the United States, continue to bomb targets in Iraq in response to a variety of alleged infractions of the no-fly zone and cease-fire accords.

As the war continues, so does the suffering of civilians. United Nations sanctions, in place since August 1990, have contributed to the deaths of far more civilians than have the bombing attacks over the same period. The Iraqi government is currently draining the historic marshes of southern Iraq, partly as a technique of environmental warfare against the Marsh Arabs and partly because UN sanctions may be forcing the Iraqis to go ahead with plans previously set a side to convert the marshes into agricultural land.[4]

From all indications, real peace in the Gulf is a long way off. Weapons still pour into countries around the Gulf. China sells missiles and nuclear technology to Iran, and billions of dollars worth of U.S. jets, tanks and other equipment are being purchased by Saudi Arabia. Despite two major wars in less than two decades—wars that resulted in millions of casualties—the world community's answer to the volatility of the region is to give it more arms.

This is the second volume in ARC/Arms Control Research Center's *Hidden Casualties* series on the human, environmental and political impacts of wars. The purpose of the *Hidden Casualties* series is to reveal both the overt and the hidden environmental, economic and social consequences of wars, combat and military activities. The series is called *Hidden Casualties* because, in any war, the direct combat deaths are only the most obvious casualties. The less obvious environmental and long-term health effects of a war can prolong suffering for years, often planting the seeds of future conflict. Sometimes these effects can be felt by people far from the combat zone.

Over the coming years, ARC/Arms Control Research Center hopes to present a series of prospective assessments and retrospective impact statements on combat and wars. It is our hope that as the public and national governments become more fully informed about the consequences of combat, they will grow more reluctant to go to war. By documenting the numerous effects of warfare, the *Hidden Casualties* series will provide the international community with report cards on the costs of failing to find peaceful solutions to political differences. The *Hidden Casualties* series is dedicated to the proposition that humanity, through education appealing to enlightened self-interest, can evolve away from war.

THE HIDDEN CASUALTIES OF WAR

In the past, wars were fought without regard to their potential environmental effects. Then the prospect of nuclear war shocked us into realizing that we have the technological ability to destroy our planet, and the effects of the defoliant Agent Orange on the Mekong Delta in Vietnam showed that we have nonnuclear means of destroying the ecosystems of entire countries.

But the public's perception of war is easily managed. The more antiseptic and remote the image of war, the less likely it is that the public will be alarmed. This was clearly demonstrated by the version of the Gulf War televised in the United States (aptly dubbed a "Nintendo War")—newspeople in comfortable surroundings saw video images from computerized bombs being guided to tanks or buildings which then disappeared in a sudden brilliant flash. Absent were the horrifying images, like those from Vietnam, of children running naked down the road, crying from the pain of napalm searing their skin. Through Grenada, Lebanon and Panama, the U.S. military had learned the lessons of modern media management. Nevertheless, those pictures from Vietnam are closer to the reality of the Gulf War than the ones presented on the nightly news. Two years of investigation by the Arms Control Research Center indicate that tens of thousands of children died in Kuwait and Iraq, struck not by napalm but by shrapnel, malnutrition, or waterborne diseases.

Wars have always harmed the environment and killed or wounded noncombatants. However, modern technology has greatly increased the scope of the violence. The targeting of industrial facilities like oil fields, refineries and nuclear reactors can have unprecedented environmental and health impacts. Congressional reports indicate that there are some 52 wars currently going on around the world. Modern weapons may be more accurate in their aim, but they can be even more deadly than those used in wars of the past. The numbers of hidden casualties continue to mount.

HIDDEN CASUALTIES, VOLUME I—THE BEGINNING OF THE SERIES

As the countdown to the war began in the fall of 1990, ARC became deeply concerned about the impact that renewed regional combat could have on the Gulf's environment and inhabitants. ARC Development Board member Philippa Winkler approached me regarding our response. We agreed that ARC's best response would be to offer arguments against the military option, by focusing our research and organizing activities on the environmental and human consequences of the impending war. This seemed logical because, since 1983, ARC had been investigating the environmental and human health consequences of military activities, and in 1988 and 1989, we had been considering beginning a series of publications on the impacts of war. Our experience in the issue enabled us to quickly launch a two-pronged effort. One element of the campaign would focus on developing a prospective assessment of the war's potential effects. The second element would focus on organizing opposition to the war within the international environmental community. In late October 1990, I asked the coordinator of our International Clearinghouse on the Military and the Environment, John M. Miller, to begin interviewing experts for the pre-war assessment, and in November we brought Ross Mirkarimi on board to coordinate outreach to the environmental community.

The projects moved quickly. By December 1990 the Arms Control Research Center and Clearinghouse had finished the manuscript of the prewar assessment, *Hidden Casualties, Volume I: The Environmental Consequences of the Persian Gulf Conflict.* Copies of the manuscript were distributed to members of the U.S. Congress and governments internationally. Together with a local San Francisco Bay Area collective, the Political Ecology Group, ARC organized the Global Environmental Alliance for Peace in the Persian Gulf. The alliance produced a "Call to Action" that was signed by a number of leading international environmental organizations, including Greenpeace, Earth Island Institute, Friends of the Earth, the Ecologist and Environmental Action. Eventually some 200 organizations would sign the Call.

The public version of Volume I was released in New York on January 11, 1991—just five days before the war began—at a press conference co-hosted by ARC, Mobilization for Survival, the British American Security Information Center and the British Greens. At the press conference, several scientists, including nuclear physicist Frank Barnaby; Abdullah Toukan, director of the Jordanian Ministry of Science; oil industry analyst Richard Golob; oil industry engineer John Cox; and William Monning, the executive director of International Physicians for the Prevention of Nuclear War, warned the world's media of the environmental and health effects of the looming war.

Volume I covered a wide range of possible impacts, from the potential effects of the widespread dispersal of depleted uranium in the desert, to the loss of marine life from oil spills. Based on the analysis presented in Volume I, ARC concluded that tens of thousands of people and animals would die and the region would be devastated.

Volume I pointed out that the history of past wars in the Gulf gave reason for grave concern about the possible environmental impacts of the pending conflict. Saddam Hussein had already, during the war with Iran, demonstrated his willingness to use ecoterrorist tactics. In 1983, Iraqi missile attacks on the Nowruz and Ardeshir oil fields resulted in a four-billion-barrel oil spill.[5] The 1983 Nowruz spill disrupted fishing, forced a temporary closing of desalination plants and caused the deaths of many marine animals. Saddam Hussein refused to allow blow-out experts safe access to the wells he had destroyed unless Iran agreed to a cease-fire. Only after colossal ecological damage had been done were the Iranians able to cap the wells.[6]

In retrospect, many of the predictions in Volume I were chillingly accurate. John Cloudsey-Thompson predicted that troop movements in areas where grazing occurred would accelerate desertification. Other interviewees pointed to the long-term problems of unexploded anti-personnel bombs. Bombs from the World War II German blitz occasionally explode at construction sites in London today; leftover unexploded ordnance is a cause of death for children on many former battlefields who pick up shiny cluster bomblets to play with. Vietnamese civilians are still being killed by unexploded ordnance from the Vietnam War, and a generation of Iraqis, Kurds, Kuwaitis and Bedouins will now face the same problem.

Two major concerns in the fall of 1990 were that the Iraqis had mined the oil fields of Kuwait and that both nations' oil wells could be set on fire and burn for over a year, and that massive oil spills would cause catastrophic damage to the Gulf's marine environment. John Cox, an oil industry engineer and vice president of Campaign for Nuclear Disarmament in the United Kingdom, warned that if Kuwaiti and Iraqi oil wells burned for a year, the Asian monsoons might be influenced. Oil pollution expert Richard Golob asserted that extensive ecological destruction would result from massive releases of oil into the Gulf—and pointed out Saddam Hussein's use of such ecoterrorist tactics during the Iran-Iraq War.

We now know that the issues of oil fires and spills had been under intensive review by the U.S. Department of Energy and the Defense Nuclear Agency at the same time the Arms Control Research Center was preparing Volume I. The environmental assessments of the coming war were carried out by the U.S. and its Coalition allies before the war started. Like Manhattan project scientists betting on whether the first test of an atomic weapon would set the atmosphere on fire, the Western governments assessed the possible impacts of the Gulf War and decided to risk them.

Ultimately, *Hidden Casualties, Volume I* did what we had hoped. It identified the potential environmental and human consequences of the war and helped raise international awareness. Congressmember Nancy Pelosi used Volume I when preparing her statement arguing that modern technological combat could irrevocably harm the Fertile Crescent (including southern Iraq), which the UN Environment Programme has called "one of the most fragile and endangered ecosystems in the world." Excerpts from Volume I appeared in numerous publications, and the sound bites from the press conference reverberated throughout the national televised media over the course of the war.

Beginning *Hidden Casualties, Volume II*

After the cease-fire agreement of February 1991, ARC refocused its Gulf campaign on producing the second volume of the *Hidden Casualties* series, which would assess the consequences of the war. ARC also began organizing opposition to the continuation of nonmilitary economic sanctions against Iraq. Articles by our Gulf campaigners Ross Mirkarimi and John M. Miller appeared in newspapers and magazines around the country. Speaking engagements helped bring ARC's analysis to a number of college campuses in the United States. In April of 1991, John briefed members of the Italian press and Parliament on the possible consequences of the then-raging oil fires. In September 1991 ARC sent Ross and environmental contractor Al Picardi to Iraq to provide an analysis of the war's environmental impacts for the International Study Team, which was organized by researchers from the Harvard School of Public Health. Their findings appeared in the October 1991 IST report and are excerpted in this book. In May 1992, Ross returned to Iraq to represent ARC on another fact-finding tour.

Research for the follow-up report continued apace, and in June 1992 Philippa Winkler joined the staff to coordinate the research necessary to complete Volume II. ARC's international research associate, James Warner, joined the project in the fall of 1992, completing the editorial team.

Compiling a study like Hidden Casualties is never easy. The number of related topics and details to review are enormous. Further complicating the matter was the lack of funding the project had to contend with. The major peace, environmental and social justice foundations in the U.S. were not interested in the project, despite the continuing upheaval in the region. The lack of funding caused financial hardships for our staff, but they persevered nonetheless, aided by a dedicated group of volunteers. As the director of ARC, I take no small amount of pride in the commitment of the *Hidden Casualties* staff, and it is with a deep sense of gratitude to them that I present this document.

HIDDEN CASUALTIES, VOLUME II

While Volume I speculated on the potential impacts of war in the Gulf, this second volume attempts to document and analyze the actual impacts. In the manner of an environmental impact statement, *Hidden Casualties, Volume II*, attempts to analyze comprehensively the outcomes of the war. Volume II provides a baseline assessment of the prewar environmental conditions in the region, reviews events that led up to the war, examines the impacts of the combat, and discusses the still unfolding aftermath.

The consequences of the war are often difficult to assess because of the absence of baseline data, political and scientific censorship, and the slow time frame for environmental research. We have sought to present the information necessary for a comprehensive picture of the effects of the war. We have made an effort to provide a forum for alternative, nongovernmental perspectives.

The book's format is a melange of interviews, observational reporting, technical surveys and previously published studies. We gave voice to experts who represent the broadest cross section of work in the field. These experts are employed by institutions such as the U.S. Departments of Defense and Energy, the United Nations Special Committee on Iraq, the University of Amman in Jordan, Harvard University, the University of California's Livermore and Lawrence Berkeley laboratories, Friends of the Earth, Greenpeace, the Royal Society for the Preservation of Birds and the U.S. Congress.

ARC/Arms Control Research Center cannot guarantee the accuracy of the details of claims made in interviews or previously written materials appearing in this volume. Many of the environmental effects of the early war were not catalogued, some data were sequestered, and many effects are still evolving. One of the experiences we have had in compiling this report is that what is accurate and accepted today may not be so tomorrow. Nor do all the opinions presented herein reflect those of

ARC. The purpose of the series is to give voice to a wide variety of sources and perspectives. We may not agree with every contributor, but to truly understand the event we felt it essential to provide a very wide sampling of perspectives. It is important to keep in mind that Volume II is a series of snapshots over a period of roughly two years. The importance of the findings presented herein lie in the totality of the picture, not in the individual elements.

To some readers this book may seem biased against the United States. From the perspective of the editors, this is not the case. We have attempted to treat all the protagonists in the war equally, because in ARC's opinion there were no "good guys" in this conflict. The governments of Iraq and Kuwait continue to exhibit a brutal lack of appreciation for human rights, democracy and the due process of law. Similarly, the extreme number of civilian casualties, the continuing suffering of civilians, especially children, under economic sanctions, and the lack of international collective action to free other nations suffering the same fate as Kuwait—all expose the hypocrisy of the members of the U.S.-led Coalition of 1991. But if this book seems more biased against the U.S. than against any other nation, it is to a certain extent a testament to the tradition of freedom in this nation. The U.S. government allows greater freedom of official information than do the governments that rule Iraq, Kuwait, or Saudi Arabia—or even than those of France and Great Britain. As a result, far more information is available and therefore more is known about the U.S. role in the conflict. This imbalance of available information is reflected in this book.

The book is organized into several sections, grouped according to the major topics of the war. Chapter One provides an ecological and historical overview of the region and the war. The Gulf region, as the World Conservation Monitoring Centre and Boyce Thorne-Miller make clear, contains many important, albeit stressed, habitats. We present the reader with these reports so that the ecocidal impacts of the war can be understood in the context of preexisting environmental conditions. Similarly, the interview with Clovis Maksoud, former representative of the League of Arab States to the UN, is intended to give the reader a historical overview of the region and a sense of the complex politics behind the Gulf crisis from an Arab perspective.

Chapters Two, Three and Four take a deeper look at the environmental devastation that made headlines around the world. Chapter Two assesses the impacts of the Mina Al Ahmadi and other wartime oil spills, in the course of which, according to the Saudi Arabian Meteorological and Environmental Protection Agency, some eight million barrels of oil entered the Gulf. Chapter Three asks what the immediate impacts of the oil fires were on Kuwait and its inhabitants, and investigates whether the fires contributed to the anomalous weather events of 1991: the floods in China and the monsoon in Bangladesh, which killed over 100,000 people.

Chapter Four examines the impacts of both the ground war and the oil fires on the desert plain between Iraq, Saudi Arabia and Kuwait. The oil lakes are a little-publicized legacy of the war: Many times more oil spilled onto the Kuwaiti desert than into the waters of the Gulf, and, even today, the oil lakes stretch for tens and even hundreds of miles on the desert's surface, some several meters deep. Another legacy of the war is the low-level radioactive depleted uranium left behind in shards of shrapnel throughout the desert combat zone.

Next we move on to issues of human ecology. Chapters Five and Six explore the impacts on the human environment and Iraq's infrastructure, and the ways in which the war changed the lives of ordinary people. The people of industrialized nations depend on electrical power grids and water treatment facilities for their survival. The destruction of the infrastructure in Iraq has led to widespread malnutrition and increased infant and child mortality. The reports on industrial pollution, waterborne diseases and chemical emissions from bombed sites are the result of fact-finding missions to Iraq conducted by ARC/Arms Control Research Center as part of the International Study Team.

Chapter Six begins with the controversy over the exact number of Iraqi war dead in 1991. We go on to look at the effects of the war on the psychological health of those who survived it. Post-traumatic stress in children, an inevitable impact of war, is rarely raised as an issue in the debate that precedes the decision to wage war. The Gulf crisis also led to some of the largest-ever refugee movements in history. Chapter Six conveys how Iraqis, including Shiites and Kurds, have been impoverished by the bombing and the sanctions, and how the terror of the Gulf War spread throughout the region, threatening the lives of civilian Kuwaitis, Palestinians, Saudi Arabians and Israelis.

The last three chapters examine the military and policy implications of the Gulf War. The growth of Iraq's nuclear, chemical and biological weapons arsenal was one of the stated reasons for going to war with Iraq. Chapter Seven asks how much of a threat Iraq's unconventional weapons program was and how much can be learned from the UN's unique experience of forcibly disarming a country.

Chapter Eight documents the continuing flow of arms into the Gulf region, and discusses some of the legal implications of the war and its aftermath. In Chapter Eight we present the point of view that both the Iraqi and the Coalition high command were guilty of war crimes, and raise the question of whether stricter legal safeguards are necessary to protect the environment in time of war.

Chapter Nine presents a detailed, extensive chronology of how the world armed Iraq and, together with Chapters Seven and Eight, raises questions about the strategies of elected officials who use the arms trade as a foreign-policy tool and as a way to buttress domestic economies.

The book's appendices include reprints of relevant UN Security Council resolutions, a list of organizations to contact for more information, a bibliography and more information about ARC, our campaigns and publications.

THE NEED FOR ONGOING STUDY

As the interviews and reports in this publication reveal, scientists have had little experience dealing with the complex and synergistic effects of a war of the dimensions of the Gulf conflict. Long-term monitoring is needed to answer many of the questions that remain, and many of the effects of the war will be difficult to separate from the continuing degradation of the environment of the region.

Several significant questions remain:

- How will the oil lakes change the desert ecosystem?
- Will there be serious long-term regional impacts from the Coalition's bombing of hundreds of Iraqi petrochemical plants, oil refineries, factories and unconventional weapons factories? Will contamination from depleted uranium cause long-term health impacts? What of the long-term health effects for Kuwaitis and Coalition soldiers who lived under the smoke clouds from Iraq's destruction of Kuwait's oil fields?
- What will be the consequences when the younger generation of traumatized Iraqis and Kuwaitis, and the Iraqi children impoverished as a result of the war, become adults?
- Given that particles from the oil fires may have aggravated the storms that devastated Bangladesh in 1991, will other combatants deliberately attempt to effect the regional and global climate as a tactic in future conflicts?
- How many other Iraqgates are going on now, waiting to explode with deadly result at some future point?

Why Be Concerned?

There are quite a number of reasons for the international community to remain concerned about the ongoing crisis in the Gulf. Here are four of the main points.

A. The War Continues

There have been approximately a half-dozen skirmishes between Iraq and the United States since the beginning of 1993. In January of 1993, for example, Iraqi soldiers threatened a UN peacekeeper and seized property at a former base, which is on the Kuwaiti side of the new Kuwaiti-Iraqi border drawn by the UN.

Secretary of State Warren Christopher has stated that the U.S. has achieved "stepped-up support for Iraq's opposition elements."[7] With Saddam Hussein's military nearly completely rebuilt, what are the long-term implications for peace within Iraq? Because of Kurdish and Shiite separatist aspirations within Iraq, the creation of the Kurdish enclave in the North and the no-fly zone in the South have prepared the way for violent conflicts when Coalition support is eventually withdrawn.

B. The Arms Trade Continues

The most difficult task now facing the international community is how to restrict arms sales and prevent unconventional weapons proliferation.

During the Cold War, billions of dollars in Western and Eastern weapons poured into Iraq. The U.S.S.R. provided Iraq with tanks, jet fighters and missiles. The West provided it with missiles, armored personnel carriers and munitions factories. In the 1980s these arms sales increased as a result of the Iran-Iraq War and continued even after it became clear that Saddam Hussein was using chemical weapons against both the Iranians and against the Kurdish population of Iraq. Currently, arms sales to the Middle East are at an all-time high. Will the disarming of Iraq by the UN become the first step toward establishing in the Middle East a zone free from weapons of mass destruction, as promised by Security Council Resolution 687 (see Appendix One)?

C. Suffering Continues

Since the end of the Gulf War a number of national and international peace and relief organizations have been campaigning to have economic sanctions against Iraq lifted. Lifting economic sanctions would leave in place the embargo on military equipment, technology and component hardware.

In their current formulation, sanctions against Iraq are hurting poor Iraqis, Kurds and Shiites but do not seem to be hurting the Baathist inner circle. Even with sanctions in place, Iraq's military is still operating against the rebellions in the North and the South. While Saddam Hussein is still in power, Iraq is unlikely to comply with the terms of Resolution 687, and until it does, the UN Security Council is unlikely to lift sanctions. Meanwhile, economic sanctions are preventing Iraq from importing farm implements, fertilizers and seeds for planting. They are making it difficult for Iraq to obtain equipment to restart irrigation pumps and repair sewage treatment plants. The stories of Iraqi women in Chapter Six are a powerful indictment of sanctions.

Military sanctions are justified, but economic sanctions are not. If economic sanctions are not working, why continue with them? Also, considering reports that Iraq has rebuilt 80 percent of its military, sanctions against military goods need to be strengthened and more strictly enforced, with clear penalties for violations by suppliers.

D. International Dependency on Oil Continues

Energy conservation continues to be a low priority in America and around the world. The world is still seriously dependent upon oil to run its machinery and the global economy. As long as this dependency continues, wars to defend the interests of industrialized nations in the control, production and pricing of Third World oil will probably recur.

The international community should adopt a new orientation toward energy that is environmentally, economically, and strategically sensible, focusing on conservation and environmentally responsible fuel alternatives.

Closing Thoughts

The Gulf War removed the Iraqi army from Kuwait. Gone, at least for now, is the fear that Saddam Hussein might gain control of the greatest portion of the Gulf's proven oil reserves. Gone too is the fear that Iraq could soon become a nuclear nation. But two years after Iraq's invasion of Kuwait, little else is resolved. Saddam Hussein still refers to Kuwait as Iraq's nineteenth province. The United States regularly attacks Iraq in retaliation for alleged hostile actions against military aircraft and political targets. A regional arms race of massive proportions is under way.

Given these conflicting outcomes, what lessons should the international community draw from the experience? Some say that if we were still living in the Cold War era, superpower fear and rivalry would never have allowed this war to happen. Others say that as long as the U.S. and the West remain dependent on the Gulf's oil resources, these powers will continue their historic use of military actions to stifle regional self-determination—whether peaceful or violent—if considered to be against Western interests. Still others say that the Coalition's failure to remove Saddam Hussein from power will continue the instability in the region.

What is clear from *Hidden Casualties, Volume II,* is that the numbers of casualties and refugees, the psychological effects of the war on children and adults, the traditional animosities and jealousies among various Gulf states, the tremendous number of weapons being imported into the region, the continued policy of extraregional powers seeking influence in the Gulf and the lack of a regional peacemaking apparatus mean that, unless past practices change, the region will continue to erupt with violence.

In compiling this book, we have come across a number of good recommendations for how to proceed from here. We present 18 of these recommendations as an epilogue. The main ones are also worth mentioning here.

One of the most important things we can do to stem the potential for violence in the region is to begin an arms embargo. Despite the enormous amount of money to be made from continuing to supply the Gulf states with arms, it is clear from the experience of the U.S. with Iran under Shah Mohammad Reza Pahlavi that the policy of glutting a state with weapons does not ensure its stability. One of the reasons frequently given for Saddam Hussein's attack on Kuwait so soon after he had concluded a peace accord with Iran is that he possessed the weapons and the battle-honed military to pull off such an attack. Similarly, the massive stores of weapons possessed by Iran and Saudi Arabia could conceivably lure these countries into choosing military over diplomatic options in the future.

Arms alone cannot secure a nation against aggressors. For smaller Gulf nations, the importation of great caches of weapons will not necessarily prevent an invasion by a larger power. Many Gulf states will still need to call on the United States and the United Nations for protection and/or liberation from predatory states.

What appears to have a bigger impact on peace in the region are security arrangements made with outside powers. Even larger states like Saudi Arabia rely on the presence of the U.S. military to exploit the full potential of their network of American-built superbases. Many analysts believe that the Iraqi invasion of Kuwait would not have occurred if Ambassador April Glaspie had clearly reminded Saddam Hussein of the security arrangement between Kuwait and the U.S.

If the United Nations is going to involve itself in using military forces to safeguard national sovereignty, then ARC recommends the formation of a UN-sponsored multilateral force, modeled on NATO, with a rotating leadership and an open membership.

Another recommendation is that there should be an international environmental health and refugee crisis-coordinating center. Much precious time was wasted waiting for the international community to respond to the ecological impact of the war. Refugees fleeing the conflict overwhelmed the resources of nations like Jordan and Iran. A central agency with funding, equipment and permanent staffing to monitor, prepare and execute crisis reaction plans could mitigate much of the suffering of refugees and assess the environmental needs quickly enough to mitigate some of those impacts.

Finally, efforts to peacefully resolve regional disputes should be accelerated. The UN should convene a regional peace conference to resolve bilateral issues such as the dispute between Iraq and Kuwait over shipping access, as well as broader multilateral issues. Dialogues between national governments and ethnic and religious minorities that have separatist aspirations, including the Kurds and the Shiites of Iraq, should be a component of the conference. Only by developing a mechanism to resolve these long-term, complex issues does the world community stand a chance of avoiding future wars in the region.

SUMMARY

The Gulf War continues and, to a certain extent, we are all its hidden casualties. The repercussions of wars ripple across international society, and no one escapes unscathed. Parents cannot help but feel the grief and outrage embodied in pictures of mothers and fathers comforting dying or wounded children. The costs of war are paid for in taxes that come at the expense of schools, health care and other essential services. The high-tech weapons seem marvelous indeed until their smaller cousins—assault rifles and pistols—make their deadly way though gun dealers and the black market into our neighborhoods, schools and lives.

The Gulf region is part of the international political tectonics that are in the process of remaking the world. The international community is still in the throws of postcolonial political reorganization. The Cold War may have quelled nascent nationalist and ethnic aspirations but the genie is now out of the bottle. The UN Security Council must be careful in this period of geopolitical transition not to step into the role of past colonial powers. If past practices do not change, the Gulf and other troubled regions will continue to explode with violence. It is our hope that by revealing the hidden casualties of war, we will make the world community more aware of the impacts of its choices, thereby bringing us all closer to peace.

August, 1993
San Francisco

NOTES:

1. Until the reign of Shah Mohammad Reza Pahlavi of Iran (Persia), what is now known to English-speaking peoples as the Persian Gulf was generally called the Arabian Gulf. In the text of *Hidden Casualties, Volume II*, it is generally referred to simply as the Gulf.
2. "Iraq Rebuilt 80 Percent of Prewar Arms-Making," *Reuters*, June 29, 1993.
3. "UN Lawyers Back Iraq View—Attacks Not Authorized," *Los Angeles Times*, reprinted in the *San Francisco Chronicle*, January 22, 1993.
4. *Keesing's Record of World Events*, vol. 38 no. 12 (December 1992), 39249.
5. The Nowruz spill tied with the 1979 Gulf of Mexico Ixtoc spill for the largest-ever oil spill until it was surpassed by the spill during the Gulf War.
6. Richard S. Golob, "Environmental Effects of Oil Spills," in *Hidden Casualties, Volume I: The Environmental Consequences of the Persian Gulf Conflict*, (San Francisco: Arms Control Research Center/ ARC International Clearinghouse on the Military and Environment), 1991.
7. Thomas W. Lippman, "U.S. Hails Support for Iraqi Group; Opposition Organization's Gains May Only Be Symbolic, Arabs Indicate," *Washington Post*, June 20, 1993.

The Physical and Political Environment of the Gulf

The Region

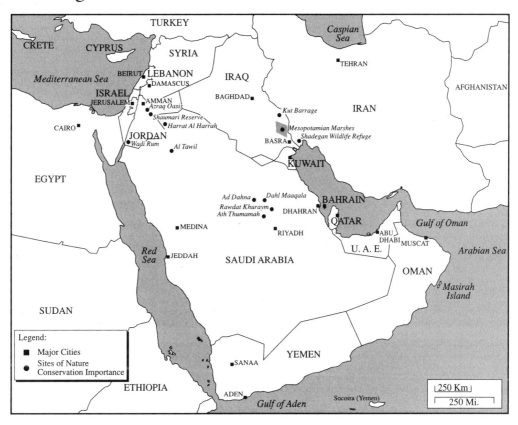

Introduction

Chapter One is intended to provide baseline information on the region surrounding the sea variously known as the Persian Gulf or Arabian Gulf.

The Gulf region includes a wide range of ecosystems, among them the Gulf sea itself, the deserts of the Arabian peninsula, and the marshes where the Tigris and Euphrates meet. Chapter One gives background information on the maritime and terrestrial environment of the areas most directly impacted by the Gulf War. Boyce Thorne-Miller gives an overview of the ecology of the Gulf sea. A 1991 report from the World Conservation Monitoring Center gives background environmental information on Iraq, Kuwait, and Saudi Arabia, and lists regional areas which in 1991 had or were intended soon to have protected area status.

Chapter One also looks at the political background to the crisis. Clovis Maksoud, a former Ambassador of the League of Arab States to the UN, gives his perspectives on the division in the Arab world caused by the invasion of one Arab country by another and on the failure of the Arab League to resolve the crisis peacefully. It emerges that divisions within the Arab League, the historical peacekeeper of the region, must be numbered among the problematic legacies of the Gulf War.

A brief account of Operation Desert Storm is included at the end of the chapter.

—James Warner

Value of the Gulf Marine Environment

Boyce Thorne-Miller

From Information Sheet on the Persian Gulf Environment, *by Boyce Thorne-Miller. Ms. Thorne-Miller was a senior scientist at Friends of the Earth when she wrote a description, excerpted here, of the ecology and marine life of the Gulf, while the Gulf War was in progress (see also Chapter Two, "Possible Impacts of the Mina Al Ahmadi Spill").*

THE PHYSICAL ENVIRONMENT OF THE GULF

The Gulf is a marine environment characterized by extremes. The coastal water temperature ranges from 10° to 36° C (50°–95° F) annually. Temperatures in the northern Gulf are cooler, by a few degrees, than the southern Gulf. Air temperatures in Kuwait range between below freezing to more than 50° C (120° F). The intertidal marine communities in the northern Gulf may be exposed to frost in January and to temperatures up to 55° C (130° F) in summer. The tidal range in the Gulf varies from about one to four meters (three to twelve feet). In areas where the slope of the coastline is very gradual, the intertidal zone may extend out a mile or more from the high-tide line. Due to high evaporation rates during the warm periods and relatively low inflow of fresh water, the salinity of Gulf water is exceptionally high, ranging from 38 to 42 parts per thousand (compared to about 35 parts per thousand in the Indian Ocean outside the Gulf). The Gulf is shallow, averaging only 110 feet in depth, with a maximum depth around 350 feet and with extensive shallow areas along the coast.

During the winter and spring, dominant winds are out of the northwest. The circulation in the Gulf is counterclockwise. Wind and circulation patterns are important to the dispersal of planktonic eggs and larvae to replenish the coral reefs and seagrass beds and other benthic communities. They will also determine the direction and rate of dispersal of spilled oil.

COASTLINE

The Gulf coast line ranges from extensive tidal mud flats at the head, forming the delta for the Tigris and Euphrates Rivers (which join to form the Shatt Al Arab waterway), to the steep rocky Iranian coast, the rocky cliffs of the Emirates and the mountains of Oman. Most of the west coast is relatively low lying, with extensive sand beaches and flats along the coast of Saudi Arabia and beyond. The western coastline is broken by numerous creek beds, but these carry virtually no freshwater runoff except during heavy rains. Bays and small offshore islands are common along this shore. The Kuwait and Saudi Arabia coastline includes areas of sandy beaches, mud flats, mixed sand and mud, and a few areas of exposed rock. The eastern rocky coast of the Gulf is indented by small rivers.

OIL FACTOR

Added to these physical conditions is the continual influx of oil into Gulf waters, both natural and human-induced. Because this is an oil-rich area there is natural seepage. For example, the island Qaruh is characterized by the constant smell of oil. In fact, the island was named for that (*Qar* meaning oil) long before human exploitation of the oil resources began. Far greater than any natural seepages are the frequent leaks and spills from the drilling, storage and shipping activities that dominate the Gulf region. Oil spills have occurred frequently since the sixties, but have increased significantly since the late seventies. The Iran-Iraq conflict, in particular, caused undetermined quantities of oil to be released into Gulf waters. Numerous small spills have occurred as well as several large spills, most notably the Nowruz spill [which occurred in 1983 during the Iran-Iraq War] which reportedly discharged about 80 million gallons into the Gulf. The frequency of spills has varied, but it is reported that during the latter years of the Iran-Iraq War, there was damage to a vessel or some oil facility at least once a week.

SEA LIFE IN THE GULF

The temperature and salinity conditions in the Gulf create a highly stressful environment for the sea life there. Access to the Indian Ocean is through the Strait of Hormuz into the Arabian Sea. Thus, marine species have populated the Gulf from more tropical waters outside; and natural communities are composed of those species that have been able to adapt to the rigorous physical conditions in Gulf waters. Because the source of species populating the Gulf is the tropical Indian Ocean, most species found there are tropical. Consequently, some of the species, such as coral and their associated reef species, are found at their northernmost points of distribution in waters off Kuwait. The temperate species found in the Gulf are generally those able to tolerate high temperatures and thus able to disperse from temperate environments in the Southern Hemisphere, across warm tropical waters and into the Gulf. However, other species have likely been introduced in ballast water from tankers that have taken on water in other ports.

The diversity of species, as expected, is not exceptionally high in the presence of these environmental conditions, but that does not negate the importance of the diversity that is there. Diversity increases from north to south with closer proximity to the Strait of Hormuz and exchange with the Indian Ocean, home to the greatest known diversity of marine species in the world. The Gulf is visited by numerous migratory species and the influx of larvae from the outside can replenish populations of Gulf species. Circulation within the Gulf is also important to the recruitment of larvae from one population to replenish another. A few species that are rare or endangered worldwide can be found in the Gulf. These include the hawksbill and green turtles, dugongs (sea cows), a few endemic reef species, and a very rare fish, the mudskipper, found on intertidal mud flats in northern Kuwait.

For the most part, the species found in the Gulf are not unique to that area, but it is reasonable to expect that many Gulf populations are genetically distinct from their counterparts in other areas. For instance, most corals cannot tolerate the maximum temperatures or the temperature range found in the Gulf, yet the Gulf populations persist, suggesting that they are genetically adapted to the temperature and salinity extremes of the Gulf. Because most species are living at their limit of tolerance to salinity, temperature and/or temperature fluctuation, relatively small additional environmental stresses could cause populations to collapse. For example, an occasional combination of exceptionally low tides and exceptionally low temperatures has been known to kill off the shallow portion of some coral reef communities. The extensive mud flat ecosystems would also be susceptible to unusually stressful conditions during periods of very low tides, although many of the species in those areas are likely tolerant to large oscillations in their environments. We do not have information as to how long it takes to re-establish a community in the Gulf once it has collapsed. Related to that, it is also not known to what extent these Gulf communities rely on outside waters for replenishment and how well or how rapidly invading populations from outside the Gulf can adapt to the extreme conditions found there. There are several types of habitats with their associated communities common in the Gulf, including those characterized below:

Dugong. Artwork by Carol Melnick.

1) Intertidal mud flats: There are extensive areas of mud flats exposed at low tide. These are inhabited by a variety of invertebrates (snails, crabs, marine worms, etc.) that can tolerate long periods of exposure. The upper reaches of the mud flats are exposed to the air longer than they are covered by water. These areas are feeding grounds for a number of shorebird species that eat the mud flat fauna. Some fish are also found on the wet mud flats, including the mudskipper. Mangroves and saltmarshes may be associated with the mud flats, especially in embayments and river estuaries.

2) Rocky shore: Rocky shores with their attached flora and fauna are more common along the east shore than the west, although there are small areas of rocky outcrops in Kuwait and Saudi Arabia. These exhibit sharp patterns of zonation relative to the length of exposure as the tide recedes, and offer a variety of habitats, each with their own set of species—e.g., tide pools, rock faces, protected undersides of rock, etc.

3) Seagrass beds: This type of habitat is found along most of the western coast and in certain locations along the eastern coast of the Gulf. These are submerged meadows of flowering plants known as seagrass or turtlegrass. They harbor a variety of animals that feed directly on the grass, on the decaying pieces of grass, or on the algae associated with the grass; other animals may feed higher on the food chain but find refuge in the grass. The seagrass beds of the Gulf are important in their role as nursery grounds for numerous offshore species including many economically valuable species such as shrimp, mullet, mackerel, seabream, etc. Dugongs and sea turtles are among the rare or endangered species that are found here.

4) Coral reefs and islands: The coral reefs of the Gulf are not the most diverse in the world, but they are, nevertheless, pockets of relatively high diversity in the Gulf. A few very rare reef species have been identified here, but the reef communities here are most interesting because they are at the northernmost limit of their range, and they have adapted to unusually harsh temperature conditions. The coral islands associated with the reefs are sanctuaries for a number of sea birds, including cormorants, several species of gulls, and others.

5) Subtidal bottom (soft and hard bottoms): Offshore from the seagrass beds, the bottom community is dominated by several seaweeds that provide shelter for the adult stages of shrimp as well as other bottom-dwelling animals. Much of the Gulf is shallow enough to allow light to reach the bottom to support the growth of algae.

6) Pelagic/planktonic communities: The water column supports a moderately productive phytoplankton community. The plankton combined with the seagrass beds provide the base of a food chain productive enough to support a viable fishery of a number of kinds of fish and shell-fish, including shrimp, grouper, mullet, mackerel, seabream, butterfish, tuna, anchovies, sardines, and several others. All the countries around the Gulf fish these waters both for local markets and for the export market.

7) Microbial communities are important in the Gulf. An important part of seagrass bed ecology is the decomposition of dead plant matter. This is a significant pathway by which the seagrass production enters the marine food chain. In addition, the presence of natural oil seepage zones in the Gulf has allowed a natural community of microbial oil-consumers to be established.

FISHERIES IN THE GULF

More than a hundred species of fish and shellfish in the Gulf are exploited on a commercial basis. At least in Kuwait and Saudi Arabia, the traditional subsistence fishermen have largely been replaced by commercial boats owned by nationals but operated by foreign crews. This is less true in Iran, where artisanal fishermen still ply the waters, particularly off the southern Iranian coast. The UN Fisheries and Agricultural Organization (FAO) yearly statistics list about 50 species or classes of animals that are fished, including groupers, snappers, grunts, croakers, mullet, seabreams, butterfish, mackerel, tuna, sailfish, sardines, sharks, shrimp, and crabs. The shrimp fishery is one of the major fisheries and accounts for many of the fish caught as well (incidental catch by shrimpers include many usable fish as well as fish that are discarded). During its peak, the shrimp fishery of the Gulf amounted to about 15,000–20,000 tons per year. Currently it is closer to 10,000 tons per year, but there is indication in the Kuwait fishery that improved management practices are increasing the yield. That country recorded a catch of over 3,000 tons last year, which represented a significant increase over only a couple of years.

The extensive seagrass beds are important nursery areas for the shrimp and many of the other fishery species. The shrimp, for example, spawn in deeper waters but the planktonic larvae drift to the grass beds and proceed through the various developmental stages until they become immature adults, at which time they settle to the bottom and most move back out into deeper water.

Mullet and many other fish actually come into the seagrass beds to spawn. Spawning season for the majority of these species is in the late winter to early spring, so during the end of January, February and March, species at the most sensitive stages in their life histories are in the seagrass beds and vulnerable to environmental hazards.

How long it takes a fishery to recover from overfishing or environmental damage depends on the species, its fecundity, its average life span, and the time it takes for outside sources (i.e. larvae or juveniles from different populations within or outside the Gulf) to replenish the depleted populations. The shrimp, for example, lives not much more than one year and produces large numbers of eggs that float in the plankton and readily disperse to various seagrass beds around the Gulf. It appears that populations of these species can re-establish themselves within a year or two, but other species may require longer.

Compared to other fisheries worldwide, the Gulf is only moderately productive. Nevertheless, the fishery represents an important source of food for the nations of the region as well as income from exports, and is the only renewable resource for the people of that region.

INTERNATIONAL LAW AND THE GULF

The Gulf is classified as a special area under two parts of MARPOL (The International Convention for the Prevention of Pollution from Ships)—those sections applying to the disposal of oily waste and of garbage at sea (Annexes I and V). This classification is given to bodies of water that are of special concern because of their oceanographic and ecological characteristics and are considered at particular risk because of the volume and nature of vessel traffic. Although the Gulf has been designated a special area under these two annexes, the designation has not yet been implemented.

Terrestrial and Freshwater Ecology of the Gulf Region

World Conservation Monitoring Center

Before the Gulf War broke out in January 1991, the World Conservation Monitoring Centre (WCMC), a joint venture of The International Union for the Conservation of Nature and Natural Resources (IUCN), the United Nations Environment Programme (UNEP) and the World Wide Fund for Nature (WWF), set up an information service on the environmental effects of the Gulf War, covering the land, sea and atmosphere. Excerpted here is a baseline description of the region's main ecological characteristics, based on WCMC's report "Gulf War Environmental Information Service, Impact on the Land and Atmosphere" written as the war was still in progress, February 7, 1991.

TERRESTRIAL ECOLOGY OF THE REGION

DESERT

In northwest Saudi Arabia, Kuwait and southeast Iraq, most of the land is sand and gravel desert plain. This supports a sparse vegetation of drought-adapted scrub and perennial herbs which typically have a substantial fibrous root system to tap deep water. The ecological value of this habitat had already been degraded before the arrival of troops, due to the disturbance caused by oil installations,overgrazing by livestock and uncontrolled shooting of wildlife.

DESERT WETLANDS

Marshes and wetlands are scattered throughout the desert, particularly towards the Gulf coast. The proposed nature reserve of Khawr Al Muffateh, some 15 kilometers north of the Kuwait-Saudi border and 25 kilometers from Khafji, comprises a rich area of mud flats around the An Nap creek, which during the winter months supports large numbers of migratory waterfowl. Similar important wetlands occur around Kuwait Bay and opposite Bubiyan Island.

RIVER MARSHES

The terrestrial area of greatest importance both for nature conservation and as a productive natural resource is the extensive Mesopotamian Marshes of the Euphrates and Tigris river basin in Iraq. These wetlands cover some 5,000 square kilometers and support a highly productive freshwater ecosystem with a diversity of fish species and bird life. Some 55 percent of Iraq's fish production is from freshwater sources. The wetlands are the home of the people vividly portrayed in Wilfred Thesiger's *The Marsh Arabs*.[1] The Eastern Marshes, between the Tigris and the Iran border, were seriously disturbed during the Iran-Iraq War, when large areas were flooded to prevent tank movements, which damaged local agriculture. The Central and Southern Marshes are still ecologically viable, although manipulation of the river flow for irrigation, coupled with extensive land drainage, has reduced the spring flooding.[2]

VEGETATION

KUWAIT

The majority of Kuwait is desert plain covered in sparse scrub with perennial, and often salt-tolerant, herbs and ephemerals. The vegetation type and density are controlled primarily by the amount of precipitation. As there is a marked seasonal and yearly variation in rainfall, the desert tends to be either covered in a rich green mantle in the rainy years or devoid of vegetation in dry years. Kuwait is estimated to have about 300 species of vascular plants.

There are primarily three types of plant communities found in the desert plains which are controlled by soil characteristics as well as rainfall. There are:

1) *Cyperus* [cypress grass] steppe: This is found in the area immediately south and southwest of Kuwait City. It is dominated by *Cyperus conglomeratus*, but the millet species *Panicum turgidum* occurs here and there. Where the soil is gravelly or disturbed, *Cornulaca leucacantha* [no English name] gains importance.

2) *Rhanterium* steppe: This occurs in the center and in the extreme northeast of the country. The dominant species is *Rhanterium epapposum* [*arfaj* in Arabic] which is frequently associated with the bindweed species *Convolvulus oxyphyllus*, *Moltkiopsis ciliata* [*halam* in Arabic], and *Stipagrostis plumosa* [*dawat* in Arabic], as well as many other species.

3) *Haloxylon* steppe: This type of desert is found in the northern, northwestern and southern part of the country. The soil is shallow, and nearly pure stands of *Chrozophora* [tournsole] are the dominant vegetation type.

In the extreme west of the country there is a gravel desert plateau which is more or less devoid of vegetation. Where there is accumulation of sand, *Haloxylon salicornicum* [*rimth* in Arabic] occurs. Playas are barren depressions or low portions of a desert region that periodically collect rainfall and sediments. Playas in Jal Al Zhor national park in Kuwait typically contain communities of *Iris sisyrinchium* [crocus-rooted iris] and also *Malva parviflora* [an edible mallow], both species being dormant in the summer in the form of seeds and bulbs.

Along the coast of the Gulf there is a system of low coastal dunes from Al Dbaiyyah southward. These dunes are usually dominated by the bean caper *Zygophyllum coccineum* and/or *Seidlitzia rosmarinus* ["wormbush"]. Coastal salt marshes and saline depressions are fed by the shallow saline water table and tidal action. The salt marshes fringe Kuwait Bay and Khawr Al Sabiyah and are also on Bubiyan.

IRAQ

The vegetation in Iraq shows a transitional character between that of Africa and Asia. Four vegetation zones have been distinguished which show a relationship between the climatic and the topographic features of the land. There are: 1) desert and steppe, 2) river-system and adjacent formations, 3) the Assyrian higher plains and Kurdish foothills, and 4) the mountains. The desert steppe zone forms the largest part of Iraq; in the southwest near the Saudi border true desert conditions occur, but further north the steppe changes gradually from arid to more humid conditions.

Iraq has 2,937 vascular plant species, of which 190 are endemic to Iraq. At least one species, the *Acacia gerrardii*, protected in Saudi Arabian reserves, is known to be at risk as a result of the war.

Two types of vegetation communities are found in the desert steppe area: annuals and perennials. The annuals appear after the winter rains for a few weeks and produce seeds which are dormant in the hot summer months. The perennials survive either by having deep roots able to reach deep groundwater or by having swollen underground storage organs or drought-resistant features. Perennials are often salt-tolerant, as the ground water is often saline. The vegetation is strongly influenced by the amount of rainfall and is sparse in the South, being mainly *Poa* [meadow grass], *Carex* [sedge grass] and *Artemisia* [wormwood] steppe. Further north the steppe becomes less arid and flora becomes richer, turning into open savanna mainly dominated by *Pistacia* [pistachio]. In the North of the country the humid steppe zone gradually gives way to the Assyrian uplands and the Kurdish foothills. These areas are largely impoverished by thousands of years of overgrazing and overcutting of the tree cover. The area was covered with *Quercus aegilops* [oak] and *Pinus brutia* [fir] forest between 500 and 2,750 meters in elevation, which has been largely destroyed. Above this level the peaks become treeless and only bushes of *Daphne* [laurel herb], *Euphorbia* [milkwort], *Astragalus* [astragal] and *Acantholimon* [prickly thrift] form thorn-cushions.

The Mesopotamian Marshes of the lower reaches of the Tigris and Euphrates north of Basra are some of the largest in the world, covering an area of about 20,000 square kilometers. The marshes consist of a series of shallow lakes and periodically inundated land. Dominant vegetation includes the emergent *Phragmites communis* [common reed] and *Typha angustifolia* [narrow-leaved reed mace] plus many submerged and floating plants such as *Vallisneria* [eel grass], the pondweed *Potamogeton*, and water lilies *Nymphea* and *Nuphar*. To the north the marshes have been reclaimed and are the site of agriculture supported by irrigation. Much of the agricultural production is from large rice fields and small holdings growing cereals and vegetables, as well as citrus orchards.

SAUDI ARABIA

The majority of Saudi Arabia is desert, about one-third of it being mobile sand, mainly in the empty region of the South and West. The north and central areas are predominantly a mosaic of steppe and dwarf shrub communities being dominated by *Rhanterium epapposum*, [*arfaj* in Arabic] which is a perennial dwarf shrub. It is abundant over a wide area and extends eastward to within a short distance of the Gulf coast of Kuwait. The feather grass species *Stipe tortilis* is the most abundant of the cool season annuals and is found in a wide area to the north of central Arabia. Saudi Arabia is estimated to have 3,500 species of vascular plants, of which 23 taxa have been identified as endemic.

THREATENED SPECIES

Very little is known about the number of plants that are threatened in this region. As a consequence only five plant species are [listed as] threatened in the area. (See Table 1-1 below.) Of these none is known to be directly threatened in any of the three countries, but all are known to occur in the region and are considered threatened at the world level. This in no way should be taken as an indication of the total number of plants threatened in the region but reflects more the lack of knowledge about the status of the flora of the area.

TABLE 1–1. THREATENED PLANT SPECIES OF THE GULF REGION			
COUNTRY	SPECIES	NONENDEMIC TAXA	IUCN WORLD CATEGORY
Kuwait	Leguminosae	*Acacai gerrardii*	Vulnerable
Iraq	Iridaceae	*Iris assadiana*	Rare
		Iris gatesii	Rare
		Iris heylandiana	Endangered
Saudi Arabia	Euphorbiaceae	*Euphorbia fractiflexa*	Rare

MAMMALS

KUWAIT

Only 30 species are listed: the majority are rodents (nine species), bats (three species) and insectivores (three species) which are too small to be severely affected by the war. Of the large mammals, four are already believed to be extinct in Kuwait (the Asiatic cheetah and the Dorcas, mountain and Arabian sand gazelles), three are marine mammals, and two (the gray wolf and the caracal) are listed as occurring, but probably only as occasional vagrants from Iraq and Saudi Arabia. The honey badger and the Fennec fox are the only species left in Kuwait likely to have suffered from the large-scale troop movements and artillery and aerial bombardments.

IRAQ

The main species likely to suffer in the Gulf conflict are the larger mammals. Gazelle populations in Iraq have been more intensively hunted than those in Saudi Arabia and very few are thought to survive in the desert and sub-desert areas along the Iraqi/Saudi Arabian border. The dorcas gazelle may already be extinct, but small numbers of the mountain and Arabian sand gazelles may survive, all very vulnerable to military activity.

Fennec Fox. Artwork by Carol Melnick.

The disjunct population of the smooth-coated otter *Lutra perspicillata* in the marshes of southern Iraq, and populations of the Eurasian otter *Lutra lutra* in the marshes and the Tigris-Euphrates river system may be adversely affected by oil or chemical contamination as a result of war activities.

Saudi Arabia

The only mammals likely to suffer in the conflict are two of the three mainland species of gazelle, and possibly some carnivores.

Dorcas Gazelle. Artwork by Carol Melnick.

The Saudi subspecies of the Dorcas gazelle *Gazella dorcas saudiya* was still considered common in the north of the country in the 1960s, but possibly has been extinct in the wild since the 1970s. The Arabian sand gazelle *Gazella subgutturosa marica* is found in sandy areas throughout Saudi Arabia, but within the last 20 years numbers have decreased considerably, particularly in the North, where herds of 50–100 used to be seen. The species probably only persists in low numbers and is the only local mammal species endangered internationally. All the gazelles have declined mainly due to over-hunting by people in motorized vehicles. Since they are mainly diurnal and live entirely above ground, gazelles suffer more from bombing than do desert carnivores.

The presence of land mines in the desert may have had a positive impact on gazelle populations by deterring hunting.

Birds

Over 400 species of birds have been recorded in the northern Gulf region, comprising Kuwait, Iraq, eastern Saudi Arabia and western Iran. Of these, 19 are considered to be internationally threatened. However, the only resident species with significant populations within the war zone is the Houbara bustard, which has an important Arabian breeding population between Riyadh and Kuwait. Some birds from more northern populations also move into the Gulf region to overwinter.

The Tigris-Euphrates marshes south of Baghdad are the most important area in the region for threatened birds. There are large colonies of pygmy cormorants (these marshes are the stronghold of the species in the south of its range) and scattered colonies of marbled teal. In winter the area is visited by significant numbers of Dalmatian pelicans, red-breasted geese and lesser white-fronted geese, and the numerous raptors preying on the abundant waterfowl include white-tailed and imperial eagles.

There are also three species which, although not listed as internationally threatened, are restricted to the region and could therefore be seriously threatened by widespread habitat destruction. The Basra reed warbler *Acrocephalus griseldis* is a summer visitor to the region and only breeds in reedbeds in the marshes of southern Iraq from north of Baghdad to Basra and Faw; its current status is unknown but its total population is unlikely to be very large. The Iraq babbler *Turdoides altirostris* is a resident in reedbeds and riverine thickets, occurring in five apparently disjunct areas in south and central Iraq from Basra north to Khanaqin, and also in adjacent parts of southwestern Iran; although it was described as common in 1981 there are no quantitative population estimates. The gray hypocolius *Hypocolius ampelinus* is almost entirely restricted as a breeding bird to south and central Iraq and southwestern Iran; in winter virtually all birds of the species move to Saudi Arabia, and one of the main wintering areas is along the Gulf coast.

The region is also important as a migration route for huge numbers of birds of a great variety of species. It has been estimated that some two to three billion migrants move in a southerly direction across Arabia each autumn. The great majority of these birds pass directly over the region without stopping, but adverse weather conditions can ground migrating birds in large numbers.[3]

FRESHWATER FISH

KUWAIT

The only species present may be the salt-tolerant *Aphanius dispar*, a killifish, recorded in coastal lagoons; little information is currently available.

IRAQ

Approximately 84 species, few of them endemics, are reported to occur in the Euphrates-Tigris system. Some species endemic to the system are likely to be restricted to the upper reaches (partly outside Iraq). Many of the groups of fishes present are in need of taxonomic revision.

Caecocypris basimi [a recently discovered fish with no English name] and the barbin *Typhlogarra widdowsoni* are both categorized as rare in the 1990 IUCN Red List. Both are blind cave fish endemic to Iraq and apparently restricted to subterranean waters near Haditha, adjacent to the Euphrates.

SAUDI ARABIA

Only nine freshwater fish species are known from the entire Arabian peninsula; only four species are recorded to occur in Saudi Arabia. *Aphanius dispar* occurs along the Gulf coast.

REPTILES

KUWAIT

The reptile fauna is known to be relatively depauperate, with no endemic species, although 20 species have been recorded at Jal Al Zhor National Park.

IRAQ

The reptile fauna comprises approximately 48 lizards (including amphisbaenians), 30 snakes, and three chelonians.

SAUDI ARABIA

There is a species-rich reptile fauna, with around 65 lizard species and more than 25 snakes; approximately three species appear to be endemic to Saudi Arabia. Three lizards (a gecko *Stenodactylus khobarensis* and the fringe-toed lizards *Acanthodactylus haasi* and *A. gongrorhynchatus*) are largely restricted to the northeast sector of the peninsula; the *Stenodactylus* occurs mainly on coastal mud flats.

Most lizard species in the Gulf region are desert forms with relatively wide geographical ranges. Many new species, particularly of lizard, have been described in recent years.

No terrestrial reptile species currently identified by IUCN as globally threatened appears to occur in southern Iraq, Kuwait or northeast Saudi Arabia.

AREAS OF NATURE CONSERVATION IMPORTANCE

KUWAIT

Before August 1990, Kuwait was in the final stages of preparing a detailed protected areas system. Three sites had been officially established from a series of nature conservation areas which were proposed in its Master Action Plans, the most well known of which is the Jal Al Zhor National Park near Kuwait City.

JAL AL ZHOR NATIONAL PARK

This site was surveyed extensively as a part of the procedure prior to being designated Kuwait's first national park. By spring 1990, the site had been fenced. In addition to biological surveys, detailed information has been gathered describing the weather, hydrology and soils of the area. Moving away from the coast, the four main habitat types that have been described are: the coastal zone, incorporating tidal mud flats, *sabkhas* [salt flats] and sand dunes; the debris slope; the escarpment; and the desert plain above this with its deep depressions with some unique plant communities, wadis, playas and the desert flat. Thirty-nine species of vascular plants have been described from the coastal plain; 89 species have been described from the other habitat types in the park. Twenty-one mammal species have been described within the park, including wolf, honey badger, the Fennec fox, the Indian gray mongoose and three species of bat. One hundred and fifty species of bird have been listed and 20 species of reptile. Certain parts of the national park have been singled out for further protection, as reserves where no interference from humans or livestock is permitted.

There were radar units and other military equipment located on the escarpment (to take advantage of the altitude), thus there would have been military activity in the area even prior to invasion. The escarpment also overlooks the military base at Jahra; hence, the site has strategic importance. There was considerable human impact in the park before the war, arising from off-road driving, which destroys the vegetation and compacts the soil, and also from people camping in the park and burning material suitable for firewood. The park was badly damaged during the war by Iraqi troop emplacements, carpet bombing, and oil fallout.

NATURAL HABITATS AND SITES OF CONSERVATION INTEREST

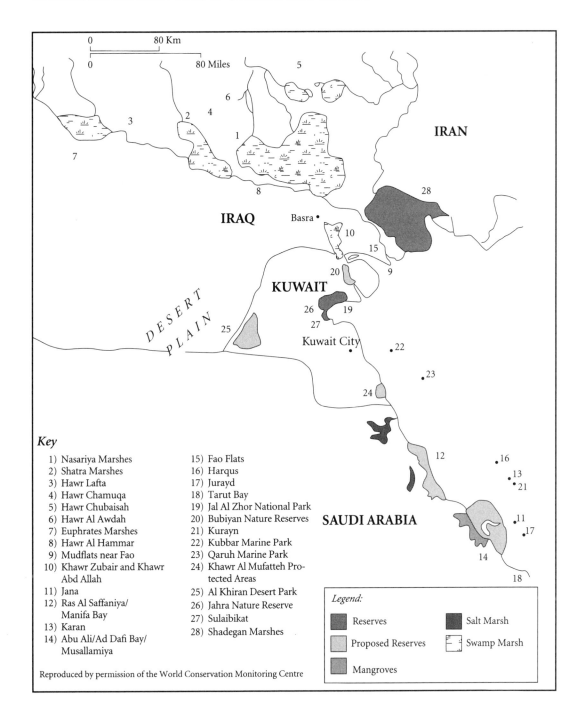

IRAN

IRAQ

Basra

KUWAIT

Kuwait City

SAUDI ARABIA

DESERT PLAIN

Key

1) Nasariya Marshes
2) Shatra Marshes
3) Hawr Lafta
4) Hawr Chamuqa
5) Hawr Chubaisah
6) Hawr Al Awdah
7) Euphrates Marshes
8) Hawr Al Hammar
9) Mudflats near Fao
10) Khawr Zubair and Khawr Abd Allah
11) Jana
12) Ras Al Saffaniya/ Manifa Bay
13) Karan
14) Abu Ali/Ad Dafi Bay/ Musallamiya

15) Fao Flats
16) Harqus
17) Jurayd
18) Tarut Bay
19) Jal Al Zhor National Park
20) Bubiyan Nature Reserves
21) Kurayn
22) Kubbar Marine Park
23) Qaruh Marine Park
24) Khawr Al Mufatteh Protected Areas
25) Al Khiran Desert Park
26) Jahra Nature Reserve
27) Sulaibikat
28) Shadegan Marshes

Reproduced by permission of the World Conservation Monitoring Centre

Legend:

■ Reserves

▨ Proposed Reserves

▨ Mangroves

■ Salt Marsh

▨ Swamp Marsh

Jahra Nature Reserve

This reserve is centered around a number of freshwater pools arising from a treated sewage outlet, and some of the pools nearer the shore are brackish. There is no real outlet to the sea; the water seeps through the mud flats. The site includes high reedbeds and is important for birds.

This site, which was fenced by May 1990, is located between the military base at Jahra and the Dohah peninsula (a site of potential military significance). It has been suggested that the site may have been virtually destroyed by vehicle movements between the two.

The following four sites in Kuwait have been recommended for protection and were under consideration, but had not been officially designated prior to the invasion.

Al Khiran Desert Park

An arid desert area and salt marsh saline depression area with *sabkhas*, the area is only about five meters above sea level. Before the Iraqi invasion in August 1990, Khiran was relatively undisturbed and considered a rich habitat for plants and animals, with several plant communities observed. The site was highly recommended for protection, particularly because of the *sabkhas*, which were regarded as a unique habitat for many saline-tolerant species. It suffered damage not just from the occupying forces stationed in the area but through bombardment and from atmospheric pollution due to its proximity to the burning Al Wafra oilfield.

Al Batin Desert Park

Wadi Al Batin is a deep depression running along the western border of this park. It is an important geological feature which is associated with vital reserves of underground fresh water. Several plant species have been identified in the region, *Haloxylon* making up the major plant community.

Khawr Al Mufatteh Protected Area

This site consists of marshlands and mud flats supporting large populations of wintering shorebirds and waterfowl from Europe and northern Asia.

Um Niqqa Desert Park

The most important habitats in this proposed park are sand dunes up to five meters high and salt marshes.

Iraq

The majority of the critical nature conservation areas in the country are unprotected, although many have been recommended for designation. The marshes of southern Iraq are of greatest conservation importance.

Hawr Al Hammar

This is one of the most important wetlands, probably the most crucial wintering bird area in the country, and the largest eutrophic lake in Iraq. It has been recommended as a national park to cover some 270,000 hectares. It has the biggest waterfowl concentrations in autumn, winter and spring with hundreds of thousands of shorebirds. Species observed include ducks, cormorants, kingfishers, flamingos, pelicans, and egrets. The population of Dalmatian pelican in the Hammar lake system was decimated during the Iran-Iraq War, and the remaining population could be severely threatened by shooting for food. The large marshes to the north of Hawr Al Hammar are the home of the Marsh Arabs, of whom there were approximately 100,000 in the late 1970s.

Nasariya Marshes

These are a series of wetlands often formed in "dead" branches of the Euphrates. The area is actually continuous with the Hawr Al Hammar system. The two major wetlands lie about eighteen and twenty kilometers from the town of Nasariya, and have been recommended for protection.[4]

Shatra Marshes

East of the town of Shatra there are two lakes. The northernmost is almost drained, but the southern lake is still present; it has an extensive vegetation of *Typha* [reeds] and large populations of shorebirds and kingfishers. It is an important waterfowl site and has been recommended for protection.

Marshlands around Basra and Kuw

The internationally important marshlands around the ports of Basra and Kuw are under extreme threat from seepage of chemicals and oil pollutants as a result of bombing during the Gulf War. This rich natural ecosystem, in the confluence of the Tigris and Euphrates, contains a vast complex of marshes, one of the largest in the world, once covering 20,000 square kilometers but now threatened by drainage. The region is of international importance for waterfowl for its rich *Phragmites* [reeds] and *Typha* plant communities.

Mesopotamian Marshes

The Mesopotamian Marshes of the Euphrates and Tigris river basin in Iraq, extending from Basra halfway to Baghdad, are extremely rich and fertile, supporting an abundance of bird species and spawning grounds for several commercial fish species.

Breeding Stations

Iraq at present has a series of protected areas which it classes as breeding stations. Most are smaller than 100 hectares in size. One of the major purposes of these reserves is for the breeding of game, and most reserves contain species imported from abroad. Three of the breeding stations lie in the South close to Baghdad (Kusaybah, Sab Al Nisan and Rawdat Al Maha), and five in the northern provinces (Zawtah in Dohuk, Hajran in Irbil, Days in Ta'meen, Darr Bandar Bazyan in Sulaymaniyah, and Sanjar in Nineveh.)

Iran

Iran has had protected areas since 1927.

Shadegan Wildlife Refuge

With an area of 296,000 hectares on the Iran-Iraq border, this Ramsar site is part of the largest lowland wetland in Iran (3.8 million hectares). The marshes are internationally important wintering and breeding areas for over 125 waterfowl species and are of particular importance for duck species, including a large percentage of the world population of marbled teal *Anas angustirostris*. During the Iran-Iraq War the wetland was reported to be severely polluted by chemical weapons.

SAUDI ARABIA

The Saudi Arabian Government through its National Commission for Wildlife Conservation and Development (NCWCD) in association with IUCN has drawn up an extensive list of important nature conservation areas in the country.

HARRAT AL HARRAH RESERVE

This is a very large reserve, some 13,775 square kilometers, in the northwest of Saudi Arabia, near the Iraqi border. It consists of desert steppe and volcanic rock, hills or jebels and lava fields, with some *sabkhas*. Important mammal species found in the reserve include Arabian and sand gazelles, the Arabian wolf and desert sand cat. The reserve also contains important wintering and breeding grounds for the Houbara bustard, cream-colored courser, dotterel, golden eagle, and many other bird species, including nine species of lark.

AT TAWIL

This site contains typical sedimentary, medium-altitude mountain biotypes, with rugged hillsides and canyons. It is virtually surrounded by sand desert including the Nafud desert. There is a rich and varied natural vegetation with some acacia and dwarf shrub in wadis. A viable ibex colony is found at the site, and the site may be used for the reintroduction of other species in the future.

AL AHASA

This 270,000 hectare site of typical sandy, gravelly desert interspersed with *sabkhas* lies between Hofuf and the Gulf. The site contains some of the few remaining undisturbed natural artesian wells in the country, containing fossil water some 30,000 years old. The *sabkhas* east of Hofuf are important for the conservation of carnivores, especially the locally threatened jackal, and for numerous endemic arthropod species. It is an important wetland for breeding birds and large numbers of migrants during passage and overwintering. The site is also of considerable archaeological interest due to the presence of artifacts of the Dilmun and paleolithic periods.

RAWDAT KHURAYM

This is a large, well-vegetated depression with ephemeral pools at the edge of the Dahna sand dunes. The site includes part of the dunes themselves, with their characteristically sparse vegetation and superarid conditions. At 140,000 hectares the site is of special zoogeographic and ecological significance with many endemic or threatened animal species, including the Houbara bustard. It is the only known locality for the acacia or wattle species *Acacia gerrardii najdensis*.

DHAL MAAQALA

An area of 1,900 hectares, this site contains old underground karstic watercourses in cretaceous limestone strata, most of them dry-dahl. The watercourses are often inhabited by numerous endemic and highly specialized animal species, such as white blind fish, arthropods, and amphibians.

AD DAHNA

This site lies in the northern desert, approximately halfway between Riyadh and the Iraqi border. It consists of typical sand dune biotypes, but with a large number of well-formed sand dunes, some up to 80 meters high. The sand gazelle has been recorded in the region.

ATH THUMAMAH

A limestone plateau with a small but steep escarpment, deeply incised with wadis, these biotypes, coupled with the sandy and stony deserts found at the site, all typify the central regions of Saudi Arabia. The site also includes the farm of the late King Khalid, notable for its collections of Arabian gazelle and ibex.

JORDAN

AZRAQ WETLAND

The Azraq wetlands in eastern Jordan, another Ramsar site, may have been severely affected by refugees fleeing the war. The oasis lies in a large drainage basin, with a large central playa fed by wadis, and freshwater springs which flow through a well vegetated marshy area designated as the Azraq wetland reserve. Before the influx of Iraqi refugees, the site was already deteriorating because of groundwater extraction, and this problem was exacerbated by the refugee transit camps set up there in 1991.

NOTES:

1. Wilfred Thesiger, *The Marsh Arabs* (New York: E.P. Dutton and Co.), 1964. See also Minority Rights Group, *The Marsh Arabs of Iraq*, Report, London, February 1993.
2. The Marshes are now extremely threatened. December 1, 1992 saw the inauguration of the Saddam River, a 565 km. canal between the Tigris and the Euphrates south of Baghdad. The believed purpose is to prevent the use of the Marshes as a refuge by Shiite rebels and to enable development of oil reserves underneath the Marshes. *Keesing's Record of World Events*, vol. 38 no. 12 (December 1992), 39249. Water pollution has severely reduced the supply of fish on which the indigenous population relies. Middle East Watch, *The 1991 Uprising in Iraq And Its Aftermath*, Report, Human Rights Watch, New York, June 1992.
3. See Chapter Two, "Impacts on Bird Populations."
4. Since July 1991, the Iraqi government has launched major offensives in the marshlands between Nasariya, Amara and Basra. Middle East Watch, *The 1991 Uprising*. The marshlands in Nasariya and Amara have now become the scenes of offensives by opposition forces, who use speedboats to attack the regime's positions. *Voice of The People of Kurdistan* (periodical in Arabic), May 14, 1993.

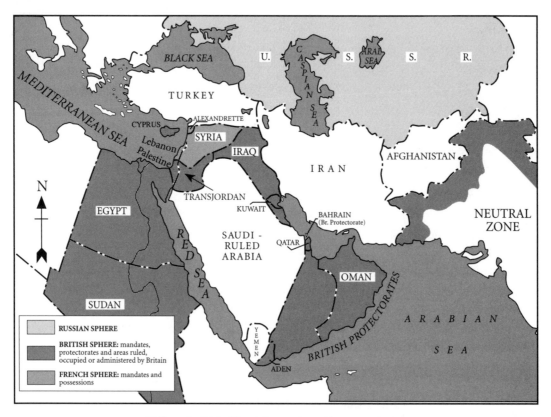

The Middle East in the 1920s

Arab States, Arab Nationalism and the Gulf War

Interview with Clovis Maksoud

On August 10, 1990, the League of Arab States voted on whether to call for armed intervention from abroad to remove Iraq from Kuwait. A split then arose between the 12 member-states that voted for war and the nine member-states that sought an Arab-negotiated solution. Professor Clovis Maksoud, the League's ambassador at the United Nations, resigned from the League in protest at its inability to deal with the crisis. Professor Maksoud is now Director of the Center for Global South School of International Studies, at The American University, Washington, D.C. Clovis Maksoud was interviewed by Saul Bloom and Philippa Winkler in May 1993.

Saul Bloom: What are the origins and functions of the League of Arab States? What role has it played historically?

Clovis Maksoud: Arabs consider themselves to be one nation of many states. During the Ottoman Empire, there was the concept of the nation of Islam. In the aftermath of the Ottoman Empire, the Arab national patrimony was divided to accommodate the varied geopolitical interests of the major powers, mainly Britain and France. The Balfour Declaration by Britain established the homeland for the Jewish people in 1917. The British-French Sykes-Picot agreement of 1917 divided the Arab nation into protectorates, colonies, mandates—a variety of structures. Some countries were under French and British mandates, such as Palestine, Lebanon and Syria, while others were treated as provinces of a European country, as Algeria was by France.

France and Britain planted the seeds for the division and the disintegration of the region and pre-empted the emergence of an Arab nationalist movement. Nevertheless, a pan-Arab nationalist movement did emerge, albeit local and fragmented, and attempted to delegitimize the post-World War I boundaries.

After the Second World War, there were seven independent sovereign Arab states: Saudi Arabia, Yemen, Iraq, Lebanon, what was at that time Transjordan (present-day Jordan), Egypt and Syria. In 1945, these countries organized themselves, with the encouragement of the British who were at that time the prevailing influence, into a league of Arab states, as an attempt to harness the community of the Arab countries into one framework. The function of the League was not only to coordinate their activities and policies, but to enhance their diplomatic and political leverage in order to expedite the process of decolonization of the rest of the Arab world: Algeria, Tunis, Morocco, Libya, Sudan, South Yemen, and the Gulf countries were still British protectorates.

This decolonization process led to a situation in which two legitimacies emerged.

On the one hand there was the legitimacy of Arab nationalism, based on a unified culture, a prevailing unified language, broadly speaking a unified religion (although there is a substantial minority of Christians and others), a sense of spiritual identity as Arabs, and a feeling of common destiny and solidarity. This was Arab nationalism that made all the Arab states feel that they were accountable to each other.

But on the other hand, the different time frames of independence also created a vested interest in the sovereignty of individual states, and so the sovereignty of states became the other legitimacy.

The goal of the Arab League throughout its historical development over the last 48 years was to reconcile these two legitimacies and coordinate their functions—to ensure that the legitimacy of state sovereignty and the legitimacy of Arab national unity should complement each other, rather than conflict with each other. The coordinating efforts were not always successful. There is a record of failure as well as a record of success. But the Arab League remained as a framework reconciling the imperatives of the two legitimacies.

SB: What about ethnic differences, before the arrival of the British and the French, and since?

CM: Arab nationalists consider that the prevailing Arab "stock" and the prevailing Islamic religion historically facilitate cohesion rather than exclusion. Of course, there were tribal, religious and ethnic differences but many of these were subsumed, although they were potent factors as they are in every part of the world. According to the Arab nationalist culture or Arab nationalist position, ethnic minorities are part of the Arab nation. They are entitled to a large measure of cultural autonomy and a recognition that as long as they are voluntarily willing to be Iraqi citizens, Libyan citizens, or Algerian citizens, their non-Arab ethnicity should not deny them equal rights.

Arab nationalists are disposed to recognize the right of self-determination, provided that it does not break up the unity of the Arab countries. If the Kurds want self-determination, they are entitled to it, but in as much as self-determination for the Kurds would constitute a geopolitical explosion in four countries (Iran, Turkey, Russia and Iraq) it becomes an international concern rather than exclusively an Arab concern.

Arab nationalism shares the historical characteristics of the national liberation movements and the decolonization process throughout the Third World, or global South, as I would call it.

SB: The border between Kuwait and Iraq was drawn by the British in 1922, when the British were a colonial power in the region. Does this mean that the border is illegitimate?

CM: The Arab League Charter has recognized the legitimate rights of the sovereignty of states—not the absolute sovereignty, the legal sovereignty. Many of the local borders were artificially imposed in order to accommodate a plethora of colonial claims or to accommodate the perpetuation of certain forms of colonial control. However, after these various states became independent, the Arab League ensured the mutual recognition of the Arab states towards each other's sovereign rights. Now this does not mean, in the ethos of Arab nationalism, that these boundaries must remain artificially imposed. Yet the boundaries are legally accepted. This ambivalence is still one of the determining intellectual and political factors in the Arab world.

And in that sense, the invasion by Iraq of Kuwait constituted a violation of the Charter of the Arab League. Whatever the complaints Iraq had about Kuwait, which we shall discuss later, the sovereignty of states must be mutually respected by all the Arab states, and if there is to be unity among two Arab states, it has to be a consequence of the will of the people, as in the case of the two Yemens in 1990, and in the case of Syria and Egypt from 1958 to 1961. These were cases of merging sovereign states into one, as a consequence of voluntary popular will. In the case of Iraq occupying Kuwait, it wasn't so.

OIL AND THE WEST

SB: To what extent did the Western industrialization of Arab oil resources impact the region? [1]

CM: Let me give you the overall context in terms of recent history.

The Arab states are a rich nation of poor people. They're rich because they have large reserves of oil which many of the industrialized countries are dependent on. But they are also a nation of poor people, in Egypt, Sudan, Somalia, the Palestinians, etc.

In the nationalist concept, Arab wealth should be addressing and ameliorating Arab poverty. Yet the Arab nationalist reality does not lend itself to this level of united resources and destiny, and therefore the responsibility of the rich toward the poor is not ingrained in the Arab state system at this moment. There is a notion that Arab brothers should help Arab brothers, but that

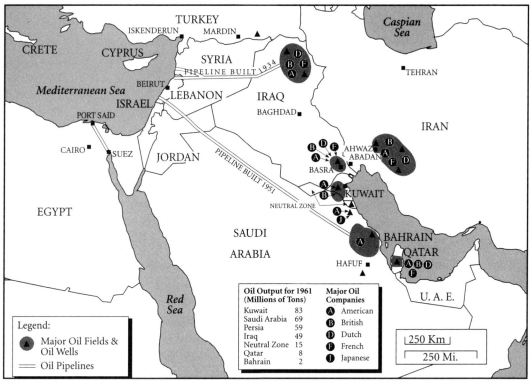

Oil in the Middle East—1961

From Martin, Gilbert, *Recent History Atlas* (London: Cox and Wyman, Ltd.), 1966.

The following appears within the map image:

TURKEY
ISKENDERUN   MARDIN
CRETE   CYPRUS
SYRIA
PIPELINE BUILT 1934
Mediterranean Sea
BEIRUT
LEBANON
ISRAEL
PORT SAID
CAIRO   SUEZ
JORDAN
PIPELINE BUILT 1951
EGYPT
NEUTRAL ZONE
KUWAIT
SAUDI
ARABIA
HAFUF
Red
Sea
Caspian Sea
TEHRAN
IRAQ
BAGHDAD
IRAN
AHWAZ
ABADAN
BASRA
BAHRAIN
QATAR
U. A. E.

Legend:
Major Oil Fields & Oil Wells
Oil Pipelines

Oil Output for 1961 (Millions of Tons)		Major Oil Companies	
Kuwait	83	Ⓐ	American
Saudi Arabia	69	Ⓑ	British
Persia	59	Ⓓ	Dutch
Iraq	49	Ⓕ	French
Neutral Zone	15	Ⓙ	Japanese
Qatar	8		
Bahrain	2		

250 Km
250 Mi.

has emerged from the sovereign prerogatives of the rich countries rather than from national responsibility toward each other.

The Western industrialized powers are dependent on having a regular, continuous, ongoing supply of oil without interruption at a price that is commensurate with Western industrial interests. In order to achieve that, the thrust of Western policy was to diminish the level of united Arab consciousness, so that the primary goal of the oil-producing countries would be to meet Western economic needs, rather than to meet the basic and fundamental needs of recovery and development of the poorer Arab nations.

Vertical relations developed among most of the Arab Gulf countries on the one hand and the Western world and the United States on the other, frequently at the expense of the horizontal relations among the Arab states. That weakened the Arab world and enabled the West to fashion a level of strategic dependency in many Arab states, so that the separateness between the Arab groups was further reinforced. This has been strongly emphasized in the aftermath of the Gulf War. Also, arms sales have kept up a high level of tension in the area.

The Arab countries did not use their oil wealth to build an overall Arab institutional infrastructure. Wherever there was some development in that respect it was to accommodate Western industrial interests and satisfy localized requirements.

Philippa Winkler: It seems that Iraq was one country that had nationalized its resources and built an infrastructure, regardless of Western industrial interests.

CM: In other countries too, the public sector in the seventies and the eighties was beginning to play a more dominant role through nationalization and through a mixed economy. This ensured that social welfare programs became part of the state ideology and state function. However the war between Iran and Iraq and the Gulf War partly destroyed this. Economies were put on a war footing and, in the aftermath, economic energy went towards reconstruction.

SB: How did the West react to the nationalization of oil resources in the eighties?

CM: I think many of the Western countries realized that nationalization was inevitable, or at least allowing a national government to have a controlling influence, even in Saudi Arabia.

Think what the oil corporations did to persuade governments to let them retain managerial influence, if not total control, instead of confronting the governments and, therefore, triggering a nationalist upsurge which would probably have led to the ultimate loss of influence of these oil companies.

But in each country, it was different. There are different levels of control, but basically, many of the Western companies realized that they could not sustain absolute and total control, so they made the necessary adjustments. Either they diffused the thrust of total nationalization through a new partnership, or they chose to confront—as they did in the Suez aggression in 1956, when the Suez Canal was nationalized.

Or as [the Western powers] did for different reasons in Iraq in 1991, when the invasion of Kuwait was seen as a threat to America's hegemony in the region, warranting military intervention. The Western powers determine what constitutes a threat to their vital interests.

THE CARTER DOCTRINE

PW: According to the social scientist Eqbal Ahmad, "Almost every post-World War II American president has had a doctrine on the Middle East, and has also seen his grand design challenged by Middle East nationalists—Mossadegh in Iran, Nasser in Egypt, Qassem in Iraq"[2] After the Soviet invasion of Afghanistan and the fall of Shah Mohammad Reza Pahlavi from power in Iran in 1979, President Carter in 1980 introduced the Carter Doctrine, which was meant to prevent the Soviet army from seizing the oil fields in Iran. What made it different from the Eisenhower and Nixon Doctrines and British or French policies towards the region?

CM: The U.S. assumed the geopolitical, quasi-imperial hegemony of both the British and the French after 1956 with the introduction of the Eisenhower Doctrine in 1957. The Carter Doctrine established that the rapid deployment force is to be used when the United States considers that one of its allies is threatened or the interests of the United States or its allies are threatened in the Gulf. The Carter Doctrine was the embryo of the strategic dependency that is now almost the prevailing condition. It led to the reflagging of the Kuwaiti ships, [when Kuwaiti ships were escorted by the U.S. Navy in the Gulf] during and after the Iran-Iraq War,[3] and to the formation of the Coalition in 1990. Although the U.S. became the vicarious representative of Western interests, the British and the French had certain differences with the U.S. For example, the French maintained that they had a special role in Lebanon, and the British had their historical ties with the Gulf countries and wanted to maintain a significant presence, yet both realized they had to defer to the United States as the superpower shielding their interests, and that they would be strategic partners instead of strategic competitors.

SB: How did the Carter Doctrine affect Arab policies towards the Gulf region?

CM: Some of the Gulf countries acquiesced to it, which gave it a modicum of regional approval.

The Arab League intended the regional powers to remain nonaligned, and so sought to coordinate their diverse reactions to the superpowers that were competing for influence in the Arab world. The superpowers impeded the growth of a nonaligned Arab national policy and prevented the Arab League from enforcing coordination among the Arab states. This was particularly evident in the aftermath of the Camp David agreement when the largest, single most important Arab country signed a unilateral peace treaty with Israel, resulting in the suspension of the Egyptian government from the Arab League.

PW: Which countries in the Arab world retained a policy of nonalignment, and which supported the Carter Doctrine?

CM: Syria, Iraq, the Palestinians, Yemen, South Yemen, Algeria, Libya and Sudan maintained a policy of nonalignment, as did to a much lesser extent Egypt, Kuwait (especially prior to the U.S. reflagging), the United Arab Emirates, and other states where there was an active political constituency and relative freedom of the press. They tried to avoid coming under total American hegemony. Saudi Arabia was technically a nonaligned country and protested the Carter Doctrine because it didn't want to lose its influence with the Arab countries that wanted to maintain a genuine nonaligned policy. Saudi Arabia had a very strong understanding and links with the United States because of the economic oil interests and the strategic relations. Some of the other Gulf countries were in agreement with the establishment of the rapid deployment forces.

PROPPING UP SADDAM HUSSEIN'S REGIME

SB: In the late eighties, Iraq launched its Anfal *campaign to depopulate the Kurdish countryside. In 1988, 5,000 are thought to have died in the chemical gas attack on the town of Halabja. Kurdish sources estimate that between 100,000 and 200,000 Kurds disappeared during the* Anfal *operation and there have been numerous reports of torture by Iraqi security forces.[4] Yet, from 1982 up until the invasion of Kuwait, the U.S. was loaning agricultural credits to Iraq, and Britain and other countries were providing technology and weapons. Why did the U.S. overlook Iraq's record of aggression and human rights violations?*

CM: Because during the eighties, human rights was not a consideration in the calculus of American foreign policy, and the United States had to decide who was more of a challenge to its geopolitical and economic interests, Iraq or Iran.

Because of the tremendous emotional outburst caused by the hostage taking and other aspects of the Iranian regime, it was considered in the U.S. that Iran was the more immediate danger.

The traditional allies of the United States—Kuwait, Saudi Arabia, all the Gulf countries—were supporting Iraq at that time. Iraq acted as a bulwark against Iranian geopolitical power projections in the area and against Iran's efforts to export its brand of revolutionary Islamic ideology.

There was not so much a Western commitment to Iraq, as a policy of letting both bleed each other into weakness. Weakened oil-producing countries suit Western industrial interests in the area.

PW: Why did the United Nations fail to condemn Iraq for the invasion of Iran in September 1980?

CM: The UN at that time considered this to be a dispute between Iraq and Iran, not an invasion, from a legal point of view, as did both Iran and Iraq. They maintained for the first four or five years of the war, that it was not a war but an armed dispute, and they maintained embassies, in their respective capitals, albeit at the lower level of *chargé d'affaires.*

SB: Did U.S. policy in the eighties lead Saddam Hussein to believe he would be permitted to invade Kuwait?

CM: I think that Saddam Hussein must have believed that U.S. permissiveness towards his war with Iran would apply to his other policies. He should have realized that Iraq was not considered a pivotal country underpinning American policy, while Saudi Arabia was. Hussein must have misread the nature of the growing dependency which was emerging between the Gulf states and the U.S., and misread the capability of the U.S. to mobilize troops in order to prevent such a takeover. He should have realized that the U.S. had reflagged Kuwaiti ships and considered Kuwait a strong ally, and that neither Iraq nor Yemen were invited to be part of the Gulf Cooperation Council (GCC) formed in 1981, which was conceived to accommodate the strategic shield that the U.S. provided for the Gulf countries. The members of the GCC are Saudi Arabia, Kuwait, Bahrain, Qatar, the United Arab Emirates and Oman.

SB: Was U.S. policy at all to blame for Saddam Hussein's misreading of the situation?

CM: The United States did not make its policy towards the region very clear during the Bush and Reagan Administrations, except in two ways, on the one hand, the tilt towards Iraq in its war against Iran, and on the other hand, treating Iraq as a recipient of assistance from Gulf countries that were the principal allies of the U.S.

INFLUENCE OF THE SOVIET UNION

SB: When did the Soviet Union begin to lose influence in the region, and what were the geopolitical impacts of that?

CM: The Soviet Union acted as if it were a potential countervailing force and, rather than trying to challenge American hegemony directly, tried to prevent the United States from establishing exclusive hegemony in the region. After Nasser's death and President Sadat's assumption of power, the Soviet Union's influence in the region was weakened, and yet it remained a major supplier of arms to Syria and Iraq. The special relationship that existed between the United States and Israel continued to be a pretext for the Soviet Union to supply the arsenals of some of the Arab states. Around 1986, 1987, Gorbachev began to redefine the Soviet Union's priorities. He pursued a more accommodating policy toward Israel, he attempted to persuade President Assad to be more accommodating toward Israel's relations with the U.S., and he attempted to downplay the confrontational aspects of the Arab-Israeli conflict. As a result, between 1987 and 1990 the Soviet Union's influence was waning along with its commitment to the Palestinians, in return for a growing level of approval from the Reagan and Bush Administrations.

PW: Hasn't the demise of the Soviet Union left the U.S. and its allies very powerful in the Middle East?

CM: Yes, in the UN there is no longer a countervailing force. In the period leading up to and during the Gulf War, the U.S. was able to dictate the agenda of the Security Council.

THE IRAQ-KUWAIT DISPUTE

PW: When the Iran-Iraq War ended, Iraq alleged that Kuwait and Saudi Arabia were keeping oil prices too low so that Iraq could not make a profit, and that Kuwait was overproducing oil, contrary to OPEC agreements. Also, Iraq owed a huge debt to Kuwait but was resentful that it had to pay the loan, on the grounds that the war with Iran had also served to protect Kuwait and the other Gulf States from Iranian expansionism. Can you comment on Iraq's grievances towards Kuwait?

CM: Iraq undoubtedly had certain legitimate grievances, but they did not warrant an invasion and an annexation of the sovereign state of Kuwait into a nineteenth province of Iraq, renaming the airport of Kuwait Saddam Airport, for example.

Iraq's demand for access to the Shatt Al Arab waterway and the Warba and Bubiyan Islands, even on a lease basis, and its demand for a share in the Rumalia oilfields, to which they were perhaps legally entitled, constituted elements of a dispute that should have been addressed by the proper Arab authorities, which should have been the Arab League.

WAS AN ARAB SOLUTION POSSIBLE?

PW: What examples do you have of the Arab League being able to intervene and broker negotiated solutions in the type of dispute that Iraq had with Kuwait?

CM: The Arab League has always been expected to deal with inter-Arab disputes, and there is a record of the Arab League successfully intervening to bring about inter-Arab solutions: between Iraq and Kuwait in the early sixties, to some extent successfully[5]; in 1972 between the two Yemens; in 1988 and 1989 the League was instrumental in preparing the ground for agreements inside Lebanon and allowed Syrian forces to be deployed to Lebanon as deterrent forces. That doesn't mean it has been successful at all times. But the case of the invasion of Kuwait was unusual. It was the first time that an invasion and annexation of one Arab state by another took place and the first time that the Arab League had to intervene in the aftermath of an invasion.

PW: General Norman Schwarzkopf records that when Kuwait was invaded, his first reaction was that "as long as the Iraqis went no further [than Kuwait], it seemed to me that the diplomatic community and the Arab nations would figure out a way to resolve the crisis peacefully."[6] Which Arab countries were actively trying to bring about a negotiated solution to the dispute between Kuwait and

Iraq, both prior to and after the invasion of Kuwait by Iraq? And why wasn't a negotiated solution possible?

CM: Prior to the annexation of Kuwait, Egypt and Saudi Arabia were trying to make inter-Arab arrangements that failed. The Kuwaitis were not as forthcoming as the Iraqis expected. Kuwait was determined not to forgive some of the loans, and even exhibited some provocative behavior. For example, at the Jiddah meeting arranged by King Fahd in July 1990, prior to the invasion, the Kuwaitis in a cavalier way announced they would give a very, very limited sum of money to forgive the debt and the attempt at conciliation broke down.

When the invasion took place, the Secretary-General of the Arab League, King Hussein of Jordan, and the leaders of Yemen, Algeria and the PLO were extremely involved in finding a formula which would both lead to an Iraqi withdrawal and address the legitimate claims that Iraq might have had for access to the Gulf and the Rumalia oil fields. There is evidence that King Hussein was given some assurance by Saddam Hussein that Iraq would withdraw from most of Kuwait to facilitate mediation efforts, conditional on the Arab League refraining from any outright condemnation of Iraq's invasion.

I think that the Arab League should have been much more persistent in attempting to bring about a political, legal, diplomatic and economic settlement. What happened was that the Arab League's foreign ministers condemned Iraq for the invasion, and Iraq insisted that the Arab League lift the condemnation as a condition preceding any kind of negotiation. I suggested at that time that an Arab League summit delegation of around five heads of state go to Baghdad to propose the withdrawal of Iraqi troops from Kuwait and the redeployment of the troops to the disputed islands and the Rumalia oil field, with Arab League observers, pending an adjudicated outcome of the disputed claims. In return, the summit would agree not to confirm the Arab League foreign ministers' condemnation of the invasion of Kuwait, so that the condemnation would no longer be on record. My suggestion was not acted on.

It was hoped that the Arab League summit scheduled for August 10 would bring about a solution to diffuse the crisis. Unfortunately, by August 10, Defense Secretary Dick Cheney had convinced the Saudis that they were Iraq's next target of aggression.[7] Exactly what happened at the August 10 meeting is not clear and needs to be further documented. Egypt, because of Camp David, was excessively deferential to American pressure. The Egyptian president, Hosni Mubarak, and the Saudis argued that the threat posed by Iraq to Saudi Arabia and the other Gulf states was too imminent to allow an Arab solution. The Americans persuaded Egypt that Arab League approval of American deployment in Saudi Arabia was necessary, and that was when the division within the League took place—it voted 12 to 9 to approve the deployment.

I think that the collectivity of the Arab League should have been much more persistent in at least attempting to bring about a political, legal, diplomatic, and economic settlement. Essentially, we were seeing the U.S. policy of strategic dependency come to fruition.

Now, whether the Arab solution would have succeeded or not, in view of the mindboggling intransigence of Saddam Hussein, remains a question that cannot be answered at this juncture. If he had not responded, and still insisted on rejecting the collective will of the Arabs in finding an Arab solution, then his policy would have been totally isolated without any appeal to the Arab population, and we would have avoided the breakdown of the Arab states' diplomatic system that we are experiencing today.

PW: Was there any real threat of an invasion of Saudi Arabia by Iraq, as the U.S. claimed?

CM: I don't think so, because Iraq did not have the strategic or military capacity to do so. Defense Secretary Cheney allegedly had the satellite pictures to show there were Iraqi troops mobilizing on the Saudi border. I would challenge that Iraq wanted to go into Saudi Arabia, but the way the annexation of Kuwait took place heightened the level of anxiety on the part of Saudi Arabia and other Gulf countries so that they were no longer willing to question the veracity of such claims.[8]

SB: Was there a risk of Iraq becoming the main economic and military power in the region through the control of both Iraqi and Kuwaiti oil? If so, what would have been the consequences for the Middle East?

CM: With the addition of Kuwaiti oil reserves, Iraq would have become a power equal to Saudi Arabia. From my perspective as an Arab nationalist, I am in favor of Arabs pooling their resources, as in the case of the unification of the two Yemens, but not as a consequence of an involuntary union, as in the case of the annexation of Kuwait.

PW: What did you think of the proposals that Iraq offered in the six months preceding the outbreak of war on January 16? For example, on August 12, Iraq offered to withdraw from Kuwait if Israel withdrew from the occupied territories and Syria from Lebanon; on August 23, Iraq offered to withdraw if sanctions were lifted and if it could remain in control of the Rumalia oilfields; on January 2, there was another offer to withdraw from Kuwait if the U.S. pledged not to attack as Iraqi soldiers pulled out, with no linkage to other regional issues.[9] Do you think these were good faith proposals?

CM: They were part of President Saddam Hussein's misreading of the overall international scene. After he polarized the situation by the annexation of Kuwait and declaring it a nineteenth province of Iraq, I think it became easier for some of the Gulf states as well as the U.S. to project these proposals as gimmicks, however well intentioned they might have been.

He started the collision course, and when the response was another collision course, that is, the formation of the Coalition and the deployment of U.S. troops in Saudi Arabia, there was no stopping the process of collision, except through the United Nations, and there were attempts through the UN. Each of Iraq's offers always came after the Coalition had assumed a progressively more hostile position. Also, Iraq's attempt at hostage taking consolidated Western opinion against him, so that Hussein's subsequent offers to be more malleable to mediation efforts came much too late.

Let me put it this way: you had two simultaneous developments—on one hand, Western public opinion which had assimilated the images of the hostage taking, the show towards the children, all these images, and on the other hand, in the Arab world, throughout the Third World in general, and the Muslim world in particular, there was the presence of the American forces in the area which began to raise all sorts of issues.[10]

The origins of the conflict were being submerged. On the one hand, the Western leaders and President Bush thought that this was an opportunity to consolidate American hegemony in the region. On the other hand, the situation gave many of the dissatisfied and disgruntled Arab masses the false hope that this was an opportunity to open a Pandora's box of issues that had been frustrating them for 50 years: Why were Security Council resolutions eagerly pursued and implemented when it came to Iraq, when other resolutions pertaining to southern Lebanon, the occupation of the Golan Heights and the rights of the Palestinians to self-determination, have not been pursued or implemented by the Security Council? If it wasn't for the oil, the U.S. would not have deployed half a million troops, which means that the U.S. and the oil rich countries are in an alliance that excludes the poor countries, the large majority of the Arab countries such as Sudan, Mauritania, and Egypt. This led to the question, why doesn't Arab oil belong to the Arabs? Why are profits from the oil invested abroad—shouldn't they be invested in ameliorating conditions in the Arab world?

This questioning wasn't support for Saddam Hussein. It was a reaction to the double standard that has been applied.

So every side considered the crisis to be an opportunity: the West wanting to consolidate hegemony in the region, Israel thinking that Iraq was an enemy state that could be weakened, the Arab population thinking—why not linkage to the Palestinian question? and why not dump the Western powers and their double standard?

For the record, I must note that Kuwait had a development fund which was the principal funding agency for many of the developing countries inside the Arab world. Kuwait is still bitter towards the Yemenis, Palestinians, Jordanians and others it had helped before the invasion, because their governments promoted a nonmilitary solution to the crisis. That bitterness feeds the division within the Arab world today.

THE REACTION OF THE WEST TO THE INVASION OF KUWAIT

PW: Do you think that sanctions would eventually have forced Iraq out of Kuwait?

CM: I think so, but I think the unilateral decision-making in Iraq, whatever might be the cause, means that the leadership is also insulated from options analysis. Hussein's policy makers, or those perceived to be his policy makers, gave him what he wanted to hear. So he provided ammunition to those who wanted to strike at Iraq. Here in the U.S., 48 senators were debating against the military option, as were retired military leaders such as Admiral William Crowe, who testified in Congress in favor of sanctions and against a military course of action.[11] Yet Hussein misread the debate in the U.S., thinking it was a license for him to continue to defy.

PW: It has been reported that the U.S. bought votes in the UN Security Council to ensure that the U.S. policy to use force as well as sanctions against Iraq would be implemented. Reportedly, China was promised its first post-Tiennamen Square meeting at the White House, and the U.S.S.R., Columbia and Zaire were promised aid packages.[12]

CM: There is no doubt that the U.S. used every means at its disposal, whether financial incentives or providing remuneration, in order to bring about this Coalition, or to prevent people from articulating their own policy judgements, whether China or the Soviet Union, or even France, in order to silence dissent and control the agenda at the UN in the Security Council.

PW: Can you elaborate on the specific motivations of the U.S. during the crisis?

CM: This crisis was an opportunity for the U.S. to assert its hegemony not only in but beyond the Gulf region. I think that President Bush believed that the potential economic hegemony of the U.S., a military-strategic, unipolar power, was being challenged by the rise of economic powers such as Germany, the European community, and Japan.

By asserting control over the Gulf countries, which sit atop major reserves of oil (and Germany and Japan and Europe are quite dependent on these reserves), America's ability to influence decision making in these countries would be strengthened. The U.S. would be in a position to determine how to channel the oil from these Gulf countries. This would prevent the emerging economic powers from challenging the superpower role of the U.S.

PW: Doesn't the U.S. also need petrodollars to keep its banking system stable? Wouldn't that be another reason why it might be important to maintain control over the oil-producing Gulf states?

CM: Yes.

SB: Of all the Western nations, the United Kingdom gave the most support to the U.S. Why?

CM: Thatcher, the British Prime Minister, pushed Bush to accelerate the pace of the mobilization of the Coalition. One reason was that the Gulf countries have always been in the past an extension of Britain's imperial power. Another reason was that public opinion in the U.K. was aroused by the execution of the Iranian-born British journalist from the *Observer*, Farzad Basoft, for allegedly spying on nuclear facilities in Iraq.

PW: Why were French and Soviet Union last-minute peace plans rejected by the United States?

CM: The United States realized that these were attempts by the French and the Soviet Union to distance themselves from the United States' Coalition. The French and the Soviet Union wanted to show that they could not be co-opted instantly by the U.S., and they also had a great deal invested in Iraq. Within their respective governments there were strong forces that did not want to break with Iraq. If their peace proposals had succeeded, they would have restored a sort of joint hegemony with the U.S. over the Gulf region. But they were overwhelmed by the U.S.' determination to pursue the military option.

SB: Why did the Soviet Union eventually join the Coalition?

CM: The Soviet Union failed to get Iraq to comply with its peace-making efforts, and joined the Coalition symbolically by withholding its support at the last minute from Iraq.[13]

SB: Why did France join the Coalition? How did the U.S., as you say, prevent France from articulating its position in the UN Security Council? Why did Germany and Japan join the Coalition?

CM: France has a strategic alliance with the United States, although it wants to maintain a modicum of independence. Membership in the Coalition became the criteria for enduring relations with countries in the West. The U.S. was keen to prevent the judgment of France from being articulated in the Security Council, so it created a roller-coaster atmosphere through diplomatic pressure, through the escalation of the deployment of troops. And some aspects of Iraqi behavior—the hostages, for example—facilitated the U.S.' task. Pressure became persuasion. France resisted at first but then ultimately joined the Coalition.[14] The same thing happened with Germany and Japan, which were under pressure from the United States, but showed their distance by supporting the Coalition financially rather than militarily.

ARAB PARTICIPATION IN THE COALITION

PW: Why do you think some of the Arab nations, such as Saudi Arabia, Syria and Egypt, went to war with Iraq?

CM: The Gulf countries were bound to go to war because of genuine anxiety on the one hand, and contrived, engineered paranoia on the other hand. Syria joined the Coalition because of its antagonism towards the Iraqi regime, and vice versa, and Egypt joined partly because it was prompted by the U.S. to play a role, and partly because of the anticipated economic benefits, although, according to one report I've seen, there has been a great deal of disappointment because Egypt did not get the economic rewards it expected for supporting the Coalition. Both Egypt and Syria, the Arab countries in the Coalition, sent troops but made it clear that they were doing so to help restore Kuwaiti sovereignty, and not to strike at Iraq. In fact, none of the Arab troops went into Iraq.

LEGAL QUESTIONS

PW: Can you comment on the legality of the UN's prosecution of the war against Iraq in 1991?

CM: I agree with Karen Parker's analysis. [See Chapter Eight, "International Legal Issues—Part Two."] Resolution 678—sanctioning the use of force against Iraq—was in compliance with Article 42 of the UN Charter, but, as she says, Articles 46 and 47 were intended to be in compliance with Article 42, and the implementation of Security Council Resolution 678 was out of compliance with Articles 46 and 47 of the UN Charter. [Resolution 678 is reprinted in Appendix One.] Javier Perez de Cuellar, who was Secretary-General of the UN at the time, has expressed concern about the way in which the Security Council did not guide, supervise or control the prosecution of the war. He has also warned that the veto power of the five permanent members was being used in a way that promoted an imbalance in the international community. Additionally, the destruction of the Iraqi civilian infrastructure was in violation with the intent of the Security Council, as Ms. Parker says. Currently, the UN community is wary of authorizing operations without having UN involvement in the operation itself, even in a symbolic way.

PW: What were the reactions of the Arab world to the destruction of Iraq's infrastructure?

CM: That the deserved punishment of Iraq was taken far beyond humane limits, with deliberate indifference to the fate of the Iraqi people. There has been acceptance of the humbling of Iraq's regime, but not of the humiliation of the Iraqi people.

THE ARAB LEAGUE AND THE GULF WAR

PW: What has happened to the Arab League since the split vote on August 10?

CM: With the Arab League failure in this challenge to shoulder its responsibilities under its Charter, the Arab League became marginalized as the anchor of the Arab states. It has proven ineffective in a major crisis. Most Arab states allowed their parochial loyalties to gain precedence over Arab national consciousness and collective responsibility.

PW: Since the war, what has been the policy of the Arab League?

CM: The Arab League has failed to attempt to bring relief to the Iraqi people suffering from the sanctions. Its total absence from the peace talks, its failure to respond instantly to the tragedy that has befallen Somalia, a member of the Arab League, and to bring about a relief effort before the Americans and the UN, all mean that the Arab League has become factionalized and marginalized.

PW: There have been other major crises in the Middle East. Why did this particular crisis have such a terrible impact on the Arab League?

CM: There have been two main crises in the history of the Arab League: the suspension of Egypt's government from the Arab League in 1979, when Egypt undertook a unilateral peace treaty with Israel, and the Iraqi invasion of Kuwait, which was the first time one Arab state openly invaded and annexed another country against the will of the government and people of that country. The Iraqi invasion of Kuwait was quite unlike the various disputes and conflicts that existed and still exist today among many Arab countries.

In the case of Egypt, it took more than 10 years to restore the Egyptian government into the Council of the Arab League. In the situation with Iraq, the Iraqi government was not suspended because there was not a unanimous resolution, as there was in the Egyptian case. However, the fact was that there was a war, sanctioned by some of the Arab states and prosecuted by other Arab states, against an Arab state. This caused the split in the Arab League. Currently, the Iraqi government is eager to get the Arab League functioning again, and so is Egypt, yet the Gulf countries are still distrustful of those Arab states that refrained from joining the Coalition. This is further complicated by the fact that Egypt and Syria have distanced themselves from the Coalition.

So subregional groupings have formed that pay lip service to the Arab League temporarily, which only further marginalizes it. This might be a blessing in disguise. It might lead to reform within the Arab League.

POSTWAR INTERVENTIONS IN IRAQ

The U.S. has intensified its interventionist approach in Iraq with the no-fly zones and the almost de facto partitioning of Iraq. Intervention for humanitarian reasons is growing in favor as a policy instrument, but, after the war, the U.S. was not only interventionist but intrusive.

For example, the Kurdish problem: the U.S. would have probably wanted to see some sort of partition of Iraq during the Bush Administration, but having a Kurdish autonomous state of Kurdistan in northern Iraq would have generated a geopolitical explosion in Turkey, which is a member of NATO, and in Iran and other places. Although I personally believe that the Kurds are entitled to self-determination, it cannot be confined to Iraq. It would have to involve citizens from other countries—ten to eleven million Kurds in Turkey, and around four million in Iran. That is why the intervention of the U.S. was tentative rather than all-out.

This, plus the fear of many Gulf countries, especially Saudi Arabia, of having an Iranian influence in Shiite southern Iraq, is why the whole system froze into the state we find ourselves in now.

PW: Can you comment here on the no-fly zones that the Coalition enforced in Iraq above the 36th and below the 32nd parallel?

CM: They are the French, British and U.S.' unilateral interpretation of Security Council Resolution 688, which contains no reference to implementation measures.[15] [Resolution 688 is reprinted in Appendix One.] Humanitarian assistance requires negotiation regarding access, corridors, with the government itself.

The fact that this undertaking is managed exclusively by Western powers strikes a raw nerve in the Arab psyche. It strengthens the view that what the West is really after is humiliation of the Arabs. Such anxieties on the part of Arabs might seem far-fetched to outsiders; nevertheless, they can be transformed into serious political forces.

SB: Do you think that, today, Saddam Hussein is a popular role model in some sections of the Arab population?

CM: No. I think he became reckless in the way he pressed some of his valid claims. Too much bloodshed in Iraq has tainted his regime, as was not the case with Nasser's Egypt, for example.

At least, Iraq under Saddam Hussein was perceived as organizing a modern sort of secular society, in contrast with Iranian theocracy. But the recklessness of the Iran-Iraq War (without going into that war's causal factors) and the invasion of Kuwait cancelled out much of the progress that had been achieved in the early seventies, which had previously given Iraq the appearance of a role model.

PW: A goal of the Bush Administration was to depose Saddam Hussein through a military coup. What would have been the reactions of the Iraqi people to such an eventuality?

CM: President Bush personalized the issue excessively. I think that the Clinton Administration's principal focus on the domestic agenda leads the Administration to remain involved, but to depersonalize the issue. And not to engage in personal vendettas and to be a bit more modest in projecting global power.

Although there will continue to be a constant policy on Iraq, it will be more subtle, and will focus on finding credible democratic forces in Iraq, rather than encouraging any kind of element which might not hit a responsive chord with the Iraqi body politic. If Saddam Hussein were removed by an American-engineered coup, there would be a rallying around him, even by people who oppose him. But like anywhere else, there is the possibility of a genuine opposition from within.

When President Bush lost the elections, there was relief in the Arab world, because even at the peak of antagonism against Saddam Hussein, Iraq is still a part of Arab consciousness. There is a great deal of sympathy in Egypt and Syria and even Saudi Arabia, for the people of Iraq who suffered during the war and continue to suffer. Grassroots organizations all over the Arab world, even in the U.S., are sending medicines, slipping goods in as much as they can, although the U.S. forced Jordan to close their borders with Iraq.

There was a gut feeling that people did not want Saddam Hussein to be removed while Bush was in power. But if Hussein is removed from power now, there won't be a great deal of sadness in the Arab world, as there was, for example, when Nasser died. I feel that Arabs at this moment are a people without a leadership anchor, and so their positions, aspirations, attitudes and rights are not being articulated. Islamic fundamentalists are trying to fill this void in the intellectual firmament.

When Bush lost the elections, there were two excessive reactions. You had excessive sadness among the Kuwaitis, and excessive jubilation in Baghdad, when Saddam Hussein started firing bullets at the sky. After all these illnesses come to the surface, a more rational discourse must be introduced. That is the present challenge.

PW: Can you elaborate on your view of the Clinton Administration's policy towards the Gulf?

CM: During the eighties, the U.S. still considered the Gulf to be a vital strategic necessity, a vital adjunct to its geopolitical interests. Now I think perhaps this is diminishing. During the Clinton Administration, although one cannot be sure, at least there are certain hints of a revised policy taking place, albeit in a very intermittent way. For example, the Clinton Administration's recognition of the Angolan government, abandoning Jonas Savimbi, is, I think, a very positive signal. This policy could later on be applied in other areas. The more authentic, rooted movements should be recognized rather than fought.

However, being involved in many new global issues, the Clinton Administration has not had enough time to revise U.S. policy towards Iraq. The Clinton Administration is maintaining the Bush Administration's policy towards Iraq. This is because Saddam Hussein's regime provides the U.S. with an opportunity to project power, when projecting power is necessary for domestic or foreign-policy reasons.

The June 26, 1993 missile attack on Baghdad, ostensibly as a retaliation against an alleged plot to assassinate former President Bush, undermined the credibility of the court in Kuwait, besides stretching the interpretation of Article 51 of the UN Charter to its breaking-point. The attack brought about strong opposition throughout the Arab world, and eroded the credibility of the United States among the Arab parties to the Middle East peace process.

SB: Why would the U.S. not want to continue to maintain its military foothold in Saudi Arabia? Doesn't it seem unlikely that the U.S. would want to abandon access to the superbases in Saudi Arabia, which were built with U.S. expertise in the eighties? [16]

CM: I think that the momentum continues in that direction, but there is also simultaneously a process of policy revision. I don't want to exaggerate what is taking place in the Angolan situation except to indicate that it constitutes a signal of a possible revisiting of the old strategic objectives of the United States.

PW: Iran recently made the point that the West was eager to pursue a military solution to protect Muslims in Kuwait, but not to protect Muslims in Bosnia-Herzegovina. What's your view?

CM: The Western powers want to protect the Muslims, but as a matter of humanitarian, not military, intervention, and they are debating the level of military force to be used in a humanitarian endeavor. There are no vital strategic interests in the region, according to the Clinton Administration. That is where the whole concept of global governance has to be redefined. In Somalia, because of the intolerable images we have seen, there was a humanitarian intervention, but it was easy to do, there was no controversy.

PW: Didn't the U.S. intervene in Somalia because of a possible future interest in its oil fields?

CM: No, I don't think so. The Somali and the Kampuchea interventions are good examples of global governance.

LESSONS FOR THE FUTURE

SB: Given the fact that Saudi Arabia and Iran are arming themselves to the hilt, do you see the need for a regional peace conference with or without Iraq?

CM: The arms sales in the region are due first of all to the one and only regional conflict, which is the Arab-Israeli conflict. The tensions between the Arab countries are manageable in the context of regional arrangements or UN mediation.

If the peace process succeeds in bringing a resolution of the Palestinian question based on their right to self-determination and if Israel withdraws from the occupied Arab territories, I think more than 50 percent of the need for arms would be eliminated. Israel's arsenal of nuclear weapons must be part of the regional disarmament process.

SB: Is there a possibility of healing the rift within the Arab world? Should there be a Gulf regional peace conference focused on the aftermath of the Gulf War? How do you bring the players back to the table and work for change based on Arab nationalism, and to solve the environmental, economic, and political problems that are the legacy of the war?

CM: First, the charter of the Arab League should be reinvigorated, since it is the only Arab national institution. The Arab League needs to amend its charter to make resolutions binding only if adopted by a two-thirds majority, and it needs to have at its disposal an early-warning monitoring system and an Arab rapid-deployment force attached to the office of its secretary-general. In addition, the Arab League needs to broaden the scope of its development funding so that it is used for the purpose of need-based and not politically-motivated aid.

Second, oil, the wealth of the Arabs, although geologically placed in certain areas, must be considered a national wealth, and the role of the development funds in the wealthier Arab nations should be enhanced. Millions of Arabs live in abject poverty in countries such as Sudan, Somalia, Egypt, Mauritania, etc. The more than one billion dollars in Arab wealth that went to the war effort against Iraq could have gone to alleviate their situation.

Thirdly, we need to restore the dialogue between secular nationalists and Islamic fundamentalists in the Arab world.

Fourth comes the development and growth of nongovernmental organizations (NGOs), especially those focusing on the environment, health and women's rights. Most NGOs in the region are still embryonic, but human rights organizations do exist in Tunis, Algeria, Morocco, Egypt and Yemen. These have tremendous potential as a political corrective, rather than as a direct political challenge, whenever they can shame regimes into full or partial compliance. Women's NGOs are very important, because, in many places in the region, there is an attempt to hide the marginalization of women under the cloak of religious rights.

In terms of the environment, the oil-producing countries are not eager to adopt the standards that the new Agenda 21 established at the Rio Summit, in June 1992, when Saudi Arabia in particular fought the new measures protecting the environment. (In Lebanon, the militias were paid to allow polluters to dump off Lebanese shores, which are now completely contaminated.)

Fifth, we must speed the process of democracy in the Arab world. We cannot afford unilateral decision-making, however charismatic the leader is.

Sixth, as developing countries, we cannot go through the stages of a loose economy. I advocate a mixed economy, that is, with a complementary role between private and public sectors. India during Nehru's period is a model for this. Democratic socialism remains the comprehensive, credible solution for the problems of developing countries, and would satisfy the general yearnings of the Arab masses for empowerment.

Public sectors in Egypt, Syria and in Iraq, and in other places, have been burdened with the dead weight of political bureaucratic mismanagement, and some bureaucracies have obstructed innovation. This has made it possible to challenge public sectors in the name of privatization and market economy. While this is the new fashion at the moment, I think the public sector will continue to be a necessity because it is important to have a viable economic development plan, while avoiding bureaucratic coercion and mismanagement.

At the same time, private capital should not remain unchecked, because that can lead to obliviousness towards social problems and a lack of training programs. We need an adaptable—not dogmatic—democratic, socialist approach. This includes a uniform educational program in which the needs of the Arab world are addressed by directing students into programs, especially technical training programs, where they can be most useful.

Seventh, Arabs must consider themselves as part of the global South, not adjunct to the Western world and not in confrontation with the North.

In terms of lessons to be learned by the international community, I would say that a new world order must not be based on a double standard or a North-centric order. The UN must play a role in correcting this fundamental bias. This task is facilitated by the fact that most of the world's regional organizations encompass the countries of the South: The League of Arab States, the Organization of African Unity, the Organization of American States, and the Association of Southeast Asian Nations. These regional organizations, in partnership with the United Nations, should be the building blocks of the new world order, but they must face up to their own shortcomings.

NOTES:

1. The exploitation of the Gulf's vast oil reserves began in the years leading up to World War I. The 1914-1918 war prompted the first extensive use of oil to fuel the newly developed submarines, battleships, blimps, tanks and airplanes. Since the Second World War, the development of oil resources in the region has been of vital importance to the development of the military and domestic economies of the world.

2. Eqbal Ahmad, "Introduction—Portent of a New Century" in *Beyond the Storm—A Gulf Crisis Reader* (New York: Olive Branch Press), 1991, 12.

3. "The reflagging operation in 1987-88, when the largest U.S. naval armada assembled since World War II operated in the Gulf region, provided experience in operation in the very special environment of the Gulf, with its space constraints in waterways and harsh climatic conditions. It facilitated an expanded accord with the Saudis for U.S. operations: as the Iran-Iraq War intensified and appeared to threaten tankers, Administration officials persuaded the Saudis to agree to the stationing of a KC10 aerial tanker to allow U.S. fighter-bombers to attack Iranian assets in the northern Gulf." Sheila Ryan, "Countdown for a Decade," in *Beyond the Storm—A Gulf Crisis Reader.*

4 See, for example, "Unearthing Past Abuses," in *Endless Torments: The 1991 Uprising in Iraq and its Aftermath*, Middle East Watch, New York, June 1992; and "Saddam's Killing Fields," *Frontline*, PBS-TV, June 21, 1993.

5. When Kuwait became independent from Britain in 1961, the Iraqi prime minister Abdul Karim Qassem announced his intention to incorporate Kuwait into Iraq, and the Kuwaiti ruler requested British troops for protection. After Qassem's assassination in 1963, the new Iraqi government recognized Kuwait's independence, partly in return for a large loan from the Kuwaitis. Another incident occurred soon after the conclusion of the 1972 Iraqi-Soviet Friendship Pact, for which Saddam Hussein, then secretary-general of the ruling Iraqi Baath party and vice-president of its Revolutionary Command Council, had some personal responsibility. In 1972 the Iraqis asked the Kuwaitis for a substantial loan, and were refused. At the outset of negotiations on a draft treaty sent to the Kuwaitis, proposing that Iraq build an oil terminal on Bubiyan island in partnership with the U.S.S.R., Iraqi troops massed on the Kuwaiti border. The Kuwaiti government rejected the draft treaty, and in March 1973 Iraqi tanks attacked two Kuwaiti borders posts. Saudi Arabia moved troops to the Kuwaiti border as a gesture of support, and the Arab League appealed to the two sides to seek an accommodation. Iraq offered to withdraw its claims to sovereignty over Kuwait in return for the cession of Warba and Bubiyan islands. In April 1973 the Iraqis withdrew from Kuwaiti territory and subsequently received a large loan from the Kuwaitis. J. B. Kelly, *Arabia, the Gulf and the West* (London: George Weidenfeld and Nicolson, Ltd.), 1980, 277, 282–4.

6. General H. Norman Schwarzkopf, *It Doesn't Take A Hero*, Bantam Books: New York, 1992, 302.

7. On August 6, Defense Secretary Cheney persuaded King Fahd and his advisors to allow U.S.-Saudi military cooperation against Hussein. On August 7, President Bush ordered thousands of troops in the Gulf. U.S. News & World Reports, *Triumph Without Victory: The History of the Persian Gulf War* (New York: Random House), 1992, 86-89.

8. The interpretation of the satellite pictures meant to depict a massing of Iraqi troops on the Saudi border may be questionable. See Jean Heller, "Public Doesn't Get Picture With Gulf Satellite Photos," reprinted from the *St. Petersburg Times*, in *In These Times*, February 27, 1991.

9. For a list of Iraq's proposals, as published in U.S. newspapers, see "Mismanagement of the Crisis" a chronology compiled by Marshall Windmiller, Professor of International Relations at San Francisco State University. An account of the diplomatic activity between

August 1990 and January 1991 on the question of Iraq's withdrawal from Kuwait appears in Pierre Salinger and Eric Laurent, *Secret Dossier: The Hidden Agenda Behind the Gulf War* (New York: Penguin Books Ltd.), 1991. See also Noam Chomsky, "After the Cold War," in *Beyond Desert Storm*.

10. To protest the deployment of U.S. and Coalition troops on Arabian soil, tens of thousands participated in street demonstrations in Arab countries including Tunisia, Algeria, Jordan, Morocco and Egypt, and also in countries with large Muslim populations: Indonesia, Bangladesh, Pakistan, India, and the Philippines.

11. The process of decision-making at the top, however, did not reflect the extent of the debate. Bob Woodward, in *The Commanders* (New York: Simon and Schuster, 1991), describes how President Bush's top advisors were mostly reluctant to present options different from the "force Iraq out of Kuwait" option favored early on by their boss. Public resistance in the U.S. to war as a policy option was significant, as evidenced by opinion polls and huge public demonstrations numbering up to 200,000 people each in New York, San Francisco and other major cities. In Europe, popular protest was equally fervent, and hundreds of thousands took to the street to register their disapproval. Although the Constitution of the United States requires the consent of Congress for offensive military operations, President Bush made it clear that he was prepared to go to war without congressional assent, and then forced the decision of Congress by using whatever tactics he could to achieve UN Security Council support for the war, prior to formal congressional debate. U.S. News, *Triumph Without Victory*, 414-5. There was no congressional debate until January 12. The Senate's vote granting Bush the authority to go to war was fairly close, 52-47, while the House vote was 250-183.

12. "A day after the UN vote [on November 29, authorizing military force against Iraq], Gulf states pledged a $6 billion in financial aid to the USSR in consideration for their support. In separate deals, Columbia, Ethiopia, and Zaire were offered new aid packages, access to World Bank credits or IMF loans in return for their vote. Yemen . . . held out against U.S. pressure and voted against the resolution . . . and within days, Yemen's $70 million in U.S. aid and vital financial aid from the Gulf states was terminated." Steve Niva, "The Battle is Joined," in *Beyond the Storm*, 64. When the Yemeni foreign minister voted no to Resolution 678, U.S. Secretary of State James Baker apparently wrote a note to the Yemeni ambassador—"That is the most expensive vote you have ever cast." U.S. News, *Triumph Without Victory*, 181.

13. The Soviet Union had traditional ties with Iraq, and a large Muslim population whose feelings had to be taken into account. As late as February 21, 1991, President Gorbachev of the Soviet Union attempted to arrange a Coalition cease-fire in return for unconditional Iraqi withdrawal. In a half-hour telephone conversation, Bush told Gorbachev that this offer was unacceptable, and that Iraq would have to withdraw prior to suing for peace. U.S. News, *Triumph Without Victory*, 279-80. Sources close to President Bush suggested that one reason Bush called the cease-fire as early as he did, leaving the strongest parts of the Iraqi army intact, was to protect Gorbachev. "In Moscow, Mikhail Gorbachev was under increasing pressure from Kremlin hard-liners as the war continued. Some advisers [to President Bush] worried that if all of central Baghdad were reduced to rubble, it might be enough of an excuse for Gorbachev's opponents in the military and the KGB to move against him. With no strong dissent from Schwarzkopf on the timing of the cease-fire, these aides said, the real reason for Bush's decision to quit early might have been to protect Gorbachev." U.S. News, *Triumph Without Victory*, 401.

14. At the time of the Iraqi invasion of Kuwait, the French defense minister was Paul-Jean Chevénement, a founding member of the French-Iraqi Friendship Society who had opposed France's Security Council vote authorizing the use of force against Iraq. He

resigned on January 29, 1991, and was replaced by Pierre Joxe, a vocal opponent of the Iraqi aggression. U.S. News, *Triumph Without Victory*, 314.

15. "The United Nations' legal department says it sees no language in existing UN resolutions that would give the United States, Britain and France authority to enforce the no-fly zones they have imposed on Iraq." "UN Lawyers Back Iraqi View—Attacks Not Authorized," *San Francisco Chronicle*, January 22, 1993.

16. Scott Armstrong's "Eye of the Storm," *Mother Jones*, November-December 1991, gives an account of this policy.

Operation Desert Storm

Background Information

U.S. air superiority proved decisive for the Coalition's victory over Iraq, something Saddam Hussein seems not to have anticipated.[1] Starting on January 16, an unrelenting air war took out military and civilian facilities all over Iraq, in an onslaught that lasted 43 days. The Coalition air campaign made an average 2,555 sorties a day. According to the U.S. Air Force, U.S. planes alone dropped 84,200 tons of bombs.[2]

U.S. technical superiority over the Iraqis was convincingly demonstrated. Within twenty-four hours of the start of the war, electricity to most large Iraqi cities had been cut off by "strategic bombing."[3] By the end of the war, only fifteen percent of Iraq's electricity-delivery grid remained functional.[4]

As he had threatened in December 1990, Saddam Hussein's first counter-attacks were against Israel, on January 18, 1991. Iraqi Scuds also attacked Saudi Arabia. Within a week of the start of the war, the oil slick anticipated by Sandia National Laboratories (see Chapter Two, "A Prewar Environmental Assessment") began to travel down the Gulf coast. On February 15, the outmatched Iraqi army began the process of setting fire to 700 oil wells. Coalition intelligence at this time indicated that Iraqi front line troops were likely to surrender in large numbers once a ground war began.[5]

The ground war did not begin until February 23, largely because the Coalition Commander in Chief, General H. Norman Schwarzkopf, was anxious to postpone it until sufficient damage had been done to the Iraqi army that Coalition casualties would be minimal. Iraqi defensive lines stretched south from Kuwait City along the coast, in case of a naval attack, and then followed the Kuwaiti-Saudi Arabian border towards Iraq. The Iraqis had mine fields backed up by artillery, oil-filled "fire ditches" that could be ignited by remotely detonated explosives, and anti-tank guns.[6]

To break the lines, the U.S. fired line charges of high explosives that detonated the mines. Most Iraqi soldiers ran away under heavy attack from the air. On February 24, M1 tanks with mine plows and engineer vehicles of the U.S. 1st Mechanized Infantry Division crossed the trenches at one point in the Iraqi desert, burying alive those Iraqi soldiers who had not fled.[7] Although it had been feared that the Iraqi army would use chemical weapons against Coalition soldiers, as they had against Iran and against Kurds, officials on both sides deny that this happened. (However, see Chapter Seven, "Nerve Gas Linked to Gulf War Syndrome.")

Superior U.S. weapons meant that Iraqis could usually be killed at a considerable distance, long before they were in a position to fire back. On the other hand, the difficulty of distinguishing friend from foe at a distance meant that there was a high rate of Coalition casualties from "friendly fire." Iraqi and Coalition unexploded ordnance was also a major cause of death.[8]

On the night of February 26, the Iraqis began retreating out of Kuwait towards Basra. According to the U.S. Air Force's own report:

> . . . They had every kind of vehicle imaginable: tanks, armored personnel carriers, school buses, trucks, delivery vans, ambulances and "confiscated" Mercedes, many stacked high with looted goods—televisions, radios, refrigerators, clothes, jewelry, computers, anything that caught their fancy. So dense was the road traffic that the individual radar "hits," which looked like little crosses superimposed on a map readout on the J-Stars moving target display, merged into thick lines, becoming themselves a roadmap of desperation. It was imperative that these forces not be allowed to retire so that they could regroup and threaten Coalition ground forces; air power had to intervene. The J-Stars called in the first air strikes, cutting the causeway. Then Strike Eagles began hitting the road congestion.
>
> Coming unseen out of the night, relying on their LANTIRN pods to turn night into day, flying under miserable weather, the F-15E crews hit these targets repeatedly with cluster bombs, precision-ground munitions, and general purpose bombs. Other strikers, including Navy and Marine aircraft, continued the attacks by day. They attacked into the morning of the 27th, first the Kuwait City-Basra road, and then other roads that had jammed up as well. When the jams became too great, many Iraqis simply fled away into the desert. To do otherwise, to stay with their vehicles, to fire back, was to risk certain death. Strike video showed this, and from the perspective of the aircraft: racing towards vehicles like predatory sharks, the Iraqis running away into the desert and relative safety, and then cannons, rocket, and bomb hits up and down the road, blowing vehicles in half, blasting them off the road, or melting them in their own fuel-fed conflagrations. Nothing could have more dramatically illustrated just how total air power's victory over the Iraqis had been than this example.[9]

By February 27, President Bush was under considerable pressure from the Saudis to conclude the war quickly. King Fahd was concerned that if Iraq was weakened further, the Shiite population of southern Iraq would be successful in setting up its own pro-Iranian state right on his border.[10] For whatever reason, the Bush Administration chose to call a cease-fire, on February 28, which allowed many Iraqi divisions to escape unscathed. Saddam had sacrificed large numbers of his conscript troops, largely Shiites and Kurds,[11] and his remaining army was able to put down Shiite uprisings in southern Iraq after the cease-fire. The terms of the cease-fire allowed the Iraqi army the use of helicopters, which aided them in putting down a Kurdish rebellion in the mountains of northern Iraq. Some in the U.S. military resented having to leave Saddam in command of the most powerful army in the region, when they had been in a position to inflict substantial damage on the Iraqi army.[12]

As a move to protect Saddam's rebellious citizens, the Coalition set up "no-fly zones" along the 32nd and 36th parallels, holding that this action was justified under UN Security Council Resolution 688. The Coalition also established a small "safe haven" for Kurds.[13]

A recent congressional staff report has said that Saddam Hussein's army has returned to eighty percent of its prewar military strength.[14]

—James Warner and Philippa Winkler

NOTES:

1. Most of the ground troops that fought for the U.S.-led Coalition against Iraq were provided by the U.S., the U.K., Saudi Arabia and Egypt. Other combat units came from France, Italy, Canada, Kuwait, Bahrain, Oman, Qatar, the United Arab Emirates, Syria, Morocco, Afghanistan, Bangladesh, Pakistan, Niger and Senegal. Facilities were provided by Saudi Arabia, Oman, Qatar and the United Arab Emirates. Air forces were provided by the U.S., the U.K., Saudi Arabia, France, Italy, Belgium, the Netherlands, Canada, New Zealand and Kuwait. Ships were provided by the U.S., the U.K., France, Italy, Canada, Belgium, the Netherlands, Portugal, Spain, Greece, Australia and Argentina. Bulgaria, Czechoslovakia and New Zealand provided medical units, and Hungary, Romania and Czechoslovakia provided chemical warfare experts. Germany and Japan provided funds. Turkey was not officially part of the Coalition, but provided it with support. Frank Chadwick, *Desert Shield Fact Book* (Bloomington, Illinois: Game Designer's Workshop), 1991; Harry G. Summers, *On Strategy II: A Critical Analysis of the Gulf War* (New York: Deal Publishers), 1992; Dilip Hiro, *Desert Storm to Desert Shield: The Second Gulf War* (London: Routledge, Chapman and Hall, Inc.), 1992.

2. U.S. Air Force, *Reaching Globally, Reaching Powerfully: The United States Air Force in the Gulf War*, Report, Washington DC, September 1991, 29-31. The report concludes that "the Gulf War was not, as some alleged, an exercise in massive bombing unparalleled in recent war history," after comparing the average per month tonnage of Air Force bombs dropped in the Gulf War with the average per month of combined Air Force and Army Air Force bomb tonnage dropped in other wars. The comparison did not include the tonnage dropped by the Army Air Force in the Gulf War and presumably also excluded the Navy planes' tonnage. (It is not clear whether the term "American airmen" in the report includes those flying Army and Navy planes.) If the authors of the Air Force report had cited their own estimate of 84,200 tons dropped by "American airmen" in the Gulf conflict and compared that figure with their estimates from previous wars, they would have had to conclude that the per month tonnage of bombs dropped in the Gulf conflict was the largest for any war to date: 47,777.78 (World War II, 45 months), 12,270.27 (Korea, 37 months), 44,014.29 (Vietnam/Southeast Asia, 140 months), and 56,133.32 (Gulf War, 1.5 months). The total tonnage of explosive ordnance dropped on Iraq may have been far higher—the Concord Naval Weapons Station in California reported shipping 80,000 tons of explosive ordnance, which "amounted to 30 percent of all the ammunition, bombs and missiles expended by U.S. and Coalition forces in the war," which gives a total of around 240,000 tons of ammunition. "Naval Weapons Station Concord Named Top Bay Area Military Installation," Press Release issued by Naval Weapons Station, Concord, California, May 28, 1991.

3. U.S. News & World Reports, *Triumph Without Victory: The History of the Persian Gulf War* (New York: Random House, Inc.), 1992, 274. General Merrill A. McPeak stated that only 7,400 tons of the bombs dropped on Iraq were precision-guided or "smart" bombs. General Merrill A. McPeak. Chief of Staff of U.S. Air Force, Briefing, March 15, 1991, Transcript, 6, quoted in Human Rights Watch, *Needless Deaths in the Gulf War: Civilian Casualties During the Air Campaign and Violations of the Laws of War; A Middle East Watch Report*, New York, Human Rights Watch, November 1991. There has not been an official estimate of the total amount of expended Coalition munitions.

4. U.S. News, *Triumph Without Victory*, 410.

5. General H. Norman Schwarzkopf, *It Doesn't Take A Hero* (New York: Bantam Books), 1992, 377.

6. U.S. News, *Triumph Without Victory*, 290.

7. U.S. News, *Triumph Without Victory*, 312.

8. U.S. News, *Triumph Without Victory*, 373.

9. U.S. Air Force, *Reaching Globally, Reaching Powerfully: The United States Air Force in the Gulf War*, Report, Washington DC, September 1991, 50–51.

10. U.S. News, *Triumph Without Victory*, 395.

11. Ahmed Hashim, a Washington-based expert on the Iraqi army, has argued that about 70 percent of Saddam Hussein's front line army were Shiites, and 20 percent Kurds. He called these forces Saddam's "throwaway divisions." U.S. News, *Triumph Without Victory*, 404.

12. U.S. News, *Triumph Without Victory*, 400.

13. See Chapter Six, "The Iraqi Kurds."

14. "Iraq Rebuilt Eighty Percent Of Prewar Arms-Making," *Reuters*, June 29, 1993.

The Oil Spills

The destruction of pipelines at the Mina Al Ahmadi oil refinery by the Iraqi occupation forces. UN Photo 158158. Courtesy of the United Nations.

Introduction

Chapter Two focuses on the effects on the marine environment of oil released from tankers and oil terminals because of the war.[1]

Prior to the Gulf War, the U.S. government carried out a secret environmental assessment of the probable effects of the demolition of hundreds of Kuwaiti wellheads. Among their predictions were, "Oil 77 times the amount of the Exxon *Valdez* spill, discharged from tankers, pipelines or on-stage storage tanks into the Gulf, will cause major damage to the marine economy, to the fishing industry, and to desalination facilities in four countries."[2] The Sandia National Laboratories report is excerpted at the start of the chapter.

During the war the Iraqis dynamited Sea Island Terminal and five tankers and released oil at three oil ports, Mina Al Ahmadi, Abu Halifa, and Shuaiba. The Coalition was probably responsible for spilling about 1,600,000 barrels, as a result of bomb attacks on the Iraqi tanker *Al Mutanabbi* and on Mina Al Bakr, Iraq's offshore loading terminal.[3]

Saudi estimates put the total spill at a maximum of 8,000,000 barrels,[4] around 30 times the volume of the Exxon *Valdez* spill. By all accounts, this was the largest marine oil spill in history. A major exacerbating factor was fallout from the oil fires, which added to the marine spill a quantity of oil about equal to that from the other sources combined.[5]

After the cease-fire, when satellite data were no longer classified, researchers used Landsat satellite pictures and computer-controlled side-looking radar to find that around 600 kilometers of Saudi coastline were severely affected—the bulk of the oil had continued south along the shoreline until March 1991, when it was blocked by the Abu Ali/Ad Dafi Bay/Musallamiyah complex. The oiled stretch of coastline received little or no protection, because all available resources had been gathered south of Abu Ali in order to protect the desalination plants at Al Jubail and Al Khobar.[6]

With help from the International Maritime Organization (IMO), the Saudis recovered a record one-and-a-half million barrels of floating oil from the affected coastline. Converted oil tankers collected oil out in the Gulf, while cleanup crews using booms corralled some of the oil into natural catchments, and shoveled the oil/sand mixture that washed up on the beaches into pits.[7] According to one source, cleanup crews sunk another several million barrels of oil by spraying them with a coagulant.[8] The over $6 million donated to the IMO for the cleanup amounted to only a third of one percent of the Exxon *Valdez* cleanup costs.[9] The U.S. was not among the 12 nations which contributed money to the IMO.[10]

The unusual width of the intertidal zone exacerbated the damage caused by the spill. In many areas, the spring high tides can pull Gulf waters two or more kilometers inland from the normal high tide line. Here oil remains trapped in the sediment, unreachable by the air and bacteria that might otherwise enable it to biodegrade. The U.S. National Oceanic and Atmospheric Administration (NOAA) *Mount Mitchell* research ship expedition which visited the Gulf in 1992 estimated that a total of 1,500,000 to 2,500,000 barrels dispersed in estuaries, tidal salt flats, marshes and beaches,

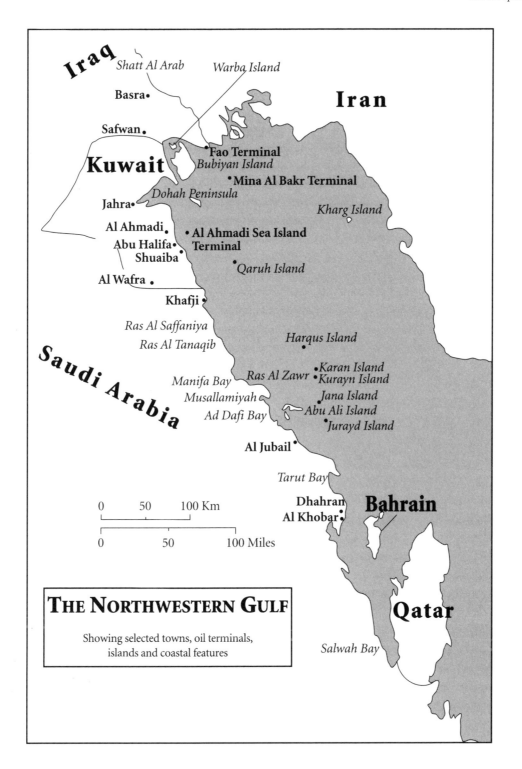

THE NORTHWESTERN GULF

Showing selected towns, oil terminals,
islands and coastal features

some of which are "paved" with a tarmac-like substance from this and previous spills.[11]

Chapter Two contains first-hand accounts of the impacts of the spills. Burr Heneman, author of the initial International Council of Bird Preservation report[12] on the spill, describes the scene in March 1991. Mike Evans talks about the impacts on birds and James Perran Ross discusses the effects on sea turtles. Finally, Sylvia Earle describes what she saw on recent trips to the Gulf. In 1992, NOAA and several UN agencies organized a research ship expedition to the Gulf. The 100-day cruise of the *Mount Mitchell* provided baseline scientific data for the Gulf region and field observations of the oil still remaining from the spill. The *Mount Mitchell* expedition workshop met in Kuwait on January 24–28, 1993 to discuss the findings of the cruise in January 1993, and another conference is set to meet under the auspices of ROPME (Regional Organization for the Protection of the Marine Environment) in November 1993. The hidden casualties of the spills are only beginning to emerge.

—Philippa Winkler and James Warner

NOTES:

1. Burr Heneman and Sylvia Earle in their interviews also refer to the oil lakes in the desert. These lakes were formed by unburnt oil from the oil wells set on fire during the war, which gushed forth in quantities exceeding by two orders of magnitude the amount of oil released into the sea. The oil lakes are discussed both in this chapter and in Chapter Four.

2. Sandia National Laboratories, *Potential Impacts of Iraqi Use of Oil As a Defensive Weapon*, Report, Albuquerque, 1991.

3. T.M. Hawley, *Against the Fires of Hell: The Environmental Disaster of the Gulf War* (Orlando: Harcourt Brace Jovanovich), 1992, 47.

4. Saudi Arabian Meteorology and Environmental Protection Administration, *National Report on Oil and Air Pollution*, Jiddah, 1991.

5. U.S. National Oceanic and Atmospheric Administration, Mount Mitchell *Expedition to the ROPME Sea Area February-June, 1992*, Report, Intergovernmental Oceanographic Commission of United Nations Educational Scientific and Cultural Organization, Paris, January 1993.

6. T.M. Hawley, *Against the Fires of Hell*, 55–70.

7. Greenpeace International, *The Environmental Legacy of the Gulf War*, Report, Amsterdam, February 1992.

8. Adam Trombly, *Interim Environmental Damage Assessment Report for the Persian Gulf Region*, Aspen Institute for Advanced Studies, July 1991.

9. T.M. Hawley, *Against the Fires of Hell*, 64.

10. Greenpeace International, *The Environmental Legacy of the Gulf War*.

11. NOAA, Mount Mitchell *Expedition*. See also interview with Sylvia Earle, this chapter.

12. Burr Heneman, *The Gulf War Oil Spills: The ICBP Survey of the Saudi Arabian Gulf Coast, March, 1991*, Report (to International Council for Bird Preservation and the Saudi Arabian National Commission on Wildlife Conservation and Development), Bolinas, California, 1991.

A Prewar Environmental Assessment

Sandia National Laboratories

Prior to the Gulf War, the Bush Administration commissioned its own secret environmental assessment of the likely damage caused by a 20-million-barrel oil spill in the Gulf—a spill over 77 times larger than that of the Exxon Valdez. In January 1991, this report was prepared by the Sandia National Laboratories for restricted distribution for the United States Department of Energy under Contract DE-AC04-76DPOO789, Office of Foreign Intelligence. The sections of the report excerpted here show that that the U.S., and probably its main Coalition partners, had a very good idea of the possible ecological and health impacts of Operation Desert Storm.

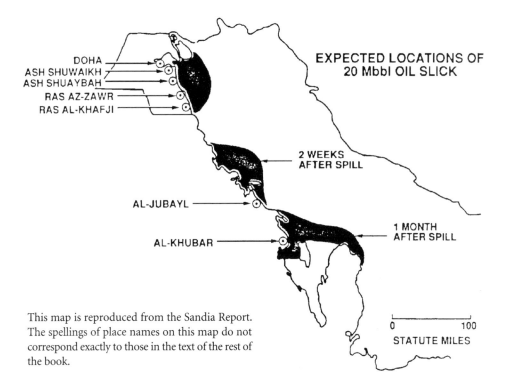

This map is reproduced from the Sandia Report. The spellings of place names on this map do not correspond exactly to those in the text of the rest of the book.

ECOSTRESSES

Oil releases from damaged Kuwaiti oil fields, tank farms, and offshore tankers can potentially disrupt both terrestrial and marine ecology. Unburned oil flowing over and pooling on the ground will have toxic effects on native desert vegetation near the oil fields. It can pollute nearby shallow freshwater aquifers important to Kuwait's agriculture (which is quite limited) and the hydrogen sulfide release can have toxic effects on people and animals near oil fields. If the oil is burning, it can affect vegetation, humans, and animals because of sulfur dioxide (SO_2), carbon dioxide (CO_2), soot, and heavy metals in the combustion products. Unburned oil released near the coast can damage salt marshes, the marine ecology, and desalination plants.

MARINE EFFECTS

Based on information we have received, a 20-million-barrel crude oil spill into the Persian Gulf is possible near Kuwait's coast. Ten million barrels could be released in the first 24 hours, followed by another 10 million in the next 36 hours. The potential source is a combination of pipelines, tankers and on-shore storage tanks near the Kuwaiti coast. The magnitude of this potential oil spill is 77 times that of the Exxon *Valdez*. Such an oil spill could disrupt the important fishing industry in the Gulf, shut down water desalination plants in Kuwait, Saudi Arabia, Bahrain, and Qatar that supply a large share of the area's water, and cause long-term damage to the Gulf's ecology.

The Nowruz spill, tied for the world's largest, put four million barrels of oil into the Persian Gulf over several months in 1983. We have been unable in the short term of this project to obtain accounts of scientifically determined quantitative effects from this spill, but news articles reported a paralyzed shrimp industry and suspended operation of two Saudi desalination plants. Damage from this spill was probably minimized because it was in the northeastern part of the Gulf and a combination of northwesterly wind and currents carried the oil down the Iranian coast away from the Saudi coast.

We estimate that a 20-million-barrel spill off Kuwait can spread to cover an area about 90 kilometers wide and will probably travel south along the Saudi coast due to natural Gulf circulation patterns. It will probably interfere with the operation of several desalination plants along the coasts of Kuwait, Saudi Arabia, Bahrain, and Qatar. These areas are dependent on desalinated water.

An oil spill in the Persian Gulf will have relatively serious effects on marine life because the Gulf is small and shallow, has slow circulation, and is very biologically productive. The Arabian Sea, which includes the Gulf, is the area with the highest marine life productivity in the world. Much of the oil will degrade by biodegradation or photochemical reactions relatively quickly (over a few days) because of warm temperatures. Oil sediments, on the other hand, will persist for a long time and will enter the food chain through species such as shrimp, which feed on the Gulf bottom. Thus, there is the potential for long-term fishing industry disruption as well as general ecological disruption.

Consideration should be given to igniting the oil spill. Burning the oil, even at the cost of creating more atmospheric pollutants, is probably better for the marine ecology and desalination plants than not burning it because burning helps to remove the most volatile oil compounds that are the most soluble in water and hence the most toxic. Dispersants, while effective in deep water, cannot be used in the shallows of the Gulf or over reefs because they are more toxic than the oil.

TERRESTRIAL EFFECTS

Oil discharged across the desert's surface will kill vegetation by smothering and poisoning. The destruction will be limited to areas immediately around the oil fields. Some recovery is expected over time because seeds will survive the oil and germinate when conditions are favorable. In most places, the oil will not penetrate to deep aquifers because of hardpan [layers of water-impervious soil]; however, shallow coastal wells fed by percolating rainwater could be polluted by releases from the Burgan oil field or coastal storage tanks. The huge groundwater field at Rawdatain has a nearby shallow, freshwater aquifer at a depth of 30 to 60 feet, which is partially recharged annually by rainfall and which could become polluted by oil flow from the northern oil field. Also, large areas of beach sand marshes southeast of the Burgan oil fields would be destroyed by an oil covering.

[Despite this foreknowledge of the possible impacts, the Coalition itself bombed Iraqi oil refineries and an oil tanker, causing some 1,600,000 barrels of oil to enter the Gulf. Press briefings by the government of Saudi Arabia say that a total of 8,000,000 barrels eventually oiled Gulf waters off the Saudi Arabian coast.]

Possible Impacts of the Mina Al Ahmadi Spill

Boyce Thorne-Miller

From Information Sheet on the Persian Gulf Environment, *by Boyce Thorne-Miller. Ms. Thorne-Miller was a senior scientist at Friends of the Earth when she wrote a description, excerpted here, of the ecology and marine life of the Gulf, while the Gulf War was in progress (see also Chapter One, "Value of the Persian Gulf Marine Environment").*

1983 NOWRUZ OIL SPILL

We do not have much information on the effects of chronic oil pollution or how many species have been eliminated by its presence. Nor do we know to what extent the animals that persist in this environment are unusually tolerant to chronic low-level hydrocarbon pollution. We do have some information about the effects of some of the larger oil spills, such as the Nowruz spill in 1983, which killed marine mammals (porpoises and dugongs), sea turtles, sea birds, sea snakes and fish. The oil spill continued for several months, beginning at the end of January. Especially during the hot summer, the highly toxic volatile portion of the oil evaporated rapidly, leaving behind the heavier component, which drifted and sank in large mats and tar balls and worked its way into sediments.

1991 MINA AL AHMADI SPILL

Add to the normally stressful conditions an oil spill of as great a magnitude as the spill at the Mina Al Ahmadi oil port and you have a formula for disaster—whole communities of species could collapse. Besides the immediate asphyxiation and oiling of numerous animals, the system will be harmed by dissolved hydrocarbons that are deadly to sensitive larval stages in the water this time of year and by the solid phase that settles and is mixed into the bottom sediments where it can retard the re-establishment of healthy communities for years. The victims of this and possible other spills will be a diversity of species and ecosystems (coral reefs, seagrass beds, mud flats and open water communities) that are amazing in their ability to thrive under such seemingly adverse conditions. How rapidly they can recover is difficult to say. Some species may recover within a year or two, other species and ecosystems may be affected for years to come.

The species fished by the countries surrounding the Gulf may suffer great losses, particularly among juvenile and larval populations, which will affect the catches for the next year to several years. Local fisheries, while not dominating the economies of these countries (what could compete with oil?), do provide a significant source of local food and a surplus for the export market. This is the only renewable resource these people have, and, prior to oil, the finfish, shellfish and pearl fisheries formed the basis of the regional economy.

Air-breathing sea life is particularly vulnerable to the evaporating toxins, pelagic and planktonic life is vulnerable to dissolved hydrocarbons, and benthic life is vulnerable to any toxic materials ending up in the sediments. The relative toxicity of these three components decreases from the volatile to the dissolved to the solid phases. The damage caused by past oil spills to less obvious submerged and planktonic plants and animals has not been documented, but larval stages are known to be especially susceptible to the toxic effects of dissolved hydrocarbons.

Furthermore, the quality of the fish or shellfish would become questionable due to added loads of hydrocarbons in the tissue.

A gigantic oil spill such as the current Mina Al Ahmadi spill, occurring during late winter, can be expected to take a toll on both adult and larval stages of important fishery species, which could affect the catch for several years. Oil spills are also lethal to intertidal areas such as the broad mud flats. The small invertebrates in the muds die or become contaminated with oil, and the wading birds feeding there ingest these contaminated animals so that they in turn die or become ill. Coral reefs exposed at very low tides would be smothered by oil left behind by the receding water.

In shallow areas of restricted exchange with ocean waters the effects of an oil spill may be more extensive and longer lasting, at least from the perspective of those measuring the effects. The Gulf is shallow and well mixed, so much of the oil is mixed and dissolved into the water column, and some of it is finally mixed down into the sediments where it can reside for years, inhibiting growth of benthic organisms. The extensive seagrass beds are particularly vulnerable, as they serve to trap the oil. Much is made of the fact that the highly toxic volatile fraction evaporates rapidly, especially in warm waters. However, the Gulf waters are not very warm in the winter (50°–55° F) and the dynamic mixing processes will maximize the dissolution of hydrocarbons. Thus, while a large portion does evaporate (killing many air-breathers as it does so), the damage that can be caused by the remaining dissolved and solid material should not be underestimated.

In addition, organisms contaminated by hydrocarbons (ingested or absorbed) often become less resistant to other environmental stresses. Since this is an environment of extremes and many of the species are functioning very close to their tolerance limits, the effect of the oil contamination in reducing their physiological tolerance to their natural environment could be devastating. If communities collapse from the added stress, it is not known how long it would take for them to become re-established with their same level of diversity—a year? a decade? several decades?

General Observations

Interview with Burr Heneman

Burr Heneman, environmental consultant, visited Saudi Arabia for the International Council for Bird Preservation (ICBP), February–March, 1991 and returned on a visit for Friends of the Earth, in late May–June 1991. Both trips were for fact-finding and to advise the Saudi Arabian National Commission on Wildlife Conservation and Development (NCWCD). Interviewed by John M. Miller May 1991 and July 1991. Interview revised and updated by Burr Heneman February 1993.

John M. Miller: Why don't we start with the spills?

Burr Heneman: Let's start with the size. In their briefings to the press in May–June 1991, the official MEPA (Saudi Arabian Meteorological and Environmental Protection Agency) numbers were six to eight million barrels. NOAA used those numbers in their press releases. The people in the U.S. Coast Guard acquiesced to that estimate. It is not at all clear where those numbers came from. I really don't think anybody has a very good idea.

I think to get the six-to-eight million barrel total, they were including the estimate on continuing spills. When I left in mid-March, NOAA talked about tens of barrels a day in continuing spills from the various sources. Not long after that, a new NOAA guy got there, and suddenly there was talk about 1,500 to 6,000 barrels a day. The most commonly quoted figure was 3,000 barrels a day in continuing spills.

JMM: Where were these estimates coming from?

BH: From various sources in either the Mina Al Bakr Iraqi offshore terminal or Kuwait. Those numbers have bounced around quite erratically. In June I was able to fly over all the sources of oil and see them firsthand. Some of those estimates were clearly just fantasy land: I know from talking to Coast Guard pilots who flew the flights that they were based on SLAR (Side Looking Aerial Radar). SLAR can't distinguish between sheen and thick oil.

Oil Lakes

So some of these estimates were based on that SLAR. Then they would go up there the next day and wouldn't see anything. The puzzling thing to me was how it could go on day after day at 1,500 to 6,000 barrels a day of spills, and nothing came down the coast. Clearly there was something wrong with those estimates. And in fact, they never did find any significant quantities of new oil anywhere in the northern Gulf. So the estimates on the size of the spills is probably quite unreliable. What's clear is that they added up to a very large spill—millions of barrels—and very likely the largest spill from any source ever.

In terms of threats from other sources in Kuwait—I wasn't on the ground in Kuwait; in June I was on a low-level flight that covered all of the areas with burning wells and oil lakes—but talking to the other members of our group, one of the things we were concerned about were the oil lakes we were hearing about, some of which were estimated to be quite large and quite deep, and whether these had a chance of making it to the Gulf. We were able to get some information about the ones in the Burgan field, and we felt those weren't a threat to the Gulf. One that we are concerned about is up on the northern field that's west of Bubiyan Island.

There's Bubiyan Island's narrow waterway, which we flew over, and on the landward side we didn't see any evidence of oil lakes. But we talked to people who were concerned that if there were oil lakes in that field, oil might make its way through old water courses, wadis, down into the narrow waterway between Bubiyan Island and the mainland. We didn't see any evidence of that.

Subsequently we learned what a terrible toll the oil lakes have taken in bird life. Swallows and ducks and these incredibly beautiful birds called bee eaters were hard hit. On migration, they mistook the lake for water and tried to drink from them, or landed in them. The dead and dying birds trapped in the oil attracted large numbers of migratory hawks that would try to scavenge them and become oiled in turn. For many migratory birds, we don't know what percentage of the world population use that flyway. Unfortunately, there is no way to assess this problem accurately because of the size of the lakes, their inaccessibility, the length of time that they were attracting birds, and the fact that most of the evidence—the dead birds—disappeared in the oil.

Catching Oil

JMM: What have the spills done? What did you observe?

BH: In March, we covered pretty much the whole coast or at least sizeable samples of it from just below Khafji to well below Dhahran. And we got to five of the offshore islands: Jurayd, Jana, Kurayn, Karan and Harqus. Along the mainland coast, we spent most of our time along the oiled section from Abu Ali north. Abu Ali used to be an island, but is now one of their big fill projects; it is connected to the mainland by a huge causeway.

JMM: Is that the peninsula where the oil is caught?

BH: Yes, that peninsula and the bay behind it, Ad Dafi Bay, is where the oil has been mostly caught. There was a little bit of oil—the best I could find out from all my sources: sheen, tar balls, some little patches of mousse— that has gone on south as far as Bahrain and Qatar, but I did not hear of any more than that getting past Abu Ali and the islands.

Having flown quite a bit over the Gulf in that area, I would say there wasn't a lot of oil to go south offshore. It was essentially sheen. And that was the same thing that the NOAA and MEPA people were finding as well, and what their maps showed at daily NOAA briefings in Saudi Arabia.

JMM: Sheen would be fresher oil?

BH: You get sheen for a long, long time. You are still getting sheen on Prince William Sound, two years later. That can happen for a quite a while. Sheen is molecules thick.

The mousse (a mixture of water and somewhat weathered oil) was quite scattered. I saw patches offshore. The stuff that would be out beyond Abu Ali was from half a meter up to some two meters in diameter. Those patches would be a couple of hundred meters apart on average. There may have been some areas where there were more, because we didn't cover every area. But the pilots that were flying to look for it weren't seeing it distributed any more densely than that offshore. Since I left, some larger amount may have gotten around Abu Ali, in one incident, but apparently not a huge amount. There is some oil south, and I know shorebirds are getting into it.

The oiled section of the coast is less used by shorebirds than the unoiled or very, very lightly oiled section. South of Abu Ali at Tarut Bay, the Gulf of Bahrain, Salwah Bay would be where the biggest concentrations of shorebirds are. The same for dugongs and sea turtles. All of these areas of superior habitat were spared.

When we got there in early March, the oiled coast up near Khafji was remarkably clean. The big beach south of Khafji that goes on for miles is the same area that we were seeing on TV at the beginning of the spill with the waves of oil coming in. And this was all exposed sand beach, relatively steep by local standards, and therefore with a narrow intertidal zone. It is clear that what had happened is that there was a lot of natural cleaning going on. The wind, waves and tides are refloating the oil and the wind is pushing it offshore and along shore, moving it south.

This had been going on for five weeks when we got there. That northern part of the coast nearly as far south as Ras Al Saffaniya (Saffaniya Point) was pretty much clean. South of there, especially from Ras Al Tanaqib, the oil was really heavy when we were there. Also south of there is where you get more protected coast, the coast gets more complicated. There are more bays and deeper bays, with more protected waters that wind and waves don't clear. The oil just sits there coating the shore. And the slope of the coast is very gentle, which means the intertidal zone can be a half-mile or more wide. And many of those expanses are still under a heavy coat of oil.

JMM: Places where the oil can get caught?

BH: Once it gets in, you are not going to get it out, although even in some of those areas we saw natural cleaning action like at Manifa Bay, which is a small bay that was completely full of oil the first time I saw it, and is perfectly open to the northwest winds which are the predominant winds. When we went back a few days later (the wind had shifted to the southwest the night before) the oil was just streaming out. We saw the last remaining part of that streamer of oil sliding out of the bay. Of course, the shoreline of the bay remained heavily oiled, and it still is today. The coast runs sort of east-west there, and it was following that coast and heading a little way out to sea.

Then the wind changed back to the northwest. A day or two after that, we were flying over the area from Ras Az Zawr to Jana Island to Abu Ali and there was a lot of oil just offshore. I suspect that was the oil that floated out of Manifa a couple of days earlier floating down the coast. It had hit Jana Island really hard, and there was a big patch of it offshore that was heading toward Abu Ali. And a little oil a few days later got around Abu Ali.

JMM: The bulk of the cleanup and recovery happened further south.

BH: Other than some ARAMCO (Arab American Oil Company) facilities, it was a real mixed story. There was little cleanup since the middle of March, 1991. ARAMCO had some heavy equipment on Karan Island getting some oil off there. But I didn't know the details of what ARAMCO was doing at its plants. It was not easy to get onto their property.

JMM: They were basically trying to protect their machinery.

BH: ARAMCO was apparently busy pumping away, where they've pumped. MEPA credited them with a million-and-a-half barrels of oil—that supposedly was oil, not oil and water. I don't think they had a very good handle on how much oil they actually got. Then they went through a weird exercise of trying to go back and reconstruct that from the volume of oil pits.

JMM: So they weren't keeping track of it as they pumped it?

BH: They were giving us figures all along which would indicate that they were keeping track of it. If they were keeping such good track of it, why go back and try to reconstruct it from the volume of oil pits? It seemed rather imprecise, because you really wouldn't have any idea of water content, and you wouldn't have any idea how often the pits were filled and emptied.

The important thing is there is no doubt that they got a lot of oil off the water. In essence, they got all the oil off the water. The problem was that they did that from a limited number of locations, didn't do it very aggressively, and waited for the oil to come to them. They were fortunate that the configuration of the coast limited how far south the oil went. They were fortunate in the wind pattern that kept the oil along the shore moving south to where they eventually recovered it. Meanwhile, my estimate from the map is that there is 600 kilometers of actual Saudi shoreline from Abu Ali north to the Kuwait border, probably 500 kilometers of which was moderately to heavily oiled. The NOAA estimate from the subsequent *Mount Mitchell* research cruise in 1992 was 570 kilometers, so I was pretty close.

JMM: The Saudis announced early in July 1991 that everything was cleaned up, everything was fine.

BH: I saw that. The reporter must have misunderstood something. I think what they were saying is that they were wrapping up the cleanup operation, not that the coast was cleaned up. They stopped because they had gotten all the oil off the water. I am sure that's what they were referring to. All the shore that was oiled is still oiled.

HABITATS

There is a range of problems on the 500 or so kilometers that are still oiled. Some of the exposed oil is cleaned up pretty well by wave action; at most areas there is still quite a heavy coating of oil in the intertidal zone, from moderately protected coasts to bays to salt flats and mud flats. There are these pathetic little salt marshes, maybe a few hundred acres scattered along the coast. Some of them have what passes for mangroves, three-foot tall black mangroves that are fairly well spaced apart. This is not dense mangrove growth, but that's all they've got, and all of those have been pretty well oiled. It will be interesting to see how well they do. The *Mount Mitchell* cruise in 1992 found that some had survived.

I was able to get back to the salt marshes in June 1991. It gave me some hope that the vegetation, the individual plants, are surviving. Commonly, there was a central plant that sprawls out in a pad that is maybe three to six or eight feet in diameter. The foliage would be dead in much of the outer area of it. Presumably, the branches are dead; we don't know for sure, it is too soon to tell just looking at it. But there was new growth in parts of the plant toward the center, which would seem to indicate those plants were alive, which is a very good sign rather than having to wait for recolonization. . . .

You could clearly see from looking at them that some of the beaches were still heavily oiled. Others looked lightly oiled. Some looked as though virtually all the oil was gone, and in some, you could dig down and the sand was pretty clean. Or you could dig down and discover a sort of brown sugar underneath. In some cases, you could dig down and create a hole in the intertidal zone and immediately oil and water started oozing out of the sand and it wasn't brown sugar, just dark gray-brown with oil. Those were coarser sands in moderately protected shore lines.

JMM: Oil doesn't sink so much into sandy beaches?

BH: Yes, if you are going to have it coming ashore, it is certainly a hell of a lot better than something like Prince William Sound, where it sank down a meter into the gravel.

JMM: One of the concerns had been that not much was being done to protect some of the more sensitive habitats, such as the coral islands and seagrass beds.

BH: That is an interesting question. I have heard that when oil is more than a few days old it is not terribly toxic to coral. Certainly in the concentrations that get more than a few centimeters below the surface the main risk would be from the smothering effects of the oil that sank. And we didn't see evidence of sunken oil on the corals when we visited the main coral areas off Saudi Arabia. That's fortunate, but I don't know what might have happened earlier when the oil first passed through there. If there had been some very low tides when the oil was going through, that might have affected some coral.

NOAA divers visited the Gulf in 1992 [the *Mount Mitchell* research cruise] and found a lot of the coral was dead in the north, near Kuwait. This was reported at the January 1993 conference organized by ROPME. They don't really know when it died or why. Was it toxicity from the spills? Or was it cooler water temperatures caused by the shading of the oil fire smoke? Or was it some other cause from before the war?

All of the islands had been oiled to at least a slight extent. By the time we got to the exposed beaches they had cleaned up naturally, by wave action. There was some oil on the northwest beach of Karan Island, one pretty big patch that was a few meters wide and maybe a hundred meters long on the east side. Other than that it was sort of a wash of small tiny bits of mousse. So the islands, which are important for sea turtle and seabird nesting, were largely spared.

JMM: The cleaning of the islands was through natural action?

BH: Yes, similar to what had happened up near Khafji. So the islands cleaned up quite well, other than little flecks of mousse, some tar balls, and sheen offshore. The sheen was coming from some of the few remaining oil patches onshore. A little more oil hit Karan after we left, and that and some of the earlier oil was cleaned off with a piece of heavy equipment that they took out to the island, just working on the exposed beach.

JMM: They were just scraping off the top layer of beach and the oil with it?
BH: Yes.

JMM: One concern is how much oil is sinking into the water versus floating and washing up on shore. Are there any estimates?

BH: The NOAA team did some sampling in 1992 and found submerged oil in some areas, but it would be difficult for anyone to estimate the extent of it. I saw some areas along the shore where I am quite sure there is a fair amount of sunken oil. From the shore it can be hard to distinguish grass beds from sunken oil. I know it wasn't just grass beds, because we waded out into it.

You ought to understand that the habitat along the oiled section of coast is not the most exciting thing I have ever seen, even up along the underdeveloped coast north of Abu Ali. I think a lot has changed in terms of dredge-and-fill development down along Tarut Bay and Gulf of Bahrain. There is huge development there. Up north there is not much except at a couple of ARAMCO facilities. But there are some grass bed areas. And there is a tiny mangrove island that is a few acres in size; it is pretty much the northern limit for them. These are mangroves that are maybe a meter high, all black mangrove, *Avicennia marina*. I think there are bits left. And there is some low grade salt marsh in a few places, a couple that are pretty good size and a couple of smaller ones, and that is about it.

There are quite a few sand flats and mud flats, though not that many mud flats to the north, where it is mostly sand flats and *sabkhas,* which are salt flats that may or may not connect with the Gulf. The ones that connect with the Gulf are only flooded a little bit on very high tides, maybe once or twice a year, perhaps not that often. Or they only get wet when you have a heavy rain.

Shorebirds were using some of those quite a bit. There had been some unusually heavy rain, so there were up to a few inches of water at many of these *sabkhas.* They get these blooms of shrimp and crustaceans of various kinds that draw in the shorebirds, flamingos and what not.

There is salt marsh, there is mangrove, but we are talking about a very minor amount on that coast.

JMM: How about in the near shore. Is there a lot of seagrass?

BH: In a few areas there is a good extent of seagrass. . . . That is probably the most exciting habitat. From the Gulf of Bahrain on up to Ras Al Tanaqib, there would be occasional areas, either big or small grass beds.

I am confident that the seagrass beds were not hit hard. The best seagrass beds were south of the spill area. The only oil on the bottom would be close to shore, so that's a limited area where there is oil on the bottom compared to the area of the seagrass bed. That oil on the bottom is going to move around, seep down.

THE LONG-TERM RESPONSE

JMM: Were there any plans by the Saudis or others to clean up any of those beaches?

BH: They made plans for practically everything; what actually happened is quite something else again. They began a salt marsh experiment that was just a study in chaos. There were six strips in a marsh that they bermed off (a berm is a long low mound or dike) where they were going to try different approaches. They chewed that over, and increased to eleven the number of things they were going to try on different strips. Some of them the Saudis actually let the contractors proceed with: scraping the oil off, floating the oil off, etc.

On the other hand, they never did give approval for nutrient augmentation, which is the favored term, rather than bioremediation (applying nitrogen fertilizer to encourage naturally occurring bacteria to eat the oil). The Saudis seemed to be afraid to try bioremediation of the variety of just fertilizing, adding nutrients! All the Saudis you talk to say yes, we really need to do that, and it's always somebody else who is the bottleneck on that decision. It never really gets sorted out who is blocking it. Some of the concern is rumored to be the fear that: "Oil is our life and we are talking about encouraging oil-eating bugs? What if they get into our oil formations?" I never heard the Saudi scientists say that, other than suggesting it was the concern of people higher up in government.

JMM: They were afraid that the bacteria would get in their reserves and eat their oil wealth?

BH: Yes, but it's never the person you are talking to—it's someone else's concern. And the decision was never made to try it, although this spill was the perfect opportunity. Everybody seemed to be in favor of putting nitrogen and phosphate on the oil, at least on an experimental basis. It has not happened, or had not by the time I had left, in June 1991.

Meanwhile, in this one main experimental marsh area, the Dutch contractor who was supposed to do that under a contract funded by IMO gave up and left when the contract came to an end and they still did not have permission to carry out some of the most useful parts of the experiment. They did as much as they could before they ran out of time and money. The rest was supposed to be continuing; I doubt that it did. It was supposed to be monitored to find out the results. But King Fahd University has two biologists who were stretched paper thin before the spill, and all this was added on to their normal responsibilities. There is just no way they are going to be able to do this without help.

Years from now they may still be proposing new things to study the effects of the spill and experiments. It is impossible to predict what of it will ever be done and how useful it will be, considering how late they were starting.

There were all sorts of politics going on, infighting between Bechtel and Crowley and the other contractors who were in there. There was consistent backbiting and suspicion, and a lot of money at stake for those who got major responsibility for the cleanup, and a lot of competition for responsibility. The Saudis portioned out coordination and direction to different individuals and companies in a really inefficient way.

But no country could have handled the oil spill and fires alone, and the West did next to nothing to help. We walked away and left the spill cleanup and the fires to countries that certainly weren't competent to deal with them.

Anyway, where it will all end up, nobody can say, in terms of how much is cleaned up, how much actual research is done on the effects of the spill, what kind of experimentation is done: effective, real experimentation on spill response technique, cleanup technique. I am not optimistic about any of those things.

OILED BIRDS

Diving sea birds (e.g. grebes and cormorants) in the spill area were virtually wiped out in the first weeks of the spill. These birds are most vulnerable to oil spills because their instinctive response is to dive, and so they become too oiled to fly. Gulls and terns are adept at avoiding oil, and their casualty rate was low.

Shorebirds, or waders, are hardest to estimate, because when their feet and tail feathers are oiled they may still fly hundreds of miles away. Even if a shorebird is not killed, reduced fitness after oiling may lead to failure to breed. Oiled shorebirds have skin coming off. You can tell when you have them in the hand.

JMM: That is an indication of how oiled they are? How toxic the oil is?

BH: Not necessarily toxic, but these birds do spend

Oiled cormorant. Artwork by Carol Melnick

a huge amount of time preening, and just one of the ways it can affect them is they spend too much time preening. It is an additional energy drain that they are not equipped to deal with. But, whether it is toxic effects of the oil, irritation from the oil or that plus the preening that the birds do, it has quite an effect on the skin of the ones the ICBP team netted.

Also, there was definitely evidence that some of the birds picked up the oil by flying through the soot. There were birds I was seeing along the Saudi coast that I had trouble identifying, because they were so sooty. They apparently were picking it up by going through the foliage, little shrubs along the coast. There was a rain in late April or in May along the Saudi coast that was quite sooty and turned everything gray, including the foliage on the shrubbery. You could wipe your hands on this year's grass and come away with gray streaks on your hands. The resident birds apparently picked up soot that way, but there was also evidence of birds picking up soot from flying through it. There was oily soot on the undersides of their flight feathers, their secondaries and primaries, which, presumably, they could not pick up any other way, at least the migratory birds. Some birds may have been prevented from migrating by the soot from the oil fires.

I flew over the islands again in June 1991 but did not land on them. They still seemed to be clean. Karan Island got hit with some oil after I was there in March. A Dutch outfit under IMO contract went out there with their equipment and scraped that oil up and dug pits and buried it in the interior of the island and covered the pits back over. There is a ground cover that grows all over Karan Island except on the beach and the tops of these pits. The lesser-crested terns favor bare areas, so they have suddenly got more breeding habitat on the island. They were crowded onto some of these covered pits where the vegetation was gone.

But they got the cleanup done before turtle nesting season got well under way, which was good, so from that standpoint, the islands are in pretty good shape.

LONG-TERM PROBLEMS

JMM: In your report,[1] you talk about finding evidence of previous war-related spills.

BH: Yes. They were very evident on Abu Ali and a number of other places. Around Manifa, Ras Al Zawr, Salwah Bay, I don't remember where else, but on the exposed beaches particularly there were these asphalt pavements that would be the width of the intertidal zone, maybe 10, 12, 20 feet wide. They would be hundreds of meters long, of very old, weathered, hard oil that might be up to several centimeters thick. You could walk on it. Other places, fresher oil had soaked into the sand to a depth of perhaps a foot. Over the years, it has become as hard as some sedimentary rock formations and just as permanent. We were told that it was left over from the 1986 Iran-Iraq War spill.

JMM: Was that because there was no cleanup effort launched?

BH: Apparently. The best we could find out was that the response then was pretty much to protect the power plant intakes, the refineries, the industrial plant intakes, the desalination plants. I think that has traditionally been the response, with the Nowruz spill in 1983, or with some of the other chronic spills they have had.

JMM: So in a sense, however little may have been done to protect the environment for the environment's sake, this time there was more than in the past.

BH: Yes. Richard Golob came up with this incredible estimate for the 1980s of maybe a million barrels a year spilling into the Gulf, just sort of operational type stuff. Not war stuff, just normal operations, with maybe 60 percent of that being transportation-related and most of the rest of it production-related.[2]

JMM: Given all this attention to these spills and environmental protection, might there now be more consciousness about normal operations?

BH: I kind of doubt that unless somebody convinces them of the need for that. . . .

None of the Gulf states is a signatory to MARPOL Annex 1. MARPOL is the International Convention for the Prevention of Pollution from Ships. That is the convention for regulating and setting standards for oil pollution from vessels. And it is one of the International Maritime Organization conventions. It is ridiculous that none of the Gulf states is signatory to that. More oil goes through the Gulf than any place in the world, and virtually every other country that does anything with oil—produces it, ships it, receives it—all nations of any consequence at all are signatories to the provisions of MARPOL Annex 1. It would make a huge difference if the Gulf states signed on and implemented MARPOL, which they can well afford to do. The only signatory state in the region is Oman, which is very progressive environmentally.

DEVELOPMENT

JMM: In your article you talk about development perhaps in the long term being a greater threat than the spills.

BH: About 40 percent of the Saudi Gulf coast has been developed just since 1973. Most of that has involved at least some dredge-and-fill land reclamation. And there are many areas where there are large reclamation projects, many square miles.

JMM: They filled it because they can?

BH: Yes. It is hard to know what inspired some of this. One thing we were told in terms of residential construction and land for industry was that it was cheaper than acquiring existing land. Land in the desert is owned by someone and is expensive. I don't know if that is the reason for it. From what we saw ourselves, and from the limited references available, Tarut Bay and the Gulf of Bahrain are some of the best habitat in the Gulf for shorebirds, dugongs, sea turtles, shrimp and fish. And that is the area that had the most development pressure in the past 15 years. And there is the additional concern on the part of the few Saudis who have been looking at it, about the effects of the development on the areas that haven't been dredged and filled, industrial pollution, and urban pollution on those areas. The Saudis know from their fisheries data that their biggest fishery, shrimp, has had declining catches for the last ten years or so. One thing they think it may be is overfishing, but the question arises how much of it has to do with the best shrimp breeding areas being destroyed.

JMM: It seems a bit of luck has been involved that the damage is not greater.

BH: Oh yes, definitely some luck. The story to me is not so much this spill, it's the other spills and the other environmental prices that the Gulf is paying without our really being aware of it, in spite of our level of unwitting involvement in it as major customers for the Gulf states' oil.

NOTES:

1. Burr Heneman, *The Gulf War Oil Spills: The ICBP Survey of the Saudi Arabian Gulf Coast, March, 1991*, Report (to International Council for Bird Preservation and the Saudi Arabian National Commission on Wildlife Conservation and Development), Bolinas, California, 1991.

2. R. Golob and E. Brus, "Statistical Analysis of Oil Pollution in the Kuwaiti Action Plan Region and the Implication of Selected Worldwide Oil Spills to the Region," in *Continuing Oil Pollution in the Kuwait Action Plan Region*, United Nations Environment Programme Regional Seas Reports and Studies No. 44, 1984.

Impacts on Bird Populations

Interview with Mike Evans

Mike Evans is coordinator of the Important Bird Areas in the Middle East Project of ICBP, Cambridge, U.K. Interviewed February 1992 by John Miller. Revised and updated by Mike Evans February 1993.

APRIL–MAY 1991 SURVEY

John M. Miller: What have you found out about how bird life has been affected by the oil spills and oil fires?

Mike Evans: Let's start with the survey in April–May 1991. There was an eight-man team that worked with the NCWCD (Saudi Arabian National Commission on Wildlife Conservation and Development) on the Gulf coast to study the effects of the oil on wader migration. We found that the oil came ashore along about 560 kilometers of shoreline between Abu Ali and Khafji.

Not taking into account its toxic component, but just through smothering, it seemed to have killed virtually all invertebrate life in the intertidal mud flat all along that stretch, which is about 50 percent of the Saudi gulf coast shoreline. All the invertebrate life appeared to have been temporarily wiped out. And so the value of this area as a feeding and refueling area for shorebirds had been very severely reduced. We found there were very few shorebirds (waders as the British call them) along this area of coast during this spring migration period. You could drive 20 kilometers and not see any birds at all sometimes.

JMM: And there would normally be?

ME: It is difficult to say. There has only been one previous study five years ago.[1] Through the study of about 30 scattered sampling sites, it came up with an extrapolation of a total shorebird population along that coast in winter. They estimated about 260,000 shorebirds all along the Saudi gulf coast. Since about 50 percent of the coastline was very heavily impacted by the oil, you can only estimate that 50 percent of the shorebird population had its feeding grounds very severely reduced in value. That would be over 100,000 shorebirds.

However, because the previous estimate of 260,000 may for various reasons have been a little too high, to be more conservative one can estimate that before the oil spill there were up to 65,000 shorebirds present (25 percent of 260,000). But aerial and ground surveys along the entire oiled coastline in April and May in 1991 found fewer than 1,000 shorebirds present at a time, indicating a reduction of more than 98 percent compared to estimated numbers of shorebirds present in January/February. One would expect April/May population figures to be of the same order of magnitude as winter figures.

It is difficult to know for sure how many were killed, because the oiling event happened during the war, and nobody was allowed near there until March 1991. The war ended February 28, 1991, but the actual impact of the oil all along that shore occurred in early February. So the biologists got in there for the first time a month later.

The initial ICBP survey, in March 1991 by Burr Heneman, found that at least 50 to 75 percent or more of the shorebirds found in the oiled zone were oiled.[2] The trouble is that we could see that shorebirds, even when they were totally oiled, didn't die immediately; they didn't drop dead conveniently on the shoreline to be counted. They can fly very strongly and disperse, so long as their fat reserves last. They could have dispersed anywhere in that month. We found very few corpses along the beaches and inland. We did find a few corpses of oiled shorebirds, but they had obviously been sheltering from the cold in the bushes and salt marshes. It is incredibly difficult to know the actual direct mortality from the oil.

JMM: I have seen figures that run from 15,000 to 30,000 birds. Is that just people talking out of their hats?

ME: In March 1991, an average of 30 percent of all species of shorebirds were observed to be oiled along the whole Gulf coast of Saudi Arabia, not just the oiled zone. Given the estimate of over 100,000 in the oiled zone, then with 30 percent oiled, you come up with a minimum figure of 30,000 oiled in the oil zone. Any kind of severe oiling is probably fatal to the shorebirds and most other birds.

TERNS

After the shorebird survey, we stayed for the breeding terns on the offshore islands in the Gulf. There are four of these islands. They hadn't been affected by the oil at all. Overall there were larger numbers than the previous survey five years before. Of all the birds that were there, extremely few showed signs of oiling, and those that did just had small spots that hadn't appeared to have affected them directly.

What the effects of this mass death of the intertidal flat on the overall ecosystem and fisheries productivity will be in the next few years, nobody knows. Then some effect on the terns' food supply may become apparent, but at the moment it seems that they were unharmed by the oil. They spend the winter in the Indian Ocean, and they only migrate into the Gulf around April. In fact, they moved in after most of the oil had beached. As for the offshore colonies, two out of the four islands had been heavily oiled along the shore, but they had been cleaned by a contractor who had managed to clean up the coastline before the terns arrived en masse on the breeding islands. That was good news.

Soot

We did a banding project in April and May of 1991 to study the spring migration through the Gulf northwards. We basically found that individuals were getting covered in soot by flying through it or by brushing against it while feeding in bushes. It tended to coat anything and everything on the ground. When you felt it with your fingers it was still greasy. It seemed like there were unburned microparticles of oil in this stuff. Individuals were being sooted.

Sooted birds were showing significantly lower weight than unsooted birds. And sooted birds were spending significantly longer on the ground feeding and fattening up compared to unsooted birds. The unsooted birds were coming down after a migratory journey to fatten up.

Wildlife Rescue

JMM: There were some well-publicized bird rescue efforts. NCWCD set up their first-ever rescue center, near Al Jubail, on February 8, 1991. How useful or successful was it?

ME: Its main value was symbolic. It treated only about 1,300 oiled birds. Most of those were cormorants and grebes which tended to wash up along the shoreline, covered in oil, weak and quite easy to catch. They had an overall cleaning and release success rate of 30 percent. It wasn't amazingly successful, nor is any oiled wildlife cleanup operation like that. It didn't make any difference at all compared to the vastly greater numbers of oiled birds out there which could not be caught or which died way out of sight.

JMM: And some of those that were released did not make it either?

ME: Yes. There is one interesting observation: quite a lot of great cormorants were cleaned and released, and all the birds that were released had a colored band put on their leg. In November of 1991, a couple of these great cormorants were sighted again along the Saudi Gulf coast, probably very close to where they were originally oiled and picked up. So they obviously had survived the cleaning process. They were released in the spring. They breed in wetlands in Iran and southern Russia and they had obviously made it up there, survived that and migrated back to the Gulf successfully for the winter. That suggests for the cormorants anyway that the cleaning operation was successful.

The main value of that wildlife rescue center was in capturing the attention of the public around the world. There was a lot of media that emanated from that center. Also in Saudi Arabia, it was very good publicity for the wildlife cause. It resulted in Saudis volunteering to help clean up. Saudi men and Saudi women were actually working side by side, which is quite unusual.

NOVEMBER 1991 SURVEY

Another four-man ICBP team went to the Gulf in November 1991 for one month, and they were monitoring the shorebird population again to see how quickly the oiled coastline was recovering, and there were large numbers of shorebirds moving back onto the oiled shore. They found that on the oiled half of the coastline the oil was no longer visible, because it had been covered either by windblown sand or a fine layer of new sediment. Basically, the oil was no longer apparent along the shore, but all you had to do was scrape the surface, and it was there not far underneath, and it was still liquid. One thing that surprised a lot of people was how liquid the oil remained. When we were there in April and May, the oil was still heavy liquid, like mutton sauce that had been spilled. It wasn't showing that much sign of congealing. And I think once it is buried it will remain liquid; it probably needs weathering from the atmosphere, wind and waves to turn it hard.

JMM: How will the buried oil affect the birds directly?

ME: In November of 1991, there were still very reduced numbers of shorebirds all along the oiled coastline. They basically weren't frequenting that area even though the oil was covered with a fine layer of silt. That was because the invertebrate population was showing very few signs of recovery. It had only been a few months since April, and I think they perhaps saw a little more crab activity.

JMM: So the birds were going elsewhere to find things to eat?

ME: One would think so. They would go elsewhere in the Gulf. No doubt that would cause the population to move, but that was beyond the realm of what we were able to investigate. Anyway, these two surveys found or confirmed what we suspected: that Tarut Bay in the southern, unoiled sector is the most important chunk of the coastline for shorebirds. It basically has the richest intertidal sediments, richest in food. It certainly has the remaining areas that haven't been oiled and probably even before the oil spill it would still have been the most important. It has the best remaining examples of salt marsh and mangrove ecosystems on the Saudi Arabian Gulf. Unfortunately, it is also the area most threatened by coastal development. . . .

OIL LAKES

JMM: Have you looked into the oil lakes and their impacts on bird life?

ME: Two teams went to Kuwait, one in May and one in November again, in 1991, and both of them found abundant evidence that birds of all species were mistaking these lakes for water. They are very reflective. They are flat and they basically look like water. They are visible at night by moonlight. Ducks are landing on them; swallows are trying to drink from them. Flamingos land in them and wade about. The shores of these lakes were littered with corpses of birds of all species. Large waterfowl were probably the most conspicuous. If they land in the middle of the lake, get oiled and can't take off again, they, more than other birds, have the strength to paddle to shore where they collapse and die. Small birds tend to just sink.

The corpses we found around the edges of the lakes are rapidly disintegrating in the oil, sort of coming apart. The corpses these teams found along the edge were very recent.

Water birds were basically dying by flying down and landing directly on the oil lakes. Other birds were dying by landing beside the lakes and walking up to them with the intention of preening or drinking or bathing. A lot of those may have just been oiled and flown off again. But the oil then has the possibility of poisoning or killing them or knocking them out of their annual cycle, reducing breeding.

The trouble was they [the teams] didn't have easy access to these lakes. In May 1991, they managed to visit two or three fairly small ones. In November 1991, they managed to visit only one small lake. The density of dead large waterfowl found around the edges of these lakes indicates that 20,000 large waterfowl had died around the lakes. I suspect the actual total must be vastly higher. In May, the team flew over a lot of these oil lakes, some of them more than one kilometer wide.

I was talking to a guy from the *Wall Street Journal* who had been there in September or October 1991 and had been flying over the lakes with independent consultants that the Kuwaitis had hired. These consultants were saying they reckoned that the volume of oil in these lakes was hundreds of millions of barrels. One guy reckoned that just one had a hundred million barrels in it. The official Kuwaiti figures which we saw in November 1991 were that there were six to nine oil lakes covering about 20 square kilometers. For birds, what is important is the actual surface area. From the reports we were getting from our team and other reports, those were rather conservative figures.

In November of 1991, the Kuwaitis said they were in the process of choosing which people to award the contracts to. They had a big line of companies waiting to do the job of draining the lakes. The time frame for completion of the job is unknown.[3]

CONCLUSIONS AS OF FEBRUARY 1993

The most current estimate [February 1993] is that a minimum of about 25,000–30,000 pelagic [oceanic] seabirds were killed by the spill while it was still drifting in the open sea, based on tideline corpse counts. The vast majority (more than 95 percent) of these were of four species: great crested grebe *Podiceps cristatus*, black-necked grebe *Podiceps nigricollis*, great cormorant *Phalacrocorax carbo*, and Socotra cormorant *Phalacrocorax nigrogularis*. The last species (endemic to the seas fringing Arabia) was the most numerous in the beached corpse counts and is thought by ICBP to have suffered a mortality greater than one percent of its world population (estimated one percent is 4,000 birds), which is one reason for calling this event an environmental disaster.

We also now estimate that the shorebird species that were worst affected (both by direct oiling and loss of feeding grounds) at the flyway-population-level were Terek sandpiper *Xenus cinereus*, broad-billed sandpiper *Limicola falcinellus* and Mongolian plover *Charadrius mongolus*. It seems certain that more than one percent of the flyway populations of these species were affected, and in the case of Terek sandpiper perhaps 10 to 15 percent.

Many other species of waterfowl, especially flamingos, herons and spoonbills, have also lost their feeding grounds and faced direct oiling.

The joint Gulf Wildlife Sanctuary Project of NCWCD and the Commission of the European Communities (CEC) is currently studying the effects of the oil pollution and monitoring recovery of the marine ecosystem, based in Al Jubail on the Saudi Arabian coast, and aims to establish a protected area in the Ad Dafi Bay area, one of the worst-hit parts of the coast.

NOTES:
1. International Union for the Conservation of Nature and Natural Resources, *Saudi Arabia: An Assessment of Biotypes and Management Requirements for the Saudi Arabian Gulf Coast*, Report (prepared for the Saudi Arabian Meteorology and Environmental Protection Agency), 1987.
2. Burr Heneman, *The Gulf War Oil Spills: the ICBP Survey of the Saudi Arabian Gulf Coast, March, 1991*, Report (to International Council for Bird Preservation and the Saudi Arabian National Commission on Wildlife Conservation and Development), Bolinas, March 1991.
3. In March 1993, OPEC News Agency reported that the Kuwait Petroleum Corporation was just beginning to evaluate an operation to remove the oil lakes. OPEC News Agency, "Kuwait Committee to Look at Removal of Oil Lakes," March 17, 1993.

Sea Turtles

Interview with James Perran Ross

James Perran Ross, Ph.D., is a biologist and a specialist in sea turtle conservation at the Florida Museum of Natural History, Gainesville. Interviewed in February 1991, by John M. Miller.

John M. Miller: You once worked on an environmental restoration plan for the Gulf?

James Perran Ross: In 1983, there was a big oil spill in the Gulf as a result of the Iran-Iraq War—the Nowruz spill. There was a lot of publicity in this country about disastrous effects of offshore wells that were blown up and spouted oil for a while. In response, MEPA invited a number of experts to come and advise them. . . .

The thing that surprised me in those first surveys—and these were in 1984–1985—was the very large amount of pristine habitat in the northern Gulf. We were able to do an aerial survey north of Dhahran, Saudi Arabia, and then south around Bahrain and into Qatar. And there are extensive areas of very attractive-looking seagrass and small coral reefs and several offshore islands. While there is local environmental degradation, mostly due to industrial activities there, certainly a good bit of the habitat is intact and functioning.

Sea Turtles

We did identify two islands that had significant nesting grounds for sea turtles. Those are Karan Island, which has 800 to 1,000 green turtles nesting each year, and an adjacent island, Jana, which has about 100 hawksbill turtles nesting every year. . . .

The turtles will not be there in large numbers at the moment because this is not their nesting season. The turtles will be distributed throughout the Gulf. Those that happen to be in the path of this particular spill will be seriously affected, but the bulk of the population is probably scattered all over.

The biggest problem I see for sea turtles is that, if those beaches become heavily oiled, as they are likely to do, then when the turtles come to nest in the summer months, the adults will be somewhat affected.[1] There is some information from the University of Miami indicating that crude oil is quite toxic to sea turtles. Exposure to quite small amounts does things like mess up their liver enzymes.

The Green Turtle. Artwork by Carol Melnick

The biggest problem, I think, will be to the eggs. Sea turtles dig a hole in the sand and lay eggs, so exposure to even small amounts of crude oil will probably kill the eggs. If any of the eggs survive that hazard, then when the small turtles hatch (they are quite small, only the size of a matchbox or so), they will not be able to crawl down the beach if it is covered in oil. So, I see the most drastic effect being on those nesting beaches. Unfortunately, sea turtles will not change their nesting beach; they are completely committed to particular locations. . . .

JMM: Did you look at the restoration issue at all?

JPR: We sort of diverted away from restoration per se. I think in the present

The Hawksbill Turtle. Artwork by Carol Melnick.

instance there are a few factors of the animals' biology that will help. All the turtles don't nest every year. In very crude terms, roughly a third of the female adults nest each year. What that means is that you could perhaps get two years in a row of unsuccessful nesting, but there are still going to be some adult females in the third year that could come up. If the beaches, by that time, return to some normal state, they could nest successfully.

Sea turtles also take a very long time to reach maturity. And what that means is that, in addition to the adults that are out there somewhere, there are numerous generations of sub-adults. As an example, if they take 30 years to reach maturity, which is an average sort of figure, along with all the 30-year and older adults who are coming to the nesting beach, there will also be the 29-, 28-year olds, and so forth, and there are quite a lot of them. So, even if there is no successful nesting for several years, it is conceivable that, if there are some areas of the habitat that remain, then sub-adults will grow to maturity and eventually be there as a nucleus to re-establish the nesting population, even though it may not successfully produce any hatchlings for several years.

In the long term, I think total extinction of that group of sea turtles is not likely. The biggest pervasive problem will be the destruction of their habitat. If you have nesting grounds, and you do some damage on the feeding grounds, they will probably survive. If you destroy the nesting grounds for a period of time but the feeding grounds are intact, they will probably survive. If you hit them both at once, then there are no options left. The effect could be very severe.[2]

NOTES:

1. Greenpeace International reported that eighty percent of the beaches of Karan and Jana were covered with oil. See Greenpeace International, *The Environmental Legacy of the Gulf War*, Report, Amsterdam, February 1992. See also the interview with Burr Heneman in this chapter.

2. For more information on turtles in the Gulf, see Greenpeace International, *The Environmental Legacy of the Gulf War*.

The Voyage of the *Mount Mitchell*

Interview with Sylvia Earle

From February 21 to June 20, 1992, 142 marine scientists from 15 countries took part in an unprecedented cooperative venture to explore and research the environmental aftermath of the Gulf War. The Mount Mitchell *expedition traveled the waters of the State of Bahrain, the Islamic Republic of Iran, the State of Kuwait, the Sultanate of Qatar, the Kingdom of Saudi Arabia, and the United Arab Emirates. The 100-day cruise, as it was called, was led by Drs. Robert Clark and Sylvia A. Earle of NOAA and was sponsored by NOAA, the International Oceanographic Commission (IOC), the United*

Nations Environment Programme (UNEP), and the Gulf-Area ROPME. A follow-up workshop took place in Kuwait, January 24–28, 1993.

Sylvia A. Earle, Ph.D., is a marine scientist who was NOAA's chief scientist from 1990 to 1992. She is currently an advisor to NOAA, and was interviewed by James Warner and Philippa Winkler, February 1993.

Philippa Winkler: The Gulf War ended two years ago, on February 28, 1991. During the war, you were NOAA's chief scientist, you flew into the oil fire smoke, your photos of the postwar devastation appeared in National Geographic, *and you've returned to the Gulf many times since to assess the damage. Can we begin this interview with a chronology of your visits to the region?*

Sylvia Earle: My first visit to the Gulf region was in March 1991. I was part of a group invited by the ambassador of Kuwait to the U.S. It included U.S. Secretary of Commerce Robert Mosbacher and U.S. businessmen and congressmembers. The principal goal was to look at ways of restoring the economy of Kuwait, obviously stricken because of the effects of the war. That was my first look. I stayed with the group much of the time, then I left them for a day and went down to Bahrain and met up with a group from NOAA that was there to study atmospheric effects. I was able to do a fly-around on a Saudi Navy viewercopter to look, photograph and document the oil as it was at that point along the western side of the Gulf, and south to Saudi Arabia. We started at about Abu Ali and went northward very close to the Kuwait border and then returned along the same way. I had a chance to fly through the fires with scientists who were studying the effects of the great plumes of smoke.

Then I visited the region in late spring and early summer of 1991, once with a small group from NOAA, four of us, and once with the then-administrator of the Environmental Protection Agency (EPA), Bill Reilly, and a group he pulled together, eight or nine of us. And in both cases, the goal was to meet with people about the nature of the environmental impact and to look at air, land and sea. I was also there in August 1991. During most of these trips, I've had a chance to dive in various parts of the Gulf, and in the Abu Ali area several times. I was there for a conference in February 1992 in the United Arab Emirates where I mostly met scientists from all over the region as well as elsewhere in the world to talk about their assessments. Then I was back for the *Mount Mitchell* cruise in May 1992. I've just returned from the follow-up workshop in January 1993. I again went diving off the coast of Kuwait, and I went to the desert. And I've tried to really immerse myself in others' findings.

POSTWAR IMPRESSIONS

PW: Going back to the situation right at the end of the war, can you describe what you saw in March 1991, when you flew through the smoke?

SE: That was my very first introduction, and the combination of the fires, oil spills, and the oil in the sea, was certainly awe-inspiring. It was unlike anything I'd seen before. I'd seen other oil spills of course. I've been to the Prince William Sound spill, but that was 250,000 barrels as opposed to six to eight million barrels. And the difference was not just limited to volume, but also the terrain was substantially different. The shallowness of the Gulf area means that at low tide there may be a near-tidal space exposed as much as a kilometer wide, and I observed during this time as much as a kilometer of oil in this intertidal area. Of course, when the water returns, some of it floats off and some of it does not, it stays on the bottom. And also, some penetrates deeply into the substrate below depending on the kind of substrate. But in this area, flats are penetrated by many small organisms: crabs, polychaete worms and many things. Under normal circumstances, there have been as many as a hundred thousand individual creatures per square meter, but after the spill the number dropped to zero to a dozen or so. In follow-up studies that have been done, recovery is not happening in that area very swiftly. The marshes were really hard hit.

James Warner: And that could have a long-term impact on bird populations?

SE: It certainly does have a long-term impact on the invertebrate populations typically associated with these intertidal areas along the coast of Saudi Arabia, from about Abu Ali northward to the coastal areas of Kuwait. Parts of Kuwait were affected but not nearly as badly as the downstream areas. The impacts to the birds are a little harder to assess because they are in and out and we don't really have a good yardstick against which to measure the changes. The numbers that were killed directly as a result of being trapped by the oil were hard to come by. There were educated guesses but some birds are still being trapped, especially in the oil lakes in the desert.

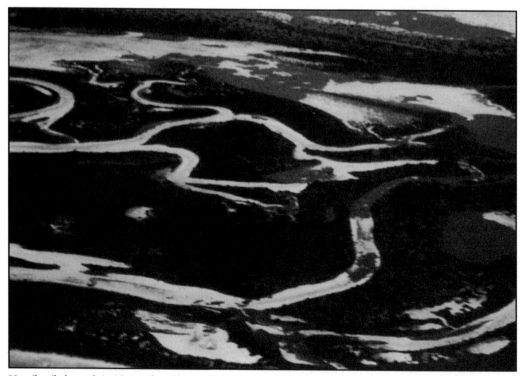

Heavily oiled marsh inside Dawhtat Al Musallimiyah, just north of Abu Ali Island, Saudi Arabia. Photo by Sylvia Earle, from the *Mount Mitchell* expedition report, 1992.

OIL FALLOUT

I certainly didn't think of this, and most people don't realize this, but the fallout of oil from the sky was at least as great as the amount of oil deliberately released into the Gulf, six to eight million barrels. That seems preposterous, until you realize that six to eight million barrels a day was going up in smoke. Even if five or ten percent of that fell out over the Gulf, the amount over the period of time the fires were burning is really phenomenal.

I've heard estimates that 60 to 100 million barrels of oil were lost on the face of the desert. It is said that within the first few days 40 to 50 percent of the volume may have gone into the atmosphere. Those who were there testify that there was raw oil falling from the sky. I have clothing which after repeated washing still has evidence of being spattered by that oil.

JW: *That would presumably have impacted the marine environment as well.*
SE: Yes, it's like acid rain, it falls indiscriminately.

OIL LAKES IN THE DESERT

There are vast pools of lakes. Just a few weeks ago I witnessed evidence of birds and insects and small mammals still being trapped in contact with the oil. [For more on oil in the desert, see Chapter Four.]

CLEANUP

I gather that some of the lake oil has been recovered, but once it sits for a while, the grade of oil becomes less desirable. That's true for the oil that was recovered by the Saudis along intertidal areas, so I was pleased, and really astonished, by the amount of oil that was recovered, more than a million barrels of oil, perhaps as much as two million. That is in itself four or eight times as much as in the Exxon *Valdez* spill.

JW: *Did you think there should have been a more aggressive cleanup overall?*
SE: The first priority went to protecting the desalinization plants at Al Jubail and Al Khobar. The war effort depended on fresh water supplies. There were also health and well-being reasons for doing this. So the booms that were available were mobilized to go straight to serve that purpose first and foremost.

It's unfortunate, and it's easy to say in retrospect, that a modest amount of effort to help protect the marshes could have had a magnified impact. It's easy to see now that if they had blocked off certain areas, huge tracts of the marshes would have been saved instead of being inundated by the oil that was allowed to go in. It went in through certain channels and then fed into a wide area behind these narrow channels, but once it is there, the cleanup effort is very difficult to know how to engineer. In some cases, it's likely that the cleanup effort could be more damaging than just leaving it alone. That was discovered at Prince William Sound. It was a very different situation, with a rocky, pebbly beach, but even just as a general principle there were some circumstances where, as painful as it may be, the best course of action is to leave it rather than sacrifice whatever may be remaining. To get rid of the oil in the marshes means bulldozing down in some cases to as much as a meter below the surface. Any residual life or any sign of restoration that might be taking place naturally would be set back. The net result would be a cleaner surface but it would be a very different habitat. It is going to be a very different habitat no matter what happens. The change is a fact.

MARSHES, SEAGRASS AND CORAL REEFS

During the 100-day *Mount Mitchell* cruise in 1992, scientists looked at the marsh areas, especially around Abu Ali and the marshes north of Abu Ali, and it was from that assessment that we know that oil has deeply penetrated into the substrate below, following in some cases channels created by the invertebrates, especially the crabs. That will be a legacy in the long term. Also during that time, they made a lot of dives in the seagrass beds and other areas adjacent to the shore and found that offshore there wasn't much oil in the bottom. There's some that was apparently derived from the intertidal oil. The old tradition of saying oil floats but doesn't sink is by and large borne out here but there is oil in some places heavily [concentrated] on the bottom. It's oil that has washed back and forth largely from the intertidal area. It's mixed with sand and it does get heavy and sink, and that has happened in some broad areas as well.

We found in our exploration of the coral reef—starting in Qatar and moving up the coast, looking at some places in Bahrain and several along the coast's offshore islands off Saudi Arabia and finally the shore and offshore islands of Kuwait—that there was little evidence of oil beneath the surface, that is, on the bottom around the coral reefs. The one exception is Karan Island, where there are some near-shore reefs—the coral comes almost up to the shore—and in that very shallow water, there was evidence of soft oil, probably from the 1991 spill, at the base of some of the coral. We could reach down with our hands and pull up big globs of it.

That was an area where an extensive cleanup effort had been organized in the spring of 1991, because it was a well-known nesting site for birds and turtles. But despite these heroic efforts to remove large quantities of oil from the beach, there is still a lot of oil around there. It's the only place I saw a substantial amount of sheen, because it keeps on getting released from the intertidal and subtidal areas. The marshes also continue to generate sheen. Scientists on board the *Mount Mitchell* observed that substantial amounts would come up with the tide and flow over the affected areas. Oil will continue to leach out and create more than just the evidence of this multicolor rainbow sheen. That will go on for a long time.

DEAD CORAL OFF KUWAIT

JW: We heard that a lot of coral died off Kuwait.

SE: We observed last spring during the *Mount Mitchell* expedition the deterioration of many of the places we visited. It seemed obvious that during the recent past these reefs have been in good condition, that is, the dead or dying corals were still sharp-edged, not eroded. Because coral is calcium carbonate, after a reasonably short period of time any dead coral becomes smooth and also bloated. It becomes a substrate on which other things can grow. The deaths of the corals that we observed appear to be by and large fairly recent, and we were unable to make a hard and fast cause-and-effect tie between the oil spill as such and the deterioration of the reef, but it is clear that these reefs are stressed and they've been recently stressed. It may also relate to the cooling, which in part could be influenced by that oil plume that reduced the overall temperature in that area. The corals there are living under cooler circumstances than in most places. Temperatures get well below 15 degrees centigrade down to a low of nine degrees. As one who is a longtime observer of coral reef around the world, I think that is just phenomenal. A few species in the northern Gulf of Mexico can tolerate a drop in temperature for some period of time, down to as low as nine to ten degrees, but they can't sustain it for long. It could be that sustained low temperatures as opposed to an occasional nip below a critical level could have caused some of these corals to respond in the way they have or just make them more susceptible to other ills. Very few things are just black and white, this leading directly to that. What is much more likely to be the case in almost any ecosystem is that the effects are synergistic. That's what makes science so interesting. But it is also pretty unsatisfactory because people want to have a straightforward answer to a straightforward question. Did the oil harm the coral? The answer is still elusive.

Acropora is one of the more conspicuous members of the reef communities there. When they're in trouble it's like the whole reef is in trouble. In fact, they may be more sensitive to circumstances than others. Certain species are understandably more hardy than others, even within a single species there are individuals more susceptible and others less so, as in a population of human beings.

We saw places during the spring of 1991 where most of the *Acropora* were either dead or dying off the coast of Kuwait, and other species of coral were necrotic, or in a state of decline. There's some controversy over these findings because a noted scientist, Dr. Downing, visited the same area the *Mount Mitchell* visited and pronounced the area to be in good health. I'm not at all disputing his observations. I gather that later in 1992, since the *Mount Mitchell* cruise, he went back and found things not to be in as bad a condition as when we observed them last spring. I don't think it's a matter of disputed findings—I think there was some recovery. We have ample video and film evidence of the bad shape those reefs were in, close-up images showing dead coral—and a few places where the coral has bleached, and yet the polyps are still alive, but the corals themselves are in bad shape. The bleached coral, if still alive, has some hope of recovery, and perhaps that's what Dr. Downing observed.

MANGROVES

The mangroves have been badly impacted because they are also near the low temperatures, so it doesn't take much to push them over the edge. In Bahrain, where historically mangroves have been very noticeable, they're mostly gone because of shoreline development as they call it. Only in a few places where they are explicitly protected are there still mangroves in Bahrain.

TURTLES AND DUGONGS

JW: Have you heard anything recently on the turtle species?

SE: No, I've not. I'm very curious to know. We saw a few turtles on the *Mount Mitchell* cruise, but it wasn't the nesting season. We did see evidence that they had come up on the beaches in Karan Island. Tarballs were all over the beach. It's hard to know what effects the loss of the traditional beaches will have, and what will be the effects on the turtles of the beaches where they can still gain access.

JW: *How about the dugongs?*
SE: We witnessed a few in the course of our visit last spring. I saw none during previous visits.

Impacts on Fisheries Hard to Ascertain

JW: *How have the fisheries been impacted?*
SE: There's a lot of controversy about that. One of the problems, of course, is that it's hard to know when you don't have a reliable baseline against which to measure change. And even if you're out there trying to measure what's going on right now, the techniques are very primitive. It's hard enough if you're looking at populations of something you can see like deer or elk or caribou on the land, but working in a three-dimensional realm, where the best means you have available are blindly deployed nets that are dragged in what seem to be appropriate places, in the hope that you're going to catch something—it's hit or miss and not, in my view, something that can be taken seriously. You can make generalizations based on the subjective reports of fishermen who are suggesting that the catches are down. It's true with the shrimp. It's true with certain species of fish. But whether that is directly related to the spill, or there are other factors, for example, other toxic materials, whether there has been a slight, in some cases, cooling of the area because the pool of smoke reduced radiation for that year of 1991, that has caused a chain of reaction of events that might have an impact on the plants that in turn might have had an impact on the small organisms, that in turn might have had an impact on the fish—but in certain areas there have been reports that some of the species are more abundant than they've been before. That would be a reflection of reduced taking during 1991 because they had not been out fishing as much as before the war. It may have given certain species a breathing spell. There aren't any clear-cut answers.

JW: *Is the fish safe to eat?*
SE: The samples suggest that chances of any negative effect from eating the muscle tissues are probably very slim. You would have possible problems if you're inclined to eat the internal organs, the liver or such.

JW: *What were the most important findings of the 100-day cruise?*
SE: This was the first look at the Gulf in this way, to look at the currents, the temperature, the solidity, the general physical and chemical nature of that body of water. Nothing has been as comprehensive as this, over so broad an area with near-simultaneous efforts, in the Gulf. A nice twist was that the space shuttle was up in the sky during part of the cruise. The astronauts were able to talk with those aboard the ship. And that communication was more than just a handshake, more than just a nice gesture. It proved the concept of being able to have an overview

from the sky above coincident with making certain kinds of measurements at sea levels and below. And while it was proof of concept rather than actual work accomplished, it was a very elegant twist to add to the agenda.

Important findings did come in on all fronts explored, but baseline information is vital to draw conclusions. There needs to be a network of sampling stations that are permanently monitored, both in the chemical-physical and biological side of things, to look at the impacts of the oil. We need to follow up in a coordinated fashion.

LONG-TERM EFFECTS OF OIL

PW: How has the habitat changed?

SE: Well, there are substances now in the environment that were not there historically, i.e., large quantities of oil. And, some components of that oil in the short term have a toxic influence, and in the long term, depending on the nature of the substrate, it's going to be changed. Where the oil has formed tarmac you have a flat surface rather than a sandy surface.

JW: Some people say that the ecosystem is quite resilient to oil because there have been so many spills in the past.

SE: That's like saying you've had one automobile accident and, after six accidents, you'll be able to build up resistance to them. There are crabs and some organisms that prosper in the presence of oil and these conditions may cause a larger concentration of them. They can react speedily to an oil spill in the future. And there is some oil natural to the area, like off Santa Barbara in California, oil has been known historically, but not in this volume. Oil is not toxic to some things; in fact, certain organisms can help break down the oil, to make the environment more hospitable for a whole series of other things. That's what is happening now. But that happens only on the surface. When the oil is deep into the substrate below, with little hope of being moved around through the new areas that are being exposed over time, then the oil is likely to become a permanent fixture. It's geological change, long-term change.

JW: Won't the oil eventually naturally biodegrade?

SE: If exposed to the air and to organisms that can then get at it and process it and utilize it as a source of nutrients, yes. But these sediments are first of all very deep and far removed from areas where bacteria are likely to act on them. Digging down into the beaches, it's possible to see repeated layers of previous spills, and in some places the oil was still soft, in some places it formed a tarmac-like thing. Now, geologically speaking, maybe within the next thousand years there will be storms that will shift those sediments around and expose those oil-bearing sediments again to bacteria—blue algae and the like—but once they become really hard and rock-like, it's less likely to be degraded. And there are places like that where they are like organic rock, hard rock, and very difficult to break through with a shovel.

Overall Conclusions

PW: You were there from 1991 to 1993. What are your overall conclusions about change you have seen in the last two years?

SE: I am encouraged by the resilience of nature. There is evidence of some recovery of certain things along the shore. One misses elements of the underwater realm. If you didn't know beforehand what to expect, their absence might not be noticeable, but if you've seen some of the creatures in the past, you wonder where they went. Some are more sensitive to changing chemistry as a result of oil. In the spring of 1991, there were numerous small mollusks that were dying—olive shells in particular—and certain small plants. Whether they were oil-related is hard to say. There were substantial die-offs of various organisms, which acted like little cleaning stations. The diversity of the small subsets of the ecosystem were far more apparent in the offshore islands off Saudi Arabia. It's clear that the inshore reefs were stressed. You don't see the diversity of life that is normal. Plants and animals were showing signs of not being well.

There have been spills both before and since the war, relatively small spills. It's clear that it's an environment that up to 25 years ago enjoyed a long period of being what can be referred to as a wilderness state, but in recent times the pressures have been swift and strong, from fishing techniques applied with a much heavier hand to the introduction of massive amounts of oil, coupled with fallout from the sky, not just of oil, but of other atmospheric pollutants; the groundwater seeps some materials into the sea that are unfriendly to life, and so on; also, shoreline modification creates turbidity. There is a loss of organisms such as mangroves that under normal circumstances would help maintain the good health of these systems.

The small creatures—birds, crabs and little invertebrates—are squeezed in small spaces. You probably know Thomas Lovejoy's work on minimum critical size of habitats in places like the Brazilian rainforests. He asks, how small an area can you have and maintain a healthy ecosystem? It's fine to have protected areas, but they must be of a certain size. The payback can be enormous in maintaining the health of the area as a whole. This is an area where oxygen is generated and where carbon dioxide is absorbed, where organic materials are generally processed in a healthy ocean as a result of such activity. The absence of that means that the systems are more vulnerable to swings one way or another.

Need for Ongoing Monitoring, Sanctuaries

There needs to be a network of sampling stations that are permanently monitored, both in the chemical-physical and biological side of things, to look at the impacts of the oil. Are we really going to be surprised if some of those areas are destined to be modified, or is there likely to be some unforeseen mode of recovery and restoration? Not likely, but we need to keep an open mind. But we need to follow up in a coordinated fashion.

One aspect is that the magnitude of the catastrophe made people think of the good health of the air, land and sea, which may not have come to their attention before. It has been creeping up on them fast, as it has in other areas of the world, here in the U.S. as well. The importance of taking care of the place, the fact that the misbehavior of, in this case, Saddam Hussein, Iraqis generally, can have a huge impact on everyone, including the Iraqis. Nobody wins when anyone misbehaves. Everyone gains if the converse is true. Any place set aside for sanctuary of birds, coral reefs, turtles will contribute to the magnitude and good health of the whole system.

JW: Have you the impression from talking to people in the region that they are more environmentally conscious since the war?

SE: Yes, more sensitized and absolutely more interested in trying to work together in cooperative solutions. I'm encouraged there will be a greater dialogue between scientists who have not communicated greatly in the past.

PW: Do you think there's been enough effort on the part of UNEP or ROPME to monitor and try to remedy the situation?

SE: It's a little disappointing that more effort has not been made to establish the monitoring stations that people thought were a good idea; also to establish protected areas. It's vital that an effort is made to hold onto what remains. I hope that people will be inspired and not lose momentum to follow through, both in monitoring and keeping lines of communication open.

POSSIBLE IMPACTS OF OIL FIRES ON WEATHER OUTSIDE THE GULF

PW: Congressmember Nancy Pelosi has said that until we abolish war, we must consider its environmental costs.

SE: I agree. We too often take the environment for granted. Most people, when they think of the Gulf War, think of the cost of oil, loss of troops, but don't put on the balance sheet the resiliency of the support system. People say not to worry, the environmental damage in the Gulf is too far away and won't affect us. That's like saying your shoulder is not connected to your arm. Because everyone suffers if anybody suffers.

PW: The oil fire smoke may have impacted a region far wider than the Gulf.

SE: At the outset there were concerns over the great plume of smoke on the atmosphere beyond the Gulf area. At least in the near term, those fears proved unfounded.

JW: Some of the people we've talked to think there was an effect of the oil fires on the Bangladesh cyclone of April 1991.

SE: There may be a synergistic effect in the subtle way the system gets nudged. It's possible that things of this nature might be provoked or in some way lead to it. One thing I know is that it wasn't an insignificant impact. It created changes in the air, sea and land and impact on the people, and it will continue to do so.

Neither global warming nor cooling were greatly affected one way or another, but it wasn't without impact. You can't do anything without setting in motion a series of events that will ultimately come back and have an effect on the good health of the system. The loss of any of the resiliency of that part of the world is again a loss to the whole world. The way the birds' flyways were interrupted—channels through which they typically passed to feed on organisms—and are now modified because the traditional marshes are covered in oil and not producing the way they used to.

You think of the science of chaos as the way to understand the way the impact on one part of the planet can generate a force somewhere else. A butterfly flapping its wings over Japan can have an impact on the weather in New York in due course. It sounds extremely far-fetched, but it's not only theoretically possible, we see evidence all the time. A seemingly innocent little nudge in the system over one quarter can set in motion a chain reaction that has a magnifying impact down the other end, all around the world simultaneously. It's not just a few natural perturbations, not just a few earthquakes, fires and storms and volcanoes, which are natural; it's all of those coupled with additional stresses we are putting on the system. Life, hallelujah, is extremely resilient, so it may come out all right in the end, but it may not.

THE CENSORSHIP OF SCIENCE

PW: There have been several reports of censorship of findings regarding the environmental impacts of the war—especially the atmospheric impacts of the smoke—orders that came from the U.S. Department of Energy.

SE: It's true that because of the war there were obviously some policies in effect to keep a lid on information of whatever sort. There was still some residual attitude after the war, because if it was a secret once, people think it's got to continue to be a secret. It gradually changed, and certainly I've never felt constrained about anything I've observed. Particularly with the atmospheric measurements and findings, there was a concern about prematurely jumping into conclusions that couldn't be substantiated. It was a very crazy time. Everyone was really concerned.

Chapter 3

The Oil Fires

An oil field set ablaze by the Iraqi occupation forces. ©1991. UN photo 158124/J. Isaac.

Introduction

Prior to the Gulf War, a number of scientists publicly predicted radical changes in weather patterns if Kuwaiti oil wells were set alight. Completed just days before the war, in January 1991, an internal U.S. Defense Nuclear Agency (DNA) report predicted the probable environmental impacts should there be major oil well fires in Kuwait. It warned, "This would be a massive and unprecedented pollution event. It would impact the ecology of the Persian Gulf, and fall out on a wide swath across Southern Iran, Pakistan, and Northern India. The impact on human population and desert ecosystems from such prolonged soot fallout is unknown."[1] The DNA report is excerpted in this chapter.

At the beginning of the war, the first smoke over the Gulf probably came from oil fires set alight by Coalition bombing. According to the U.S. Air Force, Coalition forces bombed 28 Iraqi oil refineries, leaving Iraqi refined oil production at zero early on in the war.[2] On February 15, the retreating Iraqi army began dynamiting facilities located in seven oil fields mostly south of Kuwait City. Over 700 oil wells were set alight.[3]

The Kuwait Oil Company claims that three percent of its prewar oil reserves of 100,000,000,000 barrels were lost in the fires. Eyewitnesses estimated that between a third and a half of the oil burned, and therefore at least 1,500,000,000, and possibly 2,000,000,000, barrels of oil returned to Earth unburned.[4]

According to the U.S. National Science Foundation (NSF), roughly three percent of the oil that burned turned into soot, the part of the plume about which there was the most concern.[5] However, huge quantities of carbon dioxide (CO_2), sulfur dioxide (SO_2), salt and a wide range of hydrocarbon compounds (some of them carcinogenic and mutagenic) were also emitted. Small oil droplets fell out of the plume within a fifty-kilometer radius of the fires.[6]

The hundreds of millions of barrels that did not burn after they spilled out of the ground are the cause of the oil lakes, black rain and other forms of fallout through the territory downwind of Kuwait. Evaporation may quickly have reduced the amount of oil in the oil lakes by half. Some of the remaining oil seeped into the ground, and some biodegraded. An unknown amount, estimated recently at 100,000,000 barrels, constitute the oil lakes that still remain.[7] The effects of this legacy of the fires have hardly been studied.

Fire-fighting crews from all over the world, hired by the Kuwait Oil Company, took nine months to put the fires out. During this time the Kuwaiti people lived under black skies and experienced continual oil fallout.[8] The U.S. Interagency Air Assessment team, staffed by the National Oceanic and Atmospheric Administration (NOAA) and the Environmental Protection Agency (EPA), monitored pollutant levels in Kuwait soon after the fires were started, and reported that there were no significant acute health risks to people with normal respiratory capacity, but that more data were needed to determine long-term health risks.[9] Halûk Özkaynak, a specialist on the effects of air pollution on public health, and Paul Horsman of Greenpeace International were in the Gulf in 1991, and both argue in this chapter that there is not yet enough technical knowledge and baseline data to judge the extent to which the oil fires carried long-term health risks.

The NSF team found that particle concentrations approached background levels within 1,000 kilometers of the fires.[10] However, according to Michael Renner of Worldwatch Institute, "Satellite pictures showed that by mid-March, clouds of toxic smoke were stretching from Romania and Bulgaria to Afghanistan and Pakistan."[11]

Black snow fell in the Himalayas that year, 2,000 kilometers from Kuwait, and smaller quantities of smaller soot particles traveled longer distances. Researchers who found soot over Japan deduced that it had circumnavigated the Earth one-and-a-half times.[12]

At least at the beginning of the war, the U.S. government issued a gag order on scientists with regard to the fate of the soot that traveled around the world. Lara Hilder, an aerosol chemist employed at Lawrence Berkeley Laboratory, comments on how scientists experienced this censorship. Abdullah Toukan, who at the World Climate Conference in Geneva in November 1990 was one of the first to draw attention to the possible environmental impacts of the war, discusses the UN response to the crisis.

The rest of the chapter presents conflicting opinions about the effects of the oil fires on the weather, including the responses to a questionnaire which, in January 1993, ARC/Arms Control Research Center sent to several experts who have studied the possible effects of the fires on the global climate. Those interested in reading more about the technical aspects of the fires are directed to the proceedings of three conferences: The Health Impacts of Kuwaiti Oil Fires, held in Birmingham University, England, October 1991; the Kuwait Oil Fire Conference, held at the Harvard University School of Public Health, August 1991; and the Environmental Dimensions of the Gulf: Policy and Institutional Perspectives, held at Al Ain, United Arab Emirates, April 19–22, 1992.

—*James Warner and Philippa Winkler*

Notes:

1. R.D. Small, *Environmental Impact of Damage to Kuwaiti Oil Facilities*, Report, (prepared for the U.S. Defense Nuclear Agency), Pacific-Sierra Research Corporation, Santa Monica, January 1991.

2. U.S. Air Force, *Reaching Globally, Reaching Powerfully: The U.S. Air Force in the Gulf War*, Report, Washington D.C., September 1991, 31. See also James F. Dunnigan and Austin Bay, *From Shield to Storm* (New York: William Morrow and Co. Inc.), 1992, 181. Also see Chapter Five for environmental assessments of three oil treatment facilities bombed in Iraq.

3. Saudi Meteorological and Environmental Protection Administration, *Environmental Impact of Oil Burning in the Kuwaiti Oil Fields; A Preliminary Evaluation*, Report, (prepared for the Geneva World Meteorological Organization expert meeting on the atmospheric part of the emergency response to the Kuwait oil field fires, April 27–30, 1991), Jiddah, 1991.

4. T.M. Hawley, *Against the Fires of Hell: The Environmental Disaster of the Gulf War* (Orlando, Florida: Harcourt Brace Jovanovich), 1992, 142.

5. Peter V. Hobbs and Lawrence F. Radke, "Airborne Studies of the Smoke from the Kuwait Oil Fires", *Science*, vol. 256 (May 15, 1992): 987–990.

6. Peter V. Hobbs and Lawrence F. Radke, "Airborne Studies."

7. Interview with Sylvia Earle in Chapter Four. See also T.M. Hawley, *Against the Fires of Hell*, 143.

8. T.M. Hawley, *Against the Fires of Hell*, 128–129, 147–148.

9. EPA and NOAA, *Kuwait Oil Fires; Interagency Interim Report*, Washington DC, April 3, 1991.

10. Peter V. Hobbs and Lawrence F. Radke, "Airborne Studies."

11. Michael Renner, "The Environmental Aftershock of the War," *The New Economy*, April/May 1991.

12. Kikuo Okada et al., "Extremely High Proportions of Soot Particles in the Upper Troposphere Over Japan," *Geophysical Research Letters*, vol. 19 no. 9 (May 4, 1992): 921–924.

Oil Fields at Risk.
This map is reproduced from the DNA report. The spellings of place names on this map do not correspond to those in the text of the rest of the book.

Prewar Environmental and Health Assessments

Pacific-Sierra Research Corporation, Sandia National Laboratories

The Bush Administration knew five days before going to war at midnight GMT on January 16, 1991, that the destruction of the Kuwaiti oil wells and refineries was likely to produce disastrous consequences throughout the Gulf and beyond. The following is excerpted from two sources: a January 11, 1991, report, Environmental Impact of Damage to Kuwait Oil Facilities, *by Richard D. Small, of the Pacific-Sierra Research Corporation in West Los Angeles, for the Defense Nuclear Agency; and a report prepared by the Sandia National Laboratories in January 1991 for restricted distribution for the United States Department of Energy under Contract DE-AC04-76DPOO789, Office of Foreign Intelligence.*

FROM THE DEFENSE NUCLEAR AGENCY REPORT

In 1989, Kuwait produced 1,593,000 barrels a day rom 363 producing wells in seven fields. Over 80 percent of the production is from the Burgan (210 wells) and Magwa (71 wells) fields. There are in addition another 380 nonproducing wells.

Kuwait's oil facilities include three refineries with a combined capacity of 670,000 barrels a day. They are Mina Abdullah (capacity 200,000 barrels a day), Mina Al Ahmadi (270,000 barrels a day) and Shuaiba (200,000 barrels a day). An estimated 13,000,000 barrels are stored.

Destruction of the wells will cause fires that are likely to continue until extinguished. These fires are isolated "point" fires supported by the natural flow rate of each well. The fires would not merge, but, until the pressure is reduced, they will continuously add smoke to the atmosphere. The refinery fires will be difficult to extinguish, but the burning and smoke production is limited to the stock at hand. Because of the natural flow rates in Kuwaiti wells and the refinery inventory presumably still on hand, the potential exists for a massive environmental event.

In a 30 day period, 450,000 metric tons of smoke could be added to the atmosphere. This mass would be supplemented by smoke from the refinery complexes should they also be set on fire.

The potential for environmental damage depends on both the smoke mass and the injection height. In general, smoke from the refinery fires will be injected higher than smoke from the burning wells. Smoke from burning refinery stocks could reach 1 to 3 km, while smoke from the oil fields generally will stay below 1 km.

A number of impacts have been projected. These include smoke clouds covering 20 percent of the Northern Hemisphere, cooling of the earth's surface similar to a "nuclear winter," failure of the Asian monsoons, and heating of the atmosphere due to increased CO_2 production. Such consequences are serious and should be neither advocated nor dismissed without cause.

Even though the wells may continue to burn and produce smoke (450,000 million metric tons a month) for a prolonged period, the dispersion is likely to be regional rather than continental because the injection is so low. Most of the fallout will probably occur over the Persian Gulf, Southern Iran, Pakistan and Northern India.

The estimates we develop in this note of the smoke mass produced by the destruction of Kuwait's oil wells and refineries and the injection height of the smoke do not support any of the purported climate impacts. The amount of smoke is not injected high enough to spread over large areas of the Northern Hemisphere, nor is a large enough amount of smoke produced to cause a measurable temperature change or failure of the monsoons.

Nevertheless, a large amount of smoke could be produced. This would be a massive and unprecedented pollution event. It would impact the ecology of the Persian Gulf and [would] fall out on a wide swath across southern Iran, Pakistan, and northern India. The impact on human population and desert ecosystems from such prolonged soot fallout is unknown.

FROM THE SANDIA NATIONAL LABORATORIES REPORT

Based on concentration analyses and toxicity data, the effects of airborne contaminants on mortality are expected to be small, except possibly downwind of burning trenches, where concentrations may be adequate to produce nausea and eye and respiratory irritation. Carbon monoxide, carcinogens and heavy metals are not expected to have a significant effect. The largest effect is expected from SO_2. Some increased mortality in a small, sensitive population, especially newborns and the elderly, is expected and will be most severe at 10 kilometers from a burning field. The largest effect will occur if the wind is from the south, putting Kuwait City in the path of combustion products from the Burgan oil field. Winds from the south occur infrequently. Even with winds from the south, SO_2 concentrations are probably not large enough to affect nonsensitive people in Kuwait City seriously. Hydrogen sulfide is expected to have a negligible effect except in the immediate vicinity of the oil fields. For personnel in the vicinity of trenches or wells, respiratory protection is recommended because the fumes and toxins may cause debilitating nausea.

Oil Fires, Air Pollution and Regional Health Effects

Interview with Halûk Özkaynak

Halûk Özkaynak, Ph.D., is an expert on air pollution and public health, and a Research Associate and Lecturer in the Department of Environmental Health at the Harvard School of Public

Health. He visited Saudi Arabia in June 1991 for Friends of the Earth. Interviewed September 1991 by John M. Miller. Transcript revised by Halûk Özkaynak in February 1993.

John M. Miller: William Reilly, the head of the EPA, said that the oil fires pose no health problem, and the Pentagon thinks it's not a problem. You disagree?

Halûk Özkaynak: There are two issues: what is seen or reported, versus what is not known. One can get a false sense of security if one over-interprets the limited number of observations made on the environment and hospital data, because there is too much uncertainty. I was surprised that the EPA took this approach and readily jumped to conclusions.

Existing information on air pollution is not comprehensive in terms of available air monitoring. The EPA has reached the conclusion that there is no significant concern. They could have presented the same findings in a different fashion. For example, they could have said that we are assured that a lot of the pollutants that we were worried about were measured in concentrations that were not high, but we still need to collect more information and study the extent of the problem and the nature of health impacts further. I think they kind of missed that caveat in what they reported.

By contrast with their caution about coming to conclusions on other, domestic issues, such as the acid rain problem, the EPA took a much less conservative approach this time, claiming that the information available right now tells us there is nothing to worry about.

My principal concern is that there are certain types of pollutants that we have not yet measured. There are certain atmospheric conditions that we have not measured, namely the situations from direct plume impact, which do not happen every day—the episodic events. Also, the characterization of what is in the plume in terms of pollutants has not been done. Some of that information is currently being gathered; additional information should be gathered as well. Until we know the answers from such studies, I think it is somewhat premature to say that there is really no atmospheric or health impact to worry about from the oil well fire emissions.

JMM: The EPA has made some measurements of some things?

HÖ: They have measured the standard set of criteria particles and gases, including respiratory particles: sulfur dioxide (SO_2), hydrogen sulfide (H_2S), carbon dioxide (CO_2), nitrogen dioxide (NO_2). However, organics, acids, size-fractionated particle mass, chemical composition and elemental characterization of particles have not yet been studied. I know that EPA researchers are planning on conducting those measurements, who have the equipment and the know-how to do that. At the time that EPA administrator William Reilly visited the Gulf, those studies were not yet made or completed. Knowing that additional data were being obtained, the EPA administrator could have been a little more conservative and prudent about claiming that there is nothing to worry about.

The health effects issue is a different matter. There is hardly anything being done on the health end of things. We have no information on the increase and exacerbation of respiratory conditions due to the oil fire plume effects. There have been anecdotal reports in the local papers, and I heard from talking to various people in the region that the number of visits to hospitals or clinics for respiratory symptoms, eye irritations, and nose irritations have probably increased since the war. However, nobody has systematically and scientifically collected all of this information. This is one area where we urgently need to start gathering data. It should have happened right away but it has not.

JMM: So this would be door-to-door, or hospital admissions?

HÖ: Mostly hospital-based studies, working with physicians and having them take the lead on getting the data from clinics, hospitals, even private physicians. Door-to-door studies are more community-oriented health studies and could support more rigorous epidemiologic studies. They are useful, but I think that, since there seems to be socialized medicine and people do use the hospitals and clinics, one should try to get information from those central sources.

The epidemiologic approach is a much more refined and sharper method. We rely on it in this country a lot, and it's essential for situations in this country because we don't often experience major impacts. But in the Gulf region we are talking about definitely measurable impacts that you can probably find out by examining data from archives at hospitals and clinics. One would make comparisons of prior-to-plume impacts with after-the-plume impacts and try to make approximate, if not qualitative, comparisons that way. So far, anecdotal information exists which should not be readily dismissed. As a person who is worried about health effects and works in the field of environmental epidemiology, I would be extremely cautious about claiming that there is nothing to worry about from air pollution impacts.

JMM: What sorts of health effects would you expect, aside from a raw throat and cough?

HÖ: Children and adults in Al Ahmadi, who have been getting a lot of these oily particles falling on their bodies, are having a bronchitis type of reaction, difficulties in breathing, asthmatic-type responses and so on. People who are young and have pre-existing respiratory ailments, and people who are old are obviously going to be immediately feeling the impacts of respiratory effects of particle pollutants. If you go farther away to Saudi Arabia where the plume is noticed on a more episodic basis, you are probably going to experience to a lesser degree some of the more subtle effects like eye burning, nose irritation, sore throats and things like that. I heard people telling me that they had colds that didn't go away for weeks and months. So those types of effects could conceivably happen.

It is not, unfortunately, a field where we know exactly what relationships to expect between x number of micrograms per cubic meter of oil particle pollution and a given type of health response. A unique set of exposure conditions do exist in Kuwait and Saudi Arabia, and the concentrations in some cases are very high. The health responses could vary by exposure level, from severe reactions by asthmatics and people who have bronchitis, to some minor irritations and simple headaches or nausea. There could be a whole host of symptoms, and there are acute versus chronic effects that could come into play in this kind of exposure situation.

Those are some of my concerns, and what I would like to see is not only more extensive pollution monitoring, but for them to begin collecting health data. I know that there was not much happening in Saudi Arabia in terms of epidemiologic or health effects studies.

JMM: I don't know if you saw today's New York Times *where it was reported that the National Toxics Campaign had analyzed some of the smoke from the fires and found five toxic hydrocarbon compounds that were not being measured at all.*

HÖ: Measuring organics is not that easy. There are particle-phase organics and gas-phase organics. You need, in some cases, sophisticated chemical support facilities, laboratory facilities on site, and to be able to store the samples right. That is why organic measurements have not been among the first set of things to be measured and monitored by EPA and the other groups, including our group, because of the difficulty in sampling and analysis. So I am not at all surprised at what you are saying because oil particles contain a lot of different organic constituents, and they are going to be condensing as they cool off and coat the particles that are out there. The King Fahd Research Institute has been analyzing hydrocarbon particles in Saudi Arabia. Harvard School of Public Health is also evaluating the relative toxicity of oil fire particles. Results indicate that these particles are in fact toxic and not as benign as dust particles; they are more mutagenic than pure coarse particles.[1]

Given the course along which we expect the information to develop, I would not yet make definitive statements on whether we have any effects or not from oil fire particle impacts.

JMM: What kinds of effects do the organics have?

HÖ: Most of our information will not tell us if a particular oil fire chemical is going to cause a nosebleed or a cancer. We don't have that kind of sophistication in terms of pinning down each type and level of organic with a given type of health response. However, quite a few of the organics are mutagenic or carcinogenic. If you have long-term exposures, I would not be surprised if the carcinogenic risks would be significant. But that is going to vary depending on the duration and the amount of exposures. People who live in Al Ahmadi, for example, may be at higher risk than individuals living in Saudi Arabia who are maybe zapped by lower concentrations once a month.

Carcinogenic impacts are obviously something that everybody worries about, but noncarcinogenic effects have been really difficult to characterize for a lot of the organic substances. The data most often come from animal bioassays and from studying various types of genotoxic effects and systemic effects and also from occupational situations. Researchers then try to extrapolate that information to the general population and lower concentrations. Systemic reactions, respiratory irritations, reproductive effects, and other effects could be associated with some of the organic species. There could be a whole host of responses to a lot of the organics. We are dealing with mixtures, of course, of which little or hardly anything is known.

NOTES:

1. Howard Lieber, "Mutagenicity of Soot: A Comparative Analysis," *Proceedings of the Harvard University School of Public Health Kuwait Oil Fire Conference,* August 1991.

Testimony of the U.S. Interagency Study Group on the Kuwait Oil Fires

Peter V. Hobbs

Peter V. Hobbs, Ph.D., a professor of Atmospheric Sciences at the University of Washington, Seattle, testified before the U.S. Senate Environment and Public Works Committee (Gulf Pollution Task Force) on July 11, 1991.

The following is a summary of the preliminary results of a U.S. interagency study of the atmospheric effects of the smoke from the Kuwait oil fires, supported by the NSF, the Defense Nuclear Agency (DNA), the DOE, NOAA, the private sector, and the National Geographic Society. The team of scientists and support personnel from seven universities, National Aeronautics and Space Administration (NASA), NOAA and NCAR conducted a five-week airborne field study in the Arabian Gulf, using two specially equipped research aircraft.

OBJECTIVES
- To measure the nature and the quantities of the various particles and gases in the smoke.
- To determine the effects of the smoke on the atmosphere on local, regional and global scales.

NATURE OF THE EMISSIONS

Some 500 oil fires are still burning in Kuwait, spread out over an area about the size of greater New York City and roughly centered on Kuwait City (although most of the fires are south of Kuwait City, which is fortunate since northerly winds are dominant in that area, and these carry the smoke southward away from the city, down the Arabian Gulf).

These fires are producing an enormous plume of black smoke. For example, if the fires were indeed located in New York City, the plume of smoke would extend all the way down to Florida, where it would be several hundred miles in width.

Based on our airborne measurements we estimate that the fires are consuming about three million barrels of oil per day (about one-half the U.S. daily import of oil) and emitting about:
- one to two million tons of CO_2 per day (about two percent of worldwide emission of CO_2 from all sources);
- nine thousand tons per day of SO_2 (about ten times the rate of emission from an average volcano);
- and five thousand tons per day of soot (i.e., elemental carbon).

LOCAL AND REGIONAL EFFECTS

Clearly the smoke is having marked effects on the Gulf region in terms of:

- air quality,
- visibility, and
- reduction in surface temperatures due to absorption of the sun's radiation by the smoke (e.g., Bahrain, which is 250 miles from Kuwait, has just had the coldest May in 35 years, to be exact, 7.4° F below average).

In these respects, the Kuwait oil fires provide a sobering demonstration, albeit on a relatively small scale, of the atmospheric effects that could accompany a larger war with widespread fires and smoke.

As the Kuwait fires are put out, most of their effects on the atmosphere should disappear. However, large areas of the desert are being covered by oil, which may affect not only the ecology of the desert but its absorption of the sun's radiation (regions of the desert are being covered with the equivalent of black asphalt).

GLOBAL EFFECTS

The good news is that our studies indicated that it is quite unlikely that the smoke from the Kuwait fires will have any significant effects beyond the Gulf region. The reasons for this are:

- the smoke is not rising very high in the atmosphere where it could be transported rapidly over large distances (our airborne measurements in May and June 1991 showed the smoke to be confined below about 20,000 feet, and in the Gulf region the base of the stratosphere is at about 45,000 feet);
- the smoke particles are such that they should be removed rather quickly from the atmosphere by cloud and precipitation processes; and
- any smoke that might be carried to high levels and transported over larger distances should be much too small in amount to produce any climatic effects.

Problems Assessing Health Risks From The Oil Fires

John S. Evans

Excerpted from testimony by John S. Evans, Sc.D., C.I.H., Associate Professor of Environmental Science, Harvard School of Public Health, before the Senate Environment and Public Works Committee, Gulf Pollution Task Force, October 16, 1991.

The human health consequences due to exposure to air pollutants from the fires cannot, at this time, be assessed with confidence. There are several reasons for this:

1) In most of the dramatic historic air pollution episodes, levels of both smoke and sulfur dioxide have been elevated. In Kuwait, high levels of sulfur dioxide have not been observed.

2) Although the smoke does not appear to be acidic, preliminary studies suggest that it is a pulmonary irritant, with a potency comparable to urban aerosols.

3) The measurements of particulate matter taken to date in Kuwait and Saudi Arabia reflect mixtures of smoke from the fires, crustal materials resuspended by the wind, and other sources. Without auxiliary information on carbon concentrations or detailed source apportionment studies, it is difficult to determine the contribution of the fires to the total mass.

4) In most of the dramatic air pollution episodes, most of the deaths have occurred among the elderly. According to the 1985 Census of Kuwait, only 3.5 percent of the population was over 65 and nearly 60 percent of the population was under 20 years old.

Despite these complexities, it would be premature to rule out significant public heath impacts from the fires.

The epidemiological studies that have been reported to date have been relatively limited in scope, size and approach. To demonstrate convincingly the absence of acute effects, it would be necessary to study the day-to-day correlations between air pollution exposures from the fires and measures of morbidity or mortality. As I mentioned previously, the air pollution measurements taken to date do not provide an accurate picture of exposure to pollutants from the fires. Random errors in exposure measurements have the effect in epidemiology of biasing toward the null, that is, failing to find effects even when they are present.

Even if better exposure information were available, it is likely that quite sophisticated time series analyses would be necessary to find the effects of the fires against the random noise in the relatively small numbers of daily deaths in Kuwait, typically four or five deaths per day, compared with 250 per day in London.

Finally, I want to note that individual risks do not need to be particularly large to be of concern from the perspective of public health. Recall that in the most severe London fog 4,000 excess deaths occurred in a population of eight million. The individual risk in that case was less than one in 2,000.

Chronology of a Coverup

Background Information

The following is based on articles by John Horgan: "U.S. Gags Discussion of War's Environmental Effects," Scientific American, *May 1991; "Burning Questions: Scientists Launch Studies of Kuwait's*

Oil Fires," and "Why are Data from Kuwait Being Withheld?", Scientific American, *July 1991; also Lara Hilder and Pete Liederman's article, "Smoke and Mirrors: EPA Slows News of Gulf Soot," in* IMPACTS, *the newsletter of the Sierra Club's Military Impacts on the Environment Committee, Summer 1991; and Andre Carruthers' article "After Desert Storm, The Deluge,"* Greenpeace Magazine, *October/November/December 1991.*

During and after the war, some satellite photographs showing smoke patterns from the region were withheld by the U.S. government. For example, the National Oceanic and Atmospheric Administration (NOAA) was kept from publishing many of its satellite photos until the president of the Union of Concerned Scientists intervened several months after the end of the fighting.

On January 25, 1991, researchers at Lawrence Livermore National Laboratory (LLNL) received a memorandum silencing discussion of the environmental impacts of the war. The memo read, in part:

> DOE (Department of Energy) Headquarters Public Affairs has requested that all DOE facilities and contractors immediately discontinue any further discussion of war-related research and issues with the media until further notice. The extent of what we are authorized to say about environmental impacts of fires/oil spills in the Middle East follows: Most independent studies and experts suggest that the catastrophic predictions in some recent news reports are exaggerated. We are currently reviewing the matter, but these predictions remain speculative and do not warrant any further comment at this time. If there are any doubts about appropriate comments, please refer inquiries to Office of Communications and Planning, John Belluardo.

Although the Gulf War ended February 28, the order was only partially lifted on March 22, when Belluardo told John Horgan of *Scientific American* that "there are no longer any restrictions." On March 28, DOE issued a memo modifying the original order. The new memo read, in part, "Laboratories may release or discuss previously released information which is in the public domain." However, the memo also required "prior approval of interviews by national media and approval of press releases prior to release." The origins of the gag order have been traced to the White House.

The gag order extended to all agencies involved in the U.S. response to the fires. In late February, the Administration hurriedly convened a task force to evaluate the effects of the burning oil wells. Researchers from the task force, headed by the EPA, began monitoring smoke from the fires in March. Agencies which were members of the Interagency Persian Gulf Task Force (IAPGTF) had to have their press releases approved by officials of the EPA, the "lead agency." In addition to the EPA, the task force included representatives from NOAA, DOE, the Department of Defense (DOD) and other government agencies.

In early April, Joyce Penner of DOE's Lawrence Livermore Labs was told not to present the results of a computer simulation of the fires at a scientific conference in Vienna.

MAUNA LOA

In February 1991, less than a month after the start of the war, NOAA researchers at an observatory on the Mauna Loa volcano in Hawaii detected elevated soot levels. The timing of the first soot "spike" is important because it occurred well before the bulk of Kuwait oil fields were set afire and indicates that the soot may have come from Coalition bombing of Iraqi oil refineries and storage tanks. A press release on the Mauna Loa findings prepared in early April, tracing the increase to the Gulf War, was withheld by John Kasper, head of press relations for EPA and spokesperson for the IAPGTF. The press release was finally issued on April 30 after inquiries from the Sierra Club and *Scientific American*. Kasper denies that suppression of the release was designed to conceal potentially embarrassing information.

In May, other DOE researchers said they were still under orders not to discuss the fires without clearance from DOE headquarters. Of ten projects studying the impacts of the war on the environment, the Sierra Club found that at least six had been subject to gags on public discussion of their data. For example, the *San Francisco Examiner* reported on May 14 that the gag order had prevented a reporter from interviewing LLNL climate expert Mike McCracken on the impact of the Mideast oil fires.

In May, after a hasty and incomplete assessment of the impacts of the fires, the EPA issued a report, whose main conclusion was that emissions in the smoke were not "at levels of concern." Moreover the EPA officials turned down press requests for interviews with task force researchers. "They're over there to do monitoring," explained Mary J. Mears, an EPA spokesperson. "We don't want them talking to the press."

According to Paul Horsman, who coordinated the Greenpeace International Expedition to the Gulf in August and September of 1991, the authorities in Kuwait undertook a massive effort to downplay the potential and actual effects of the oil fires on the population for political reasons—they wanted to prevent a panic among the residents of Kuwait. Historic public health data in Kuwait was not made available to Greenpeace International or to local health experts. They were denied access to hospitals or doctors, and there was an ongoing argument between local health professionals and Kuwait's Environmental Protection Agency over the question of access to information.[1]

A June 16 cable sent by the U.S. State Department to its embassies in the Gulf warned that predictions concerning "the risks from the oil fire smoke to human health, the environment, crop production and the global climate . . . should be considered as little more than guesswork." Meanwhile, U.S. officials continued to publicly maintain that the risks were insignificant.

At a hearing of his Gulf Pollution Task Force in early July 1991, Senator Joseph Lieberman said that the Administration promised to release all data relating to the oil fires.

—John M. Miller

NOTES:
1. Interview with Paul Horsman, December 12, 1992.

The Gag Order: Did the U.S. Government Hide Facts About the Fires?

Interview with Lara Hilder

Lara Hilder, Ph.D., is an aerosol chemist and soot specialist employed at Lawrence Berkeley Laboratory. She is a member of the Sierra Club Committee on Military Impacts on the Environment, and co-editor of IMPACTS, *its newsletter. Interviewed by John M. Miller in January 1992. Reviewed by Lara Hilder January, 1993.*

John M. Miller: It is clear that some memos were issued in January 1991 telling scientists from the Department of Energy, at least, not to talk about the environmental impacts of the war. It is not clear how long this blackout extended. What were you able to find out?

Lara Hilder: The science coordinator for NOAA's Arabian Gulf Program office, Dr. Barbara Bailey, told me in December 1991 that this memo was not really meant to be taken seriously after the war ended (February 28). The original DOE order to LLNL was dated January 25, and it was superseded by another on March 22. The March memo conditionally lifted the earlier one.

One censorship case, the government admits, occurred in early April. This involved the measurement of Mideast oil fire smoke at the NOAA observatory on the Hawaiian volcano Mauna Loa.

During March and April many journalists and even scientists were disallowed copies of satellite photos of the fires. Pressure from Henry Kendall, president of the Union of Concerned Scientists and a Nobel Prize winning physicist, is credited with convincing authorities to release the first ones in April. Within a few days of my talking with the source of the gag order on the Mauna Loa story [John Kasper of the Environmental Protection Agency, press officer for the IAPGTF], a watered-down press release appeared. That was April 30. Pressure on the White House may also have been applied by Senator Joseph Lieberman's office. His staff told me on April 25 that they were having trouble getting information on the environmental impacts of the war and felt that a well-placed call might help.

Carl Irving, a reporter for the *San Francisco Examiner,* said that in early May, DOE had not granted LLNL personnel permission to talk to him. John Horgan of *Scientific American* told me on May 15th, 1991 that Mike McCracken of LLNL had had to get permission from DOE in Washington to talk to him. Release of information from the monitoring flights over Kuwait mid-May to mid-June had to be approved by government representatives of the U.S., Kuwait and Saudi Arabia, according to a participant. At a meeting at Harvard University in mid-August, a LLNL scientist [Thomas J. Sullivan] whose calculations indicated possible involvement of the Kuwait soot particles in the Bangladesh storms, was told not to alarm the public with his opinions. [The text of Sullivan's speech to the Harvard oil fires conference appears later in the chapter.]

The EPA Kuwait czar told me in April that there was never an attempt to stifle legitimate scientific discussion. On September 30, the IAPGTF had a meeting with nongovernmental organizations to discuss the environmental impact of the Kuwait oil fires. One Sierra Club staffer described the presentation as a "dog and pony show" meant to respond to charges of government suppression of information.

John Horgan's disclosure of the gag order in April embarrassed the government, and I think it helped speed release of information. Efforts of Kendall, Lieberman's staff, the Sierra Club and others helped expose the gag order too. But there is a fundamental problem with the government's continuing efforts to minimize the environmental and human impacts of the war.

JMM: You said that this media blackout was more or less intended to last just through the war, the actual fighting. Why would all these scientists and bureaucrats just have assumed that it should continue until somebody actually formally said that it was over?

LH: Normally, scientific results are announced by publication in refereed, peer-reviewed journals, with coincident press releases if the scientists, their organizations and funders think the studies are newsworthy. This process is time-consuming; it's typical for six months to elapse between the time of submission of an article and its publication. A year would not be at all unusual. So, in the normal publication time span, the gag order would have been irrelevant. Some scientists with projects relating to environmental effects of the war may have found the restrictions on public discussion a convenient shield to keep them out of the limelight.

A number of colleagues have told me that dealing with the media has been a real headache, with constant work interruptions and embarrassing newspaper stories with misinterpretations of their work. Given the constant struggle to get government funding for research, many investigators would prefer not to rock the boat by complaining about the restrictions. In spite of this, many scientists were very angry about the restrictions.

Dr. Bailey at NOAA told me her impression that restrictions were only meant to last during the war, but she said it was rather difficult for people at her level to get information from the Persian Gulf Task Force until they were "introduced" to the right people.

The Extent of Censorship

My work leads me to believe that decisions were made in the White House to control environmental and health information, and they were enforced by the IAPGTF. It was easy to do because they coordinated ground-level measurements in Kuwait soon after the war. Scientists and technicians from Task Force agencies made some measurements of particles and gases in early March. These were the basis of the report released in early April that there was no acute health risk from the oil fires.[1]

JMM: That was the Interagency Persian Gulf Task Force report. You mentioned that the team had some technical limitations. Would you mind expanding on that point?

LH: I learned that people were deputized by their organizations to participate in the monitoring effort. I was told by Kasper and others that there wasn't very much time to plan the trip or assemble equipment, because there was a sense of extreme urgency. My assessment from what he told me is that they did a fairly sloppy job.

It is hard enough to organize a field expedition when you are not under stress, because you have to get together all the nuts and bolts, fittings and pumps, and you can forget things. When you have to do things in a hurry, you might forget to calibrate instruments properly or forget to bring a crucial component, and then you would have to make do. So they might not have a great technical basis for their conclusions. Now, presumably there were competent people making the measurements, but there is a possibility of sloppiness. Preparation was better for the flights of May and June because there was more time to get organized, and participants included many people whose professional reputations might depend on acquiring decent data.

The data of the March sampling expedition went through political channels. In other words, decisions were made at the White House level about how they were going to handle environmental impacts.

JMM: Are you saying the White House implemented some spin control?

LH: Yes, spin control. That happened before the ground war started, and it continued long after it ended. After all, the Pentagon had an effective press strategy in place for months. My guess is that people near the top of various government agencies, as part of the Interagency Persian Gulf Task Force, sat down together in Washington and said, "This is how we are going to manage the findings."

The policy applied to the work of agencies close to the executive branch like DOD, DOE, EPA and NOAA, which is part of the Department of Commerce. NSF mostly funds university research, and NSF, as far as I know, never received a gag order the way DOE did. There was already the pattern of how to deal with the media established before the war by the Pentagon.

The nixed press release on the Mauna Loa soot would have upset the information control and brought a lot of questions about the atmospheric impact of the fires, questions the government did not want asked in public, let alone answered.

Kasper was not at all happy that I called him. I think he spoke to me only because he was afraid of what the Sierra Club would do. I am sure he was afraid of what I could say about the censorship. Same with the head of the press at NOAA, Reed H. Boatright, who was quoted in the first *Scientific American* article.[2] However, many NOAA scientists expressed indignation at the gag order because their agency could not get proper credit for its research.

Interestingly, when I talked to the head of public information at Lawrence Berkeley Laboratory, which does no classified work at all, I asked, "Did you get this memo, and does it affect our work here?" I said this very innocently. I had just talked to a person whose work had been gagged, and I knew (this was in the middle of April) that censorship was widespread. Arthur Tressler said to me, "I got that memo too, but I did not tell anybody about it. I just put it in a file marked 'DOE Nonsense.' I knew that if I published that, all hell would break loose, and it would be very embarrassing for the University of California, which manages Livermore Laboratories and LBL (Lawrence Berkeley Laboratory), if the memo was made public."

JMM: The censorship seems to have gone beyond just keeping information from the media. Somebody from LLNL was told not to present certain findings at a meeting in Europe?

LH: Joyce Penner, a physicist who does atmospheric modeling at LLNL, told other people at a meeting in Vienna in early April that she was allowed to show her results to other scientists informally, but she was not allowed to participate in the panel that was going to be discussing the impacts of the soot on the environment. (During that panel, an edited version of the Mauna Loa work was first reported. Because the authors had asked for permission to discuss their findings, NOAA in Boulder reviewed the work and decided to do the draft press release which was later scratched by Kasper.)

JMM: In Geneva in late April there was a meeting of the World Meteorological Organization (WMO). That was a meeting where everyone was discussing various plans to monitor and measure the smoke.

LH: Probably very little of that has happened. LLNL used up-to-date meteorological data to model the soot plume while the fires were burning. Their results were given to interested government agencies and the WMO, I believe. Now that the fires are out, there is very little political will or interest to continue to study their impacts. To some atmospheric scientists, especially those who did measurements during the flights, the fires remain academically fascinating.

OUTSIDERS AND INSIDERS

JMM: Is it your sense, after all this publicity and politics, Senate inquiries, etc., that whatever information there is, is now available?

LH: I don't know of completed work that is being prevented from discussion. At the American Geophysical Union (AGU) meeting in December '91, lots of people who were involved in the flights put forth their results.

JMM: That was true at Harvard [the Harvard oil fires conference in August 1991] also.

LH: An attendee told me speakers reported enormous regional devastation but presented very little data. Nobody was considering that there would be any long-term atmospheric impact at the time. That was not the focus of the conference, but the idea was dismissed at the very beginning. One atmospheric modeler [Thomas Sullivan of LLNL], who talked about potential short-term, region-wide climate effects, like with the monsoons, in a very tentative way was actually told by the person from WMO that even raising these as theoretical issues was bad because people might misinterpret, misunderstand and exaggerate.

That kind of pressure was present in December at the AGU meeting, as an undercurrent or subtext. The May–June NSF flight organizers Radke [Laurence F. Radke of the National Center for Atmospheric Research (NCAR)] and Hobbs [Peter V. Hobbs of the University of Washington], as session chairs, were stern gatekeepers.[3]

The people who had detected a signal [soot] remotely, the people involved in Mauna Loa findings and also those who presented the results of balloon measurements over Wyoming, were treated like outsiders.[4] Hobbs was especially harsh and critical. The people who were in the other camp, the mainstream, were not questioned in such a grueling way about their results and interpretation. This is very interesting, because we would expect scientists to be totally objective. There were those who had the main dogma, and there were those who were presenting data which questioned parts of it.

The scientists who were saying, "Yes, we see a signal," were being attacked and made to look over the sensitivity and limits of detection of their methods. An audience member commented to me, "To speakers who said, 'We don't see anything,' Hobbs et al. did not say, 'Perhaps you did not look at the right elements, and you would not expect the ratio you measured to tell you anything anyway.'" I'm not sure why the author of the latter comment did not stand up in the meeting and make the remark himself.

BENIGN NEGLECT

JMM: I guess there are two possible explanations. In science, as in any social activity, people tend to flow with the mainstream, or it could be politically safer not to ask certain questions or explore certain issues.

LH: Scientists are people. Now a lot of new technical raw data from the flights exists on computer files. A lot of it is not going to be available because there is not enough money to analyze it. Scientists need to get paid on a contract basis to spend their time doing this work. To some extent they bootleg (sandwiching their work efforts into evenings and weekends, for example), but they can't do everything by bootlegging because they have to pay attention to the stuff that they get paid to do. Now that the fires are out, what little incentive existed for government funding of data analysis has evaporated. While not exactly open censorship, it could be seen as benign neglect.

JMM: There is an agreement within the WMO that NCAR in Colorado is supposed to have everything and make it available. So, is it a question whether anybody would have the money, resources and computer time to analyze it?

LH: Although everything is supposed to be available, the people who were on the flights, who actually operated their own instruments, don't have the funding to analyze all the data they collected. At the AGU meeting, researchers presented selected data that they had analyzed for the meeting. They probably will not analyze further because they are now working on other projects. A lot of them were involved in the climatic effects of the Mt. Pinatubo eruption, for example.

What a courageous scientist like Adam Trombly could do is to go through what was presented and what else is known and actually sort out what the evidence means. What is the quality of the evidence for and against long-range impact of the smoke? A concern of mine is lack of information about mid-range impacts of the fires. So we know something about pollution in the Gulf region, and several groups have detected possible Kuwaiti particles in Hawaii and over Wyoming, but what about in between? Radke told me that India and Pakistan refused permission for research flights over their airspace. As a result we have to rely on satellite spectroscopic data and computer modeling for estimates of mid-range distribution of the smoke plume. Direct real-time measurements could have provided higher quality data.

JMM: I think the British flight[5] is the one that went the furthest down, but most of them basically went over the Gulf.

LH: WMO may have done some monitoring on the ground. I have not been privy to the proposed sampling network of the monitoring, but my understanding is that little has been done

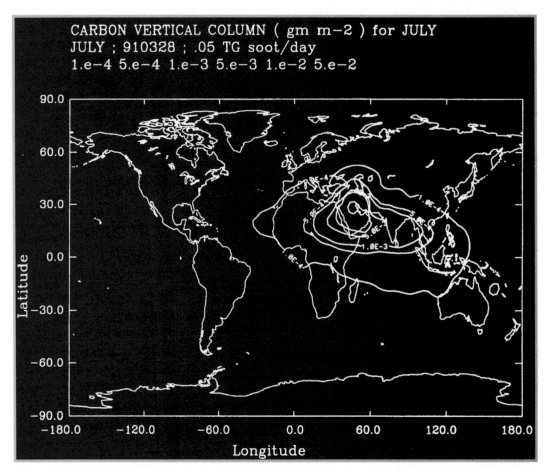

Joyce E. Penner's computer simulation shows the column abundance of soot from the oil fires in July 1991 of up to 0.05 gm^{-2} centered overe Kuwait. A large region, extending from the middle of Africa to southwest Asia, experiences column abundances of more than 0.001 gm^{-2}. The Kuwait fires appear to be capable of increasing the optical depths from soot by at least a factor of two [i.e., visibility is halved] over a large area surrounding the source region. Penner concludes that "the potential emissions of soot . . . will certainly have regional implications for climate, but its global consequences should be investigated. The smoke could either warm the climate or cool it, depending on its altitude in the atmosphere and on whether it is thermally coupled or decoupled from the surface." From "Global Model Simulations of the Long Range Transport of Soot and Sulfur from the Kuwait Oil Fires," by Joyce E. Penner, Atmospheric and Geophysical Sciences Division, Lawrence Livermore National Laboratory, California, June 1991.

beyond the Persian Gulf area. There has been attribution of climatic abnormalities to the fires by Chinese scientists[6] and others, scientists doing climate modeling. The evidence suggests that there could be a connection.

JMM: That is what Thomas Sullivan had presented at the 1991 Harvard Oil Fires Conference. The model was showing smoke and soot being sucked into a vortex that created the cyclone over Bangladesh that turned out to be so devastating.

FLOODS IN CHINA

LH: And there were devastating rains in China. Perhaps, while their people were dying in flooding, the Chinese did not feel the need to go along with the U.S. spin. Some Chinese scientists contacted Farn Parungo of NOAA in Colorado and asked her group to do air trajectory modeling for the time period of the storms. At the AGU meeting she said the results were consistent with a connection between the rains and the smoke trajectories. Her electron microscopy results also suggested that the oil fire particles had more water-loving (hydrophilic) character from sulfate than had been expected before the war, based on laboratory studies of burning Middle East oil. Hydrophilic particles could lead to more clouds and possible rain. She thought it was consistent with that.[7] I found it interesting that Parungo was not challenged by supporters of the main dogma the way the people who were presenting data from Mauna Loa or Wyoming were. Maybe it was because her interpretation was too farfetched even to bother to comment on it. Or maybe because she was right?

JMM: The Hawaii and Wyoming measurements apparently detected evidence for the oil-fire smoke, because these people measure this sort of thing on a regular basis. There must be many other sites around the world that do that?

LH: I don't know of others, but the atmospheric scientists who pick up signs of urban pollution particles in remote places like the Arctic would know. One problem, however, is finding sampling sites which are not influenced by local traffic, power generation and heating. Everybody burns oil from the Middle East for their cars, and in some places oil is used for heating. So you could collect soot anywhere, even black soot on your windshield, and you could analyze it, but you couldn't say it came from the Kuwait fires. Too many local sources exist, and extremely low concentrations from the fires would reach us because of the dilution effects.

If there were more data available from sites between the Middle East and China or Hawaii, then the questions of the fire's impacts would be easier to answer. Maybe WMO-related studies will yield such data. At remote sites the soot is very dilute. If the tracers are below the limit of detection, no one can answer the question. Present knowledge about the elevated particle concentrations at Mauna Loa, for example, can't say conclusively that the particles came from the fires, because even the elevated levels contained trace metal concentrations below the limits of detection for the significant chemical species. That's why data from intermediate sites are needed, then the plume would not have been so diluted. Chemical tracer studies for Mauna Loa and Wyoming particles were hotly debated at the recent AGU meeting.

The best analytical equipment and expertise for addressing the questions of long-range transport and climatic effects are probably in the U.S. But if for political or funding reasons they can't be used, we will not get any answers.

If it were a bigger research priority of the national laboratories, for example, to see how far the smoke went, then I am sure that the DOE or the EPA could have negotiated a contract through the WMO or local agencies, like they have done in Kuwait, to help local people set up an analysis network. I don't think it has happened. If we had an open climate and if this was more important to the community at large, this kind of information could be gathered and analyzed. It is not clear to me whether it is appropriate now to do it.

POLITICS OF SCIENCE

JMM: Politically appropriate? If it is there, we really don't want to know because that will affect interpretations and evaluations of the war?

LH: I'm not sure that much benefit could derive from atmospheric measurements that could be made right now, because the fires are out. However, this winter's [Winter 1991–92] soot data from Mauna Loa will be very useful as baseline information for further interpretation of last year's data.

Scientists doing these kinds of measurements are thrilled at an opportunity to measure something, to look for something. Scientists, regardless of their political interpretations, would like to be able to make measurements and answer questions and solve problems. Scientists are usually not paid for censorship. Scientists hate censorship, even reactionary ones. We are paid to think and create, not to figure out whether what we are saying fits into a political dogma or not. At the benchscale, that is how scientists operate.

When scientists are trying to get money to do projects, they have to interact with the political will to convince government agencies to put the research money in certain areas. My boss jokingly calls that kind of proposal hustling "sales and marketing." The atmospheric community could be more skilled politically in getting the executive branch and the public to listen and act, although the global warming issue now has a lot of attention and some funding.

JMM: But they are not failing to get research dollars.

LH: They should be getting more. As far as the fires are concerned, a lot more data analysis could be done, but the scientific community may not be willing to risk rocking the boat to secure the funding, since the fires are out and the government doesn't want to hear any bad news about possible environmental effects of the Gulf War.

The enormity of the ecological damage to the earth and the suffering of its inhabitants cannot be understood if the information is not available. Partly because of the spin control, attention is not being directed to ecological problems that really should get long-term study and corrective action.

JMM: I think that may be starting to change at least in the region. People at least want to look at it and want to know more. I think in the global debate, as important as that is, sometimes the regional environmental crisis has gotten lost.

LH: The government's only concern about the fires was their potential long-term worldwide climatic impact. Since long-term impacts are likely to be negligible, we have nothing to worry about. Who cares about the local and continental impacts? Not the U.S., apparently.

NOTES:

1. U.S. Environmental Protection Agency, Public Health Service and National Oceanic and Atmospheric Agency, *Kuwait Oil Fires; Interagency Interim Report*, Washington DC, 1991.

2. John Horgan, "U.S. Gags Discussion of War's Environmental Effects," *Scientific American*, May 1991, 24. "NOAA researchers were ordered to withhold satellite information or other information on the Gulf region after the war ended . . . NOAA spokesperson Reed H. Boatright speculated that the restriction was related to demands for reparations expected to result from the war."

3. As a result of their airborne measurements over Kuwait in May–June 1991, Hobbs and Radke concluded that there would be no significant climatic effects of the soot fires. Their results were published in Peter V. Hobbs and Lawrence F. Radke, "Airborne Studies of the Smoke from the Kuwait Oil Fires," *Science*, vol. 256 (May 15, 1992): 987–990.

4. The increase in soot at Mauna Loa and Wyoming in March 1991 implied long-range transport of the soot, albeit in very small quantities. See D. Lowenthal et al., "Evidence for Long-Range Transport of Aerosol from the Kuwaiti Oil Fires to Hawaii," *Journal of Geophysical Research*, 97 D13 (September 20, 1992): 14573; T. Deshler, "Measurements of Unusual Aerosol Layers in the Trophosphere over Laramie, Wyoming in the Spring of 1991; Evidence for Long-Range Transport from the Oil Fires in Kuwait," *Geophysical Research Letters*, vol. 19 no. 4 (February 1992): 385-388.

5. See K.A. Browning et al., "Environmental Effects from Burning Oil Wells in Kuwait," *Nature*, vol. 351 (May 30, 1991): 363-367.

6. See Zhou, J.M., "Report of Severe Rainfall in China," (in Chinese), *World News*, July 12, 1991, 10.

7. Farn Parungo's responses to ARC's questionnaire on the climatic effects of the oil fires appear later in this chapter. See also Farn Parungo et al, "Aerosol Particles in the Kuwait Oil Fire Plumes: Their Morphology, Size Distribution, Chemical Composition, Transport and Potential Effect on Climate," *Journal of Geophysical Research*, 97 D14 (October 20, 1992): 15867–15882.

International Response

Interview with Abdullah Toukan

Abdullah Toukan, Ph.D., is chief scientific advisor to King Hussein of Jordan, and Secretary-General of the High Council for Science and Technology. Dr. Toukan was among the first to warn of potential extra-regional impacts of the oil fires, if Saddam Hussein carried out his threat to destroy Kuwait's oil wells. His calculations formed the basis of a speech given by King Hussein of Jordan at the Second World Climate Conference in Geneva, Switzerland, November 6, 1990. Dr. Toukan was first interviewed in Hidden Casualties, *Volume I. Interviewed for this publication in January 1992 by John M. Miller.*

John M. Miller: In terms of the climate, you and others were making some strong, some would say alarmist, predictions. How do you evaluate those concerns in light of what actually happened? The number of fires was twice what you were talking about last December and January, and they have not burned as long as many people feared.

Abdullah Toukan: All I can say to that is thank God. Although nobody really knows the final effects of all of this.

JMM: But the U.S. scientists and Administration and others are saying that there never should have been any concern about global effects or even long-term regional climate effects. What is your thinking?

AT: That's typical. I mean that went on for a long period of time, so that does not surprise me. Remember when EPA head William Reilly went down there and said the most absurd things.

JMM: If the potential for long-term climate effects is being dismissed, does that mean it will not be investigated? It seems that has been the case in this country. Is that true in the U.S. or elsewhere? Is it true in the Gulf region?

AT: One has to look at them. I was talking to a friend yesterday who had come back from Kuwait, and it finally hit them apparently, even those in the environmental agency in Kuwait, that one has to now look into the long-term effects, to keep monitoring to see what could possibly be the long-term effects, or the environmental impact.

JMM: Have they formulated plans to do that?

AT: No, that is one thing they have not done. They are saying it should not have taken them as long as it did, that kind of talk to start with.

JMM: It should not have taken so long to put out the fires or start studying?

AT: To put out the fires and to get the equipment. The second point is how much is this going to affect them overall? How much is going to be a long-term effect?

JMM: Are there or will there be political difficulties in trying to do that?

AT: In Kuwait? Certainly. As you know, everybody wants to cover the whole thing up and show that it was not as bad as everybody thought it would be. But now that things are calming down over there, obviously, people and the environmental agency are re-evaluating the Gulf, the Gulf waters, what is happening there: what is left behind, the soot and garbage that's all over the place, all over the land in Kuwait.

JMM: What about the UN response to the environmental crisis itself? They were pressured by you and others to deal with it before it happened. Are you satisfied with what the UN environmental agencies have done since?

AT: Oh no. They came in much later. They should have prepared a little bit more, they should have put more international effort into it. No, I was not personally very happy with the role of the UN as we went along and I think that showed quite clearly, even with the meetings in Switzerland and Europe, trying to get the equipment there as soon as possible. No, I was not the least bit impressed, and I think the UN can and should have played a bigger and more important role than what we saw.

JMM: *At your initiative, Jordan introduced a proposal at the UN to strengthen the protection of the environment in wartime. What happened to it?*

AT: We were going to give it to the International Committee of the Red Cross (ICRC), to look at ENMOD (Convention on the Prohibition of Military or any other Hostile Use of Environmental Modification Techniques, May 18, 1977) and look at Protocol 1 Additional to the Geneva Conventions of 1949, June 10, 1977, to analyze them, but that was all postponed because of internal delays. . . . In the UN General Assembly about 22 countries gave a good reply; obviously the two that did not were America and Kuwait. That was expected, but the rest, the other countries, were very positive.

JMM: *The proposal was to strengthen international law in terms of environmental damage done in the war, and Kuwait got the brunt of that damage. Why would they . . . ?*

AT: There are two aspects to the environment: one is using the environment in times of war (covered by ENMOD,) and the other is impact on the environment. The impact on the environment comes within the additional Protocols to the Geneva Convention, and the U.S. is not a signatory to that, so it was very clear to me . . .

JMM: *That any strengthening of this could affect U.S. military actions, as well as what the Iraqis might have done in Kuwait.*

AT: The Canadians and the Germans were all ready to sponsor a resolution with us absolutely, but as always, they wanted a preamble that condemns Iraq. I told them, sure, go ahead and condemn Iraq as much as you want, you will never get anything out of it. The whole point is, let's look toward the future.

The Downwind Impacts of the Oil Fires

Thomas J. Sullivan

Thomas J. Sullivan, Ph.D., is a computer modeler at the Atmospheric and Geophysical Sciences Division, LLNL, Livermore, California, operated by the DOE. The following is excerpted from a presentation before the Harvard Kuwait Oil Fires Conference, August 13, 1991.

I am just a spokesman for the ARAC group [Atmospheric Release Advisory Capability, which advises the U.S. government]. We are a group of 24 people in assessment meteorology. We are an operational emergency response organization, primarily for nuclear accident modeling, and that was our charter in life until very recently.

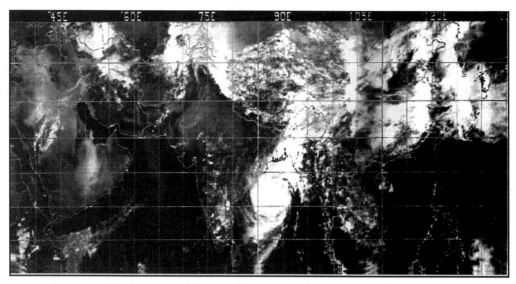

Composite photo of NOAA weather satellite visible images for April 28, 1991, during the period just prior to the landfall of the Bay of Bengal cyclone. As indicated in Atmospheric Release Advisory Capability (ARAC) model calculations, there is and has been a clear path from Kuwait to the cyclone with essentially no cloud systems to capture the Kuwait oil fire soot. Source: Thomas J. Sullivan, ARAC Group Leader.

Just conceptually, so you understand our modeling, in the briefest sense, we have a terrain-influenced, mass-consistent flow modeling capability, driven by wind [data], provided by the Air Force Global Weather Center.

We can emulate the material being transported and distributed by thousands of microparticles. We can ascribe various properties to particles—size, deposition velocities and so forth. It can be either gaseous or particulate. For these particular calculations, everything we have modeled is in terms of particulate.

Just so you know, there are lots of different properties, capabilities and modeling sources . . .We do have dry and wet deposition processes; however, I must confess that we do not have any good sources for precipitation at this time, so we really are not doing any wet deposition modeling . . .

Again, modeling is imperfect. Dependent upon the winds that are provided to us, they can give a very consistent overall picture of what happened.

We are getting calculations for carbon soot on the order of 100 micrograms per cubic meter at 1.5 meter elevation, in other words, respiration level, right near the sources. Downwind over Saudi Arabia, we are seeing on the order of a maximum of 10 micrograms per cubic meter.

What is interesting is that if you come down the coast, you see the highest concentration again reported along the coast. And this is where that fumigation is taking place and is being modeled. So you see the plume dispersion in the vertical comes down and leads to the higher concentration. When you look at the 2,000 meter results, then you see more of a coherent plume structure that is analogous to what you see in the satellite imagery, and it is more representative of the integrated plume.

Very quickly, I want to show a few things we have been doing on the hemispheric scale. We started some calculations in May and early June to go back and basically look at the longer-range transport from this fire that started on the 21st of February.

This is kind of a large-scale synoptic picture of what we see involved. Here we are at 180 hours [after the fire started] in late February. You see the plume out over the Arabian Gulf. The swell is switching direction here. This is, I think, consistent with what you just saw before, in some shots from the past of the plume going across the Gulf and into Iran. That in fact was a time when there were black rains in Iran.

Here we see a pick-up of the plume again at 360 hours certainly, coming down through the south to transport across the subcontinent. I would like to go on and talk now about some of the effects that I am beginning to suspect, and I have to label these as purely speculative at this time. But we are beginning to see some interesting and curious things developing.

Seeding the Clouds

First of all, the predictions before we got any measurement data were that these would be hydrophobic [water repelling] particles, we would not see any rain interaction. Since the aircraft have been out measuring, they have now determined they are hygroscopic [water seeking], potentially an agent for cloud seeding and precipitation enhancement. It is basically a speculation that I am making in terms of the mechanism that leads to something that I will discuss briefly.

Measurements from the NCAR aircraft saw CCN (cloud condensation nuclei) at least two times background in the Northern Arabian Sea.[1] Why did I mention that? Well, let's take a look at a sequence here.

First of all, this is the 24th of April. I remember this because it was a few days before I arrived at the meeting in Geneva [April 27–30 1991, Geneva, WMO, Expert Meeting on the Atmospheric Part of the Emergency Response to the Kuwait Oilfield Fires], and when I got to Geneva, we heard about the cyclone in Bangladesh. Note, looking at our calculations that there is a mass of particles in this region, the Gulf of Bengal, and there is a deficiency here, because particles had been convected off the grid, and it looks like the circulation was returning.

Watch what happens to this in a synoptic sense. Here we are on the 25th. The mass is moving toward Bangladesh. The 26th, clearly in the Gulf region here. This is about the time the heavy rain was taking place.[2] It didn't end there. As I recall, a few days later the material had moved to the west. Synoptically, I believe the rains went into Calcutta, not nearly as intense.

We see some evidence of rotation and circulation which is to be expected. The flow continues on around, and, lo and behold, on the 30th of April we saw on CNN (Cable News Network) that not only had Bangladesh had a cyclone, but a few days later intense rains returned that were not cyclone intensity, but were basically an intense convergence zone. We see evidence of that right in these calculations. These are only traces that are reflecting what is going on with the atmospheric flow. The storm was reported to be the most intense storm ever recorded in Bangladesh, to my knowledge. I would like to follow up on that and see if there is anything further.

That is not the only thing I recently learned. Here is a plot of our deposition calculation. This is from the 21st of February to the 28th of March. We are calculating deposition in these areas in the magnitude indicated. It is in a qualitative sense, so let's just step along and look at this related period.

Now, I want to show you the period from May to July. You see an increase in deposition here in West India, northwest of Bombay, with the maximum developing on the terrain in the hills of southern India on the west coast. Particle deposition on the first of May . . . with the Arabian Gulf heavily seeded with particles. On the 15th of May, most of the convection is across southern India and into the Arabian Sea, but not penetrating into Pakistan or northwest India. Again on the 30th of May, material is over southern India.

A problem in the model is that we do not have wet deposition, so we do not have a cleansing process. That is a model and data improvement that should be made. What I am looking at is the first encounter of these particles, I believe, with a moist air mass.

Take note also of what is going on over China, because I will make one closing comment. I realize this is very speculative, but I think it should not be totally discounted that there are potentially [some] impacts upon the rain. This just came across my desk last week. This is a NOAA analysis of the precipitation data for the Indian monsoon at this time. This is the period from the first of May to the seventh of July. There is a very large area of deficit in northwest India and Pakistan, and a large area of positive anomaly over the hills on the west coast of southern India. Very circumstantial. I throw that out only so the group at large knows that the long-range modeling leaves the door open for consideration that we do not have the final answer.

But my very final comment will be something that came out of the newspaper just this weekend, which I have no way to substantiate at this time but would like to look at.

Researchers at the Chinese Academy of Sciences said dense clouds rising from oil wells since the Gulf War caused patterns similar to nuclear winter that have been responsible for the country's disastrous floods this summer.[3] Very radical, but it is made by a director of the Chinese Institute of Atmospheric Physics.

I think before the year is out, we must at least look at all the anomalies throughout the subcontinent region and then draw our conclusions.[4]

NOTES:

1. Peter V. Hobbs and Lawrence F. Radke, "Airborne Studies of the Smoke from the Kuwait Oil Fires," *Science*, vol. 256 (May 15, 1991): 987–990.

2. See T. M. Hawley, *Against the Fires of Hell: The Environmental Disaster of the Gulf War* (Orlando: Harcourt Brace Jovanovich), 1992, 102. "Raging over the Bay of Bengal with 150-mile-an-hour winds, the storm drove ashore a surge of water towering 20 feet higher than normal high tides. Lands many miles inland were flooded, and between 140,000 and 200,000 people died."

3. See T. M. Hawley, *Against the Fires of Hell.* "During the latter part of June, pelting rainstorms hit areas of central and eastern China, causing catastrophic floods in the valleys of the Yangtze and Huai rivers. Press reports out of China stated that the floods affected 200,000,000 people—a fifth of the country's population—in all, about 3,000 people died in the floods."

4. For further information on the ARAC model, see Thomas J. Sullivan et al. *Modeling of Air Currents in the Gulf Region*, Report, (presented to the workshop on "Environmental Dimensions of the Gulf: Policy and Institutional Perspectives," 1992), Lawrence Livermore National Laboratory, Livermore, 1992.

Critiquing the Official U.S. Analysis

Interview with Adam Trombly

Adam Trombly is an atmospheric physicist and the co-director of the Aspen Institute for Advanced Studies. Sponsored by Friends of the Earth, he traveled to Saudi Arabia and Kuwait in June 1991, where he flew in U.S. Navy and Kuwaiti reconnaissance planes over the Gulf to assess the damage. Interviewed by John M. Miller, July 1991. Reviewed by Adam Trombly in January 1993.

John M. Miller: What was the main reason you went to Saudi Arabia and Kuwait?
Adam Trombly: We went to clarify what was happening in the region. There is a lack of information; no high-resolution satellite photographs are available.

My main concern was the atmospheric dynamics of the circulation of the plume. It had been traced all the way to Wyoming,[1] all the way across the northern half of the Northern Hemisphere. Europe had had the coldest spring on record. I had a real concern that temperatures had dropped and that I had heard nothing about that. That was one of my main concerns.

Basically, we have a meteorological phenomenon which is hemisphere wide. I wanted to find out whether what we had been told about the plume from the start was true and what global effects it might have.

Where I ended up on the issue was that from before the war, the senators and congressmembers who had voted for military action in the Gulf had been given representations about what the consequences would be by Richard Small of Pacific-Sierra Research Corporation and others, and what Richard Small wrote in that report[2] was a "blue sky" scenario . . . about the lofting, about the number of fires that might result.

OIL WINTER

There were a number of us who stood up before this whole thing and said, "This is ridiculous, this is nuts." Some people were more extreme than others, like Carl Sagan. And the thing is that what Carl Sagan and others said was that this could precipitate a "nuclear winter." And, unfortunately, it is kind of like everything else in this area of the science: people think that the greenhouse effect means that you add greenhouse gases to the atmosphere and everything gets warmer. That's not the way it happens. You add greenhouse gases to the atmosphere and a lot of different things happen. You end with greater differentials between high pressure and low pressure systems; you end up with higher wind velocities. We have been fighting the simplicity of consensus science for years. And the same thing pertains to the "nuclear winter" effect. We may well have a very cold winter as a result of these fires combined with the horribly exacerbating effect of Mt. Pinatubo. And, of course, the people who say it is not the plume will say it is Mt. Pinatubo that is causing the deep cold.

But the people who have been watching this from the beginning with open eyes . . . will recognize that the temperatures in Europe and across the Northern Hemisphere above certain latitudes certainly do reflect that this has had an impact. In fact the temperatures seem to indicate a very severe global attenuation of thermal transfer from the equator to the pole.

We have had an attenuation; we have had a slowing down of, an impediment of, the transfer of heat from the pole and, therefore, things have been colder the further north you get. And that doesn't mean that things are going to be extremely hot to the south, because all that hot air impinging upon the equatorial region still has to go somewhere, and that means that you have more and more violent differentials between high pressure and low pressure fronts. You have more storm activity, for example. You have more violent winds.

PLUME HEIGHT

We heard months ago about black snows in Kashmir, and we were told by various people in the scientific community that there was no causality that could be traced back to Kuwait. Those are the kind of absurd comments that have followed on this coverup. In point of fact, it is obvious that the smoke from the Kuwaiti oil fields is what caused the black snow, not just in Kashmir, but across the entire Himalayan range.

It is a point of fact noted by *Scientific American*,[3] for example, that even though the NSF team came back and said this would have no global climatological consequences, the soot is falling on Japan[4] and has been measured all the way across into Wyoming in the United States.[5] We are being told it is a regional phenomenon, but somehow or other the smoke is making it all the way around the world.

JMM: You have talked about measurements released by NOAA and your measurements the next day that came up with a big difference in the height of the plume.

AT: On June 7, 1991, NOAA was saying the top of the plume was 6,800 feet, from satellite reconnaissance. This was the professed height of the plume that day. You have to understand that the top of that plume varies dramatically depending on what time of day you happen to fly over it because it is like a giant black wing in some ways. It rises and falls cyclically.

People are not familiar with this scale of phenomena. Hardly anybody knows about large-scale, self-growing inversions. It is a very rarely studied subject, because most of the inversions we study may be as big as a city. A self-growing inversion that has a steady state source of effluent, in terms of these fires in Kuwait, is unlike any phenomenon we have seen. The closest we have seen to it is the large-scale forest fires in Brazil and Africa. I had studied those under a Reynolds grant for two years so I was more familiar with the phenomenon than a lot of people.

When Hobbs [Peter V. Hobbs of the NSF] was asked in the Senate for example, whether the plume rose and fell, he said he didn't think it rose and fell significantly.[6] They flew mainly early in the morning. Well, by 1:30 in the afternoon, instead of most of the smoke being concentrated between 1,000 and 10,000 feet like their report claims, the smoke was concentrated between 13,000 and 16,500 feet 200 kilometers south of Kuwait.

Fly further south of Kuwait and you will find that the lofting trajectory is even steeper, because the further you get down-plume the more it fans out, the more ground effect you have. It reaches maximum lofting at about 3:30 to 4:00 in the afternoon and begins to fall again.

They also talked about being surprised about the low levels of evaporation. Well, you can't judge evaporation levels at 10:30 in the morning. You judge evaporation levels throughout the day, because the more time that has gone by since sunrise, the more time you have had the sun impinging upon the plume, the more time you have had for the evaporation of volatiles. We clearly saw and filmed a distinct upper strata of volatiles that had evaporated off the top of that plume. I am sure that many of these volatiles and the very light particulate will loft into the upper troposphere. This is exactly what is indicated by the findings at the University of Wyoming.[7]

The smoke from Kuwait had been found over the U.S., over the Midwest at high, very high tropospheric altitudes like 11,000 meters. Once you get up there into the tropopause, the probability of transport into the stratosphere increases dramatically, although no one is talking about the Japanese and others having measured signatures in the stratosphere. I haven't seen enough data yet to really talk about that. But once there is lofting into the tropopause, the probability increases dramatically that some small percentage of this, only one percent according to the Max Planck Institute model,[8] will have to leak into the stratosphere to cause severe and long-term (meaning lasting several years) climatological impact. . . .

I was first told how high people had seen the thick smoke by a NOAA employee who was stationed in Saudi Arabia at the time, and he came up to me and was very forthright and said, "I'm concerned about this issue too, and I have personally seen this very thick smoke up to 18,000 feet."

This is significant when the NSF is making representations that the smoke is concentrated between 1,000 and 10,000 feet. It is just not true. It is not even that they were lying about it. It was very possible, and Hobbs confirmed this in his testimony, that they flew in the early morning. What can you tell about the lofting of a plume in the early morning?

GLOBAL IMPACTS

JMM: So you expect that a few years from now, many of these people will . . .

AT: No, what will happen years from now is probably that any terrible effects will all be attributed to Mt. Pinatubo, the volcano. And all the guys will hide behind the dust of the volcano, and they will ignore the fact that the coldest temperatures recorded since the 1600s were recorded prior to that volcano [erupting] and that wasn't just in Europe and that wasn't just in the western portion of the Soviet Union where the effects were the most obvious, this was also true even where I am in Aspen; this is the coldest spring that they ever had. Of course if people don't look at the worldwide meteorological data base, if they don't look at the data, if they don't look at the temperature profiles, if they don't look at the storms, if they don't look at as many things as possible, then they miss what is happening. . . .

Hobbs was pretty good in his testimony.[9] I have to give credit where credit is due. He was the NSF spokesman at the hearings. While under oath, if you contrast that with what was said at their news conference, he said that basically they agreed with all of our findings except for the global impact. They agreed that the oil well fires were extremely dangerous, they agreed that they needed to be put out immediately.

There are a lot of people who believe that the jury is still out on the global impact. I was quoted in one publication, saying the same thing. The fact that the jury is still out does not mean that the crime has not been committed.

JMM: You are saying that the extent of the global impact is a question, but there has been some.

AT: The extent of the global impact is something that a lot of people are going to have to put their heads together and have real-time data to determine. In other words, we have to have an open forum. . . .

JMM: At the Senate hearing [in July 1991], one of the senators said that he had talked to the government people responsible and said that from now on whatever information people wanted would be available.

AT: Senator Lieberman. We are in the process right now of testing it. I can't tell you what the final results are. And it is going to be impossible to tell in some ways how much of the historical data we get is accurate. In other words, this is digital information sent down from a satellite and spit out by a computer according to a program that interprets it. And to get that data unedited, without the conditional branches put into the computer, based on somebody's assumptions, is very difficult.

In the region we are talking about, the entire Indian subcontinent is affected. There are a billion people there. This [the plume] is lofting over the Himalayas; they are seeing it in Japan. It is going to affect temperatures in China. Watch the crop failures in China. Has anyone noticed that China has had more torrential downpours since this war than ever before in their history, that China is requesting, for the first time, international aid to help them with the flooding from the unprecedented torrential downpours? Do we know why those torrential downpours are there? People need to find out if this is nucleation from this plume.

JMM: Nucleation is?

AT: In other words, the particulates from the plume act as cloud condensation nuclei (CCN). Precipitation follows on that.

People are saying that it is no problem because a majority of the plume is being precipitated out as rain. Ask the Chinese people, if that is a very pleasant experience. That is ecological disaster on a grand scale. . . .

NOTES:

1. T. Deshler, "Measurements of Unusual Aerosol Layers in the Troposphere over Laramie, Wyoming in the Spring of 1991: Evidence for Long-Range Transport from the Oil Fires in Kuwait," *Geophysical Research Letters*, vol. 19 no. 4 (February 1992): 385-388.

2. R.D. Small, *Environmental Impact of Damage to Kuwaiti Oil Facilities*, Report, (prepared for the U.S. Defense Nuclear Agency), Pacific-Sierra Research Corporation, Santa Monica, January 1991. See Chapter Three, "Prewar Environmental and Health Assessments."

3. John Horgan, "Science and the Citizen. Burning Questions: Scientists Launch Studies of Kuwait's Oil Fires," *Scientific American*, (July 1991): 17.

4. Kikuo Okada et al., "Extremely High Proportions of Soot Particles in the Upper Troposphere over Japan," *Geophysical Research Letters*, vol. 19 no. 9 (May 4, 1992): 921–924.

5. T. Deshler, "Measurements of Unusual Aerosol Layers."

6. U.S. Congress, Senate Environmental and Public Works Committee, Gulf Pollution Task Force, *Testimony* by Peter V. Hobbs, 102nd Congress, 1st sess., July 7, 1991, 8.

7. T. Deshler, "Measurements of Unusual Aerosol Layers."

8. S. Bakan et al., "Climate Response to Smoke From the Burning Oil Wells in Kuwait," *Nature*, vol. 351 (May 30, 1991): 367-371.

9. See U.S. Congress, *Testimony* by Peter V. Hobbs.

The Global Impacts of the Oil Fires: Six Questions

INTRODUCTION TO QUESTIONNAIRE RESPONSES

In the days preceding the Gulf War, a number of scientists from around the world voiced concern regarding the potential effects on the local, regional and global environment of large-scale oil-field fires, involving Kuwait's more than 700 wells. Some scenarios included low temperatures over wide areas due to the shading effects of the soot, a significant exacerbation of global warming, and the failure of the monsoon in Bangladesh.

Many of these predictions were based on the oil fires continuing to burn for as long as two years. In fact, the fires were started in January and February and extinguished by November. The first scientific conference on the Kuwaiti fires was held by the World Meteorological Organization in April 1991 in Geneva. By May, several groups had produced computer models of the fires' atmospheric effects, which were in agreement that the fires would not have a significant effect, that is, one exceeding the bounds of natural variability, on the global climate.[1,2,3] These models and available evidence from satellite photos suggested that most of the soot stayed in the lower stratosphere where its effects would only be short-term.

However, during a run of the climatic model developed by Hamburg's Max Planck Institute, it was discovered that with an assumed figure of fifteen million barrels a day burning, instead of

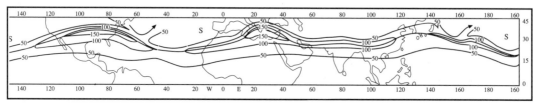

The subtropical jet stream. Wind speeds shown in knots. Source: T. N. Krishnamurti, *The Subtropical Jet Stream of Winter*, Report, University of Chicago, 1959.

the WMO estimate of five million barrels a day that were believed actually to be burning, the model predicted highly significant global effects, including extreme highs and lows in temperature and precipitation and unusually frequent storms.[4] One of the modelers told *Scientific American* that *if* Saudi Arabian oil wells had also been ignited during the war, this scenario could "easily" have come to pass.[5] In fact, exceptionally low temperatures were recorded in the Middle East after the war (although these may have had more to do with the disruption of the desert surface than with oil fallout[6]) and also in Europe.[7]

None of the predictions made prior to the war had anticipated that the Kuwaiti soot particles would be effective cloud condensation nuclei (CCN), as they proved to be. This led to a new concern: could the anomalous intensity of the April 1991 cyclone in Bangladesh be a result of the oil fires? The Max Planck Institute model predicted that the monsoon might arrive earlier and more forcefully than usual because of the fires.[8] The British Meteorological Office model indicated regions of increased rainfall over India in May.[9]

The U.S. Interagency Airborne Study of the Kuwait oil fires took measurements over Kuwait in May and June 1991. The conclusion from these studies, published in *Science* in May 1992,[10] was that the smoke probably had insignificant global effects. One reason for this was that soot appeared to be concentrated in the lower troposphere and so would be rained out within weeks.

THE ARC/ ARMS CONTROL RESEARCH CENTER QUESTIONNAIRE

In January 1993 ARC sent a questionnaire to several experts. The answers we received should give the reader an indication of the problems involved in determining the effects of the oil fires. Weather interactions are highly complex, and few measurements were taken outside the Gulf region itself.

We asked whether soot could have gone higher than the lower troposphere and whether any could have entered the subtropical jet stream. We asked this because the jet stream is known to pass over Northern Arabia and Kuwait, and then over Bangladesh and China.[11] Then we asked about the quantity of soot that would have to enter the jet stream to cause meteorological effects.

Our next question was intended to resolve our uncertainty about whether the U.S. Interagency Study[12] measured the full range of particles within the smoke plume that might affect climate.

Finally, we asked whether the oil fires could have impacted the Bangladesh cyclone, the floods in Eastern China, or subsequent events.

An ethical question also needs to be raised here. If the oil fires did contribute to the intensity of these storms, then a percentage of the victims are also casualties of the war. That the fires could have affected the storms in Bangladesh and China indicates the possible environmental hazards of modern warfare, even when there is no use of nuclear, chemical or biological weapons. This raises serious questions for those who believe in the possibility of a just war using conventional weapons.

—James Warner and Saul Bloom

NOTES:
1. S. Bakan et al., "Climate Response to the Smoke from the Burning Oil Wells in Kuwait," *Nature*, vol. 351 (May 30, 1991): 367-371.
2. K.A. Browning et al., "Environmental Effects from Burning Oil Wells in Kuwait," *Nature*, vol. 351 (May 30, 1991): 363-367.
3. John Horgan, "Science and the Citizen: Burning Questions," *Scientific American*, July 1991, 17.
4. S. Bakan et al., "Climate Response."
5. John Horgan, "Science and the Citizen."
6. T.M. Hawley, personal communication, March 29, 1993.
7. Adam Trombly, *Interim Environmental Damage Assessment Report for the Persian Gulf Region*, Aspen Institute for Advanced Studies, July 1991.
8. S. Bakan et al., "Climate Response."
9. K.A. Browning et al., "Environmental Effects from Burning Oil Wells."
10. Peter V. Hobbs and Lawrence F. Radke, "Airborne Studies of the Smoke from the Kuwait Oil Fires", *Science*, vol. 256 (May 15, 1992): 987–91.
11. T.N. Krishnamurti, *The Subtropical Jet Stream of Winter*, Report, University of Chicago, 1959.
12. Peter V. Hobbs and Lawrence F. Radke, "Airborne Studies."

QUESTIONNAIRE RESPONSES

RICHARD SMALL, HUGH CHURCH, FARN PARUNGO, THOMAS SULLIVAN, ADAM TROMBLY AND JOHN COX

Richard D. Small

Richard D. Small, Ph.D., is Director for Thermal Sciences at the Pacific-Sierra Research Corporation in Los Angeles, and is the author of the report to the U.S. Defense Nuclear Agency excerpted earlier in this chapter. His research on smoke production from global nuclear exchanges was a focal point of the nuclear winter debate. He answered our questions by phone in January 1993.

QUESTION 1

In view of the evidence shown to you, how likely is it that soot from the Kuwaiti oil fires could have penetrated into the jet stream?

Some soot could have penetrated into the jet stream. Some could have been transported long distances. Most did not. Firm experimental evidence from Interagency experiments[1] and contemporary satellite photos showed the smoke plume at low altitudes dissipating over the Gulf.

QUESTION 2

How much soot would have had to have entered the jet stream to produce significant climatic effects? In view of the evidence known to you, how likely is it that this quantity of soot could have entered the jet stream in the region around and above Kuwait?

You have to consider the overall effect of smoke emitted by several hundred wells for several months. On a particular day smoke could have been injected higher than normal, or the more energetic plumes could have been higher than the norm, but to do the climatic assessment you need to look at the average from all the wells. That most of the smoke was at low altitudes was verified by experiment.[2,3]

QUESTION 3

Can particles that are not visible affect climate? If so, could soot constituents not detected by the aerial and satellite observation performed over the Gulf have risen above 22,000 feet?

The British[4] and Interagency[5] experiments measured particles in a range of size from submicron to larger sizes, including concentrations that could not be detected visually.

QUESTION 4

In view of the evidence known to you, do you think it possible that the Kuwaiti oil fires affected the unusual intensity of the cyclone in Bangladesh?

There is no evidence to show that the cyclone intensity is outside a normal fluctuation. Moreover, there is no evidence to support large smoke concentrations being transported beyond the Persian Gulf region.

QUESTION 5

In view of the evidence known to you, do you think it possible that the Kuwaiti oil fires affected the intensity of the July floods in China?

Relating the July floods to Kuwaiti oil smoke is pure speculation. There is no experimental basis and there have been no observations to support a linkage. There were no effects in Japan and other neighboring areas, so it's a little far-fetched to attribute what happened in just one area to the smoke from Kuwait.

QUESTION 6

How likely is it that further climatic effects could still occur as a result of the oil fires?

Some soot was no doubt mixed upwards to the stratosphere, but not nearly enough to cause any climatic effect.[6]

NOTES:

1. Peter V. Hobbs and Lawrence F. Radke, "Airborne Studies of the Smoke from the Kuwait Oil Fires," *Science*, vol. 256 (May 15, 1991): 987–990.
2. Peter V. Hobbs and Lawrence F. Radke, "Airborne Studies."
3. D.W. Johnson et al., "Airborne Observations of Physical and Chemical Characteristics of the Kuwaiti Oil Smoke Plume," *Nature*, vol. 353 (October 17, 1991): 617–621.

4. K.A. Browning et al, "Environmental Effects from Burning Oil Wells in Kuwait," *Nature*, vol. 351 (May 30, 1991): 363-367.

5. Peter V. Hobbs and Lawrence F. Radke, "Airborne Studies."

6. See also Richard D. Small, "Environmental Impacts of Fires in Kuwait," *Nature*, vol. 350 (March 7, 1991): 11–12.

Hugh W. Church

Hugh W. Church of Environmental Monitoring Systems, Sandia National Laboratories, is one of the authors of the report to the U.S. Department of Energy excerpted in Chapters Two and Three. He answered our questions in writing in April 1993.

QUESTION 1

In view of the evidence known to you, how likely is it that soot from the Kuwaiti oil fires could have penetrated into the jet stream?

At various times during the nine months of fires, soot could have penetrated to the jet stream through the action of ambient convective activity that mixes air between the lower and upper troposphere where the jet stream resides.

QUESTION 2

How much soot would have had to have entered the jet stream to produce significant climatic effects? In view of the evidence known to you, how likely is it that this quantity of soot could have entered the jet stream in the region around and above Kuwait?

The impact of soot (in whatever quantity) in the jet stream, or elsewhere, on climatic effects is poorly understood. Calculations for various "nuclear winter" scenarios have produced a wide range of estimates. For weather effects, the presence of soot may affect the precipitation process through altered cloud condensation phenomena, again, for which quantification is poorly understood. The lack of success by weather modification efforts through artificial cloud seeding is an example of this lack of understanding.

QUESTION 3

Can particles that are not visible affect climate? If so, could soot constituents not detected by the aerial and satellite observation performed over the Gulf have risen above 22,000 feet?

Yes, subvisible particles can affect climate. Yes, they could ascend above 6,700 meters altitude, see answer to Question 1.

QUESTION 4

In view of the evidence known to you, do you think it possible that the Kuwaiti oil fires affected the unusual intensity of the cyclone in Bangladesh?

Yes, it is possible that oil fire-injected particles affect far-off storms, but with what probability or even of what sign (intensification or diminishment) is unknown.

QUESTION 5

In view of the evidence known to you, do you think it possible that the Kuwaiti oil fires affected the intensity of the July floods in China?

See answer to Question 4.

QUESTION 6

How likely is it that further climatic effects could still occur as a result of the oil fires?

My opinion is that subsequent effects on climate would be very small compared to volcanic stratospheric injections and anthropogenic influences, such as land use diversion and contaminant injection as a result of population pressure and development. I don't agree that jet stream soot could easily be transported into the stratosphere.

Farn Parungo

Farn Parungo has a Ph.D. in Chemistry from the University of Colorado and has worked for NOAA since 1970. She answered our questions by phone in February 1993.

QUESTION 1

In view of the evidence known to you, how likely is it that soot from the Kuwaiti oil fires could have penetrated into the jet stream?

I don't think that possibility can be ruled out. Hobbs and Radke found that the fire plumes were concentrated at low altitudes,[1] but they were only there for one month–they flew for a couple of hundred hours to take the measurements. That was in May and June, and the fires started in February and lasted to November. I don't think they're justified in concluding from their study that there was definitely no long-range transport.

QUESTION 2

How much soot would have had to have entered the jet stream to produce significant climatic effects? In view of the evidence known to you, how likely is it that this quantity of soot could have entered the jet stream in the region around and above Kuwait?

The soot we (NOAA) measured in the plane was sometimes over 103 particles per cubic centimeter (cc). The measurements covered only 600 kilometers, and at that distance the soot deposited, and decreased a lot, down to 10 per cc for large soot particles. Three groups did the measurements on black carbon mass concentrations–maybe they could tell you the quantity.[2,3,4]

QUESTION 3

Can particles that are not visible affect climate? If so, could soot constituents not detected by the aerial and satellite observation performed over the Gulf have risen above 22,000 feet?

The smallest particles involved here are sulfates, formed when SO_2 from the fires converted to sulfate particles. These can be very small and transport a long distance. They function as cloud condensation nuclei (CCN), which initiate haze, fog and clouds, and affect rainfall. A point I made in my paper[5] is that they could have profound impact on climatic change. These particles are not visible from satellites.

Small size particles were present in 10,000s (10^4) per cc, and those could be raised by what we call orographic lifting. Over the Tibetan plateau and the Himalayas, the jet stream is lifted by the mountains, and here particles can get into the jet stream. The higher up they go, the further they can travel. And, thus, they could have long-range and long-term effects on cloud amount and precipitation amount.

QUESTION 4

In view of the evidence known to you, do you think it possible that the Kuwaiti oil fires affected the unusual intensity of the cyclone in Bangladesh?

I don't know. Sullivan's model indicated that most of the plume was deposited in the Gulf, but some came down over India and China,[6] and he was shut down by a lot of people at many meetings for being too speculative.

At the May 1992 WMO meeting in Geneva [the Second WMO Meeting of Experts to Assess the Response to, and the Atmospheric Effects of, the Kuwaiti Oil Fires, Geneva, May 25–29, 1992], an Indian scientist argued that there was no effect to the environment of the Indian subcontinent because overall in those few months India didn't have an increase in rainfall. When you look carefully at his report, he used the average Indian rainfall to reach this conclusion. If the plume got to India, it affected just one area, so using an average removes any perturbation from the data.

QUESTION 5

In view of the evidence known to you, do you think it possible that the Kuwaiti oil fires affected the intensity of the July floods in China?

The rainy season usually occurs in June and July in East China, but in 1991 it started in May, and there were the most severe floods in 50 years. If the soot and sulfates got to China, they could have enhanced the rainfall and caused the flooding. The jetstream travelling from northwest to southeast converged in East China with the subtropical cyclone traveling from southeast to north. If additional CCN were available for moisture condensation, rainfall could be enhanced.

This is a possibility, but there is no data to support it. Few measurements on black carbon or sulfates were conducted in China at the time. Some high concentrations of carbon were detected in Northern China, but when the fires ceased they also found high black carbon occasionally, so it's not clear where the carbon came from. I'm giving you my personal opinion; the official opinion of NOAA about this is the same as Peter Hobbs' opinion.

QUESTION 6

How likely is it that further climatic effects could still occur as a result of the oil fires?

Sulfate particles and carbon particles coated with sulfate are very hygroscopic, so they have a high wet deposition rate and don't stay long in the atmosphere. The aerosol particles from Kuwait were still a small amount compared with a volcanic eruption. In my opinion, the effects of the fires wouldn't have lasted more than a few months, or a year at most.

NOTES:
1. Peter V. Hobbs and Lawrence F. Radke, "Airborne Studies."
2. S. Bakan et al., "Climate Response to the Smoke from the Burning Oil Wells in Kuwait," *Nature*, vol. 351 (May 30, 1991): 367–371.
3. D.W. Johnson et al., "Airborne Observations."
4. Measurements available from Anthony Hansen, Lawrence Livermore Laboratories.

5. Farn Parungo et al., "Aerosol Particles in the Kuwait Oil Fire Plumes: Their Morphology, Size Distribution, Chemical Composition, Transport, and Potential Effect on Climate," *Journal of Geophysical Research*, 97 D14 (October 20, 1992): 15867–882.

6. Thomas J. Sullivan, et al., *Modeling of Air Currents in the Gulf Region*, Report, (presented to the workshop on "Environmental Dimensions of the Gulf: Policy and International Perspectives" sponsored by the United Arab Emirates and the World Bank, April 19–22, 1992), Atmospheric Release Advisory Capability, Lawrence Livermore National Laboratory, Livermore, April 1992.

Thomas J. Sullivan

Thomas J. Sullivan, Ph.D., is head of the ARAC group at LLNL. He answered our questions in writing in January 1993.

Before answering your questions, allow me to take a minute to clarify that there is no necessity for the Kuwait oil fire soot to be transported by the jet stream in order to have it (potentially) involved in the Bangladesh cyclone and China floods. There is sufficient transport in the lower atmosphere. Also, as the enclosed paper indicates,[1] our ARAC modeling system was able to very consistently match the satellite views of the visible plume over the Gulf region.

QUESTION 1

In view of the evidence known to you, how likely is it that soot from the Kuwaiti oil fires could have penetrated into the jet stream?

It is extremely unlikely that any soot from the Kuwaiti oil fires could have penetrated into the jet stream. Satellite photographs and aircraft observations consistently indicated that the smoke plume remained in the lower troposphere. Reports by the NSF research flight program,[2] the WMO meeting of experts[3] and our own ARAC modeling and data collection here at the LLNL[4] are very consistent in this regard.

QUESTION 2

How much soot would have had to have entered the jet stream to produce significant climatic effects? In view of the evidence known to you, how likely is it that this quantity of soot could have entered the jet stream in the region around and above Kuwait?

Concerning how much soot would have had to enter the jet stream for significant climate effects, I cannot answer. Certainly this unknown quantity did not enter the jet stream because there were no significant climatic effects of the Kuwaiti fires soot.

QUESTION 3

Can particles that are not visible affect climate? If so, could soot constituents not detected by the aerial and satellite observation performed over the Gulf have risen above 22,000 feet?

The atmosphere contains a large number of particles of a variety of types and sizes all the time. In order to have an effect on climate, they must be of sufficient quantity and lifetime (e.g., years, seasonal, etc.) to alter normal physical conditions. To my knowledge this quantity of particles would always be visible/measurable by the normal eye or measurement instruments.

QUESTION 4

In view of the evidence known to you, do you think it possible that the Kuwaiti oil fires affected the unusual intensity of the cyclone in Bangladesh?

Yes, I think it is possible that a significant quantity of hygroscopic soot particles did feed into the late April 1991 Bay of Bengal/Bangladesh cyclone, possibly increasing its intensity. This would be possible based on the lower atmosphere trajectories of the soot particles from the Kuwaiti oil fires which the ARAC group modeled.[5,6]

QUESTION 5

In view of the evidence known to you, do you think it possible that the Kuwaiti oil fires affected the intensity of the July floods in China?

Once again I believe it is plausible, and our lower atmosphere trajectories show that it is possible, that the Yangtze Valley floods of early July 1991 were enhanced or exacerbated by the influx of additional hygroscopic soot particles/condensation nuclei transported from the Kuwaiti oil fires. The jet stream was not involved at all, but rather the west-to-southwest seasonal monsoon windflow and a stagnant stationary cold front that remained over the Yangtze Valley for about a seven-to-ten-day period.

QUESTION 6

How likely is it that further climatic effects could still occur as a result of the oil fires?

Soot did not get into the jet stream or the stratosphere. It is virtually impossible that any climatic effects occurred or will occur because of the injection of the mass of soot particles into the atmosphere. The half-life of hygroscopic particles in the atmosphere is on the order of five to fourteen days, depending on the distribution of sufficient water vapor to lead to condensation. Since the atmosphere is constantly being cleansed by the condensation/precipitation process, it is highly improbable that any soot particles remained in the atmosphere more than a few weeks after the last fires were extinguished in November 1991. Long before that it was virtually impossible to differentiate the Kuwaiti soot particles from the daily mass injection from the combustion of oil and coal from throughout the world.

NOTES:

1. Thomas J. Sullivan et al., *Modeling of Air Currents in the Gulf Region.*
2. Peter V. Hobbs and Lawrence F. Radke, "Airborne Studies."
3. World Meteorological Organization, *Report on the Expert Meeting on the Atmospheric Part of the Emergency Response to the Kuwait Oilfield Fires*, Geneva, April 27–30, 1991.
4. Thomas J. Sullivan et al., *Modeling of Air Currents in the Gulf Region.*
5. Joyce Penner, *Global Model Simulations of the Long Range Transport of Soot and Sulfur from the Oil Fires*, Report, (prepared for the Geneva World Meteorological Organization expert meeting on the atmospheric part of the emergency response to the Kuwait oil field fires, April 27–30, 1991), Lawrence Livermore National Laboratory, Livermore, 1991.
6. Thomas J. Sullivan et al., *Modeling of Air Currents in the Gulf Region.*

Adam Trombly

Adam Trombly, a research physicist and climatologist, is a Fellow of the Aspen Institute for Advanced Studies. His answers were excerpted from a phone interview conducted in February 1993.

QUESTION 1

In view of the evidence known to you, how likely is it that soot from the Kuwaiti oil fires could have penetrated into the jet stream?

It's not only likely, it happened. I flew in the stratosphere in December 1991, all the way across the Atlantic, and without a shadow of a doubt a relatively contiguous layer of petroleum effluent, in the flight path we took, stretched nearly all the way across the Atlantic.

A NOAA source is quoted as saying in the *National Geographic* that [the smoke] got up as high as 22,000 feet,[1] but you've got to realize that all of these surveys were done within the Persian Gulf Region itself,[2] and the longer the plume, the longer the effluent itself is exposed to instant solar radiation. The further you got from the source, on the day side of the earth, the longer the exposure to instant solar radiation was. As you went further down the plume, you began to notice stratification happening, and, as you flew down the plume further, that stratification became more profound. People who say that 22,000 feet isn't that significant in terms of stratospheric penetration or intrusion–if it stopped there that would be true. But we were feeding into jet stream type of activity and into the stratosphere with the more volatile elements of this plume.

In his testimony before Congress,[3] Peter Hobbs was willing to admit that they had seen traces of smoke up to 22,000 feet. A couple of NOAA people I talked to in Saudi Arabia had observed quite thick strata at 22,000 feet. Going over the flight logs for the NSF team, by far the vast majority of their flights[4] were early morning flights, and the plume, despite what was said before Congress, did have a significant lofting cycle. It rose and fell.

The plume was circling the earth. This was acknowledged by the astronauts from the Space Shuttle mission that returned in the middle of April 1991. They stated publicly on CNN, with video footage, that the plume had circled the earth several times. Plumes that don't get above 22,000 feet don't circle the earth several times.

QUESTION 2

How much soot would have had to have entered the jet stream to produce significant climatic effects? In view of the evidence known to you, how likely is it that this quantity of soot could have entered the jet stream in the region around and above Kuwait?

Deep stratospheric intrusion is a concern of mine, not primarily because of climatological change, but because Kuwaiti oil has a very high content of polychlorinated hydrocarbons, polynucleated hydrocarbons, and some quantity of relatively free chlorine. We have had a significant input of chlorine from the Kuwaiti oil fires, and a dramatic increase of chlorine in the stratosphere is very bad for the ozone layer. Bromine is worse, and I don't know what eventually will be discovered about how much bromine Safety Boss from Canada used to put out the fires.

We forecast at our press conference when we came back from Kuwait [the press conference to present the Friends of the Earth-sponsored study of the environmental impacts of the Gulf War, Washington, DC, June 1991] that we would see significant exacerbation of ozone depletion and of chlorine monoxide concentrations in the stratosphere as a result of these fires, a significant exacerbation of an already horrible problem.

The other thing was an increase in turbulence in the stratosphere after the war. A British Air Concorde got its tail blown off because of the intensity of these winds. There's nothing in the literature yet about this.

QUESTION 4

In view of the evidence known to you, do you think it possible that the Kuwaiti oil fires affected the unusual intensity of the cyclone in Bangladesh?

LLNL scientists have stated publicly that the plume was observed to go directly into the Bangladesh area. The plume was observed to feed directly into the Bay of Bengal. No matter how many lies are told about it by others, there's no doubt that the effluent from Kuwait exacerbated that horrible, profoundly destructive storm that killed so many people over there.

QUESTION 5

In view of the evidence known to you, do you think it possible that the Kuwaiti oil fires affected the intensity of the July floods in China?

Again, you have a tremendous input and a tremendous increase in nucleating particulate. The heaviest particulate precipitated out over the Gulf or relatively proximate areas. But you also have the middling type of particulate that took longer to precipitate and to begin to fall, and, of course, it nucleated, and cloud-building occurred, and you had torrential downpours. Any time you have a source of effluent, whether from African forest fires, or dust storms off of Africa, or Brazilian forest fires, or oil fires, any time you have a significant input in the atmosphere of particulate aerosols, then you inevitably have profound increases in the populations of nucleating particulates. And cloud condensation nuclei make clouds.

QUESTION 6

How likely is it that further climatic effects could still occur as a result of the oil fires?

Ambassador James George, in his testimony before Senate Environment and Public Works Committee, raised the question whether the dramatic increase in tornado activity we saw in 1991 was also associated with cloud-building from the Gulf War that had resulted from nucleation of particulate that had been emitted by the fires. Of course, you have other things that were also very bad that year. You had terrible, terrible fires in South America, Brazil in particular. You had very bad fires in Africa, you had the worst forest fires in 1991 that we've had in Africa for a while. We also had very, very severe wind storms.

As late as December 1991, at 56,000 feet we saw significant brown effluent. This is not an albedo that you can associate in any way, shape or form with Pinatubo or any other volcano. This is a petroleum albedo, albedo meaning the reflectivity which affects the color and the absorption rate.[5] That's really important to note, because these things will continue to fall out of the upper troposphere and the stratosphere and nucleate, and this is, of course, affecting cloud-building and other processes. Cloud-building, of course, affects our weather.[6]

NOTES:

1. Sylvia Earle, "Persian Gulf Pollution: Assessing the Damage One Year Later," *National Geographic*, February 1991, 122.
2. Results of the NSF flights made from May 12 to June 15, and from May 19 to June 4, were summarized in Peter V. Hobbs and Lawrence F. Radke, "Airborne Studies."
3. U.S. Congress, Senate Environmental and Public Works Committee, Gulf Pollution Task Force, *Testimony* by Peter V. Hobbs, 102nd Congress, 1st sess., July 7, 1991, 8.
4. Peter V. Hobbs and Lawrence F. Radke, "Airborne Studies."
5. Adam Trombly also told us this could be seen from STS 43 satellite photos for August 1991.
6. For more detail, see Adam Trombly, *Interim Environmental Damage Assessment Report for the Persian Gulf Region*, Aspen Institute for Advanced Studies, July, 1991.

Correspondence With John Cox

John Cox, Ph.D., an oil industry engineer and the Vice President of CND (the British Campaign for Nuclear Disarmament), was among the first to warn the public of the possible environmental impacts of the Gulf War (see ARC/Arms Control Research Center's previous study, Hidden Casualties: The Environmental Consequences of a Persian Gulf Conflict, *January, 1991). Instead of answering our questionnaire, he sent unpublished material which addresses the questions we asked.*

MeteoSat and other observations in May 1991 showed a visible plume, often 100 kilometers wide and usually extending over 1,000 kilometers from Kuwait. Its normal height was five kilometers (16,825 feet) and, by calculating the soot volume in the cloud, its lifetime can be shown not to exceed twenty days. This, it is claimed, refutes fears that soot could have stayed aloft long enough to reach the stratosphere and cause major climatic variations.

The limitation of such measurements is that no one actually observed where the soot went. Dispersal goes in three directions: downwards with rainfall, laterally by diffusion and (at higher altitudes) easterly with the subtropical jet streams. There is no reason to believe that all the soot left the visible cloud and returned to earth.

Whereas low-level rainfall was responsible for most visible pollution around Kuwait (and confirms that most soot particles were hydrophilic), the deposition of oil and soot in the Himalayan snow in April demonstrates that, even under relatively humid conditions, the cloud height exceeds five kilometers. Similarly, the twenty-fold increase in dust in Hawaii[1] (recorded before Mt. Pinatubo exploded) can be explained only by transportation in the subtropical jet streams.

Reality has exposed the limitations of the theoretical climatic models used by climatologists. For example, the "Hamburg global coupled ocean-atmosphere general-circulation model"[2] predicted an average cloud rise of only two kilometers (6,730 feet), so what credence can be given to its estimates for stratospheric intrusion?

The silliest claim by the no-danger-to-the-stratosphere school is that visible cloud is synonymous with the presence of soot. In reality, the top of a cloud is sheared by high-altitude, high-velocity air currents which disperse its contents around the globe. Even a lowly 2,000-foot smoke cloud is capable of sending some of its soot to the stratosphere.

MONSOONS

On this aspect, the reporting of my views (though not the actual words of my article) overstated my fears. I did not suggest that the Asian monsoons were the most sensitive of the microclimatic phenomena at risk and, in retrospect, regret that this aspect received so much publicity. My key statement was "even a few degrees drop in daytime temperatures could cause crop failures on a massive scale."[3] This is an incontrovertible reality.

Agronomists emphasize that harvests fail with temperatures only five degrees Celsius below normal for two to three weeks in the germination period. On the monsoon issue per se, two of the more popular climatic models suggested that the short-term effects of the smoke would increase rainfall—exactly as did occur.[4,5]

These, and other problems raised by climatologists and agricultural experts, confirm my pre-war fear that a "prolonged conflagration" might "influence the onset, duration and character of the Asian monsoons" and support my plea that climatic perturbations should have been assessed before taking the military option.

GLOBAL WARMING

In this important respect, my presentation in January 1991 understated the problem. When the issue was highlighted by King Hussein's warning (in November 1990) that an oilfield conflagration could accelerate global warming, I felt, in common with other scientists, that other problems were more important. So I distanced myself with "the resulting fires could burn almost three million barrels/day. This adds under five percent extra CO_2 to worldwide emissions which, though undesirable, hardly rates as a global eco-catastrophe. In reality the main dangers arise from the major by-products of uncontrolled combustion: CO_2, SO_2, oxides of nitrogen (NO_x) and, above all, smoke."[6]

In retrospect, this was too dismissive. CO_2 is not the only gas emitted by the fires, and several unburnt hydrocarbons have a greater greenhouse effect. If only two percent of the oil remained unburnt as methane, this would have a greater effect than the 98 percent converted to carbon dioxide. Moreover, many oil well emissions were mainly gaseous and discharged for weeks without ignition.

Another omission was consideration of the potential greenhouse contribution of smoke and soot, reducing infrared radiation from the earth by absorption and thus raising ground temperatures. An accentuation of the greenhouse problem could prove the most serious and longest-lasting legacy of this wholly futile war.

NOTES:

1. D. Lowenthal et al., "Evidence for Long-Range Transport of Aerosol from the Kuwaiti Oil Fires to Hawaii," *Journal of Geophysical Research*, 97 D13 (September 20, 1992): 14573.
2. S. Bakan et al., "Climate Response."
3. John Cox in *Environmental Protection Bulletin*, No. 10 (January 1991), Institution of Chemical Engineers, U.K.

4. K.A. Browning et al., "Environmental Effects from Burning Oil Wells."

5. S. Bakan et al., "Climate Response."

6. John Cox in *Environmental Protection Bulletin*

Chapter 4

Desert Impacts

U.S. vehicles in the desert in Kuwait, with oil fires burning on the horizon.
Photo courtesy of United Nations.

Introduction

In this chapter, desert ecologist Tony Burgess and former National Oceanic and Atmospheric Agency chief scientist Sylvia Earle describe the effects of the war on the sand and gravel desert plain constituting most of Kuwait, Iraq south of the Euphrates, and northern Saudi Arabia.

As we estimated in the Introduction to Chapter Three, as many as 2,000,000,000 barrels of oil (prior to evaporation) may have spilled out onto the Kuwaiti desert, producing one of the most dramatic legacies of the war, the oil lakes. It is only now, two years after the end of the war, that the Kuwait Petroleum Corporation committee has begun the process of evaluating the removal of (in their estimate) a remaining 9,500,000 barrels of oil from the Kuwaiti desert.[1]

John M. Miller describes the radioactive residue of depleted uranium (DU) that was left behind on the desert plain in Iraq and Kuwait. DU is used to harden the casings of ammunition designed to pierce armored vehicles, and also to strengthen the protective armor of tanks and armed personnel carriers. The Gulf War was the first time that the U.S. and Great Britain used depleted uranium shells in combat.[2]

The *Army Times* reports that up to 62 U.S. soldiers were exposed to DU during the conflict. At least one U.S. soldier, who spent 45 days helping to prepare tanks damaged by friendly fire for reshipping to the U.S., has since complained publicly about the resulting damage to his health.[3] Because of the DU shrapnel that still contaminates the desert, local inhabitants, such as the Bedouins, could be exposed to low-level radiation for long periods to come.

Much of the unexploded ordnance (UXO) left by Iraqi and Coalition forces on the desert plain has yet to be cleared up. According to one estimate, in the six months following the end of the Gulf War an average of six people a day were killed in Kuwait by picking up or standing on UXO.[4] Unexploded ordnance is a serious problem not only on the desert plain, but also in most of the areas of Iraq that were bombed by the Coalition.

—*James Warner*

Notes:

1. Organization of Petroleum Exporting Countries (OPEC) News Agency, March 17, 1993.
2. Grace Bukowski et al., *Uranium Battlefields Home and Abroad,* Report, Rural Alliance for Military Accountability, Carson City, Nevada, 1993.
3. Soraya S. Nelson, "Radiation, Storm Illness Link Alleged," *Army Times,* October 12, 1992.
4. Paul Brown, "Kuwait's Keening Fields," *The Guardian,* November 5, 1991.

Desert Ecology

Interview with Tony Burgess

Tony Burgess, Ph.D., is a desert ecologist who worked with the University of Arizona Desert Laboratory in Tucson, Arizona, and serves as a consultant to numerous public and private organizations. He is currently doing research at the Geosciences Department at the University of Arizona. He visited the Gulf in June 1991 for Friends of the Earth (FOE). Interviewed July 1991 by John M. Miller.

John M. Miller: What impacts has the war had on the desert?

Tony Burgess: First and foremost, of course, are the oil fires. My area of expertise [for the FOE tour] was the effect of the fire on the desert, and it is manifold.

There were soot deposits on the plants up to 200 kilometers downwind, to the extent that they would blacken our fingers when we would rub the stems of the grasses. But the plants themselves looked very healthy, because there had been unusually good winter rains and the smoke clouds had kept daytime temperatures cooler than normal. So they stayed greener longer than they would have been expected to. By June, they should have been fairly dried up, I was told, but instead they were still pretty green and growing. So, a great distance downwind the effects of the fires were offset by what you might call ameliorating effects.

Of course in the immediate vicinity of the burning oil fields, the environment has been trashed. There is a film of oil over everything that blackens plants and soil, the whole landscape. A few plants look like they were surviving, but I am not sure that most plants will be able to survive that kind of coating. It is very likely to suffocate them if nothing else.

JMM: I have heard that the fires have caused more rain and therefore a lot more plants to bloom in Saudi Arabia.

TB: Yes, but the point is—which is what you learn when you start looking at the globe—for every area where there is excessive rain, there will be a downwind area where there is deficient rain. That is of course the natural balance between rainforest and the areas on the downwind side of what we call a Hadley Cell in the tropics where you get very dry areas. It is normal, but it is a zero-sum game.

JMM: So if the moisture falls elsewhere, there won't be enough left to fall where it normally would?

TB: Exactly. Unless you heat up the whole globe and evaporate more water. It is complicated, but there is sort of a balance there. Of course the more unbalanced the situation, the more the natural ecosystems are going to be stressed.

OIL ON THE DESERT

Another problem we saw in Kuwait was not only the oil fires, but the oil lakes. Even for wells that had been extinguished, there was a period in which some of them were not capped. Some of the wells that were still burning were also putting out oil, seeping through other areas in the pipes, I guess. Lakes were forming, and in some areas were beginning to catch fire and burn with a more smoky, polluting kind of smoke than was produced by the high-pressure wells. The lakes seem to attract some of the birds. The oil lakes themselves will pose a serious problem, not only to the local fauna, but also to the migratory fauna funneling in there from all over Asia.

JMM: Dust had covered some of the oil?

TB: On aerial photos there had been indications of blackened areas that actually looked covered. It turned out that oil had coated the grasses and the surface of the ground, and then windblown dust had coated the oil, so that it looked like the environment was clean, when in fact the oil was still there but was covered with a thin layer of windblown sand and dust.

We saw a similar situation on some of the beaches. The beaches in Kuwait looked fairly clean, and some of the beaches, even in the heavily polluted areas of the northern Saudi Arabian coast, looked remarkably clean, but what we found was, when we dug below the surface of some of these beaches, there was a veneer of clean sand covering a stratum of oil that ranged from a couple of centimeters to a half meter thick as best we could judge. It was not visible on the surface, but the oil was still there and still affecting the intertidal ecosystem.

Bombs and Mines

In terms of other effects of the war, again you have the phenomenon that some of the effects we view as bad may actually serve to benefit the desert, such as the cluster bomb fragments, mines, and grenades. These are clearly disastrous for humans trying to go out there and do whatever, whether it is grazing stock, repairing fences or any of those duties. A high priority will naturally be to get the bombs and things out.

The problem is that a lot of the ordnance left around by the retreating Iraqis in Kuwait has now been covered by windblown sand. I saw several of their trenches and bunkers almost completely filled in with windblown sand, and of course there is no telling what lies underneath them. I doubt if they will ever be able to clean up all that ordnance. It will probably continue to be unearthed for hundreds, if not thousands, of years.

JMM: So, the companies coming in to take care of the unexploded ordnance are working in the more populated areas?

TB: No, because one of the worst sites I saw was on the north shore of Kuwait Bay at the point opposite Bubiyan Island, where you had antipersonnel mines scattered along the upper intertidal area of the beach. It seemed like every 10 or 15 meters there was one. Certainly, we could not go near the beach to inspect it. We would not dare with all those antipersonnel mines there. Those definitely need to be cleaned up and will be, I am sure, because fishermen or sea turtles coming ashore could set them off.

JMM: A sea turtle could set off a mine?

TB: Yes. They weigh 80 to 100 pounds. Floating logs could set those mines off, and they have a kill radius of, I understand, well over 20 meters. So, this has to be dealt with. It is not only in the cities, but in these coastal defense areas where so much of that kind of thing is concentrated.

By the same token, some areas I saw in Kuwait have barbed-wire entanglements and defense bunkers and stuff like that to keep the livestock out. You are dealing with an ecosystem, especially in Saudi Arabia, that has been devastated by excessive levels of grazing for at least two or three decades now. So in regard to a system that was already so degraded before the war, anything that can keep people and livestock out, for even a limited amount of time, may actually benefit the recovery of the desert.

Under normal conditions—conditions that could be sustained by the climate—the diversity and biomass of the vegetation would be much greater than what is there now. If it is a question of restoring the desert to what it was before the war, it won't take much, because there was not that much there. It was a "desertified" desert. But in terms of restoring it to what it potentially could be, that would require a major effort.

RESTORING THE DESERT

JMM: More than just keeping human activity out?

TB: More than just keeping stock off; you would have to reintroduce plants that may have gone extinct in the region and therefore have no seed source in the immediate area anymore. In fact, it would probably take a considerable amount of effort just to reconstruct what potentially had been there before the use of grazing began.

You really have a system that has been hammered by livestock for thousands of years, with a consequent alteration in the biology and even the soil. While things had been pretty devastated in Kuwait, some areas actually had pretty good pasture because the stock had not been able to get in there at the time of our June visit.

On the Saudi side, the Coalition forces left pretty clean campsites. About all I saw was communication wire and a little bit of barbed wire, not a lot of trash, although there was some. A few diesel spills and other fuel spills were reported. We did find one complex with lots of ammunition left behind by the Egyptian army, but they may have been planning to send some trucks in to clean it up eventually. It was not clear that it had been abandoned or left behind, it was just unguarded.

Where the Coalition forces had camped, you do have huge complexes of berms two to three meters high enclosing the areas where the camps were and smaller berm complexes enclosing what I guess were artillery emplacements. You also have, of course, trenches and sandbags and things like that. These complex topographic modifications could actually be turned to advantage. With some modifications you could conceivably turn these trenches and berms into water harvesting devices that would actually promote the establishment of vegetation.

The area where most of this action occurred is a very flat plain called the Northern Plain that has been pretty badly overgrazed. These local topographic alterations could actually funnel runoff and allow the vegetation to recover to a level that would be better than it had been before. This would require some sustained protection from livestock damage while the vegetation was becoming established.

EROSION

JMM: Will the berms eventually erode?

TB: They will, but given the low rainfall, it will take hundreds, if not thousands of years. For example, Patton's tank tracks are still visible in the California desert. You can still see signs of the impact of war maneuvers up to 40 years after abandonment there. Some of the work that Howard Wilshire and Bob Webb have done on recovery of compacted soils from off-road vehicle activity suggests that if the soil is compacted, you are talking several human lifetimes. In fact in some sites it may take over a thousand years for the recovery of the soil and vegetation to pre-compaction states.

Certainly the areas within the compounds that had been camped on, driven over and pretty effectively denuded will be visible for a long, long time. Several human lifetimes, I think, is reasonable. What had been predicted with a lot of this denudation is a lot of sand and blowing dust. To some extent, especially in the extensively denuded areas around Hafar Al Batin [site of Coalition encampment on the desert plain, in Saudi Arabia near the Iraqi border], that is the case. But, in some of the areas I looked at, the soil had a fairly high content of clay and gypsum and had already formed a crust on it that will pretty effectively impede any more wind erosion—unless the crust is disturbed again by animals or vehicles or something like that. So the wind erosion where I saw it was not as bad as we had expected.

JMM: Won't that crust also keep the plants from growing back?

TB: Sure. And again, that crust, in keeping plants from growing back in one place, funnels the run-off into another place which makes more water available. So in some ways the crust could promote plant growth on another site by focusing the run-off. The problem is, will there be serious erosion and gullies? In the landscapes I saw, this was not a problem because the terrain was so level that there was not much potential for deep erosive activity, but I am sure there would be places where it is a problem.

I did see an area with sandier soil, such as the big troop encampments on the peninsula near Manifa [in Kuwait], where it looked like there had been a lot of denudation of stabilized dunes next to the coast. That could set up an erosive cycle especially by wind that could go on for some time. The effects of wind erosion are fairly dependent on the texture of the soil, and if it is fine sand as in Kuwait and some parts of the Saudi coast, then I think you are going to see some pretty serious wind erosion. In fact, we have already.

CONTAMINATION

There was some limited evidence of heavy metal contamination in Saudi Arabian soils near the Kuwait border, with diminished concentrations of metals as you traveled away from the Kuwait border. One of the highest levels of these metals was titanium, which of course is a strategic metal, and I think it is used in bomb casings. So there may be residual chemical pollution of the surface of the soil just due to byproducts of explosives, fuel burning and things of this nature, but this needs a lot more analysis and sampling before we could get any kind of a conclusive picture about it.

JMM: And the Saudis were doing that?

TB: They were trying to. They were hampered by a lack of information about exactly what to look for. The U.S. Department of Defense had not released any information to them about the make-up of jet fuel or what the likely pollutants would be as byproducts of explosives and so forth. I guess a lot of this is classified information, so it is not readily available. They were sort of searching in the dark for different kinds of pollution that would be at low levels or difficult to detect by conventional means.

JMM: Aside from whatever toxic garbage gets left by armies, there is sewage, food waste, paper. . . .

TB: Actually, I did not see much of that. If it was there it has been buried. In fact, compared to what I remember of what we left behind when I was in Vietnam, I was impressed with the areas where the Coalition forces had camped. I guess the sloppiest camps, based on a very general inspection, were left by the Egyptians. The ones where the Americans and British had been were remarkably clean. There was communication wire, some C-ration packages blowing around, a few gun magazines, but on the whole it was remarkably clean. But certainly there is that potential.

I think the worst thing they left behind—and I did not see this—but it was reported that there had been some major fuel spills at some of the refueling places that had not been cleaned up, so there was diesel-soaked ground around. But put it in the context of the fact that you have a big oil industry in place there and a lot of stuff just being dumped or left lying around by the various oil workers, it is really hard in many of those places to tell what is damage due to military activity and what is damage that is just a byproduct of industrial development and especially of the oil industry.

JMM: Were data destroyed that were needed to restore some of the environment in Kuwait?

TB: Restoration depends on having some baseline data as to what was there. In the case of the Kuwaitis, the Iraqis had sent down personnel from the Iraqi universities who then stripped all the equipment possible from Kuwait University and the Kuwait Institute for Scientific Research. Once all the equipment was taken that the Iraqi universities and professors wanted, all remaining files, records and books were then burned. Then they turned the artillery on the physical structures.

The situation in Kuwait was especially tragic in the national park they had recently set up north of Kuwait Bay [Jal Al Zhor National Park], where the vegetation looked like it had been starting to recover under the protection from livestock grazing. There were some fires up there, so a lot of the vegetation was blackened, but also the fences were down.

So you have essentially all of the scientific infrastructure there gone or destroyed. It takes time to build this kind of information base, and my hope is that copies of some of the important information were out of the country at that time or in obscure files. But it will take time to reassemble all that into something coherent, as well as to re-establish the whole scientific community in Kuwait.

Depleted Uranium: Radioactive Residue in the Desert and the U.S.

Background Information

In July 1991, the U.S. Central Command reported that 26 Americans had been killed or injured in tanks and armored vehicles hit by depleted uranium weapons. Only the North American and British militaries use depleted uranium in their antitank munitions, so the discovery of radioactive residue in tanks forced the Pentagon to revise its tally of casualties from "friendly fire."[1]

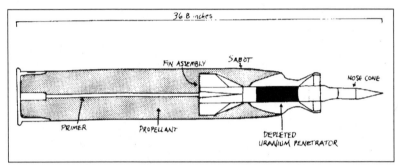

A depleted uranium weapon. Disposal methods have been described as "unloading the gun by pulling the trigger." Source: Grace Bukowski et al., *Uranium Battlefields Home and Abroad*, Report, Rural Alliance for Military Accountability, Carson City, Nevada, 1993. Artwork by Carol Melnick.

In January 1993, the official number of U.S. friendly fire casualties rose when the U.S. General Accounting Office (GAO) released a report concluding that 35 soldiers had been injured inside Bradley Fighting Vehicles or Abrams tanks penetrated by DU rounds fired by Abrams tanks. The GAO stated that all 35 had been externally exposed to depleted uranium, either through wounds, ingestion or exposure, and that their health may be at risk in the long term. In response, the Pentagon said the 35 soldiers would be medically evaluated over several years, beginning in July 1993.[2]

A 1991 report by the United Kingdom Atomic Energy Authority (AEA) said that at least 40 tons (36,000 kg.) of DU were left behind in Kuwait and Iraq by Coalition armies. The report calculated that this was enough to cause 500,000 deaths "potentially, if it were all absorbed," going on to say that the actual casualties would be far less. (For one thing, most of the DU was in uninhabited areas.) The secret report, prepared in April 1991, was revealed seven months later by the British newspaper, *The Independent.*[3]

WHAT IS DU?

Depleted uranium is a byproduct of the uranium enrichment process for nuclear weapons and reactors. Uranium 235 is the isotope used in nuclear weapons and reactor fuel. The enrichment of uranium concentrates the percentage of U-235 (a more radioactive and less stable isotope of uranium), leaving behind large amounts of the less radioactive U-238. The U-238 is considered to be "waste." DU consists of 99.8 percent U-238, which decays slowly, emitting primarily alpha radiation. The alpha particle emissions of DU are the same as that of plutonium, though much less intense. The General Accounting Office in its January 1993 report says that depleted uranium is about half as radioactive as natural uranium.

The reason why the military likes DU is its great density—two-and-a-half-times that of steel. DU easily pierces the armor in tanks and other military vehicles. When a DU shell hits the armor it sends molten fragments through to the inside of the vehicle. DU shrapnel may penetrate the body, or uranium oxide may be inhaled, leading to "unacceptable body burdens" in the words of the AEA report.[4]

DU is molded into the armor-penetrating shells to be fired by M1-A1 tanks, A-10 Wart Hog attack planes and Apache antitank helicopters. Navy warships use DU shells in their anti-aircraft guns. Because DU is so dense it is also used to harden the armor of M1 tanks and Bradley Fighting Vehicles. During the Gulf War, only DU shells pierced the M1 tanks' DU-hardened armor.

A recent estimate is that U.S. Air Force A-10 aircraft fired some 940,000 30-millimeter uranium-tipped bullets, about half of them into Iraq and half into Kuwait, while U.S. tanks fired about 4,000 rounds, and that 300 metric tons (300,000 kg.) of depleted uranium fragments remain in Kuwait and Iraq in the form of shrapnel.[5]

HEALTH RISKS

The U.S. Food and Drug Administration has stated that troops in vehicles loaded with DU shells receive the equivalent radiation dose of about one chest X-ray every 20 to 30 hours.[6]

DU is especially dangerous when inhaled, or enters the body through a wound or by swallowing. While U-238's alpha radiation does not travel far (a piece of paper or the skin can stop it), it can cause cancer and genetic defects once it enters the body.

Unlike an X-ray, which provides a brief exposure, the radiation from ingested or inhaled depleted uranium continues to assault the body's cells and their nuclei. Children are especially vulnerable because their cells are dividing rapidly as they grow. In addition to its radioactive dangers, uranium is also chemically toxic like lead. The body deals with uranium as it does with calcium. Large doses can cause heavy metal poisoning; lower doses can damage kidneys or the lungs. The uranium is permanently deposited in the bones and can migrate into the placenta.

The AEA report describes the potential hazards to desert inhabitants:[7]

> The DU will be spread around the battlefield and target vehicles in varying sizes and quantities from dust particles to full size penetrators. It would be unwise for people to stay close to large quantities of DU for long periods and would obviously be of concern to the local population if they collect this heavy metal and keep it.[8] There will be specific areas in which many rounds will have been fired where localized contamination of vehicles and soil may exceed permissible limits and these could be hazardous to both cleanup teams and the local population.

RECYCLING RADIOACTIVE TANKS

After the war, 10 M1 tanks and 15 Bradley fighting vehicles were returned from the desert to be decontaminated for reuse or disposal at the Defense Consolidation Facility of the radioactive waste dump in Barnwell, South Carolina.[9]

When interviewed in August 1991, army spokesman Major Padilla said these vehicles were "brought back not because they posed a danger, but because we have to account for the DU under our license with the Nuclear Regulatory Commission." The concern was nuclear proliferation, he said, "because somewhere down the road there may be a method of gathering low-level uranium" for weapons.

DEPLETED URANIUM TESTING

U.S. communities where DU weapons testing takes place are worried about health risks. This practice threatens the health not only of soldiers, but civilians, livestock and wildlife, according to Geoffrey Sea of In Vivo, a radiation health research group, who says, "Depleted uranium munitions have caused serious contamination problems in every community in which they have been tested."[10]

Groundwater contamination has been found near a test site in Minnesota. In Socorro, New Mexico, another test site, U-238 has contaminated a pond used to irrigate a golf course. The Stillwater, Nevada, wildlife refuge sits next to Bravo 20, a Navy bombing range. A high radionuclide count has been measured at the refuge. In 1986, the entire area was flooded, flushing contaminants from Bravo 20 into the refuge.

In 1980, workers at a Jonesboro, Tennessee, plant that handles only DU had the highest radiation exposures of any nuclear workers in the nation. A similar plant near Albany was forced to close in 1980 by the state of New York because it regularly exceeded its radioactive emission limit.

The military, convinced that DU poses little threat, is taking no initiative to monitor its health effects on communities near the testing ground, much less estimate the long-term impact of production and use.

DESERT CLEANUP UNLIKELY

The closing of the Albany, New York, site raises a red flag for those concerned about the danger of radiation in the Kuwaiti and Iraqi deserts. Leonard Dietz, who was a scientist at Knolls Atomic Power Laboratory, N.Y., asks in a letter to *Chemical and Engineering News:*

> If New York state is greatly concerned about the equivalent of one or two uranium projectiles being released as fine particles to the Albany environment in a month, why isn't the U.S. government concerned about tens of thousands of these projectiles being fired in a few days of war?[11]

An indication that the Pentagon remains oblivious to rising concern about DU is the postwar export of Abrams tanks to Kuwait.[12] The AEA in its report offered to develop a DU desert cleanup plan—an offer which has yet to be accepted. DU will continue to take more than its due of hidden casualties.

—John M. Miller

NOTES:

1. Richard H. P. Sin, "Friendly Fire," *The Baltimore Sun,* August 10, 1991.

2. Thomas W. Lippman, "Gulf War Vets Were Exposed to Uranium From 'Friendly Fire'," *Washington Post,* January 28, 1993. Dorothy Brooks of the Military Families Support Network based in Buies Creek, North Carolina, compiled reports of over 1,000 soldiers who returned from the Gulf War with mysterious ailments, and found that about 75 percent of their spouses had related health problems. Probable causes include exposure to toxics from the oil fires, the sexually transferable parasitic disease leishmaniasis, and DU exposure. Chronicle Wire Services, "Spouses Share Gulf Vets' Ailments," *San Francisco Chronicle,* March 9, 1993.

3. Nick Cohen, "Radioactive Waste Left in Gulf by Allies," *The Independent,* November 10, 1991.

4. Nick Cohen, "Radioactive Waste Left in Gulf."

5. William M. Arkin, "The Desert Glows—With Propaganda," *Greenpeace Bulletin,* May 1993.

6. James Ridgeway, "Using Nuclear Bullets," *Village Voice,* January 15, 1991, reproduced in G. Bukowski et al., *Uranium Battlefields.*

7. Nick Cohen, "Radioactive Waste Left in Gulf."

8. William Arkin calculates, based on a cancer rate of one in 1,000 per cumulative rem of exposure, that an individual would have to carry one of the DU bullets in question, which emit 15 millirems per hour of gamma radiation, for a whole month to have a one percent chance of incurring a cancer from the exposure. William M. Arkin, "The Desert Glows—With Propaganda." However, a child suffering from malnutrition would be at greater risk than an ordinary individual, and there have been reports of Iraqi children using DU shells as playthings.

9. Charles Pope, "Armored Casualties Doctored in Barnwell," *The State,* August 14, 1991.

10. Geoffrey Sea, "Depleted Uranium Health Effects: Background Paper," *In Vivo Radiation Response,* Oakland, California.

11. Leonard Dietz, letter to *Chemical and Engineering News,* February 4, 1991.

12. *The Associated Press,* "Kuwait Will Buy Abrams Tanks," October 14, 1992, reproduced in G. Bukowski et al., *Uranium Battlefields.*

Unexploded Ordnance (UXO)

Background Information

Like many of this century's battlefields, Iraq and Kuwait are now littered with unexploded bombs and land mines—commonly called unexploded ordnance (UXO)—that will long pose a threat to human and animal life. Much of the UXO is now hidden beneath swirling sands and oil lakes.

Iraqi forces laid millions of mines to prevent Coalition recapture of Kuwaiti territory. According to a 1993 U.S. Department of State report, there are approximately five to seven million uncleared land mines in Kuwait. These mines are scattered throughout the country, but are concentrated in the South, in sandy desert terrain. Minefields crisscross oil fields and roads, and in some cases were laid parallel to power lines.[1] The number of mines sown by the U.S. is classified information and still unknown, but the total amount of ammunition, bombs, anti-tank mines and missiles expended by the Coalition forces was approximately 240,000 tons, according to a press release from the Naval Weapons Station, Concord, California.[2] Artillery, naval guns and tanks fired additional shells. Naval ships in the Persian Gulf and Red Sea fired land attack cruise missiles with conventional explosive warheads into Iraq.

Not all of this ordnance exploded: "At least 600 bombs, rockets and artillery shells dropped or fired every day of the war will have failed to explode and thus constitute a continuing hazard somewhere in the war theater," one U.S. expert told the *Washington Post*.[3] Kuwaiti officials said that 200 people were accidentally killed and over 1,000 others wounded by land mines after the war ended (as of December 1991)—a third of them children.[4] The Medical Educational Trust in the U.K. reports that six people on average have been killed every day since the end of the war by picking up or standing on unexploded ordnance (as of November 1991[5]) yielding the higher figure of around 1,000 deaths.

Much of the unexploded ordnance consists of cluster bombs. The cluster bombshell holds hundreds of small explosive bomblets which disperse over a wide area, increasing the weapon's destructive power many times over. The remaining shiny spherical bomblets are highly sensitive to jarring. Special equipment and training are needed to find and render harmless many of the weapons that Coalition aircraft rained down on Iraq and Kuwait. The chief method for getting rid of UXO is to blow it up. The effort to rid the desert of one hazard has contributed to another, as bombs used to clear the minefields have pulverized topsoil and destroyed nearby vegetation.

Iraqi mine-laying and Coalition bombing of the area surrounding Kuwait's oil fields slowed the process of extinguishing the oil fires. British and Australian demolition teams spent months working in advance of the firefighters, identifying and destroying both Iraqi mines and allied ordnance.

The randomness of the bombing adds to the difficulty of the task. While the Kuwaiti government estimates it will take two or three years to clear unexploded ordnance in their country, teams working on the job say it could take decades. The Iraqi government, more concerned with its own survival, has yet to begin an operation to clear unexploded ordnance in southern Iraq.[6] Some areas in Kuwait and Iraq, especially those away from populated and industrial areas, may ultimately have to be fenced off.[7]

The Kuwait Government may now place 1.3 million mines along a ditch and rampart the length of the Kuwait-Iraq border, construction of which is scheduled for completion in the summer of 1993.[8]

—*John M. Miller*

NOTES:

1. Bureau of Political-Military Affairs, *Hidden Killers: The Global Problem of Uncleared Land Mines*, U.S. Department of State, 1993.
2. Naval Weapons Station press release, "Naval Weapons Station Concord Named Top Bay Area Military Installation," May 28, 1991.
3. Ken Ringle, "After the Battles, Defusing the Debris," *Washington Post*, March 1, 1991.
4. Jennifer Parmelee, "Environmentalists Survey the Blackened Wasteland That Was Kuwait," *Washington Post*, December 20, 1991, A41.
5. Paul Brown, "Kuwait's Keening Fields," *The Guardian*, November 5, 1991, quoted in Medical Educational Trust, *Continuing Health Costs of the Gulf War*, Report, London, October 1992.
6. Scores, possibly hundreds, of Kurds have also been injured from mines and unexploded munitions along the Iran-Iraq border left over from the long war between the two countries. U.S. Senate Subcommittee on Immigration and Refugee Affairs, *Summary Statement of Physicians for Human Rights; Report from Iran-Iraq Border*, Washington D.C., May 1991.
7. Earl Lane, "Two Americans Killed by Iraqi Mines," *Newsday*, March 2, 1991.
8. Edmund Epstein, "Kuwait Digs In Against Iraq," *San Francisco Chronicle*, May 14, 1993.

Desert Update

Interview with Sylvia A. Earle

Sylvia A. Earle, Ph.D., was interviewed in Chapter Two about the Mount Mitchell *maritime survey of the aftermath of the war's environmental destruction. Here she talks about impacts to the desert, which she visited most recently in January 1993. Interviewed by James Warner and Philippa Winkler, February 1993.*

Philippa Winkler: Even after the oil fires were put out, oil kept on gushing out from the oil wells. How much oil is left in the desert?

Sylvia Earle: I've heard of anything from 60 to 100 million barrels of oil lost on the face of the desert. Some of the oil has already gone into the atmosphere and more will over time. It is said that within the first few days 40 to 50 percent of the volume may evaporate and go into the atmosphere.

PW: How large are the lakes and how many of them are there?

SE: They were apparent from the 1992 Space Shuttle but I don't have the measurements yet. There are vast pools of lakes—certainly very dramatic-looking. I do know there were hundreds of square miles involved, and in some cases, lakes were several meters deep. In other areas they were spread widely but thinly and the oil mist that landed on the face of the desert in some cases has been biodegraded.

DESERT MAMMALS

SE: In January 1993 I witnessed evidence of birds and insects and small mammals still being trapped in contact with the oil. There are very few of the traditional desert carnivores present now. I asked many people if they had in their lifetimes seen a desert cat; they're sacred animals. They had been seen—in zoos—but not recently. One species is supposedly the ancestor of the domestic cat, another similar to the North American bobcat and lynx. They're endangered species and so is the desert fox. And they were certainly victims of the war. So were the kangaroo rats. But I was impressed by the number of small mammal tracks I saw during recent visits, such as small mice and gerbils. Many of these were victims of the oil lakes. Black beetles that normally burrow into the face of the desert got smothered by the effects of the oil.

James Warner: Don't the mines kill animals too?

SE: They do.

PW: I thought there's quite an effort to defuse those mines or blow them up?

SE: It's true in areas where people are likely to go, but there are vast areas where it's not only going to take a long time, shifting sands may cover them more deeply than the sensing equipment can detect.

PLANTS

PW: What have been the effects of the oil on the plant life in the desert?

SE: The oil has served to help hold the desert sand in place and allow some plants to get established. That's good or bad, depending on how you read these things. The existence of more plants means historically that the surface sand is more likely to be kept intact but also means that when the winds blow, each of these hillocks formed by the plants creates a miniature dune . . . so it means the desert is changing. It's changed and will continue to change as a result of what took place in 1991.

RIPPING UP THE SURFACE

SE: It's not just the oil lakes that are the problem, it's the ripping up of the desert surface. In a historically healthy desert, it looks like little elves have been out there neatly fitting grains together to make a surface that is slightly more solid than what is below. You can take your hand and lift up the crust of these grains that look like beautiful little gems polished by the wind, and after a time, they really seal off the desert so that the sand is not stirred from below. But when sheep move across they break up the crust. When jeeps and trucks move across, the surface is disrupted, and it was substantially disrupted during 1990 and 1991. As a result, much more sand and dust have blown around. But it's offset by the additional holding power of the oil, so it's hard to know yet from these unsatisfactory assessments. The bottom line is that there has been change, lots of change.

JW: How large a section of the desert was impacted by these changes?

SE: I don't know, but it's not trivial. It's also the impact of our increased dependence on machines instead of camels, which make big, soft, pad-like impressions and don't break the crust. Just a few trucks careening through the crust of the desert can make a profound impact.

Cleanup Efforts

JW: Has there been any attempt to clean up the oil lakes?

SE: There has been an effort to recover this oil, but it depends on the circumstances. If the lake is very shallow it really becomes more like tarmac as it does on the beaches. In areas where it's still really deep, several meters deep in some places, then some of it is at least recoverable, so it could be pumped out. I gather that some of it has. It's probably a relatively small amount, given the volume, and once it sat for a while it became mixed with sand, and with volatile compounds evaporated, the grade of oil becomes less desirable, and it becomes harder to work with.

JW: Is there a solution? Covering up the oil lakes . . . ?

SE: With sand? Some of that is happening naturally. In the shallow lakes that's certainly an effective way of rendering them not as damaging, but with the deep lakes, it's not practical.

Burning oil wells at the Al Maqwa oil field in Kuwait. Photo credit: UN Photo 158168/J. Isaac..

Chapter 5

Human Ecology

Residents of the Ma'kel neighborhood of Basra collecting water and washing clothes at a pond created when a water tower (background) was struck by Coalition bombs. © March 1991, Louise Cainkar and Folklens, 6635 N. Sacramento, Chicago, IL 60645.

Introduction

As an industrialized country, Iraq relies on a complex network of power plants, electrical grids, sewage and water-treatment plants, highways and mass transportation and communication systems. The damage to this infrastructure caused by the Coalition bombing was a catastrophe for the people of Iraq. UNICEF described the 43-day war as having "near-apocalyptic consequences to [Iraq's] economic and social infrastructure."[1]

As part of our development of this volume, ARC/Arms Control Research Center sent a contract environmental analyst, Al Picardi, and our Gulf Campaign Coordinator, Ross Mirkarimi, to Iraq with the International Study Team (IST). The IST was a group of 85 scientists, economists and public health experts who visited Iraq between August 25 and September 5, 1991 to investigate the impacts of the war. ARC's task was to assist the IST with the development of the environmental impact section of its report. The investigations of water quality and agricultural impacts and the assessments of bombed sites undertaken by ARC-sponsored IST members are included in this chapter. The IST report concluded that "unless Iraq quickly obtains food, medicine, and spare parts, millions of Iraqis will continue to experience malnutrition and disease."[2]

The bombing attacks on different components of Iraq's infrastructure had a combined effect worse than the sum of their individual impacts. For example, after the destruction of the electricity-driven sewage system, bacilli reproducing in the accumulated sewage caused epidemics of cholera and typhoid. The epidemics were exacerbated by a simultaneous steep drop in domestic food production and a breakdown in medical services as a result of the bombing, and by economic sanctions which cut off supplies to Iraq.

The chapter ends with an update on the situation, based on 1992 and 1993 reports. Since the Gulf War the Iraqi government has rebuilt its army and repaired Baghdad, its capital, but hospitals, agricultural machinery and sewage treatment facilities are functioning at a far lower level of efficiency than they did before the war. Shortages of basic medicines, food and drinking water continue to plague many Iraqis.

-Philippa Winkler

NOTES:
1. UNICEF and the Government of the Republic of Iraq, *Children and Women in Iraq: A Situation Analysis*, New York: UNICEF, October 1992.
2. International Study Team, *Health and Welfare in Iraq After the Gulf Crisis: An In-Depth Assessment*, Report, October 1991. This report, funded by Oxfam (U.K.), UNICEF and others, was a follow-up study to *Public Health in Iraq after the Gulf War, May 1991*, published by members of the Harvard School of Public Health.

Defense Department Critical of Bombing

United Press International

This report was released by United Press International February 23, 1992.

WASHINGTON (UPI)—A Defense Department analysis of the U.S. air campaign during the Persian Gulf War concludes that a breakdown in communications resulted in greater-than-intended damage to Iraqi civilian facilities, a published report said Sunday.

The New York Times reported that restrictions set by the military command in bombing Iraqi electrical plants were not passed on to pilots, leading to unintended damage in the 1991 war that drove Saddam Hussein out of Kuwait.

The *Times* said the Pentagon report also notes that deficient radios used by American airmen made it easier for Iraqi troops to capture downed pilots, and cites problems in clearing away mines and in distribution of intelligence.

The Defense Department report, commissioned by Congress and circulating in the Pentagon in draft form, represents its most complete analysis yet of the U.S. war effort.

The air war was waged to cripple Iraq's command structure and military operations by attacking communications, electrical installations, oil installations and transportation links without doing long-term damage to the civilian infrastructure.

After the war, critics said the air raids didn't much affect Iraqi military performance but succeeded in devastating some power plants, leading to long-term shutdown of sewage treatment and water purification facilities and hampering medical services, which jeopardized the health of Iraqi citizens.

The new Pentagon report acknowledges greater damage was done to Iraq's electrical network than planned.

The military generally wanted to knock out electrical service by hitting transformers and switching stations without destroying plant generators, which produce power and are difficult to rebuild.

The *Times* said the report acknowledges that senior commanders made deliberate exceptions to the policy of limiting damage to certain power installations. But in some cases, restrictions against targeting generators were simply not passed on to tactical air units, the report said.

Defense Department officials say that Al Hartha, an electrical plant near Basra, and two nearby substations were hit by air to ensure they could not be repaired during the war.

Details as to why the breakdown in communications developed were not included in the segments of the report seen by the *Times*, the newspaper said.

The draft report also concluded that radios provided to American airmen before the war for contact with search-and-rescue teams were not secure, allowing Iraqis to monitor the broadcasts for downed pilots and more easily capture them.

It concluded that America's mine-clearing ability was limited. Two U.S. ships were seriously damaged by mines in the Persian Gulf during the war.

Intelligence gathering was hamstrung, too, the report said. In some cases, aerial photographs of Iraqi targets did not reach Allied ground units assigned to attack them.

Bombing Civilian Facilities

Background Information

While the Pentagon has not yet released a list of its targets during the war, the U.S. Air Force has admitted to incapacitating the electrical power grid, as well as 28 oil refineries and 41 railway and highway bridges.[1]

Human rights groups went to Iraq immediately after the bombing to itemize the civilian facilities that had been damaged or destroyed. Here we summarize findings from two reports. The first is *Needless Deaths in the Gulf War*,[2] published by Human Rights Watch, which found:

- that bombs were dropped on bridges and other targets in populated areas of Iraq during the daytime, killing hundreds;
- the apparent use of unguided bombs when attacking urban areas;
- the attack on Al Ameriyah shelter in Baghdad, killing between 200 and 300 civilians (other estimates are of 900 deaths);
- the crippling of the electrical grid. The lack of power disabled the sewage system, water and wastewater treatment plants, agricultural production, food distribution and the health care system; and
- the targeting of food, agricultural and water-treatment facilities, attacks on civilian vehicles on highways, Bedouin tents, 400 homes, 19 apartment buildings, several hotels, two hospitals, two medical clinics, two schools, one mosque, restaurants and markets. "By far the greatest number of civilian objects damaged in Iraq during the war were residential buildings."

Initiated by former U.S. Attorney General Ramsey Clark, the Commission of Inquiry to the International War Crimes Tribunal held hearings in over 20 countries throughout 1991, and identified even greater damage. The Commission heard testimony from eyewitnesses representing U.S. congressmembers and such groups as the Institute for Peace and International Security and the International Physicians for the Prevention of War. Their findings are detailed in full in Ramsey Clark's book *The Fire This Time*[3] and are partially summarized here:

- eight dams repeatedly hit, and heavily damaged;

- four of Iraq's seven water pumping stations destroyed;
- 31 municipal water and sewage facilities hit causing the sewage system to collapse in Basra and water purification plants to be incapacitated nationwide;
- six broadcast stations, twelve television stations and five radio stations lost;
- the telephone system put out of service;
- 139 automobile and railway bridges damaged or destroyed;
- agricultural and food-processing, storage and distribution systems attacked directly and systematically;
- all of the irrigation systems—storage dams, barrages, pumping stations and drainage projects—attacked;
- food warehouses destroyed;
- grain silos hit methodically, and hundreds of farms and farm buildings attacked;
- grain and wheat fields hit with incendiary bombs;
- 28 civilian hospitals and 52 community health centers bombed;
- 676 schools, 56 mosques, the 900-year-old Church of St. Thomas in Mosul, and the Mutansiriya School, one of the oldest Islamic schools in Iraq, damaged; and
- manufacturing plants, including seven textile factories, five engineering plants and four car assembly plants hit.

The health of the Iraqi population will also be affected by the toxic chemicals contained in Coalition missiles. Solid propellants such as hydrozine and ammonium perchlorate are contained in missile exhaust fumes and in the unburned waste contained in missile shards. The explosion fumes contain other toxic chemicals, and, subsequent to impact, explosive and binder particles are spread by the wind. Given the enormous quantity of ordnance dropped, the titanium, beryllium and other metals contained in the missiles also have a significant contaminating effect.

According to a note verbale dated June 1, 1993 (A/Conf. 157/4), from the Permanent Mission of Iraq to the United Nations Office at Geneva to the Secretary-General of the World Conference on Human Rights held in Vienna, June 14-25, 1993:

> It is estimated that the volume of petroleum products set on fire [by the Coalition bombing of Iraq] was 65 million liters, including 24 million liters of heavy oil and 39 million liters of fuel oil. 2.25 million cubic meters of natural gas and 30 million cubic meters of hydrogen sulphide were burned. As a result of the bombing, the liquid, solid and gaseous waste treatment plants in these installations were destroyed and remain destroyed at the present time. The bombing caused the outflow and discharge of 22,320 cubic meters of polluted waste per day to adjacent land and surface water.
>
> Military operations in desert areas damaged 18,978,614 *donam* (1,186,000 acres) of desert land. The disappearance of the desert's vegetation cover led to the proliferation of rodents—mice and rats—and wild boar, which have attacked the crops causing heavy losses. The burning of petroleum tankers and installations and the ensuing crude oil spillage caused thick clouds of black smoke, the formation of black and acid rain and atmospheric pollution over the whole country. This acid rain has contaminated the soil, destroyed the vegetation cover throughout the country and adversely affected harvests and market-gardening production.

The destruction of electric power stations caused a stoppage of the pumping stations which diverted drainage water from the secondary circuits to the main circuits, producing a rise in the level of this water and causing it to ebb towards the land that had been drained. This land has reverted to its original salinity and 4,762,625 *donam* (257,700 acres) have been damaged.

—Philippa Winkler

NOTES:

1. U.S. Air Force, *Reaching Globally, Reaching Powerfully: The United States Air Force in the Gulf War*, Report, Washington DC, September 1991, 30.
2. *Needless Deaths in the Gulf War: Civilian Casualties During the Air Campaign and Violations of the Laws of War; A Middle East Watch Report* (New York: Human Rights Watch, 1991), 95-227. Virginia N. Sherry had overall responsibility for the report. See also report from WHO/UNICEF Special Mission to Iraq, February 1991, UN Security Council S/22328, March 4, 1991.
3. Ramsey Clark, *The Fire This Time: U.S. War Crimes in the Gulf* (New York: Thunder's Mouth Press, 1992), 64-65.

One of seven homes destroyed and 12 damaged by Coalition bombings in the Adhamiya neighborhood of Baghdad. Residents said that about 40 civilians were killed in the attack. © Louise Cainkar, March 1991.

On the Road in Iraq—The First Field Trip

Ross Mirkarimi with Saul Bloom

In this section, Ross Mirkarimi, ARC's Persian Gulf Campaign Coordinator, provides a first-person account of his visit to northern Iraq.

We arrived in Baghdad after a brief visit to Amman, Jordan, where additional preparations were made. By the time we left Amman, our International Team had grown to 85 people, including interpreters who accompanied us from the University of Jordan.

In Iraq, we were greeted by our host, a representative from the Ministry of Foreign Affairs. The Iraqi government, although uncomfortable, in most cases resisted the temptation to interfere. Assessing the impacts was going to be difficult enough; arguing about credibility due to Iraqi involvement wouldn't help anyone's cause. We particularly did not want to be accompanied by Iraqi government representatives during interviews with civilians who might be influenced as a result of their presence.

Nevertheless, in the name of Moslem hospitality and safety, the Ministry insisted that each team of two to four people travel in a government car with an assigned driver. When I came out of my Baghdad hotel (the Al Rashid of Cable News Network fame), I noticed a fleet of white mid-1980s Chevrolets. The cars resembled a United States General Services Administration carpool. The cars made an impression and this troubled us. As we departed Baghdad, I noticed that our government vehicle caught the attention of civilian and military passers-by.

The IST was divided into specific areas of investigation. The primary focus of the ARC/Arms Control Research Center's team was the assessment of the quality and quantity of Iraq's agricultural and water resources and sanitation. Our secondary focus was to determine the impact of the war-generated pollution on civilians and wildlife. The trick was distinguishing between prewar industrial environmental practices, the residual effects of Iraq's ten-year war with Iran, and conditions that were the result of this most recent war.

ENTERING KIRKUK

Iraq is divided into 18 governorates or states. The governorates of Irbil, Dohuk and Sulaymaniyah are now under Kurdish jurisdiction, which is currently being negotiated by both war and diplomacy. My trip to the Ta'meen Governorate and the city of Kirkuk was in the direction of the area where some of the most intense fighting occurred between Iraqi and Kurdish forces. My colleagues on this trip were a hydrologist and a public health specialist.

About an hour northwest of Baghdad on our way to Kirkuk we encountered a heavily fortified checkpoint. Tanks and machine gun outposts were dug into the surrounding dunes. The soldiers

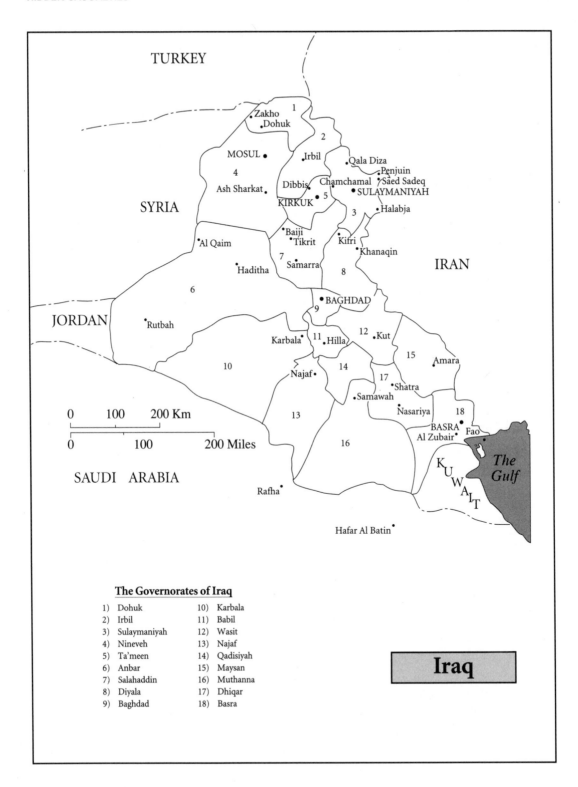

TURKEY

•Zakho
•Dohuk

1

2

MOSUL •

•Irbil

•Qala Diza
•Penjuin
•Saed Sadeq

4

Chamchamal
•SULAYMANIYAH

Ash Sharkat•

Dibbis•

5

•Halabja

SYRIA

KIRKUK

3

•Al Qaim

•Baiji
•Tikrit

•Kifri

•Khanaqin

7

Samarra•

IRAN

•Haditha

8

6

•BAGHDAD

JORDAN

•Rutbah

9

12

11

Karbala•

•Hilla

•Kut

15

•Amara

14

10

Najaf•

17

•Shatra

•Samawah

•Nasariya

18

13

16

BASRA•
Al Zubair•

•Fao

0   100   200 Km

0   100   200 Miles

The Gulf

SAUDI   ARABIA

K
U
W
A
I
T

•Rafha

Hafar Al Batin•

The Governorates of Iraq

1)	Dohuk	10)	Karbala
2)	Irbil	11)	Babil
3)	Sulaymaniyah	12)	Wasit
4)	Nineveh	13)	Najaf
5)	Ta'meen	14)	Qadisiyah
6)	Anbar	15)	Maysan
7)	Salahaddin	16)	Muthanna
8)	Diyala	17)	Dhiqar
9)	Baghdad	18)	Basra

Iraq

were ready for combat. We slowed down for the security check and maneuvered around the charred human corpses, trucks and armored personnel carriers that littered both sides of the highway.

When we arrived in Kirkuk, the town was riddled with bullets and fallen buildings were everywhere. It was dusk and the roads into the city were becoming empty and still. The destruction we were seeing was from a combination of recent civil strife and Coalition bombings.

B-52s had pummeled residential blocks. The buildings left standing had been used as cover during the skirmishes with the Kurds. Iraqi security forces had repelled Kurdish advances by obliterating the remaining blocks and the meager cover they offered. The battle was recent and people everywhere were on edge. A nearby field was littered with bomb fragments. Sewage was contaminating the water.

FROM FERTILE FIELDS TO ROTTING FISH

Kirkuk is part of the most fertile crop-producing area in Iraq. Thousands of acres of crops were destroyed by direct Coalition bombing or, in some cases, due to unexploded bombs that were blown up after fields were slashed and burned. I interviewed several farmers in this region. One man had lost his farm and two family members, his brother and cousin, in a bombing raid. Their car had been hit as they tried to drive off.

I talked to another farmer who was fishing. He boasted about the size of past catches and how fishing had brought him a little extra income from the early morning market. When we spoke, he hadn't caught anything in days. He was worried because he has a large family to feed and needs extra food. He spoke of the contrast between life before and after the Gulf War. His confidence was clearly gone. He said his life was over.

I went upstream a few kilometers to see if any fish were present. There were none. Rotting fish killed by industrial spills lined the bank; free-roaming cattle drank and defecated into the river that provided the water for the town.

There was also significant industrial damage around Kirkuk. We visited a 285-megawatt electrical power station at Dibbis. Nothing was left but huge sculptures of twisted metal. The North Oil Company, a refinery, was dismantled after two attacks and 30 days of oil fires.

We recorded and photographed the destruction in this area for two days. Under the governorate's directive, we had to be back at our hotel by sundown, when snipers came out. We were quite willing to comply with this directive, and when we returned to our downtown hotel, we would fall into its restaurant's chairs and ease our fatigue with whiskey that came in little airline-sized bottles with a Johnny Walker label. The rest of our waking moments we spent discussing our findings and comparing notes to see if we had missed anything.

"BROKEN COALITION PROMISES"

The Kirkuk officials tried to dissuade us from going to the autonomous region of Sulaymaniyah, where the Kurdish Peshmergar forces and Iraqi security forces were supposed to collectively govern, but the relationship was tenuous.

I arranged alternative transportation with the UN High Commission on Refugees. They sent us two four-wheel drive vehicles with drivers who were comfortable traveling in this region.

Near the 36th parallel, Iraqi security forces had dozens of tanks, artillery and countless machine-gun posts aiming their guns at the road like a gauntlet. When we arrived in Sulaymaniyah, the ubiquitous murals of Saddam Hussein were replaced with pictures of Kurdish leaders. We also felt an immediate difference in the political climate, as we were welcomed by the Peshmergar Border Guard. Iraqi security guards were also present but silent.

When we got into town, the carnage was everywhere. It looked like news pictures of Beirut: bombed-out hotels, cars, homes and offices. "None of this was directly related to the Gulf War or the Coalition," said one Peshmergar officer, "unless one considers the broken Coalition promises that drove us to kill for an independent state we will not get. Now all we can fight for is coexistence."

Halabja

In some cases determining the difference between the impacts of Operation Desert Storm and Iraq's other recent war was not that difficult. A small monument stands at the entrance to Halabja. The monument is a sculpture of a mother shielding a child with her body from deadly gas. According to a UN report, Iraqi government forces used chemical agents on the Kurds twice in early 1988. The monument was a chilling introduction to a community trampled by the fortunes of history.

In Halabja I was able to witness the discovery of another monument to the effects of that war against the Kurds, the unearthing of a macabre tomb. The tomb was the basement of a family home which had become a gas chamber when chemical weapons settled onto the ground nearly four years ago.

The Chemical Consequences of Independence

In 1982, Iraq was involved in a full-scale war with neighboring Iran. The continuing Kurdish rebellion forced Hussein to divert military resources northward away from the Iranian front. Between 1983 and 1985 Hussein appeared to be willing to negotiate with the Kurds. Talks broke down in 1984 because the Kurds wanted Kurdistan to include the rich oil fields of Kirkuk. By 1985, elements of the Kurdish uprising were cooperating with the Iranians.

In 1988, Saddam Hussein lashed out with a campaign designed to drive the Kurds from their homelands. Government planes bombed the civilians of Halabja with chemicals. I went to Halabja because of UN-intercepted reports indicating that residual effects of the chemical attacks might still be plaguing the village. The UN provided a car and a Kurdish-speaking driver.

The types of chemical weapons the Iraqi army used to force the Kurds from the village included nerve and blistering agents and blood gases. Nerve agents are organophosphate compounds that enter the body through the skin and inhalation. They kill by interfering with the nervous system, causing paralysis and suffocation. Blistering agents destroy the cells of target tissues in their victims. They can burn the skin, lungs, and harm other organs. The most famous blistering agent is mustard gas. Hydrogen cyanide is a blood gas, which interrupts cellular respiration.

When the Kurds got pictures of the chemical bombing to the international media, it stunned the world. Pictures of entire families who had fallen where they stood flooded the newspapers, corpses of the elderly along with the young, with their mouths wide like fish gasping for air.

A Town Destroyed

The town of Halabja was rubble. Before the 1988 bombing, an estimated 60,000 people called this place home. When I visited Halabja, between 9,000 and 12,000 remained. First, Iraqi warplanes had bombarded the town with chemical weapons; later, troops had dynamited buildings.

As late as March 1991, government troops, tanks and helicopters had surged north from defeat by the Coalition, to push the Kurds out of Iraq. Two villagers who had just returned from the mountains after fleeing this most recent engagement told me that in 1988 thousands had retreated to their basements to escape the gas. They didn't. The gas sank, trapping everyone who was underground or on the ground.

I was escorted to a makeshift hospital. Three nurses were on staff; the facility was gravely overcrowded. The ailments ranged from malnutrition, to shrapnel wounds, to cholera and typhoid. Other prominent ailments were residual flesh burns and respiratory inflammation caused by the contact in 1988 with mustard gas and other chemical weapons.

I spoke to a woman in the hospital who had not yet recovered from the effects of the chemical bombings. She told me that when the planes came she had tried to seek shelter in a shack near the field she was harvesting. She recalled hearing the impact of seven bombs all around town, that day in March 1988. The impact was unlike a normal bomb because there were no deafening explosions. Instead a white smoky cloud emerged covering the site in a deadly ground fog. The gas hit her within minutes. She was wearing the traditional body cover garb of Kurdish women, but some skin on her ankles and face remained exposed. Her skin began to burn. She ran in pain, tearing her clothes away only to expose more skin to the agent. She fell unconscious and was eventually revived in a Peshmergar field hospital.

The attendants at the field hospital weren't trained for chemical warfare. They didn't know what to do about the burns or her respiratory problems. The most they could do was give her painkillers. She was hospitalized for months, but as the conflict between the Kurds and the Iraqis intensified, she was evacuated to the Iranian border. While she was there, Red Crescent and Iranian doctors succeeded in saving her legs, but they could not restore her beauty and she will have pain for the rest of her life. When photographed, she held cardboard in front of her face to protect her from reprisals by Iraqi agents.

Nowhere to Hide

I was led to the ruins of a house. It was from here that some of the malodorous fumes of chemical agents were seeping. The villagers were excavating the ruin, stone brick by stone brick. They had just lifted a portion of the roof. After a while an opening to the basement was cleared, revealing six bodies. The stench rose thickly. It was a small basement, barely large enough to be a crypt for two people, let alone a family of six. The bodies were removed and buried in what was once their backyard. I jumped into the hole only to find that the odor was not caused by the decaying corpses but rather by chemicals that were the source of their demise. My eyes began to burn and my skin itch. I donned my respirator and protective clothing and went back to obtain some samples of the residue. I wasn't prepared to find the skull and jaw fragments of a six-year-old child. When I climbed back out, some of the townspeople wanted to know if the chemical agents were still active. Their requests for information had gone unheeded by the Iraqis, and new families had moved into the vacant dwellings of the dead.

I visited three basements that day. People surrounded me on the survey demanding to know if the odors they were smelling in nearby basements and ruined buildings were from chemicals. Twelve bodies had been pulled from one basement the previous week. UN peacekeeping officials speculated that various chemicals like tabun, sarin (nerve agents) and cyanide were still present.[1]

THE LEGACY OF WAR

A colleague from the International Study Team noted that eye infections, in particular conjunctivitis and recurrent infections, are common in some Kurdish villages. The cause of the problem was alleged to be chemical agents polluting the water supply. According to local sources, eight tanks of Iraqi chemical agents were stored near the Kurdish town of Khore. A Kurdish worker with the UN reported that someone had dosed the water supply with some chemical or biological agent. The saboteur had been apprehended and stated that he had been paid to do it by the army. The story could not be confirmed and the identity of the chemical is unknown.

The aftermath of the First World War planted the seeds of the Second and the current crisis in the Gulf. It is not inconceivable that the last war in the Gulf has planted the seeds for the next. Buried mustard gas from World War I still occasionally effects farmers and city dwellers in Belgium and other European nations. Every now and then a ruin is excavated or an unexploded bomb detonated that creates new casualties for a war that ended 73 years ago. The situation in Halabja is yet another example of the long-lasting effects international games of power have on the people least able to respond.

BACK ON THE ROAD

We didn't allow enough time for our drive back to Sulaymaniyah from the UN refugee camp of Penjuin. We risked the drive in the dark playing REM and Peter Gabriel tapes. Just as our driver turned up the volume, a grenade launcher lobbed one over our vehicle. There was no mistaking it and we didn't care where it came from. We reduced our speed to half, tilted our bent UN car flag upright and reminded ourselves to breathe.

In Mosul I did an extensive examination of the agriculture. The agricultural conditions in Iraq have been worsened by shortages of fertilizers, seed, pesticides and spare parts for farm machinery. Animal wealth has been reduced by 60 percent. I interviewed one worker at a slaughterhouse who told me of livestock kills from Coalition bombings, and a lack of veterinary medicine due to sanctions. The livestock declines in Mosul mirror similar findings throughout northern and central Iraq.

The Nimrud Agriculture Technical Institute south of Mosul was bombed in four separate Coalition attacks. The craters left by the B-52s pockmarked the campus as far as the eye could see. The campus sits between a military installation and a sulfur mine. The mine was not bombed and the military post incurred minimal damage. I brought several people with me to search for indications of this vocational school's role as a military site. We interviewed several locals to see if there was any rationale for bombing this institution.

I found ten teachers sitting together in a dilapidated conference room that had been part of the administration building, discussing future plans. I slipped into the room with my interpreter, listening to these gentlemen make their plans. It took me a couple of minutes to realize that they were in a state of shock. Their speech was slow and they had a lost look in their eyes.

The teachers appeared pleased to have a foreign delegation hear their story. Two of the faculty members escorted us outside, and everyone followed. They first showed us the spot where the assistant dean was killed in the initial air raid. He was trying to escape to his car and was blown in half. One teacher grabbed my arm and walked me 500 yards to where the other half of the car and body were found days after. One of my faculty guides broke down and cried. Everyone went silent; it was one of those moments in which words would be meaningless.

We came to the library. Books were scattered everywhere and the desks were smashed to kindling. It was ironic to see American journals on livestock and related agriculture issues. I began to dig into what used to be the biology laboratory because industrial plants with similar facilities, such as the controversial baby milk formula factory outside Baghdad and the Al Qaim Fertilizer Factory, were suspected of doubling as chemical weapons factories.

I broke through to a classroom laboratory that yielded no evidence of having a military purpose. Another classroom held an extra surprise for us all. A bomb had fallen right through the roof of the one-story building and, without exploding, had embedded itself into the ground floor, its tail barely visible. A video crew was climbing onto the roof where the bomb made initial contact, trying to get the sexy shot. All I could think of was that there was too much activity in the immediate area of this bomb and it was time to leave.

NOTES:
1. See Chapter Seven, "Chemical and Biological Weapons Background Information," on the persistence of tabun, sarin and cyanide in the environment.

Waterborne Diseases and Agricultural Consequences

International Study Team-ARC/Arms Control Research Center

Presented here is the environmental assessment team's report on the health and agricultural impacts of the destruction of Iraqi infrastructure. Alfred Picardi, Ross Mirkarimi, and Mahmoud Al Khoshman all contributed to this report. Statistical peer review for the agricultural study was provided by Lydia Gans, Ph.D.

The overall findings are:

1) The destruction of electric power facilities and water and wastewater treatment plants has created a cycle of contamination. Untreated waste flows into rivers that supply drinking water, which leads to high levels of water- and waste-borne disease among consumers, which is eventually cycled back into the river in the form of untreated human waste.

2) Agricultural productivity has been sharply reduced due to the inability to operate the electricity-reliant irrigation network, high soil salinity, and acute shortages of fertilizer and seeds. Neither fertilizers nor seeds are available because the main fertilizer plant at Al Qaim was bombed and destroyed, and most seeds were imported.

HEALTH CONSEQUENCES OF THE DESTRUCTION OF IRAQ'S WATER SYSTEM

For many Iraqis, it is difficult to escape disease. Pathogenic microbes contaminating water supplies are creating epidemic levels of disease. Prevention is hampered by incapacitated water and sewage treatment facilities and the paralysis of disease vector control programs due to lack of pesticides. Treatment is hampered by shortages in medical supplies and overcrowded facilities.

In all seven southern governorates surveyed, the onset of unsanitary conditions and the increase in waterborne disease followed the loss of electric power in the first days of war. Sewer systems depend on electric-powered pump stations to move the contents of the sewers to the wastewater treatment plants.

The loss of 80 percent of Iraq's electric power-generating capacity from the air war resulted in the backup of the sewers at the pump stations, causing sewage to overflow into the streets. This problem is compounded by solids settling in the now-stagnant pipes.

Although electric power has been partially restored in all of the cities, serious problems remain due to damaged pipes, lack of spare parts to repair pumping equipment, and chronic periodic power outages. Over 60 percent of the population in five of the seven governorates surveyed have no tap water available in their homes because of low water pressure caused by the incapacitation of the delivery system.

Direct sewage contamination of the water supplies was observed by two routes:

1) wastewater treatment plants not adequately chlorinating their discharges, or bypassing treatment entirely; and

2) infiltration of contaminants through breaks in the water mains.

In order to obtain water, people carry it from the river, which is often far away, or they dig wells in their yards. In some areas, people have dug down to the water main, broken a hole in it, and inserted a hose to collect water.

In five of the seven cities surveyed, breakage of the water mains and insertion of hoses was a common practice. People often have to bail raw sewage out of these holes in order to access the hose stuck in the hole in the water main pipe. The raw sewage that collects in the holes dug to the water mains can infiltrate into the water main itself. Moreover, the practice of breaking into the water mains lowers the pressure in the water supply system further.

Most of Iraq's population of 18 million is directly exposed to waterborne disease in their drinking water supply. Team members took tap water samples from a total of 158 randomly selected households in all 18 governorates. Each sample was tested for coliform or fecal coliform contamination.

Of the samples taken, 106 were positive for gross coliform contamination, 25 were confirmed negative, and 27 were unconfirmed negative. Roughly half of the areas tested showed positive evidence of gross fecal contamination. Only in Baghdad, where coliform media sampling was used, did over half of the samples test negative.

Team members documented unsanitary water and waste disposal conditions in all of the cities surveyed in seven governorates. Common conditions observed include:

- solid waste accumulating in the streets due to the lack of collection and landfilling equipment;
- raw sewage overflows in the street and around homes;
- raw sewage dumped directly in rivers due to impaired or inoperable wastewater treatment plants;
- children bathing and playing in these rivers;
- people with little or no tap water supply because impaired or inoperable water treatment and distribution plants cannot generate adequate line pressure;
- people drawing drinking water directly from contaminated rivers; and
- people drawing drinking water from holes dug to water mains, often contaminated from sewage overflows.

The situation is bound to worsen as the public health system continues to break down and food shortages diminish the population's resistance to disease. To break this cycle of water contamination, the infrastructure of public health and water sanitation must be brought back on line. This would require restoration of electric power, access to spare parts and replacement equipment, repair and replacement of damaged sanitation systems, and increases in medical supplies, chlorine, other essential water treatment chemicals, and laboratory analysis supplies.

CONSEQUENCES OF THE DESTRUCTION OF IRAQ'S AGRICULTURAL RESOURCES

The Ministry of Agriculture administers the agriculture sector in Iraq. They coordinate food intake and food distribution for all of Iraq's 18 governorates. The three governorates of Irbil, Dohuk and Sulaymaniyah are considered autonomous under Kurdish control. Each governorate has an agriculture director who supervises field managers that vary in staff numbers according to the size of the farmable land. The field managers are required to report on the following conditions: crop production, water and irrigation, farm machinery, seed, fertilizer and pesticide supplies, animal wealth, weather and farmer confidence. Prior to the war, their reports were expected to be submitted to the governorate agriculture director on a weekly basis, and in return, the director would submit their report to the Ministry every two weeks.

A census taken every two years determines the state of Iraq's agricultural economy. The last complete census was taken in 1989; the 1991 census has been delayed due to the crisis. Census figures from 1989 indicated that 35 percent of Iraq's population was employed in agriculture, while 20 to 25 percent was employed in services related to the agricultural industries.

As farming is practiced in Iraq, a healthy harvest depends on a combination of proper irrigation, a sufficient supply of fertilizer and pesticides, and the availability of farm machinery.

AGRICULTURAL DESTRUCTION: PRINCIPAL FINDINGS

The destruction of the electric power system in Iraq and the continuation of sanctions have significantly impacted Iraq's food production. Fields could not be irrigated because the irrigation pumping system ceased to operate when the electricity was cut off. Sanctions have prevented all but a tiny fraction of pesticides, fertilizers, seed and farm equipment from entering the country.

As a result, the total number of tons for 1991/1992 crop production was only 17 percent of 1989/1990 crop production (see Table 5-4). The prospects for 1992/1993 crop production look even worse.

IRRIGATION

Limited-duration flood irrigation is used to supply water to the agricultural areas. Soil fertility throughout central and southern Iraq depends on the irrigation system. Most of the water used for irrigation comes from the Tigris and Euphrates rivers and is saline. The system regulates the flooding to prevent crop drowning and limit the concentration of salt in the soil.

Saline deposition is reduced by: (1) a short period of inundation, to minimize salt concentration through evaporation, and (2) in many areas, extensive field drainage systems.

When a field is inundated, the water leaches through the soil to a system of subsurface field drains. The relatively saline water is then carried away by the drainage system. This wastewater is discharged into the marshes located between the Tigris and Euphrates, not back to the rivers.

Electric power is used to regulate the system. Power outages have resulted in the long-term flooding of a good percentage of agricultural land, resulting in immediate crop losses and an increase in soil salinity. As power supplies are restored, flooding is being brought under control, but the lack of spare parts and replacements for damaged pumps is once more putting increasing stress on the system. Huge areas of formerly productive agricultural lands have been rendered unproductive or infertile.

Team members estimate that the irrigation network is, as of September 1991, operating at 40–50 percent of prewar capacity. A preliminary assessment made in May by the Agriculture and Electricity Ministries determined that 70 percent of the irrigation systems were inoperable. This assessment has been corroborated by subsequent investigations by UN Envoy Prince Aga Khan's special missions and international relief organizations.

PEST CONTROL

Current restrictions have prevented the Ministry of Agriculture from limiting pest infestation through aerial crop-dusting. In the past, farmers would contract with local government agents for the aerial crop-dusting. Since the war, the central government must contract for these services with member UN nations. According to regional directors, crops have not been sprayed for pests because of the administrative difficulties of this process (See Table 5-1).

TABLE 5-1.
AREA SPRAYED AGAINST AGRICULTURAL PESTS
(IN 1000S OF *DONAM*)

1988	2,694*
1989	7,73*
1990	10,561*
1991	1,000†

A *donam* is approximately 1/16 of an acre.

*Areas sprayed are recorded in the Ministry of Agriculture, Baghdad and the Agriculture Governorate Field Offices.

† Statistics reflect agriculture field reports in northern Iraq and UN monitoring of aerial spraying to date by UN Envoy Prince Aga Khan, July 15, 1991.

TABLE 5-2.
PESTICIDES PROCURED
(QUANTITY IN TONS)

1989/1990*	59,000
1990/1991†	11,220
1991/1992‡	500

* Annual Abstract of Statistics, 1990, Central Statistics Organization, Ministry of Planning, Republic of Iraq.

† Initially forecasted by UN Envoy Prince Aga Khan, July 15, 1991, verified by subsequent examination of data by team members in September.

‡ Forecasted by Study Team members, September 1991.

FERTILIZERS AND SEED STOCK

In addition to the inability to protect crops from pests, fertilizer and seed are in low supply. The Abu Ghreib potato seeds factory in Baghdad and the Al Qaim fertilizer factory[1] were targets of the bombing.

As the following chart indicates, the embargo has halted the import of fertilizers and seeds. Note that the annual crop season is counted from June to May, which includes two planting and harvesting cycles.

TABLE 5-3. AGRICULTURAL IMPORT REQUIREMENTS AND PROCUREMENT

Commodity	1989/90*	1990/91†	1991/92‡
Projected Requirements			
Fertilizers	269,000	290,000	300,000
Seeds	6,700	6,925	7,000
Procurement			
Fertilizers	269,000	48,000	0
Seeds	6,700	1,155	0

* Annual Abstract of Statistics, 1990, Central Statistics Organization, Ministry of Planning, Republic of Iraq.

† Initially forecasted by UN Envoy Prince Aga Khan, July 15, 1991, verified by subsequent examination of data by team members in September.

‡ Forecasted by Study Team members, September 1991.

CROPS

Iraq's main crops are wheat, maize, barley, rice and other grains. Fruits and vegetables vary in abundance.

Following the embargo in August of 1990, the Ministry of Agriculture recommended that farmers increase the planting of wheat and rice by 30 percent in order to cushion anticipated shortages. However, agricultural production has declined precipitously.

The projections presented in Table 5-4 are based on information collected randomly from farmers in 16 governorates regarding their ability to plant for the October 1991 season. Table 5-4 shows that the 1991/1992 harvest will be 17 percent of the 1989/1990 harvest, according to the IST's projections.[2]

TABLE 5-4. CROP PRODUCTION
(AREA IN 1,000S OF HECTARES, PRODUCTION IN 1,000S OF TONS)

Crop		1989/90*	1990/91†	1991/92‡
Barley	Area	1,995	2,389	1,990
	Production	1,854	520	400
Maize	Area	59	40	30
	Production	185	74	59
Wheat	Area	1,196	2,512	900
	Production	1,196	525	290
Rice	Area	85	88	62
	Production	1,854	125	88
TOTAL	Area	3,335	5,029	2,982
	Production	5,089	1,244	837

* Annual Abstract of Statistics, 1990, Central Statistics Organization, Ministry of Planning, Republic of Iraq.

† Initially forecasted by UN Envoy Prince Aga Khan, July 15, 1991, verified by subsequent examination of data by team members in September.

‡ Forecasted by Study Team members, September 1991.

ANIMAL WEALTH

LIVESTOCK

Estimates based on interviews with 74 randomly selected farmers in 15 governorates and on records from the Ministry of Planning indicate a severe decline in animal wealth. Table 5-5 below shows projections that the total number of animals by December 1991 will be 50–60 percent of the total number in 1986.

Several factors have caused this decline in animal wealth. The principal causes are the contamination of the water supply, which has caused a high incidence of waterborne diseases among the animal population, and the lack of veterinary medicines and vaccines to treat the animals. In addition, there is a shortage of animal feed due to crop failures and import restrictions, resulting in malnourishment and higher incidence of death among the animals; the cycle of livestock births has dropped precipitously and many animals were smuggled into Iran and Turkey.

| TABLE 5-5. ANIMAL WEALTH (IN 1,000s) | | | |
Kind	1986*	1989†	1991‡
Sheep	8,981	9,038	4,160
Goats	1,476	1,882	752
Cattle	1,578	1,495	747
Buffalo	141	169	85

*Annual Abstract of Statistics, 1990, Central Statistics Organization, Ministry of Planning, Republic of Iraq.
† Initially forecasted by UN Envoy Prince Aga Khan, July 15, 1991, verified by subsequent examination of data by team members in September.
‡ Forecasted by Study Team members, September 1991.

FISH

Prior to the war, Iraq nursed its fish population for food markets through fisheries or fish farms. Records from the Ministry of Statistics and Planning indicate that there were 1,684 fish farms before the war. Presently, only 237 farms are in operation. The primary reasons cited for the destruction of the fish farms are the shortage of electricity and the lack of foodstuff.

CONCLUSION

According to official Iraqi figures prior to the war, 28 million *donam* (1.73 million acres) of arable land yielded an annual harvest that satisfied the food needs of approximately 30 percent of the population. Iraq imported the remaining 70 percent of its food needs, primarily from the United States and New Zealand.

The vast destruction of Iraq's agricultural resources, crops, livestock and animal wealth has impeded Iraq's ability to produce food domestically. Whereas Iraq produced 30 percent of its food needs domestically before the war, today it produces between 10 and 15 percent of its needs.

NOTES:

1. The Al Qaim fertilizer plant was built in 1976 by Sybetra, a Belgium engineering firm. Sybetra helped mine phosphate deposits essential to the production of chemical agents tabun and sarin, the precursors of nerve gas. The mine, at Akashat village in western Iraq, was later linked by a railroad line to the Al Qaim plant 150 miles away and concrete fortifications were raised around certain plant buildings. Kenneth Timmerman, *The Death Lobby: How the West Armed Iraq* (New York: Houghton Mifflin Company, 1991), 51, 52.

2. "Black rain," fallout from the oil fires, adversely affected pollination and yield in several areas in March of 1991. See *Report to the Secretary-General on Humanitarian Needs in Iraq* by a mission led by Sadruddin Aga Khan, Executive Delegate of the Secretary-General, dated 15 July 1991.

TABLE 5.6
CHEMICAL RELEASES FROM BOMBED INSTALLATIONS

Quantities of chemical substances which have been discharged from bombed installations. Source: Note Verbale Dated June 1, 1993, from the Permanent Mission of Iraq to the United Nations Office at Geneva addressed to the Secretary-General of the World Conference on Human Rights held in Vienna, June 14-25, 1993.

Bombed Installation	Quantities	Substances
State Sugar Refinery	95,191 kg*	Pesticides
State Organization for Geological and Mining Surveys	7874 kg	Mercuric nitrate, potassium nitrate, mercuric chloride, arsenic oxide, potassium cyanide, ammonium thiocyanide and potassium thiocyanide
	2 liters	Concentrated solutions of sulfuric acid and nitric acid
Iraqi State Cement Factory	4.5 kg	Ammonium thiocyanide and potassium thiocyanide, potassium nitrate
State Organization for Fertilizer Production	700,000 kg	Ammonia
State Organization for Phosphates	5,606,000 kg	Concentrated solution of sulfuric acid
	5,000,000 kg	Concentrated solution of phosphoric acid
	180,000 kg	Fluosilicic acid
	53,600,000 kg	Liquid sulfur dioxide
State Organization for Electricity (Production and Transport)	1,350 kg	Alun
	150,000 kg/200 liters	Hydrochloric acid
	1,360 liters	Anti-rust solution
	75 kg	Polyelectrolyte
	164,000 kg	Caustic soda
State Organization for Pharmaceutical Products and Medical Supplies	200,000 kg	Polythene and polypropylene
	100,000 kg	Wrapping and packaging products
Al Nu'man Factory	328,371 kg	Plastics (granules and residue)
	7,476 kg	Pigments
	400 kg	Fiberglass
	67,500 meters	Low-density polyethylene pipes
	9,960 kg	Resin
	350 kg	Solid and liquid wax
	19,925 kg	Black graphite
	600 kg	Dyes
	500 units	Used tires

* 1 ton = 907.18 kg

Environmental Assessments of Bombed Sites, and Field Notes

International Study Team-ARC/Arms Control Research Center

While in Iraq in September 1991, Mahmoud Al Khoshman and Ross Mirkarimi inspected 19 installations that had been bombed by Coalition forces. Here we present their reports on five bombed sites: an electrical power plant, an oil pretreatment plant, two oil refineries, and the controversial baby milk formula factory. Jorge Emmanuel, Ph.D. in Chemical Engineering and a member of the Technical Advisory Board of the Arms Control Research Center, reviewed the data after Ross' return. His analysis of the data follows each site report.

DIBBIS ELECTRICAL POWER PLANT

Governorate: Ta'meem
Type of industry: Power generation
Location: 35 km. northwest of Kirkuk
Person interviewed: Adnan Abdullah, Technical Manager
Description of the plant: The plant consists of two parts:
 1) Steam generator plant built in 1958; and
 2) Gas turbine plant built in 1982.
Dates of attacks: 5 attacks between January 27 and February 19, 1991
Description of attacks:
 1) Attack directed to the gas turbine by bombs;
 2) Attack directed to the gas turbine by missiles;
 3) Attack directed to the steam generator by bombs;
 4) Attack directed to the steam generators by missiles; and
 5) Attack directed to everything by more than 200 huge bombs.
Level of damage: 60–100%
Current condition: Not operating
List of material damaged, emitted to the air and spilled to the water and soil:
 1) Gasoline;
 2) Naphtha;
 3) Crude oil;
 4) Demulsifier;
 5) Tofloc 300; and
 6) Sulfuric acid 99.6%.
These materials burned for two days, January 27–29, 1991.

Estimated time until the plant will be fully operational: depends on the period of sanctions.

Surroundings:

> East: water injection center
> North: water channel
> West: Small Zab River
> South: the town of Dibbis

Environmental impacts:

1) Hydrocarbons, sulfur oxides (SO_x), carbon oxides (CO_x), nitrogen oxides (NO_x), and hydrogen sulfide (H_2S) were emitted to the atmosphere, causing serious air pollution.
2) Spilled oil and chemicals from both tanks and the nine transformers contaminate the soil and water in the nearby water pool.
3) Solid wastes generated from the damaged equipment, concrete and fiberglass cause serious problems for the workers—especially the fiberglass, which causes breathing problems.

Short-term environmental effects:

1) Smoke generated from the burned oil caused "black rains" contaminated with hydrocarbons.
2) The damaged transformers emitted pollutants for seven days.

REVIEW AND ANALYSIS

According to this report, two bomb and missile attacks on the gas turbine, two bomb and missile attacks on the steam generator, and a 200-bomb attack on the plant in general caused 60 to 100 percent damage—presumably, this is the range of damage at various parts of the power plant. Gasoline, naphtha, crude oil, etc., burned for two days, resulting in the fallout of "black rain." Chemicals and oil from tanks and transformers spilled into the soil and nearby water pool.

Comments: The general description given of the environmental impact at this site is plausible for a large electrical power plant. Apparently, almost 30,000 barrels of fuel burned at this plant. That would amount to a significant emission into the atmosphere of carbon dioxide (CO_2) (with possible effects on global climate) and major pollutants such as carbon monoxide (CO), SO_x, volatile hydrocarbons and NO_x as products of combustion. However, I would expect most of the H_2S to have been oxidized to sulfur dioxide (SO_2). The phenomenon of "black rain" would refer to the fallout of carbonaceous particles or soot, which was also a consequence of combustion; these particles could have toxic metals and organic chemicals (especially some toxic products of incomplete combustion) adsorbed on their surfaces. The environmental impact from the sulfuric acid (less than two gallons) would be vastly overshadowed by the results of fuel combustion and spillage. In addition, I would be concerned with possible adverse effects from the apparent spillage of these fuels, oils, chemicals and transformer fluids (which for a plant built in 1958, may or may not contain PCBs) on the Zab river, surrounding groundwater and the population of Dibbis and other areas. With regard to damaged fiberglass, exposed workers typically experience itching and skin and eye irritation, as well as respiratory problems if the levels of fiber dust are excessive.

North Oil Pretreating Plant

Governorate: Ta'meem
Type of industry: Petroleum refining
Location: 12 km. northwest of Kirkuk
Person interviewed: Serop S. Sirkissian
History of plant: The plant was built in 1933 by the British Petroleum Co.
Date of attacks: January 26, 1991, 11:30 pm
Description of attacks: One attack by bombs
Level of damage: 50–55%
Current condition: Not operating
List of material damaged, emitted to the air and spilled to the water and soil:
1) 10 bbl of tetraethyl lead (TEL); and
2) 2 bbl of hydrazone (causes lung cancer).

Spare parts: Various types of mechanical and electrical equipment
Supplier: Germany, France, U.K. and U.S.
Impact of Sanctions: Estimated time until the plant is fully operational depends on the period of sanctions.

Surroundings:
East: oil field
North: mountains
West: army site
South : water channel

Environmental impacts:
1) Directly after the bombs hit, a huge black cloud formed and the oil spilled to the soil.
2) A water treatment unit was destroyed and the spilled oil continues to go into the water channel where people swim and cows drink.
3) A pile of sulfur (about 2.3 tons) was directly hit and burned, so large quantities of SO_2 and sulfur trioxide (SO_3) were emitted to the atmosphere. The damaged tanks burned for 27 days until all the oil (140,000 cu. ft.) was gone, which caused the huge black cloud.
4) There were gaseous emissions, such as CO, SO_x, NO_x, H_2S.

Short-term environmental effects: water pollution of the nearby stream and "black rain." Because of sanctions there is a lack of chemicals used to purify water, and of spare parts for treatment equipment.

Long-term environmental effects: the large quantity of SO_x emitted to the atmosphere may cause acid rain.

Review and Analysis

According to this report, one bombing attack resulted in 50 to 55 percent damage. Tetraethyl lead and hydrazone were released. Spilled oil contaminated the water channel, a potential source of human and animal exposure. A pile of about 2.3 tons of sulfur was hit directly and burned, while tanks containing 25,000 barrels of oil burned for 27 days, causing a fallout of "black rain."

Comments: The general description given is plausible for an oil pretreatment plant. As in the case of the Dibbis power plant, the burning of 25,000 barrels of oil would result in a large release of particulate matter (precipitating "black rain"), CO_2, SO_x, NO_x, and products of incomplete combustion such as CO and small amounts of toxic organic compounds. The burning of the sulfur pile would have discharged about four tons of SO_2 into the air. The release or combustion of tetraethyl lead (TEL) should also be of concern, since lead adversely affects the nervous system, blood cells, kidneys, and other organs. The area adjacent to the oil pretreatment plant, however, does not appear to be heavily populated. Nevertheless, the 10 barrels of TEL amount to almost two tons of lead which apparently have been released into the air, water and soil.

BAIJI OIL REFINERIES COMPLEX

Governorate: Salahaddin

Type of Industry: Oil refinery

Location: 40 km. north of Tikrit

Person interviewed: Ahead Mowfaq, Technical Manager

History of the plant: The construction of the complex was began in 1982 by three international companies.

Date of attacks: January 22 and February 7–9, 1991.

Descriptions of attacks:

1) January 22: cruise missiles
2) February 7: directed bombs
3) February 7: bombs
4) February 8: bombs
5) February 8: bombs
6) February 8: bombs (B-52)

Level of damage: 60–100%

Current condition: operating at 30%

List of material damaged, emitted to the air and spilled to the water and soil:

1) Different types of catalysts;
2) Tetraethyl lead (TEL);
3) Methyl ethyl ketone (MEK); and
4) Toluene.

Chemicals used in refining: Catalysts and additives

Supplier: Different sources. Sanctions impede supply of the above chemicals. Undamaged quantities are now being used.

Estimated time before plant will be fully operational: About three years after the end of sanctions.

Surroundings:

> East: Dijjla river
> North: desert
> West: residential area
> South: Baiji Power Station

Environmental impacts:

1) The damage to chemical stores caused an environmental disaster wherein about 100 chemical substances burned, were emitted to the air and spilled to the water and soil.

2) The wastewater treatment unit was destroyed causing water to discharge without any treatment.

3) Gaseous emissions include CO, SO_2, SO_3, NO_x, H_2S, chlorine gas (Cl_2) and lead oxide.

4) Directly after the hits, the area was covered by black clouds, and a "black rain" fell in different areas.

5) Operators are sometimes forced to burn excess oil because of damage to equipment.

6) The sulfur recovery plant was damaged, causing large quantities of H_2S to be emitted.

REVIEW AND ANALYSIS

According to the report, six bomb and cruise missile attacks destroyed 60 to 100 percent of the plant. About 100 different chemicals were burned or leaked into the soil and water including catalysts, tetraethyl lead, methyl ethyl ketone (MEK) and toluene. The area was covered by a black cloud and "black rain" fell. It seems that soil and wastewater samples were taken to test for contamination. (As with the other reports, no results of water and soil tests are provided.)

Comments: Again, the general description of the environmental impact is plausible for an oil refinery complex. Although no mention is made of fuel oil, one might assume that gasoline, distillates, heavy residuals and other oils were among the chemicals that burned, and that these chemicals were in large enough quantities to produce the black cloud and fallout of "black rain." Also emitted along with the particulates are the other combustion products mentioned above (CO_2, CO, hydrocarbons, etc.) Apparently, in addition to lead and sulfur, chlorine gas (possibly from chlorine products) was released but the amounts could not be deduced from the report. H_2S, and also possibly carbonyl sulfide (COS) and carbon disulfide (CS_2), could have been released into the air as fine particles. Toluene is a volatile solvent which, if spilled, could have been absorbed in the soil and may have long-term effects on aquatic life in the Dijjla river. MEK is also a common volatile solvent which easily breaks down in the atmosphere and dissolves in water; it is, however, a potential contaminant in the surrounding groundwater. Unfortunately, the nearby area west of the refinery complex is apparently a residential area.

BABY MILK FORMULA FACTORY

Governorate: Baghdad

Type of industry: Food

Location: 20 km. west of Baghdad

Person interviewed: Ahmad Tameem

History of plant: The plant was built in 1976 and began testing production in 1984, then closed until 1990.

Date of attacks: January 20 and 21, 1991

Description of attacks: Two massive hits over two days

Level of damage: 100%

Current condition: Totally destroyed

List of material damaged, emitted to the air and spilled to the water and soil:

1) Lubrication oils;
2) Grease;
3) CFC-12 from Freon refrigeration cylinders; and
4) Huge quantities of fiberglass.

Surroundings:

East: military site

North: residential area

West: highway interchange

South: residential area

Environmental impacts:

1) The damaged fiberglass causes breathing problems for workers.
2) The damaged CFC-12 emitted to the atmosphere will contribute to ozone layer depletion.
3) The burned oils and grease emitted large quantities of CO_x, SO_x, and NO_x, and also hydrocarbons.

REVIEW AND ANALYSIS

According to the report, two massive hits over two days completely destroyed the baby milk factory. The destruction resulted in the release of lubrication oils and greases, as well as Freon (CFC-12) and large amounts of fiberglass. Residential areas are found north and south of the facility, with a highway running on the western side.

Comments: I cannot imagine a baby milk factory having huge amounts of lubricating oil and grease; however, burning of the oils and grease would likely result in the formation of the air pollutants mentioned above (particulate matter, SO_x, NO_x, CO_x, etc.) but not in massive quantities. It is possible that the factory had many refrigeration units which used Freon as a coolant and fiberglass for insulation. I do not expect the Freon to have been in large enough quantities to significantly contribute to stratospheric ozone depletion. However, as mentioned above, the damaged fiberglass could cause skin irritation and possibly some respiratory problems at high enough levels, thereby affecting exposed workers and nearby residents.

[Matthew Meselson, in his interview in Chapter Seven, speculates that a baby milk formula factory might be making tryptone broth for microbiological work, thus raising suspicion that it was part of a biological weapons factory. Ramsey Clark in his book *The Fire This Time* says that he believes that the attack was "simply part of the deliberate targeting of Iraq's food production."]

AL DOURA OIL REFINERY

Governorate: Baghdad
Type of industry: Oil refining
Location: 12 km. southwest of Baghdad
Person interviewed: Mowafaq Khalil, Technical Manager
History of the plant: The plant was built in 1955, and expanded many times.
Date of attacks: January 19 and February 7, 1991.
Descriptions of attacks:
   1) January 19: bombs; and
   2) February 7: bombs and missiles.
Level of damage: 10–60%
Current condition: The refinery operates at 100% of its designed capacity and the lubricating oil plant at 50%.
List of material damaged, emitted to the air and spilled to the water and soil:
   1) Crude oil spilled into the water drainage system and soil.
   2) A huge cloud of smoke covered Baghdad.
   3) H_2S was emitted to the atmosphere.
Impact of sanctions: Sanctions ban the import of chemicals, catalysts and spare parts.
Surroundings:
   East: residential area
   North: residential area
   West: military sites
   South: military sites
Environmental Impacts:
   1) Crude oil from damaged tanks burned, emitting a large quantity of NO_x, CO_x, and SO_x.
   2) The kerosene desulfurization plant was totally damaged and now the high sulfur content in kerosene causes health problems in houses where kerosene burners are still used.

REVIEW AND ANALYSIS

According to the report, two bomb and missile attacks destroyed 10 to 60 percent of the refinery (10 to 60 percent is presumably the range of destruction level at various parts of the plant). Crude oil in storage tanks was burned. The kerosene desulfurization plant was totally destroyed. The immediate impact was the release of air pollutants resulting from the burning of crude oil and the release of some of the oil to the soil and surface water. A longer-term impact was associated with the use of high-sulfur kerosene for domestic use as a result of the damage to the desulfurization plant. Residential areas are found north and east of the facility.

Comments: The general description of the environmental impact is plausible. The burning of crude oil would result in the release of particulate matter, CO_2, SO_x, NO_x, CO and other products of combustion. Even though no figures are provided, one could probably assume that large amounts of crude oil were burned at the refinery resulting in the huge clouds over Baghdad. As mentioned earlier, I would expect any H_2S to have been mostly oxidized to SO_2. Depending on the meteorological conditions at that time, large numbers in the densely populated city of Baghdad could have been exposed to these pollutants. Because of the damage to the desulfurization plant, widespread use of high-sulfur kerosene may lead to elevated urban concentrations of SO_2. If so, high SO_2 levels coupled with weather patterns such as atmospheric inversions could lead to classic "smog" conditions with potential risk to public health. I am surprised that the refinery can manage to operate at 100 percent capacity after the destruction and with the lack of chemicals, catalysts, or spare parts.

FIELD NOTES

The following are field notes taken by Ross Mirkarimi and Alfred Picardi, who each visited several bombed sites during the IST tour, August 25–September 5.

AUGUST 26, 1991: KUT DAM

Inspected: the Falahia Dam on the Tigris in Kut. Iraqi government officials and a dam engineer were interviewed.

BACKGROUND

The Kut Dam is the regulator of irrigation and water supply systems upstream to the north of the Tigris as well as downstream. The dam services the governorates of Wasit, Maysan, and Dhiqar. The irrigation system regulated by this dam shifted water from north to south for seasonal planting of wheat, barley, and vegetables.

OBSERVATION

The dam was bombed twice during the war. At night on January 30, the east end was hit and damaged. In the morning of February 5, the dam area was bombed, damaging the central section of the dam; a military hospital, 12 houses, and 33 shops on Al Xura street along the Tigris near the dam were also hit.

As a result of bomb damage to the dam, the irrigation system, which operates on gravity flow, could not function, and water supplies could not be shifted north for planting. The electric system that raises and lowers the floodgates was rendered inoperable by bomb damage; the inability to regulate flow prevented irrigation supplies from reaching the higher elevations of the system. Sedimentation is now a problem upstream of the dam. The money allocated for dredging has now been used for other priorities. Many resources were used drilling wells in an effort to replace lost irrigation waters. However, the groundwater used was more saline than the Tigris waters, limiting the crops which were subsequently planted. Public water supplies are also drawn from the irrigation canals.

After the bombing, a fish kill of thousands of shabut, a native fish around 28 inches long, was observed in the river. Studies on the possible causes of the fish kill, carried out by Dr. Abdul Ameer Al Thamiry of the Institute of Food Study, have been inconclusive. Studies have included both bacteriological and chemical analyses.

By August 26, team members observed that the electric system for seven gates had been repaired; 14 gates out of 56 were damaged in the bombing. Water levels in the system are now reaching design levels and only one area to the north is still not getting the required supply of irrigation water.

AUGUST 28, 1991: BASRA

Inspected: water and sewage treatment facilities in the city of Basra, including a sewage pump station and several residential areas. A Basra environmental health official, the sewage pump station operator and local residents were interviewed.

OBSERVATION

Acres of sewage pools and sewage overflow in several residential areas. The local sewage pump station currently operates only from 7:00 a.m. to 7:00 p.m. Only one out of four pumps at the station is in working order; the other three were damaged by vandalism during the civil uprising.

Solid waste is accumulating in the city, with an increase in disease vectors. Solid waste was previously transported out of the city by trucks, but most are now out of order. The government currently relies on volunteers in municipalities to bury garbage at local dumps. Bulldozers are unavailable.

A local resident explained that sewage began to overflow into the streets as soon as electric power was cut. In addition, tap water was stopped. The resident was currently receiving his drinking water from a hose stuffed in an intentionally broken water main.

Another local resident reported that his sister had contracted cholera four days earlier, and that his children had diarrhea and were vomiting. None of the children had been vaccinated because the hospitals no longer have vaccines available.

Dr. Saud, Director of the Department of the Environment, reported drinking water in the governorate is currently below WHO standards for the following reasons:

1) limited operation of water treatment and wastewater treatment plants because of erratic power supply;
2) broken water supply and sewage pumps that cannot be repaired because of the lack of spare parts and interrupted maintenance, and
3) infiltration of sewage into the water mains when the sewers back up and flood.

Inspected: Basra Oil Refinery. The assistant director of the refinery was interviewed.

OBSERVATION

The assistant director reported that the refinery was set on fire by Coalition aerial attacks starting January 17. There is a residential area near the refinery for employees. Some family members of employees were killed in the attacks, and some were killed by suffocation from the massive fires.

The air pollution from the fires has largely subsided; when the spills first occurred there was evident revolatilization from the spills. A large area of soil, approximately two kilometers square, is still contaminated by petroleum spills. The volume of the spill is estimated at 250,000 cubic meters. Spills originated from process and storage equipment, traveled through the facility sewer system and overflowed at the separator.

A huge lake of petroleum product remains standing on the soil. According to facility personnel, in the winter months when the spill occurred there was a rainwater component as well that filled the area of the spill up to the level of the road grade. Groundwater is used in the vicinity for irrigation. If the groundwater represents a resource in current or potentially future use, the oil spill represents a serious potential for extensive environmental damage. Environmental damage could also result from contaminated ground water discharge to local surface water. This is the worst case of environmental contamination resulting from war damage documented during the survey of the southern section of Iraq.

On the Road in Iraq—The Second Field Trip

Ross Mirkarimi

From April 24 to May 6, 1992, Ross Mirkarimi visited Iraq for a second time. Here are his personal observations, beginning with a walk through the wards of a major hospital in the city of Karbala.

A physician took me by the hand and guided me through the poorly lit corridors of Karbala General Hospital in this large city about 75 miles south of Baghdad. The nauseating odor of plaster, formaldehyde and fresh paint wafted by as I walked with a handful of physicians to the infant ward. In each of the eight makeshift cribs was a gaunt infant, reduced to a sack of skin and bones from malnutrition and severe diarrhea. Mothers dressed in black stood by; the only comfort they could give was to swat the flies from the skeleton-like faces of their dying children.

In another bed was a woman named Zana who was watching her 18-month-old child die. The child was making the motions of crying, but no sounds were coming out. She lay bundled waiting for the inevitable. The mother was also silent; in February another one of her children had died from diseases that were uncommon in Iraq just last year.

As we watched breathlessly, the child expired. Zana dropped her head next to her deceased baby. The doctors could do nothing. Even such basic supplies as antibiotics are rationed carefully. Patients requiring extensive procedures, such as Zana's infant, have little hope of receiving them.

Across the ward was another unit for children. One young mother was so undernourished that she had stopped lactating. The only milk she could find, she said, was on the exorbitantly priced black market. Sugar water was the best she could do for her six-month-old baby.

Dr. Hassan, the physician in charge of the ward, posed a question: "What will be the future of this infant? If he survives, which seems unlikely," said Hassan, "the child's growth will be stunted and probably he will suffer permanent damage."

During my trip to the hospital in early May, many doctors clearly were frustrated by the number of children dying from what previously were minor ailments, such as the flu or diarrhea. Other than in some isolated rural areas, diarrhea never had been a health problem in pre-Gulf War Iraq.

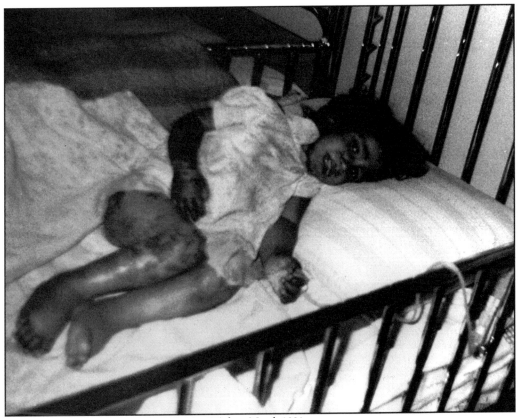

Child burned in Coalition attacks. © Louise Cainkar, March 1991.

In hospitals throughout Iraq, doctors were bracing for an increase in cases of cholera and typhoid fever. The Iraqi Minister of Health reported 825 cases of typhoid and cholera in March and April 1992 in Karbala, Najaf and Basra, among the cities hit hardest by the Coalition. A couple of international relief agencies stationed in Baghdad concurred with the reported cases.

While Hassan gave me a sobering report about the infant mortality rate, a government official was eager to display the repairs made on the hospital since the end of the fighting. He reminded me that "what the Coalition left standing, the civil unrest finished."

The hospital, along with two holy shrines, was one of the last bastions of the Shiite insurrection in Karbala. According to the nongovernmental sources and foreigners trapped during the March 1991 uprising, more than 2,000 patients, staff, and military personnel were killed on the hospital's premises alone. (It's believed that a total of 14,000 people died throughout the city during the two weeks of combat between the Shiites and Saddam Hussein's 80th Infantry Unit.)

Outside Baghdad, most of the water supply is still contaminated with raw sewage. While waterborne diseases have waned in some cities, sewage is still flowing into the water throughout the South, especially in Basra. The Basra Petrochemical Plant, built by Loomis-USA, was the largest producer of chlorine in Iraq—45,000 tons per year, 90 percent of it used for water purification. The plant was destroyed in three separate Coalition attacks, though Loomis employees interviewed by the International Study Team in September said they couldn't understand why a plant that couldn't be converted to chemical weapons production was bombed. Iraq now relies on relief agencies to supply chlorine for water treatment.

An Iraqi farmer named Musa, who lives outside Najaf, told me he lost his wife, his brother and his farm during the Coalition bombing. His wheat field also was destroyed when local civil defense was forced to detonate an unexploded cluster bomb that fell there.

Musa, who also lost a son during the Iran-Iraq War, gave me the impression that he had given up on life, and only went on for the sake of his two remaining children.

The Continuing Impacts

Background Information

Considered a nearly developed, industrial society before the Gulf War, Iraq is now on a downward slide into bankruptcy and chaos. A virtual news blackout on postwar Iraqi society has shielded from public view 1992 and 1993 reports from international humanitarian organizations. What follows is a summary of some of those reports. For a view of the current status of sanctions, see Chapter Eight, "Update on Sanctions."

FOOD AND NUTRITION

Before the war, Iraq imported 70 percent of its food. Even though it is exempt from the UN sanctions, food delivery is slow, and restrictions on Iraq's cash supplies have helped prevent bulk purchasing. UNICEF reports that by January 1992, food prices had increased 20 to 40 times over pre-Gulf War prices.[1] Dr. Eric Hoskins, a Canadian physician who has been monitoring the effects of the Gulf crisis on Iraqi women and children, reports that from August 1990 to April 1993 the food price index had increased 50 times and that most prices increased by an additional 50 percent or more during the first three months of 1993 alone. Before the war, most Iraqis spent half their income on food. Today, their income goes to little else.

Government food rations provide 1,500 calories per day, not the 2,700 calories per day recommended for adults.[2] As a result, malnutrition has been and continues to be a major problem in Iraq. According to Dr. Hoskins, pregnant women are subject to anemia because their diets are deficient in iron and folic acid, leading to abnormal rates of miscarriages, premature labors, and low birth-weights of newborn infants. The number of newborns with low birth-weights climbed from four percent in August 1990 to seventeen percent by late 1992. Adding to these problems is a continuing lack of infant formula, with protein and micronutrient deficiency the cause of growth retardation, anemia, goiter, and rickets, and other illnesses related to the health of infants. Malnutrition, touching all groups of Iraqi society, has especially affected children one to three years of age. Government attempts to supplement food supplies ran into trouble when the 1992–1993 cereal harvest fell far short of expectations. Damage to crops resulted from the lack of pesticides and spare parts for irrigation pumps and other agricultural machinery, another consequence of UN sanctions.

THE ECONOMY AND UNEMPLOYMENT

The Iraqi economy has virtually collapsed. Dr. Hoskins reports that returning Iraqi war veterans faced a 70 percent industrial unemployment rate. Sanctions have absorbed the middle class into the poverty-class majority.[3] Per capita gross national product has sunk from $2,367 in 1988 to $65 in 1991. The government spends more than 30 percent of its cash on defense and security, twice the global average.[4] Street vending has increased as a means of survival, and often children of primary-school age are forced to sell goods at roadside stalls in order to supplement family income. Dr. Hoskins says that this may account for a rise in primary-school dropout rates from three percent before the Gulf crisis to fifteen percent during 1992. The government is encouraging the fabrication of alternative, homemade items to replace imports, and has initiated ambitious public works projects such as an artificial river and a communication tower, but eventually the country is expected to run out of raw materials.[5]

WATER AND SANITATION

By the late 1980s, 96 percent of the urban population and 31 percent of the rural population had access to safe drinking water.[6] The intense U.S.-led Coalition bombing campaign against Iraq led to electrical power being cut back to three percent of prewar capacity, so that water treatment and sewage facilities dependent on electrically run pumps were shut down. Untreated sewage was backed up and began to flow into the streets and homes of urban centers. Wastewater contaminated with bacteria and fecal matter was dumped into Iraq's major river systems which provide drinking water for the population. Dr. Hoskins reports that, in January of 1993, it was found that 35 percent of the water samples taken in the governorates of Maysan, Basra and Najaf were contaminated. The production of chlorine and aluminum sulfate, used to purify water, was shut down by the bombing. Now chlorine and aluminum sulfate can only be obtained through UN agencies, principally UNICEF, according to the sanctions rules and regulations, but UN agencies can only provide a small fraction of what is needed.

While Iraq's prewar sewage systems had not been up to Western standards, UNICEF found in 1992 that the solid waste collection and disposal system had deteriorated to less than 25 percent of prewar capacity.[7]

The health of the Iraqi people has been directly affected by waterborne diseases related to the breakdown of sanitation controls. According to Dr. Hoskins, in January 1993 it was reported that the number of typhoid cases in the Kurdish city of Sulaymaniyah had increased by 500 percent, compared to the same month the previous year. This recent outbreak follows other illnesses affecting children since the war, which are also due to poor sanitation, including outbreaks of malaria, cholera, gastroenteritis, intestinal parasites, excessive diarrhea leading to dehydration, infectious hepatitis and respiratory tract infections.

HEALTH SERVICES AND SUPPLIES

Prior to the war, Iraq had made steady progress in providing health services for its people. According to the London-based Medical Aid for Iraq, immunization coverage for all children one year old in Iraq was 95 percent by 1990.[8] But the war and UN sanctions reversed this trend. Based on hospital observations from its seventh trip to Iraq in January and February of 1993, Medical Aid for Iraq reports that there is a shortage of vaccines for mumps, measles and rubella, despite these childhood illnesses being potentially fatal because of the intervening problem of malnutrition.

This has led to a greater shortage of medical supplies in 1993 than in previous postwar years. Today, there is an observable lack of medicines, vaccines, syringes, anesthetics, surgical materials, and laboratory and diagnostic equipment. Dr. Hoskins reports that in 1992 a measles epidemic spread throughout Iraq. There were some 20,000 reported cases of this normally treatable illness.

During the Nongovernmental Organizations Conference held in Baghdad April 28-30, 1992, Dr. M. Fakhoury from the German-based Direct Assistance Organization described the typical problems medical staff face in treating their patients because of poor hospital conditions and lack of medical supplies:

> Operations are normally done in sterile surroundings. Is this possible when the windows are broken, air-conditioning is not working, sterilizing equipment is out of order for different reasons, be it for only a small missing spare part? So the first rule before you start an operation is not fulfilled, because you should work sterile. The result is wound infection, gangrene, osteomyelitis, sepsis, all of which could be prevented. The surgeon needs special tools for operations. The simple things were missing: sterile disposable scalpels. Because of this the doctors were forced to use them as often as possible and only throw them away when they did not cut anymore. There was no gauze, bandages, surgical yarn, and even now the available amount is not according to the standard Iraq was accustomed to before the embargo. Normally operations are done under total

anesthesia. How can you do it if the drugs are not available, the narcotic gas is missing? This is the reason why many patients, including children, had limbs amputated without anesthetic as well as painful wound dressing without painkillers."[9]

APPEAL TO WORLD CONFERENCE ON HUMAN RIGHTS

The following is excerpted from a note verbale dated June 1, 1993 (A/Conf. 157/4) from the Permanent Mission of Iraq to the Secretary-General of the World Conference on Human Rights held at Vienna, June 14-25, 1993:

The Government of Iraq wishes to draw the attention of the international community to the grave violations of Iraq citizens' human rights resulting from the continued economic blockade, on the basis of the principle of the interdependence of civil, political, economic, social and cultural human rights as emphasized by United Nations resolutions, the most recent one being General Assembly resolution 47/137.

Owing to a variety of interrelated factors, infant and child mortality increased considerably following the Gulf War. First, there is a severe shortage of food and basic medicines as well as drinking water. Second, poor medical services have led to an increase in diseases resulting from polluted water, such as cholera, typhoid, dysentery and gastritis. Hepatitis has spread considerably in all parts of Iraq, increasing by 100 percent in some part of the country. Meningitis is now common in the south of Iraq. Lack of vaccines and precarious health conditions have led to the reemergence of children's diseases such as poliomyelitis, measles and dysentery, which had been previously brought under control through vaccine programs. The total number of deaths of infants and children due to the economic blockade caused by selected factors is 264,738 by the end of April 1993.

Children account for 43.9 percent of the total number of Iraq's inhabitants. When we add women over the age of 15 (28 percent of the population) and persons over the age of 60 (5.5 percent), the total percentage of children, women and the elderly stands at nearly 77 percent. Taken together these figures give a clear indication of the grave damage Iraqi society, especially women, children and the elderly will incur in the future.

In spite of the fact that the resolution adopted by the Security Council and the Sanctions Committee allows Iraq to use its funds frozen in banks throughout the world for the purchase of medicines and food, most of the States where such funds are held have prevented the banks from accepting open credit lines made available for medicines and medical supplies by the Central Bank of Iraq.

There is only one route for travelling to and from Iraq and transporting goods and medical supplies into the country, the highway to Amman (in Jordan), which is 1,000 kilometers long. The journey takes 17 hours. The delays caused by the transportation of foodstuffs and medicines to Iraq have direct repercussions on Iraqis' daily lives.

—Daniel Robicheau

NOTES:
1. UNICEF, "Children and Women in Iraq; A Situation Analysis," Report, UNICEF and the Government of the Republic of Iraq, Baghdad, October 1992.

2. Quaker Service, "Effects of Sanctions in Iraq," Draft Report, Baghdad, December 31, 1992.

3. Quaker Service, "Effects of Sanctions in Iraq."

4. John Roberts, "Iraq: Saddam's Land 'Statistically' the Poorest in the World," *InterPress Service,* February 3, 1993.

5. Quaker Service, "Effects of Sanctions in Iraq."

6. UNICEF, "Children and Women in Iraq" .

7. UNICEF, "Children and Women in Iraq."

8. Medical Aid for Iraq, *Report On Medical Aid For Iraq's Seventh Convoy, Delivering Medical Supplies to Hospitals in Southern Iraq During January and February, 1993,* London, February, 1993.

9. *Save The Children In Iraq,* Proceedings, Nongovernmental Organizations Conference, Baghdad, April 28–30, 1992.

Chapter 6

Human Casualties

A mother holds up a photograph of her son killed in the Al Ameriyah Shelter Attack.
Photo: Chris Martin.

Introduction

No matter how one feels regarding the justification for the Gulf War, its brutality should be a matter of some reflection for the governments of both the Coalition countries and Iraq.

Articles in this chapter look at the effects of Scud missiles on Israeli civilians; describe the current situation in the area of Iraq now held by the Kurdish Regional Government; document the situation of Palestinian and Kurdish refugees and the impacts of the war on Kuwaiti and Palestinian children; analyze the UN response to the crisis; and attempt to assess the continuing impacts on poor Iraqis, who remain the worst-hit victims of the crisis.

The Coalition armies did not suffer heavy casualties in the Gulf War. Of the 355 U.S. soldiers who died in the Gulf from August 1990 to March 1991, 207 died in noncombat accidents.[1] The total number of Coalition deaths during the war itself was only 343.[2]

Iraqi military casualties were far heavier. Kurdish and Shiite conscripts in the Iraqi army were routed and killed by the Coalition while in disorderly retreat.[3] Some Iraqi soldiers, 80 to 250 according to one estimate, considerably more according to others, were buried alive in their trenches by Coalition bulldozers.[4] Iraqi soldiers fleeing Kuwait were incinerated on the "Highway of Death" by Coalition strafing and bombing.[5] Although the number of Iraqi military deaths is a matter of controversy, with estimates ranging from 30,000 to 115,000, the disparity between Iraqi and Coalition death tolls give some idea of the extent to which the Iraqis were outmatched as a fighting force.

The Iraqi and the Coalition governments have been equally reluctant to estimate the number of Iraqi troops killed in the air and ground war. Some analysts believe that the Pentagon fears that a high number would make the U.S. look murderous and a low number would smack of a whitewash. Trevor Dupuy, a military analyst and retired U.S. Army colonel, suggests that the Pentagon has avoided estimating the number of Iraqi military deaths for two reasons: "Part is the legacy of the Vietnam body count, and part is they are reluctant to reveal how little they know."[6]

The task of estimating Iraqi civilian deaths during the war has fallen to nongovernmental organizations and the Iraqi Ministry of Health. Civilian deaths were placed no higher than 2,500–3,000 by Middle East Watch in November 1991.[7] On February 17, 1992 the Iraqi government claimed that 8,000 civilians died in the Coalition air raids.[8] Ramsey Clark has calculated that there were 25,000 deaths due to Coalition bombing.[9]

In Iraq, the casualties escalated after the cease-fire. During the Kurdish and Shiite rebellions that followed the end of the Coalition campaign, tens of thousands of civilians were killed by Saddam Hussein's security forces, and about a tenth of the country's population fled temporarily: about one-and-a-half million people to Iran, half a million to Turkey, and smaller numbers to Kuwait, Syria and Jordan.[10]

In early 1992, Beth Osborne Daponte, a U.S. Census Bureau demographer, was nearly fired for releasing estimates on Iraqi casualties that the Bureau did not want the public to see. She was hired temporarily by Greenpeace to continue her research, and now believes that 60,000 Iraqi deaths are "missing" from official Census Bureau counts for 1991. In Ms. Daponte's interview in Chapter Six, she estimates the Iraqi military deaths, the civilian deaths during Coalition bombing and, allowing for refugee movements, deaths during the postwar violence. We have also reprinted the Census Bureau report, which Ms. Daponte criticizes in her interview.

Chapter Six includes several excerpts, taken from the International Study Team's report of October 1991, (according to UNICEF still the most comprehensive documentation to date of the postwar nutritional and psychological status of women and children in Iraq). The IST reported in 1991 that over 25 percent of Iraqi children were malnourished, and that mortality rates had quadrupled.[11] Most recent reports indicate that the numbers of child deaths have risen even higher in 1992 and 1993.

In 1992, UNICEF estimated that the increase since the war of the under-five mortality rate had risen from the threefold increase reported by the International Study Team to a fivefold increase.[12] The Iraqi Ministry of Health attributed 41,000 deaths—including 14,000 children—to direct impacts of sanctions in the first four months of 1992.[13] In early 1993, the Minister of Trade, Dr. Mohammed Mehdi Saleh, said that the average mortality rate of children under five had increased seven times, from 27 per thousand, before the sanctions, to 189 per thousand, with the rate of deaths of children one to two years old rising sharply, mainly due to the shortage of baby milk formula.[14]

The Paris-based International Physicians Commission of Inquiry, a delegation of physicians who visited Iraq from April 10 to 14, 1993, reported that compared to a monthly average of 712 deaths among Iraqi children under five years of age from August to December 1990, 5,112 children from the same age group had died in the month of January alone in 1993.[15]

As we go to press, there are hearings in the U.S. on the continuing health effects on U.S. Gulf War veterans. Thousands of veterans in the U.S. have complained of memory loss, muscle and joint pain, fatigue and other symptoms—their condition is described at the end of this chapter. It is not known whether Iraqi war veterans are being monitored for continuing effects, which in any case would be hard to detect amongst the health impacts due to the collapse of the Iraqi economy since the war.

—James Warner and Philippa Winkler

NOTES:

1. James F. Dunnigan and Austin Bay, *From Shield to Storm* (New York : William Morrow and Company, Inc.), 1991, 342.
2. Medical Educational Trust Report, *Continued Health Costs of the Gulf War*, London, February 1992.
3. Medical Educational Trust Report, *Continued Health Costs.*
4. Patrick Sloyan, "U.S. Tank-Plows Said To Bury Thousands of Iraqis," *New York Times,* September 12, 1991; U.S. News, *Triumph Without Victory: The History of the Persian Gulf War* (New York: Random House, Inc.), 1992, 312.
5. Steve Niva, "The Battle is Joined," in Phyllis Bennis and Michel Moushabek, *Beyond the Storm—A Gulf Crisis Reader* (New York: Olive Branch Press), 1991.
6. "Iraqi War Dead Exaggerated?" *The Oakland Tribune,* March 3, 1993.

7. Human Rights Watch, *Needless Deaths in the Gulf War: Civilian Casualties During the Air Campaigns and Violations of the Laws of War; A Middle East Watch Report*, New York, Human Rights Watch, November 1991, 19.

8. *Keesing's Record of World Events*, vol. 37, no. 2 (February 1992), 38789.

9. Ramsey Clark, *The Fire This Time: U.S. War Crimes in the Gulf* (New York: Thunder's Mouth Press), 1992, xxvii, 83. Ramsey Clark's estimates are that: 25,000 Iraqi civilians died during the bombing; another 25,000 died of the indirect effects of the bombing, embargo, shattered infrastructure, and damaged safety and health services by the end of the war; and a further 150,000 civilians had died from these causes by May 1992. In early 1993, Ramsey Clark concluded that approximately 2,000 Iraqis a week were dying due to the ongoing impacts of sanctions against Iraq. *Keesing's Record of World Events*, vol. 39, no. 2 (February 1993), 39342.

10. Middle East Watch, *Endless Torment: The 1991 Uprising in Iraq and its Aftermath*, Report, Human Rights Watch, New York, June 1992.

11. International Study Team, *Health and Welfare in Iraq After the Gulf Crisis; An In-Depth Assessment*, Report, Cambridge, Massachusetts, October 1991.

12. John Roberts, "Iraq: Saddam's Land 'Statistically' the Poorest in the World," *Interpress Service*, February 3, 1993.

13. *Keesing's Record of World Events*, vol. 38, no. 6 (June 1992), 38743.

14. "Iraq: Saddam's Land 'Statistically' the Poorest."

15. "Delegation to the WHO Headquarters in Geneva, Monday, May 24, 1993," Press Release, International Physicians' Commission of Enquiry, Paris, May 27, 1993.

Censorship at the U.S. Census Bureau

Interview with Beth Osborne Daponte

Beth Osborne Daponte, a U.S. Census Bureau demographer, was nearly fired in early 1992 for releasing unclassified estimates of Iraqi war deaths. After her research notes for the estimates were taken away from her, she hired a lawyer to defend herself and told the press that the Census Bureau was deliberately suppressing politically embarrassing data about the war dead.[1] She took a leave of absence from the Bureau and in the summer of 1992, worked with William Arkin, Director of Military Research at Greenpeace, to arrive at an independent estimate of the 1991 Iraqi death toll (see Table 6-1). She is a visiting faculty member at the University of Pittsburgh. Interviewed December 1992, by Lydia Gans, Ph.D., Professor Emerita, who taught statistics and mathematics at California State University, and Philippa Winkler.

Following this interview, we publish the January 1992 report written by the Census Bureau.

LG: In their January 1992 report on the 1991 Iraqi death toll, the U.S. Census Bureau listed in their attachments media sources such as CNN (Cable News Network), Washington Post, *and*

Newsweek, *primarily. [See Table 6-2.] My sense is that they would not be reliable sources, given the Pentagon's media management of the war and the widespread editorial bias in favor of the Coalition forces. What would you use as good sources for data?*

BD: Let me try to explain why the Census Bureau went to these sources. In the fall of 1991 there was very limited data available on casualties from the Gulf War and in some ways press reports were all the sources the Bureau thought they could get. There just weren't the documents yet to go through, and to provide a more systematic approach to the problem, which means creating a data set. What I did [in research sponsored by Greenpeace] was to rely on surveys of the 1987 Census similar to what the Census Bureau did, but I also relied on surveys that were taken on the eve of the invasion of Kuwait that were done in 1989 and 1990 in Iraq. Then, to obtain postwar estimates, I put together a data set of incidents, mostly of missed bombs and how many civilians were killed from each incident, and summed up the numbers. In Middle East Watch's *Needless Deaths*,[2] they go through incident after incident of bombs that did not hit their intended target, but instead hit marketplaces and homes. So I think when you consider sources you have to consider the timing of the estimate, and whether data was available.

LG: *But didn't the Census Bureau have access to the same data as you did?*

BD: Well, they should have, I believe, done a better job of estimating what the population of Iraq was like on the eve of the war. They should have pursued the 1989 and 1990 surveys conducted in Iraq. I pursued them. I actively pursued them. They were hard to get, especially the 1989 survey (that was the survey done in Iraq by the Gulf Council of Health Ministers), which was very difficult to obtain. Demographic information is hard to get from Middle Eastern countries. They don't want to give out what their populations look like.

LG: *So how did you get the Iraqi demographics?*

BD: I don't want to get into that. I was sworn to secrecy!

LG: *Okay. But the Census Bureau could have gotten the same information if they had tried.*

BD: To my knowledge, they didn't try. I was told not to worry, when I did the estimates for the Census Bureau under the direction of my superiors, about the prewar population. They should have worried more about the prewar population because estimates of mortality after the war really depend on what you think the population would have looked like had there been no war. And that's the biggest difference between my estimates and the Census Bureau's estimates. And I spent a lot of time trying to figure out what the population would have looked like had there been no war. I think the Bureau's work was—I shouldn't say sloppy—they did well with the sources they had—but they should have pursued sources that didn't happen to come across their desks. They should have gone out of their way.

THE JANUARY 1992 CENSUS BUREAU REPORT

LG: *In looking at the Census Bureau report I notice their summary results don't reflect their quoted sources. For example, the Bureau quotes 40,000 Iraqi military deaths, based on the Defense Intelli-*

gence Agency's estimate of 100,000 military deaths, Newsweek's *estimates of between 70,000 and 115,000, and military analyst Trevor DuPuy's estimates of between 30,000 to 50,000. [See Table 6-2.] Why did they pick such a low number?*

BD: This report has an interesting history. Basically, the estimates that I did under the direction of my superior [Frank Hobbs, Chief, Population Studies Branch] in the fall of 1991 went through the review in December, when everything was approved. At the Census Bureau the way things operated was that once the projection files were approved they were part of the public domain. William Arkin at Greenpeace called me in the beginning of January and asked me what I had come up with. Part of my job was to answer any questions the public had on the demographics of a country. Analysts were encouraged to use the projections file once it was in the public domain, once it had gone through approval. So I pulled up the projection file that was sitting on my desk and told him the answers to his question. That was a normal part of my job. The projection file had 13,000 civilian deaths and 5,000 postwar military deaths. William Arkin had a press conference a couple of days later and the whole thing got into the public limelight and the Census Bureau decided that they were going to quash any more information about Iraqi mortality. So the files were taken from me, and all hell broke loose at the Census Bureau, at least with respect to me, and I was made off limits. My calls were screened, files disappeared. But then, there was an outstanding question. They had taken a research note from me, which I had done mostly on my own time, and I asked for it back. They said they would not give it back to me because they thought they owned it. And I thought that they did not own it. I hired an intellectual property rights attorney to look into the question of who owns the research note, this little two-page, three-graph document. My attorney and the Department of Commerce attorney decided that it was very unclear who owned the research note but that Frank Hobbs and I together would write a research note on Iraqi mortality. I agreed to that. Frank was my branch chief at the time and he was my immediate superior and I trusted him. But then the next morning (at this time I was in Pittsburgh writing my dissertation) they faxed me a copy of the research note which looked nothing like my research note, although it had my name on it. And then they asked me if I had any comments on the research note and my main comment was to take me off as author and to instead cite my original research note. They never publicly put it out, their research note, you had to know it existed to get a copy of it. The report changed the number of civilian wartime deaths from 13,000 to 5,000, and omitted the category of postwar military deaths, which made the number zero. My original research note was written so an educated layperson could understand the results of the work, meaning it included graphs and comparisons in life expectancy and infant mortality with other countries. The [January 1992] note the Bureau "released" reads like technical documentation. It included no graphs, and countless caveats about data "quality." My impression of the Census Bureau research note is that it is intentionally vague and complicated. If you read the first two pages of it, you would think that Iraq never had a census. They would have you think that Iraq had the worst quality data in the world. It was pretty clear to me that this was done to address the comments the Department of Defense had made, saying that they could not do a body count. So, that was the history of the January 1992 Census Bureau report.

LG: When I read the Census Bureau's report, and it talks about how hard it was to obtain data, I was surprised because Iraq has a good enough infrastructure to the point where they were probably keeping pretty good census data.

BD: Iraq to my knowledge had better census data than Saudi Arabia. They had a 1977 and a 1987 census that were of reasonable quality. They weren't great but they were okay for a developing country.

MIGRATION ESTIMATES

LG: On the question of emigration estimates for Iraq, I notice the Census Bureau's figures are strange. [See Table 6-2.] They talk about Iraqis who fled, and then others are called refugees. In the sources they use "approx" for some figures, yet all the figures are estimates. Under their sources for foreign population, they include Iraqi nationals as well. Two out of three of the sources say that the foreign population who left Iraq were either Kuwaiti or Iraqi. You have to have correct migration figures in order to make projections on future populations, right?

BD: Net migration is always the most difficult component of a population to account for. Even if you take the U.S. for example, we don't have closed borders, there is a lot of illegal immigration, and so migration is a difficult component to address. Given that it is so difficult, sometimes a demographer is better off assuming, even though they know the assumption is wrong, zero net migration. For Iraq, the migration data, I can't go into how bad it is—for example, the International Labor Organization (ILO) put out a table of the people, foreign workers and their families, who lived in Iraq in August 1990 on the eve of the invasion. And I assume that most of those people left the country after the invasion. Then the State Department put out a map with a chart showing the numbers of emigrants who returned to different countries, Sri Lanka, India, etc. At times, the State Department has more people going back to these countries than the ILO ever thought had left. And these aren't minor figures. These were differences of a hundred thousand for a particular country. So you start to ask why you should believe any of this data. I discuss how bad the data is, and then I say that I assume that net migration was zero. A big problem with the Iraqi census, and demographers are very split on this issue, is whether or not foreign workers were even included in the census to begin with. So if they weren't included, and if you're projecting the population from 1987, you shouldn't be taking them out later. If they were included and you don't take them out, then you're overestimating the population. I don't know how many foreign workers and their families were in Iraq in 1987. I asked the Iraqis directly, and they insisted that foreign workers were never included in their census. I talked to the UN mission, and they thought it was a strange question, of course, and that foreign workers weren't included. I don't think it compromises the result of my research because the age and sex distribution of migrants is heavily skewed toward those with relatively low probabilities of dying. The ILO had 1.1 million foreign workers in Iraq and the great majority of those are young males. There were 100,000 family members, wives and children and perhaps parents of migrants, those people who would be greatly affected by the change in mortality rate. But

I think it doesn't compromise the results of the research at all. And actually I think it's a much safer assumption than trying to guess a number.

LG: In terms of the population projections in the Census Bureau's report, again of January 1992, there is an enormous decrease in the projected population, both in 1991 and 1992. In 1991, they project a decrease of 1,231,480 people. [See Table 6-3.]

BD: I don't know if they took out the migrants.

LG: I think they did. It obviously includes migration, since they estimate 145,000 excess deaths, and the decrease in infant mortality was apparently factored into that figure.

BD: I don't include migration. A lot of people who left were Iraqis who returned shortly after the war after going to Iran and Turkey. The question is, do you really take them out of the population? I don't. I didn't want to take them out intentionally because these people were also affected by the great change and the risks to their health. So I want to consider them also. I do think it's important to consider the Kurds in the mountains of Turkey, even if they're across the border.

PW: You left the bureau on leave of absence, and in the summer of 1992, you and William Arkin worked together to come up with a more accurate 1991 Iraqi death toll. [See Table 6-1.] There is really a large difference between the Census Bureau's 1991 death toll estimate—145,000—and the estimate for the same period, of 205,500, which you and William Arkin did. That's a difference of 60,000 Iraqi civilian and military deaths in 1991.

BD: In terms of military deaths, the Bureau took the lowest figure. Bill Arkin put together a database on battles of the Gulf War, and he tried to account for desertion and weapon intensity, so I would believe his estimate of 56,000 because it's based on an analysis, which is actually much

TABLE 6-1. IRAQI 1991 DEATH TOLL ESTIMATE

110,000	Deaths expected without war	Number of deaths arrived at by starting with the 1987 Iraqi census, then projecting the population using a component method, taking into account fertility, migration and other probabilities. Also takes into account a 1990 UNICEF survey and a Gulf Council of Health Ministers 1989 survey.
3,500	Civilian deaths during the war	Figure extrapolated from data from *Needless Deaths in the Gulf War*, published by Middle East Watch; Middle East Watch internal memos, the International Study Team, and the Iraqi Minister of Defense.
56,000	Military deaths during the war	Includes 12,000–15,000 deaths from air attacks on Iraq, 20,000–25,000 from air attacks on Kuwait, and 17,000–23,000 deaths during the ground war. Estimates based on a reconstruction of the war.
35,000	(30,000 civilian, 5,000 military)	Deaths after the war from postwar turmoil. Estimate for civilian deaths is from U.S. Census Bureau ("the weakest estimate," according to Daponte).
111,000	Postwar deaths due to health effects of the war	Estimate derived from applying the International Study Team's child mortality rate to the adult population, based on Model Life Tables.
205,500	**Total excess deaths**	

Source: Beth Osborne Daponte, from her research on civilian casualties and research by William Arkin on military casualties. Sponsored by Greenpeace U.S.

lower than the Defense Intelligence Agency's estimate of 100,000.[3] So it's still a very low end of that estimate. Fifty-six thousand is not high at all. The Census Bureau originally had 13,000 wartime civilian casualties, which was based on nothing and then went down to 5,000. I have no idea what that was based on. I was kept in the dark about that estimate. And I estimated 3,500, much lower. I put together a data base based on any document I could get my hands on. I organized it by place of death, time of death, number of people killed in an incident. So I would believe the 3,500 over any of their other figures. In terms of the military postwar violence, the Bureau did originally have 5,000 deaths and for some reason they reduced that to zero. That's an absurd number because we all know there were purges of military personnel in Iraq after the war. I believe any positive integer over zero. As for the postwar civilian deaths due to violence, none of us really know how many died. Thirty thousand seems reasonable, especially given the report to Congress about how deaths occurred in the tens of thousands. Excess deaths from health effects: they estimate 70,000. I estimated 111,000. Those differences are based on the most part on having different prewar mortality figures. They also had used the International Study Team infant mortality study for their postwar deaths from health effects.[4] I did also, but in the fall of 1991, the Harvard team still had a coding error in their data. By the time I did my work the coding error was corrected.

PW: When the International Study Team released their April 1992 infant mortality report?[5]

BD: Yes. So the differences between the Greenpeace estimates and the Census Bureau's estimates are mainly in the categories of health effects and wartime military deaths and to some extent the postwar military deaths. I'm not saying the Bureau intentionally misestimated, but I do believe there was intentional suppression of the information in the public domain afterwards.

PW: At the press conference you held with the American Civil Liberties Union in April 1992 in Washington, DC, you were quoted as saying that the Bureau had effectively kept the public ignorant of the effects of the Gulf War, and that it was suppressing politically embarrassing information. Were you quoted accurately and is that the way you still feel?

BD: The exact quotation is, "I find it extremely disturbing that the U.S. Census Bureau tried to suppress and delay the release of information that was embarrassing to the current [Bush] Administration. By trying to do so, the Bureau was effectively keeping the public ignorant of the full impacts of U.S. actions in the Gulf area." Yes, I said that, and it's absolutely true.

PW: Has the Census Bureau suppressed information before?

BD: There have been other incidents. For example, the John McNeil report of the number of workers in the U.S. work force who are earning some paltry sum of money per hour, went up from 13 to 18 percent from 1980 to 1990. The Public Information Office told John McNeil (around the same time as my incident) there was nothing new in the report and they didn't want to put it out. McNeil had to go through a long, drawn-out battle to get that information into the public domain. An analyst should not have to do that.

PW: You're on leave of absence with the Census Bureau. How do you feel about returning?

BD: I would never want to go back into the same situation. One of the reasons I decided to take a leave of absence was that I hoped that things would calm down and be cleaned up in my absence. Barbara Torry, who was head of the Center for International Research, has since left, which I think is very good for the Bureau. And Frank Hobbs and I no longer work together. So a few changes have been made, whether or not they're substantial in practice I don't know. I can only hope that the Bureau is being cleaned up, because I found it very, very politically influenced.

PW: Why weren't other Bureau employees more outspoken about this?

BD: I was forced to be outspoken. Actually, I'm not a whistleblower. I don't understand government corruption. Usually the stakes are so small.

PW: In this case what was at stake was the public perception of the war and the damage it caused.

BD: Yes, but the smartest thing the Bureau could have done was to say the data isn't that good and maybe next year we'll do a better job. The stupidest thing they could have done was try to fire the analyst who did the estimates. And why they did this is beyond me. They ended up retracting everything a month later. When I left I thought there was a very dangerous situation. The brother-in-law of Pat Buchanan [a conservative candidate for the Republican Presidential nomination in 1992] was head of the Public Information Office (it was a political appointment) and they wanted all information about the U.S. population to go through Pat Buchanan's brother-in-law. That's unusual for the Bureau. In the past, it had been an open organization. Analysts were free to talk to the press. It was my incident that made them start keeping analysts off limits to the press. After March 1992, memos started to be sent around about how everything had to go through the Public Information Office. You couldn't even refer people to the correct books that information was in without going through the PIO.

NOTES:

1. 'Gulf War Death Toll Disputed,' *Associated Press,* reprinted in the *San Francisco Chronicle,* April 14, 1992.

2. Middle East Watch, *Needless Deaths in the Gulf War,* Report, Human Rights Watch, New York, November 1991.

3. On January 15, 1992, the U.S. estimate of Iraqi military deaths was adjusted down from 100,000 to 10,000. *Keesing's Record of World Events* (Cambridge, U.K.: Longman) vol. 38, no. 1 (January 1992), 38743. On March 11, 1993, the U.S. Defense Intelligence Agency further reduced its estimate of Iraqi military deaths to 1,500. *Keesing's Record of World Events* vol. 39, no. 3 (March 1993), 39390.

4. International Study Team, *Health and Welfare in Iraq After the Gulf Crisis; An In-Depth Assessment,* Report, Cambridge, Massachusetts, October 1991.

5. International Study Team, *Infant and Child Mortality and Nutritional Status of Iraqi Children after the Gulf Conflict,* Cambridge, Massachusetts, April 1992, excerpted later in this chapter.

▌raqi War Deaths

U.S. Census Bureau

Excerpted from Population Estimates for Iraq, *by Frank Hobbs, Chief, Population Studies Branch, Center for International Research, Bureau of the Census, United States Department of Commerce. This "note" was issued January, 1992. This is the Census Bureau report discussed above, in the interview with Beth Osborne Daponte. Frank Hobbs was Beth Osborne Daponte's supervisor at the Census Bureau.*

BACKGROUND AND DATA QUALITY

. . . Not only are the available population data on Iraq limited and of less than desirable quality, but the country has gone through a period of two wars in the past 12 years . . .

To estimate the population of Iraq, the Center for International Research (CIR) performed a literature review and contacted experts thought to have information and knowledge on Iraq (particularly on the mortality and migration aspects related to the Gulf War), military affairs, mortality of wartime populations, or mortality given various health conditions. These contacts included persons in international organizations, the media, research institutions, the military, government agencies, and private individuals.

Even among knowledgeable sources, there clearly is considerable uncertainty with regard to the impact of mortality and migration during and after the Gulf War on Iraq's population. The wide range of estimates of mortality and migration during this period reflects this uncertainty and is presented in [Table 6-2.]

The estimates of mortality used by the Center for International Research were selected considering the range of estimates available, and assuming an age and sex pattern of mortality (including separate age and sex distributions of deaths expected in the absence of war, and war-related military and civilian deaths), and a general level of infant mortality. The migration assumption used by CIR also considers the various levels of population movements presented by alternative sources, and relies heavily on a document prepared by the U.S. Department of State in 1991.

For the projections of the population of Iraq, more than the usual level of uncertainty pertains to the demographic estimates. While the data and estimates of population parameters are already subject to considerable uncertainty for many developing countries, the effects of the Gulf War and its aftermath substantially exacerbate the difficulties demographers face in their attempts to accurately portray the population situation in Iraq.

TABLE 6-2. RANGE OF MORTALITY AND MIGRATION ESTIMATES FOR IRAQ, U.S. CENSUS BUREAU

Mortality	Estimate	Source
Deaths Expected Without War	133,000	Center for International Research (U.S. Census Bureau) estimate
War Losses	Subtract 1 year from projected life expectancy 150,000 to 250,000 9,000 homes 100,000 military deaths Infant mortality rate, 80 per 1,000 in 1991 30,000 to 50,000 military deaths 70,000 to 115,000 military deaths, 2,500 to 3,000 civilians (air war only)	United Nations *Cable News Network* *Washington Post* Defense Intelligence Agency International Study Team Trevor DuPuy, Military Analyst *Newsweek,* 1992
Postwar Losses	20,000 to 30,000 civilians 100,000 to 120,000 civilians (civil unrest and war-related ailments combined) 10,000 to 20,000 in South, 10,000 to 20,000 in North, from civil violence 243,000 civilians	International Study Team *Newsweek,* 1992 Thomas McNaugher, Brookings Institute *Newsweek,* 1992 (Wilkinson)

Migration	Estimate	Source
Total	Net migration = 0	United Nations
Iraqis	150,000 to 180,000 non-Kurd Iraqis fled to Jordan 10,000 (approx.) refugees still in Turkey; 120,000 (approx.) refugees still in Iran; 35,000 (approx.) refugees in Saudi Arabia (will probably never return to Iraq)	U.S. Department of State (Iraq desk) U.S. Department of State (Refugee desk)
Foreign Population	600,000 (approx.) Egyptians fled Iraq and Kuwait combined (about half from Iraq); 16,000 (approx.) Vietnamese fled; 1,000,000 (approx.) total fled Iraq and Kuwait combined (about half from Iraq) Number of return migrants and country of origin (returning to): Egypt, 250,000; Jordan, 50,000; Lebanon, 50,000; Syria, 70,000; Turkey, 60,000; Soviet Union, 10,000; Iran, 20,000; India, 150,000; Pakistan, 100,000; Bangladesh, 100,000; China, 10,000;Philippines, 90,000; Vietnam, 17,000; Sri Lanka, 90,000.; total, 1,067,000. 1 million total from Iraq and Kuwait	U.S. Department of State (Refugee desk) U.S. Department of State, 1991, "Middle East: Foreign Workers Face Uncertain Future," Geographic Notes, No. 14 (October) U.S. Department of State, 1991, "Crisis of Refugees and Displaced Persons of Iraq," *Dispatch,* Vol. 2, No. 16 (April)

RESULTS

Iraq's population in July 1990 was estimated to be 18.4 million persons. Without taking into account effects of the Gulf War, the population was expected to grow to 19.1 million by July 1991. Assuming 1990 mortality conditions, a male infant born in Iraq could have expected to live 65 years and a female infant could expect to live 67 years. For every one thousand infants born in Iraq in 1990, approximately 67 would not have lived to see their first birthday.

The estimated population decreased from 18.4 million at midyear 1990 to 17.9 million by midyear 1991. Two factors decreased the population of Iraq—people fled from Iraq and people died. After Iraq invaded Kuwait in August 1990, over one million non-Iraqis who had been living in Iraq returned to their countries of origin (U.S. Department of State, 1991). In 1991, approximately one million Kurds temporarily left Iraq.

Estimated deaths in 1991 for Iraq were determined using several assumptions regarding the number and age/sex structure of specific components of war-related deaths, and combining these deaths with those "expected" in the absence of war. There were four components of war-related mortality. These were military deaths during the war, civilian deaths during the war, military deaths in the postwar period, and civilian deaths during the postwar period. Considering the mortality ranges cited in [Table 6-2], the following assumptions were made for each component. Military fatalities during the Gulf War were assumed to amount to approximately 40,000, while civilian casualties during the war were assumed to total 5,000. The postwar period was assumed to account for another 100,000 civilian deaths. These civilian deaths were further divided into two subcomponents, those due to the violence surrounding the postwar uprisings and those due to health effects. This additional breakdown was required since the civilian deaths of each subcomponent would be expected to have markedly different age and sex patterns.

Considering the available data and the reported infant mortality rate from the International Study Team, the breakdown of the assumed 100,000 postwar civilian deaths was 30,000 due to postwar violence and 70,000 due to health conditions following the war. These assumptions imply that the war had large and detrimental effects on the health of the Iraqi population. The sum of deaths from each of these components [100,000 postwar civilian deaths plus 40,000 military fatalities, plus 5,000 civilian casualties of the war] totals to an estimate of 145,000 "excess" deaths—deaths that occurred either directly or indirectly from the Gulf War. In addition to these "excess" deaths, there are "expected" deaths that would have naturally occurred in the absence of the war. Of the total 1991 deaths, 133,180 were "expected." Combining the 133,000 "expected" deaths with the 145,000 "excess" deaths results in a total estimated deaths for 1991 in Iraq of 278,000.

EMIGRATION

In addition to mortality, a high level of international emigration had a considerable impact on the population of Iraq. There are two aspects of migration to consider—movement of Iraqis and movement of foreign workers and their families who were living in Iraq prior to the Gulf crisis. As for mortality, considering the available data [see Table 6-2], assumptions were made regarding each aspect of migration. For Iraqis, net emigration in 1991 was assumed to be 125,000 persons. This total includes Iraqis migrating to Turkey, Iran, and Saudi Arabia. Foreign workers and their families were assumed to have emigrated after August 1990 and prior to the start of 1991. The level of foreign workers' net emigration (1,067,000 persons) as reported by the U.S. Department of State (1991) was accepted as Iraq's 1990 level of net emigration.

TABLE 6-3. PROJECTIONS OF THE POPULATION OF IRAQ GIVEN DIFFERENT SCENARIOS, U.S. CENSUS BUREAU

No War Effects Taken Into Account

Year	Mid-Year Population Total	Life Expectancy			Infant Mortality Rate
		Total	Male	Female	
1987	16,543,189	62.0	58.3	66.0	72.3
1990	18,425,268	66.5	65.5	67.6	67.4
1991	19,149,559	67.0	65.9	68.0	65.7
1992	19,896,924	67.4	66.3	68.5	64.0
1993	20,667,391	67.8	66.7	69.0	62.3
1994	21,460,466	68.3	67.1	69.5	60.7
1995	22,275,670	68.7	67.5	70.0	59.0

All War Effects Taken Into Account

Year	Mid-Year Population Total	Life Expectancy			Infant Mortality Rate
		Total	Male	Female	
1987	16,543,189	62.0	58.3	66.0	72.3
1990	18,425,268	66.5	65.5	67.6	67.4
1991	17,918,079	52.7	47.2	58.4	80.6
1992	18,463,095	63.8	63.2	64.4	79.1
1993	19,161,956	65.0	64.2	65.8	71.8
1994	19,889,666	65.7	64.9	66.7	67.1
1995	20,643,769	66.5	65.5	67.6	62.4

Note: The low levels of life expectancies at birth for 1991 when all war effects are taken into account may be explained as follows. These levels, while extremely low, are temporary, as evident by the large increase in life expectancy from 1991 to 1992. Life expectancy at birth, when calculated for a single year, is greatly influenced by unusual events. The levels shown above for 1991 would only be obtained if the cohort born in 1991 experienced the estimated 1991 mortality levels at each age throughout their lifetime. Since a war, or any other catastrophic mortality event, is a singular experience, the effect on life expectancy is temporary. For this reason, life expectancy at birth levels based on data for a single year must be interpreted with caution.
Source: U.S. Bureau of the Census, Center for International Research, unpublished worktables.

Not only did the war and its aftermath affect the 1991 population in Iraq, but it will affect the size and age-sex distribution of Iraq's population far into the future. People who left Iraq will not have their progeny in Iraq, nor will those who died before completing their childbearing years. Without war effects, Iraq's population in the year 1995 was projected to be 22.3 million. Once the war is accounted for, the projected population is 20.6 million, a difference of nearly two million persons. These effects are expected to continue to have future ramifications.

In summary, the effects of the war on Iraq's population were considerable. The population decreased in size because of mass out-migration and a large number of deaths. The Gulf War crisis will continue to show demographic effects far into the future.[1]

NOTES:
1. Demographer Arjun Adlakha currently compiles Iraqi statistics at the U.S. Census Bureau Center for International Research. He says that since the Hobbs Report there has not been any change in the projections of Iraqi mortality rates, but that estimates might change should new data become available. Interview with Arjun Adlakha, September 10, 1993.

Child Mortality, Nutrition and Health Care

International Study Team

This article is excerpted from The Iraq Infant and Child Mortality and Nutrition Survey, *published in April 1992 by the International Study Team (IST), sometimes known as the Harvard Group. The data is a re-evaluation of preliminary analysis presented in October 1991 by the IST in* Health and Welfare in Iraq After the Gulf Crisis: An In-Depth Assessment. *A child mortality survey carried out between August 23 and September 5, 1991 included approximately 9,000 Iraqi households. A public health team independent of Iraqi officials, comprised of international supervisors and Jordanian surveyors, was involved in the design, collection, and analysis of the data. The data were edited, input, and analyzed at the Harvard School of Public Health.*

The intent of the IST study was to provide a description of the effects of the Gulf War on the public health situation in Iraq, and specifically on children under five. A retrospective mortality survey interviewed women between the ages of 15-49 who had given birth to a living infant since January 1985. An estimated 16,076 live births and 768 deaths were included in the mortality analysis. The risk of death for the period 1985-1990 was compared to that in the post-conflict period. Similar studies were done for infants aged 1-11 months and 12-59 months.

Another survey assessed the nutritional status of 2,676 children between the ages of 3 and 59 months, by comparing their weight-height-age profiles with the National Center for Health Statistic's average values for height-for-age, weight-for-age and weight-for-height.

Members of the team included Drs. Alberto Ascherio, Robert Chase, Tim Cote, Godelieve Dehaes, Jilali Laaouej; and Saleh Al Qaderi, M.B.B.S., Saher Shuqaidef, M.B.B.S., Dr.P.H., Mary Catherine Smith, M.Sc., and Sarah Zaidi, M.Sc. For more information, see the New England Journal of Medicine, *September 24, 1992.*

BACKGROUND

Iraq, with its oil revenues, had launched a rapid industrialization program during the 1960s. Between 1960 and 1988, the urban population had grown from 43 to 73 percent of the total.[1]

The per capita gross national product had more than doubled between 1975 and 1987.[2] Investments had been made in capital-intensive heavy industries as well as in public services, that involved improvements in the health care infrastructure and other basic needs, such as clean water, adequate food, education, etc. The proportion of the population with access to clean water had doubled and free primary health care reached 93 percent of the population in 1988.[3] According to the UNICEF (1990) infant and child mortality survey, infant mortality was estimated to have been one of the lowest in the region, 42 per 1,000 in 1987.[4] Thus, before the Gulf conflict, most of the Iraqi population was accustomed to and dependent upon a fairly "developed" lifestyle with electricity for water purification and distribution, sewage treatment, and a health care system with extensive coverage.

In addition to investments made in health care, a strong public-sector food marketing system was set in place that subsidized consumer prices for staple items. Prior to the conflict, food imports comprised approximately 70 percent of the total caloric needs of the population. The war disrupted both its private and public passage of foodstuffs.[5]

ECONOMIC SANCTIONS

A series of resolutions that limited Iraq's access to global markets was passed by the UN Security Council after the invasion of Kuwait. The first of such measures implementing an embargo was Resolution 661 (UN Security Council, August 6, 1990), which excluded from the sanctions list items that were intended strictly for medical purposes and, in the case of humanitarian crisis, foodstuffs. Resolution 666 (UN Security Council, September 13, 1990) which was passed a few weeks later, deemed that the Security Council, acting on behalf of the Sanctions Committee, would determine whether humanitarian circumstances had arisen in Iraq such that assistance could be provided. From August until March, the Sanctions Committee had made no decision recognizing the existence of a humanitarian crisis.

During and just after the conflict, humanitarian supplies and assistance were limited, or almost unavailable, because of bombings and sanctions. Moreover, climatic conditions were inhospitable (i.e. extremely cold in the North) and living conditions were inadequate. Coalition bombings had reduced electric power to three percent of prewar capacity, which affected water and sewage treatment plants. The results were evident throughout the country in the raw sewage that flowed into houses, streets, and rivers.[6] It was not until the public had seen the flashing television images of the Kurds, hungry and freezing in the mountains near the borders of Turkey and Iran, that humanitarian assistance was launched on a large scale without violating economic sanctions. Even so, during this time, the delivery of medical supplies was limited.

In April 1991, when a humanitarian crisis had been identified, the Security Council passed Resolution 687 that allowed for a review, every 60 days, of sanctions on imports with respect to policies and practices of the Iraqi government. [Resolution 687 is quoted in Appendix Three.]

POSTWAR MORTALITY

The probabilities of dying in the first year or first five years of life were 32.5 and 43.2 per thousand live births, respectively, before January 1991, and rose to 92.7 and 128.5 per 1,000 live births after the conflict. When extrapolated to the population of Iraq, these increases translate into 46,897 excess deaths for children under five years of age during the first eight months of 1991.

The data were further stratified by maternal age, sex of child, maternal education, residence and region. There were no differences in mortality by maternal age or sex of child, thus these estimates are not included in the report. But there were differences in mortality by maternal education and region.

From January to August 1991, both infants and children experienced a rise in mortality rate, with the exception of the 0–1 month group, in the central region of the country compared with before the conflict. Stratifying by maternal education for the 0–1 month age group, the relative risk of mortality increases most for children of mothers with primary or secondary plus educational levels after the conflict. In the age group 1–11 months, relative risk of death is most notable for children of illiterate mothers, but mortality rates also increased for children of mothers with either primary or secondary plus education levels. For the 12–59 months age group, relative risk is highest for children of mothers with primary education.

Stratifying by residence, the effects of conflict on mortality are greatest for the displaced children for all age group categories. The relative risk of mortality by region was greatest for infants, both 0–1 month and 1–11 months, in northern regions of Iraq. The next highest relative risk is for infants residing in the South. For children 12–59 months of age, the relative risk of mortality was highest for southern governorates.

Information on the cause of death was available for 583 (75.9 percent of 768) children. The age-adjusted mortality rate from diarrhea rose from 2.1 per 1,000 person-years before the onset of the conflict (reference period 1988–1990) to 11.9 per 1,000 person-years after the onset of conflict (January to August 1991). The age-adjusted mortality rate from injuries rose from 0.55 per 1,000 person-years before the onset of the war to 2.25 per 1,000 after the onset of the war. Before the conflict 20.7 percent of deaths were due to diarrhea and 8.8 percent were due to injuries; comparable proportions after the onset of conflict were 38.0 percent and 7.2 percent.

EFFECTS OF BOMBINGS, CIVILIAN UPRISINGS AND MASS EXODUS

Of singular interest is the marked mortality increase for infants (under one year of age) in northern Iraq, especially for the displaced populations.

In the North, the effect of conflict, war and civilian uprisings that led to the mass exodus of Kurds to Iran and Turkey, in combination with lack of food and cold climatic conditions, were all important contributions to increased mortality. Interviewers were encouraged to collect qualitative data which included additional comments provided by mothers. Such dialogue indicated that in the North many infants died from cold (i.e., hypothermia) and hunger (malnutrition). This observation is consistent with the highest prevalence of malnutrition noted in the North among displaced children.

In southern Iraq, relative risk of mortality was highest for children 12–59 months of age. In the South, it is most likely that epidemics of disease that occurred in conjunction with the destruction of the infrastructure due to bombing, especially water and sewage, and the lack of basic medical supplies contributed to the observed increases in child mortality. In the central part of Iraq, mortality rates also doubled, with the exception of the 0–1 month age group. Age-specific mortality rates also increased in Baghdad, but the rise was not so dramatic as in either northern or southern regions of the country. It seems likely that acute shortages of food (especially infant formula), essential medicines, lack of water and poor sanitation due to the breakdown of the electrical infrastructure were major contributors to the observed rise in mortality.

CONCLUSION: MORTALITY

This survey conducted after the Gulf conflict showed a dramatic increase in the under-five mortality rate. The neonatal mortality rate approximately doubled after the conflict, and for both 1–11 month and 12–59 month age groups, mortality rates quadrupled and tripled, respectively, after the conflict compared with before the conflict (see Table 6-4).

MALNUTRITION

Another goal of the study was to assess the nutritional status of children under the age of five. Unfortunately, no national baseline data on nutritional status exist for Iraq prior to the war; therefore, drawing conclusions regarding the effect of the conflict is difficult. In the present sample, the prevalence of wasting [deficient weight-for-height] by age that was observed is similar to that seen in several developing countries where chronic malnutrition and infectious diseases, rather than acute famine, determine the nutritional status of children. A nutrition study limited to infants 0–11 months old conducted by Mahmood and Feachem (1987) in Basra during 1983 and 1984 provides a possible baseline.[7]

Severe malnutrition was noted among children under five: stunting [deficient height-for-age] (7.3 percent), underweight [deficient weight-for-age] (2.3 percent) and wasting (0.4 percent). Stunting was highest among children 18–23 months of age (38.5 percent) and wasting (6.1 percent) among children 12–17 months of age.

Children 18–23 months of age were 3.3 times more likely to be stunted than children 3–17 months, and two times more likely to be stunted than children 24–59 months of age. The 12–17-month age group appears to be at highest risk of being underweight. Children 12–23 months of age were 2.4 times more likely to be underweight than children 3–11 months, and 1.6 times more likely than children 24–59 months. The highest risk for wasting was seen among the 12–17-month age group.

The prevalence of stunting increased as the level of education of the mother decreased. A similar pattern was noted for underweight and for wasting children. With respect to urban/rural differences, children living in rural areas were 1.3 times more likely to be stunted than urban children.

However, there were no urban/rural differences for the prevalence of underweight and wasting. Children in the North that were part of the displaced population were most likely to be at an increased risk for stunting, wasting, and underweight, compared with children in urban areas. Children of displaced residence were 2.4 times more likely to be stunted, 3.9 times more likely to be underweight,

and 1.9 times more likely to be wasted than children in urban areas. An increasing prevalence of stunting was noted for the following regions: Baghdad, Central Iraq, South, and North (excluding areas in the North temporarily populated with displaced people). There is a similar trend for underweight. However, for wasting no significant trend was observed.

There were no statistically significant differences between males and females for stunting, underweight, and wasting. The presence of diarrhea at the time of the survey (defined as three loose stools within 24 hours during the past 48 hours) was associated with stunting, underweight, and wasting.

POSTWAR HUMANITARIAN CRISIS

Since the inception of economic sanctions, the food price index has increased 1,500 to 2,000 percent despite a constancy in wages (Dreze and Ghazdar, 1991). Such a dramatic decline in purchasing power has made food

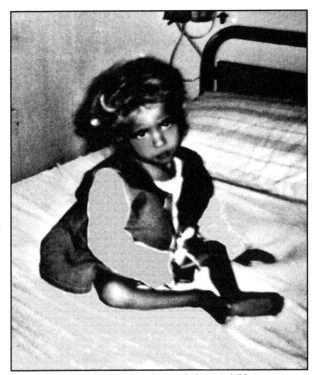

Malnourished and wounded Iraqi child.
© Louise Cainkar and Folklens.

scarcity a substantial problem, and, unless reversed, may gradually lead to an acute food shortage.

War has never been good for health. The greater than three-fold increase in infant and childhood mortality is a result that dramatically contradicts the widely publicized view that use of modern weapons and selection of strategic targets have limited damage inflicted on the civilian population. What is clear from our analysis is that the casualties of war go far beyond those immediately intended by warfare. In this case, the added effect of sanctions prevents any type of recovery or reversal of the public health situation faced by children under five years of age. Information collected by several other members of the International Study Team (1991) suggests that the destruction of the electrical power supply, with subsequent disruption of water and sewage systems, the paralysis of health services, and food scarcity may have contributed to the increased risk of death for children. In the North and the South the situation was further exacerbated by the civilian uprisings and subsequent fleeing of the Iraqi population (about 2 million persons), Kurds and Shiites, into the mountains and the marshes.

RECOMMENDATION: UN HUMANITARIAN RELIEF

In light of the results presented in this report, the tragedy of a case such as Iraq is our limited understanding of the complex and ever-changing definitions of conflict. We need to re-evaluate current definitions of jurisdiction concerning sovereignty and individual human rights. Perhaps the greatest tragedy is that political factors have in this case limited the response of the international community, which in other circumstances might have been substantial when faced with such evidence regarding the public health situation of children. We recommend that a humanitarian solution for Iraqi children should be the responsibility of the international community and the Iraqi government, under the auspices of the United Nations.

NOTES:
1. UNICEF, *State of the World's Children,* 1991.
2. UNDP and World Bank, *Human Development Report,* 1990.
3. UNICEF, *State of the World's Children,* 1991.
4. UNICEF, *State of the World's Children,* 1991.
5. Jean Drèze and Haris Gazdar, *Hunger and Poverty in Iraq,* Report, (sponsored by World Institute for Development Economics Research and London School of Economics), London, September 1991.
6. International Study Team, *Health and Welfare in Iraq After the Gulf Crisis; An In-Depth Assessment,* Report, Cambridge, Massachusetts, October 1991.
7. D. Mahmood and R. Feachem, *Feeding and Nutritional Status Among Infants in Basrah City, Iraq; A Cross-Sectional Study,* 1987.

Psychological Impacts of the War on Iraqi Children

International Study Team

A study of the psychological impacts of the war on Iraqi children was another task for the International Study Team on its visit to Iraq, August 23 to September 4, 1991. Atle Dyregrov, Ph.D. is the director of the Center for Crisis Psychology in Bergen, Norway. Magne Raundalen is the Center's director of research. Assisted by Arabic-speaking, non-Iraqi psychology students, they conducted a total of 341 in-house interviews. The authors note that their study reveals "a level of psychological stress that is the highest the authors of this report have seen in 10 years of conflict-related research."

INTRODUCTION

Children experiencing conflict at close range are invariably forced to endure conditions of severe hardship and stress, leading to long-term psychological manifestations. Despite the serious impact of conflict stress, there are few examples where researchers have sought to investigate and quantify such exposure and its subsequent effect on child behavior. Recent events in the Gulf have generated what may well be an unprecedented level of anxiety and post-conflict stress among children residing throughout the Middle East.

METHODOLOGY

From August 23 to September 4, 1991, a total of 214 Iraqi children of primary school age were interviewed. The caregivers of an additional 127 children were questioned to ascertain the children's post-conflict behavior.

One hundred seven children were sampled from each of two locations within Iraq:

1) Al Ameriyah neighborhood, Baghdad (site of the shelter bombing); and

2) City of Basra.

Finally, more intensive child and caregiver interviews were conducted on an ad hoc basis, to elicit in-depth information regarding the child's experience of conflict. This procedure includes the use of picture drawing, play and story writing.

ASSIMILATING THE SIGHTS, SOUNDS AND SMELLS OF WARFARE

The children interviewed strive to frame and to understand what they saw: planes bombing, houses collapsing, fires burning, soldiers fighting, mutilated and crushed bodies, and burned-out trucks. The children fight to forget what they heard: people screaming, desperate voices, planes, and explosions.

The children are haunted by the smell of gunfire, fuel from planes, fires, and burned flesh. Many children are still struggling with the memories of what they touched: remains of planes, blood, dead bodies, and wounded relatives.

And every night these children go to bed with memories of the terrible sounds, shaking ground, and the fear of the whole family being buried in the ruins of the house.

TABLE 6-4. EXPOSURE TO THE PHYSICAL HAZARDS OF CONFLICT

Question Asked of Event	% Answering "Yes"	Question Asked of Event	% Answering "Yes"
Did the child experience:		**Has the child lost close family members during the war?**	
shelling	79.7%		
air raids	79.5%	mother	8.7%
shooting at close distance	61.9%	father	2.5%
own home destroyed	25.6%	others	33.6%
being shot at	13.0%	**Has the child's behavior changed**	
being wounded	13.5%	**after the war?**	82.4%
Due to war, was the child separated from:		more anxious and fearful	81.5%
the mother or primary female caregiver	5.0%	more depressed and sad	76.6%
the father or primary male caregiver	39.5%	more angry and irritable	79.8%
both mother/father or caregivers	2.5%		

THE WAR EVENT SURVEY: TRAUMA, SEPARATION AND LOSS

The survey [asked of 214 children and caregivers of 127 children, see "Methodology"] focuses on the child's actual exposure to the physical hazards of conflict (bombing, shelling, shooting) as well as temporary and permanent separation from family members.

It is important to note that these behavioral disturbances remain more than six months following the cease-fire declaration. This component of the study clearly shows a highly exposed child population in which probably none of the children were unaffected by the Gulf crisis.

THINKING AND BEHAVIOR CHANGES

The Impact of Event Scale (IES) is currently the most reliable and valid instrument for assessing the impact of traumatic events on individuals. It has been used to measure the impact of various disasters throughout the world and is considered a sensitive instrument, as well as an effective means of assessing the psychological consequences of disaster. Unfortunately, only a few studies consisting of small samples of traumatized children have been published. The scale was administered to 107 children in the Al Ameriyah neighborhood of Baghdad, site of the bombing of an air-raid shelter, and a further 107 children in the city of Basra. In addition to using the Impact of Event Scale, the authors also used questions from an inventory compiled by the "Bergen-Columbia" Group.

One of the most worrisome features of the results is the high proportion of interviewed children who were experiencing sadness and worry. Seventy-five percent of the children feel sad and

Iraqi child's drawing of the Coalition bombing. Source: International Study Team.

unhappy, worry for the survival of the family, and need the company of an older person to feel safe. Nearly four out of five children interviewed expressed fear of losing their family through death or separation.

During the interviews, the theme of survival guilt was also brought up. Although this question was not part of the systematic study, a vast majority of those children asked felt the burden of depression and guilt because they had survived and their friends had not.

Below is a sample of questions and responses.

TABLE 6-5. SAMPLE QUESTIONS AND RESPONSES
(ASKED OF 107 CHILDREN IN AL AMERIYAH AND 107 CHILDREN IN CITY OF BASRA)

Question Asked	Percent Answering "Yes"
Do you think about the event when you don't mean to?	92.1%
Do you avoid getting upset when you think about the event or are reminded of it?	76.4%
Do you have sleep problems (i.e., problems staying or falling asleep) because of pictures and/or thoughts about the event coming into your mind?	73.9%
Do you have waves of strong feelings about the event?	88.8%
Does any reminder bring back feelings about the event?	91.4%
Are your feelings about the event sort of numb?	66.1%
Do you often think about the events now?	86.7%
Since the event happened, do you enjoy playing with friends, doing sports, or enjoy participating in other fun activities less than before?	74.7%
Since the event happened, do you jump at loud noises or at unexpected things?	75.5%
Do you feel sad or unhappy?	76.3%
Are you afraid of losing your family (through death or separation)?	78.4%
Do you feel helpless?	36.3%
Do you get irritable easily?	63.8%
Is it hard for you to concentrate on your schoolwork?	52.1%
Since the event happened, is it more difficult for you to pay attention or concentrate on things than before?	62.5%
Since the event happened, does the child seem worried that she/he might not live to become an adult? (asked of parents/caregivers)	62.0%

THE "OFFICIAL" VERSION

When children were asked about the reasons behind the conflict, they generally began by stating that it was an attack from the U.S.A., personified by the name Bush. Even six- and seven-year-old children talk about Bush. When asked, some of the younger children would recount how Bush was sitting in a plane from which he bombed Iraq. Older children complete the anti-Bush version by declaring victory for Iraq in the future, with some children also talking about revenge.

THE "SECRET" VERSION

Some interviewed children recounted a version of the following story:

"Saddam Hussein took Kuwait and that was wrong and then Bush helped Kuwait and said it was because it was a very little country, but that was wrong because he was interested in controlling the oil and then he took Kuwait back and attacked Iraq and that was wrong also, but this is a secret."

Although this part of the study was not systematically chosen, detailed discussions with the interviewed children generally arrived at the above description of events.

THE VIEW ON SANCTIONS

The authors of this report clearly got the feeling that it is the sanctions much more than the war itself that create aggression, feelings of revenge, and negative anti-American attitudes in the population. This must be carefully interpreted.

CONCLUSION

The results of the various studies reported above reveal that the majority of Iraqi children interviewed suffer from:

1) emotional reactions—depression, sadness, anxiety and fear; 2) cognitive reactions—sleep and concentration problems; and 3) prospective reactions—worries about the future.

The most significant impression from the interviews of the children, in both Baghdad and Basra, was their lack of "life," their deep depression, sad appearance, tiredness, and lack of joy. Iraqi children are affected in their cognitive functions by fatigue, lack of energy, concentration problems, and confusion about what happened and why. They are deeply disturbed in their prospective thinking and many seriously consider it likely that they will not survive to adulthood.

The most serious conclusion to be drawn from this material is that what happened to these children—the severe psychological trauma—may cause them serious problems for years to come. For some children, these problems may endure for their entire lifetime.

Recent studies from Finland investigating the after-effects of the "Winter War" of 1939 reveal serious effects even 50 years following the event itself. The children studied in Iraq all have signs of being seriously disturbed by their traumatic experience and by the current difficult situation. They are affected in their emotional life by grief, sadness and desperate fear.

The current study also reveals the widely observed fact that adults constantly underestimate what their children have, in fact, experienced, and how children suffer psychologically from such experiences.

[A soon-to-be-published follow-up study by Magne Raundalen and Atle Dyregov notes that, for a significant proportion of the children they studied in 1991, trauma has since increased. Raundalen and Dyregov have just established a child psychology support unit in Baghdad, the first of its kind in Iraq, and are planning three more in other regions of Iraq. Felicity Arbuthnot, "Study Finds 'Most Traumatized Child Population' in Iraq," *Peace Works*, September 1993.]

The Experience of Children In Kuwait: Occupation, War, and Liberation

James Garbarino

A 1993 report[1] issued by the U.S. State Department to the United Nations details a gruesome catalogue of atrocities committed by Iraqi troops against Kuwaitis, including genital mutilation, removal of 120 newborn children from incubators,[2] eye gouging, acid baths, rape and killing. Iraqi troops killed more than 1,000 Kuwaitis, the report said, including 153 children under 13 years of age.

James Garbarino, Ph.D., is president of the Erikson Institute for Advanced Study in Child De-velopment in Chicago. The following excerpt was reprinted from The Child, Youth, and Family Services Quarterly, *the newsletter of the American Psychological Association, Division 37.*

On February 22, 1991, I received a call from UNICEF asking if I would travel to the Persian Gulf with the Chief of Emergency Operations, Carl Tinstman, as a volunteer consultant. My mis-sion: to conduct an assessment of the psychological impact of the occupation and war on chil-dren in Kuwait. Three days later, we were on our way, and on March 1, 1991, we arrived in Kuwait City in the company of a United States army convoy.

Over the next few days, I was able to conduct a preliminary assessment of children resident in Kuwait City during the period of Iraqi occupation (August 1990 to February 1991) and the war (January 16 to March 1, 1991), and on that basis to recommend measures designed to provide "psychological first aid."

During the period of March 1–4, 1991, in the wake of the liberation of Kuwait City, I con-ducted interviews with 45 children–25 boys and 20 girls ranging in age from 5 to 13—and in many cases their parents or other adult relatives. These children were identified in two hospitals visited by the UNICEF team, in two neighborhoods of the city, and in the beach area where many thousands of families came to celebrate the end of the Iraqi occupation. Thus, while not sys-tematically random, this "convenience sample" may be taken to be at least somewhat represen-tative of the child population that experienced the occupation and war.

There are many adults in Kuwait who speak English, so I was able to conduct the interviews with children in English, using adult interpreters (who in many instances were parents). Given the short period of time available, the ad hoc procedures used, and the difficult conditions in Kuwait City at the time (no electricity or running water, uncertain civil authority, unexploded grenades, rock-ets, and ammunition strewn around the city, etc.), these interviews were of necessity brief (per-haps 10–15 minutes) and informal (sometimes one-on-one, sometimes in small groups).

The interviews focused on the following areas:

1) Did the child directly experience a traumatic event such as seeing an execution, witness-ing a kidnapping, discovering a victim's body, or being present at a war-related incident such as a bombing?

2) Did the child suffer loss of a family member through death or disappearance?

3) Was there evidence of psychological effects, e.g., repetitive dreams, a clear pattern of fear related to the occupation/war, a clear change in behavior or personality, etc.?

4) Had the child changed his or her aspirations for the future? ("What do you want to be when you grow up?")

In several cases, I asked children to draw pictures of the worst things they had seen, and in about half the cases, asked parents about the child's reactions (e.g., changes in behavior, sleep disturbances, fearfulness, etc.). These interviews, the pictures children drew, and the observations of parents produced some disturbing conclusions.

- A majority of children (62 percent) reported direct experience with a traumatic event. This is probably an underestimate. Many children had seen bodies either hanging from lampposts or "dumped" in their neighborhood. Often this was someone known to the child. Because the Iraqi forces fled the city before Coalition forces entered, most children were spared from directly witnessing military combat. Some children did witness deaths and injuries related to munitions. Two boys had seen a cousin killed while playing with a grenade, and a little girl was in a house that was bombed.

- Many children (at least 20 percent of the sample) experienced loss of a close relative due to death or kidnapping—with death still a possibility at the time of the interview. In some cases, children witnessed the kidnapping (e.g., a 12-year-old boy who was in a car with his father when Iraqi soldiers stopped them and removed the father and three other men in the car, or a seven-year-old girl who was at home when Iraqis came to take her father away). Kuwaiti officials claim some 33,000 people were killed or kidnapped by the Iraqis. Weeks later, few of these individuals were accounted for.

- More than half of the children described what appeared to be psychological effects of trauma. Prominent among these were repetitive dreams related to a traumatic event or generalized fear of the Iraqis. One 10-year-old girl who had seen the body of an executed neighbor dumped in their alley said she had the same dream at least once a week in which he is sitting on her head asking why she didn't cover him up. Among younger children (six and under), fear of going outside, generalized fear of people in uniforms, uncontrollable crying, and sleep disturbances were common. Parents commonly reported differences in their children as a result of the occupation: "She became so quiet and stopped eating," or "He cries a lot now," or "He wakes up at night talking in his sleep."

- Nearly all of the boys interviewed indicated that they wanted to become soldiers when they grow up. In most cases, this was a change from a year ago, when they aspired to civilian occupations. Most girls wish to become doctors, teachers, or nurses—not a dramatic change from a year ago, but where there was a change, it was from "mother" or "clerk" to "teacher" or "doctor." These occupational aspirations presumably reflect the salience of careers that indicate the strength—social and personal—needed to protect family and country in the future.

I was able to make some additional observations:

- Girls were more sheltered during the occupation (kept inside all of the time) and thus were less likely to witness traumatic events—50 percent of girls did so versus 72 percent of boys.
- Several children had stories to tell about collaborators (particularly Palestinians) and the anger they felt toward them. This will be one of the postwar issues for children—reconciling Kuwaitis and non-Kuwaitis.
- The dramatic and positive conclusions of the occupation/war may help children, coupled with the joyful public celebrations that followed (daily parades involving long convoys containing many thousands of celebrating Kuwaitis). All this gives great positive social meaning and closure to the events of the occupation/war, even while it became a source of physical danger, as numerous people in the city were injured or killed accidentally from bullets being fired in celebration.

However, some children expressed concern that the Iraqis will return. What is more, the occupation/war has left a very large pool of children made vulnerable to future harm. If there is a breakdown in civil order in Kuwait with political violence, these children would be at increased risk (not "immune," as one might assume naively).

The children of Kuwait need an ongoing opportunity to "process" their traumatic experiences. It will be tempting for adults to close off this processing: "It's over. Let's put it behind us. We survived, so now let's go on with our lives." Such an approach would work against the best interests of Kuwait's children. It would risk compounding the problems of traumatized children by "driving them underground" through a process of denial.

All that the children have experienced means that they will need a program of "psychological first aid." This means opening the schools as soon as possible. It means helping teachers and parents learn how to help children express and clarify their thoughts and feelings. It means being patient over the coming months and years as kids try to work through the images that will return to them—sometimes as daydreams, sometimes as nightmares. We have seen all of this before in our visits in war zones around the world.[3]

NOTES:

1. Sid Balman, Jr., "U.S. Gives UN Iraqi War Crimes Investigation," *United Press International,* March 19, 1993.
2. This is controversial. In 1991, an Amnesty International team found no reliable evidence that Iraqi forces had removed babies from incubators. Amnesty International U.S.A., "Kuwait: Amnesty International Calls on Emir To Intervene Over Continuing Torture and Killings," Press Release, April 18, 1991.
3. Jasem M. Haija, a Kuwaiti psychologist, estimates that as many as 80 percent of Kuwait's 700,000-strong population suffer forms of post-trauma stress syndrome traceable to the seven months of Iraqi occupation. Mark Fineman, "Violence Flares in Kuwait," *Oakland Tribune,* August 10, 1992, reprinted from *Los Angeles Times.*

Palestinian Youth in Kuwait

Mohamad Marzoued

*Many hundreds of people in the region were arrested and tortured because of alleged opposition to
the Gulf War. Victims included Yemenis in Saudi Arabia and Egypt, and Palestinians, Yemenis and
Sudanese in Kuwait. See Amnesty International reports* Update on Amnesty International Human
Rights Concerns in Countries Involved in the Gulf Conflict, *February 18, 1991,* Egypt: Arrests of
Opponents of the Gulf War, *February 19, 1991, and* Saudi Arabia: Torture, Detention and Arbi-
trary Arrests, *September 9, 1990.*

*Because the Palestine Liberation Organization supported Iraq against the U.S.-led Coalition, between
250,000 and 500,000 Palestinian workers and their families were expelled from Kuwait in the wake of
the war, and many were killed and tortured. Here we excerpt from an account by Mohamad Marzoued,
a Palestinian diplomat in Kuwait, as told to the Reverend Bassam Abdallah, an Evangelical Lutheran
Church pastor from Hammond, Indiana. Reprinted from* Children at Risk in the Middle East, *published by Division for Church in Society, Evangelical Lutheran Church in America, in 1992.*

In the summer of 1991, Kuwaiti officials started detaining Palestinian children and teens between
the ages of 10 and 17. The young are being arrested and tortured by the government of Kuwait. They
are forced to confess that their fathers and older brothers collaborated with the Iraqi invaders.
Many a father and older brother have been arrested as a result of these confessions.

Most of these children are taken to a prison such as the Sixth Circle (Al Daiery Al Sades), which
is a detention facility for the National Security Intelligence Department. The prison is located in
the desert. The building has no roof on it. It looks more like animal stalls. In the region of Farrouniah,
building 18 of the Addon Hospital has become another children's detention center.

A boy who suffered great abdominal pains in the Sixth Circle prison was taken to building 18
of the Addan Hospital. After his appendix ruptured, he was finally operated on at Al Mubarak
(Blessing) Hospital under strict guard. Following the operation, three men entered his room and
with a sharp blade, wrote on his forehead in English: "Kuwait is free."

In the region of Al Salemeyah, a 16-year-old Palestinian was detained at Maroush Restaurant.
His family found his body in a garbage dump. Autopsy reports showed that the young boy was
tortured, severely molested and raped.

Abu Nasir, a Palestinian returning to Amman from Kuwait, reported the murder of a bride and
groom in the region of Farrouniah. The couple was shot for no apparent reason other than getting married during the period of martial law. A Kuwaiti confessed to the crime. He stated that he
had entered the home of the Palestinians, whereupon he shot the bride three times in her neck
and the groom twice in the head, killing them both. He offered no explanation for the murders.

Unheard Voices: Iraqi Women on War and Sanctions

Bela Bhatia, Mary Kawar and Mariam Shahin

Excerpted from Unheard Voices: Iraqi Women on War and Sanctions, *published by Change (U.K.) in* Thinkbook VIII *in March, 1992. This study is a contribution to the International Study Team (IST) report. By Bela Bhatia, Mary Kawar and Mariam Shahin.*

The Gulf War and the ensuing internal conflicts and continued sanctions have had a devastating effect on Iraqi people and society. In the aftermath of war, the people of Iraq are still fighting a daily battle against the hardships imposed upon them by the ongoing sanctions. This impact on the Iraqi people cannot be fully understood until one encounters them inside their homes.

The war and sanctions have a direct impact upon the roles that have been traditionally assigned to women in Iraqi society and culture. Bearing in mind the status of women in Iraq, as in many Third World countries, one expects that women have borne and are still bearing the brunt of recent upheavals in family, economy and society.

The aim of this study was to understand the impact of the war and sanctions as experienced and perceived by Iraqi women. We believe that, aside from shedding light on the experience of war on the Iraqi people as a whole, these testimonies will bring out particularly forcefully how this experience has affected women and their roles and status in society.

By carrying these voices of the Iraqi women to the public at large, we also hope to inform the current debate on economic sanctions.

METHODOLOGY

The research for this study was carried out between August 24 and September 7, 1991. Two of the researchers are Jordanian, thus requiring no interpretation, while the third carried out the first part of her field work with an interpreter from Jordan and the second part with another interpreter from Baghdad. Both interpreters were women of her own choice. During this period we traveled extensively throughout the country without any restriction and were able to carry out our field investigations independently.

The basis of our study was not quantitative analysis but in-depth testimonies, which we thought would usefully illustrate the lives of Iraqi women and their families during and after the war. We conducted 80 in-depth interviews with individual women. Aside from this, group discussions were encouraged. First-hand observation was also an important part of our field work.

The areas explored in the questionnaire were:

1) Economic conditions, food and subsistence; 2) Health and sanitation; 3) Social aspects of family and society; 4) Psychological impact; and 5) Future aspirations.

The composition of the sample was guided by certain categories including geographical area, urban-rural distribution, and economic condition. In order for the sample to be as representative as possible, we selected our respondents in a way that the main areas in the North, center and the South of Iraq were covered. Similarly, it was essential that the urban-rural distribution in the sample should roughly correspond with the national distribution of the Iraqi population.

Accordingly, 27.5 percent of the total sample is from the North, 37.5 percent from the center and 35 percent from the South of Iraq. Out of the 80 households interviewed, almost 69 percent are from urban areas, reflecting the high degree of urbanization in the country. Most of the interviews were conducted with middle- or low-income families on the premise that these families are likely to be most drastically affected by this disaster.

The interviews were conducted with women heads of households. In many instances, the adult male members were found to be absent. However, more often than not, men in the house or the immediate neighborhood would be curious and show interest. Most of the time, having understood the purpose of our visit, they would leave us alone. There were instances, however, when they would stay on and such times were used productively for general discussions.

Similarly, instances of female neighbors coming in during the interview were very common. We saw this as more of an asset than a liability. Although we would get interrupted sometimes, we would continue the thread of conversation with our respondent. On a particular theme, we would elicit the response of our interviewee as well as those of other individuals present. Very productive group discussions were held.

The length of individual interviews ranged from one to three hours. We felt that it was necessary to spend some time building rapport with our respondents, to encourage them to speak without inhibition. We tried to put them at their ease by carefully explaining the purpose of our research.

Besides interviews with women in the households, we had discussions with women doctors in various hospitals, representatives of the government, various aid agencies, and bodies such as the General Federation of Iraqi Women.

PROFILE OF THE RESPONDENTS

The profile of the interviewees involves consideration of the following aspects: age, marital status, education, occupational status, number of children and the household size.

Among the women sampled, 56 percent were below 40 years of age, 28 percent were in the 40–50 age group and 16 percent were above 50 years of age.

Most interviewees were married women. Of the 80 respondents, 60 were married, 14 were widows, two were divorced, three were single and one was abandoned. Age at marriage of most of the respondents was between 15 to 19 years (see Table 6-6).

Almost half of them had not received any formal schooling. Those who had gone to school had discontinued their education after the fourth or fifth grade. This standard of literacy is somewhat lower than for the female population as a whole, possibly reflecting the relatively low incomes of the respondents (see Table 6-7).

Half the respondents had more than five children. This high fertility rate reveals the expectations that the society has of women and the roles assigned to them. Women are seen as child-bearers and expected to have children soon after marriage.

In the past decade, state policy has consciously favored and encouraged higher fertility among women. Contraceptives were declared illegal during the eight-year-long Iran-Iraq War. Moreover, immediately after the Gulf War, this campaign was reinforced. According to one woman gynecologist, this pro-natalist policy was modified in April 1991 and the ban on contraceptives has now been lifted. However, due to the sanctions, these are not available except on the black market.

As far as household size is concerned, almost 40 percent of the sample had 11 members or more. An equal number had six to ten members. Besides children, another important reason for large family size is the extended nature of households. More often than not, women were found to be living with husbands' relatives, mainly parents and brothers, and sometimes their families, too.

Despite large families, most of the homes consisted of only two to three rooms with a courtyard in the center. We observed that the social organization within such households was based on seniority. Accordingly, younger women in the family were found to bear a greater work burden than older women.

The occupational status of the interviewees was predominantly that of housewives (90 percent). In spite of the fact that, during the Iran-Iraq War, female participation in the labor force was encouraged by the state, the proportion of women in the total economically active population was still as low as 11.6 per cent in 1987.

Only nine women in our study were engaged in paid work outside the household. These women worked in informal-sector activities such as selling vegetables, or in service-sector activities such as teaching and the medical professions. They were either equal contributors to the family income or (in five cases) the only income earners in the family. Among the women who identified themselves as housewives, 11 were actually unpaid family workers on the farm or in the shop. Several reasons accounted for the low involvement of women in labor outside the household. First, as most women who did not have any paid employment pointed out, cultural barriers and stereotypes are very strong. Secondly, some women stated that the domestic work burden did not allow them to take up any paid employment (particularly at this time of increased domestic responsibilities). Thirdly, some of those who did consider taking up a job complained of the lack of employment opportunities, particularly in view of their lack of capital and—in some cases—limited skills.

Average household income was very low in real terms. For the total respondents, the average monthly income was as follows: 58 percent had an income below 200 *dinar* (14 of the families were destitute), 30 percent had an income between 200 and 400 *dinar*, four percent in the range of 400 to 600 *dinar* and six percent had income above 600 *dinar*. [At the time of this report, one U.S. dollar could be exchanged for eight *dinar*.]

ECONOMIC CONDITIONS AND FOOD SUBSISTENCE

The war and sanctions have had a disastrous impact on the economy of Iraq. Since August 1990, earnings have not increased for most people, while the prices of basic commodities have increased on an average by a factor of 15 to 20. As a result, the purchasing power of Iraqi households has dramatically declined. The average food basket purchased by a family of six used to cost about 66 *dinar*, at today's prices, the same purchases cost more than 1,000 *dinar*. By contrast, the salaries of unskilled and semi-skilled laborers have remained at their pre-crisis level of 150 to 200 *dinar* per month. Most households in Iraq today earn an income well below what is needed to satisfy elementary needs.

It is not the aim of this report to provide a detailed analysis of the macroeconomic situation; however, on the basis of intensive fieldwork across the country, we can say with some confidence that, aside from some households in the rural areas (e.g., those with good harvests) or from a small minority of others who have made capital out of crisis (e.g., wealthy merchants), no household in Iraq today is spared by this recession.

There have been major changes in the lives of ordinary people of Iraq. Day-to-day existence has become a struggle for survival. The Iraqi people have been plunged into poverty, an affliction with many faces—hunger being one of them. *Hasar,* as the sanctions are known in Arabic, is now a household term, and was perceived by our respondents to be the root cause of their plight. We are witnessing today the pauperization of a people and society.

In the last thirty years, Iraq made rapid progress in development and public services. This was reflected in the standards of living of the people and the fact that very few people were below the poverty line. Those who were in the "destitute" category were provided with a pension of 54 *dinar* which, at today's prices, would be equivalent to 800 *dinar*. Presently, very few people are above this destitution line. These same people, for whom acquiring bread did not pose any significant problem before the war, now regard it as a major preoccupation.

This section examines the plight of the Iraqi people today and during the time of the recent crisis. The section has been divided into the following parts:

1) Employment and Incomes; 2) Financial Crisis; and 3) Food and Subsistence.

EMPLOYMENT AND INCOMES

War and sanctions have led to a sharp deterioration in formal employment. During the war and the internal conflicts that followed, most sources of employment came to a standstill. In the aftermath of the war, the destruction of industries, power and telecommunications systems in the Coalition bombings and shortages of spare parts due to the economic blockade have prevented a speedy recovery from taking place. A visit to a factory shows evidence of this—row upon row of idle machines. The condition of these machines gives an idea of the predicament that their operators must be in. A large percentage of the industrial workers have lost their former jobs.

Employment patterns in our study revealed the army to be the main employer. However, the salaries of most soldiers are very small. Moreover, immediately after the war, large-scale demobilization of soldiers took place. Many of these soldiers joined the ranks of the unemployed and their families suffered a further decline in income. As a woman in the Al Khaliliya quarter in Basra remarked, "My father has just been discharged from the army. There are no jobs available. My husband is also jobless. He was a laborer and also a mechanic. I have three children and do not know how to feed them. I have just registered my son in the school, but I have no money to get school clothes for him."

Government employees fared better only to the extent that they had stable jobs. However, the worth of their salaries (unchanged in money terms) has been greatly reduced by price increases on the order of 1,500 to 2,000 percent since August 1990. Only the salaries of officials in senior positions had increased.

The condition of casual laborers is no better. Even though their daily wages have increased a little in money terms, their work opportunities have been reduced by about 50 percent.

A large number of families in Iraq seem to be surviving on pensions. There are different categories of pensions for retired government employees, war widows, parents of soldiers killed or missing in war, and the destitute.

In the state of near-total collapse of real income from wage employment and pensions, many people have started finding ways and means of being self-employed. Distress sales of assets and indebtedness, besides being necessary to basic food needs, have also been used to raise capital for these alternative sources of employment. As Alia, a 35-year-old woman from Amara, speaking about the plight of families in her neighborhood reported, "Men came back from the army and women had to sell their gold. My neighbor had to sell her gold to get 2,000 *dinar* so that her husband could set up a shop."

In Baghdad, we saw many signs of this type of activity. Small stalls with young people (often educated and unemployed) have been erected in every street, selling various home-cooked food items like vegetable and lentil stews. There were hardly any roadside stalls in the prewar days.

While traveling from Baghdad to nearby towns, one is struck by the number of small children who should have been in school but instead are selling cans of soft drinks and mineral water. It is an irony that they sell bottled water to make a little money to help their families while having to drink unpurified water themselves due to the scarcity of chlorine (essential for purification), which is embargoed as a chemical.

On the way to Basra, we found young Iraqi women, their faces veiled, selling fish. Similarly, in market places in towns all over Iraq, it is very common to find women selling an assortment of items like baked bread, tea, cigarettes and especially vegetables.

HADEEL'S MOTHER

Many of the women who are the sole income earners in their families have great difficulties feeding their children, as the story of Hadeel's mother reveals.

Hadeel's mother is a 45-year-old widow, who has been providing for her four children for the last 16 years by vegetable vending. It is a hard day's work, at the end of which she sometimes has made five *dinar*, sometimes 10. She goes every day at 4:30 in the morning with four other women, who are also vegetable vendors, to an area called Khamsameel, which is a half-hour away from her home in the Al Muraba quarter in Basra. This morning drive to Khamsameel and back costs her two-and-a-half *dinar*. Depending on her *kabiliyat* (capacity), determined by how much money she earned the previous day, she buys vegetables worth 25 to 50 *dinar*. Most of the vegetables she buys are green leafy vegetables and beetroot rather than onions, potatoes and tomatoes, which are too expensive.

Showing bundles of these green leafy vegetables, Hadeel said, "My mother buys each bundle for 200 *fils* and sells them for 250 *fils* [1,000 *fils* to a *dinar*]. After coming back from Khamsameel, she carries these vegetables in a basket on her head and walks to the *sukh* (market) which is 15 minutes away. If she is lucky, she is able to find a shaded place in the crowded *sukh*. If not, she sits under the sun. She waits until she has sold all her vegetables before she returns, often alone, at around 8:00 or 9:00 in the evening. Yesterday she made five *dinar*.

She could not sell during *harb* Bush (Bush's war), especially during the last two weeks of the war and during the whole month of the riots."

With a smile Hadeel continued, "She was hiding under the blanket out of fear! We were telling her at that time that she is supposed to protect us, but she said that she cannot help feeling nervous when she hears the planes." She added, "But fear or no fear, she has to work under any conditions. Our only source of income is our mother's income. We have only God and my mother to take care of us."

KARIMHA

There were other women who had to surrender to the circumstances created by the sanctions and the war and could not continue. Such is the situation of Karimha.

Karimha is thirty-six years of age and has been a widow for the last nine years. Since her husband died, she and her seven children have been living with her parents, who are a strong source of support for her. She comes across as a fiercely independent woman. Her whole presence represents strength.

For the last four years, ever since she was able to get a license from the government, Karimha has been baking bread to be used for making sandwiches. She explained, "For the license, I applied through the manager of a wheat factory and supported it with evidence that I am a widow. This license is only for the poor and the needy. In this locality, there are more than 200 women bakers—among them many who have orphans to feed.

"With the license, before the war and sanctions, I used to buy a bag containing 85 kilograms of wheat flour for two *dinar* and 750 *fils*. In the open market, it was available for half a *dinar* more. I would utilize 12 to 15 such bags in a month." For baking, Karimha uses a *tanoor* (a big oven) which operates on gas. She continued, "I sometimes used one gas cylinder a day. My whole chest would become red due to the constant heat and the sweat. My one married sister, Yaze, used to help me. Her husband used to get only 20 *dinar* a month as a trainee soldier. But now how can I continue baking? One kilogram of wheat costs two-and-a-half to three *dinar*. In addition, we have a fuel crisis. We have to stand in line for a long time, sometimes for a whole day, to get our monthly quota of one gas cylinder. On the black market, it is very expensive."

Suddenly, Karimha got up and went inside a room and got a sack which was marked "50 kilograms." Pointing at it she said, "The last portion of my savings was finished in order to buy this sack of rice. It cost me 200 *dinar*."

SIHAM AND WAHIDA

The force of circumstances has, in more ways than one, alienated the women from their earlier sources of income. Many stories such as those of Siham and Wahida confirm this fact.

Siham lives with her seven daughters and her husband, a retired school teacher, in a small town called Safwan on the border of Kuwait and Iraq. Presently, the only source of income in the family is the pension of her husband. He gets 200 *dinar*. Siham said, "Before the war, I used to supplement the family income by sewing clothes. But now there are no orders. There has been no work ever since the war started. Due to the strategic position of Safwan, most of the people got scared and fled. When they came back, they found their houses looted and damaged. People do not have money for food; who can afford new clothes?"

Wahida, a Kurdish woman, has a similar story to tell. She is a fifty-five year old widow from Zakho, the northernmost tip of Iraq, bordering Turkey. She comes across as an extremely forthright, strong and confident person. In the course of our conversation with her, she remarked, "I became a widow when I was twenty-five. Since then I have been a seamstress and this is how I raised my children. But now, for the first time, there is no demand. Moreover, in my family we needed money urgently, especially as my two sons are unemployed, and so I had to sell my sewing machine. In the last two months, I have taken up a job as a cleaner in the newly opened UN office. But I find that I have less status now as a cleaner than I had as a community seamstress."

Unlike Wahida, most women have been unable to find new jobs to replace the ones they have lost. This has increased the vulnerability of these women and made them more dependent on their families or neighbors.

We learned from some of our respondents that female employees in the service sector are increasingly threatened with job losses in favor of males. Zahira is a young, educated and independent woman from a middle-class family who lives in the southern town of Najaf. Losing her job is the fear which is uppermost in her mind now. She has been working in an insurance company for a few years and has been on maternity leave for the last few months. She is worried that the policy might change and she might find that she has lost her job once her leave ends.

Many women in Iraq today are driven to take up humiliating ways of earning in order to assure the survival of their dependents. They have had to compromise with the traditional notions of honor and shame. These include women who can be seen begging at street corners, hidden completely in the anonymity of the *abaya* (the traditional black garment covering the entire body).

Women respondents in the city and villages around Mosul, in the governorate of Nineveh in northern Iraq, admitted that they had heard that prostitution had increased in their own city as well as in Baghdad. This fact was corroborated in a conversation with an official in the Ministry of Trade in Mosul who said, "Social problems have increased. Morality has declined. People are selling themselves to feed their families." He was, it seemed, referring to women.

Verbal reports also confirmed such occurrences in Basra. However, among the respondents to whom we posed this question, a majority said that they had not heard of any incidence or increase in prostitution. Some of them said that they are *sharaf* (self-respecting) and would rather die than contemplate such an action.

FINANCIAL CRISIS

> For ten years during the war with Iran we have felt nothing. But after two months in the war with Bush, we are suffering like never before. Every day is getting worse. I have sold all my gold, including my wedding ring. This was not enough so we sold our furniture and kitchen utensils. Even our water tank had to be sold. This too was not enough. So my son borrowed 1,000 *dinar* two days ago.
>
> *Majida Hamid, 60 years, Baghdad*

Almost half (48 percent) of our respondents have incurred debts from loans, and 55 percent have sold gold and other household items such as refrigerators, televisions and furniture as a result of economic need. Many of those who did not sell any household items were among those who had nothing to sell.

We found that the first item to be sold was always the woman's jewelry. In Iraq, gold is given to every woman upon marriage as a dowry. It guarantees her social status and her financial security. A woman's gold ensures her involvement in decision-making in the household, especially if she is required to use it for any sort of investment. The surrender of gold has a long-term impact on the status of women. It means that women are losing this financial security; without it they are totally dependent on men and have no involvement in decision-making.

The fact that women are forced to sell their gold due to the economic crisis within the Iraqi household is a telling indication of the extent of poverty in the household. Most of our respondents reported that they had sold their gold and other assets and incurred debts to buy basic items. As one respondent put it, "I sold my gold to buy wheat flour for my children." However, as often happens in periods of crisis, she was not able to get the market value of the gold.

Besides meeting basic needs, we found that distress sales were also made in order to raise capital to assist the setting up of petty trade or business of relatives demobilized from the army, prisoners of war who have returned, or those who are seeking to be self-employed. However, many Iraqi families have used up their resources and are today below the destitution line.

FOOD AND SUBSISTENCE

> Every waking moment I worry about how will I feed my eight children. It is the hardest thing for a mother not be able to feed her child.
>
> *Saeda Bani Dana, 32 years, Bartella, Mosul*

> We never eat meat anymore. The last time we bought meat in our house was a month ago when a suitor came to ask for my daughter's hand. We cooked chicken for him. He and his family ate it all and the marriage did not even work out. The next day we had chicken-bone soup!
>
> *Siham Al Kader, 48 years, Safwan, Basra*

Food has become the main preoccupation of most Iraqi women. The food consumption pattern of the Iraqi family has been severely affected. The two main sources of food are government food rations and the open market, which is often called the "black market."

Iraqi family sitting among the rubble of part of their home, destroyed by a Coalition bomb, Basra, April 1991.

After the economic sanctions were imposed, ration cards were issued by the Iraqi government to each family without any kind of discrimination. Under this scheme, each family member is entitled to identical monthly rations of basic food items, including wheat flour, rice, sugar, tea, and cooking oil. Besides, a few other items, like lentils, dairy products, razor blades, etc., are occasionally distributed. The public distribution system (PDS) has become the lifeline of a majority of Iraqi families.

In the course of our field work in 10 different governorates in Iraq, we found that the PDS was administered very effectively. While the people were very grateful for its existence, they felt that there was some scope for improvement, mainly on two fronts. First, the quantum allocated was felt to be insufficient and second, the quality of wheat flour was sometimes sub-standard.

On average, rations last for 10 to 15 days each month. For the rest of the month, people have to rely on market purchases for their needs. The prices of food commodities have increased 15 to 20 times on average since August 1990, while the price of wheat flour has increased nearly 50 times.

As was mentioned earlier, due to the increased pauperization of middle- and low-income Iraqi families, destitutes are found in thousands in many governorates. Many families have become totally dependent on rations and charity for survival. This is especially the case in households headed by women such as widows, and divorced and deserted women.

Considerable variations are found between southern, northern and central regions of Iraq with respect to food consumption. The South, especially Basra, is the worst hit. Currently, most families in the South subsist on bread and occasionally seasonal vegetables such as okra, tomatoes, potatoes and eggplants. In many households, meat was last eaten before the war. In some areas even drinking water has to be bought at high prices. In Baghdad, there are variations. In some households, basic necessities were found to be accessible, even if dietary habits had changed. Many of these households literally spend all their income on food. In other low-income areas like Saddam City, the situation is just as bad as in the South. People subsist on bread and occasional vegetables, and the consumption of meat, for many formerly eaten once or twice weekly, has ceased altogether.

The picture in the North differs, though only to a small extent. Many people have agricultural land which has helped their subsistence. For instance, home-produced bulgur (cracked wheat) and seasonal vegetables are an important part of their diet. However, low-income groups in the North, especially displaced communities, seem to be as poverty-stricken as in other parts of Iraq.

As for the Kurds, their food consumption was adversely affected during their flight to the mountains. Women interviewed stated that they lived on boiled water and bulgur until the emergency relief arrived. After two months in the mountains, thousands of Kurds still live [as of September, 1991] in refugee camps and scattered shelters. Those who returned found their homes and property stolen or vandalized. Many men lost their income source. Today, although their situation is somewhat improved, malnutrition is still common, especially among children. This is partly because many pockets of the Kurdish areas where the government is not in control are not receiving the ordinary food rations. Food rations from the UN were supplied for two months (June and July) but according to our respondents have ceased.

The present state of the people is a warning of the critical situation that might develop if the sanctions are not lifted. In spite of the fact that the food distribution system meets at best one-half of the family requirements, it seems to be making a major contribution in averting starvation and famine.

In general, food-related worries had become the main subject of interaction between women. This is because the management of food within the household is women's main responsibility. Their helplessness weighs heavily on them. It was interesting to note that most of the women's awareness of international politics toward Iraq was sparked by the economic sanctions, which the women perceived as the root cause of their plight.

> I am a widow with seven children. I receive my late husband's pension of 100 *dinar* per month. I pay 70 every month for rent. I used to sew for my neighbors but now nobody is sewing. My daughter was killed by the Coalition bombings of Basra. Now I take care of her two children because their father is a soldier. The landlord wants to throw me out. He comes twice each day to threaten me. He says he wants to sell the house or rent it for more. I have sold everything I own. What can I do—sell my children?
>
> *Kamila Ali, 40 years, Saddam City, Baghdad*

CHILDREN'S HEALTH AND WOMEN'S ROLES

> Just take a look at this child. They told me his mouth is infected but gave me nothing to treat it. Now he just cries all day long.
>
> *Zahira, 39 years, Karbala*

Only a few respondents (one of whom was from a semi-nomadic family) reported a complete absence of health services. Most complained that available facilities were inadequate.

Of the women interviewed, 49 percent stated that there was an increase in illness among their children and among themselves. The same observation was made with reference to children in the neighborhood. Illnesses most commonly identified are diarrhea and typhoid. Some also reported instances of malnutrition. Cases of infant deaths were also reported. This was especially relevant among Kurdish families, most of whom had suffered child deaths during their stay in the mountains. The ill health of children put great stress on women, who were helpless to provide safe water for their children, and unable to feed them properly, or to immunize them due to the scarcity of vaccines.

In most of the households visited we found the children suffering from diarrhea. Women expressed concern and were aware of the serious consequences. In these cases, the women had the additional burden of acting as the health caretakers. In the pediatric ward in both Babylon and Dohuk hospitals, it was common to find dehydrated children. The mothers usually stayed with their children in the hospital.

One mother in the Dohuk hospital said that when she took her child to a nearby health center there was no medicine available for diarrhea. Things got worse and after two days she brought her child to the hospital. This is a typical case where either health centers have been incapacitated due to lack of medicines or have been temporarily closed. The private sector has ceased to be an alternative for many families since they cannot afford it.

Another mother in the Babylon hospital, from a rural area, whose two-month old son was malnourished and was suffering from marasmus, indicated that her family ignored her concern for her child, until one morning, after severe diarrhea, she convinced her husband to take her and the child to the hospital. She had not returned home since. The mother had identified the danger to her child before her family, and greater persistence on her part might have saved her child's life.

WOMEN'S HEALTH

> Most women suffered terribly from trauma of miscarriages during the war and the disturbances. Many could not find medical treatment at the time and have continuing problems with their health. Effective treatment seems unavailable for most women. A doctor friend of mine estimated that 7,000 women had miscarriages because of shock in Najaf alone.
>
> *Alia, 21 years, Najaf*

Dr. Liela Abed Al Amir, head of Babylon Pediatric and Maternity Hospital, expressed her concern for women's health situation. Most women patients in the hospital, she stated, are found to be anemic due to lack of proper nutrition. The incidence of miscarriages, premature labor and low-birth-weight babies is very high compared to before. Dr. Abed Al Amir stated that this might be due to physical and psychological pressures, lack of medicines or needed prenatal care, or difficulty in reaching the hospital due to transportation problems.

Only emergency operations are being performed. The hospital's average number of operations per week was 200 before the war. Now it is around 50 operations per week. Many Caesarean operations are being performed with the minimum of anesthetics.

Dr. Abed Al Amir also expressed concern at the lack of contraception. Due to scarcity and legal restrictions, contraceptives are given only to women with medical needs and in rare cases to older women who have had many children. One hospital patient we met, who had had her second Caesarean in one year due to lack of contraception, was anemic and in a generally weak condition. We also met a teenage girl who had a bleeding problem that could only be controlled by the birth control pill, which could not be obtained at the time.

A woman gynecologist from the town of Hilla claimed that there was an increase in illegal abortions. Although she did not state the number, she claimed to know of several maternal deaths that had resulted from these abortions. Poverty was the reason that motivated most women to abort. Often the husbands encouraged their wives to abort, fearing that they could not support another child.

Among the respondents in our sample, 57 percent claimed that they are suffering from health problems caused by physical and psychological hardships. A significant example is disturbance in menstruation. A large number of women stated that they and/or their daughters have had irregular menses or excessive bleeding or severe pains. Other problems cited were hair loss, skin problems or other psychosomatic symptoms such as insomnia and weight loss.

A mother of ten children in a household visited in Najaf was in the hospital. The husband, who was in a desperate situation due to his wife's illness and his own lack of employment, was eager to talk. He said that his wife was under so much stress and fear that in the end her body collapsed. The neighboring women were taking care of the children. He commented, "By God, if I can return my children to where they came from, I will," alluding to the chaos that ensues in a mother's absence.

The availability of medicine was a major concern, especially for those women with permanent health problems such as diabetes, rheumatism, or high blood pressure. Among the women interviewed, 61 percent said that medicine was scarce and, if obtainable, unaffordable for the average household. In such cases, women consulted with each other on home and herbal remedies. One such medication used for diarrhea was dried lime with tea.

WOMEN'S DOMESTIC ROLES

Almost all women claimed that their lives had changed since the Gulf War. They usually contrasted this war with the Iran-Iraq War, during which the impact within the household was minimal, according to most women. Of the 80 respondents, 80 percent mentioned that they had extra domestic responsibilities due to the destruction of infrastructure, such as water supply and electricity, and because of fuel shortages.

Most women started to bake their own bread after the war, as buying bread had become too costly. Many of them have to gather firewood daily in order to bake and cook, since gas for the ovens is also expensive. Women also have to plan and ration their food so that it is enough for the month. They have to be aware of market prices and of what is most cheaply available.

Some creativity is required in cooking since the women are obliged to use limited ingredients. For example, some women said that they added cheap barley to wheat while baking bread to increase the quantity. Whenever women receive "black" (adulterated or low quality) flour from the public distribution system, they mix it with some white flour from the open market. In periods of severe shortages, women (especially in Basra) even use the left-over unrefined flour in the sieve. In normal times, this residue would be used only to feed cattle. Others said that they now pick some wild edible green leaves to use as soup.

When asked how inadequate amounts of food would be distributed in a household which included children, pregnant women, the old and adults, women were unanimous that the children would be fed first. Often mothers reported that they went hungry and gave their share of the food to the children. Priority to pregnant women was given in very few cases.

Water is another major worry now and its acquisition differs according to different locations. While in some rural areas women are used to fetching water from wells or rivers, many Iraqi villages are in fact equipped with water pipes; fetching water became an added responsibility for many women after supplies of piped water were disrupted.

Some households now have nearly regular water supply, after at least three months of erratic delivery. In some areas such as Basra, water supply is still erratic, with water being available for as little as an hour each day. During this hour the women fill up as many containers as they can and carry out all their washing and cooking.

In the rural areas south and north of Basra, water is bought from tanks or supplied free by organizations such as the Red Cross. The women in these areas have to carry large water containers and stand in line for hours before carrying them back home. By mid-August most women were no longer heavily dependent on river water, which had been a main source of water since mid-January.

The safety of the water is questionable and a few women do boil their water. However, in such cases of scarcity the availability of water is the issue for most women and not its safety.

Women's constant worry about food and household management in such a dire situation leaves little free time as compared to before the crisis. Women stated that they socialized outside their home more often before the war, or engaged themselves in such things as sewing. According to 46 percent of the respondents, there is now less time for leisure; but as many women put it, "the matter is not a question of time as much as a troubled state of the mind."

> We went to the neighbors' house during the war. Their house was safer. It was like we were one family. We shared our food and our water. We were so scared we all stayed in one room and did not move for days.
>
> *Abisa, 40 years, Karbala*
> *9 children*

> When we fled to Turkey it was very difficult to get food. All the younger men ran fast and got all the food the Americans were handing out. We only had my husband with us and he can't run—so we ended up as a family without food. This happened to all the women who fled without their men— we were just left out—as if we weren't there. Three of my grandchildren died in those mountains.
>
> *Fatimah, 68, Amadia (Dohuk district)*
> *Returned Kurdish refugee*

> Every woman I know in this town fights with her husband or son on a daily basis. They have no work and they are in the way. When they go out of the house they spend the little money that they have on coffee, tea or some beer, so that's not the solution either. Our men need jobs and we need a break.
>
> *Um Faris, 46, Karameles, Mosul*

Women's added responsibilities are largely seen as their duty. Eighty percent of the women reported that their work burden has increased. When asked whether these responsibilities are more than the men bear in the household, 74 percent of the women responded that this was natural. When probed further whether this was appreciated by the males or the rest of the family, the women reacted in a surprised way and largely did not give a clear answer.

On the question whether there has been an increase in marital problems after the war as a result of increased pressures, 17 percent of the women related such cases. However, they were rarely open about these matters. Some women expressed the view that their husbands were more nervous, and said that whenever the women or the children approached them regarding any of their needs, they would scream and leave the house avoiding any answers. Two women, whose husbands are unemployed and sit idly at home or in the coffee shops said that whenever they approached their husbands and urged them to seek work more actively, the husbands threatened them with a second wife.

In the Iraqi houses visited that had daughters of marriageable age, marriage was increasingly becoming an issue. Iraqi society is a married society. In 1987, 50 percent of Iraqi women above the age of 12 were married (see Table 6-6). One twenty-year-old woman from the Marshes expressed her concerns: "Some of the eligible young men were killed and many others have left. The only ones who stayed are the children and the old people."

The fact that many young women remain unmarried is largely due to economic reasons. Young men are mostly unemployed and their families cannot provide for them, as is traditionally the case. Marriage customs include a dowry given to the bride, mainly of gold jewelry. When asked why young women did not compromise on their gold dowry, several mothers expressed their concern that in that case their daughters would not have a good social standing among their new in-laws.

Women's Interfamily and Community Relations

Community relations with neighbors have consolidated during and after the Gulf crisis. Sometimes neighbors move in with each other if they find others' houses to be safer.

Women stated that their relations with each other were very important to them during the war. They shared their fears and worries with each other. Besides helping one another with foodstuffs and medicines, they stayed in each others' houses or shared rooms in the shelters. After the war they fetched water together from the rivers or went to get their monthly rations together. Those who did not know how to bake were taught by the neighbors. Often one *tanoor* (oven) would be shared by many families.

Social solidarity was, however, more fragile among the Kurds, perhaps due to the extreme hardship they experienced. According to three Kurdish women respondents, during their flight to the mountains the situation was so bad that everyone fended for themselves in order to survive. One woman claimed that there was a lot of competition over scarce items.

PSYCHOLOGICAL IMPACT

Iraqi society as a whole, today, gives an impression of despondency and fatigue, aggravated by the fact that it has just emerged from an eight-year war with Iran. Life seems to have become a struggle for survival for every Iraqi individual. As one woman asked, "Until when will the sanctions continue? We are tired. We want to go back to what we were before the war."

The psychological health of the individual and society as a result of war and related hardships is also of concern. However, determining the psychological and emotional impact on women and their families (especially children) is not an easy task. In this section the women will speak for themselves.

Of the women respondents, 39 percent said that they feared that members of their family either at home or at the front could face danger. Forty-seven percent said that they left their homes for the provinces or cities fearing bomb attacks or other forms of war violence. Those who remained behind were often the very old, those who could not afford the expense or those who had no place to go.

> To hear the bombers flying over your house was almost unreal. In moments of fear, you pretend that it is all over and you are already dead, looking at the sky from your grave.
>
> *Um Jassim, 45, Basra*

Sixty percent of the respondents felt that they were suffering from psychological side-effects as a result of the war and sanctions. Most of them related symptoms like depression, anxiety, insomnia, weight loss and health problems such as with menstruation, high blood pressure or increased smoking (this was not common among women). Many pregnant women miscarried and others could not breastfeed.

> I dream about Samir all the time. I see him as a grown-up. I dream of him on his wedding day or in his army uniform. The doctor has written a letter to my employer saying I need a sick leave because of psychological problems (depression). But when I sit at home all day I remember Samir even more.
>
> *Um Samir, 25*
> *Baghdad mother of a nine-year-old who died*
> *in the Al Ameriyah shelter bombing, and an*
> *Iran-Iraq War widow*

> From terror, my two daughters-in-law miscarried during the war. One was three months preg-
> nant and the other was seven months pregnant.
>
> *Jamila, 39 years, Al Ameriyah, Baghdad*

Iraq being a traditional society, most women refused to answer questions pertaining to the issue of increased moral problems, such as sexual harassment of women or increasing prostitution. Some respondents expressed anxiety about the safety of daughters. One respondent in Amara described the anxiety that she used to feel for her daughters during the civil disturbances in the South. During that period several rape cases were reported. Consequently, she sent her daughters to Baghdad only to realize that it was just as unsafe.

In the Kurdish refugee camp of Penjuin, Kashwar, 22 years, revealed that she was upset to have left her middle-class life and her teaching job in Kirkuk. Apparently the Peshmergars (Kurdish guerrillas) urged her family to leave with the approach of the Iraqi army. "They will kill you and rape your daughters," they told Kashwar's father. This prompted the father to leave everything behind and become a refugee.

The future expectations and aspirations of the women reflected their psychological distress. Almost all women believed that the war and the sanctions had brought permanent changes in their lives. Forty percent of the women said that they are living one day at a time. Another 41 percent are pessimistic about the future, especially because of the continuation of sanctions. Only 19 percent of the women were optimistic about the future—mainly because they believe that things cannot get worse than they are now.

> Even if I were to wish anything, it would not come true. All I want is a nice home and a good liv-
> ing. That is all.
>
> *Salima, 27 years*

> Life was better before, but things cannot get worse. They have to get better.
>
> *Ramla, 33 years*

CONCLUSIONS

After viewing the situation in Iraq from the inside, one has a closer understanding of the human consequences of war as a solution to international conflicts. Certain issues emerge that are critical to the well-being of Iraqi society as a whole. The effect on the Iraqi family and the women in particular is a cause for serious concern.

The following is a summary of the most salient findings:

1) The Gulf War and the economic sanctions have, on the one hand, forced women to adopt roles and responsibilities traditionally assigned to men, and, on the other hand, have made their own roles harder to fulfill.

2) From the point of view of Iraqi women, the most serious consequence of this crisis is their greatly reduced ability to feed their families. Hunger is the foremost preoccupation among low-income groups in Iraq.

3) Sanctions have resulted in large-scale unemployment. Female employees are increasingly vulnerable to losing jobs in the wake of competition from males.

4) Impoverishment has led households to sell their assets, beginning with women's jewelry. This has increased women's dependence and vulnerability. In the worst cases, women have been driven to begging and prostitution.

5) Women's physical well-being has been greatly reduced not only through economic hardship but also due to the lack of medical care and clean environment.

6) Women have also greatly suffered from psychological and emotional stress related to war and sanctions, including the trauma of bombings and internal disturbances, the loss of loved ones, and constant anxiety about the well-being of their families.

7) Social life is another casualty of the war. Iraqi families are so dispossessed and demoralized that they cannot celebrate marriages, welcome guests or enjoy any kind of social entertainment. Women's mobility has been greatly reduced by fear of sexual harassment and theft. Women frequently express these social losses in their testimonies.

8) Marital problems are reported to have increased as a result of economic and psychological pressures. Women, due to their physical and financial powerlessness, are the prime victims of increased discord.

9) The condition of widows, divorced and deserted women is the worst of all. One important reason is that price increases have undermined the real value of the pensions that widows receive from the state.

10) Iraqi women see the lifting of sanctions as the only hope for a return to normal life. This, if anything, is the central message of their testimonies.

Iraqi women have experienced this whole crisis not only as victims, but also as crucial actors who have sustained the family and the society against the forces of violence and destruction. The basis of the Iraqi society, the home, has been held together by their ingenuity and strength—despite their own economic, social, emotional and psychological deprivation. Their central role both as victims and as actors makes it all the more important to listen to their unheard voices.

[In May 1993, in a follow-up study funded by OXFAM, CAFOD (the British Catholic Fund for Overseas Development) and Christian Aid, Mariam Shahin reinterviewed 40 of the 80 women surveyed in 1991. She found that one of the 40 women had died from ill health, and a child had died in one out of 10 of the 40 re-surveyed households. There had been a sevenfold increase in miscarriages and a threefold increase in skin and eye problems. Cases of more serious illnesses had risen by a third. Thirteen more families had sold assets to supplement income. In 32 households, family members over one year old had not drunk milk in over a year. On the positive side, the availability of clean drinking water had increased by 44 percent.]

The following tables are based on interviews by IST members with 80 Iraqi women August 24 to September 4, 1991.

TABLE 6-6. PERSONAL HISTORY

Age group of interviewees		Marital Status		Number of children	
15–24 years	7	Married	60	None	2
25–29 years	13	Widowed	14	1–4	36
30–39 years	25	Single	3	5–8	25
40–49 years	21	Divorced	2	Above 8	15
50+ years	14	Abandoned	1	Not available	2
Education		**Age at marriage**		**Size of Household**	
Illiterate	38	12–13	7	1–5	18
Primary	24	14–15	27	6–10	31
Intermediate	14	16–17	22	11+	31
Diploma	1	18–19	13		
Bachelor	2	20–21	5		
Master's	1	22–25	1		
		25–28	2		
Occupational status		Not available	3		
Employed	9				
Housewives	64				
Unpaid labor outside home	8				

TABLE 6-7. ECONOMIC CONDITION

Monthly family income (In dinars)	(%)
No income	14%
Below 200	44%
200–400	30%
400–600	4%
Above 600	6%
Not available	2%
Assets	
Home owners	66%
Additional property	28%
Distress sale, debt	
Sold gold or other items	55%
Incurred debt	48%
Food subsistence	
Received food rations	90%
Felt food rations were insufficient	100%

TABLE 6-8. HEALTH

5-kilometer proximity of health service	77%
Problems getting access to medicine	61%
Ill/dead family members in last 12 months	68%
Illness/death in neighborhood in last 12 months	77%
Negative health impact on women (menstrual disturbance, hair loss, skin disease)	58%
Don't have access to clean water	42%
Don't have access to garbage collection	41%

TABLE 6-9. SOCIAL IMPACT

Added responsibilities	80%
More responsibilities than men	74%
Long absence of male members of household	68%
Leisure time decreased	46%
All family members currently not at home	35%
Marital problems	17%

TABLE 6-10. PSYCHOLOGICAL IMPACT

Believed self or family members will die or are in danger	39%
Psychologically affected	59%
Family members left home during war or civil disturbances	47%
Members of family psychologically affected	73%
Bad dreams	46%

TABLE 6-11. FUTURE ASPIRATIONS

God knows	40%
Pessimistic	41%
Optimistic	19%

The Iraqi Kurds

Cyrus Salam

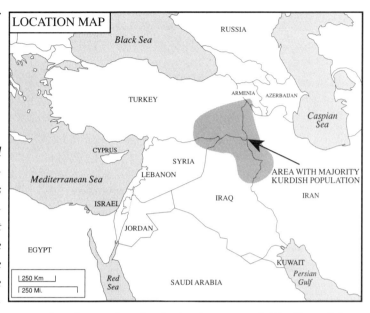

LOCATION MAP

Inhabiting the plateaus and mountains of Iran, Turkey, Armenia, Iraq and Syria, Kurds have been a linguistically, culturally and racially distinct people for millennia. In the twentieth century, when the Middle East was divided by the British and the French, Kurdistan didn't become an autonomous province; later, when decolonization occurred, Kurdistan did not become a nation-state. Instead, the Kurds were brought under the control of the surrounding states, which have tried to assimilate them through the use of forced population transfers.

The accompanying map shows the area with a majority Kurdish population, referred to in this article as Kurdistan. The parts of this area that are within the formal borders of Iraq and Turkey are referred to in this article as Iraqi Kurdistan and Turkish Kurdistan. Sixty percent of Iraqi Kurdistan is currently controlled by the Kurdish Regional Government; the current dividing line between Kurd and Arab forces in Iraq is shown on the map "Kurdish Area of Iraq."

This article was written in May 1993 by Cyrus Salam, a computer software developer who has traveled to Kurdistan since the end of the Gulf War. He is a member of the Kurdish National Congress, a North American organization working to publicize the situation in Kurdistan.

Over a period of weeks in April 1991, with dozens of poison gas attacks during the mid-to-late 1980s fresh in their minds, 2.25 million Iraqi Kurds fled to the Turkish and Iranian borders. This mass exodus occurred after the recapture by Iraqi Arab forces, through the use of indiscriminate shelling of civilian areas by air and artillery, of the major Kurdish cities following the Kurds' 1991 rebellion against the central government in Iraq.

In what is believed to be one of the largest-ever mass displacements of people in such a short period of time, an estimated 750,000 Kurds fled to Turkey and 1.5 million fled to Iran. Even though a larger number of Kurds fled to Iran, it was the Kurds who fled to Turkey who received the most attention from the Western World.

The lack of attention paid to the Kurds who fled to Iran was partly due to Iran's reluctance to allow foreign journalists into the country. Another factor was that, whereas Iran allowed Kurds to descend from the mountains before detaining them in camps, Turkey would not allow the Iraqi Kurds to descend from the high mountain passes that predominate on the Turkish-Iraqi

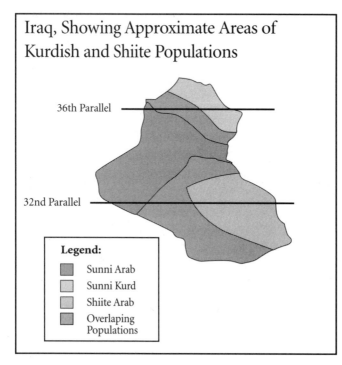

Iraq, Showing Approximate Areas of Kurdish and Shiite Populations

36th Parallel

32nd Parallel

Legend:
- Sunni Arab
- Sunni Kurd
- Shiite Arab
- Overlaping Populations

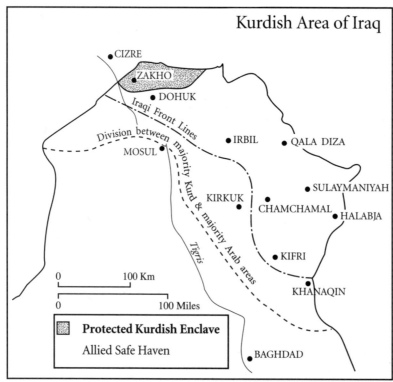

Kurdish Area of Iraq

CIZRE

ZAKHO

DOHUK

Iraqi Front Lines

Division between majority Kurd & majority Arab areas

MOSUL

IRBIL

QALA DIZA

SULAYMANIYAH

KIRKUK

CHAMCHAMAL

HALABJA

Tigris

KIFRI

KHANAQIN

0   100 Km

0   100 Miles

Protected Kurdish Enclave

Allied Safe Haven

BAGHDAD

border. This is because throughout the 1980s Turkey has been involved in an increasingly violent war against resurgent Kurdish nationalists in Turkey. Turkish leaders were worried that the presence of over a half million additional Iraqi Kurds in Turkey wearing their traditional dress (still forbidden by Turkish law) would further incite their own Kurds.

The result was hundreds of thousands of Kurds huddled and dying in the snow-covered mountains at elevations up to 10,000 feet in full view of television cameras. The subsequent public sympathy generated in the West coupled with Turkish insistence that the Kurds not be allowed into Turkey convinced the Coalition forces to create "safe havens" inside Iraqi Kurdistan.

Originally, the safe havens did not include a single major Kurdish city. Instead, they represented two token cities, Zakho and Amadiyah, both of which had pre-war populations of under 100,000. Coalition troops occupied these cities and warned the Iraqi regime against use of fixed-wing aircraft north of the 36th parallel. Within six months this token force, combined with the gradual reassertion of control over 60 percent of Iraqi Kurdistan and two of its three major cities by the local Kurdish militias, convinced almost all Iraqi Kurdish refugees to return to a precarious existence in Iraqi Kurdistan. Anything was better than the freezing mountaintop camps on the Turkish border or the ill-supplied camps in Iranian Kurdistan.

Three months after the establishment of the "safe havens," all Coalition troops were removed from Kurdistan. The havens are now protected only through occasional over-flights by Coalition planes based in Incirlik and Batman, NATO bases in Turkish Kurdistan. These flights are subject to cancellation without notice by the Turkish Parliament, which may soon decide against continuing the Coalition protection of Iraqi Kurds.

In the two years since the end of the Gulf War and the withdrawal of Coalition troops, a 350-mile front line of trenches and troop emplacements roughly following the Kurdish foothills has separated Iraq into two regions, one controlled by the Kurdish Regional Government based in Irbil and the other controlled by the Arab government in Baghdad. Up to 300,000 Kurds from Kirkuk, which is under the control of the Iraqi army, remain refugees, primarily living in refugee housing or tents in and around the Kurdish-held city of Sulaymaniyah. Perhaps another 100,000 Kurds from other lowland Kurdish regions under the control of the Iraqi army are similarly displaced.

In the meantime the Iraqi government has systematically been destroying most of the housing of Kurds from Kirkuk who fled to the Kurdish-controlled zones, and/or forcibly transfering Shiite Arabs from the south of Iraq into the city in an effort to outnumber the reduced number of Kurds who live there under government control. Low-level conflict continues between the Kurds and Arabs with frequent shelling of border villages by the Iraqi army.

Currently, 16 Iraqi Army divisions are situated on the front lines facing Kurdistan. It is estimated that in the event of an Iraqi offensive, the area south of the 36th parallel will bear the brunt of the attack. In this area live over one million Kurds.

Sulaymaniyah, with a total population of about 900,000, lies south of the 36th parallel and far outside the formal safe havens on the Turkish border. Analysts do not expect an automatic Coalition response if Sulaymaniyah is attacked.

In addition to military harassment by the Iraqis, during the past two years the Kurds of Iraq have been subject to a dual economic embargo, the UN embargo on Iraq coupled with an Iraqi embargo on Iraqi Kurdistan. This dual embargo, which effectively bans the transfer of all food and fuel, has led to a tenfold increase in prices and a quadrupling in the unemployment rate, with over 60 percent of the working age population without jobs. While prices have also increased in Arab Iraq, the cost of fuel in Iraqi Kurdistan is still thirty times higher than in Arab-held areas. Malnutrition is increasing and the infrastructure is deteriorating due to UN import restrictions on spare parts and chemicals for industrial and agricultural activities.

Hardship in the private sector is being matched by that in the public sector. During this period the nascent Kurdish administration has been dependent upon customs duties from illegal cross-border trade (in contravention of UN sanctions) from Turkey and Iran into Iraq. This trade was tolerated by the Coalition as a means of supplying essential goods to the Iraqi people but more importantly as an economic reward to Turkey for its cooperation in the Gulf War. In the winter of 1992, in order to prevent the collection of customs duties, both Turkey and Iran cancelled such cross-border trade (or in the case of Iran rerouted it through other non-Kurdish-controlled regions.) The result has been a cancellation of salaries for 90 percent of Kurdish civil servants and further impoverishment of the region.

While Iraqi Kurdistan has faced many challenges in the past two years, a few positive developments have occurred. In the summer of 1992 the first free elections in Iraq were held in which three million Kurds, including women, voted for the first Kurdish Regional Parliament. In what has been acknowledged by international observers as a remarkably free and fair election—the first in the Middle East in which the voting franchise has been universally extended to all voting age citizens—105 members were selected, of multiple ethnic and religious makeups, including five or six women.

In addition, with the recent freedom of Western journalists and scientists to travel in Kurdistan, impartial documentary evidence has emerged detailing the crimes and policies of the Arab Iraqi administration towards the Kurds during the 1980s. The word *Anfal* is now more generally known to the outside world as an Arab campaign to extinguish the Kurds as a separate and viable community within Iraq's borders.

Scud Attacks Drive 4,000 From Israeli Homes

Hugh Orgel

Iraq's Armed Forces General Command attacked targets in Israel and Saudi Arabia during the Gulf War. Middle East Watch reported that Iraq launched 37 missiles at Saudi Arabia; one civilian was killed and 77 were injured. A missile attack on U.S. Army barracks in Dhahran on February 25 killed 28 U.S. soldiers and injured 97.[1] Iraq launched 18 missile attacks on Israel between January 18 and February 25, 1991.

The following is excerpted from an article by the Jewish Telegraph Agency, published in the Northern California Jewish Bulletin, February 1, 1991. Reprinted with permission.

Tel Aviv—Some 4,000 people have been evacuated from thousands of damaged homes in the greater Tel Aviv area, and temporarily are being housed in local hotels.

Officials say that most of the damage—including broken window panes and door frames, cracked walls and marred roofs—is repairable. Some structures, however, have to be totally razed. For example, the municipality of Ramat Gan, the Tel Aviv suburb struck by a direct hit January 22, began work Sunday demolishing seven structures severely damaged by the impact of one Scud warhead. One of the buildings contained eight apartments.

As of press time Wednesday, 273 people had been injured—most not seriously—by the six Scuds that had landed. Two people had died as a direct result of the missile attacks, and 12 others had died of accidental causes such as incorrect use of gas masks. Five more had died of heart attacks during air raid alerts.

Also, 500 people had sought treatment for stress and anxiety, and another 220 had been treated for the painful side effects of atropine, a self-administered nerve gas antidote included in the gas-mask kits.

Last Friday night, shortly after Shabbat began, Iraq fired seven Scud missiles at Tel Aviv and Haifa. Five of them were destroyed, with the other two being diverted in the air by Patriot anti-missile defenses.

As the debris from a destroyed Scud came down over the city, a two-story house took a direct hit and completely collapsed. Next door, a house was partially destroyed, and adjacent homes had their roofs ripped off and windows broken. On the streets, cars were smashed and set aflame.

Across the street from a synagogue, a piece of missile ripped through four apartments. An eight-foot-deep crater was left where a wall of a school for disabled children collapsed.

In one house, two people survived because they took refuge in a basement bomb shelter in direct disregard of civil defense orders to avoid basement shelters and to stay instead in rooms sealed against poison gas.

But debris raining down on Tel Aviv proved lethal. One man, Eitan Grundland, 55, of Ramat Gan, died from a severe head wound. Some 69 others were wounded, including one person reported to be in critical condition.

Saturday night, the air raid sirens sounded again as two successive waves of Scuds came down, a change in Iraqi tactics. Three Scuds were reportedly fired towards Tel Aviv and one at Haifa. All were intercepted by the Patriots, with no casualties and only minor damage.

Monday night, a Scud missile targeted at Tel Aviv exploded instead on the outskirts of the Arab village of Deir Balut in the West Bank.

[According to a final official count, 13 Israelis were killed: one directly by a missile and another 12 by indirect causes including heart attacks. Between 165 and 334 Israeli civilians were wounded.[2]]

NOTES:

1. Middle East Watch, *Needless Deaths in the Gulf War: Civilian Casualties During the Air Campaign and Violations of the Laws of War; A Middle East Watch Report*, Report, Human Rights Watch, New York, November 1991, 385.
2. Middle East Watch, *Needless Deaths in the Gulf War*, 348.

Aftermath of the Gulf Crisis: Refugees, Stateless People and Returned Migrants

British Refugee Council

Excerpts reprinted, with permission, from the Gulf Information Project Information Pack, *produced by British Refugee Council, October 1992. The Gulf Information Project is supported by British NGOs Oxfam, Quaker Peace Service, Save the Children Fund, Christian Aid and the Catholic Institute for International Relations.*

Note: Most figures are estimates and in a constantly changing situation, they are only valid for the period specified.

IRAQI REFUGEES

United Nations High Commission for Refugees (UNHCR) figures are used for this section unless otherwise specified.

In the immediate aftermath of the 1991 Persian Gulf War there were short-lived uprisings in the Kurdish areas of northern Iraq and in the South. As a consequence of the suppression of these rebellions, an estimated two million refugees fled the country in the course of a few weeks during March and April 1991. By the end of December 1991, about 1.8 million had returned voluntarily to Iraq, mostly from Turkey and Iran.

IN TURKEY

Situation of Iraqi refugees at the beginning of August 1992:

Total: 22,939, of whom 18,909 are 1988 refugees. By early October 1992, some 15,000 refugees, mostly from 1988, were reported to have returned to Iraq as part of the UNHCR's repatriation plan.

Some 400,000 refugees from northern Iraq fled to the mountainous border with Turkey after Iraqi troops launched their counter-offensive at the end of March 1991. (The Turkish government gives a figure of 450,000.) Most were Kurds but some Assyrian Christians, Turkomans and Arabs also fled. Some 55,000 Iraqis from the North had already fled to Turkey during the Iraqi army's *Anfal* operations of 1987–1988.

Turkey is a signatory of the 1951 UN Convention on the Status of Refugees but it has limited its obligations to cover only refugees from Europe. It did not therefore regard the fleeing Iraqis as refugees. At first, Turkish troops prevented them from crossing the border, so that they remained on the mountainsides in freezing conditions. When they were allowed to cross they were at first housed in tents near the border. Only later were they moved to more permanent shelter. The Turkish Red Crescent was the main provider of relief to the refugees.

The Turkish authorities regarded them as seeking "temporary" shelter rather than as asylum-seekers. Since mid-1991, there have been a number of cases of forced returns (*refoulements*) to Iraq by the Turkish authorities. UNHCR has not always been able to prevent this.

By 1992, the vast majority of 1991 refugees had returned to northern Iraq. Most of the remaining refugees live in camps administered by the Turkish authorities. UNHCR has maintained a presence in the Haj camp at Silopi, where most of the remaining 1991 refugees live. Some refugees have opted for temporary residence permits but these disqualify the holders from refugee benefits. Some third-country resettlement has been arranged, mainly for 1988 refugees. UNHCR is now supervising repatriation for, it is hoped, the majority of the remaining camp populations in Turkey. However, this program was delayed from the early summer 1992 by problems in the Iraqi Kurdish areas. After a visit from members of the new Iraqi Kurdish parliament and encouragement from UNHCR, the repatriation began only in August. Now the refugees are returning as winter approaches. UNHCR is planning to provide basic shelter for the returnees and the World Food Programme will provide rations.

In Iran

Situation of Iraqi refugees at the end of June 1992:

Total: 89,180

Kurds: 59,557, of whom 44,627 are 1988 refugees, and 14,930 are 1991 refugees

Refugees in the South: 29,623

In early 1991, Iran received between 1.2 and 1.4 million refugees in the course of two months. The majority came from northern Iraq, but UNHCR recorded 68,000 refugees in the South. These people had fled to southeastern Iran from southern Iraq after the uprisings in March/April. Most were placed in 15 camps in the border vicinity. Others settled in local communities. There was already a large Iraqi refugee community in Iran (about 44,000 in camps and many others living elsewhere). These were both political refugees and groups of people expelled from Iraq during the 1970s and 1980s. In all, Iranian estimates suggest that up to one million Iraqis currently live in Iran.

A large proportion of the refugees from northern Iraq had returned home by the end of 1991. In the South, most of the returns occurred before the Iraqi amnesty for civilians and noncommissioned officers, which ended in December 1991. Since then, the military clampdown and difficult economic conditions in southern Iraq have probably deterred people from returning.

A substantial number of refugees from southern Iraq do not live in camps. They can move from camps to live in the community if they can prove that they can support themselves. In the northern, predominantly Kurdish camps, conditions have been more restrictive. The refugee camps are administered by the Bureau of Alien and Foreign Immigrant Affairs at the Ministry of the Interior. The Iranian Red Crescent and Iraqi groups based in Iran also provide services.

In Saudi Arabia

Situation of Iraqi refugees in August 1992:

Total: 28,000 (approx.)

Rafha camp—18,000

Artawiyeh camp—10,000

After the uprising in the South, some 22,000 Iraqis fleeing from government forces were air-lifted from camps on the border of Iraq by the U.S. Air Force. They were housed in a camp near the Saudi city of Rafha, close to the Iraqi border. A second camp was established for Iraqi prisoners of war at Artawiyeh, near Riyadh. This camp now houses former POWs who opted not to return to Iraq after the deadline established by the International Committee of the Red Cross (ICRC). After August 1991, they were classified by ICRC as civilian refugees entitled to protection under the Fourth Geneva Convention.

Saudi Arabia is not a signatory of the 1951 Convention on Refugees and UNHCR had never operated there. Only as of 1992 did UNHCR receive official recognition from the Saudi government, establishing an office in Riyadh and a permanent presence in the camps. The camps were established under the control of the Saudi Ministry of Defense and Aviation. A new camp is now being built close to the existing Rafha camp.

There were concerns that some cases of involuntary repatriation occurred in 1991 and early 1992, particularly from Artawiyeh camp. Conditions for the former POWs in this camp were reported to be harsh and there have been a number of allegations of ill-treatment by Saudi guards.

Resettlement has been agreed upon for small groups of refugees. Iran has accepted about 5,000 refugees. The U.S. announced in October that it would be accepting up to 3,000 refugees from these camps and about 1,000 will go to Nordic countries.

In Syria

There are some 4,000 refugees from Iraq in Al Hol camp. Over half of this population are said to be Assyrians, the remainder are mostly Kurds, and a few third-country nationals.

In Kuwait

Twenty thousand Iraqi nationals are reported to remain in Kuwait (July 1992). They are not housed in camps. UNHCR estimates that some 85,000 Bedouins are alleged by the Kuwaiti authorities to be Iraqis, though their nationality has not been clarified. UNHCR states that it is "assisting the Kuwaiti authorities to clarify the situation of the Bedouins." In May 1992, ICRC estimated that about 2,500 people had been deported from Kuwait, along with some 5,000 dependents since ICRC began monitoring deportations in July 1991. Hundreds more were thought to have been deported before that date. For the most part the deportees have been Iraqis, Bedouins, and Palestinians, with a few Sudanese and Yemenis.

In May 1991, the Kuwaiti government gave its acceptance of a UNHCR *chargé de mission* and support staff in Kuwait.

IN JORDAN

An undefined number of Iraqis (probably tens of thousands), many of them Christians from Baghdad and the North, went to Jordan in 1991 seeking emigration or asylum in third countries. Few were accepted as refugees, or as immigrants, and many were forced to return to Iraq, having used up their savings. Others still remain in Jordan.

REFUGEES AND DISPLACED PEOPLE WITHIN IRAQ

DISPLACED IRAQIS IN NORTHERN IRAQ:

Some 100,000–150,000 people from the city and region of Kirkuk still under Iraqi control remain within the Kurdish areas of Iraq. The UN has been unable to establish a presence in Kirkuk because of opposition from the Iraqi government. Displaced people have been afraid to return without UNHCR supervision and protection.

In addition, thousands of people have been displaced temporarily or on a longer-term basis from villages which have been shelled or cleared by the Iraqis since September 1991, when the army withdrew from much of the predominantly Kurdish North. In late 1991, some 200,000 were displaced from the environs of Chamchamal, Kifri and Qala Diza. In March and April 1992, some 40,000 were displaced by heavy shelling from the area around Khalah and Khabat, north west of Irbil. Most of this group subsequently returned to their homes.

DISPLACED IRAQIS IN SOUTHERN IRAQ

After the 1991 uprising, larger numbers of people in southern Iraq fled to the marsh areas between Amara, Nasariya, Basra and the Iranian border. Precise figures have never been established. Initial estimates of up to 500,000 appear to have been too high, but certainly tens of thousands were internally displaced. Since the end of 1991, further forcible displacements have taken place in the Marshes. The displacements have been the result of Iraqi artillery bombardments and aerial attacks destroying homes and means of livelihood. The cordon of troops and checkpoints surrounding the Marshes has restricted trade, food, and medical supplies. No reliable estimates are available of the numbers who have been forced or induced to move from the Marshes.

REFUGEES/DISPLACED PERSONS

In Iraq, it is estimated that there may be 6,000 to 10,000 Palestinians displaced from Kuwait, mostly people from the Gaza Strip with Egyptian travel documents. Some 3,500 people from Kuwait, mostly Bedouins, registered with ICRC in Baghdad after the 1991 war. Of those requesting repatriation, only a few hundred have been allowed to return to Kuwait.

KUWAIT

MISSING KUWAITIS

In May 1992, the Kuwaiti government estimated that some 850 Kuwaitis were still missing since the war. Most are thought to be held in Iraq. The Kuwait Association for Defending War Victims put the number at 770. The Iraqi government does not admit to holding any Kuwaiti POWs and consequently has not produced any list of prisoners.

TABLE 6-12. MIGRATION ESTIMATES, BRITISH REFUGEE COUNCIL

Estimates of foreign nationals and their dependents in Kuwait, Iraq
and other affected countries in mid-1990, and of returnees from the area in 1990–1 (thousands).

Country of origin	Kuwait		Iraq		Returnees
	Workers[1]	Dependents	Workers[1]	Dependents	
Egypt	180	35	850	50	500–700
Yemen	7	16	1	1	750–800[2]
Jordan/Palestine	110	400	5	22	350[3]
Lebanon	20	20	15	5	60
Sudan	12	3	190	10	35–200
Syria	(Unknown)		(Unknown)		50–130
India	130	42	7	2	180–200
Sri Lanka	79	21	1	0	73–101
Pakistan	77	13	7	2	90–142
Bangladesh	70	4	15	0	64–90
China	(Unknown)			60[4]	60
Philippines	38	7	7	2	30–55
Vietnam	(Unknown)		16[5]		8–16
Thailand	(Unknown)		(Unknown)		10

Notes:
1. Migrant workers or economically active foreigners.
2. The People's Democratic Republic of Yemen and the Yemen Arab Republic united in 1990 to form the Republic of Yemen. All figures cited here refer to the combined total. Most Yemenis returned from Saudi Arabia.
3. Not all the returnees were from Iraq or Kuwait.
4. Total number of workers reported to be in Iraq and Kuwait.
5. Total number of workers, mainly in Iraq.

Sources: International Labor Office; U.S. General Accounting Office; International Organization for Migration; United Nations Development Programme.

Meanwhile, ICRC has been trying to obtain information from the Kuwaiti Ministry of the Interior on the whereabouts of at least 100 people reportedly missing in Kuwait since liberation.

RETURNING MIGRANTS

This section is derived from Dr. N. Van Hear's Migrant Workers in the Gulf—Update, *published by the Minority Rights Group (U.K.).*

The 1990 Iraqi invasion of Kuwait caused major disruption for the many migrant workers in the Gulf area, where most countries, including Kuwait, were heavily dependent on imported labor. By the end of 1990, some two million foreign workers had left Iraq and Kuwait, having lost their jobs or fearing the outcome of the invasion. The largest groups of workers came from the Arab world—Jordan, Egypt, Yemen, Lebanon, Syria and Sudan; and from South and East Asia: India, Pakistan, Bangladesh, Sri Lanka, and the Philippines.

By the end of 1990 more than one million of those who left Iraq and Kuwait had entered or passed through Jordan: some 250,000 with Jordanian nationality (mainly Palestinians) and 865,000 third-country nationals. A further 220,000 foreign nationals were evacuated through Turkey, Iran and Syria. Many of these involuntary migrants lost their assets and were harassed en route.

The International Response to the Refugee Crisis

Background Information

This article is based on Larry Minear and Thomas G. Weiss, "Groping and Coping in the Gulf Crisis: Discerning the Shape of a New Humanitarian Order," World Policy Journal, *Fall/Winter 1992.*

In August 1990, 850,000 third country nationals and 300,000 Palestinians fled Kuwait. At least a million refugees, many without travel documents, were accepted into Jordan in a few months. Within a month of the Iraqi invasion, an extra 14,000 refugees were arriving in Jordan daily.

UN organizations and NGOs were slow to respond to this crisis. Less than 1,000 metric tons of food arrived by the end of August 1990, and only 9,000 tons by mid-November.

Jordan's critical humanitarian contributions, totalling $55 million, which saved hundreds or thousands of lives, were ignored by the Western media. The Jordanian government was reimbursed by the international community for only $18 million of its contribution.

As of March 1991, 1.5 million Iraqi Kurds fled to the Turkish border and Iran, a population displacement on an unprecedented scale. Whereas Iran took more refugees than Turkey, the Turkish government received more compensation from the international community.

In March 1991, recognizing that the UN had been unprepared for such a huge population displacement, the Secretary-General created the Department of Humanitarian Affairs and appointed a humanitarian coordinator with a revolving fund of $50 million at his disposal. With Resolution 688 in April 1991, the UN Security Council set a precedent by insisting that the Iraqi government allow access for humanitarian organizations, and authorizing the use of force to create the safe haven for the Kurds.[1]

The UN also had the Iraqi government sign a memorandum of understanding detailing the kinds of services to be provided and the number of international personnel to be involved. A year later, however, when these arrangements expired, there was little continuing international pressure on the Iraqi government to allow access to humanitarian organizations. Minear and Weiss suggest that, in retrospect, it would have been better to include in Resolution 687, as one of the conditions for the lifting of sanctions, the demand for the Iraqis to allow access for humanitarian groups.

In its overall handling of the Gulf crisis, the UN Security Council set a number of precedents. Its actions against Iraq, the freezing of assets, the disarming of unconventional weapons plants, and the establishment of a reparations fund all break new ground. This gives grounds for hope that the UN is entering a period of institutional restructuring which will equip it for a more effective role.

CRITICISMS OF THE INTERNATIONAL RESPONSE

The UN did not anticipate the huge scale of the refugee problem. In August 1990 and again in March 1991, the UN response to refugee problems was too slow. Delays of a few weeks in the transmission of pledged aid created major problems for humanitarian workers on the scene.

International agencies imported unnecessary foreign personnel. For example, although there are unemployed doctors in Jordan, many foreign doctors were imported, at a far higher cost, to deal with the crisis in Jordan.

Many competing UN agencies, including the Office of the UN Disaster Relief Co-ordinator (UNDRO), UNICEF, the World Food Programme, the UNHCR, UNDP and WHO, were involved in the response, each with its own staff and fundraising channels. There was a lack of institutional resources for coordinating the response. Donations were received specifically earmarked for particular projects and institutions, or particular villages or NGOs, at a time when shortage of funds made greater flexibility essential. NGOs also lacked a framework for coordinating their efforts.

A major obstacle for UN organizations with a humanitarian function was the Security Council's determination to enforce sanctions. Inevitably, one result of this conflict was that Iraqis distrusted UN humanitarian organizations, and to a lesser extent Western NGOs. Iraqi Ambassador Riyadh Al Qaysi stated in Baghdad that, throughout the Gulf crisis, "political considerations and interests were the prime motivation for the aid that was given, articulated and implemented by the international community." In this respect the International Committee of the Red Cross (ICRC) had the advantage over other NGOs, having credibility with the Iraqi government because of its assistance to Iraqis during the Iran-Iraq War.

Minear and Weiss argue that "the inconsistencies between the humanitarian and political-military aspects of the United Nations have yet to receive serious attention." These inconsistencies explain the failure to compensate Jordan or Iran for their humanitarian aid to refugees, and the failure to provide humanitarian aid to Iraqis in the same measure as to Kurds. The maintenance of sanctions continues to negate the effects of humanitarian aid to Iraq.

OBSERVATIONS

Minear and Weiss make the following observations.

The slowness of response to the humanitarian crisis in the Gulf indicates excessive centralization within the UN. UN field staff should have more power to make on-the-spot decisions and commit resources. The UN should appoint one individual in a given region who has the power to coordinate UN resources in a crisis situation.

The case of Iraq suggests that sanctions may sometimes be an even crueller solution to a crisis than the use of military force to topple a regime. The population of Iraq got the worst of both worlds. Minear and Weiss hope that in future the UN will be able to coordinate its various powers more effectively. Sanctions in late 1990 could have been more effective if coupled with an effective naval and land blockade. Once the war had begun, the Coalition might have pressed on to depose Saddam Hussein, preventing the subsequent repression of the Shiites and Kurds.

Coordination between the political and humanitarian divisions of the UN might result in a less contradictory response to future crises. In the future, before a decision is made to impose sanctions, the views of UN organizations with humanitarian competence and responsibilities, such as UNICEF and the World Food Programme, should be consulted. If the Security Council decides to proceed with sanctions, funds should be collected from governments at once to ameliorate their consequences.

—*James Warner*

NOTES:

1. This interpretation of UN Security Council Resolution 688, included in Appendix One, is controversial. UN lawyers have said that no language in existing resolutions gives the U.S., Britain and France authority to enforce the no-fly zones. "UN Lawyers Back Iraq View—Attacks Not Authorized," *Los Angeles Times,* reprinted in the *San Francisco Chronicle,* January 22, 1993.

The "Gulf War Syndrome"

Background Information

Since returning home, thousands of U.S. soldiers have suffered from muscle spasms, joint and muscle pains, rectal bleeding, respiratory problems, fatigue, headaches, nausea, sleep disorders, weight loss, memory loss, skin rashes, fevers, impotence, miscarriages and birth defects—a set of disparate symptoms the media have dubbed the "Gulf War Syndrome." A number of secret or little-publicized reports, now becoming available, indicate that the Bush Administration knew prior to the war of a number of factors other than combat that might endanger the health of troops serving in the Gulf.

One veteran told the U.S. House Veterans Affairs Committee on Hospitals and Health Care, at a hearing held on September 21, 1992:[1]

> I was a healthy, high-spirited individual prior to serving in the Gulf. I now live daily with shortness of breath, choking, and wheezing. For reasons unknown, I suffer from chronic diarrhea and continue to lose weight. I have fevers of 103 degrees, recurring sores and a tingling sensation in both arms, especially when my heart rate is high. With little or no exertion, I suffer from extreme fatigue.
>
> *Sgt. Frank Landy, Nashua, New Hampshire*

Multiple Causes

The potential causes of the Gulf War Syndrome are numerous, including the Kuwaiti oil fires and exposure to depleted uranium and Iraqi chemical warfare agents.[2] A number of other possible environmental causes for the veterans' illnesses are currently under consideration. The following list was supplied by Todd Ensign, the director of Citizen Soldier, a G.I./veterans' rights advocacy group based in New York City:[3] aerial spraying of pesticides over U.S. military bases in Saudi Arabia, spraying of diesel oil to control dust around U.S. military bases in Saudi Arabia, radiation exposure from depleted uranium,[4] portable heaters that used leaded gasoline and diesel fuel inside unventilated tents, and the detonation of Iraqi ammunition depots.

Other possible causes are infectious diseases indigenous to the Middle East and the alarming possibility that the soldiers are suffering from the side-effects of drugs given to them that had not been approved for general civilian use by the U.S. Food and Drug Administration (FDA).

Drugs Given Without Informed Consent[5]

Chemical and biological warfare agents were one possible cause of the ailments. Iraq had used chemical weapons in its war with Iran, and threatened to use them against Israel and the Coalition. Ironically, the drugs administered to U.S. troops to counteract these weapons may also have been damaging to their health.

Three drugs were administered to U.S. troops as antidotes for biological or nerve-gas weapons. Only one, an anthrax vaccine, had passed the review of the FDA; the other two had not. Pyridostigmine bromide tablets were approved by the FDA only for the treatment of myasthenia gravis, a disease of faulty nerve conduction, characterized by muscular weakness and fatigue. A botulism (botulinum-toxoid) vaccine had not received licensing approval from the FDA. Botulism is poisoning resulting from a toxin sometimes found in improperly canned or preserved foods, and can cause muscular paralysis and disturbances of vision and breathing.

Normally, drugs which have not been cleared by a FDA review must by law be administered only to an individual who gives his or her informed consent. An individual is said to have given informed consent when he or she has been fully informed of the consequences of an action and has agreed to it in the light of that knowledge. After the Iraqi invasion of Kuwait, the FDA bypassed these requirements by issuing a new general regulation. Rule 23(d) declared that consent "is not feasible in a specific military operation involving combat or the immediate threat of combat."

At the outset of the war, Ralph Nader's advocacy organization, the Citizen Health Research Group, went to court to stop the military from giving unapproved drugs to the troops. A U.S. District Court judge denied an injunction to stop the drug program, citing a number of precedents in which the courts have refused to obstruct military operations. The case went to the Court of Appeals, which, in a two-to-one opinion written by Judge Ruth Ginsburg in July 1991, defined the issue not as an action challenging military decisions, but one challenging the authority of the Food and Drug Administration. Although rule 23(d) raises the troubling issue of human experimentation, the Court of Appeals upheld the lower court's decision, stating among other issues that the administration of unapproved drugs did not violate the Fifth Amendment interest of service people.

Involuntary Vaccinations[6]

General Norman Schwarzkopf issued an order that the botulinum toxoid vaccine was to be given on a voluntary basis, despite the FDA waiver saying that informed consent was not required. However, several veterans complained of forcible administration of vaccines, both to Todd Ensign of Citizen Soldier and to a congressional hearing:

> They said that if I didn't take the vaccination, then I was under UCMJ (Uniform Code of Military Justice) action [subject to court-martial].
>
> *Phillip J. Abbatessa, East Boston, Massachusetts, who served with the 101st Airborne Division, an active-duty unit*

Sergeant Venus Hammack, of Lowell, Massachusetts, a veteran with 16 years in the military, told the 1992 House Veterans Affairs Committee that she had been held down and forcibly given the vaccine against her will. Paul Perrone, of Methuen, Massachusetts, said he was told only two weeks after his vaccination that it was supposed to be voluntary.

One Army Reserve doctor, Captain Yolanda Huet-Vaughn of Kansas City refused to serve in the Gulf, in part because she did not want to vaccinate soldiers without their consent. Sentenced to 30 months, the mother of three was later released after serving eight months, thanks to pressure from Amnesty International's international membership.

Todd Ensign believes that most of the troops that were in the immediate combat zone received the unapproved drugs without their informed consent.

Risks of Oil Fires Covered Up

A secret 132-page report to the Bush Administration prior to the war suggested that smoke and pollution ingested or inhaled from the Kuwaiti oil fires could pose health problems to those downwind of the fires. The Sandia Report was prepared for the United States Department of Energy, under a contract with the Office of Foreign Intelligence, and is quoted from below:

Burning oil or fumes from a breached well would generate a plume containing a number of potentially hazardous components, including carbon monoxide and products of incomplete combustion, such as polyaromatic hydrocarbons, sulfur dioxide, and heavy metals. . . . It is probable that a small sensitive population consisting of the elderly, infants, individuals with cardiovascular or pulmonary impairments, and some hypersensitive individuals would exhibit clinically detectable symptoms if exposed to the plume at optimal distances. Symptoms would include irritation of eyes and throat and aggravation of bronchitis and asthma. . . . Any increase in cancer incidence would be undetectable by current statistical methods. . . . The primary toxicological effect would be a possible increased mortality in a small sensitive population from inhalation of sulfur dioxide and particulates. Because of the low exposure level and the small target population, the increased mortality may not be obvious except by retrospective analysis. Downwind of the trench, however, short term exposures to soot and sulfur dioxide would result in an appreciable impact to the respiratory system of personnel without protective apparatus.[7]

Major General Ronald R. Blanck of the U.S. Army told a congressional hearing in June 1993 that the Army is responding to the insufficiency of data about the effects of the Kuwaiti oil fires with studies that include environmental monitoring, a health risk assessment, and a biologic surveillance initiative.[8]

INFECTIOUS DISEASES

Soldiers in the Gulf were given drugs to protect them against infectious hepatitis and malaria, and their medical records were reviewed to ensure that they had current immunizations against polio, typhoid, diphtheria-tetanus, influenza and meningococcal meningitis.[9] However, there are many other endemic diseases for which there are no preventive measures.

One month after the cease-fire, a group of doctors practicing in the Walter Reed Army Medical Center published an article in the *New England Journal of Medicine* to alert physicians to be on the lookout for these diseases in returning service people.[10] The article summarized the risks involved in military service in the Gulf:

Whenever Americans spend time in foreign lands, they may become infected with pathogens alien to the United States and bring these pathogens back with them. Mass deployments of the U.S. armed forces abroad amplify this risk since military personnel are more intimately exposed than ordinary travelers to each other, to local people, and to the natural environment. The breakdown of public health measures, hygiene, sanitation, and nutrition that inevitably accompanies warfare further magnifies this peril. Since August 1990, more than 500,000 Americans have been sent to the Middle East, where they have encountered a variety of infectious diseases endemic to the area. . . . In terms of incidence, gastrointestinal illnesses pose by far the largest threat to Westerners visiting the Middle East. Incidence rates have been as high as 50 cases per 1,000 American troops per week in Saudi Arabia. . . . Although most of the consequent illness will be treated by military physicians, some will undoubtedly occur outside the purview of the military health care system. This will be especially true for the thousands of reservists recently called from civilian life to active military service and sent to the Middle East. Some will return to their civilian communities with diseases that only become evident after their homecoming, sometimes after months or years, and others will pose a risk of secondary transmission to people with whom they come into contact.

The physicians concluded that:

> Although the majority of servicemen and servicewomen returning from the Middle East are not
> likely to have contracted infectious diseases other than enteric infections, several principles should
> guide physicians who evaluate them. First, a limited number of infections that are uncommon in
> the United States may be rapidly fatal and should be specifically excluded. Second, broadly resist-
> ant enteric pathogens and Congo-Crimean hemorrhagic fever pose a risk of secondary spread to
> contacts. Third, certain infectious agents (e.g. sandfly fever virus and the leishmania species that
> cause cutaneous disease) may cause chronic, indolent syndromes. Fourth, various agents, including
> leishmania, brucella, *Coxiella burnetii* (the agent of Q fever), and echinococcus (causing hydatid
> disease), may emerge years after exposure and may pose their greatest risk to persons who become
> immunosuppressed as a result of other illnesses. Persons presenting a variety of illnesses after de-
> ployment to the Middle East should alert clinicians to these possibilities. Questions about the man-
> agement of suspected infectious diseases in returning personnel may be referred to the Walter
> Reed Army Medical Center, Infectious Disease Section (202-576-1740, 1741, or 1742).

Of these diseases, leishmaniasis, transmitted by the bite of sandflies, has emerged as a paramount problem in returning troops, according to one of the article's authors, Major Alan J. Magill, M.D., U.S. Army, who says: "There are eight published cases of leishmaniasis so far, but we are seeing only the tip of the iceberg. The current diagnostic is woefully insensitive in picking up cases of leishmaniasis, and there could be thousands of infections."[11] The disease can affect the bone mar-row, spleen and liver, causing symptoms that include chronic fatigue, joint pain, diarrhea, gastro-intestinal complaints, coughs and fevers.

POST-TRAUMATIC STRESS DISORDER

The Department of Veterans Affairs has found that Gulf War veterans were twice as likely to suffer from Post-Traumatic Stress Disorder (PTSD) as soldiers who were called up at the time of the war but never went into battle.[12] Department of Veterans' Affairs spokesperson Terry Jemi-son points out that people who are in potentially life-threatening situations, or who have seen charred bodies of Iraqi soldiers, might suffer from stress, which could make them subsequently more susceptible to environmental exposures.

Some critics think the military is too ready to blame veterans' disorders on PTSD. However both Terry Jemison and critics of the Department of Veterans Affairs, including Todd Ensign, are in agreement that the symptoms of the so-called Gulf War Syndrome may be caused by a multi-tude of synergistically related factors.

VETERANS DESCRIBE GWS SYMPTOMS

Several veterans described their illnesses to the House Veterans Affairs Committee hearing on Hospitals and Health Care, held on September 21, 1992:[13]

> I was sick with a high fever, had a hard time breathing and [experienced] constant vomiting and
> dysentery. In the past I had set records in physical training; now, I couldn't get back in shape. In
> February 1992, rectal bleeding [began], I couldn't digest food and my skin got scaly and blotchy.
>
> *Phillip J. Abbatessa, East Boston, Massachusetts.*

> Since returning [home], I've had to be rushed to the hospital for prolonged bleeding several times.
> If you view my civilian and military medical records, you'll find no previous history of these disorders.
> *Venus Hammack, Lowell, Massachusetts.*

Of the 231,000 U.S. troops discharged after the Gulf War, 72,000 have come to Veterans' Service Hospitals to receive treatment since August 1990, when the deployment of U.S troops to Saudi Arabia began, and of these, 4,100 left the service as a result of conditions typical of military service, from scars to back injuries, and 32 as a result of environmentally related disabilities.

In 1992 the Bush Administration set up the Persian Gulf Registry primarily for veterans with medical problems who believe they were exposed to environmental hazards, or are concerned that they might have been. The program tracks patterns in diagnostic data that could offer directions for research and policy review. The program also keeps veterans informed about new scientific findings and policy developments. As of June 1993, 6,125 veterans had signed onto the Persian Gulf Registry.

The Department of Veterans' Affairs has also established special environmental medicine referral centers at its hospitals in West Los Angeles, Houston and Washington, D.C., but only 20 Desert Storm veterans had been admitted to these centers by March 1993.[14] The numbers of troops who may still step forward with GWS symptoms is expected to increase considerably in future years. Terry Jemison points out that 250,000 Vietnam veterans have signed onto the Agent Orange registry that was set up 20 years ago.[15]

Mike Ange, of the Military Family Support Network in Buies Creek, North Carolina, says that 3,000 veteran s and their families so far have contacted the network to complain of Gulf War Syndrome symptoms.[16]

CRITICISMS OF THE GOVERNMENT RESPONSE

Critics of the government's response claim that efforts thus far have been inadequate. In their view, symptoms are neither being defined or tested correctly, nor are the proper questions being asked to establish exposures to environmental factors and diseases, which vary from unit to unit and from person to person. In response to the latter charge, Department of Veterans' Affairs spokesperson Linda Stalvey says that although the Persian Gulf Registry is meant to be all-inclusive, the questionnaire changes as more information becomes available.[17]

Reserve Major Richard Haynes of the 415th Civil Affairs Battalion in Kalamazoo, Michigan, believes that the basic blood test, chest x-ray, and basic physicals by Department of Veteran Affairs doctors are insufficient to deal with the complexity of the possible problems. Major Haynes has spent the bulk of his savings to set up a database for Gulf veterans suffering from a host of symptoms. He suggests the use of brain scans and specialized tests involving hair analysis, blood analysis, fat cell biopsies, and bone analysis, to determine the nature of the illnesses, which he believes may include brain damage, central nervous damage, immune damage, liver damage, gland or hormone damage, severe metabolic imbalance and chemical hypersensitivity.[18] Mike Ange says that some soldiers linked up to the Military Families Support Network have been found to have elevated white cell counts, unusual amounts of minerals, and other signs that Army physicians do not typically look for.

One of the main limitations of the government response is that the Persian Gulf Registry does not keep records on troops still serving in the armed services. Active duty troops are also not covered by pending legislation that may give veterans priority for treatment for possible Gulf War impacts, even if they cannot prove their symptoms are due to the war. Active duty troops are also less likely to admit to having these symptoms, since there is still a lot of "impatience in the military" about the environmental illnesses, according to Terry Jemison.

Critics of the Pentagon say that even if it is proved conclusively that the government concealed information about health risks, soldiers cannot sue the military because of a 1951 Supreme Court decision known as the Feres Doctrine.[19] In the past, service people who were involuntarily dosed with LSD and who suffered health effects from Agent Orange have been unable to sue because of the Feres Doctrine.

However, it is encouraging to note that the official response to those suffering from Gulf War Syndrome has been faster than in previous similar cases, such as those related to Agent Orange. Despite their drawbacks, the programs to help veterans provide long-awaited official recognition that the veterans' environmental exposures can produce disabling illnesses. This governmental acknowledgment should be cause for much concern for the people of Iraq, Kuwait and Saudi Arabia who were also exposed to the unquantifiable toxic hazards of the war.

—*Philippa Winkler*

NOTES:

1. Todd Ensign, "Guinea Pigs and Disposable GIs," *CovertAction*, Winter 1992-1993.
2. See Chapter Seven, "Nerve Gas Linked to Veterans' Illnesses."
3. Todd Ensign, "Guinea Pigs and Disposable GIs."
4. See Chapter Four, "Depleted Uranium: Radioactive Residue in the Desert and in the U.S."
5. Information for most of this section comes from George J. Annas, J.D., M.P.H., "Changing the Consent Rules for Desert Storm," *The New England Journal of Medicine*, March 12, 1992.
6. Information for this section comes from Todd Ensign, "Guinea Pigs and Disposable GIs" and interview with Todd Ensign, August 10, 1993.
7. H. W. Church et al, *Potential Impacts of Iraqi Use of Oil as a Defensive Weapon*, Sandia National Laboratories, January 1991, 120-121. See Chapter Two, "A Prewar Environmental Assessment."
8. Statement by Major General Ronald R. Blanck, Commanding General, Walter Reed Army Medical Center, before the Subcommittee on Oversight and Investigations Committee on Veterans' Affairs, House of Representatives, June 9, 1993.
9. Statement by Major General Ronald R. Blanck.
10. Lt. Col. Robert A. Gasser, Jr. et al., "The Threat of Infectious Disease in Americans Returning from Operation Desert Storm," *The New England Journal of Medicine*, March 21, 1991.
11. Interview with Major Alan J. Magill, M.D., U.S. Army, August 20, 1993. See also Magill et al., "Visceral Infection Causes by *Leishmania Tropica* in Veterans of Operation Desert Storm," *New England Journal of Medicine*, May 13, 1993.
12. Department of Veterans' Affairs Fact Sheet, "Distribution of Selected Diagnostic Groups for 4,514 Persian Gulf Veterans and 4,325 Era Veterans Treated in VA Hospitals on an Inpatient Basis," May 1993.
13. Todd Ensign, "Guinea Pigs and Disposable GIs."

14. Department of Veterans' Affairs Fact Sheet, "VA Health Care for Persian Gulf Veterans," May 1993.

15. Interview with Terry Jemison, Public Affairs, Department of Veterans' Affairs, August 8, 1993.

16. Interview with Mike Ange, August 20, 1993. The network does not have a publicly listed phone number and can only be reached by word of mouth.

17. Interview with Linda Stalvey, Public Affairs, Department of Veterans' Affairs, August 17, 1993.

18. Major Richard H. Haines, Memo to Ray Parrish, veteran and activist with the Midwest Committee for Military Counseling, March 9, 1 993. Dr. Theron Randolph, who is considered a founder of modern epidemiology, believes that some Gulf veterans may be suffering from "Multiple Chemical Sensitivity" (MCS), a diagnosis that he created. Terry Jemison, the spokesperson for the Department of Veterans Affairs, believes that MCS has not yet been subjected to systematic study with placebos and controls to develop medical protocols as demanded by the American Medical Association, but that further research should be encouraged.

19. Feres v. United States, 340 U.S. 135 (1950). Congressmember Barney Frank has introduced legislation to either overturn or modify the Feres Doctrine.

Destroying Iraq's Nuclear, Biological and Chemical Arsenal: Implications for Arms Control

The Tammuz II Reactor at Tuwaitha destroyed by Coalition bombing. Photo: United Nations.

Introduction

Nuclear, chemical and biological weapons and their delivery systems are sometimes called unconventional weapons. The difference between conventional and unconventional weapons is in orders of magnitude. For example, while missiles armed with conventional high explosives can destroy a skyscraper with hundreds of civilians in it, nuclear explosives destroy cities with hundreds of thousands of inhabitants. This capacity for massive human and environmental destruction is what makes a weapon unconventional.

Because unconventional weapons cause such severe damage, are difficult to control and are often indiscriminate in their destruction, they are of little military value. Their value lies in the fact that possessing them confers on the owner a regional superpower status. With sufficient quantities and long-range delivery systems, regional powers can become global powers.

While the use of these armaments is unusual, it is not unknown. Chemical weapons, particularly mustard gas, were widely used by both sides in World War I. In 1920 Britain dropped chemical bombs on the insurgent tribes of the Euphrates, killing 9,000 people.[1] Germany killed millions of Jewish civilians in gas chambers during World War II. Some maintain that the widespread spraying of Agent Orange and its consequent impacts on the environment in Vietnam constituted use of a chemical weapon. Iraq used chemical weapons against Kurds in Halabja in 1988.

The use of biological weapons is even more rare. After the 1925 Geneva Protocol banning "bacteriological weapons," they were used by the Japanese against Chinese civilians in 1940–41.[2] Cuba blamed an outbreak of swine fever in the early 1980s on U.S. use of biological weapons.

Only the United States has actually used atomic weapons against another nation, with the bombing of Hiroshima and Nagasaki in 1945.

The Persian Gulf War was the first war in which a nation possessing unconventional weapons had its production and storage infrastructure targeted for destruction, with potentially serious impacts on the surrounding community and ecology. Quoted in the *Washington Post,* President Bush made it clear that the bombing of Iraq's nuclear and chemical facilities was one of the highest priorities of the early stages of the war.[3] F111s, F117A Stealth fighter-bombers and sea-launched cruise missiles carried out the attack. According to a map accompanying the *Post* article, Iraqi targets stretched from the southern Iraqi city of Basra to the cities of Mosul and Irbil in the North. Also hit were the sites near the central and eastern urban centers of Iskandariya, Salmanpak, Samarra, Tikrit, and Baiji. To the west, sites were bombed near Akashat and Al Qaim on the Iraqi-Syrian border.

The *New York Times* reported that two research nuclear reactors, Tammuz II and IRT-T2000, both safeguarded under the International Atomic Energy Agency, had been among the first targets hit by Coalition forces. Also hit were nuclear fuel enrichment test laboratories at Zaffarina and Al Fallujah, southwest of nearby Baghdad.[4]

The destruction of these facilities involved significant environmental risks. Prior to the war, as can be seen from *Hidden Casualties*, Volume 1,[5] ARC/Arms Control Research Center was extremely concerned about the contamination that might result if these installations were destroyed. Throughout the war, ARC heard intermittent, unconfirmed reports of trace contamination from the destruction of these bombed sites. One of ARC's principal interests in accompanying the International Study Team (IST) to Iraq was to investigate the possibility of such releases.

However, this was not to be. The Iraqi government made it clear to our IST contacts that they would not be able to visit the sites in question. As a result, all confirmation of the environmental implications of the destruction of these facilities comes from the UN itself. This presents a conflict, since it is fundamentally not within the interests of either Iraq or the Coalition to admit to widespread contamination resulting from the war. Statements from the United Nations Special Committee (UNSCOM) should be viewed in this light.

Chapter Seven looks at the impacts of these bombings, and the postwar inspection and destruction of Iraq's unconventional arsenal. Jay Davis, a nuclear physicist with Lawrence Livermore National Laboratory, describes Iraq's nuclear weapons complex and the effects of the Coalition attacks on it. In a reprint of an *Arms Control Today* article, David Albright, a senior scientist with Friends of the Earth, and Mark Hibbs of *Nucleonics Week* provide their perspectives on the lessons to be drawn from Iraq's quest for entry into the "nuclear club."[6]

Because nuclear reactors can be involved in the production of weapons material, and because Coalition forces bombed them during the war, we have incorporated an interview with Bennett Ramburg, Director of Research at the Committee to Bridge the Gap. Bennett Ramburg discusses the impacts and policy implications of the first bombing of active nuclear reactors in history.

Matthew Meselson of Harvard University discusses Iraq's chemical weapons, the history of chemical weapons,[7] and the new international Chemical Weapons Convention and raises some important questions regarding U.S. policy toward the convention. Bryan Barrass of the United Nations Special Committee (UNSCOM) discusses the UN's program for destroying Iraq's chemical weapons. Both Meselson and Barrass briefly discuss Iraq's biological weapons. However, as of this writing, Iraq's biological capability remains something of a mystery, although there is evidence that biological warfare was used against the Kurds in the late 1980s.[8] The development of Iraq's long-range ballistic missile system is covered in Chapter Nine, "Iraqgate Chronology."

Chapter Seven paints a disturbing picture of the environmental, political and logistical difficulty of putting the unconventional genie back in the bottle.

—Saul Bloom and Daniel Robicheau

NOTES:

1. Medical Educational Trust, *Chemical and Biological Weapons; Background Papers*, Report, updated May 1991.
2. Medical Educational Trust, *Chemical and Biological Weapons; Background Papers*.
3. Rick Atkinson and David Broder, "Air War Against Iraq Continues," *Washington Post*, January 17, 1991, A1.

4. Eric Schmidt, "A Search and Destroy Priority: Unconventional Iraqi Munitions," *New York Times,* January 30, 1991, A9.

5. ARC/Arms Control Research Center, *Hidden Casualties, Volume I: The Environmental Consequences of the Persian Gulf Conflict* (San Francisco: ARC/Arms Control Research Center), 1991.

6. According to the U.S. Arms Control Disarmament Agency, countries with declared nuclear arsenals include: U.S., Russia, Kazakhstan, Ukraine, Belarus, U.K., France, China and India. Countries with undeclared nuclear arsenals: Pakistan and Israel. Countries suspected of trying to build nuclear weapons: Iran, Iraq and North Korea. Countries believed to be backing away from nuclear ambitions: Argentina, Brazil, Taiwan and South Africa. Countries that have the capability of building nuclear weapons: Australia, Canada, Japan, Germany, Netherlands, Chile and South Korea.

7. Chemical-weapons capable countries include: U.S., some states of the former USSR, China, France, U.K., Egypt, Iraq, Iran, Israel, Libya, Syria, Afghanistan, Burma, India, North Korea, Pakistan, Philippines, Taiwan, Thailand, Vietnam, Angola, Ethiopia, Somalia, South Africa, Sudan, Argentina, Chile, Cuba, El Salvador. Medical Educational Trust, *Chemical and Biological Weapons.*

8. In November of 1992, Middle East Watch obtained a top secret Iraqi government document, dated August 1986, in which the commander of military intelligence in Irbil ordered division units to count their stocks of "biochemical materials." The same document had been quoted in a report privately published in England in January 1991, *Death Clouds: Saddam Hussein's Chemical War Against the Kurds,* by Dlawer Ala'Aldeen, a Kurdish microbiologist and doctor at the University of Nottingham Hospital and Medical School in England. In 1988, Dlawer Ala'Aldeen had accused the Iraqi government of starting an outbreak of typhoid in Sulaymaniyah—his evidence was that the outbreak stemmed from a single strain of bacteria, rather than from several diffent strains, suggesting that it was the result of an artificially produced agent. Judith Miller, "Evidence Grows On Biological Weapons," *New York Times Magazine,* January 1993, 33.

What UNSCOM Found in Iraq—Part One

Interview with Jay C. Davis

Jay C. Davis, Ph.D., is a nuclear physicist who is Director of the Center for Accelerator Mass Spectrometry at Lawrence Livermore National Laboratory, Livermore, California. He was a member of the early UNSCOM and International Atomic Energy Agency (IAEA) teams inspecting the Iraqi nuclear program. The interview took place by submitting the questions in written form. Dr. Davis' responses appear here verbatim. Interviewed by Saul Bloom via fax, November 1992.

Saul Bloom: Could you, in as detailed a fashion as is reasonable (given intelligence issues), outline the objective of the mission you directed, the number of sites visited and their locations?

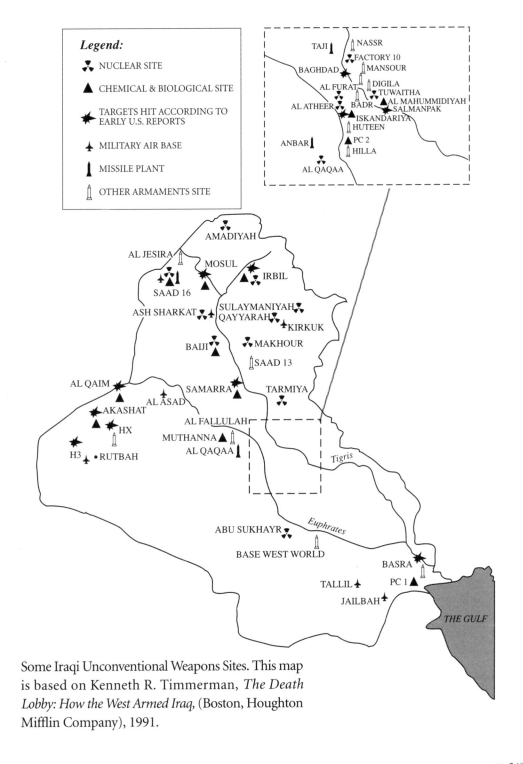

Some Iraqi Unconventional Weapons Sites. This map
is based on Kenneth R. Timmerman, *The Death
Lobby: How the West Armed Iraq,* (Boston, Houghton
Mifflin Company), 1991.

Jay C. Davis: I participated in UNSCOM/IAEA Nuclear Inspections Two and Four; approximate dates were the last two weeks of June and July 1991, respectively. As a nuclear physicist, accelerator and mass spectrometer expert, I was added to UNSCOM/IAEA Two on short notice to evaluate the rumored Iraqi Electromagnetic Isotope Separation (EMIS) program. Primary sites visited on that mission were Tuwaitha (declared nuclear site), Tarmiya (suspected nuclear site), Zaffarina Dijjla (electronics fabrication site), Abu Gharib (barracks compound, materials concealment site) and Al Fallujah (motor transport compound, materials concealment site).

I returned to Iraq on UNSCOM/IAEA Four to evaluate the human, fabrication, and technical aspects of the Iraqi uranium enrichment program as part of determining its origin, progress, and degree of success. Sites visited on this trip included Tuwaitha, Tarmiya, Al Amir, Al Radway and Badr (these last three are mechanical fabrication sites) and the State Heavy Engineering Establishment. All of these are within 150 kilometers of Baghdad. We additionally went 500 kilometers north to inspect the feedstock preparation plants at Al Jesira (UF6, UCI4) and to search for hidden materials near the Saddam Dam. The Iraqis took us to Babylon on one free day and showed us the reconstruction in progress at two bombed power plants.

SB: Could you characterize the facilities you investigated? How many people would you estimate were employed by these programs?

JD: The general character of the Iraqi facilities mirrors that of equivalent U.S., British, and other European nuclear facilities I have visited. Given slight differences in contracting and landscaping styles, the Iraqi buildings could be inserted into our sites without notice. The newer secret facilities, built as part of the enrichment program, were essentially state-of-the-art with respect to design of support systems, process equipment, and environmental controls.

The official IAEA estimate is that 20,000 people were (and still are) employed in the secret programs. Partition of them among the various sites is difficult to do because many were being turned on and staffed in parallel. I have heard estimates that up to 50,000 more people were employed in the general purpose industrial complex that provided support to the secret programs but had no direct knowledge of them.

SB: Where did Iraq obtain its supplies for constructing these programs? To what extent were Security Council member nations involved in provisioning—with or without their knowledge—the Iraqi unconventional weapons programs? A number of reports have appeared indicating that U.S. components were also used in the Iraqi nuclear weapons program. How important were these components to the production of these weapons? Can you comment on the U.S. Administration's role in the supply of this material, and if so, what was it? With regard to the Iraqi nuclear weapons program, where did they get their uranium? Were the sources solely domestic mining or did they receive supplies of ore, refined uranium, and/or uranium hexafluoride from other countries?

JD: In general, Iraqi supplies came from the U.S., Western Europe and Japan as is appropriate for high technology equipment. The five-layered Iraqi procurement activity makes it difficult to establish either national or corporate complicity in these activities, in many cases. Major civil engineering support (design and construction) for the multibillion-dollar facility at Tarmiya came from a Yugoslav firm. The U.S.'s role in allowing the export of dual-use equipment is still being explored.

SB: A number of articles printed in the U.S. pointed to a surprising level of sophistication in the Iraqi nuclear weapons program. Do you have any specific comments on this subject you can share with us?

JD: Our best estimate is that they were 18 to 30 months from having sufficient material for one or two nuclear weapons. The records of their weapons design program suggest that they could have converted the material to a workable weapon very quickly. Although they said they intended to develop a weapon suitable for delivery by ballistic missile, we in fact know of neither delivery system nor use doctrine.

Chemical weapons were in production and literally litter the countryside. Anecdotally, the biological weapons program was said by those team members to be much less developed.

SB: Did your investigation reveal anything regarding the status of the development of complete unconventional weapons systems by Iraq, including intermediate range ballistic missiles?

JD: Other than the status of the nuclear weapon program outlined above, I have no direct knowledge of the other programs. Anecdotally, the ballistic missile teams are reported to have expressed surprise at the relatively primitive state of the Iraqi missile program.

SB: How would you characterize the environmental and safety issues related to the sites you investigated? Did the Iraqis take the necessary precautions to ensure that their personnel and the surrounding environment were protected from exposure to hazardous substances, such as enriched uranium or chemical agents?

JD: Environmental control and safety practices at the Iraqi sites, particularly the newer ones, were generally excellent. As virtually all their facilities are built in the combined drainage region of the Tigris and Euphrates, they express great concern about the consequences of accidents that would affect their primary water supplies and agricultural areas. On the scale of the chemical agents they were abundantly manufacturing, enriched uranium may be regarded as a negligible hazard. The extraordinary efforts to suppress its release that were designed into the facilities at Tarmiya and Ash Sharkat were intended to prevent detection of the existence of highly enriched uranium, not necessarily to guard against environmental or personnel hazard.

SB: We understand that these facilities were primary targets for attack and that General Schwarzkopf stated that they had been taken out in the initial sorties. To what extent do you have knowledge or can you comment on the success of these operations in containing releases of contaminants? Do you have any evidence, based on the sites you have visited or information you have reviewed, that indicates that breeches of containment and releases to the environment of unconventional weapons' constituent substances had occurred? To what extent, if any, has monitoring taken place to determine if there were any releases to the environment?

JD: Onsite monitoring of the nuclear facilities indicates that negligible release of radioactive materials and hazardous compounds has occurred at Tuwaitha and Tarmiya, the only active nuclear sites. The Iraqis created a minor combined industrial and radiation hazard near the feedstock preparation plant at Al Jesira by trying to conceal acidic process fluids in a petroleum tank farm. The chemical and biological team members should have more relevant information since, unlike in most nuclear inspections, accurate monitoring was essential for their survival. Destruction of Iraqi chemical stocks is now in process under UN monitoring; presumably, that includes considerable environmental oversight.

SB: How effective was Coalition intelligence in identifying unconventional weapons targets, both before and after the war? How much of the elephant has been revealed thus far?

JD: Assessment of intelligence effectiveness is controversial and ongoing. At present, we know that all major components of the Iraqi nuclear program (including many fabrication facilities) were targeted and effectively destroyed during the war. Some components of the centrifuge program were not hit (perhaps because they were unknown), and some fabrication facilities were spared because of their proximity to civilian housing. Inspections continue to seek a hidden reactor and a centrifuge cascade. If these facilities do exist, the inspections inhibit their use, completion, or restart.

SB: You were involved in a number of confrontations with the Iraqi government and its soldiers during your investigation of Iraq's unconventional weapons capability. How do you feel the investigation has gone so far? What problems do you anticipate, if any, in the future?

JD: The investigations have been an iterative process in which Iraqi military and civilians as well as UN inspectors have been learning and modifying their roles. When the Iraqis wish to frustrate an inspection by denial of access, they can always succeed locally and for a limited time. The ability to seize the initiative from them, as occurred at Al Fallujah last year when we photographed a fleeing convoy, is unlikely to recur. Steady pressure from the Security Council has led repeatedly to Iraqi retreat and disclosure when threatening peaks. As the inspection mission shifts from discovery to inhibition and frustration, and as the present regime remains in power and feels distress from the embargo, these missions will become progressively more hazardous for the participants. While the Iraqi military have been cordial and even friendly, it must be understood that they will not hesitate to seize or execute an inspection team if ordered to do so. Under this regime, their personal survival, and that of their families, depends upon such obedience.

SB: The process of destroying Iraq's unconventional weapons production system can be rather complex. Can you illustrate any of the complexity of the process for our readers and the problems one encounters? What, if any, environmental issues are taken into consideration when these facilities and systems components are destroyed? If environmental protection is a requirement of the process, what procedures are used to accomplish this? Who is responsible for ongoing monitoring of these issues?

JD: The nuclear facilities were generally in the early stages of activation, had low inventories of materials, and are being progressively destroyed at a very low level of hazard. Fuel from the two reactors at Tuwaitha has been difficult to remove from the country for economic and political reasons (the Russians don't want it back[1]), and the fuel-holding ponds and the reactor pools themselves will have to be carefully closed and sealed. Targeting of the two reactors at Tuwaitha appears to have been done to drop buildings around the cores without damage to them. This was successfully done.

SB: As someone who has just been involved in exposing the breadth of a serious covert nuclear weapons production program, how effective do you think international conventions—like the Nuclear Non-Proliferation Treaty (NPT)—are in curtailing the spread of this dangerous technology? In the early 1980s, Israel bombed Iraq's nuclear power plant, claiming that the reactor was being used to enrich uranium to weapons grade. Is it possible for world commerce in nuclear power components to exist without creating the possibility for that technology to be marshaled into nuclear weapons programs?

JD: The Iraqi experience has shown that the present implementation of the NPT inspection and technology control protocols by the IAEA is wholly inadequate to deter a proliferator with the resources and advantages of a closed society that Iraq possessed. Presumably, renegotiation of the NPT in 1995 will include far more intrusive and aggressive inspection rights, perhaps create new bodies to carry out inspections (including having access to the sort of intelligence that has guided the UNSCOM) and encourage penalties for closed societies. The improved U.S.-Russian relationship, the current U.S. testing moratorium and the nature of the Iraqi scare may all contribute to this possibility. Note, however, that any NPT only deters national states. Prevention or discouragement of terrorist organization access to or possession of nuclear weapons will require significant relaxation in the territorial, ethnic or religious tensions that provide the motivation for such activities.

SB: What other observations have you taken from your involvement in investigating Iraq's unconventional weapons program?

JD: A great pleasure of the Iraqi inspections is that ad hoc, multinational teams assembled very quickly (and provided with minimal equipment and training) could be effective in adversarial inspection and discovery in a tightly controlled, albeit recently heavily bombed, police state. The constant and effective support of the UN Security Council was an essential element of the success. A lesson perhaps not yet learned from Iraq is that future successful arms control efforts will be inherently multinational and driven by unprecedented sharing or disclosure of intelligence information.

NOTES:

1. The IAEA has since awarded a contract to reprocess Iraq's nuclear waste to the Russian Mayak Combine at Kyshtym in the Urals, considered the world's most radioactive site as a result of several serious accidents and the uncontrolled dumping of nuclear wastes in the 1940s and 1950s. "IAEA Sends Iraqi Nuclear Waste to World's Worst Plant," *Interpress*, June 25, 1993.

Iraq's Quest for the Nuclear Grail: What Can We Learn?

David Albright and Mark Hibbs

Excerpted, with permission, from Arms Control Today, *July/August 1992.*

For just over a year, IAEA inspectors, working with the UNSCOM under the UN Security Council's Gulf War cease-fire resolution, have been systematically uncovering and destroying Iraq's clandestine nuclear weapons program. With a year's experience—and with the emphasis of the inspection job about to shift from investigation to long-term monitoring—it is now possible to draw back and assess the overall picture of Iraq's nuclear weapons effort, and the lessons to be drawn for strengthening international efforts to stem the spread of nuclear weapons.

Over the course of the spring and summer of 1991, the inspectors found a multibillion-dollar, Manhattan Project-style atomic bomb program in Iraq, aimed at establishing the knowledge and infrastructure to build several nuclear bombs a year. For over a decade, Iraq had devoted massive economic and technical resources to its bomb effort, which had made considerable progress toward its ultimate goals of enriching uranium to weapons-grade and fashioning it into nuclear weapons.

But Iraq's decade-long bomb program was not going smoothly. Lack of technological and industrial infrastructure, increasingly stringent trade restrictions and poor management all slowed progress. If Iraq had not invaded Kuwait in 1990, experts now believe it would have needed three or four years to produce its first nuclear weapon.

It is still sobering that with determination and financial resources, even a country with little industrial infrastructure such as Iraq was able to flaunt international non-proliferation efforts and come as close as it did to gaining a nuclear weapons capability. There can be little doubt that the inspectors' finds in Iraq warrant modification to the body of international norms, rules, and agreements which constitute the nuclear non-proliferation regime.

INSPECTIONS: THE STATE OF PLAY

Since the Gulf War, the IAEA "Action Team"—the small group charged with managing inspections in Iraq—has conducted 13 on-site inspections, searching out secret facilities and activities and destroying key buildings and equipment. The team has also inventoried and tagged hundreds of pieces of "dual-use" industrial equipment, which was or could have been intended for nuclear weapons development.

Most work in the field has been routine. But inspectors became the focus of international media attention when they had to confront their Iraqi hosts to get information and access. In

June 1991, warning shots fired by Iraqi soldiers at inspectors forced the IAEA team to back off from a convoy of trucks carrying uranium enrichment equipment from a military base. During four days in September, Iraqi security forces prevented inspectors from leaving the Baghdad headquarters of Petrochemical Three (PC-3)—the code name for Iraq's nuclear weapons program—after they had uncovered a cache of secret documents. At the end of the standoff, the inspectors were allowed to leave with the documents.

These mostly Arabic documents, totaling more than 50,000 pages, have provided detailed glimpses into the Iraqi nuclear weapons program, and some parts of its vast foreign procurement network. The documents uncovered in Iraq have been key to understanding the overall Iraqi program and judging whether additional significant parts of it might remain hidden. More information, particularly on the international network of companies that provided critical technologies for the program, will be needed before the IAEA can make that judgment definitively.

After a year of digging, IAEA officials believe that the most important aspects of Iraq's program have been uncovered. IAEA officials believe that they have found the key facilities and traced out the main lines of the Iraqi effort. If they can get long-term monitoring firmly in place, they are confident that no major nuclear weapon effort could resume without detection.

Although Iraq followed IAEA and UN orders to destroy buildings and equipment clearly linked to its nuclear program during the twelfth inspection in late May and early June, Iraqi officials tried to stop or limit the team's efforts to take photographs and place "tags" on critical equipment. Transportation to sites was often slow, and meetings were delayed.

Iraq refused UNSCOM inspectors access to the Iraqi Agriculture Ministry, which they believed contained documents relating to Iraq's weapons programs. At the time of this writing, although Baghdad has agreed to allow inspectors inside the ministry, Iraq and the UN Security Council remain at odds over Baghdad's refusal to submit to anytime-anywhere inspections, as called for under the Gulf War cease-fire resolution.

According to IAEA officials, Iraq has little interest in cooperating with the inspections. Economic sanctions have remained in effect, and the Bush Administration said in the past that it will seek to continue them as long as Saddam Hussein remains in power, whether the Iraqis cooperate with inspectors or not. [More recently, the Clinton Administration has also linked the continuation of sanctions to Saddam Hussein's remaining in power.] Most of the high-tech equipment in Iraq has been subsequently destroyed. Moreover, at least one inspector was told by a senior Iraqi official that Iraq does not want to reveal its procurement networks because it is now using them again. Iraqi intransigence has only strengthened the IAEA's resolve to step up efforts to track down Iraq's suppliers.

The summer of 1992 will mark an important change in the inspection effort, as the IAEA and UNSCOM plan to shift the focus from a "search and destroy" mission to long-term monitoring of Iraq's industrial activities, to ensure that it does not resume its quest for weapons of mass destruction. Thus long-term vigilance is critical, as CIA Director Robert Gates has testified that Iraq could have its nuclear program back in business in two years if international surveillance were lifted.

But Iraq has so far refused to accept the long-term monitoring program required under UN Security Council Resolution 715. Scheduled to start in August, this monitoring program would provide ongoing verification of Iraq's compliance with Resolution 687, the Gulf War cease-fire, which forbids any restart of the nuclear weapons program. The Iraqi authorities claim that the conditions imposed under Resolution 715 would be too intrusive and would violate Iraq's national sovereignty. IAEA officials, however, are hopeful that much of the monitoring they seek can be put in place even without formal Iraqi acceptance of the Security Council's demands. But UNSCOM officials insist that Iraq formally accept the resolution, since Iraq could easily disrupt the inspections by refusing to support transportation or access to key buildings and equipment, or once again physically threatening the inspectors.

IRAQ'S BOMB EFFORT: AN OVERVIEW

The IAEA Action Team has put together a detailed picture of the Iraqi nuclear weapons program. As with any other nuclear weapons program, Iraq had to accomplish two key goals: acquiring the nuclear weapons material—highly enriched uranium or separated plutonium—needed to build a bomb, and turning that raw material into a working device, a task known as "weaponization." Iraq was working hard on both jobs, but had encountered significant obstacles.

Iraq may have first pursued the plutonium path to the bomb. But Israel's bombing of Iraq's Osiraq reactor effectively stymied that effort [see interview with Bennett Ramburg, this chapter]. Suspicions linger that Iraq might have subsequently started building an underground nuclear reactor to produce plutonium, but the combination of a year's intensive inspections, information from defectors, and the reams of seized documents has not revealed such a project.

After the Osiraq bombing, Iraq simultaneously pursued several means of producing highly enriched uranium. Postwar revelations of Iraq's most developed enrichment route, based on archaic calutron electromagnetic separation technology, startled the world. Western intelligence agencies had been fully aware that Iraq was attempting to develop the means to enrich uranium, but had focused on the gas centrifuge enrichment effort—which matched current approaches used in several developed nations—and missed the calutron effort completely. These two approaches were the central focus of Iraq's uranium-enrichment program, overshadowing chemical enrichment, a path Iraq was also pursuing but at a slower pace.

CALUTRONS: UNDETECTED PROGRESS

The biggest surprise about the Iraqi nuclear program remains its calutrons. The United States developed this technology during World War II to enrich uranium for the bomb that destroyed Hiroshima, but had long since abandoned it in favor of more cost-efficient enrichment approaches. In a calutron—a shortening of "California University magnetron"—uranium is formed into a beam of ions, which is bent by huge magnets. The slightly lighter ions of U-235—the type of uranium needed for a bomb—are deflected more by the magnets than are those of U-238, the dominant type in natural uranium, allowing the two to be separated.

By the mid-1980s, the Iraqi research and development program, which was located at the Tuwaitha nuclear research center near Baghdad, was in full swing. The program consisted essentially of duplicating the U.S. calutron program, which had been largely declassified years ago. Some inspectors believe that the program started as early as the late 1970s, before the bombing of the Osiraq reactor.

The war led to the defection of members of this program and to intensive inspection of many sites, including both Tuwaitha and Tarmiya, located 40 kilometers north of Baghdad. When finished, the Tarmiya complex, which includes some 100 buildings, was slated to be Iraq's principal calutron enrichment site.

During the first inspection of this site in May 1991, the inspectors were unsure of what they had found. To find the purpose of the facility, the IAEA invited John Googin, a U.S. calutron specialist from Oak Ridge, Tennessee, to Vienna. As he studied the picture of the buildings' interiors, showing water-cooling systems, electrical distribution systems, and large chemical processing areas with extensive ventilation, a startling composite image began to emerge. Tarmiya looked like the Y-12 Plant at Oak Ridge, where the United States built hundreds of calutrons during World War II.

At the time of the Gulf War, Iraq was at least a year behind the calutron installation and operation schedule laid out in a 1987 report by an Iraqi engineer, and the IAEA concluded that up to that point, Iraq had produced less than a kilogram of enriched uranium, and no weapons-grade uranium. If Baghdad had followed that report's schedule—and there is no evidence it had been accelerated—Iraq might have been able to produce one bomb's worth of weapons-grade uranium by early 1994, assuming it was starting with natural uranium feed, rather than uranium that had already been somewhat enriched by other means. But the 1987 study also shows that if Iraq had diverted stocks of low-enriched uranium under IAEA safeguards as feedback for the calutrons, it might have been able to produce enough weapons-grade uranium for one bomb by the end of 1992. [A "safeguard" is an inspection to ensure no nuclear material is being diverted to weapons work.]

IAEA officials are confident that they would have detected a significant diversion of the low-enriched uranium in less than one year, although other officials have questioned how soon detection would have occurred. But the fact that Iraq had considered diverting the low-enriched uranium as a shortcut to the bomb highlights the importance of safeguarding even relatively small quantities of low-enriched uranium, such as those on hand in Iraq.

The fact that low-enriched feed can dramatically increase the productivity of calutrons might also explain why Iraq pursued so many other enrichment technologies. Most of the weapons-grade uranium produced in U.S. calutrons was first pre-enriched at a nearby gaseous diffusion enrichment plant.

How much weapons-grade uranium could Tarmiya have produced each year once it was fully operational? In the plan outlined in the 1987 document, the plan could have produced about seven kilograms of weapons-grade uranium a year, assuming it was using natural uranium feed, and not low-enriched uranium. Other, more current documents and declarations by Iraqis indicate that as Iraq gained operating experience, it might have been able to increase Tarmiya's output by operating at higher currents, and keeping the calutrons running a large fraction of the time, making as much as 15 kilograms a year of weapons-grade uranium.

CENTRIFUGES: DESIGN PROBLEMS

Gas centrifuges were the other major enrichment technology Iraq was developing. In a gas centrifuge, spinning rotors whirl uranium hexafluoride gas at high speed, leading to the separation of the heavier U-238 molecules from the lighter U-235 molecules. Getting the technology of these high-speed rotors right is a challenge. Pakistan and Brazil each took a decade to develop small pilot-scale plants. To enrich enough uranium to produce a few weapons per year, several thousand centrifuges must be linked by pipes into "cascades."

At the time of the Gulf War, the Iraqi gas centrifuge program was nearing the capability to make centrifuges but no decision had been reached on a final design. According to enrichment experts, design problems made the centrifuges inefficient and mechanically unreliable. An inspector said that Iraq appears to have had a set of drawings that it was working from, but Iraqi centrifuge experts had not solved all the design problems. Iraq would probably have overcome these difficulties, but resolving them would have taken a significant amount of time. Iraq, moreover, would have faced a stiff learning curve in first mastering the manufacture of individual centrifuges, and then constructing cascades of interlinked centrifuges able to produce weapons-grade uranium.

Although the West was aware that Iraq was trying to master gas centrifuge enrichment before the war, the extent of the program was made clear only after the IAEA and UNSCOM began to unearth the program. Even though it was not ready to begin mass-producing large numbers of centrifuges, Iraq bought thousands of centrifuge subcomponents and tons of raw material whenever an opportunity presented itself and it determined it needed them. Despite this assistance, the IAEA has established that Iraq remained several years away from being able to use centrifuges to produce significant quantities of weapons-grade uranium, or even low-enriched uranium to feed into the calutrons.

Iraq has refused to provide critical information about its foreign procurement of key components and know-how, and the IAEA has been only partly successful in cracking the foreign network without Iraqi help. As a result, important questions remain about the program. Without answers to these questions, the IAEA cannot be certain that Iraq is not hiding parts of its centrifuge effort, or planning to use these supply networks again for a nuclear weapons program.

The three most important unresolved issues concern the suppliers of high-grade maraging steel, an advanced material important for centrifuge rotors; the origin of Iraq's carbon-fiber rotors, intended for more sophisticated centrifuges; and Iraq's source for centrifuge design information.

Maraging Steel

Iraq has declared, and the IAEA has verified, that it received about 100 metric tons of high-grade maraging steel, enough to construct about 2,500 centrifuge rotors at Al Furat, a manufacturing facility 30 kilometers south of Baghdad. If fully operational, this number of centrifuges could produce up to 30 or 40 kilograms of weapons-grade uranium a year. A Western intelligence agency has found indications, however, that Iraq might have received as much as 400 tons of maraging steel—meaning that it could still be hiding enough material to make 7,500 rotors. Iraq has so far refused to tell inspectors where it got the maraging steel, or admit that it has received more than it has declared.

Carbon Fiber Rotors

Twenty carbon-fiber rotors are known to have been in Iraq, one of which was used successfully in single-machine tests to enrich minute quantities of uranium. Without knowing the origin of these rotors, the IAEA cannot verify that Iraq does not have more. Inspectors worry that Iraq might have linked a small number of carbon rotors into a test cascade of perhaps 10 to 15 machines before the war. If successful, such a step would put Iraq closer to production of significant quantities of enriched uranium than is currently believed.

Iraq has declared that it obtained the rotors overseas from a "dealer," and some information obtained by the IAEA indicates that they may have been imported. Other information, however, suggests that the Iraqi experts made the rotors themselves—an unexpected accomplishment. IAEA investigations are continuing.

Centrifuge Designs

The third unanswered question is who supplied Iraq with centrifuge designs. Baghdad has steadfastly refused to provide any names, and several companies which provided important subcomponents or manufactured equipment for Iraq's centrifuge program have refused to cooperate.

The centrifuge designs at issue are for early machines built in the 1970s at Almelo in the Netherlands by the European uranium enrichment consortium, URENCO. A German engineer who visited Iraq in the autumn of 1988 and again in early 1989, said that the Iraqis showed him general designs for one of these machines, although with some modifications.

In addition to centrifuge designs, foreign experts provided Iraq with specific and detailed guidance on accomplishing certain centrifuge manufacturing steps. Besides providing useful know-how, they also told Iraq what kind of manufacturing equipment it would need and the names of companies which could supply it.

With design information on specific centrifuge parts, Iraq was able to give its European corporate suppliers enough data to enable them to build sophisticated centrifuge manufacturing equipment. For example, the Swiss firm Schaublin SA and the British company Matrix-Churchill sold Iraq advanced computer-numerically-controlled (CNC) machines able to make key centrifuge parts with significantly less worker input and skills. Many of these machines were in fact sent to Iraq, where they were subsequently found by the IAEA and put under seal.

WEAPONIZATION: THE WEAK LINK

An atomic bomb requires more than plutonium or highly enriched uranium; it also requires a workable bomb design, and means to test and build a weapon. Making nuclear explosive material is generally considered more difficult than fashioning it into a bomb. But Iraq's weaponization efforts were taking considerably longer than initially expected. At the time of the Gulf War, many pieces of the puzzle simply eluded Iraqi scientists.

Iraq's weaponization program was slowed in part because its leaders were buying more equipment and demanding higher standards than really needed. As one inspector put it, "The program was not very good; it was too grandiose."

The *New York Times* reported that a secret gathering of nuclear weapon designers from the United States, Britain, France and Russia, had concluded the bottlenecks in the program would have delayed completion of a working bomb for years.[1] In an interview, one participant at the meeting said that the group had not agreed on a firm estimate of how long Iraq would have needed to complete a design. He said, however, that with the approach that the Iraqi scientists were taking, Iraq would have needed more than two years, perhaps significantly longer, to execute a design.

But if the Iraqi political leadership had become aware of the problems, and pressured the program to accelerate its efforts, the time to complete a design and produce components could have been reduced considerably.

Iraq apparently copied approaches in the open literature and bought plants and equipment it hoped to operate successfully. In some cases, Iraq picked a more difficult solution than necessary, lengthening the time needed to attain the goal at hand. For example, while uranium bomb components can be molded relatively simply, the Iraqis were planning an exotic and complicated approach involving a Swedish-supplied hot isostatic press using cerium sulfide. Inspectors believe that Iraq learned about this method from an unclassified article advocating the advantages of cerium sulfide, published by Lawrence Livermore National Laboratory a few years earlier.

LESSONS FOR THE FUTURE

Had Iraq's own decision to invade Kuwait not intervened, Iraq might well have succeeded in building nuclear weapons despite having signed the NPT. That likelihood has forced the international community to re-examine existing non-proliferation mechanisms and find ways to strengthen them.

EXPORT CONTROLS

Some analysts have argued that Iraq's reliance on unclassified calutron technology suggests that there is now little that controls what the technology and materials can do. In the case of Iraq, however, because Baghdad was so dependent on foreign suppliers, technology trade restrictions on equipment and technologies slowed Iraq's program substantially, despite inadequate controls in some areas and spotty enforcement in others. The evidence shows that Iraq could not import crucial centrifuge components in sufficient numbers to build enough centrifuges to produce significant amounts of enriched uranium, and failed to procure key components and test equipment to build nuclear bombs. Efforts to get help from German experts were hindered by the intervention of the German government. Unable to import ready-made components, the Iraqis were forced to try to obtain materials, machinery, and other equipment for making the centrifuges and bomb components themselves. Because its industrial infrastructure was weak, however, Iraq had difficulty creating the necessary manufacturing capability.

The UN-mandated economic embargo, imposed in late 1990, hindered the Iraqi effort even more. While the Bush Administration moved toward a military solution to the Persian Gulf crisis, UN trade sanctions prevented an entire list of equipment, from spectrometers to centrifuge valves to half-finished calutron magnets, from reaching Iraqi scientists. For example, unfinished calutron iron pieces weighing many tons apiece were to be shipped to Iraq by truck via Turkey. But the embargo stopped the trucks, and the iron pieces were put into storage in Turkey, where they remain.

Though export controls slowed Iraq down, the fact that much slipped through, and that only a complete economic embargo stopped some vital equipment and components, highlighted weakness in the pre-Gulf War international export regime. While existing controls on centrifuge enrichment effectively hindered Iraq from procuring finished components, for example, the absence of effective controls on other important items permitted Iraq to obtain maraging steel, sophisticated CNC machines, and other dual-use equipment for centrifuge manufacture. Likewise, controls on nuclear weapons components and testing equipment did not stop Iraq from buying presses, lathes, and other equipment that would have been used to create an infrastructure to make nuclear weapons components.

Moreover, export controls rarely covered equipment Iraq imported for its calutron program. Western governments overlooked calutrons because they saw them as too slow, too costly, and too electricity-intensive. U.S. national laboratory scientists, however, worried as far back as the early 1980s that a country with lots of cash, excess electrical energy, and a large labor pool might find the technology attractive.

SPECIAL INSPECTIONS

Iraq's activities highlighted a major weakness of IAEA safeguards—namely, that inspectors may routinely visit only facilities that the inspected country has declared, regardless of whether activities are ongoing nearby. At Tuwaitha, for example, inspectors regularly visited a few research reactors and nuclear material storage locations. But within the same complex, behind heavy security, Iraq was running laboratory-scale calutrons, engaging in centrifuge research, and developing the infrastructure for making nuclear weapons.

A related problem involves the systematic sharing of intelligence information with the IAEA. According to IAEA Director General Hans Blix, the IAEA's discoveries in Iraq "were totally dependent on the intelligence information given about particular sites by member states." In the past the United States provided the lion's share of information on nuclear activities in other states, partly out of concern that IAEA member states—including proliferators—could use this information for their own purposes, to the detriment of U.S. security.

ROUTINE SAFEGUARDS

The fact that the IAEA's routine safeguards in Iraq failed to detect anything untoward going on has led to much criticism of the IAEA's efforts. Iraq's development of nuclear weapons, however, was hindered by IAEA safeguards. Safeguards prevented Iraq from irradiating significant amounts of fuel in reactors and recovering the plutonium. If Iraq had diverted its safeguarded low-enriched uranium to the calutron program—which might have put bomb material in its hands as much as two years sooner—such a diversion could have triggered an international confrontation and the exposure of the secret calutron program.

But postwar inspections also revealed that Iraq took advantage of loopholes in the standard safeguard agreement, thereby gaining nuclear expertise relevant to military use. In light of what has been learned about Iraqi activities using safeguards, practices should be tightened to eliminate loopholes:

- The safeguards agreement allowed Iraq to exempt small amounts of spent fuel from safeguards and then separate gram quantities of the plutonium in a laboratory—a key process for Iraq to learn, if it were ever to return to the plutonium path to the bomb.
- Iraq irradiated bismuth in a safeguarded reactor, without detection, to produce polonium-210 for use in researching neutron initiators that would have triggered the chain reaction in a nuclear explosive.
- Iraq was not clearly required to give the IAEA design information on an enrichment facility it was building, and it failed to notify the IAEA that it was producing enriched uranium in laboratory facilities.
- The safeguards agreement allowed Iraq to obtain large quantities of natural uranium (in the form of yellowcake) outside of international inspection, which would have been used as feedstock for clandestine production of enriched uranium.

Elimination of loopholes and stricter safeguards will require more funding from member states, but because the states of the former Soviet Union cannot pay the Soviet contribution to the 1992 IAEA general budget, the 1992 safeguards budget was slashed 13 percent from the 1991 level, and officials are pessimistic that these states will make a contribution until the mid-1990s.

Meanwhile, affluent advanced nuclear states, such as the United States, Germany and Japan, which have paid lip service to strengthening IAEA safeguards, have also refused to significantly increase funding. Some countries' voluntary contributions to the IAEA budget have even declined since the Iraqi program was revealed by the Action Team. Recent revelations that two other NPT parties, North Korea and Romania, separated plutonium outside of safeguards have only served to highlight the necessity to eliminate safeguards loopholes. Underscoring the importance of increased safeguards activities, however, the Board of Governors approved a slight increase in the 1993 safeguards budget at its June meeting.

THE PEOPLE PROBLEM

Inspectors have concluded that certain foreign individuals in search of financial remuneration supplied key know-how to push the Iraqi program ahead. Nonetheless, lack of knowledge slowed enrichment and weaponization programs, suggesting that additional assistance provided by outside experts could have greatly speeded the Iraqi program. In the future, nuclear experts from the former Soviet Union might sell their services abroad. Industrialized nations have responded to that possibility by providing funds for research centers in Moscow and Kiev to co-ordinate peaceful employment for these scientists.

THE USE OF FORCE

Unofficial statements from Washington this year suggested that the nuclear-armed U.S. military should now prevent others from acquiring nuclear weapons. Global reaction to such a prospect, however, has been strongly negative. Although the success of the military in the Gulf War is ultimately responsible for having forced Iraq to allow destruction of its nuclear infrastructure, the world has not given the United States a license to intervene at will to stop the spread of nuclear weapons. Indeed, talk of U.S. attacks on potential proliferators is likely to be counter-productive, only adding to the arguments of those factions in states considering the nuclear option that U.S. global power poses a serious threat for which nuclear weapons are the only effective response.

Ultimately, however, if a country is determined to build the bomb, export controls and inspections can only slow it down. The non-proliferation system in place today cannot guarantee that a nation with sufficient resources and ambition will not acquire nuclear weapons.

But the recent cases of Argentina and Brazil teach the value of slowing a program down. These programs were hindered by outside controls, offering time for the nations' leaders to change their minds and renounce the nuclear option. Convincing states to take that nonnuclear road must be a major non-proliferation priority for the future. In other regions, such as South Asia, the Korean Peninsula, and the Middle East, doing so will require sustained and creative efforts to resolve the conflicts and security threats that lead nations to try to get the bomb in the first place.

These efforts would be helped if the nuclear weapons states would accept restraints on their own programs, including a global ban on the production of fissile material for nuclear weapons, and a halt to nuclear testing. The non-proliferation regime can be effective only if the nonnuclear weapons states see constraints as being in their interest and cooperate in their implementation.

The events leading to the Gulf War show the link between nonnuclear weapons states, such as Iraq, that perceive they are threatened by others' nuclear weapons, and the few states that already possess them. As long as states possess nuclear arsenals, we must expect that some states which do not have these weapons will seek to develop them.

A vigilant international inspection and export control regime must go hand-in-hand with an international effort to delegitimize nuclear weapons, and eventually eliminate them. Only then can the spread of nuclear weapons be permanently stopped and reversed.

NOTES:

1. Paul Lewis, "UN Experts Now Say Baghdad Was Far From Making an A-Bomb Before Gulf War," *New York Times*, May 20, 1992, A6.

Bombing Nuclear Reactors: Warfare Takes an Ominous Turn

Interview with Bennett Ramburg

Bennett Ramburg, Ph.D., is the author of the book Nuclear Power Plants As Weapons of the Enemy: An Unrecognized Military Peril, *published in 1985. He is currently Senior Research Associate at the Center for International Relations at the University of California, Los Angeles, and Director of Research for the Committee to Bridge the Gap. Interviewed by Saul Bloom, November 1992.*

Saul Bloom: You have expressed serious concern that the Coalition attack on Iraq's nuclear reactors set a dangerous wartime precedent.

Bennett Ramburg: The U.S. set a precedent by bombing reactors that were either operating or with their inventory of radioactive fuel rods in place. Previously, only reactors whose construction was not complete had been bombed. By attacking an operating reactor, the U.S. has sanctioned reactors as a legitimate target in war. This action has grave import, because if it is okay for the U.S. to bomb its opponent's reactors, doesn't it provide a justification for Serbia's threatening to bomb the reactors in other European nations if they interfere militarily in the civil war in former Yugoslavia? Not too long ago, Assistant Secretary of State Lawrence Eagleburger raised a concern that a 300-megawatt nuclear reactor in the former Yugoslavia could be attacked.

SB: Why be concerned?

BR: In 1986, the world witnessed the terrible effects of the nuclear accident at the Chernobyl nuclear power station in the Soviet Union. Thousands of people were made ill, tens of thousands were displaced and the fallout contaminated portions of Europe. The concern is that a successful military air-strike against a large civilian power reactor in the thousand-megawatt range could be worse than Chernobyl.

SB: What kind of impact does bombing a nuclear reactor have on it? Will it cause it to explode?
BR: No, because you don't have the materials concentrated into a focused weapons design.

SB: Will it cause a Chernobyl-type fire and meltdown?
BR: That's correct. The containment vessels are strong but a concerted effort would kill them. There is some speculation that if a bomb landed in the rods, the inventory would be dispersed and prevent a major meltdown. But the bottom line is that the reactors have acute vulnerabilities. They rely on offsite power generation to keep them operating—to keep redundant safeguards and pumps going. In Chernobyl they relied on turbine generators to power the facility's safety and emergency systems; that turbine failed to continue to operate and generate power and so. . . .

The important thing to note though is that in the Chernobyl situation, Moscow was able to marshal a national effort to respond to the emergency. During the chaos of war it would be virtually impossible for a country to respond to the problem, particularly if a number of bombed reactors were on fire. Without heroic remedies, the environmental and human consequences would multiply.

SB: Given the region's history of strife, were the reactors "hardened," made more resistant to attack?

BR: Smaller reactors are built to withstand internal pressures, not external attack. The reactors that were bombed weren't unusually hardened, and weren't designed to withstand a military attack.

SB: You have said that the small size of Iraq's research reactors was the reason only an insignificant amount of radiation was released as a result of the bombing; however, a 1987 U.S. General Accounting Office (GAO) report indicates that the incineration of a single nuclear warhead could have dire health effects on as many as 1,500 individuals in the area immediately near the accident site. Both research reactors and nuclear bombs have very small quantities of fissionable material in them, as compared to a commercial power reactor. Why were the impacts of the bombing minimal?

BR: There is some speculation that the Iraqis may have removed the spent fuel from the reactors before the attack.

Iraq's Nuclear Program and IAEA Safeguards

SB: Who built Iraq's reactors?

BR: I believe the French built the Osiraq Reactor, and the research reactors bombed in the Gulf War were of French or Soviet design, about the size of a GETR (a 40-kilowatt reactor).

SB: Who provided the material and technical support?

BR: The countries and companies that sold the reactors and also possibly some help from the IAEA.

SB: You have indicated that the two research reactors the U.S. bombed outside of Baghdad were IAEA-safeguarded, meaning they were inspected to ensure that no nuclear material was being diverted to weapons work. Given the now-apparent size of Iraq's nuclear weapons program, how would you characterize the effectiveness of the safeguarding and to what extent did these reactors play a role in Iraq's weapons program?

BR: There is some evidence to indicate that Iraq obtained a very small amount of plutonium from these reactors. The safeguards were inadequate and failed to detect diversion. There was some evidence of decladding (removing the outer layer of the fuel rods to get access to the plutonium and other radioactive materials within).

SB: The IAEA's mission is both to promote responsible development of nuclear power worldwide and to control the siphoning off of the radioactive materials from reactors into nuclear weapons production and proliferation. Do you think an agency can be effective in serving such a seemingly mutually exclusive mandate?

BR: The IAEA is increasing the safeguards portion of its program, but it is unclear how effective that will be. The agency's record is unclear. It relies on investigations and data provided by the countries it is monitoring, and the agency itself is completely self-monitoring, not accountable to anyone. The U.S. doesn't have oversight and the agency is somewhat close-mouthed. We clearly know that with regard to Iraq the IAEA process didn't work. Plutonium was diverted. In fact, the U.S.' own actions during the war indicate that it didn't trust the IAEA's assessment of the hazard either.

LESSONS TO BE LEARNED

SB: What lessons should the international community take from the bombing of these facilities?

BR: There are several. The American position is troubling. The official U.S. position is that we don't want any limits on targeting. At the Convention on Disarmament—an ongoing negotiation in Geneva—there are two sticking points in discussions under the "radiological" topic: radiological weapons and bombing reactors. Radiological weapons are made up of cluster bomblets that disperse nuclear materials such as spent fuel from power reactors. These are horrific environmental weapons, terror weapons that wouldn't kill a lot of folks immediately but would cause a lot of long-term health and environmental damage if used. The negotiations have been deadlocked.

The U.S. says it would agree to negotiating on radiation weapons, but none of the U.S. agencies want to ban attacks on reactors. Because bombing reactors is in the interest of the Department of Defense, the only time it comes up in the U.S. government is in the pentannual NPT review conference. But at those times the U.S. focuses on building support for keeping attacks possible. The issues will be raised in 1995 at the next NPT review. Interestingly, the Iraqis and the Iranians raised the issue in the last round. The international community needs to seriously revisit this issue given the environmental and health consequences of bombing large nuclear power stations.

Another lesson is strengthening the NPT. Stricter control of the export of nuclear or dual-capable technologies would also lessen the risk that power reactors in combination with other technologies are being used for military purposes. Until recently the Reagan-Bush Administration didn't have NPT on the front burner. It has recently become a greater concern and, hopefully, the new administration will place it on the front burner. Supplier guidelines have been strengthened. Some of the principal violators of NPT were German companies, but I don't know how much the U.S. is pressuring them to deal with it.

One option is to fashion a treaty that would create nuclear sanctuaries against military attack if the IAEA certifies that the plants are not used for military purposes. This certification would have to go far beyond current practices and require permanent unimpeded presence of IAEA inspectors. If a country doesn't open its facilities up to scrupulous inspection, the IAEA could identify the plant as a military facility. This presumes that some military action can be taken against it, should that become necessary. The U.S. opposes this option on the grounds that it would tie its hands in war. Nevertheless, such a treaty would establish a standard of behavior governing attacks on nuclear plants. It would discourage attacks on nuclear facilities, reduce the danger of war-induced Chernobyls, and provide an incentive for nations to apply international safeguards scrupulously.

Chemical and Biological Weapons

Background Information

CHEMICAL WEAPONS

The 1993 Chemical Weapons Convention (CWC), which regulates the creation and use of chemical agents that have military applications, was signed by 135 nations in January 1993, and will enter into force after it has been ratified by at least 65 states (but no earlier than January 1995). The Convention bans the manufacture, testing, and development of munitions or other devices specifically designed to cause death, temporary incapacitation or permanent harm to humans or animals through the action of chemicals on life processes. These chemicals by themselves, as well as any chemical constituent thereof, are defined by the treaty as being a chemical weapon, unless they are not intended for that use and are not produced in the types and quantities needed for weapons manufacture.[1]

While chemicals toxic to plants are not explicitly covered in the new treaty's definition, its preamble does acknowledge the 1972 Biological Weapons Convention which prohibited their use in warfare. Chemicals used for law enforcement purposes, such as riot control, are not included in the ban.[2]

WHAT CHEMICAL WEAPONS DO

The following material on chemical and biological weapons is excerpted from a background paper released by the Medical Education Trust of the United Kingdom in 1991, unless otherwise footnoted:[3]

Chemical weapons work by releasing toxins which attack the biochemical processes of living organisms. Chemicals fall into the following categories: disabling, choking, blood, blister, nerve and binary agents.

THE CHEMICALS

Disabling agents are tear gases such as CS and CN and arsenicals. These weapons are used primarily for riot control and are not defined as chemical weapons by the new convention. CN causes tearing but its effects can be avoided by keeping one's eyes closed. CS causes dizziness, coughing, breathing difficulties and sometimes vomiting. Arsenicals are used to induce violent vomiting to disable victims immediately so that they cannot put on gas masks.

Choking gases like chlorine and phosgenes attack the respiratory tract by swelling the membranes and filling the lungs with fluid so that the victim drowns; survivors can suffer life-long respiratory problems.

Blood agents include hydrogen cyanide and cyanogen chloride. These agents are absorbed by breathing and inhibit the ability of tissues to use oxygen. Blood agents kill very rapidly, within 15 minutes, but also disperse rapidly.

Blister agents include mustard gas and lewisite (Agent L). Also known as vesicants, most of these oily liquids have delayed effects (up to four hours) producing large water blisters on all exposed skin. The blisters heal slowly and are vulnerable to infection. Eyes, blood cells, and the respiratory tract can also be damaged.

Nerve agents inhibit production of the enzyme acetylcholinesterase, which allows the muscles to relax after contraction, so that the body goes into spasm and death occurs quickly through asphyxiation. The acute signs include drooling, sweating, vomiting, loss of bladder and bowel control, headache, confusion, blindness, convulsions, coma and death. Nerve agents are odorless, tasteless and colorless liquids.

The main nerve agents in use are:

- Tabun (GA) was the first nerve agent invented. It is fairly persistent (long-lived) in the environment, so that exposure can occur through contact and ingestion as well as immediate inhalation.
- Sarin (GB) is nonpersistent and impacts the respiratory tract.
- Soman (GD) is semipersistent and penetrates both the skin and the respiratory system. It also contaminates terrain and buildings and is much more toxic and rapid-acting than tabun or sarin.[4]
- VX is a persistent, skin-penetrating chemical that can contaminate the terrain for weeks. As a result, exposure comes through ingestion as well as inhalation. VX is much more persistent and lethal than the "G" agents identified above.

Binaries are weapons for which the chemicals are stored in separate containers in non-lethal form and are only mixed to make a nerve agent during delivery.

BIOLOGICAL WEAPONS

The 1972 Biological Weapons Convention, which prohibits the development, production and stockpiling of biological weapons, defines a biological weapon as:

1) Microbial or other biological agents, or toxins, whatever their origins or method of production, of types and quantities that have no justification for prophylactic, protective or other peaceful purposes; and
2) Weapons, equipment, or means of delivery that are designed to use such agents or toxins for hostile purposes or in armed conflict.[5]

WHAT BIOLOGICAL WEAPONS DO

Biological weapons represent a far greater potential for catastrophic effects, stemming from their ability to multiply once released. When a soldier breathes in a chemical agent and is killed, the material remains confined in the corpse. However, the body of a soldier killed by a germ agent can become a nursery for subsequent generations of deadly viruses. In battle, affected personnel cannot be evacuated for fear of spreading the disease; medical personnel must also be quarantined; and the germs can be spread by the winds, creating regional pandemics. Methods of delivery include aerosol spraying from planes, dropping spores in packets, fragmentation bombs, and cluster bombs.

The frightening lethality of biological weapons is underscored by this Department of Defense comparison:

TABLE 7-1. COMPARATIVE LETHALITY OF BIOLOGICAL WEAPONS (U.S. DEPARTMENT OF DEFENSE)

Casualty Agents	Lethal dose per kilogram
Modern assault rifle bullets	hundreds
Steel fragmented by high explosives	tens of thousands
Nerve gas	millions
Shellfish poison	millions
Botulism toxin (1943 weapons grade)	tens of millions
Anthrax spore slurry (1945 weapons grade)	hundreds of millions
VEE virus powder (1964 weapons grade)	hundreds of thousands of millions
Tularemia bacteria powder (1955 weapons grade)	millions of millions
Botulism toxin (pure)	millions of millions

POSSIBLE BIOLOGICAL WEAPONS

LETHAL

- Yellow fever is transmitted by blood-sucking arthropods like mosquitoes and ticks (several extensive yellow fever epidemics have occurred in the past 300 years). A three-to-six-day incubation period is followed by a sudden onset of fever, headache, backache, prostration, nausea, and vomiting and a 30–40 percent fatality rate among unvaccinated cases. Aerosol transmission has been achieved in the laboratory.
- Tick-borne, milk-borne and Japanese encephalitis are highly infectious and may lead to death within seven to ten days in 20–30 percent of cases, with serious long-term effects in non-fatal cases. Aerosol transmission and weapons-use is possible.
- Typhus, Rocky Mountain spotted fever and Q fever are rickettsial infections transmitted by lice. Typhus mortalities increase with age: three percent in infants, 50 percent in the elderly. Rocky Mountain spotted fever mortality rate averages 20 percent, but can reach 80 percent in an unvaccinated community. Q fever, though not fatal, creates severe weakness and fatigue that could last for months, with complications. The virus could be delivered through aerosol transmission.

PLAGUES

- Bubonic plague is spread by fleas from infected rodents. Symptoms are high fever, shock, confusion, acute painful swelling of lymph nodes, prostration, delirium, coma, with 25–50 percent mortality if untreated. Pneumonic plague is spread in microscopic airborne droplets and is usually fatal within 48 hours.

- Anthrax bacterial infections produce highly resistant spores. Humans are infected by contact with animals, animal products, ingestion of meat, or by inhalation of infected dust from hides, wool, etc. The anthrax mortality rate is 20 percent from infection through the skin, if untreated. With inhalation or ingestion death follows toxemia and septicemia in over 80 percent of cases within 48 hours. Dispersed through the air, its spores persist in the environment for decades.

- Tularemia, brucellosis and typhoid fever are highly contagious bacterial infections which are transmitted by contact, inhalation or ingestion. The mortality rate for tularemia is 50 percent, brucellosis two percent and typhoid 10 percent. The bacteria remain persistent in the environment.

- Coccidioidomycosis is a fungal infection that produces flu-like symptoms and was fatal in 50 percent of cases before amphotericin B.

INCAPACITATING

- Dengue is another arthropod-borne virus. Its utility is that it is marked by a sudden onset, and a highly incapacitating acute stage. Case-fatalities are approximately five percent.

- Rift Valley fever, chikungunya and O'Nyang-Nyang are also arthropod-borne viruses with severe and sudden incapacitation, although they are not fatal in humans. Aerosol transmission and weapons use is possible.

- Influenza could be spread via aerosol transmission and could incapacitate the population in one to three days. With some strains fatality could rise above the current 0.2 percent.

NOTES:

1. Matthew Meselson and Julian Perry Robinson, "The 1993 Chemical Weapons Convention: A Summary," *Chemical Weapons Convention Bulletin,* December, 1992.
2. Matthew Meselson and Julian Perry Robinson, "The 1993 Chemical Weapons Convention."
3. Medical Educational Trust, *Chemical and Biological Weapons,* Report, London, August 1990, revised May 1991.
4. GA, GB and GD are U.S. military designations which are widely used.
5. United Nations, Convention on the Prohibition of the Development, Production and Stockpiling of Bacteriological (Biological) and Toxin Weapons and Their Destruction. Entered in force March 26, 1975.

Saddam Hussein's Chemical Arsenal

Matthew Meselson

Matthew Meselson, Ph.D., is Thomas Dudley Cabot Professor of the Natural Sciences, and Professor of Biochemistry and Molecular Biology at Harvard University. Interviewed by Saul Bloom, November 1992.

Saul Bloom: In your interview in Hidden Casualties, *Volume I, you indicated that Iraq's chemical arsenal was alleged to consist of the blister agent mustard gas and the lethal nerve agents tabun and sarin. What has been learned since then?*

Matthew Meselson: About half of their arsenal is CS munitions, mainly large caliber mortar rounds. CS is a so-called riot control agent, causing pain in the eyes and the throat, vomiting at higher exposures and blistering of the skin in extremely high concentrations. The CS was produced in Iraq's factories and is now being destroyed, along with the rest of their chemical arsenal, by UNSCOM.

SB: How large and sophisticated was Iraq's chemical weapons production system?

MM: The Iraqis made GB, which is sarin, GA, which is tabun, and they were making GF, which is of intermediate volatility and has no common name. They made mustard and they made CS. Those are the main things they made.

Sophisticated? Some of their batches of mustard were very pure, they mastered that pretty well. However, many of their batches of nerve agents were quite impure or else decomposed fairly fast. Some batches were much better, so they apparently were having a problem with the manufacture of nerve agents. As far as sophistication in the actual manufacturing processes is concerned, we didn't see them actually doing it. From the way they continue to handle this stuff they appear blasé about it. They don't wear protective clothing when they go in and bore holes in the munitions [boring holes in the munitions in order to empty them of the agent is a standard decommissioning practice]. UNSCOM designed the procedures, but it's actually Iraqis who are doing it and they're very nonchalant about it.

SB: Is that because the Iraqis lack an appreciation for how dangerous it can be?

MM: It's because you can be nonchalant and not get killed. The first time somebody gets killed they'll be less nonchalant. If someone gets splashed with it or is in a closed room where the stuff is open, or if the wind is in the wrong direction, it can be very dangerous.

SB: You mentioned the "G" type nerve weapons; we've heard that they were also looking into the "V" type nerve weapons, a more potent and persistent variety of nerve agent.

MM: They were trying but I don't think they ever successfully made a V agent weapon.

SB: Did the Iraqis put any emphasis on R&D for new nerve agents, or was their program simply one of obtaining the same type of ordnance found in other stockpiles?

MM: From what I know that they've weaponized, it was all based on what had been done in the West. Germany to start with, Germany developed mustard. You go all the way back to World War I for mustard. The G agents were also developed in Germany in the late 1930s and early '40s. VX was developed in the early '50s by the British. CS was also a British development based on an American discovery.

If you're talking about where they went for their plant equipment, I don't know. I've read in the newspapers that there was a heavy German contribution and some Swiss and American and some British and French.

BOMBING THE ARSENAL

SB: During the Coalition air war against Iraq, there was a great controversy over the bombing of a baby milk formula factory because it was allegedly also making chemical munitions. Subsequently some of the increase in infant malnutrition and mortality has been linked to the destruction of that facility, which provided the vast majority of the product for Iraq. Has there been any confirmation of that facility's use in weapons production?

MM: I can offer you a speculation, which would provide a basis for asking further questions. The main substance scientists use for growing bacteria is casein hydrolysate, or tryptone broth. To make it you mix milk that you don't want to use for anything else, and cow guts. The enzymes in the cow guts decompose the casein in the milk and you get tryptone broth. You then filter, clarify, and powder it and sell it in boxes and that's what microbiologists use as a medium for growing bacteria.

So I suppose that a baby milk formula factory, for perfectly innocent reasons, might be making tryptone broth for microbiological work in Iraq legitimately. But it could also be that their biological warfare facility sent a message saying, send us tryptone broth for our work. It's conceivable that we picked up that message through signal intelligence or other means and concluded, aha! Now that's sheer speculation, but if you're looking for some scientifically plausible lead for asking further questions, one of them would be: is this a place that made the tryptone broth for a biological warfare program?

SB: In your interview in Hidden Casualties, *Volume I, you indicated that you thought the effects of bombing the arsenal would be minimal. What's your opinion now?*

MM: You can burn these things up safely. For example, the way they're getting rid of a lot of these munitions in Iraq is very simple. You dig a big trench and on the bottom you put some metal or wooden beams, and then you put down some barrels that have been sawn in two. You put aviation fuel in the barrels and then you stack on top of them some chemical rockets. You attach electrically activated detonators to the rockets and go some hundreds of yards away and turn a switch. The rockets blow up and the aviation fuel ignites and it creates a big mushroom of burning gas. Even at close range downwind you can't detect any nerve agent or any mustard. It's all burned in this big fireball. It's pretty simple and it's apparently successful and cheap. It's very good for weapons that are damaged, that you wouldn't want to try to get the agent out of, because they might blow up on you. And that's what they're doing.

SB: Are you saying the agents would break down and decompose?

MM: Not only decompose, but simply be held and slowly evaporate from the surface. Decomposition would occur primarily through bacteriological action and moisture.

SB: So you're saying these wouldn't be the same kinds of pollution problems we'd find at, say, a Rocky Mountain Arsenal [where the U.S. had built chemical ordnance for many years]?

MM: No. That problem arose because they were pumping wastes from chemical neutralization procedures and other wastes into deep wells. That was before people realized that if you do that kind of pumping where the wrong kind of geology exists you're going to start causing little earthquakes. Which is what they did, they caused little earthquakes and then they stopped the procedure and the quakes stopped. Nothing drastic ever happened.

SB: That may be so, but as far as the contamination of the soil and the groundwater is concerned, I know that the site is on the Superfund list [sites designated by the U.S. Environmental Protection Agency for immediate cleanup] and is considered very hazardous and the Department of Defense is going to spend a lot of money cleaning it up.

MM: If you're going to build on it, then you're going to have liability. With the law courts being the way they are, you're driven to doing very, very thorough cleanup before you have a commercially useful property. Now, how bad the hot spots are there, I don't know, but I've walked over that range and there are all kinds of wild animals there, so. . . . I'm sure there are some hot spots, probably those open lakes they used to use, which they had leased to the Shell Corporation later. Shell filled them with insecticide wastes which might be the worst problem, insecticide waste from civilian activity. But I don't have detailed knowledge and maybe I'm being too sanguine.

The British destroyed 6,000 tons of mustard gas by incineration in the '60s. The Germans have a modern facility for that and they spend about $10,000 per ton incinerated. The U.S. spends roughly one hundred times more per ton. The reason is the American way of making everybody rich when the government does something and going to extreme environmental standards, standards that are more strict than what industry uses when it burns toxic chemicals, and that drives the price up.

SB: Unlike organizations like Greenpeace, who oppose incineration, particularly for chemical munitions, you feel that the operation is a safe and responsible procedure to use for these weapons?

MM: Well, the proof of the pudding is actually doing it and seeing what happens. So far as I know, yes, that's true, incineration is preferable. But in places where people are worried that the incineration, which certainly can be an excellent technology, might get out of hand, you can have a batch procedure, where you can then analyze the material before you let it out. There are various ways that you can do that. One is to precede the incineration by chemical neutralization so that you end up with nontoxic or relatively nontoxic materials first—alkali neutralization or ethanolamine neutralization or other kinds of neutralization; then you have to do something with the waste. Even though it isn't very toxic, it's still waste material and you still have to deal with it.

Incineration is one of the ways of dealing with it because you reduce all the organics to CO_2 and water vapor and you scrub the flue gases and you get sulfates, chlorides and fluorides. You put the scrubber products in a landfill and that's that. There's no way to get rid of the chemical elements because they are immutable except by alchemists, and we don't have any alchemists. So you're going to end up with the elements and you're going to have to do something with it. Chemical neutralization is a nice method if you're worrying about things getting out of control.

SB: Is Iraq then a large open-air laboratory for destroying chemical weapons?

MM: No. The neutralization and incineration methods being used in Iraq have already been widely used in other countries.

The original U.S. decision to go to incineration of nerve agents was made for a number of reasons: one is that you can incinerate anything, it doesn't matter what it is. It takes care of the metal parts and, as it turns out, it is very hard to wash a piece of metal to the point where there's nothing left on it, whereas incineration will do that.

In Iraq they're using alkali neutralization for the G agents; we won't learn anything from that because we've already done lots of that. The U.S. did the neutralization with bulk GB and with GB drained out of munitions, which was a very big program in Utah in the '60s and the '70s with the M34 bomb clusters.

There's a lot of foreign experience that's very relevant—well-established, proven methods in England, Canada, Germany, and although we know less about it, Russia as well.

The British have destroyed about 20 tons of GB by neutralizing it in sodium hydroxide, the way we did, and then after they did that, they analyzed it and dumped it in the ocean. Now we couldn't do that today, but you can incinerate it instead. The British also got rid of 6,000 tons of mustard by burning and scrubbing the flue gases and getting rid of the brine in the normal city sewage system.

The Canadians have destroyed some 12 tons of mustard by incinerating it, scrubbing the flue gases, analyzing continuously for fluorides, sulfates and nitrous oxides, hydrocarbons, particulates, intermittently for TCDD and trace metals. Then the scrubber brine was evaporated in a pit and the salts were put in a landfill.

The Germans incinerate about 70 tons of chemical warfare agents a year. This is from old abandoned munitions. They've been doing it for more than ten years. That 700 tons, that's a fair amount. It's a highly automated process, they incinerate it and then they scrub and so on like other people do. Then there are the Russians: we know less about it, but they have an interesting procedure they've done with about 300 tons of G agent, GB, GD and mustard. They neutralize it with ethanolamine at a temperature near the boiling point of water and then they incinerate it. I don't think they bother to scrub the flue gas.

SB: Let's turn to biological weapons. You indicated in our last conversation that they had produced several strains of agents.

MM: Produced, I don't know. They were asked what organisms, and what materials they were working with. The four strains that were on the list were *Bacillus anthracis, Pasteurella tularensi, Clostridium botulinum, Clostridium perfingens.*

SB: So how would you rate the Iraqi biological threat?

MM: Iraq's bacteriological efforts weren't very advanced. Either that or they were very well-hidden.

SB: It's the inhalation and ingestion that is the concern regarding bacteriological warfare.

MM: The inhalatory hazard, not an ingestional hazard, would be the military route of greater interest.

SB: What about the idea of putting a bacteriological agent in the water supply?

MM: Water's a problematic way to attack anybody. For one thing, you can shut it off; two, because there are purification procedures and testing procedures, and three, you have a very big dilution effect. Air dispersal is likely to be of greater military relevance.

THE U.S., CS AND THE CHEMICAL WEAPONS CONVENTION

SB: The Conference on Chemical Weapons has recently concluded negotiations on the new Chemical Weapons Convention and it was signed by more than 135 nations in January 1993. It will enter into force 180 days after 65 states have ratified their signatures, and no earlier than January 1995. Give us some examples of the implications of implementing the Chemical Weapons Treaty.

MM: The treaty would make the manufacture, testing and development of chemical weapons an international crime.

One of the biggest incentives of this treaty is to get the big powers out of this game because they're the ones who invent new stuff, they're the ones who eventually produce it and who train technicians who know how to do it.

SB: How does the convention help the international community control chemical weapons?

MM: Article 2 of the Chemical Weapons Convention identifies which uses of toxic compounds are not prohibited. These permitted uses include medicine, agriculture, research and other peaceful purposes and also law enforcement and domestic riot control. The treaty originally used the word "domestic" in front of "law enforcement," but the U.S. wanted to leave out domestic because we see law enforcement as a worldwide issue, such as counter-terrorist activities.

The treaty requires that a country declare the component chemicals used for riot control. But the Bush Administration's policy was that we can possess riot control chemical weapons and conduct research and development of new "law enforcement" chemical weapons under the new treaty.

The problem is twofold. First the U.S. apparently reserves the right to develop, test and produce such antipersonnel weapons under military auspices in secret without any declarations at all. The second part of the problem is that I don't see the necessity of a secrecy requirement. As far as I know, the U.S. hasn't used any nonlethal chemicals for international purposes except in the case of the *Mayaguez* [a U.S. Naval ship seized by the Khmer Rouge for a short period of time in 1975].

SB: The U.S. has a large stockpile of CS rounds, including 105-millimeter CS artillery shells. Where has CS been used?

MM: Vietnam, Cambodia, Iran-Iraq, South Korea. I don't know that the CS did much that was useful to the government. Mostly it gets people pretty angry because whether you are pro- or anti-government, CS can't tell. It drifts around. The British have stopped using CS in Northern Ireland, because it only served to heat up the situation.

SB: What about Saddam Hussein?

MM: About half his stockpile is CS—a huge amount of mortar projectiles. The CS was produced in Iraq's factories and is now being destroyed, along with the rest of his chemical arsenal, by UNSCOM. But the Bush Administration maintained that CS was not a chemical warfare agent. The whole thing hinged on the definition of those toxic chemicals that are permitted for law enforcement purposes. But if a country like the U.S. has a divergent interpretation of an important international treaty, that's a real problem for the world community, and in this case, we do!

SB: Overall, you feel we're passing out of a very serious stage internationally in terms of our security and our health?

MM: Definitely. The new serious stage involves testing the proposition that you can have a global international treaty prohibiting a whole class of weapons with verification and sanctions and that it will work. Now that's a giant experiment for humankind. If that fails, it will sour the chances for this happening again for decades; if it succeeds, it will be emulated, one hopes successfully, in other areas.

What UNSCOM Found in Iraq—Part Two

Interview with Bryan Barrass

Professor Bryan Barrass was a member of the UNSCOM team and until recently was employed by the Porton-Down Chemical Biological Defense Establishment in the United Kingdom. Interviewed by Saul Bloom, November 1992.

Saul Bloom: How extensive and effective was the Coalition attack on Iraq's chemical and biological weapons (CBW) facilities?

Bryan Barrass: Not having seen them beforehand, it's not possible to do a direct comparison. There was certainly considerable destruction to the plants which had been described by Iraq as used for manufacturing chemical warfare agents. Also considerable damage to some of the bunkers where the munitions were actually stored.

SB: Were a great many additional sites discovered after the war?

BB: We have found relatively few sites additional to those which were declared by Iraq in their declarations of April 1991. They provided information on the number of sites concerned with their chemical weapons program and with the operational deployment of chemical munitions. All the declared sites have been visited, as have many other sites designated by the Special Commission.

SB: What is the list of chemical weapons that need to be destroyed?

BB: The weapons that we have found are sarin (GB), tabun (GA), and a nerve agent called GF—for which there is no common name—those are the only three nerve agents that we have discovered in quantity.

SB: Did you find any V agents at all?

BB: No. We found traces of chemicals that might have been associated with the attempted manufacture of VX, but no VX as such. We've also found considerable quantities of mustard agent and nerve agents other than those I've mentioned, but only in relatively small quantities, kilogram quantities, rather than the tens of tons of the others. That is why I am dealing with these other nerve agents quite separately, because they were in relatively small amounts.

IRAQ'S CW PROGRAM

SB: Now is that indicative of their R&D program?

BB: That I don't know. This is something we need to explore with them, why those particular three G-type nerve agents were actually made.

SB: So there were further iterations of the G-type agent?

BB: Yes. All three are analogues of sarin. It's possible that these were part of an experimental program and that they were ultimately rejected by Iraq in favor of the standard agents GB and GF.

SB: What was their goal in finding additional iterations of sarin?

BB: Well, I presume that one of the things they would be looking for is increased persistence, because in that particular climate GB would be completely nonpersistent.

SB: I understand that Iraq had a large CS arsenal; does UNSCOM consider these munitions chemical weapons, and what is it doing about them?

BB: Riot control substances have been the subject of very active discussions under the chemical weapons convention. Since it [the CS] has actually been declared by Iraq, UNSCOM is taking this material and the munitions into which it is loaded quite seriously.

SB: Is that because UNSCOM now views CS as a chemical weapon as opposed to a law enforcement weapon?

BB: That's really a political question. I'll stick with my original statement. Because Iraq listed the CS among its weapons we will treat it as described under Security Council Resolution 687, which obviously is our mandate, although we take note, fairly careful note, of the Chemical Weapons Convention. The actual mandate under which the Special Committee operates is quite clearly SC 687 and other resolutions like 707 and 715. . . . Those are our mandates; anything else is guidance. I would also point out that riot control agents such as CS are not normally dispersed by mortar bombs when used for the control of civil disturbances.

SB: How large and sophisticated was Iraq's chemical weapons production system?

BB: I get the impression that they wanted to acquire a militarily significant capability while at the same time accepting that adequate was probably good enough.

SB: So they were happy to have the same types of weapons available elsewhere, as opposed to developing new ones expected to extend persistence and things of that nature?

BB: That is probably a fair summary. They were looking at the range of known chemical agents, probably with a view to selecting those which they probably felt met their own military needs rather than getting into an extensive search for other completely novel types of agents.

SB: How extensive was their production and filling capability?

BB: Difficult to say, because the facilities were fairly well damaged by bombing during the war. My impression is they were quite sufficient for Iraq's military requirements and could have handled the munitions.

SB: How big was the stockpile?

BB: There are two answers to that, and I'll reply fairly extensively to make the situation quite clear.

As far as the chemical warfare agents are concerned, i.e., the filling—the material you actually put into the munition in order to get a weapon—there are about 600 tons in total. It probably will be somewhat more than that because we need to take into consideration how much agent was actually in munitions. We're in the process of extracting that material for systematic destruction under controlled conditions.

So when I say 600 tons, that includes an estimate of what is likely to be found, filled, in munitions. But until we've actually extracted the agent and measured it we won't know precisely.

As far as the munitions are concerned the latest figures I've seen are something of the order of 150,000 in total, including 155-millimeter artillery shells, aerial bombs, 122-millimeter rockets, and 30 Scuds with chemical or binary chemical warheads and I think it was something like 48 Scud warheads intended for chemical use which they unilaterally destroyed. There were approximately 78 Scuds intended for chemical use.

SB: Did you find equipment for dispersing aerosolized agents?

BB: No unambiguous evidence so far. We're still carrying out inspection activities in Iraq and it may be that that sort of evidence may be forthcoming in the future.

SB: So you're saying there is the possibility of uncovering new information?

BB: There's certainly the possibility and . . . let me be quite specific . . . we may in the future discover more, or be told more about their program, or we may discover more items that are covered by Security Council Resolution 687. So we are still concerned to find out the full extent of their total program.

SB: Was it possible for the Iraqis to develop their weapons without help from more developed countries?

BB: If they had received such assistance it would have helped them a lot. Whether they could have actually achieved the capability they have, as we so far understand it, without external assistance is much less clear. I think they would have found it really quite difficult to acquire that capability without assistance . . . in the form of being able to purchase various items from overseas such as equipment and that sort of thing. If you're talking about voluntary assistance, advice, etc., that's one issue I cannot comment on. However, it's difficult to see how they'd have gotten where they did without commercial purchases from overseas markets.

THE BOMBING OF IRAQ'S CW FACILITIES

SB: During the air war, there was a great controversy over the bombing of a baby milk formula factory because it was allegedly also making chemical munitions. Subsequently, some of the increase in infant malnourishment and mortality has been linked to the destruction of that facility, which provided the vast majority of the product for Iraq. Has there been any confirmation of that facility's use in weapons production?

BB: To the best of my knowledge we haven't really visited the baby milk factory. It's pretty close by the main road and it was obviously very badly damaged, virtually destroyed. But as far as I'm aware it hasn't been actually visited.

SB: With regard to bombing chemical weapons facilities, what are the ecological concerns and impacts? Have you noticed any effects on the communities neighboring the targets?

BB: We certainly haven't noticed any. I've been to their primary chemical weapons research, production, filling and storage facility at Muthanna on a couple of occasions. I think that my assessment would be that the ecological effects would be very small indeed, virtually zero. In the first place any liquid would have been very localized; we're talking a radius of maybe a kilometer at a guess, maybe half a kilometer. Any vapor would move away from that area and would become very rapidly diluted down to nonhazardous and eventually nondetectable levels of concentration really quite quickly. So, though I'm not an expert on ecology, my expectation would be that the ecological impact of any agent released into the atmosphere there as a result of Coalition action would have been very small, possibly zero.

You must also keep in mind the size of Muthanna. The overall area is about 25 kilometers square, with an inner area of about five square kilometers where the actual facilities are located. So there is a very large area of basically desert surrounding the facility.

SB: Would the use of high-temperature explosives have minimized the effects?

BB: That's undoubtably correct. High-temperature incineration is the method we have selected for the destruction of mustard agents at Muthanna. Obviously depending on the temperature that was generated, the lifetime of the agents in that sort of a fireball would be measured in one or two seconds, possibly even fractions of a second, if the temperature was high enough. So you're not talking about needing a long time to thermally destroy these agents. At temperatures in excess of a thousand degrees, which can easily be achieved in the sort of situation you are speaking of, the lifetime of these agents would be measured in a very few seconds or less.

Destroying the Remaining Stockpile

SB: Is incineration the main method of destruction for Iraq's chemical arsenal?

BB: No, it's not. We've spent quite a lot of time discussing this question of destruction of the Iraqi chemical capability. We sought advice from quite a lot of experts worldwide and we have decided, in the light of all those discussions and the advice we received, to use two methods. One is high-temperature incineration for mustard agent. This will take place in a specially designed facility. The facility was designed by Iraq with considerable direction, supervision and technical administration by the Special Commission. Iraq then built the facility, again with considerable detailed technical oversight of the construction process. Decommissioning is carried out by UNSCOM and operated by Iraqi personnel under the direct control and supervision of the UNSCOM team that was assembled specifically for that purpose.

As far as the nerve agents are concerned, for a variety of technical reasons, we decided to use caustic hydrolysis for the destruction rather than incineration. Among the many factors which contributed to the decision was the fact that in some cases they had a mixture of agents, GB and GF, and the hydrolysis process is better understood for that sort of situation than incineration. One of the other factors contributing to that decision was that their nerve agents were acidic and the last thing we wanted to do was corrode away the burners of an expensive incineration facility. Those were among the factors that led us to decide that caustic hydrolysis was the safest and most effective method.

SB: Did you do an environmental assessment of the impacts or was the discussion focused on how quickly we could proceed with decommissioning?

BB: We spent a lot of time and put in a lot of effort discussing how best to destroy these chemical agents and we sought a lot of advice from international experts. The priorities at the time for most of those discussions were related to two aspects of the project: one was safety and the other was the environment.

SB: Safe from the perspective of the safety of the operators?

BB: Safety of the operators and of the supervising UNSCOM staff is certainly one of the paramount parameters. But it's difficult to discuss environmental issues as strictly environmental. For example, if agents are released from one of these facilities into the atmosphere, would you consider it a safety issue or an environmental issue? This is one of the reasons why we have tried to deal with the issues of safety, occupational health, and the environment as quite closely related because in reality it is rather artificial to try to separate them. So we have designed those plants to contain and control the agent until it has been effectively destroyed. Any material discharged into the environment, either into the air or the surrounding terrain, is environmentally harmless.

SB: What about groundwater contamination?

BB: The bulk of the material is stored and protected up to destruction and, at any one time, is kept in relatively small quantities. The reason for that is that one very good principle underlying safety, occupational health, and environmental factors is to centralize and localize any problem sources to the maximum extent possible. This was the major reason why we took the decision to centralize the destruction activities, because localizing and controlling safety and particularly environmental problems at one site would be that much more manageable.

These materials just will not get into the water table full stop. The discharge from those two plants is channeled into concrete lagoons with plastic liners. Those lagoons are large enough not only to take the total contents of those facilities at any one time but, because of the calculated rate of through-put, they are also large enough to take the anticipated total waste contents of those facilities. They will accept all the waste that is generated during the lifetime of these destruction activities. So they're pretty big. When these are completed the waste will be disposed of in a suitable manner. Probably in situ, by sealing them [the lagoons] in concrete. So the answer is the wastes just do not get into the environment.

SB: What about in the case of the bombed facilities?

BB: At Muthanna, nothing. We looked at the hydrogeology of that area last year when we were considering how best to deal with the destruction of their CBW agents. So we did look into the hydrogeological aspects with the Iraqi experts, and any agent that would have gotten into the ground I think would have caused no problem at all. And the same would have applied at the other major storage site at Al Mahummidiyah.

SB: How long do you expect the process to take?

BB: Sorry I can't give you a simple answer. Let me explain why. I would expect the destruction of the nerve agents to be completed very early next year. I would expect the destruction of their mustard agent to be completed probably about early spring, April or May.

However, there are quite a lot of other chemicals—intermediates, precursors, solvents, etc.— which are stored at Muthanna. There are also some chemicals related to ballistic missile propellants which are there and will also be destroyed by incineration. I would expect the destruction of Iraq's chemical arsenal to be completed or very close to completed by early spring of next year. However, I would expect the destruction activities at Muthanna dealing with these other chemicals, these non-agents, to continue for probably six months beyond that, maybe a little longer. I would think that by autumn of next year all destruction activities would be either complete or very close to completion at Muthanna.

LESSONS LEARNED

SB: You've been involved in the subject matter for a number of years; what kinds of lessons are you taking from this? Has this been a useful exercise in the sense that it has given UNSCOM, the UN and the international community a better idea of the complexity of this type of disarmament?

BB: I must warn you that I have a very firm opinion on that one, so you might need to take my comments with a pinch of salt—be warned.

Yes, definitely, the experiences that UNSCOM has gone through in disarming Iraq of its weapons of mass destruction—its chemical, ballistic missile, biological and nuclear weapons—do have a number of lessons for the wider arms control/disarmament community. There is no doubt of it in my mind. Personally, I believe that the information ought to be made available to the wider arms control and disarmament community, and I'm pretty sure that UNSCOM will share that view, probably quite strongly.

It is also important to remember that the UNSCOM experience (disarming a nation under the protest of its government after a war) is unique. It's not going to happen very often. In fact, it may never happen again. So the circumstances surrounding UNSCOM's existence, actually, and its activities, are unique. That doesn't mean that the lessons we are learning aren't generally applicable. It does mean that those lessons have got to be extrapolated with some caution, taking due note of the fact that the UNSCOM situation is unique.

SB: Can you give me a couple of examples?

BB: One example: the importance of human factors. How do you take a collection of individuals from a wide variety of different countries, bring them together for the first time, and get them to operate as an effective team unit? We [UNSCOM] have done that, and I think there are quite a number of lessons to be learned on the human factors side.

Second lesson: A lot of information is acquired in the course of these activities. It is necessary to set up a good information-handling unit; almost certainly one which is equipped with a relational database, because you need to relate information obtained from different areas. There needs to be an effective information evaluation organization which can take information from various sources and collect, analyze, and correlate it with apparently quite unrelated information from different areas. So there are information handling needs. Those are just two general lessons.

The third lesson is that you need a very well-staffed, competent, professional headquarters organization. If you train, let's say, thirty people from twenty different countries, and they've all got to be in one place at a particular time, organizing their flights is not a trivial task. If you make one or two errors, they could be quite crucial depending on which team member is affected. Sometimes the obvious is so obvious that it gets overlooked. You need to have competent administrative/logistic organizational back-up support for your in-field activities. It's very important; if you didn't have that, your in-field activities could be crippled. So there are lessons of that sort to be learned.

Other lessons to be learned on a more technical level are the importance of sampling and analysis, the value of having on-site analytical equipment available—and you need very portable analytical equipment at that.

This is another lesson that has been learned: continuity is really very valuable, continuity of experience and expertise. That means you've got to employ the people rather than keep borrowing them from member states. Now, okay, there will always be the requirement to get in special expertise for relatively short periods or specific tasks from time to time and that option will have to be preserved.

There are quite a few lessons to be learned at different levels of generalization. It's quite a significant task. With the chemical weapons convention up for signature in January and the PREP-CON [Preparatory Commission] being set for around February or March, it's just these sorts of issues that I presume the PREPCON will actually need to address. Therefore, I think it is important to get these lessons, this information, more generally into the arms control and disarmament community so that it can be used. So, going back to your first comment, yes, it's been a very interesting and professionally very challenging experience, but I believe it has also been more generally a useful learning experience for quite a number of people and organizations.

SB: Are you then optimistic about the state of chemical weapons control? How do you look at it, being steeped as you are in the Iraqi experience?

BB: Ask me in a year. I would regard that with a fair degree of optimism actually, when you consider the circumstances under which UNSCOM has been operating in Iraq, with someone who was unwilling to provide information, and actually tried to withhold [information] or mislead. The UNSCOM achievement was very considerable indeed given all the circumstances that might have prevented that. I think that the CWC stands a very good chance of being very successful. Now, mind you, the proper resources will have to be allocated, and I think in any event they will not be as high as people anticipate. It won't cost that much money—and we've got quite a lot.

SB: Does it remain difficult with the Iraqis; were the pictures we see of Iraqi noncooperation accurate?

BB: Generally, they certainly have not been helpful. Not at all. In the area of the destruction of chemical weapons they appear to have taken a rather more positive and businesslike attitude than in the other areas of UNSCOM's activities in Iraq. So in the nuclear, biological and ballistic missile areas, not generally particularly forthcoming, sometimes actively not forthcoming. In the chemical area, as I said, brisk and businesslike on the destruction side. But again, when it came to inspections of chemical facilities, [when we were] looking for items they might have tried to conceal, then again not particularly helpful or forthcoming.

SB: We've seen reports of actual physical threat to UNSCOM researchers. Was it ever as serious as it was reported in the U.S.?

BB: It's not possible to give a clear-cut answer to a question like that because the situation itself is not clear-cut. People have certainly been threatened, no doubt about that, but whether there was a real physical danger to life I think is rather more doubtful. I'm not convinced that there was a real danger to life, but certainly people have been subjected to harassment, very unpleasant harassment and a lot of inconvenience, but safety . . . I'm not sure that their safety was at stake. Obviously, we keep a very close watch on the situation, on a daily basis actually. But as I say it is difficult to give a clear-cut answer because the situation varies virtually from day to day.

Biological Weapons

SB: Let's turn to biologicals. I understand that Iraq was also dabbling in some biological weapons research?

BB: They did more than dabble, a lot more.

SB: What kinds of biological agents were they working with?

BB: Anthrax, botulism, gangrene, clostridium. I'm not a BW expert although I've picked up some knowledge of it on the side. They also had seed cultures of quite a lot of other micro-organisms available to them at their research site and we've taken possession of these. Why they needed so many seed cultures, including various strains of individual micro-organisms, again is very much an open question. We need some answers to those questions. I think at this stage I would say that the BW program was probably larger than would be logically assessed based on the evidence we've actually got currently in our hands. We need a lot more information, which we're sure is there.

SB: We don't know about weaponization; but it's your opinion that there may be a lot to be learned about what their BW program was like. So would you say that we are in the very beginning of investigating their BW program and that it will take some time to develop the investigation, or is that already going on?

BB: No, we're not at the beginning. We've done a couple of dedicated BW inspections and two, maybe three, joint CBW inspections. So, no, we're not at the beginning. We have a reasonable overview of their program. For example: we know they have a program and that it was offensively oriented, we know the sort of micro-organisms they worked on, we have some feel for the type of work they carried out, we know something about the sites where the work was carried out, and we know the sort of equipment that they used in this work. So in that sense we've got a great deal of information on their program, but we feel that there is still quite a lot more information required, a lot more information to be given about the program before we can make a fully informed and complete assessment.

SB: How sophisticated would you say the Iraqi BW program was? Was it on the same level as the CW program?

BB: No. That again is only based on the information we have so far, and I might have to revise that statement in six months to a year.

Incineration: The Wisest Choice?

Background Information

A number of environmental organizations are concerned that incineration is neither a wise nor efficient method of destroying chemical weapons.

As our background section on chemical and biological weapons in this chapter indicates, extremely small quantities of nerve agents are capable of killing large numbers of people. With biological weapons, even extremely small quantities of bacteria are sufficient for replication, with potentially epidemic impacts.

Considering the environmental impacts of incomplete combustion in conventional toxic waste incinerators, the efficiency of a chemical weapons incinerator is naturally of concern. Given the potency of these agents, even 99 percent burn efficiency may be insufficient to protect health and the environment.

Greenpeace U.S. has written a critique of the incineration method in a report issued in April 1992.[1] The report focused on the United States Army's Johnston Atoll chemical weapons disposal facility.

The U.S. Army's history of chemical munitions disposal goes back to World War I. Chemical munitions have been stored on Johnston Atoll, in the Pacific about 700 miles west of Hawaii, since 1971.[2] In 1980, the Army began looking for an isolated location for chemical weapons disposal, and in 1983, released a Record of Decision designating Johnston Atoll as a facility for destroying M55 chemical weapons. In 1985, the Congress enacted Public Law 99-145, requiring the Department of Defense to destroy the U.S. stockpile of chemical weapons by September 1994. The Army concluded that high-temperature incineration was the preferred method of disposal, and in 1988 completed construction of its prototype plant at Johnston Atoll.[3]

Greenpeace is an active supporter of eliminating chemical weapons stockpiles but is critical of the impacts of the incineration method, as opposed to other methods. UNSCOM appears to share their concern, since it chose to use chemical processes, not incineration, to destroy Iraq's stockpile of nerve agents. In their report,[4] Greenpeace raise the following concerns:

> ... This technology is still practiced and promoted, not because it is a proven, mature technology, but because it is expeditious, relatively inexpensive and liability-free for the generators.

> The complexity of the incineration process, the differences in incinerator designs, and the difficulties in monitoring operating conditions make the accurate prediction of absolute incineration performance an essentially impossible task. ... Only a very small fraction of the total volume of waste needs to experience ... less than optimum conditions to result in significant deviations from the targeted destruction efficiencies (Dillinger and Lee, 1986).

For example, at this DRE [a Destruction and Removal Efficiency of 99.9999 percent], at least 3.5 grams of active agent GB were released in the LIC [liquid incinerator] stack emissions at JACADS [Johnston Atoll] when 75,000 pounds of GB were burned. Based on an acute lethal dose of 140 micrograms per adult (Picardi et al., 1991), 3.5 grams of GB, if delivered directly, is a lethal dose for 24,000 people. . . . If 1,500 one-ton containers of mustard gas are burned, with the LIC achieving a 99.9999 percent DRE at all times, approximately three pounds (1,362 grams) of mustard will be released, intact, in stack gases. Mustard is carcinogenic; it is a powerful blistering agent; and is highly persistent in the environment.[5] [The incinerator at Muthanna in Iraq burns mustard, according to the interview with Bryan Barrass in this chapter.]

One present concern for application of incineration technology is that the hazard associated with a waste stream may not be removed even though the original waste compounds are destroyed. Transformation of the waste into hazardous products of incomplete combustion (PICs) can potentially aggravate the hazard associated with the waste stream. For example, a hazardous but nontoxic waste can be partially transformed into chlorinated dibenzo-p-dioxins or dibenzofurans upon incineration (Kramlich et al, 1989).

—Saul Bloom

NOTES:
1. Pat Costner, *Chemical Weapons Demilitarization and Disposal: The Army's Experience at Johnston Atoll Chemical Disposal System,* Report, Greenpeace U.S., Washington DC, April 1992.
2. U.S. Army Corps of Engineers, *Johnston Atoll Chemical Agent Dispersal System; Final Supplemental Environmental Impact Statement,* December 1988.
3. U.S. General Accounting Office, *Chemical Weapons: Stockpile Destruction Delayed at the Army's Prototype Disposal Facility,* GAO/NSIAD-90-222, July 1990.
4. Pat Costner, *Chemical Weapons Demilitarization and Disposal.*
5. Alfred Picardi, Pat Johnston and Ruth Stringer, *Alternative Technologies for the Detoxification of Chemical Weapons: An Information Document,* Report, Greenpeace International, May 1991.

Nerve Gas Linked to Veterans' Illnesses

Background Information

Since the interviews with Bryan Barass and Matthew Meselson, the Czech government has provided the first official report that detectable levels of sarin and mustard gas were probably released early in the war following the Coalition bombing of Iraqi chemical weapons plants. The report underscores fears that Gulf War veterans may have been exposed to chemical warfare agents.

Several reports have appeared which indicate that symptoms suffered by over 4,000 U.S. Gulf War veterans could be attributed to either fallout from Coalition bombing of Iraqi chemical warfare agent facilities or to Iraqi chemical attacks on Coalition troops. Veterans have complained of a variety of symptoms including muscle and joint pain, intestinal and heart problems, fatigue, rashes and sores.

In July 1993, the Czech government provided the first official admission that veterans' illnesses may have been caused by Iraqi chemicals. Defense Minister Antonin Baudys told the Prague newspaper *Mlada Fronta Dnes* that traces of sarin had been measured by a Czechoslovakian anti-chemical warfare unit that was attached to Saudi troops during the Gulf War. Lt. Col. Lubomir Smehlik, commander of the unit, reported that the sarin was probably released when Coalition air forces attacked Iraqi chemical weapons arsenals. Details of the time and location of these incidents were not given.[1]

Also in July, the Czech News Agency interviewed Peter Zelinsky, a spokesman for Czechoslovakian Gulf War troops, who said that increased concentrations of mustard gas and sarin were noted "in the atmosphere" [in the Gulf region]. Samples of the chemicals were sent to military laboratories in the U.S., which confirmed their conclusions but kept the information secret. Zelinsky said that the chemicals were released from weapons from the chemical ammunition warehouse in the Iraqi city of Muthanna which was bombed by Coalition troops.[2]

Czech authorities say that 10 members of the 185-member anti-chemical warfare unit are suffering the same health symptoms that have been reported by U.S. and British troops. The effects of the "Gulf War Syndrome" include fever, coughing, shortness of breath, diarrhea, fatigue and aching joints. Sarin causes convulsions and difficulties in breathing. Czech researchers are investigating whether the two sets of symptoms are in fact linked.[3]

On January 27, 1991, ABC News reported that members of the 82nd Airborne Division detected traces of chemicals in the air, possibly the result of Coalition bombing of chemical plants in Iraq. A U.S. medical corpsman told reporters, "When the Air Force bombers hit all the gas places there in Iraq, there's a lot of contamination in the air. Some may have filtered down and set these things off. They're very, very sensitive."[4]

In 1993, two U.S. Senators, Donald W. Riegle, Jr. and Richard Shelby, began separate investigations into the possibility that veterans' illnesses were caused by exposure to Iraqi chemicals. A report issued by Senator Riegle's staff found that Coalition troops deployed along the Saudi-Iraqi and Saudi-Kuwaiti border were downwind of Coalition attacks on hundreds, if not thousands, of tons of bulk chemical nerve agents, mustard gas and tens of thousands of pieces of chemical munitions.

The Riegle report[5] states that it is more than likely that the Iraqis also set off chemical attacks against Coalition troops. Riegle's staff base their findings on eyewitness reports and the fact that veterans are exhibiting symptoms compatible with an attack of mixed agents, typical of the Iraqi mode of chemical warfare, which could have included biotoxins, chemical nerve agents, blood agents and blister agents.

The Riegle report contains two accounts of reported chemical attacks against two U.S. military units and concludes that "the rate of unexplained illness in both these units is much too high to be the result of random events." One attack was reported by Staff Sergeant Willie Hicks, then with the 644th Ordinance Company. Hicks said that in the early morning hours of January 17, 1991, he heard a loud explosion followed by the sounding of alarms. As he was running to the bunker his face began to burn. One member of the unit 'just dropped'. Two or three days later, Hicks began feeling ill and noticed blood in his urine. Several other members of the unit began experiencing 'problems' with their rectums. Hicks identified and described one member of his unit who was in good physical shape and suddenly died. Hicks, a former teacher and Vietnam veteran now complains of a severe problem with memory loss. His illness has been classified by the Department of Veterans' Affairs as post-traumatic stress disorder. Approximately 85 out of 110 of his unit suffered from Gulf War Syndrome, he said.

The second attack was reported by Petty Officer Sterling Symms, then assigned to the Naval Reserve Construction Battalion 24, in an area south of the Kuwaiti border. Between 2:00 a.m. and 3:00 a.m. on January 20, 1991, the Petty Officer heard an explosion overhead and saw a fireball. According to Symms, alarms went off and everybody ran towards their bunkers. Symms smelled an odor of ammonia in the air, his eyes burned and skin stung. His unit donned full chemical gear. Later, members of the unit were advised that what they heard was a sonic boom. Symms has since experienced fatigue, sore joints, running nose, a chronic severe rash and open sores. One hundred out of 725 of Naval Reserve Battalion 24 have since reported incidents of Gulf War illnesses.

In a separate account of the attack on the 24th Battalion given to the *Birmingham News*, Larry Perry, a former chief petty officer described an explosion and a substance "somewhere between a fog and a light drizzle . . . It was like a real light rain, real fine." The men ran back to their bunkers, struggling to put their gas masks on. Perry noticed his face burning around his mask. Other unit members reported burning skin and not being able to breathe normally. In the command post bunker, Dale Milsap, petty officer second-class, heard a radio report announcing that a "confirmed blister agent" had been detected. When the men emerged from their hiding places, they learned that the gas attack was "unconfirmed," and they were later ordered by their detachment commander, Lt. Lewis Harrison, not to talk about the incident.

Paul Moyers, a petty officer first-class, who was the detachment's safety officer, said that three teams of military personnel trained in chemical and biological warfare defense arrived at the base and began testing and decontamination. He said British decontamination personnel told him that all three teams found traces of mustard gas.

Many of the reservists who were there during the incident say they began getting ill a few days later and have since been chronically unwell. Perry developed pneumonia, and, when he returned to the States, was treated for a severe infection and psychiatric and other medical disorders. Mike Haynes, a former petty officer second-class, suffers from memory loss and aching joints. His son, who also served with the unit, suffers from aching joints, headaches, fatigue and rectal bleeding. Former petty officer second-class Nicholas Roberts believes there is a possible link between the "fine rain" and his cancer of the lymph nodes.[6]

The Riegle report notes that in both incidences, there were reports of FROG missiles falling in the areas where the units were assigned. FROGs and SCUD Bs are the two types of missiles into which the Iraqi military load chemical agents, according to the CIA.[7]

U.S. Senator Richard Shelby from Alabama has asked Secretary of Defense Les Aspin to investigate the veterans' charges, in the hopes that they will receive medical treatment from the U.S. government. On June 30, 1993, the Subcommittee on Force Requirements and Personnel of the Senate Armed Services Committee, chaired by Senator Shelby, opened hearings on the possibility of a chemical attack in the Gulf and its impact on the health of American veterans.

The Joint Chiefs of Staff has so far declined a request by Senator Shelby to initiate an investigation. U.S. Department of Defense spokesman Lieutenant Colonel Doug Hart denies that bombed chemical weapons were detected during the war.[8] However, the Department of Veterans Affairs announced in November, 1993, that it would test selected veterans for chemical exposure.[9]

—Philippa Winkler

NOTES:

1. "Czech Experts Say Nerve Gas Released in Gulf War," *Reuters*, July 29, 1993.
2. Letter from Jiri Majstr (Czech News Agency) to Senator Richard Shelby's office, July 2, 1993.
3. Letter from Jiri Majstr to Senator Richard Shelby.
4. *Gulf War Syndrome: The Case for Multiple Origin Mixed Chemical/Biotoxin Warfare Related Disorders*, Staff report to U.S. Senator Donald W. Riegle, J., September 9, 1993.
5. *Gulf War Syndrome*.
6. Dave Parks, "Ill Vets Suspect Chemical Weapons," *Birmingham News*, June 27, 1993.
7. *Gulf War Syndrome*.
8. Interview with Lt. Col. Doug Hart, September 2, 1993. As we go to press, there are reports that the Pentagon now concurs with the findings of the Czech anti-chemical warfare unit. Steve McGonigle and Ed Timma, "Army Admits Gulf Troops Gassed," *San Francisco Examiner*, October 30, 1993.
9. Chronicle Wire Services, "Chemical Tests Planned for Gulf War Veterans," *San Francisco Chronicle*, November 2, 1993.

Chapter 8

Arms Trade Policy and Legal Issues

The Peace Palace in The Hague, Netherlands, seat of the International Court of Justice. Photo: UN

Introduction

Arms sales to the Middle East have increased since the end of the Gulf War. Chapter Eight opens with an interview with Lora Lumpe, a senior research analyst with the Federation of American Scientists. She describes how arms sales have been used as a tool of U.S. foreign policy in the Middle East, and argues that this policy adds to political instability in the region.

Professor Francis Boyle of the University of Illinois discusses why he thinks Saddam Hussein and the Bush Administration are both guilty of violating the Convention on the Prohibition of Military or Any Other Hostile Use of Environmental Modification Techniques (ENMOD, 1977).[1] In the aftermath of the oil fires and spills there has been increasing awareness of the need to strengthen international law regarding war and the environment. This chapter includes an excerpt from the 1991 UN debate over Jordan's proposal that the General Assembly consider a treaty to prevent the use of the environment as a weapon. Environmental organizations who want to prevent the use of the environment as a weapon are now calling for a new Geneva Convention. (See "A New Geneva Convention?" in Appendix One.)

Saddam Hussein has been widely accused of war crimes. According to Professor Howard Levie of St. Louis University School of Law, Saddam Hussein's annexation of Kuwait was in violation of 1907 Hague Regulations and two 1949 Geneva Conventions, while his treatment of Kuwaitis violated provisions of the 1949 Geneva Convention on the Protection of Civilians During Wartime.[2] The oppressive actions of the Baath Regime and its persecution of minorities in Iraq are also criminal, as were Saddam Hussein's attacks against Israel, a noncombatant in the Gulf War.

The U.S. Army claims to have fought a law-abiding war. A large number of lawyers were involved in the Gulf War on the Coalition side, often as advisors to commanding officers. An article in the *American Bar Association Journal* clarifies the role of these lawyers: "As in the relationship of corporate counsel to CEO, the Judge Advocate General's role is not to create obstacles, but to find legal ways to achieve his client's goals even when those goals are to blow things up and kill people."[3] The same article notes that "in the Gulf, lawyers sometimes had to tell commanders that it was okay to do something the commanders had assumed was illegal."[4]

Interviewees in this chapter argue that, nonetheless, the Coalition forces waged the war in an unlawful manner. Karen Parker, an attorney specializing in international human rights and humanitarian (armed conflict) law, believes that Coalition attacks on retreating Iraqi forces were illegal. She also notes that the U.S. broke the law by failing to give the UN Security Council a role in planning the military action in Kuwait, and in misusing its veto power as a permanent member to avoid accountability within the UN. Both Francis Boyle and Karen Parker believe that U.S. attacks on Iraqi civilian infrastructure violated international law and served little military purpose.

—James Warner

NOTES:
1. ENMOD was done at Geneva, May 18, 1977, and ratified by the U.S. in 1980.
2. Stephanie Goldberg, "Punishing Aggression," *ABA Journal*, April 1991, 24. Iraqi atrocities against Kuwaiti civilians and U.S. POWs are detailed in *Report on Iraqi War Crimes (Desert Shield/Desert Storm) [Unclassified version]*, Office of the Judge Advocate General Headquarters, Department of the Army, Washington, D.C., January 1992. This document was sent by the Deputy Permanent Representative of the U.S. to the President of the UN Security Council in March 1993 as a move toward setting up an Iraqi war crimes tribunal.
3. Steven Keeva, "Lawyers in the War Room," *ABA Journal*, December 1991, 53.
4. Hays Parks, the special assistant for law of war matters in the Office of the Judge Advocate General of the Army, argues that all the civilian deaths caused by Coalition forces in the Gulf War were legal. He makes the point that while the role of the lawyer in wartime is to find legal ways to kill people, it is up to the commanding officer to make decisions about what actions are acceptable in terms of policy, public relations, or ethical considerations. Steven Keeva, "Lawyers in the War Room."

The Arms Trade

Interview with Lora Lumpe

Lora Lumpe is a Senior Research Analyst with the Federation of American Scientists, and the editor of its newsletter, Arms Sales Monitor. *Interviewed by Philippa Winkler, July 1992.*

Philippa Winkler: Give us an overview of the international involvement in the selling of weapons to the Gulf Region. Who are the primary sellers and who are the primary buyers?

Lora Lumpe: The five largest sellers are the five permanent members of the United Nations Security Council: the U.S., Russia, Great Britain, France and China. The U.S. is now the number one exporter of weapons to the Middle East. In 1991, the U.S. sold $12 billion worth of weapons to the Middle East, most of it to Saudi Arabia. Russian sales have decreased because of the change in the political picture there, and because their arms supply relationship with Iraq has dried up. Their arms transfers used to be on a credit and giveaway basis and now they are selling only for hard cash. The former Soviet Union's sales were to Iraq, Yemen and Syria; now there is tremendous concern that they will sell indiscriminately to Iran and Syria. I think this fear is somewhat overstated. There is such chaos now in the C.I.S. that the supply tail, that is to say, services and spare parts, might not be available in the future. Moreover, there is tremendous pressure on Russia not to make "destabilizing" sales to the region. Russia will receive far more in aid and credit from the U.S. and the West than it could ever hope to earn through arms sales. Finally, the Gulf War reinforced the perception of Western, and especially of U.S., superiority in weapon technology over Soviet weapons, which were used by Iraq. So countries now want to buy American first and foremost.

The keenest competition for arms sales in the future will be between the U.S. and European suppliers. The Europeans have been making some sales to the Gulf Cooperation Council (GCC) States, Oman, Bahrain, Kuwait, Qatar, Saudi Arabia and the United Arab Emirates. But the U.S. has been marketing so aggressively in the region that French and British sales have declined dramatically. Since the invasion of Kuwait, the U.S. has contracted to sell Saudi Arabia $16.7 billion worth of arms.

In addition to selling to the GCC, the U.S. has a longstanding military supply relationship with both Israel and Egypt. The U.S. gives $1.8 billion worth of weapons every year to Israel, and $1.2 billion worth of weapons every year to Egypt.

PW: What's the procedure for U.S. sales?

LL: The vast majority of U.S. sales are brokered by the government, specifically by an office at the Pentagon called the Defense Security Assistance Agency (DSAA). All sales above a $14 million threshold must be sent to Congress for a 30-day review before the sale can be formally made.

Notification of proposed sales are sent by the DSAA to the House Foreign Affairs Committee and Senate Foreign Relations Committee.

PW: Who are the major U.S. defense contractors selling to the Middle East?

LL: General Dynamics, McDonnell Douglas, Raytheon, LTV Corporation, United Technology Corporation. They are all very active in the Middle East arena now, since U.S. government procurement is declining.

PW: What kinds of arms and arms-related technologies are being sold to the region?

LL: Mostly equipment for air forces. One of the primary lessons of the Gulf War seems to be that an effective air force and air defense system are important. The bulk of U.S. sales to the Middle East have been advanced fighter aircraft like the F-16, F-15 and F/A-18 and associated ordnance, and air defense missiles such as the I-Hawk and Patriot. U.S. companies also sell ground force equipment such as main battle tanks, armored personnel carriers, and artillery systems. European sales have been mainly of air-to-air missiles and naval equipment. Both the European countries and the U.S. have sold dual-use technology that could be useful in developing chemical and nuclear weapons. Since most countries in the Middle East have no indigenous arms industry, they also buy repair and support services. Israel and Egypt do have a substantial arms industry. Both of these countries buy components and assemble weapons under license. Iran has some arms industry and is turning to military cooperative agreements with other Third World countries, such as China, to develop weapons systems. China has been accused of transfering technology for possible nuclear weapon and ballistic missile programs to Iran.

PW: Are there any laws or policies in place that govern the international trade of arms?

LL: There is no international law that currently governs the international trade in conventional arms. There are laws and norms that restrict and ban unconventional arms such as nuclear, chemical and biological weapons and now ballistic missiles. The U.S. certainly has domestic laws that govern arms exports, as do most other major exporting countries. For example, there are laws that forbid the arming of states the U.S. considers to be supporting terrorists, such as Iran, Iraq, Syria and Libya.

PW: Why do countries trade arms?

LL: Two reasons: politics, both domestic and foreign, and economics. For the five major suppliers, it is a mix of both rationales. The U.S. in the past has primarily exported for foreign policy reasons, in order to challenge perceived Soviet geostrategic advances in the Third World. In the last few years, the Cold War has ended and U.S. weapon procurement has declined, as has Soviet adventurism. Meanwhile, economic and domestic political motivations for arms sales have increased in the U.S. Arms sales are now being justified in the U.S. in terms of jobs in congressional districts and balance of trade benefits. Secondly, there is a gross overcapacity of arms production that is being used as a rationale to continue trading. The U.S. arms industry lobbying for arms sales in the past year has been unprecedented. They're producing videos and glossy brochures for Congress with dire warnings of the imminent demise of communities dependent on arms production if sales don't continue.

PW: What are the foreign policy objectives of the U.S. government regarding arms sales to the region?

LL: Publicly, the Administration justifies its latest arms sales to the Middle East as being "stabilizing." This attempt to balance power through arms sales is a ludicrous policy that's seen the Shah's demise [the fall of Shah Mohammad Reza Pahlavi in Iran in 1979], the Iran-Iraq War and, most recently, the Persian Gulf War. State Department officials have claimed that the reason that Iraq was able to invade Kuwait was because we hadn't transfered enough arms to Kuwait. It's the export version of Reagan's "peace through strength" maxim. They claim that it's better for the U.S. to supply weapons in order to build up a military relationship with these countries that allows us to influence their policies, and allows us to build "inter-operability" in the event of a war. The underlying assumption is that there is going to be more U.S. global military intervention.

PW: So, to what extent are U.S. arms sales inflaming or even creating a war-like situation in the Middle East?

LL: It was the arms transfers to Iraq in the past that allowed and sustained Iraq's invasion of Kuwait and threatened the region in general. The U.S. didn't transfer much weaponry to Iraq, comparatively, before the Gulf War, but we didn't discourage other countries, mainly the former Soviet Union, France, China and Brazil, from selling to Iraq, because we were trying to counter Iran's influence, which the U.S. had directly built up under the Shah. As several ongoing congressional investigations are making clear, it was the policy of the Bush Administration to reward the Iraqis, to give them an indirect military advantage, in order to "keep them in the family of nations," and to maintain our influence over them. This policy obviously failed!

The justification now for the U.S.' nearly $300 billion military budget is the "Third World threat." That includes instability in the Middle East, like potential Iraqs.

It's a "Catch-22." U.S. arms sales are perpetuating instability and an arms race in the Middle East that is then used as a justification for more arms sales, U.S. Department of Defense procurement, and interventionary policies.

PW: You raised the issue of U.S. arms sales to Iraq prior to the war. There have been a number of allegations of violations of U.S. laws regarding U.S. shipments into Iraq. What inquiries are underway currently?

LL: There are four or five congressional investigations currently underway, looking into U.S. policies toward Iraq prior to its invasion of Kuwait. The House Judiciary Committee has called for an independent counsel to investigate whether the Administration was aware of the recent development in Iraq of weapons of mass destruction, and whether credits obtained under U.S. export guarantee programs were being used fraudulently. An investigation by the House Banking Committee Chairman, Henry Gonzales, has shown that the Administration violated federal criminal statutes in trying to hide its past policies towards Iraq from Congress and the public. The Commerce Department is also being investigated by the Inspector General due to charges that it falsified information about items it has licensed and sold to Iraq. We didn't sell complete weapons systems to Iraq, so there were no violations of U.S. laws governing weapons sales.

Apparently, no other countries violated their export laws, because they didn't have any in place. But, since the Gulf War, Germany has tightened up its export policies, as have France and Russia, regarding sales to Iraq.

PW: If the policy, direct or indirect, of the U.S. and of other countries is to continue arming the region, the future looks bleak. Where do you foresee the next explosion?

LL: The next hot spot is likely to be in the Gulf again, since billions of dollars in weapons are pouring into the region. Iran is now rebuilding its armed forces, which were severely depleted during its eight-year war with Iraq. It has reportedly purchased $2 billion worth of aircraft and submarines from the former Soviet Union.

Meanwhile, the U.S. is lavishly equipping the GCC states with some $20 billion worth of state-of-the-art weapons, ostensibly to deter further Iraqi aggression and to counter this Iranian rearmament. The Iraqi arsenal was decimated in the war, and Iraqi weapons of mass destruction are being dismantled by the UN. An unprecedented arms embargo remains in effect against Iraq, with no sign that it is being violated. So while Iraq poses less of a threat than ever, the massive GCC arms buying spree is undoubtedly encouraging greater Iranian insecurity, resulting in further arms purchases.

Given the disparity in demography and geography between the GCC states and Iran and Iraq (Saudi Arabia has a population of only seven million, while Iran has 50 million people), there is no way that the Saudi armed forces could ever equal, numerically, those of Iraq or Iran. So, all the U.S. is doing now is selling the GCC weapons scary enough to prod Iran, Israel, and Yemen, for example, to buy more high-tech weapons, but we're not arming them sufficiently to defend themselves. Basically, it's a bonanza for the arms industry and a disaster for regional stability.

PW: Are there any moves towards reducing arms sales to the region, given its tinderbox quality?

LL: There is a move towards negotiated restraint among the suppliers. Since July 1991, the five big sellers have been meeting to talk about restraining "destabilizing" arms transfers to the Middle East. They've drawn up guidelines for "responsible" arms sales. But all $12 billion of U.S. sales last year would have been acceptable under these guidelines. This is because the sellers can't agree on what constitutes a destabilizing arms sale. But it is the first time that the major suppliers have sat down together to discuss the issue. Of course, it will be up to the U.S. to decide how meaningful these talks will be. Thus far, the Bush Administration has decided not to limit its arms sales because it's not yet concerned enough about conventional arms sales proliferation.

The Middle East peace process that Secretary of State Baker has been promoting has regional arms control on its agenda. There is a stated desire for progress in this area. So there is some reason to be optimistic that negotiated restraint in the region could occur.

To achieve global restraint, there must be a downsizing of the over-productive arms industry. Economic conversion is key to bringing the arms trade under control. The U.S. is helping the former Soviet Union to convert their arms industry to peacetime use. The U.S. Congress' Department of Defense Authorization Bill for Fiscal Year 1993 contains $1.5 billion in funding for conversion programs in the U.S. Although it's late, it's a beginning.

PW: It sounds like in the long term, some companies are going to lose out in arms sales profits.
LL: Yes, some companies are looking into diversifying into nonmilitary products.

PW: Finally, what can you tell the citizen activist to do that will help bring about economic conversion and a reduction in the arms trade?

LL: Citizens should talk to their political representatives. Let them know that arms sales are foreign policy and national security issues, and not a domestic jobs issue. Let congressional representatives know that their constituents understand the connection between the international arms trade and the U.S. involvement in the Gulf War, and don't want to see a repeat of past, failed U.S. policies.

[In June 1993, Lora Lumpe added the following update: The Clinton Administration has clearly indicated that at present it will stay on the Bush Administration course, with the fiscal year 1994 military aid request looking very much like the Bush Administration's last budget. The Clinton State and Defense Departments have reiterated the utility and legitimacy of arms transfers as a primary tool of diplomacy, and they appear to have abandoned supply-side arms transfer limitations, favoring instead much more difficult to achieve demand-side restraint. They have stated that the Middle East peace process is a priority, and until a lasting peace is achieved, the U.S. will continue to arm its friends to the teeth.]

International Legal Issues—Part One

Interview with Francis Boyle

Francis Boyle is Professor of International Law at the University of Illinois. When interviewed, he was serving as advisor to Congressmember Henry Gonzalez on an impeachment resolution against President Bush. Professor Boyle was also an advisor to the Commission of Inquiry for the International War Crimes Tribunal, initiated by former U.S. Attorney General Ramsey Clark. In February 1992, at a final judgment of the Tribunal in New York City, 22 judges from 18 nations found President George Bush and others guilty on 19 charges of crimes against peace, war crimes and crimes against humanity. The evidence used at the judgment is incorporated into Ramsey Clark's book The Fire This Time, *(New York: Thunder Mouth's Press), 1992. Francis Boyle was interviewed in August 1991 by John M. Miller.*

John M. Miller: Have you found any evidence to suggest that the U.S. government knew beforehand how much environmental destruction would be caused by a massive aerial bombardment in the Gulf?

Francis Boyle: Number one: based on what I have seen in the public record, the U.S. government had engaged in computer modeling, using some supercomputers, of what the environmental impact of a massive bombing campaign on Kuwait would be . . . to try to predict what precisely would be the effects in terms of pollution, because of all the soot being put up there. And it also appears that they knew full well that a massive bombing campaign would produce enormous fires and carcinogens that would affect people living downwind.[1] My working hypothesis now (with everything I have been able to see and with confirmed evidence that the computer model was done) was that the Bush people knew full well what they were doing when they launched this bombing campaign, and that they bear substantial responsibility for the environmental catastrophe that has hit the Gulf.

Now, here of course it would be difficult to segregate responsibility between the Iraqis and the U.S. In law, you can have two perpetrators of the same crime.

The key point is this: that President Bush knowingly launched a war with full knowledge and expectation that it would produce an environmental catastrophe and he did it anyway. He completely refused to engage in any negotiations for a peaceful resolution of this dispute as required by the terms of the UN Charter, Article 2, paragraph 3, and Article 33. And indeed he was even proud of it—he bragged of the fact that there would be no negotiations despite the fact that he was required to negotiate.[2] He had a fairly good idea, based on computer models, of precisely what would happen if they went over there and blew up Kuwait, and what the responses of the Iraqis would be when they did.

This is not to justify at all what the Iraqis did. But what started the environmental catastrophe was not the Iraqi invasion of Kuwait, but rather the U.S. bombing campaign of Kuwait. I think we need to keep that clear. It is recognized today by many international law experts that the deliberate infliction of severe environmental harm, to the extent we have seen in the Gulf, is a war crime.

Now if you look at it the way I look at it (of course I know this is not the way the U.S. government has presented it to the American people) it creates in my mind international responsibility on the part of the U.S. government for this environmental catastrophe. This includes the obligation to pay reparations and personal criminal responsibility on the part of high-level government officials for committing these international crimes.

JMM: Under the Geneva Protocols of 1977?[3]

FB: You have Geneva Protocol I of 1977; you have ENMOD. Many people have written that severe destruction of the environment is also a violation of customary international law—environmental consciousness has reached that level in the international community.

It also seems to me that Bush and his people knew full well exactly what they were doing but all they cared about was getting oil out of the ground . . . You'll note that the pollution is contaminating everyone in that entire region. Turkey and Iran, as I understand it, are severely contaminated.

JMM: Actually the [government] computer models run early this year were in response to some things that scientists we have been working with were talking about. The simulations said the war would be "a major pollution event" regionally.

FB: At least regionally and perhaps globally, we don't know. We are going to have to see. We [the Commission of Inquiry for the International War Crimes Tribunal] fully intend to pursue this in terms of developing more facts and then also a formal legal analysis as to both reparations and also war crimes by U.S. government officials. [Crimes were committed] not only against foreign governments, and foreign peoples, but even upon our own troops. Even our own troops are now reporting respiratory illnesses, fear of cancer down the line and things of that nature.[4]

JMM: The two explicit mentions of environmental damage in international law—the main ones being ENMOD and the Geneva Protocols—have been criticized for not being that strong. They are quite wishy-washy.

FB: I think they are strong enough as far as we are concerned. Again I think large numbers of experts on international criminal law who have looked into this matter have concluded that the deliberate infliction of severe damage to the environment, along the lines of what we have seen in the Gulf, is an international crime. I feel very comfortable with that, especially in this situation where it was modeled and they knew exactly what they were doing and they went ahead and did it anyway.

JMM: Have you thought at all about ways to strengthen those prohibitions, make them clearer? I guess one problem is that the U.S. and Iraq had not signed the Protocol.

FB: That is not the issue here. The issue is that the Protocol and the convention are indicators of customary international law. It is what happened at the Nuremberg Tribunal, where the Nazi war criminals argued that they were not bound by the Hague Regulations or 1907 or the Kellogg-Briand Pact of 1928 [because Germany was not a signatory to those accords]. Hague Regulations entered into customary international law and therefore they were convicted of war crimes under the Hague Regulations.

I think we would take the same approach here. United States government officials were on notice going back to the 1970s that severe destruction of the environment was considered by a good deal of world opinion (what we lawyers call *opinio juris*) to be an international crime. So they had notice.

JMM: I guess one of the criticisms of international law, particularly with the laws of war, is that the winner gets to decide who the criminals are.

FB: If you have a look at the *American Bar Association Journal* last month, there was an article on this issue where all sorts of legal experts were saying Saddam Hussein was guilty of various war crimes.[5] My position is, that's fine. Let's try all the war criminals together, both Iraqi and American. The same standards should apply to everyone.

JMM: Who would do that trying?

FB: . . . There is talk of setting up an international criminal court at the United Nations. Everyone is saying let's do this to get Saddam Hussein. Well, that's fine. If they set the court up, we will bring to that court our case against Bush, Baker, Cheney, Quayle, Powell, Schwarzkopf, everyone else. Let them create the court. We will go in there with our evidence, and they will have to hear it.

We need an international criminal court. You'll note the Bush people are talking about setting it up under the jurisdiction of the Security Council, because that way they can control it. I think what we need is for the UN General Assembly members to act and set it up as a subsidiary body of the UN General Assembly, which they can do. They can do that tomorrow if the votes are there, and of course I am sure that if Bush got wind that the General Assembly were trying to set this up, they would move heaven and earth to prevent it from happening.

I think the General Assembly should act preemptively here to set it up and there you would have a fair, balanced, reasonable type of court that would be controlled by the entire international community and not just by the members of the Security Council, who themselves bear responsibility for what happened.

JMM: Another aspect of the bombing campaign was the destruction of Iraqi infrastructure.

FB: That's pretty clear. The wanton devastation of cities or districts of cities is a war crime as defined by the Nuremberg Charter, the Nuremberg Judgment, the Nuremberg Principles. That's "black letter law" and there's no problem with that . . .

JMM: How about the destruction of things like the water pumping stations?

FB: Same thing. These are hitting civilian infrastructure. They are of no military utility at all. And there is more than enough authority in the U.S. Army Field Manual 27-10, in the Nuremberg Principles, in the Hague Regulations of 1907, in the Hague Rules of Aerial Warfare of 1923 to deal with this issue.

JMM: Again, if the whole point of these international laws is to prevent war from happening, why are they so ineffective? Clearly, both sides chose to ignore these rules.

FB: Well, I look at it more in terms of historical sense. There was the Nuremberg Tribunal that did have a significant deterrent effect, but you cannot expect those things to last forever. Then there was also what happened with Vietnam.

The problem with Vietnam is that when the war ended there was no effort made by the American people, Congress or even the world community to hold U.S. government officials accountable for what they did. And that was 30 years after Nuremberg. I would submit that if an attempt had been made by the American people, the Congress, the UN, and the international community to hold U.S. government officials accountable for what they did in Vietnam, we would not have seen what happened here in the Persian Gulf War.

Conversely then, if we want to prevent this from happening again, to prevent our government from going over and literally devastating an entire nation of people by means of conventional munitions alone, we must this time hold our own officials accountable, whether by impeachment or war crimes or preferably by both . . .

JMM: ENMOD and the environmental portions of the Protocols grew out of, at least on the part of some countries, concern about how the U.S. conducted the war in Vietnam, in terms of the massive herbicide use. Do you see a need for clarification of international law on the environment?

FB: We need it, sure. We need more work on fuel air bombs, napalm and many other types of conventional munitions that have a severe impact on the environment. We will ultimately have to sit down and take a good hard look at the laws of war in light of what happened in the Persian

Gulf War and try to strengthen the laws of war and make them crystal clear.

But again, like Nuremberg, the best way to do that is to first hold everyone accountable, and that is exactly what happened at Nuremberg. You establish the process of holding everyone accountable, and the rules of law that should have been upheld. To the extent that there are any gaps or ambiguities, you then proceed to draft whatever conventions need to be drafted. For example, the Nuremberg concept of crime against humanity ultimately led to the Genocide Convention.

JMM: It is fine to try to set these rules of war. But it is not really solving the problem, because so long as there are wars you will always have environmental damage and civilians will always be in the way. The only way to ensure that wars don't affect civilians or the environment is not to have wars in the first place.

FB: That is correct. And here we will also have to get into the reform of the United Nations. The UN was set up for the purpose of preventing war . . . The fact that the U.S. government was able to threaten, intimidate and bribe members of the Security Council indicates the need for major reform of the UN Charter.[6]

NOTES:

1. R.D. Small, *Environmental Impact of Damage to Kuwaiti Oil Facilities,* Report (prepared for the U.S. Nuclear Defense Agency), Pacific-Sierra Research Corporation, Santa Monica, January 1991. See Chapter Two, "A Prewar Environmental Assessment."

2. Ramsey Clark, *The Fire This Time* (New York: Thunder's Mouth Press), 1992, 32–35.

3. Additional Protocol I to the 1949 Geneva Conventions Relating to the Protection of International Armed Conflicts, done at Berne, June 10, 1977 and not yet ratified by the U.S. See Appendix One.

4. Ray Parrish, "Gulf War Vets Suffer Mysterious Ailment," *The Objector,* September/October 1992. See also Chapter Six, "The 'Gulf War Syndrome'."

5. Stephanie Goldberg, "Punishing Aggression," *ABA Journal,* April 1991, p. 24.

6. Ramsey Clark, *The Fire This Time,* 153–156; Phyllis Bennis, "U.S. Bribes, Threats Win UN War Support," *The Guardian,* December 12, 1990; U.S. News, *Triumph Without Victory: The History of the Persian Gulf War* (New York: Random House, Inc.), 1992, 180–181.

International Legal Issues—Part Two

Interview with Karen Parker

Karen Parker is an attorney specializing in international human rights and humanitarian (armed conflict) law. Interviewed by Philippa Winkler, November 1992.

Philippa Winkler: On November 29, 1990, the United Nations Security Council voted 12-2, China abstaining, to approve the use of force against Iraq. That resolution, Security Council 678, was sponsored by the United States.

Karen Parker: Security Council Resolution 678 "authorizes Member States, cooperating with the Government of Kuwait . . . to use all necessary means to uphold and implement Security Council Resolution 660 (1990) and all subsequent relevant resolutions and to restore international peace and security in the area."

Article 42 of the United Nations Charter allows the Security Council to use force if necessary to restore international peace and security. The article specifically approves action taken by military forces of Member States. In my view, Security Council Resolution 678 is in conformity with this article.

However, from my point of view, the United States violated Security Council 678 and other provisions of United Nations law and procedure in the action against Iraq. First of all, the United States went far beyond implementation of Security Council 660. SC 660 called on Iraq to withdraw from Kuwait. For much of the war, the United States military action seemed primarily directed at destroying Iraq's civilian infrastructure and its military defense capability rather than at the Iraqi military presence in Kuwait. Most military commanders would agree that bombing Baghdad and the other numerous cities and towns in Iraq was not necessary to defeat Iraqi forces in Kuwait. Then, when the United States finally directed actions at the Iraqi forces in Kuwait (and it was able to defeat those forces relatively easily, proving my point about "necessity"), the United States continued to attack. In fact, the United States attacked retreating forces—a clear violation of the rules of armed conflict.

Secondly, the United States failed to carry out its military action in conformity with Articles 46 and 47 of the United Nations Charter. These Articles provide that when there is an action taken under authority of the Security Council and its powers under Article 42, the plans for military force *must* be made by the Security Council with the assistance of the Military Staff Committee (Article 46). The mandatory Military Staff Committee *must* be composed of the Chiefs of Staff of the permanent members: the United States, France, the United Kingdom, Russia (at that time the U.S.S.R.) and China (Article 47).

As was clearly stated by the United States commanders a number of times, the United States essentially planned and carried out all significant operations. While voicing support for the

United Nations and continually referring to the situation as a United Nations action, it is patently obvious that the action was nearly unilateral. Certainly, neither the USSR nor China were parties to the plans for military operations in any meaningful way; the appearance of French or British planning was, in my view, merely token. Security Council planning according to Articles 46 and 47 fell far short of what I would consider minimum compliance.

To my knowledge, the fact that the United States went far beyond the authorized scope of military operations and failed to follow mandatory procedures is unique in United Nations history.

PW: If the United States was in violation of Articles 46 and 47 of the United Nations Charter, why did the Security Council fail to act?

KP: The United States has veto power in the Security Council and made it very clear that any attempt by the Security Council to force the United States into conformity with the Charter and procedures would be met with the exercise of the veto. Therefore, attempts (and there were attempts) to implement Articles 46 and 47 could not succeed. There was a great deal of political brokering, not the least with China, which appears to have demanded United States support for its position regarding Tibet.

PW: So a permanent member of the Security Council always has the power to veto, even when it—the member itself or its own actions—is the subject of concern? Isn't this a "who is guarding the guardians" dilemma? Can anything be done about this?

KP: In my view, the problem with the veto is more a political than a legal one. Article 27 of the United Nations Charter requires a party to a dispute to abstain from voting in the Security Council if it is the subject of concern. However, politics has prevented compliance with Article 27. The United States vetoed Security Council action arising from the United States' failure to comply with the International Court of Justice in the Nicaragua case [Military and Paramilitary Activities In and Against Nicaragua, 1986, ICJ 14]. However, no one challenged the U.S. veto. Also, no government or United Nations body has requested an advisory opinion from the International Court of Justice regarding the meaning and implementation of Article 27. As one can imagine, the other permanent members do not want to close off the possibility of the use of the veto in action involving them. Some, including especially the United States, would exercise the veto to prevent the Security Council from asking the ICJ for an advisory opinion. Even this use of the veto appears to violate Article 27, as procedural matters are not subject to veto. Asking the ICJ for a ruling on a procedural matter should be also considered a procedural matter.

If Article 27 were followed according to its clear meaning, the Security Council could have adopted a resolution ordering the United States to limit the scope of the military action to that necessary to force implementation of Resolution 660 and to conform to the plans of the Military Staff Committee and the Council. Of course, the United States would still try to convince another permanent member to veto in its stead.

PW: Can another entity ask the ICJ for an advisory opinion regarding the application of Article 27 in order to bypass a veto?

KP: According to Article 96 of the United Nations Charter, the General Assembly and the Security Council may request advisory opinions on any legal question. Other organs of the UN and specialized agencies may request opinions "arising within the scope of their activities." While theoretically possible for, say, the United Nations Commission on Human Rights to request an opinion on issues related to humanitarian or human rights law, it would be difficult, if not impossible, to frame those issues in a way to reach the Article 27 question.

PW: Is there hope for reform in this area? It sounds like a "Catch 22."

KP: Legally, it's not a "Catch 22"—only politically. Perhaps someday, the permanent members will be willing to drop their own narrow concerns in favor of true international governance. There is some talk of expanding the Permanent Members of the Security Council—Japan and Germany are making bids. Perhaps the result will be an expansion of the Security Council but the elimination of the veto. The Permanent Members would then have to be content with using control of the vote rather than the veto.

The following are excerpts from the UN Charter, with reference to the interview with Karen Parker.

ARTICLE 27

1) Each member of the Security Council shall have one vote.
2) Decisions of the Security Council on procedural matters shall be made by an affirmative vote of nine members.
3) Decisions of the Security Council on all other matters shall be made by an affirmative vote of nine members including the concurring votes of the permanent members; provided that, in decisions under Chapter VI, and under paragraph 3 of Article 52, a party to a dispute shall abstain from voting.

ARTICLE 42

Should the Security Council consider that measures provided for in Article 41 would be inadequate or have proved to be inadequate, it may take such action by air, sea, or land forces as may be necessary to maintain or restore international peace and security. Such action may include demonstrations, blockade, and other operations by air, sea, or land forces of Members of the United Nations.

ARTICLE 46

Plans for the application of armed forces shall be made by the Security Council with the assistance of the Military Staff Committee.

ARTICLE 47

1) There shall be established a Military Staff Committee to advise and assist the Security Council on all questions relating to the Security Council's military requirements for the

maintenance of international peace and security, the employment and command of forces placed at its disposal, the regulation of armaments and possible disarmament.

2) The Military Staff Committee shall consist of the Chiefs of Staff of the permanent members of the Security Council or their representatives. Any Member of the United Nations not permanently represented on the Committee shall be invited by the Committee to be associated with it when the efficient discharge of the Committee's responsibilities requires the participation of that Member in its work.

Laws of War and the Environment: A Debate in the UN

Excerpted from United Nations Press Release, 46th General Assembly, Sixth Committee, GA/L/2707-9, October 22 to 24, 1991. The Sixth Committee (Legal) of the UN met at the request of Jordan, to consider the exploitation of the environment as a weapon in war. In asking for the meeting, Jordan proposed that the General Assembly establish a committee to consider ways to prevent the use of the environment as a weapon, including the possible drafting of a new treaty. Jordan also called for the establishment of a UN environmental database. Below are excerpts from statements by various representatives as summarized in UN press releases:

Abdullah Salah (Jordan)

Introducing the [General] Assembly's item on exploitation of the environment as a weapon, Abdullah Salah said the Assembly's General Committee had unanimously approved the topic's inclusion on the agenda, thus reflecting the international awareness of environmental issues. Once harm to the environment took place, it was nearly impossible to reverse, and environmental damage in one part of the globe had implications far away; no one was immune.

The agenda item focused on the protection of the environment in times of armed conflict; the catalyst for the item had been the tragic events in the Persian Gulf. It was sometimes argued that armed conflict was not amenable to treatment within an environmental context. But armed conflict damaged combatants and noncombatants alike; the righteousness of the cause was immaterial.

Philippe de Korodi (International Committee of the Red Cross)

Increasingly destructive methods of warfare constituted a serious threat to the environment. There was reason to fear that the use of particularly devastating forms of warfare could wreak such large-scale destruction that it would prevent the implementation of provisions protecting the victims of armed conflict.

The Gulf crisis raised many questions about the content, scope and shortcomings of the rules of international humanitarian law. Several meetings in which the ICRC took part were unable to reach any conclusions because of the difficulty in establishing basic data, such as a scientific assessment of the environmental damage caused by modern warfare.

In spite of certain imperfections, existing provisions were a solid basis for the protection of the environment in time of armed conflict. A basic principle set forth in the Declaration of St. Petersburg in 1868 was that methods and means of warfare were "not unlimited." That principle had been reiterated in international humanitarian law, most recently in Protocol I of the 1977 addition to the Geneva Conventions.

The ICRC was of the opinion that certain issues on the protection of the environment deserved detailed study: the question of what constituted "widespread, long-term and severe damage" to the environment in the Protocol should be the object of concerted interpretation, and attention should be paid to the protection of the environment in noninternational conflicts.

Hans Winkler (Austria)

The large-scale damage inflicted on the environment by Iraq showed the need for strengthening existing rules and the elaboration of a new legal framework to prevent such damage in the future. Present international law was not sufficient to deal with the grave consequences of acts such as Iraq had committed in the Gulf; there were no precise legal rules to take judicial steps against those responsible for such damage. The Geneva Convention, other conventions and customary international law were inadequate to deal with acts of such magnitude as setting oil wells afire in Kuwait and deliberately spilling crude oil into the Gulf.

Nazihah Mohammed Rus (Malaysia)

The recent Gulf War had resulted in horrendous devastation. Clearly, the only way to protect the environment globally was through international cooperation. Virtually all military activities during the war had some environmental implications. Advanced technology had, however, contributed to greater systematic destruction of the environment—for example, by chemicals which destroyed forests, devastated crops and caused severe health hazards to the population. Military accidents often resulted in environmental damage.

Questions had been raised about the conduct of war when implementing resolution 678 (1990) [authorizing the use of force to evict Iraq from Kuwait]. The excessive use of force contrary to the principle of proportionality had caused harmful damage to the environment. The situation had been further aggravated by the irresponsible acts of Iraqi forces in the burning of oil fields in Kuwait. There was a need to strengthen the 1977 Geneva Convention to prevent such incidents in the future. Malaysia called upon the international community to ensure that military activities conformed to environmental norms and regulations.

James Crawford (Australia)

Exploitation of the environment as a weapon was not a new subject for international law. There was some disagreement about what the language of the different legal instruments dealing with the subject meant. For example, it was not clear what the time frame for "long-term" damage was.

There was an argument that more effective implementation of existing rules, rather than further laws on the subject, was needed. More work had to be done to clarify the issues. His delegation also welcomed Jordan's suggestion that the title of the item be broadened to "The Protection of the Environment in Armed Conflict" as the whole environmental impact of war was in question, not only its use as a weapon.

Safa S. Ahmed (Iraq)

His delegation wished to clarify its position on the environmental catastrophes which had beset the people of Iraq in the wake of the Gulf War. Adherence and accession to international conventions were very important. A letter of August 13, 1991, from the Permanent Representative of Iraq to the Secretary-General, stated that Iraq affirmed its desire to preserve the environment and national wealth. The letter stated that the environmental damage suffered by Iraq in the Gulf crisis had been ignored. That damage included the destruction of water and sewage systems, oil facilities, and power-generating plants.

The bombers of the Allies dropped thousand of pounds of explosives on bridges, farms and industrial installations. The continuation of the siege of Iraq—in place since August 1990—also threatened the environment and all living things in Iraq.

Hans Correll (Sweden)

The destruction perpetrated by Iraqi forces had revealed certain shortcomings in existing rules in that those rules did not make specific reference to environmental damage. Acts of environmental degradation were not adequately dealt with in current law. Existing laws should be strengthened.

Governments should consider identifying weapons, hostile devices and techniques that could cause particularly serious effects on the environment with a view to strengthening international laws prohibiting their use. Sweden believes the Secretary-General should be requested to solicit the views of member states on the rules and principles of international law relating to the protection of the environment and submit a report on the item.

Update on Sanctions

Background Information

The purpose of sanctions is to isolate a nation economically and culturally as an interim disciplinary measure short of war. In the case of Iraq, sanctions are in force until that country complies with all terms of surrender listed in UN Security Council Resolution 687.

A number of international humanitarian organizations are calling for an end to economic sanctions against Iraq. Denis Doyen, Assistant Director of the Middle East Peace Education Program of the American Friends Service Committee, points out that sanctions do not punish the Iraqi political elite and instead actually increase support for Hussein's government. Poor and middle class Iraqis who bear the brunt of the effects of sanctions blame the UN, not Saddam Hussein.[1]

Sanctions were projected to cripple Iraq's economy, which relies almost completely on the export of oil. But even though the Iraqi government reported a $44 billion loss in oil sales in June 1992,[2] it continues to avoid compliance with UN Resolution 687. Iraq refuses to reveal lists of its weapons suppliers, to allow for long-term monitoring of its activities, to acknowledge the new border between Iraq and Kuwait as surveyed by the UN, to release information about Kuwaiti POWs, or to discontinue its persecution of Kurdish and Shiite minorities.[3]

One of the most intractable disputes between the UN and Iraq centers around possible dual-use equipment and industry, and Iraq's desire to convert military equipment to peacetime use in order to boost its economy.[4] The UN Special Commission's efforts to destroy certain contested facilities have met with little Iraqi cooperation.[5]

Paragraph 20 of UN Resolution 687 which imposes sanctions is subject to review every two months. The UN is not likely to lift sanctions because it fears that if it concedes any disputed issue to Iraq, it will only be a matter of time and capital before that country regains its war-making capabilities. The UN especially wants to continue its monitoring of Iraq and to obtain Iraq's list of weapons suppliers, so that it can monitor the suppliers as well.[6]

Meanwhile, the Iraqi Foreign Minister, Tariq Aziz, insists that Iraq has complied with 95 percent of the requirements for weapons destruction.[7]

Negotiations, Trade, and Humanitarian Aid

So far the only trade suggested by the UN Security Council has been rejected by Iraq as an infringement of its national sovereignty. The Security Council offered, with UN Resolutions 706 and 712, to allow Iraq to sell $1.6 billion worth of oil in exchange for humanitarian aid. As part of the deal, the UN stipulated that one-third of these funds would go toward reparations to

Kuwait and the UN inspection team's costs. Only two-thirds would go toward aid for Iraq, and this money would be managed by the UN in an escrow fund.

Talks on this proposal broke down by July 1992. The Iraqi government objected to the UN's proposed administration of the proceeds on the grounds that they limited its independence. In response, the UN blamed the Iraqi government for refusing to alleviate its people's suffering.[8]

On October 2, 1992, UN Resolution 778 impounded frozen Iraqi assets to pay for aid, war compensation, and the costs of destroying Iraqi weapons. The proceeds were placed in an escrow fund, to be returned if Iraq agreed to sell oil under UN supervision.[9]

On October 22, 1992, Iraq agreed to a $200 million winter aid program serving 750,000 people in northern Iraq and 450,000 in central and southern Iraq.[10] The UN World Food Programme delivered 150,000 tons of food to Iraq in November 1992, mainly to Kurds in northern Iraq. (The Kurds in the safe haven on the Iraq-Turkey border suffer both from the effects of UN sanctions on Iraq, and from the economic embargo imposed against the Kurdish enclave by the Iraqi government.) The winter aid program expired in March 1993.

Iraq has managed to partially rebuild its economy through trade with its neighbors and the sale of gold on the international market in Switzerland. But even Baghdad, the favored city of the Iraqi government, has slipped into an economic depression after a short-lived revival.

Even if sanctions were lifted, and Iraq returned to its prewar GNP of $45 billion, it faces other costs. The war incurred approximately $100 to $200 billion worth of damage. Reparations are approximately $100 billion. Added to this is a $40 billion to $50 billion national debt.[11]

The Iraqi government views sanctions not only as financially punitive but an attempt by the UN to attack its industrial base and undermine its sovereignty. To lift sanctions, one of the requirements is that Iraq recognize the new Iraq/Kuwait border established by the UN in November 1992, replacing a border that had been in existence for 30 years. The new partition gives Kuwait six disputed oil fields, one of Iraq's naval bases, and part of its only port at Um Qasar.[12]

In June 1993, Iraq agreed to hold intensive arms talks with the United Nations. These talks, which are ongoing as we go to press in the fall of 1993, could potentially lead to substantial progress on long-term monitoring of Baghdad's weapons potential and a lifting of the Security Council's embargo on Iraqi oil sales. Security Council Resolution 687 is written in such a way that the ban on exports from Iraq, including oil, can be lifted once Iraq fulfills the UN's weapons requirements, even if Iraq does not fulfill the UN's other requirements. For the UN to lift its ban on imports to Iraq, its other demands would have to be met, including Iraqi recognition of the new border with Kuwait.[13]

—*Saul Tolton*

NOTES:

1. Interview with Denis Doyen, January 27, 1993. Denis Doyen is no longer the Assistant Director, Middle East Peace Education Program, American Friends Service Committee.
2. "Iraq's Huge Losses from Oil Embargo," *San Francisco Chronicle*, January 28, 1993, A8.
3. Interview with Tim Trevan, spokesperson, UN Special Commission to Iraq (UNSCOM), January 27, 1993; interview with U.S. State Department, anon., February 5, 1993; in-

terview with Denis Doyen. A March 1993 report to UNHCR by Max Van der Stoel reports that hundreds of Shiites were killed in death camps set up by the Iraqi government in the first months of 1993. *Keesing's Record of World Events* (Cambridge UK: Longman), vol. 39 (March 1993), 39390-1.

4. For example, the facility at Zaffarina was found by UN inspectors to have been rebuilt so as to hold equipment which could be converted to a nuclear program at short notice. *Keesing's Record of World Events* (Cambridge UK: Longman), vol. 39 (March 1993), 39390-1.

5. Interview with Doyen.

6. Interview with Tim Trevan and anon. State Department official.

7. Iraqi press conference aired on CNN, January 16, 1993.

8. *Keesing's Record of World Events*, vol. 38, no. 6 (June 1992), 38985, and no. 7 (July 1992), 39026.

9. *Keesing's Record of World Events*, vol. 38, no.10 (October 1992), 39163.

10. *Interpress*, November 18, 1992.

11. *Keesing's Record of World Events*, vol. 38, no. 3 (March 1992), 38837- 38838.

12. *Keesing's Record of World Events*, vol. 39, no. 1 (January 1993), 39291.

13. Evelyn Leopold, "Iraq, UN Make Some Progress on Monitoring Arms," *Reuters*, September 8, 1993.

R esisting the War: Conscientious Objectors and the "Stop/Loss" Order

Interview with Sam Diener

Sam Diener is a counselor for CCCO, a nonprofit agency for military and draft counseling which was founded in 1948 as the Central Committee for Conscientious Objectors. Sam Diener edits CCCO's newsletter The Objector. *Interviewed by Philippa Winkler, August 1993.*

"Stop-Loss" Order

Philippa Winkler: At the outset of the Gulf War, President Bush issued the "stop/loss" (stop the loss of personnel) order which required that the submission of all requests for discharge as a conscientious objector wait until the applicant reached the unit to which he or she was being transfered, which was in Saudi Arabia. Was this a precedent and who was most affected by the order?

Sam Diener: In the past, presidents have been reluctant to call up the reservists, but nowadays they are an integral part of the forces.[1] The "stop/loss" order was a disaster, particularly for reservists who didn't have any base to which they could apply, so there was almost nothing they could do until they got to Saudi Arabia. Because it's such a lengthy and complicated procedure, an applicant for conscientious objector status usually requires civilian counsel, a lawyer or non-lawyer advocate who can look over your written application to clarify your beliefs in the proper legal form. If a person is deployed to Saudi Arabia, there is no civilian counsel available. Plus, the closer that person got to the war zone the less likely they were to find a sympathetic commanding officer willing to process the CO application. It was devastating to our ability to help people. The order was promulgated in a way that took military commanders, reservists, and the peace movement by surprise.

Going AWOL

People who realized they didn't want to be sent to the Gulf and couldn't make their case in the U.S. went AWOL, absent without leave, which is how a lot of prosecutions were made. The U.S. refused to prosecute them as COs but as AWOL. We still haven't been able to pry from the Pentagon the number of people who went AWOL, although the General Accounting Office (GAO) is supposed to be doing a study at Congressmember Ron Dellums' request. We estimate there were thousands of AWOLs, in addition to thousands of CO inquiries, based on requests for information to telephone hotlines and military counsel networks. The reality was that if a person went AWOL and didn't say anything about being a CO, their treatment was more lenient, and certainly more lenient if they were CO but did not go public.

PW: What were the sentences for going AWOL in the Gulf War?

SD: Six months to a year, if they said they were CO, if not, 30 days or dishonorable discharges, mostly—a slap on the wrist. The African American resisters who went AWOL were treated with harsher sentences, two or three years. Congressmember Dellums has requested that the GAO look into the racism of the process, and the ethnic makeup of the COs.

PW: How many went AWOL because of being COs, and were adopted by Amnesty International as prisoners of conscience in the Gulf War?

SD: Thirty three people were ultimately adopted as political prisoners by Amnesty, including some of the most famous cases, like Tahan Jones [a Marines reserve corporal], Yolanda Huet-Vaughn [an Army reserve captain and physician] and Erik Larsen [a Marines reserve lance corporal], because the process did not honor human rights.

PW: How many registered COs were there during the Gulf War?

SD: I would say that approximately 120 people came out publicly as COs, that is, they contacted the media. We estimate that 3,000 made a step towards the CO application, but again, we're hoping that those figures will come out in the GAO report.[2] This office had to install additional phone lines because we were receiving hundreds of phone calls per day from panicked soldiers and reservists wanting to find out their rights. We probably talked to 2,000 soldiers. Many of those calls were repeat calls to follow up on their case. We don't have a precise tracking system, in part because there is danger in keeping phone records because they may be subpoenaed. Some people who did win their CO status had been mobilized and some had not been. The approval rate for CO applications went down from about 70 percent before the war to 25 percent.

PW: During the Gulf War, did the Pentagon adhere to the UN's position that the right of conscience is a basic human right?[3]

SD: No. First, the Pentagon's official policy does not adhere to the UN's position, which is that the right of conscience is a basic human right. The right of conscience would apply to selective objection to one war or several wars or total objection to all wars, although the UN has never spelled out the right of conscientious objection in a particular way, because governments around the world haven't wanted the UN to do that. The Pentagon's position is that only those conscientiously objecting to all wars on moral, ethical or religious grounds can apply for conscientious objector status. These are very narrow grounds, and only for people who are total pacifists. On joining the military, people have to sign a statement saying that they are not conscientious objectors, so if they later become conscientious objectors (COs) they have to show their beliefs have developed and changed to the point where their thoughts have "crystallized"—it's called the "crystallization point"—into an objection against all war. The fact that people are able to morally and ethically grow and examine their conscience in light of an actual impending war is something the Pentagon does not understand. So thousands of people are misinformed about their rights. At the outset of the Gulf War many were told they could not apply for CO status because they "volunteered" to enlist, and hundreds that did apply were turned down. The net effect was that thousands who did object to all wars could not achieve CO status.

PW: If a war is illegal under international law, or is not prosecuted in a legal way, does that provide enough grounds for a soldier to choose not to fight that war?

SD: One of the international laws of war (which is supposed to be binding under the Uniform Code of Military Justice in the U.S.), is that if a soldier is issued an order that violates the Geneva conventions, for example, to torture prisoners or kill civilians, they are legally required to disobey that order. If the war is illegal as a whole under international law, the law demands that the soldier must refuse to follow orders. That's theoretical, because if a soldier does refuse to follow orders, he or she is promptly court-martialed.

RACIAL BREAKDOWN OF THE ARMED FORCES

PW: What was the breakdown in ethnic background of the troops in general during the war?

SD: Forty percent of the deployed were African Americans and Latinos, and sixty percent were Caucasian and others, but easily over half of those in the front line troops were African American or Latinos. In the African American, Latino, Asian-American and Native American communities as a whole, the war was much less popular and that was certainly true for soldiers from these communities. There was a very strong awareness that they were being used as cannon fodder, that the war was being fought for oil or oil company profits and people we counseled said it was a rich man's war, or a white rich man's war, and that it was a racist war against Arabs. That made applying and winning CO status difficult because the military could argue that the real opposition was a political one, not a moral, ethical or religious one.

TODAY'S ARMY

PW: Why do people join the Army or the reserves?

SD: The military spends two billion dollars a year to convince young people that the military is exciting, a place where you can grow and be all you can be, and where you can get job training and college financial aid. What is sad about this is that the unemployment rate for veterans is higher than for nonveterans, and veterans are in a worse economic situation than before they joined. The military is designed to fight wars. The grunts are the people in the front lines and are the rifle-carriers, the tank drivers, jobs that don't have civilian applications. According to some studies, 80 percent of military jobs don't have direct civilian applications. One study concluded that only twelve percent of male veterans and six percent of females veterans are using skills they learned in the military. There is a myth, too, about college financial aid. One-quarter of soldiers don't get an honorable discharge, which disqualifies them from receiving the promised financial aid. But a person pays in $1,200 to the college fund in their first year to be eligible for the Montgomery GI bill, and it's nonrefundable. The military spent 1.5 billion dollars but received 1.6 billion dollars since 1986 on this plan. It's a scam, ripping off GIs to the tune of a hundred million dollars!

Also, military recruiters have a quota to make, they have to recruit a certain number of people, so they're motivated to lie and promise jobs, even though the military can't guarantee civilian jobs. Those are the "pull factors" to pull people into the military. The "push factors" are that we live in a racist and classist society in which job training and education are not free, there aren't many jobs for low-income youth, and that creates a "pool of available recruits," to use the Pentagon language. And people don't realize that once you join, you're stuck for eight years. It's involuntary servitude and that's scary and real. The right to resign is one reform I'd like to see. Everyone should have the right to quit their job.

PW: What's the current status of the stop/loss order?

SD: It's hard to respond to the stop/loss order. Since the war, there's been an executive order that modifies the worst of stop/loss but implements part of it. People can file for CO status here in the U.S. but that wouldn't prevent them from being deployed. Whether the stop/loss order was a proper change in regulatory policy is not certain. Different judges have ruled differently. One court has ruled that it did not go through the proper process, in which case, many of the Gulf War convictions could get overturned.

PW: What's the future for CO in this country?

SD: The CO Reform Act of 1992 was introduced by Congressmember Dellums, chair of the Armed Services Committee, and would redefine CO status. First, it would allow for selective objectors to oppose particular wars, which is more in line with the UN position. Second, when a person applies for CO status they would no longer have to prove they were sincere (the burden of proof currently is on the applicant). And third, instead of having military folks determine the outcome of CO applications, there would be a combination of civilian and military folk. Three very significant reforms....The Act would also serve as a check on military adventurism or interventionism on the part of U.S. presidents, because in an unpopular war, many more people would claim CO status.

NOTES:

1. The Department of Veterans Affairs says that approximately 657,000 active duty military service members and activated National Guard and reserve unit members served in the Gulf. Department of Veterans Affairs Fact Sheet, "VA Health Care for Persian Gulf Veterans," May 1993. According to Pentagon spokesman Doug Hart, 228,000 reservists were called back to active duty, and 106,000 served in the Gulf. This number of reservists was exceeded only during the Korean War, when most of the 938,000 reservists called up went to Korea, and during the Berlin Airlift of 1961, in which 295,700 reservists were called up. Interview with Doug Hart, August 17, 1993. Sam Diener points out that, among the reserves, 20,000-30,000 Individual Ready Reserves (IRRs) were called up to serve in the Gulf War. IRRs are those who had completed active duty service but were still liable to be re-activated. Being called up took IRRs by surprise because the IRR had not been used since the Vietnam War, and only then in negligible numbers.

2. We may never know how many resisted the war because many soldiers went AWOL without applying for CO status, according to Gerald R. Giglio, editor with Kevin Carter of *No Blood for Oil: An Oral History of GI Resistance to the Persian Gulf War*, (Trenton, New Jersey: Broken Rifle Press,) forthcoming.

3. Articles 3 and 18 of the Declaration of Human Rights and Article 18 of the Covenant on Civil and Political Rights. The Covenant is a biding human rights treaty now ratified by at least 109 states (including the U.S. as of August, 1992). Article 18 of the Covenant reads in part, "Everyone shall have the right to freedom of thought, conscience and religion. The right shall include...freedom, either individually or in community with others and in public or private, to manifest his religion or belief in worship, observance, practice and teaching." On March 10, 1993, the UN Human Rights Commission adopted a resolution which recognizes conscientious objection to military service as a human right (E/CN.4/Res./1989/59).

In the Brig

Interview with Tahan Jones

Tahan Jones was a Marine reserve corporal at the time of the Gulf War. He currently works for the American Friends Service Committee. Interviewed by James Warner in August 1993.

James Warner: Why did you take the decision to become a conscientious objector?

Tahan Jones: I had done that about three years before, but I had no way of getting out of the military. I'd never heard of CO status at that time.

I understood what my role would be in the military, that I would go out and kill, but I didn't understand the implications behind that, why I was going to kill someone. Once I became more conscious of that, I started having moral or ethical conflict with the military. I was a CO before the Persian Gulf War, but I'd never heard of the term until later, after Jeff Harrison, who was one of the first public resisters, resisting Marine active duty, went missing in Hawaii. That's how I became aware of the term. Erik Larsen [a Marines Reserve lance corporal who became a CO] told me more about it, and that's why I applied for it.

JW: Did you apply for conscientious objector status or did you go absent without leave?

TJ: I applied for CO status, and my application was being processed when I went UA (unauthorized absence). My application was being sent to New Orleans to my division, the Marine Air Wing, for them to make their decision on it. My unit was being activated for a training mission in Arizona.

JW: Why did you go missing at that stage?

TJ: There were a lot of reasons. First I felt that if I actually believed in my position, I had to make certain sacrifices, and one of the sacrifices was to put myself in a situation where either I took part in the military or I didn't. I knew I wasn't going to the Persian Gulf War.

One reason I went UA was my opposition to the war. Also, I had to reconfirm my own beliefs. I put myself in a situation where I either had to stand by my beliefs or compromise them by going to a training mission.

APPLYING FOR CO STATUS

JW: Was your objection specifically to the Gulf War or to all wars?

TJ: My objections were to all wars. When I was in the military reserves, the Panama invasion took place. The thing about being a reservist is that you're not in a military environment 24 hours a day, seven days a week. You're only in that environment two days out of a month. You're exposed to information and ideas no active duty person would be exposed to. I was trying to go back to school at the time, and I was getting hold of information. I discovered how the United States went into Panama and killed two thousand plus people just to get one man. They used Stealth fighters, F117s, on these people just to test these weapons in combat situations.

JW: Would the Army consider your objections to be political rather than ethical, which would be a problem for your CO application?

TJ: They'd say it was political, but how can you separate your political beliefs from your moral or ethical beliefs? Take for example people who support pro-life or pro-choice—these are both moral beliefs, but at the same time they're political, and the two can't be separated. The military's position was to try to separate people's ethical beliefs from their political beliefs, but it can't be done, because your ethical beliefs shape your political beliefs.

JW: When you applied for CO status, did you have a lawyer to help you make your application?

TJ: I had the person I work for now at American Friends Service Committee, Leonard Mac-Neil, he's the one who helped me prepare my statement. My statement reflected a lot of rage and anger that I had toward the military and toward war in general. My statement came out stronger than it would be if I had to do it over again. To them it came out political, but to me it wasn't political, it was more a statement of how I felt, and why I couldn't take part in the military any more.

JW: Some COs had to go to Saudi Arabia before their claims could be processed. Was there any risk of that happening to you?

TJ: No, because my unit was only being sent to Arizona, on a training mission, to train for the next phase of a missile system we'd worked on. We weren't prepared to go to Saudi Arabia. But because I was so public in my opposition toward the war, they had to make an example of me, because of other marines who might feel the way I do.

GOING PUBLIC

JW: How did you get so much publicity?

TJ: Timing and location—I came out early, before the conflict actually broke out, and I was located in the Bay Area. These two things meant I could get more exposure than most people did. Also, I could articulate my ideas, and my ideas were more focused than most people's; I could express myself a lot better. I was very active on the grassroots level, organizing a lot of young people against the war, speaking in high schools and churches. I was doing a lot of rallies around the war. Also, I would always bring in what the war meant abroad and the war at home—police brutality, homelessness, and how the military affects all this. I would always focus in on those two elements: the local war and its effects here, and the war abroad and how that impacted people.

JW: What do you mean by the local war?

TJ: For example, currently I'm doing some work around police brutality. People usually see police brutality as a civil rights violation, but it's also a human rights violation, caused by the militarization of society. The military goes abroad and commits human rights violations, like in Iraq where they attacked retreating troops, while at home a man is gunned down who's running away from the police. I talk about how the two are related to one another, and then people can start to relate more to what was happening in Iraq, because they could understand it more in terms of their experience here in their own community.

JW: How did you come to be court-martialed?

TJ: When I went UA, the military and the FBI were actively looking for me. They came to my house with an arrest warrant, and they also staked out my sister's house, because I was staying there. Also I was very public during the time that I was UA, and this probably agitated the military.

CHARGED WITH DESERTION

What happened was that I turned myself in to Treasure Island Naval Base in San Francisco. I was shipped to North Carolina. At the same time my lawyer, John Murko, submitted an injunction, a habeas corpus, to keep me here in the Bay Area to be court-martialed. Then the United States Supreme Court put the death penalty charge against me, to create the illusion that the crime I'd committed was serious—desertion in time of war, maximum penalty death or life imprisonment. They put these charges against myself, Erik Larsen and Kevin Sperik from New York City. Kevin Sperik [a Marine Reserve corporal] was only a couple of hours late for deployment. He applied for CO status but he intended to go to Saudi Arabia while his application was processed. He wasn't seeking publicity, but he told CNN he was getting married in case he didn't come back from the war. Because he was a couple of hours late for deployment, because he got married, the military decided to place these serious charges against him.

In May 1991 I was charged with desertion in time of war, and this charge was never officially dropped, but in July 1991 they brought a second set of charges against me—desertion to avoid hazardous duty in important service, for which the maximum penalty was five years.

THE COURT-MARTIAL

In January 1992, during my first court-martial, the military said they had forgotten that the first set of charges were still against me. At my first court-martial my lawyer brought a speedy trial motion against the military. Under the Fifth Amendment I had a right to be tried within 180 days. That should have had the whole case thrown out. The military claimed they had forgotten about the first set of charges against me, which isn't true, because of the fact that they were sending letters. People were writing to them about the death penalty charges, and they responded to these people.

When it was brought to the military's attention that they would lose the case, they dropped the first set of charges and initiated a second court-martial, on June 16, 1992. My lawyer brought another motion against the military, basically a speedy trial motion, but it was thrown out. I pleaded guilty to unauthorized absence and missing troop movements by design, and I was sentenced to eight months in the brig, reduction from corporal to private, forfeit of all pay and dishonorable discharge from the military. That was after thirteen months of legal battles with the military.

The right to conscientious objector status is considered a human right by the United Nations, and the U.S. was one of the signers of that treaty, the Universal Human Rights Declaration.

JW: You were also recognized as a political prisoner by Amnesty International?

TJ: Yes. A lot of the COs on the East Coast were also sponsored by Amnesty, including Erik Larsen. Amnesty did a campaign to internationalize our struggle, in Germany and England and other European countries.

JW: Who defended you at your second court-martial?

TJ: I had two lawyers, my assigned military lawyer, Captain Snyder, and my civilian lawyer, John Murko, who put up a good fight. We were able to show in the proceedings that the military was violating my fundamental rights and not abiding by the law.

But I had two prosecutors, the prosecutor and the judge, working hand in hand. My civilian lawyer was trying to show that there had been command influence, which is when commanding officers influence the outcome of a trial—for example, they tried me on the East Coast, far from where I live, so that they would have more control over the process—and that there had been selective prosecution, with COs who went public getting harsher sentences than people who went UA without going public.

My civilian defense lawyer got one of the government witnesses, a Marine officer, to get up on the stand and got him to read off a list of COs who were prosecuted. The prosecutor wasn't hip to the fact that my lawyer was doing this so that the court record would contain evidence of selective prosecution of COs. It was the judge who told the prosecutor that that was what my lawyer was doing. Then the prosecutor made an objection and the judge upheld the objection. That's just an example of how the process works.

As an African American I faced a harsher sentence than a white person for the same crime. African Americans were consistently punished more harshly for the same crime. When I was in the brig, there were mostly Latinos and African Americans there.

JW: Are you still involved in any proceedings against the military?

TW: My case is now up in military appeals court, so I can try to get my discharge changed to a general discharge.

Time in Prison

JW: How long did you actually spend in prison?
TJ: Six-and-a-half months.

JW: How were you treated in prison as a CO?
TJ: I didn't get too much harassment, partly because my case was under a lot of public scrutiny. The war had been over for a long time when I was in prison, so I was less harassed than COs who were in the brig soon after the war.

Military Resisters

JW: How many other people did you know who were in your situation?
TJ: There were probably 30 to 40 public COs, but a lot more people went UA to avoid going to Saudi Arabia. People injured themselves. Women Marines got pregnant. People shoplifted in military stores, so as to be put on legal hold at their Army bases until after the war—these cases took several months to resolve because of the backlog, because so many people were doing it. COs were only the tip of the iceberg, the most public aspect of the opposition toward the war.

When I turned myself in, there were 2,500 people still UA. Mainly they got paper discharges or were reduced in rank, and never spent time in prison.

JW: What advice would you give to other people in your situation in future?
TJ: I would tell them to think about their role in the military. When they decide to join, they should understand exactly what the military is, and the military is nothing more than an insti-

tution designed to kill people, and not just to kill people but to kill people for profit. That's the first thing I would tell them before they even decided to sign the paper.

Those already inside the military, I would tell them that they need to explore their options for trying to get out of it. They need to get legal help or military counseling to assist them, and not try to take on the military on their own, or the military will try to get them bad paper discharges (any discharge that is not an honorable discharge or a general discharge) if they can.

Chapter 9

Iraqgate Chronicles

Introduction

Since the Gulf War, the links between banking institutions and global arms trade networks have come under scrutiny in both the U.S. and Britain. Information now coming to light indicates that both U.S. and British taxpayers unknowingly helped provide Iraq with weapons which were subsequently used against their own fellow citizens. In fact, U.S. and British taxpayers may be liable for government-insured loans which Iraq defaulted on.

In the U.S., Congressmember Henry Gonzalez's Congressional Banking Committee is investigating the way banks diverted government-insured funds to finance arms transfers in Iraq. As a by-product of this inquiry, it was found that former public officials had profited from business arrangements with Iraq. For example, Kissinger Associates, headed by former U.S. Secretary of State Henry Kissinger, represented various U.S. companies that did business with Iraq. These companies also had ties with the scandal-ridden Banca Nazionale del Lavoro in Italy. On the payroll of Kissinger Associates were two officials in the Bush Administration, former National Security Advisor Brent Scowcroft and former Deputy Secretary of State Lawrence Eagleburger.

The story that unfolds is of a complex web, in which the arms business of nations leads to the preparation for war and to war itself. From 1975 to the eve of the Gulf War, governments worldwide sanctioned policies to provide Saddam Hussein with armaments, military-related materials and technology. Although Iraq had little or no domestic defense industry, these policies enabled Iraq to build up a vast arsenal of modern weapons prior to the invasion of Kuwait and the Gulf War. Many of the countries that had contributed to the Iraqi stockpile later joined the Coalition in the U.S.-led war against Iraq.

Lora Lumpe described in Chapter Eight the reasons why governments helped Iraq to gather its lethal stockpile of conventional and unconventional weapons. One reason is that the business of selling arms was and is a lucrative one. For the U.S., a second and perhaps most important reason was the Reagan Administration's "tilt" toward Iraq in its war with Iran. Iran under the Ayatollahs was regarded as hostile to U.S. interests in the region. In 1979, the Carter Administration had placed Iraq on its list of nations thought to be exporting terrorism; this resulted in a virtual embargo on all U.S. trade with Iraq. In a complete turnabout, the Reagan Administration took Iraq off the list in 1982, effectively giving the green light to the arms traders.

France sold fighter aircraft, missiles, and nuclear technology and expertise to Iraq; Great Britain sold arms-making machinery; and the U.S. offered billions of dollars in loan credits to make the arms purchases, as well as providing U.S. technology with military and nuclear applications for Iraq, helicopters, fuses for cluster bombs, and the use of a U.S. Air Force base in Spain as a transfer point for shipping bomb casings which Iraq would later fill with chemical munitions. West Germany took the lead in providing Iraq with precursor chemicals needed to produce lethal chemical weapons that released nerve gas and mustard gas. Iraq, in turn, showed its gratitude by increasing the flow of oil to these countries at bargain prices.

This chapter describes how government officials, while promising to end the proliferation of dangerous conventional weapons and weapons of mass destruction, were at the same time approving business contracts which insured that those very weapons and related technologies ended up in Iraq. Intelligence agencies regularly shared information and kept their governments informed about international sales and technology transfers.

Today, in the post-Cold War era, the arms trade flourishes. Despite the demise of the Soviet Union and the lessening of Cold War tensions, the U.S was the number one supplier of weapons to the Third World in 1990, according to the *New York Times*.[1] The *Arms Sales Monitor*, a newsletter published by the Federation of American Scientists, has listed the dollar amounts in arms sales transfers to Third World countries which have been approved by the U.S. Congress since the end of Operation Desert Storm. From late February to December 1991, there were $18.43 billion in weapons sales to the Third World, with 64 percent of these sales going to the Middle East. In 1992, the sales figure rose to $28.135 billion, or an approximate 150 percent increase in total arms sales over the previous year.[2]

In 1991, the U.S. Office of Technology Assessment stated in its annual report that:

> With decreasing East-West tensions, the focus of questions facing defense policymakers in Europe and the United States will increasingly shift from a predominantly military sphere—how to protect the Alliance from a direct military threat—to issues in which economic and commercial considerations will play a more prominent role. In particular, arms exports and their relationship to domestic high technology employment and the international balance of payments will loom larger in transatlantic armaments relations.[3]

—Daniel Robicheau

NOTES:
1. Robert Pear, "U.S. Ranked No. 1 in Weapons Sales," *New York Times*, August 11, 1991.
2. *Arms Sales Monitor*, Federation of American Scientists, November/December 1992.
3. *Global Arms Trade*, Report, U.S. Congress, Office of Technology Assessment, OTA-ISC-460, Washington DC: US Government Printing Office, June 1991.

Doing Business: The Arming of Iraq, 1974–1993

Compiled by Daniel Robicheau and Saul Bloom

This chronology is compiled from research by Daniel Robicheau and Saul Bloom and contains extracts from "Anatomy of a Scandal" by Robert Hennelly, published in the Village Voice, *August 11, 1992 (reprinted with permission) and "Forum: What the Democrats Should Do About Iraq-gate," a discussion moderated by Robert S. Boynton and Paul Tough in* Harpers Magazine, *accompanied by a chronology that excerpted from official memos and notes taken on conversations between government officials, January 1993 (all extracts reprinted with permission). Other parts of the chronology came from Kenneth R. Timmerman's* The Death Lobby: How the West Armed Iraq, *(Boston: Houghton Mifflin Company), 1991;* The London Sunday Times, The Independent, The Financial Times, The New York Times, The Los Angeles Times, The Washington Post, The Guardian *and other internationally respected newspapers. We add an important caveat: "Doing Business" is based on published reports not independently confirmed by ARC and therefore we cannot warrant the accuracy of each individual fact presented herein.*

1974

Saddam Hussein, then Deputy Chairman of Iraq's Revolutionary Command Council (RCC), outlines his view of Iraq's trade agreements with the U.S.: "There is no contradiction between our decision to sever diplomatic relations with America and to deal commercially with some American companies . . . The presence of these American companies will never open the door to a change in our political program . . . " (Hennelly, 23.)

1975

NOVEMBER 18

The Franco-Iraqi Nuclear Cooperation Treaty is signed. France begins construction of the Tammuz I breeder reactor plant at Tuwaitha and the Tammuz II experimental scale model. France agrees to train 600 Iraqi nuclear technicians. (Timmerman, 32, 33.)

1976

A Belgian engineering firm, Sybetra, based in Brussels, begins work on a phosphate mine in the western Iraqi desert region near the village of Shab Al Hiri, which is later known as Akashat. Phosphate deposits are essential to the production of chemical agents tabun and sarin, the precursors of nerve gas. Sybetra also signs a contract to build a fertilizer complex along the Euphrates at Al Qaim, which is 150 kilometers from the phosphate mine, and which later is linked by a railroad line. The one billion dollar Akashat/Al Qaim project calls for concrete fortifications around certain plant buildings. (Timmerman, 51–52.)

1977

France sells 36 Mirage F-1 advanced fighter aircraft to Iraq for $1.8 billion. The first Mirage fighters will actually be delivered to Iraq from 1980 to 1983. (Timmerman, 45.)

1978

Iraq purchases arms from the U.S.S.R. for three billion dollars, which include 138 MIG 23/27 fighter bombers, Scud-B missile launchers, troop and equipment transports, and MI8 troop transport helicopters. (Timmerman, 53.)

Iraq signs a secret 10-year nuclear cooperation treaty with Brazil. (Timmerman, 59.)

1979

FEBRUARY 11–12

The Ayatollah Khomeini rises to power in Iran, overthrowing Shah Mohammad Reza Pahlavi.

APRIL 7

At approximately 3:15 A.M., an explosion rocks a warehouse of the Compagnie des Constructions Navales et Industrielles de la Mediterranée at a seaport near Toulon, France. Inside are the completed twin Osiraq nuclear reactor cores that had been arranged to be sent to Iraq's Tuwaitha complex by the French Atomic Energy Commission, or CEA. The reactor cores are totally destroyed. A year later, Israel's intelligence network, Mossad, is implicated in the bombing. Shipment of the reactor cores from France to Iraq was to have taken place two days later, on April 9. (Timmerman, 60–61.)

DECEMBER 25

The Soviet Union invades Afghanistan.

DECEMBER 29

At Congress' insistence, President Carter places Iraq on the list of terrorist nations with whom the U.S. will not trade military hardware or aircraft without congressional approval. (Hennelly, 23.)

1980

FEBRUARY 7

The U.S. Department of Commerce approves General Electric's sale of eight gas turbine engines for use in Iraqi frigates being built in Italy as part of a huge $2 billion arms deal between the Italians and the Iraqis. (Hennelly, 23.)

MARCH

The Carter Administration charges that Italy provided Iraq with sensitive equipment for nuclear technology. Italy counters that it had done this two years earlier, after consultation with the U.S. (Hennelly, 23.)

SEPTEMBER 4

Artillery fire is exchanged between Iran and Iraq, marking the beginning of the eight-year Iran-Iraq War. Troop concentrations are deployed on both sides of the 1,200-kilometer border. (Timmerman, 82.)

SEPTEMBER 22

Hussein attacks Iran to gain control of the Shatt Al Arab waterway. The Iran-Iraq War will wear on for eight bloody years, claiming over 750,000 lives and spilling millions of gallons of oil. (Hennelly, 23.)

DECEMBER 25

The U.S. General Accounting Office reports that the proposed shipment of the General Electric-manufactured frigate engines to Iraq was approved due to bureaucratic bungling. (Hennelly, 23.)

1981

The West German company, Thyssen Rheinstahl Technology, stocks Iraq's Diyala Chemical Laboratory at Salmanpak with manufacturing equipment capable of handling extremely toxic substances. One of the chemicals produced with the German company's help is phosphorus penta-chloride, a starting chemical agent necessary for the production of nerve gas. (Timmerman, 106.)

JUNE

Months after Senator Alan Cranston (D-CA) warns of Iraq's potential nuclear capability, Israel executes a daring raid on an Iraqi nuclear power plant built by the French outside Baghdad (Hennelly, 23.) The French-built nuclear reactor, Tammuz I, at Tuwaitha, is destroyed by Israeli F-16s carrying 2000-pound "dumb" bombs, which destroy the reactor core and its containing walls. (Timmerman, 101.)

OCTOBER 28

Israeli defense minister Ariel Sharon charges that the U.S. is covertly supplying Iraq with heavy military equipment. (Hennelly, 24.)

1982

MARCH

The U.S. removes Iraq from its list of terrorist nations. (Hennelly, 24.)

APRIL

Reagan announces plans to sell Iraq up to a dozen Lockheed LL-100 transports and five Boeing jets. (Hennelly, 24.)

JUNE 19

Henry Kissinger and Brent Scowcroft start up Kissinger Associates. To avoid conflicts of interest, Kissinger promises not to lobby Washington and not to represent foreign governments. (Hennelly, 24.)

OCTOBER

A Belgian company, Six Construct International (Sixco), which had already built most of the Al Qaim chemical complex in Iraq, begins work on Project 505. With the help of a French construction company, Nord France, Sixco builds eight underground bases, which will house and protect Iraq's advanced fighter aircraft and pilots in case of a nuclear attack. (Timmerman, 118.)

Iraq announces that it has a new chemical weapon capable of killing 100,000 people at one time. (Hennelly, 24.)

NOVEMBER 21

Iraqi foreign minister Tariq Aziz accuses the U.S. of allowing American overseas companies to sell weapons to Iran. (Hennelly, 24.)

DECEMBER 15

The U.S. agrees to provide $210 million in Commodity Credit Corporation (CCC, a branch of the U.S. Department of Agriculture) loan guarantees to finance food sales to Iraq. By 1983 that figure jumps to $364.5 million. (Hennelly, 24.)

1983

JULY

The Dutch trading company, KBS, arranges purchase of 500 tons of thiodiglycol (which, when mixed with hydrochloric acid, produces mustard gas), from a Belgian subsidiary of Phillips Petroleum. The thiodiglycol is shipped from Belgium to Baghdad. (Timmerman, 134.)

DECEMBER

Yperite, or mustard gas, is used against Iranian "human wave" troops. (Timmerman, 135.) (On properties of mustard gas, see Chapter Seven, "Chemical and Biological Weapons.")

At the end of the month, sixty 500-MD Defender helicopters are sent to Iraq from Hughes Aircraft in the U.S. (Timmerman, 123.)

1984

FEBRUARY

Richard Murphy, assistant secretary of state to the Reagan Administration, makes an official trip to Baghdad to patch up U.S.-Iraqi relations, which had been severed for the past 17 years. In the same month, Iraqi forces flying Soviet, French, and German-made helicopters, dump canisters of poison gas on Iranian troops in the Howeiza marshes surrounding the strategic Majnoon

Islands. Many soldiers vomit a yellowish liquid, their skin turns red, and many are dead by the time medics arrive on the scene. (Timmerman, 143.)

MARCH

The press reports on Iraq's use of chemical weapons against Iranian troops, citing the death of 5,000 soldiers who were contaminated by nerve gas. A UN investigative team confirms Iraq's use of mustard-gas bombs and expresses concern that the nerve agent tabun was also used. German companies had led the way in providing Iraq with the chemicals necessary to produce unconventional chemical weapons. (Hennelly, 24.)

UN Secretary-General Javier Perez de Cuellar dispatches observers to Iraq in response to Iranian charges that Iraq is using chemical warfare. Observers verify Iranian troops' exposure to chemical agents. They also discover an unexploded chemical bomb, with markings indicating that it had been produced in Spain. (Timmerman, 145.)

Bomb casings had been shipped from Spain to Iraq where they had been filled with chemical agents. The point of departure in Spain for the bomb casings was the Torrejon Air Base, home of the 401st Tactical Fighter Wing of the U.S. Air Force. The casings had been manufactured by the Spanish company, Explosivos Alevesas. (Timmerman, 145.)

APRIL

Iraq's State Enterprise for Pesticide Production (SEPP) places an order with the Dutch trading company, Melchemie, for phosphorus oxychloride. The chemical had been banned by the Dutch government because of its use in producing the lethal chemical agent tabun. Melchemie attempts to purchase the chemical for Iraq from companies all over Europe, but is unsuccessful. (Timmerman, 148.)

JUNE 19

The U.S. Export-Import Bank agrees to a $484 million loan guarantee for a pipeline in Iraq to be constructed by the U.S.-based multinational Bechtel. (The U.S. Export-Import Bank is an independent agency of the U.S. government. Loans made by the bank are federally insured, hence backed by the U.S. taxpayer.) Initially, the request was refused because of concerns about Iraq's credit-worthiness. But after Vice President George Bush makes a phone call to bank chair William Draper, financing goes through. According to Congressmember Henry Gonzales (D-TX), the following high-ranking Reagan Administration officials also call the bank on behalf of Bechtel: Lawrence Eagleburger, Ed Meese, Robert McFarland, and Bill Casey. (Prior to becoming Reagan's secretary of state, George Shultz had served as Bechtel's president.) (Hennelly, 24.)

JUNE 20

Secretary of State Shultz writes Congressmember Howard Berman (D-CA) to dissuade him from his efforts to recategorize Iraq as a terrorist state: "The legislation you proposed would be seen and resented in Baghdad as a foreign attempt to dictate Iraqi policy, severely disrupting our diplomatic dialogue." (Hennelly, 24.)

OCTOBER

Bell Helicopter Textron, an American company, negotiates to sell up to 45 commercial helicopters to Iraq. (Hennelly, 24.)

NOVEMBER 13

For the first time since the 1967 Arab-Israeli War, Reagan re-establishes full diplomatic ties with Iraq. (Hennelly, 24.)

LATE NOVEMBER

Putting up a good antiterrorist front, Hussein deports several members of Abu Nidal's group. Although Secretary of State Shultz guarantees a nervous Congress that export controls will keep the volatile Hussein in check, Hussein will invite terrorist Abdul Abbas, of *Achille Lauro* fame, into Iraq. (Hennelly, 24.)

DECEMBER

Christopher Drogoul, a New Jersey native who heads the Atlanta branch of Banca Nazionale del Lavoro (BNL), meets Iraqi representatives to discuss a loan agreement. BNL is Italy's second-largest bank and a majority of the stock is held directly by the Italian government. According to Kenneth Timmerman's *The BNL Blunder* (a special report commissioned by the Simon Wiesenthal Center) the initial package offered by Drogoul was a $100 million credit line for the Iraqis to buy U.S. grain. (Hennelly, 24.)

Also in 1984, Iraq pushes to develop a ballistic missile program. A West German missile and weapons manufacturer, MBB, works with the Swiss-based Consen Group to build a missile program called the Condor Project in Argentina, with the cooperation of the Argentine military. (Timmerman, 150—7.)

MBB transfers advanced ballistic missile technology, design, manufacturing and test equipment to Argentina, and then later to Egypt and Iraq. (Timmerman, 150–7.)

Italy's largest defense contractor, SNIA Bpd, developed a solid-fuel propellant for the first product of the program, the Condor I ballistic missile. The Italian company claims the rocket fuel itself was purchased from the Baker-Perkins Company in Saginaw, Michigan. (Timmerman, 150–7.)

The French company Sagem provides the inertial guidance system for the Condor I missile. (Timmerman, 154.)

Iraq joins the Condor Project, but focuses the bulk of its funding on a longer-range missile, the Condor II, with a 1,000-kilometer range. (Timmerman, 156–7.)

In Iraq, Project SAAD 16, a missile research, development, and testing center outside the northern Iraqi city of Mosul, is built in conjunction with Gildemeister Projecta of Bielefeld, West Germany, a subsidiary of the German machine-tool company, Gildemeister AG. Thirty-eight West German companies become involved in the SAAD 16 project, providing equipment and technical assistance. A Vienna, Austria company, Consultco, provides blueprints for the SAAD 16 complex, with construction work begun by Austrian firms. (Timmerman, 158.)

According to a report published in the *Minneapolis Star-Tribune*, Ward Wheaton, the head of the Aerospace and Defense Group of the Honeywell Corporation branch in Britain, approves a 300-page study on design choices for a fuel-air explosives (FAE) system for Iraq. The FAE ignites an aerosol cloud of a liquid fuel mixture in midair, obtaining oxygen by sucking in air. The subsequent explosion is compared to that of a small nuclear explosion. FAEs had been used previously by the U.S. Air Force in Vietnam to clear jungle terrain for the construction of landing sites. Few countries possess this technology. The Honeywell U.K. study for Iraq nets the corporation $100,000. (Timmerman, 161–6.)

Carlos Cardoen of Chile organizes the transfer of cluster bomb technology to Iraq. Eighteen trips occur between Iraq and Chile in 1984. Cluster bomb fuses are purchased by the Cardoen network from a Pentagon contractor, the International Signals Corporation, and shipped from the U.S. to Iraq. A cluster bomb factory, SAAD 38, is later assembled inside Iraq. (Timmerman 167–8.)

1985

MARCH 13

Iraq initiates one of the most brutal gas attacks of the Iran-Iraq War. Thirty-two chemical attacks are launched and close to 5,000 Iranians are killed. Iran sends 70 survivors to European hospitals in order to convince the world of the ruthlessness of the attacks. (Hennelly, 24.)

MARCH 26

U.S. Secretary of State Shultz discusses the chemical attacks with the Iraqi foreign minister. The U.S. government continues to publicly denounce Hussein's chemical warfare. At the same time, trade between the U.S. and Iraq grows exponentially, from the Export-Import Bank's $35 million worth of loan guarantees in 1985 to $267 million by 1990. (Hennelly, 24.)

Beginning in March, a series of export licenses are approved by the U.S. Commerce Department authorizing sale of high-tech computers and other technical equipment which allows Iraqi engineers of the SAAD 16 complex to plot ballistic missile trajectories. (Timmerman, 202–5.)

The Commerce Department ignores Missile Technology Control Regime (MTCR) restrictions on the exporting of advanced missile technologies. The G-7 countries (U.S., Canada, France, Great Britain, Italy, Japan, and Germany) had approved the MTCR ban, but since it proved too difficult to enforce, it was not formally adopted until two years later, on April 16, 1987 in Rome. (Timmerman, 207–8, 265.)

JULY

Assistant Secretary of Defense Richard Perle pens a memo to Defense Secretary Caspar Weinberger raising the first known red flag by a U.S. official about Hussein's underhanded weapons-procurement drive. "There is a body of evidence indicating that Iraq continues to actively pursue an interest in nuclear weapons . . . In the past Iraq has been somewhat less than honest in regard to the intended end-use of high technology equipment." (Hennelly, 24.)

AUGUST 15

Iraq becomes the first nation to use laser-guided "smart" weapons in warfare as it attacks the Iranian Kharg Island oil terminal. The French-made weapon (AS-30L) also includes laser technology supplied by the U.S. company Martin Marietta. (Timmerman, 212.)

1986

MARCH

Drogoul has built the BNL's Iraqi business up to $600 million in federal CCC credits annually. (The credits are supposed to be used toward the purchase of U.S. farm surplus.) But Drogoul has a problem: a ceiling of $100 million for Iraq, imposed by his superiors in Rome. He asks to up the ante but the Italians, still fuming over warships Hussein never paid them for, refuse. Drogoul disregards the imposed ceiling and makes $5.5 billion in CCC credits and other loans available to the Iraqi government over the next five years. (Hennelly, 24.)

JUNE 11

Congressmember Charlie Rose (D-NC) writes the United States Department of Agriculture about possible improprieties regarding foreign commodities in the Export Credit program. Over at the BNL bank, Drogoul keeps a separate ledger for all Iraq transactions and pays off a handful of employees at the branch to keep quiet. According to Timmerman, author of *The BNL Blunder*, the extra $5.5 billion in loans granted by Drogoul allow him to attract numerous new companies to the bank, among them Mobil Oil, Dunavant, Universal Leaf Tobacco, J.I. Miller, W.A. Adams & Co., Dibrill Bros., Entrade, Nestle SA, Dow Chemical, Upjohn, Pacific Exports & Foodline, RJR Nabisco, and Georgia Pacific. (Hennelly, 24.)

OCTOBER 27

BBC's television program *Panorama* airs "The Secrets of Samarra," detailing Iraq's burgeoning chemical weapons capability. English audiences get a taste of what Hussein is really up to. (Hennelly, 24.)

NOVEMBER

Alan Clark, Britain's then-Minister of the Department of Trade and Industry (DTI), meets with Hassan Ali, Iraq's trade minister, in Iraq. The meeting paves the way for a new credit agreement to be financed for Iraq by DTI's Export Credit Guarantee Department. The credits give the go-ahead to British machine-tool companies to ship munitions-producing machines to Iraq.[1]

NOVEMBER 3

A Lebanese magazine, *Al Shiraa*, discloses that the U.S. sent arms to Iran. In the coming weeks it is disclosed that funds from the arms sales were sent to the Nicaraguan Contras, and the Iran-Contra scandal is born. (Boynton and Tough, 63.)

This act by the Reagan Administration—in direct opposition to U.S. stated policy—seriously compromises the U.S.' relationship with Iraq. (Hennelly, 24.)

NOVEMBER 18

Hussein sends a letter to Reagan protesting the Administration's sale of arms to Iran. The State Department's Richard W. Murphy describes the post-Iran-Contra mess in a memo to Secretary of State Shultz: "Saddam Hussein's letter . . . is a measure of the intense anger and sense of betrayal felt by the Iraqis . . . Though the equipment transferred to Iran from U.S. stock was apparently limited in type and amount, it is difficult to refute the Iraqis' underlying accusation—that the U.S. has armed Iran to kill Iraqis." Murphy discusses options to turn the situation around, including easier approval of Export-Import Bank short-term credit applications for U.S. firms doing business in Iraq. Murphy also suggests that the U.S. facilitate high-tech exports to Iraq. He bemoans the fact that Commerce has been slow to approve some export licenses and has blocked others because of Pentagon concerns that the products being offered had lethal dual uses. "In the judgment of the intelligence community as a whole, Department of Defense (DOD) concerns are exaggerated. In practice, they have meant lost sales for U.S. companies and a constant irritant in U.S.-Iraqi relations." Murphy cheerfully notes that per "our urging" Iraq paid off its American Express bill. (Hennelly, 25.)

1987

EARLY 1987

Meanwhile, as the Iran-Iraq War continues, Iraq sends Soviet-made Scud-B missiles to the Centro Technico Aeronautico (CTA) complex in Sao Jose dos Campos, Brazil, where Iraqi and Brazilian engineers, with French missile experts, upgrade the missiles according to Iraqi specifications, extending their range to hit Tehran. The French company Interspace, owned by the French National Space Agency, had trained Brazilian missile engineers and had built the CTA complex in Brazil. The actual production work of the new Scud-Bs begins at the Al Fallujah, Taji, and SAAD 16 weapons complexes in Iraq. The operation is named Project 1728. (Timmerman, 254.)

Companies that contribute to Project 1728 include Mercedes Benz, which builds 28 tractor-trailer trucks to transport the missiles. Saab-Scandia, through Saab-Brazil, provides the cabs for the tractor-trailer trucks.

In addition, a related missile-building program, Project 395, is given the go-ahead in Iraq. Leading the project is Dr. Amer Al Saadi, a chemical engineer by training, who later becomes deputy to Colonel Hussein Kamil Hassan Al Majid, head of Iraq's State Organization for Technical Industries (SOTI). He is supplied with $400 million to fund the industrial program which will build Iraqi missiles within Iraq itself. The research on missile guidance, trajectory plotting, and warhead design and manufacturing is conducted at the SAAD 16 complex. A sophisticated wind tunnel is supplied by the West German firm Aviatest, a subsidiary of Rheinmetall. Iraqi and West German ballistic missile engineers collaborate on testing missile designs. Computers are supplied by American companies, including Electronic Associates Inc., Gould, Tektronics, Hewlett Packard, Digital Equipment Corp., and the Silicon Valley-based company International Imaging which provides technology for U.S. military satellite surveillance systems. (Timmerman, 255–6.)

MARCH 3

Western banks allow Iraq, which hopes to hold onto dwindling currency reserves, to renegotiate terms for its $500 million loan repayment. (Hennelly, 25.)

APRIL 2

Reagan rejects Iraqi requests for C-130 air transports and artillery radar but agrees to share satellite intelligence on Iranian troop positions. (Hennelly, 25.)

MAY 17

An Iraqi fighter fires French-made missiles at the *USS Stark*, killing 37 Americans. There is silence from the White House. The U.S. media later report that the U.S. was gathering intelligence on Iran to share with Iraq, in which case, the *Stark* tragedy would have been viewed by the White House as a friendly-fire mishap. (Hennelly, 25.)

AUGUST 15

Saddam Hussein announces the successful firing of Iraq's new ballistic weapon named Al Hussein, which is capable of a 650-kilometer range, or over two times the range of the original Scud-B missile. (Timmerman, 267–8.)

SEPTEMBER 7

A company called Technology and Development Group (TDG) is registered in London. Previously known as Echosave, TDG is acquired by an Iraqi front company called Al Araby Trading. As an Al Araby-controlled company, TDG will set up a new front company, TMG Engineering, which will later be renamed Matrix-Churchill. Matrix-Churchill is a machine tool company which will ship lathes to the Huteen State Establishment in Iraq, where Carlos Cardoen's organization makes cluster bombs. (Timmerman, 271–2.)

1988

JANUARY 20

Britain's Minister of Trade and Industry, Alan Clark, meets with representatives of the Machine Tool Trades Association in Victoria. According to the *Sunday Times*, Clark stresses that the export applications show that machines sent to Iraq are only for "general engineering usage of machine tools." Statistics from the European-based Organization for Economic Cooperation and Development (OECD) reveal that Iraqi machine tool purchases exceeded $1.2 billion dollars in 1988, up from $800 million in 1987. (Timmerman, 282–3.)

FEBRUARY

Italian police raid a Rome-based company, Paimpex, and stumble upon 28 tons of cluster bombs headed for Iraq. Italian investigators tie the shipment to Italian firms backed by BNL financing. (Hennelly, 25.)

FEBRUARY 29

Iraq launches its first attack against Tehran (which is 550 kilometers from Iraq), using ground-based ballistic missiles. Nine missiles are fired, beginning what is later referred to as the "War of the Cities." (Timmerman, 287.)

MARCH 17, 18

Iraq uses its chemical arsenal against a Kurdish population which it accuses of aiding Iran. The Kurds are from the northern Iraqi town of Halabja, which has some 70,000 inhabitants. The hydrogen cyanide compound used against them is similar to the poison gas, Zyklon B, which was used by the Nazis to gas the Jews in concentration camps during World War II. Five thousand Kurdish men, women, and children are killed; seven thousand are maimed for life. (Timmerman, 293–9.)

APRIL 17

Iraq moves to retake the Fao Peninsula from Iran with the support of U.S. intelligence. Iran accuses the U.S. of providing helicopter cover for Iraqi troops. (Hennelly, 25.)

APRIL 18

Iraqi forces destroy half of the Iranian navy and two Iranian oil platforms, purportedly in retaliation for Iranian mining that damaged a U.S. ship. (Hennelly, 25.)

APRIL 25

Iraq successfully tests a new ballistic missile, Al Abbas, with a range of 860 kilometers. (Timmerman, 289–90.)

MAY 1

The *New York Times* reports that Iraq has fired a new surface-to-surface missile with a range of almost 600 miles. "Western military specialists have been repeatedly surprised by Iraq's ability to improvise and modify the weapons it receives from outside suppliers to fit its own needs," notes the *Times*. (Hennelly, 25.)

JUNE

Kurdish leader Jalal Talabani comes to Washington to beg for the lives of the 20 million Kurds who are the subject of merciless gas attacks by the Iraqis. (Hennelly, 25.)

JULY

The British branch of U.S.-based Bechtel gets the initial contract from Iraq for a $2.5 billion petrochemical plant. The plant will enable the Iraqis to produce mustard gas on their own. (Hennelly, 25.)

JULY 3

The *USS Vincennes* shoots down an Iranian civilian jetliner, killing 290 men, women, and children. The Pentagon fabricates a story, claiming that the *Vincennes* was in international waters at the time of the incident, that the civilian airliner was outside its designated air corridor, that it did not respond to repeated warnings, and that the U.S. ship was on a mission of mercy to help a merchant ship under attack by Iraqi gunboats. As *Nightline* and *Newsweek* reported four years after the incident, it was the *Vincennes* that was in the wrong place (Iranian territorial waters), the civilian aircraft was where it was supposed to be, the Iranian flight crew never got the warning signals, and there was no merchant ship sending a distress signal. The *Vincennes* was actually pursuing Iranian gunboats that had fired on a U.S. helicopter after it strayed into Iranian airspace. The *Vincennes* soon found itself well into the 12-mile territorial limit, mistook the airliner for an Iranian F-14 and shot it down. (Hennelly, 25.)

JULY 14

Vice President Bush makes an unusual appearance before the UN Security Council to defend the downing of the Iranian jet. Helping Bush to prepare his defense is his chief of staff, Craig Fuller. (Fuller will go on to head up Hills & Knowlton Worldwide, public relations agents for Kuwait.) (Hennelly, 25.)

SUMMER

Congressmember Charles G. Rose (D-NC), who has been questioning the U.S. Department of Agriculture (USDA) about tobacco sales to Iraq, discovers that all the tobacco dealers involved in the Agricultural Export Credit Guarantee Program were financed by the BNL. Rose also finds out—via an anonymous letter from Paris—that some tobacco brokers were cutting U.S. tobacco with foreign stock. Aside from the fact that the CCC is only supposed to be financing American products, the cheaper foreign products were allowing the shipping bulk to remain constant while the money saved went toward the purchase of high-tech "extras" and kickbacks for Iraq. (Hennelly, 25.)

AUGUST 20

The cease-fire between Iraq and Iran takes hold. (Hennelly, 25.)

AUGUST 25

An Iraqi gas attack along the Turkish border kills 200 Kurds and injures more than 1,000. (Hennelly, 25.) This gas is an insecticide which is sprayed from BO-105 helicopters made by the West German company MBB. (Timmerman, 305.)

SEPTEMBER 9

The Senate passes legislation imposing widespread sanctions against Iraq. A few weeks later the House of Representatives follows suit. Neither bill ever becomes law, thanks to Reagan's opposition. Millions of dollars in credit and tons of U.S. technology continue to flow into Iraq at an accelerated pace, despite Saddam's brutal gassing of the Kurds. (Hennelly, 25.)

FALL

The USDA issues a more liberal trade policy, loosening trade regulations between U.S. firms and foreign customers under the Export Credit program. According to Congress member Rose, these changes facilitate payment of "after-sales services," including cash. Rose describes the gifts of merchandising as "nothing less than bribes." (Hennelly, 25.)

1989

In 1989, a proposed bill, the Chemical and Biological Control Act, which includes export sanctions against Iraq, passes both houses of Congress. But President Bush exercises his presidential right of veto to prevent the bill from becoming law.

JANUARY 25

Senator John McCain (R-AZ) charges that the U.S. has sent Iraq bacteria that is 10 times more lethal than anthrax, and that can be used as a biological weapon. (Hennelly, 25.)

FEBRUARY 9

Central Intelligence Agency (CIA) Director William Webster tells the Senate Committee on Governmental Affairs that Iraq has produced "several thousands tons of chemical agents." (Hennelly, 25.)

APRIL

Department of Energy staffers Bryan Siebert and Roger Heusser deliver a memo detailing the wide scope of the Iraqi international nuclear procurement effort but are waved off by their superiors. (Hennelly, 25–6.)

APRIL 28

On Saddam Hussein's birthday, the First Baghdad International Exhibition for Military Production is held in Iraq. The slogan for the exhibition is: "Defense equipment for peace and prosperity." 148 companies from 28 countries are represented, including the United Kingdom, Bulgaria, Poland, Hungary, Romania, Germany and Austria. The Chinese demonstrate an artillery spotter used to direct counter-battery fire. (Timmerman, 331.)

Also in attendance at the Iraqi arms exhibition is the British tool-making company Matrix-Churchill, Ltd. The company will later be under investigation for transferring technology to Iraq with full knowledge that the technology was intended for arms production. (Timmerman, 332.)

JUNE

Alan Stoga of Kissinger Associates travels to Baghdad with other corporate leaders to meet with Hussein. Hennelly reports that, according to *BNL Blunder* journalist Kenneth Timmerman, Kissinger Associates helped establish the Iraqi-American business connection. (Hennelly, 26.)

JULY

The Department of Energy forms a task force to look into reports that Iraq is on a global nuclear weapons and technology shopping spree. By December, the group is disbanded due to a "lack of interest" in the department. (Hennelly, 26.)

In Britain, Lord Trefgarne swaps jobs with Alan Clark, becoming the new head of the Department of Trade and Industry, while Clark assumes the position of minister for defense procurement at the Ministry of Defense.[2]

AUGUST 3

The president of the New York Federal Reserve, Gerald Corrigan, informs Italian authorities of the FBI raid on the Atlanta branch of BNL—one day before it occurs. (Boynton and Tough, 63.)

AUGUST 4

BNL branches all over the U.S. are raided by the FBI. The Feds hit pay dirt in Atlanta. In spite of evidence of BNL-Iraq improprieties, the CCC continues loan guarantees to Iraq—to the tune of $500 million. (Hennelly, 26.)

AUGUST 17

Hundreds of Iraqis are killed when a top-secret missile plant explodes at Hilla. (Hennelly, 26.)

LATE SEPTEMBER

The CCC estimates it guaranteed $700 million in loans involving the BNL for use by the government of Iraq. (Hennelly, 26.)

OCTOBER

Attorney Joe Whitley, formerly the third highest ranking person in the Justice Department, is retained by Matrix-Churchill to push the BNL to cough up the millions of dollars in letters of credit the Iraqis owe the machine-tool maker. In September of 1990, Matrix-Churchill's Ohio subsidiary will be seized by U.S. Customs as an Iraqi front corporation—established to help Hussein acquire nuclear-weapons technology—and the connection with the BNL bank in Atlanta will be "investigated" by the Justice Department. Ironically, Whitley will be serving as Atlanta's U.S. attorney when the 1992 BNL trial is scheduled to begin and will have to excuse himself. Congressional critics will charge that having the U.S.'s top attorney disabled by a conflict of interest undermined the investigation. (Hennelly, 26.)

OCTOBER 2

President Bush signs National Security Directive 26, a top-secret directive calling for closer ties to Iraq. More than a year will pass before any member of Congress gets to see this directive. (Hennelly, 26.)

OCTOBER 3

The USDA proposes $1 billion in loan credits for Iraq. Citing the BNL scandal, the Treasury Department and the Federal Reserve Board refuse to support the program. In a compromise, the USDA agrees to an offer of $400 million in loan credits. (Boynton and Tough, 63.)

OCTOBER 6

Iraqi foreign minister Tariq Aziz meets with Secretary of State James Baker to press for an additional $500 million in commodity credits. The same day, the Senate Foreign Relations Committee passes a bill imposing trade sanctions on countries that use or supply chemical weapons. Senator Daniel Inouye (D-HI) includes specific language prohibiting export-import guarantees for Iraq. But a loophole giving the president power to waive the sanctions is inserted at the last minute. The bill passes the House and the Senate. (Hennelly, 26.)

OCTOBER 8

Iraq threatens to default on its loans if the U.S. does not extend further credit. (Boynton and Tough, 63.)

OCTOBER 11

Assistant U.S. Attorney Gail McKenzie reports to the USDA that she has found evidence of criminal complicity of Iraqi officials in the bank scandal, including use of proceeds by Iraq to buy nuclear equipment, kickbacks on the CCC guarantee, and strong indications that Iraq diverted loan guarantees to get military equipment. (Boynton and Tough, 63–4.)

OCTOBER 12

The USDA passes this information to Agriculture Secretary Clayton Yeutter. (Boynton and Tough, 63–4.)

OCTOBER 13

A State Department memo detailing 10 separate federal investigations of BNL is provided to Secretary of State James Baker. The State Department memo cites mounting evidence that Iraq is using U.S. farm export credits to purchase nuclear-related equipment, stating, "If smoke indicates fire, we may be facing a four-alarm blaze in the near future." (Hennelly, 26.) Nevertheless, at a morning briefing, Baker is reported as saying that derailing the loan credits "is a step in the wrong direction—get it back onto the table." (Boynton and Tough, 63–4.)

OCTOBER 31

Secretary of State James Baker lobbies Secretary of Agriculture Clayton Yeutter to support the loan guarantees to Iraq. (Boynton and Tough, 64.)

NOVEMBER 6

The CIA delivers a report to the Bush Administration detailing the Iraqis' use of the BNL and the USDA Commodity Credit program to procure components for nuclear, biological, and chemical weapons. (Boynton and Tough, 64.)

NOVEMBER 7

Jay S. Bybee, a member of Bush's personal legal staff in the White House, calls the chief BNL investigator, Assistant U.S. Attorney Gail McKenzie. Notes from a Treasury official, who discussed the phone call with McKenzie, will find their way to Congressmember Gonzalez three years later and only then will the public find out about this behind-the-scenes attempt to stifle the BNL probe. "McKenzie: She has been called by the White House—got impression (they are) concerned about embarrassment levels," the memo states. (Boynton and Tough, 64.)

NOVEMBER 8

The National Advisory Council (NAC) tells the Department of Agriculture that it objects to the $1 billion in loans, but eventually approves them and advises that Iraq should receive the first half for 1990. (Boynton and Tough, 64.)

NOVEMBER 9

Undersecretary of State Robert Kimitt tells Baker: "I attended a meeting Wednesday of the NAC deputies which approved USDA's proposal for a full billion-dollar CCC program for Iraq. (Your call to Yeutter and our subsequent effort with OMB [the Office of Management and Budget] and Treasury paid off.) . . . I suggest that you break the good news to Foreign Minister Tariq Aziz, since he raised the issue with you, and you promised to take a personal interest in it." Baker sends the message. (Boynton and Tough, 64.)

The British Department of Trade and Industry approves a Matrix-Churchill shipment of machines to Iraq. These machines produce sophisticated detonation fuses for 155mm Howitzer shells being manufactured by Carlos Cardoen's group in Iraq's April 7 munitions factory. Britain's Export Credit Guarantee Department (ECGD) backs up the shipment, meaning that British taxpayers will foot the bill if Iraq defaults on payments. Postwar criticisms of these loans amd of the export of arms-making machinery to Iraq will center around the fact that shells produced by British-made machines might have been used against British soldiers. At its Coventry factory, the Matrix-Churchill company built equipment to make the shells at the Taji and Huteen plants in Iraq.[3]

Other British companies involved in supplying Iraq's arms industry include BSA Machine Tools in Birmingham and Colchester Lathes (both companies are part of the "600 Group"). Royal Ordnance, which was bought by British Aerospace, sent material to Iraq to help propel large rockets. Thorn EMI supplied Iraq with sophisticated Cymbeline battlefield radar, and Racal, an electronics firm, supplied Saddam Hussein's military with battlefield radios.[4]

DECEMBER 5

Iraq launches its first three-stage space rocket. (Hennelly, 26.)

1990

JANUARY

The BNL scandal grows as investigators discover $3 billion in unauthorized loans. (Hennelly, 26.)

JANUARY 17

Citing "national interest," Bush utilizes the trade loophole to circumvent congressional legislation that would put a stop to Iraq's export-import credit. (Hennelly, 26.)

FEBRUARY 12

Senator Patrick Leahy (D-VT) writes Agriculture Secretary Clayton Yeutter asking if the CCC's agricultural credit program is in trouble, and if—contrary to its legal mandate—the program is being used to further foreign policy objectives.

FEBRUARY 20

Secretary Yeutter sends letter to Senator Leahy saying that there are no foreign policy pressures on the USDA to help Iraq. (Boynton and Tough, 64.)

MARCH 5

The National Security Council (NSC) seeks the remaining $500 million payout in CCC loan guarantees to Iraq. (Hennelly, 26.)

MARCH 11

Farzad Basoft, an Iranian national and British-based newspaper correspondent stationed in Iraq, is sentenced to death for spying. The world community begs for his life. He is hung a few days later. Margaret Thatcher calls it "an act of barbarism" but Iraq's $400 million line of British credit stays in place. (Hennelly, 26.)

MARCH 14

The USDA fights Congressmember Rose's attempt to rein in the Export Credit Guarantee Program by insisting that only minor adjustments are necessary, even as evidence to the contrary mounts. The Administration ignores abuses in the program—especially in Iraq's case—and opposes congressional legislation that would kick Iraq out of the program entirely. (Hennelly, 26.)

MARCH 22

Dr. Gerald Bull, a Canadian-born American citizen, is mysteriously shot to death in Belgium. Bull had been working with the Iraqis on the development of a "supergun" designed to project an artillery shell 720 miles. A few weeks later, British customs seizes large forged steel tubes believed to be the barrel of Dr. Bull's secret gun. (Hennelly, 26.)

Dr. Bull had promised the Iraqis in 1988 that he could build a 56-meter-long gun for $10 million, a relatively cheap price compared to other arms packages. The gun would be capable of launching satellites into space, or of firing conventional, chemical, and nuclear projectiles. The project was code-named Babylon. (Timmerman, 284.)

APRIL

The U.S. State Department asks the Department of Agriculture not to go public with news that Iraq has grossly violated CCC rules. The USDA complies but, according to Congressmember Gonzalez, insists on announcing that Hussein has been dropped from the program. When National Security Adviser Brent Scowcroft later receives a classified cable from U.S. Ambassador to Iraq April Glaspie protesting plans to cut Iraq's commodity credits, he intervenes and Iraq is quietly suspended without a formal announcement. (Hennelly, 27.)

APRIL 2

Hussein brags to the world that he has advanced chemical weapons capabilities and that he is prepared to destroy half of Israel if it attacks his country. (Hennelly, 27.)

APRIL 12

Senators Robert Dole (R-KS), Howard Metzenbaum (D-OH), Alan Simpson (R-WY) and Frank Murkowski (R-AK) meet with Hussein in Baghdad as emissaries of peace. Metzenbaum to Hussein: "I am now aware that you are a strong and intelligent man and that you want peace."

Simpson to Hussein: "I believe that your problems lie with the Western media and not with the U.S. government." (Hennelly, 27.)

APRIL 26

Representative Tom Lantos (D-CA) speaks for a growing group in Congress when he asks Assistant Secretary of State John Kelly about the Administration's endless indulgence of Hussein, asking, "At what point will the Administration recognize that this is not a nice guy?" Kelly responds, "We believe there is still potentiality for positive alterations in Iraqi behavior." (Hennelly, 27.)

MAY 12

Seventy-five tons of "supergun" parts are found in the port of Naples. They had been constructed by the Italian company Societa delle Fucine of Terni. (Timmerman, 383–4.)

MAY 17

Senators Claiborne Pell (D-RI), Jesse Helms (R-NC), and Alphonse D'Amato (R-NY) lead the fight to impose sanctions on Iraq and every country using chemical weapons. Bush and members of Congress from farm commodity export districts that have been doing a brisk business with Iraq voice their objections. Dole, Murkowski, and Metzenbaum, inspired by their recent visit with Hussein, speak out against Iraqi trade sanctions. D'Amato withdraws his amendment. (Hennelly, 27.)

MAY 23

The Department of Agriculture reports that the USDA Credit Export Program may have been used in conjunction with bribes paid to Iraqi individuals and corporations by U.S. companies. With this news, the administration's request for the additional $500 million in commodity credits for Iraq is put on hold. (Hennelly, 27.)

JUNE

The State Department warns of international implications stemming from the Justice Department's BNL investigation. A grand jury learns of the $5.5 billion BNL fraud case in Atlanta and finds out that bank officials knowingly cooperated in Iraq's acquisition of weapons technologies. (Hennelly, 27.)

JUNE 15

Assistant Secretary of State John Kelly expresses regret over the poor Iraqi human rights record but entreats Congress to refrain from economic sanctions against Iraq because it would widen the U.S. trade deficit without advancing U.S. policy in the Middle East. (Hennelly, 27.)

JULY 23

Less than two weeks before Hussein invades Kuwait there are widespread reports of massive Iraqi troop movements. The topic of trade sanctions and shutting down the loan guarantees to Iraq resurfaces in Congress. The Administration refuses to budge. (Hennelly, 27.)

JULY 25

April Glaspie meets with Hussein. She fails to give him any signal as to how the U.S. might respond were Iraq to invade Kuwait. She tactfully raises the issue of Hussein's troop deployment to the south but doesn't push. "I have a direct instruction from the President to seek better relations with Iraq," Glaspie reassures Hussein. (Hennelly, 27.)

JULY 31

The Bush Administration opposes congressional sanctions against Iraq. (Boynton and Tough, 65.)

AUGUST 2

Hussein invades Kuwait.

AUGUST 8

Bush grants conflict-of-interest waivers to 11 cabinet-level officers whose financial holdings will be impacted by U.S.-Iraq relations and the imminent war: Assistant to the President for National Security Brent Scowcroft, Deputy Assistant for National Security Robert Gates, Attorney General Dick Thornburgh, the Chief of Staff to the President (John Summer), Director of the Central Intelligence Agency William Webster, Secretary of Commerce Robert Mosbacher, Secretary of Defense Dick Cheney, Secretary of Energy James Watkins, Secretary of State James Baker, Secretary of the Treasury Nicholas Brady and the President's Chief Legal Counsel, C. Boyden Gray. Bush explains the waivers to the attorney general in a letter: "In my judgment, the nature of the current crisis and the gravity of the measures under consideration by the United States are such that even vast financial interests could not be deemed likely to affect the integrity of the services the government may expect . . . ." (Hennelly, 27.)

AUGUST 10

The exiled Kuwaiti royal family signs a contract with the U.S. public relations firm, Hill & Knowlton. By the time the war is over, Hill & Knowlton will have earned $10 million from hyping U.S. intervention to reclaim Kuwait.

In John R. MacArthur's *Second Front: Censorship and Propaganda in the Gulf War*, the connection between Hill & Knowlton and the Administration is clarified: the Kuwait contract was signed by H & K chairman Robert K. Gray, who was active in both Reagan presidential campaigns. Craig Fuller, the firm's then Washington-based president and chief operating officer, was Vice President Bush's chief of staff. (Hennelly, 27.)

AUGUST 14

Congressmember Gonzalez begins congressional hearings on BNL. (Hennelly, 27.)

AUGUST 21

In a briefing to the German Bundestag, Economic Minister Helmut Haussmann admits that U.S. intelligence agencies had knowledge of West Germany's involvement in aiding Iraq with an ongoing centrifuge project to enrich uranium. Top German scientists Bruno Stemmler and Walter Busse, both previously employed with Man Technology Gmbh of Munich, had spent several months in Iraq in 1988-89 helping Iraqi scientists develop the necessary centrifuges.

The Iraqis had vigorously pursued a second track to the processing of enriched uranium, utilizing the method of magnetic isotope separation which requires a device called a calutron.

On the road to an atomic bomb, the Iraqis had also attempted to acquire Krytrons, or nuclear triggering devices, on the open market. However, a shipment of the triggering devices was seized in London. (Timmerman, 316.)

AUGUST

The White House signs an executive order waiving the requirements of the National Environmental Policy Act (NEPA) regarding military actions in the Gulf and domestic activities in support of the mobilization. The U.S. begins covert studies of the environmental impacts of the impending war.[5]

SEPTEMBER

In the same month that U.S. Customs seizes Ohio-based Matrix-Churchill [see entry for October 1989] the Department of Commerce falsifies 68 Iraqi export licenses that were subpoenaed by Congressmember Doug Barnard's Subcommittee on Commerce. Barnard (D-GA) wanted to review the high-technology exports approved by Commerce that had potential military or "dual" uses. (Hennelly, 27.)

SEPTEMBER 6

Over 100,000 U.S. troops mass in the Gulf region. (Boynton and Tough, 65.)

SEPTEMBER 26

Attorney General Dick Thornburgh writes Congressmember Gonzalez asking him to delay House Banking hearings on the BNL for "national security" reasons. (Hennelly, 27.)

SEPTEMBER 27

Eight tobacco companies admit to lying to the Commodity Credit Corporation on their applications to trade with Iraq. In exchange for a guilty plea, the U.S. Attorney in North Carolina agrees not to pursue an investigation of the companies or their parent corporations, and simply fines them. (Hennelly, 27.)

OCTOBER

The Simon Wiesenthal Center releases *The Poison Gas Connection* by Kenneth Timmerman. The report cites 207 companies from 21 Western nations which have assisted Hussein's drive for weapons of mass destruction—18 American corporations are involved. (Hennelly, 27.)

OCTOBER 9

Congressmember Gonzalez informs the nation that U.S. taxpayers are liable for $2 billion in United States Commodity Credit Corporation loans to Iraq.

OCTOBER 16

Despite Attorney General Thornburgh's heavy-handed warnings to stay away from the BNL mess, Gonzalez holds a hearing, charging that the billions in Iraqi loans could very well have helped finance Iraq's invasion of Kuwait. Pietro Lombardi, head of BNL's American subsidiary, appears before Gonzalez's committee with his attorney, former Nixon Secretary of State William P.

Rogers, from the prestigious law firm Wells and Rogers. (Hennelly, 28.)

NOVEMBER 8

Bush announces the deployment of more troops, bringing the total to 400,000. (Hennelly, 28.)

NOVEMBER 18

The *New York Times* reports that Western intelligence sources believe that Iraq is 10 years away from a nuclear weapons capability. (Hennelly, 28.) [The generally agreed-upon figure is now nearer to 3—5 years. See Chapter Seven.]

NOVEMBER 20

A *New York Times*/CBS poll finds that most Americans don't think that oil is a good enough reason to go to war, but that they *would* support U.S. intervention to prohibit Iraq from developing a nuclear bomb. (Hennelly, 28.)

NOVEMBER 22

President Bush goes to the front to speak to the troops, announcing, "Those who would measure the timetable for Saddam's atomic program in years may be seriously underestimating the reality of the situation and the gravity of the threat." (Hennelly, 28.)

NOVEMBER 25

National Security Advisor Scowcroft and Defense Secretary Dick Cheney are forced to concede that there is no new intelligence indicating Hussein has accelerated his atomic program beyond the original assessments. (Hennelly, 28.)

NOVEMBER 29

The UN approves a resolution authorizing the use of military force if Iraq hasn't cleared out of Kuwait by January 15, 1991. (Hennelly, 28.)

NOVEMBER 30

The *New York Times* attempts to calm the nuclear-capability frenzy the Administration is whipping up, reporting that there is "a shortage of solid intelligence and definitive assessments" on when Iraq might develop nuclear weapons. (Hennelly, 28.)

DECEMBER 18

The Village Voice publishes a cover story by Murray Waas—"Gulfgate: How the U.S. Secretly Armed Iraq"—which details the U.S.'s duplicitous trade policy with Iraq. (Hennelly, 28.)

1991

JANUARY 8

Before the commencement of the air war, the *Los Angeles Times* reports that there are 530,000 Iraqi troops either in place defending Kuwait or well on their way. The Pentagon puts the number at 540,000. Only after the war will it come out that on the eve of the ground assault Iraq has 200,000 troops committed to Kuwait; the Coalition has 700,000. (Hennelly, 28.)

JANUARY 11

The Defense Nuclear Agency (DNA) releases a report by Pacific-Sierra Research Corporation which counters claims by environmentalists and scientists that the firing of the Kuwaiti oil fields could have serious impacts on the global environment."[6]

JANUARY 16

The U.S.-led Coalition initiates the air war against Iraq.

JANUARY 18

Hussein fires his first Scuds at Israel. Much of his Scud capability is the result of technology transfers and aid from almost all of the Western countries that Iraq is now fighting. (Hennelly, 28.)

JANUARY 23

To head off an anticipated beach landing by the Coalition forces, the Iraqis open oil valves, coating the Kuwaiti shoreline and fouling the waters of the Gulf. (Hennelly, 28.)

JANUARY 25

The Department of Energy issues a gag order preventing its employees from discussing war-related environmental research with the media. [See Chapter Three, "Chronology of a Coverup."]

FEBRUARY 6

ABC's *Nightline* reports that at least 40 American companies did business illegally with Iraq and that the Customs Service is investigating them. (Hennelly, 28.)

FEBRUARY

The U.S. and its allies conduct an intense air war, completing 70,000 bombing runs in less than a month. The first wave of attacks are military-related, but as the "target-rich" environment gets saturated the U.S. hits Iraqi water treatment facilities, sewer plants, highways, electrical generating stations, and manufacturing facilities. (Hennelly, 28.)

FEBRUARY 19

Senate hearings begin on BNL. A parallel investigation begins in Italy and the bank's chair, Nerio Nesi, and general manager, Giaccomo Pedde, resign. (Hennelly, 28.)

FEBRUARY 22

Former Secretary of State and head of the NSC Henry Kissinger resigns from his position on the BNL international advisory board—where he was paid $10,000 per meeting—and is later quoted by the *Financial Times* as saying, "I didn't have any idea of what BNL was doing in Iraq . . . I resigned earlier this year because I don't want to be connected, I don't want to be asked this sort of question." Kissinger's firm, Kissinger Associates, also represented a number of U.S. companies who were both getting licenses to export to Iraq and getting their deals financed through BNL. Other Kissinger Associates alumni making central decisions on U.S.-Iraq policy include National Security Advisor Scowcroft and Deputy Secretary of State Eagleburger. Kissinger's attorney, John Bellinger, denied influencing Iraqi-American trade. "Kissinger Associates never worked with any client on a particular business venture or transaction in Iraq," insists Bellinger. (Hennelly, 28–9.)

FEBRUARY 24

The Coalition ground assault begins. Press restriction tactics honed during the Grenada and Panama invasions are taken to unprecedented levels and prove effective in blocking any pictures of, or press reports on, actual combat. Protests, even a lawsuit in which *The Village Voice* is a co-plaintiff, are to no avail. This will be the first major war that Americans watch as if it were a video game, with no footage of dead bodies to interrupt the illusion. It will only be learned later, from a *Newsday* story published after the war, that on one occasion the U.S. forces employed a new and horrifying technique for smashing through the front lines: bulldozers that buried possibly thousands of Iraqis alive. (Hennelly, 29.)

FEBRUARY 27

The Coalition liberates Kuwait City after an Iraqi retreat.

FEBRUARY 28

Coalition forces are ordered to cease fire. The *New York Times* reports, "Guns fell silent across Iraq and Kuwait . . . The Pentagon chief of operations said the Iraqi expeditionary force, which once numbered more than 600,000, had been reduced to "a rabble" posing no military threat to the region. (Hennelly, 29.)

LATE FEBRUARY

A 347-count criminal indictment comes down on Drogoul and two officers of the Atlanta BNL. Government interference in the investigation becomes more aggressive. On this day the State Department secretly tells the Justice Department it has reservations about indicting Jordanian businessman Wafai Dajani because of his close ties to the King of Jordan and American grain exporters. The U.S. Attorney in Atlanta will later deny that the State Department has influenced his decision to let Dajani off. (Hennelly, 29.)

In Britain, three Matrix-Churchill directors are charged with illegally exporting machinery to Iraq that was later used to manufacture conventional and nonconventional armaments inside Iraq. One of the three who stood accused of export violations, Paul Henderson, had also been recruited by Britain's intelligence service, MI6, to provide information on Iraq's arms procurement network inside Britain. The network, which had been headed by Safa Al Habobi, who was an engineer with the Nassr State Enterprise for Mechanical Industries in Iraq, had used Henderson in its efforts to buy out front companies for the Al Araby Trading company in Britain.

Matrix-Churchill's export of machinery to Iraq had been approved by British government ministries, including Foreign Minister William Waldegrave, Alan Clark, Minister of Trade and Industry, and Lord Trefgarne, Defense Minister.

MARCH

ABC's *Nightline* and the *Financial Times* launch a joint investigation into the prewar Iraqi-U.S. relationship, including the BNL and the role of American companies in arming Iraq. The investigation turns up a 1987 cable sent by the U.S. embassy in Santiago, Chile, to Washington D.C. that describes Carlos Cardoen, a notorious arms dealer, as a "responsible recipient of U.S. products." The cable concerned Cardoen's cluster-bomb business with Hussein. It also comes out that the U.S. ambassador to Chile up until 1985, the late James Theberge, was employed both by the CIA and as Cardoen's Washington contact. (Hennelly, 29.)

MARCH 13

The *New York Times* reports on economic benefits from the war: "The United States could become a net foreign lender again, at least for a month or two, for the first time in a decade." The same day, Bush warns Iraq to stop using helicopter gunships against the Shiite and Kurdish fighters whose rebellion he encouraged. (Hennelly, 29.)

MARCH 26

President Bush abandons his pledge to prohibit Iraq from using helicopter gunships to quell the two-front rebellion he egged on. Hussein attacks the rebels and consolidates his power. (Hennelly, 29.)

APRIL 8

Former Undersecretary of Commerce Dennis Kloske blows the whistle on the Commerce Department for indiscriminately exporting $1.5 billion in high-tech hardware with potential military uses to Iraq from 1985 to 1990. Kloske tells Congress he was ignored when he raised the issue with his superiors and details his department's push for an embargo on exporting high technology and military equipment to Iraq a year earlier. Kloske claims the State Department refused to go along. (Hennelly, 29.)

APRIL 18

Amnesty International issues a report on wholesale human rights abuses in Kuwait. Citizens are summarily imprisoned, tortured, and executed without due process. (Hennelly, 29.)

APRIL 19

Secretary of Defense Cheney gets a letter from Congressmember Sam Gejdenson (D-CT) asking that he forward documents regarding U.S. government export policy for Iraq from 1979 to 1991. Defense will drag its feet for several months, forcing Gejdenson's Subcommittee on International Economic Policy and Trade to issue a subpoena. (Hennelly, 29.)

APRIL 27

The United Nations and other international relief agencies report a dramatic increase in the incidence of cholera afflicting Iraqi children. The child mortality rate is 10 to 20 times higher than usual as a result of malnutrition and the consumption of polluted water. (Hennelly, 29.)

MAY 2

Congressmember Gonzalez introduces National Security Advisor Scowcroft's stock portfolio into the Congressional Record. According to Gonzalez, Scowcroft and Deputy Secretary of State Eagleburger—former top level executives with Kissinger Associates—derived part of their paychecks from Kissinger Associates client BNL. Gonzalez points out that Eagleburger served on the board of a Yugoslavian bank with a U.S. branch partially financed by BNL, and on the board of ITT. In addition, Scowcroft had stock in 11 defense contractors. Several of the companies he held stock in did business with Iraq and have been cited as prime examples of high-technology exporters whose products had military applications. Says Gonzalez, "Consider that, together, the companies he owned stock in received over one in every eight United States export licenses for sales to Iraq." It wasn't until October 4, 1990, that Scowcroft was required to divest himself of these companies with government contracts. (Hennelly, 29.)

MAY 6

Executive branch members who have been summoned to testify before Congress on behalf of their respective agencies are called to a meeting, chaired by Nicholas Rostow, legal adviser for the NSC. According to DOD (Department of Defense) Chief Council Michael Cifrino, who attended, "the purpose of that meeting was to coordinate the responses of the various executive agencies . . . " (Hennelly, 29.)

MAY 13

At a follow-up session, the agency heads reject a proposal that the NSC represent all of them. (Hennelly, 29.)

JUNE 4

The Commerce Department admits that it changed information on export documents, in effect hiding the fact that they were providing licenses for the sale of military-related hardware to Iraq. (Boynton and Tough, 65.)

JUNE 5

A third meeting of prospective congressional witnesses is held. Cifrino, again in attendance, later tells Congress that C. Boyden Gray, the White House counsel, presided and reminded everyone of the importance of "maintaining the institutional prerogatives of the presidency through the use of executive privilege." (Hennelly, 30.)

JULY 11

Syndicated columnist Jack Anderson reports that Scowcroft was the Administration's point man when it came to the pre-Gulf War push for more U.S. trade with Iraq. Anderson draws the connection between Scowcroft's former employment with Kissinger Associates and that firm's efforts on the Iraqi front. (Hennelly, 30.)

AUGUST 1

A former attorney for Kennemetal, a Fortune 500 corporation based in Latrobe, Pennsylvania, testifies before Congressmember Rose's Agriculture Committee. Kennemetal is accused of doing military-related work for the Iraqis and using a BNL letter of credit to finance the deal. Rose wants to know exactly how BNL letters of credit, backed by the CCC and meant for the purchase of farm products, were diverted to the acquisition of high-tech equipment by Hussein. Interestingly, Kennemetal board member William Newlin is a friend of former Attorney General Thornburgh. Newlin was named the head of Thornburgh's Corporate Advisory Committee when Thornburgh was Pennsylvania's governor; Thornburgh happens to be the fellow now under fire for turning a blind eye to the Bank of Credit and Commerce International (BCCI) scandal and for permitting a slow response to the BNL scandal. In both cases critical CIA information was kept from Justice Department investigators. Most of the board of directors at Kennemetal represent companies that were also trading with Iraq and providing dual-use technologies with important military and, sometimes, even nuclear application. For example, Hewlett Packard, the Allen-Bradley Company and Westinghouse all have corporate representatives on the Kennemetal board and have been cited as doing business with Iraq. Congressmember Rose charges that even after the presidential order banning trade Kennemetal had over $1.5 million in equipment placed with Matrix-Churchill. The company denies this and insists that it promptly complied with the President's trade ban. (Hennelly, 30.)

OCTOBER 18

Senator Bill Bradley (D-NJ) attempts to block Robert Gates' nomination to head the CIA, pointing out that "Mr. Gates' misjudgments were critical in diverting the attention of the intelligence community away from Iraq in late 1988 and early 1989, just when Iraq began to show signs of strategic activities that could threaten U.S. interests in the Persian Gulf." Despite Bradley's objections, Gates is confirmed. (Hennelly, 30.)

ALSO IN 1991

International Atomic Energy Agency (IAEA) inspectors find 50 Matrix-Churchill machines for arms manufacturing at Iraqi nuclear sites. At 29 of the sites, inspectors find machinery used to make parts for a centrifugal uranium enrichment cycle, which produces material necessary for the production of nuclear warheads.

IAEA inspectors also found equipment supplied by other British and American companies at or near six nuclear sites in Iraq. The companies that had manufactured the equipment included Wickman, Harrison, Colchester Lathes, Remmshaw-Probe, Cincinnati Milacron, Bridgeport, FMT, and Morgan Rushworth.

Government sanctioning of British company exports of machinery which aided Iraq's effort to develop nuclear weaponry would later raise questions as to whether Britain had violated the 1968 Non-Proliferation Treaty.[8]

1992

JANUARY 31

Congressional investigators contend there is documentation that shows Kennemetal had worked with four different Iraqi military procurement agencies before the Iraqi invasion. Kennemetal counters that the single post-ban shipment to Matrix-Churchill in England was actually for a British steering wheel manufacturer and was fully approved by British authorities. In the late 1980s Kennemetal did supply products to Chilean arms dealer Carlos Cardoen, who made cluster bombs for Iraq. The *Philadelphia Inquirer* reported that Kennemetal's British subsidiary sold tooling packages to Matrix-Churchill based on specifications provided by Cardoen. Matrix-Churchill was the hub for Iraqi weapons development and procurement. (Hennelly, 30.)

FEBRUARY 24

Congressmember Gonzalez reveals that while National Security Director Scowcroft was working for Kissinger Associates, he flew to Rome and briefed the BNL board of directors for a fee. (Hennelly, 30.)

MARCH 6

The Census Bureau threatens to fire an analyst who puts the number of civilians who died at U.S. hands in Iraq at 13,000—double the official estimate. The analyst, Beth Osborne Daponte, told the press that she had consulted with three levels of internal bureaucracy before making her survey public. She also calculated that 30,000 people died as a result of Shiite and Kurdish uprisings and 70,000 from health problems due to allied destruction of the civilian infrastructure. (Hennelly, 30.) [See Chapter Six.]

MARCH 10

Someone breaks into the office of the Italian Senate commission charged with examining the BNL affair and ransacks the files. A senator on the commission tells the media that his investigators have established a link between BCCI and BNL: the bank account used was at the BCCI London branch through which almost $2.5 million was transferred. The money was then dispersed to BNL Atlanta employees who knew about Drogoul's Iraqi loan program. (Hennelly, 30.)

MARCH 18

Dr. Theodore Postol, a prominent weapons expert and former advisor for the U.S. military, testifies to Congress that an article he wrote exposing the Patriot's poor performance during the Gulf War was the subject of complaints from the Pentagon. Postol said that a representative from the Defense Investigative Service contacted him and told him that his article was based on classified information and that speaking out would be perceived as violating the law. (Hennelly, 30.)

APRIL 6

The U.S. government charges Chilean arms dealer Carlos Cardoen with money laundering and illegally shipping weapons-grade zirconium from the U.S. to Iraq for use in cluster bombs. (Hennelly, 30.)

APRIL 11

An aggressive response from the dismissed Census Bureau employee's lawyer—plus some decidedly bad press—results in Beth Osborne Daponte keeping her job. The bureau retracts its charge that Daponte's figures represented "a deliberate falsification." (Hennelly, 30.)

APRIL 20

Stalling until the Italian elections are over, the Italian Senate committee finally releases its report, suggesting that Drogoul's Iraqi loan activity was known by higher-ups at BNL Rome as well as by members of the U.S. government. (Hennelly, 30–1.)

APRIL 27

According to *Financial Times* reports, former deputy CIA chief Admiral Bobby Inman writes a letter to a federal judge in Philadelphia on this day on behalf of convicted money launderer and illegal arms trader James Guerin. Guerin was convicted of defrauding Ferranti, a British defense firm he worked for, of $1.1 billion. It was Guerin who brokered the transfer of defense technologies to South Africa and Iraq. At his trial he insisted he had been working for the CIA. Some of the antiaircraft radar Guerin shipped to Iraq was used against the Coalition during the war. Oddly, Inman, who served as the chair of Bush's foreign intelligence advisory board, is also on the payroll of the company Guerin defrauded. Inman's letter praised Guerin's work for the intelligence community in the 1970s. Inman told the *Financial Times* he had testified that Guerin's exploits in the 1980s were not sanctioned by the U.S. (Hennelly, 30–1.)

MAY 9

Chilean arms dealer Carlos Cardoen's attorney, Robert Martinez, is named U.S. Attorney in Miami. (Hennelly, 31.)

MAY 15

Attorney General William Barr writes Congressmember Henry Gonzalez, charging that Gonzalez "has harmed national security" by revealing details of the Bush Administration's policy toward Iraq prior to the war. (Boynton and Tough, 65.)

MAY 22

Senator Richard Lugar (R-IN), ranking Republican member of the Senate Agriculture Committee, closes ranks with Committee Chairman Patrick Leahy (D-VT) in requesting that the Bush Administration turn over the reams of documents covering U.S. prewar policy on agricultural-financing aid to Iraq. Leahy made the request after the General Accounting Office was denied access to the documents. (Hennelly, 31.)

MAY 30–31

The government initiates a plea bargain with Drogoul, allowing him to plead guilty to only 60 of the 347 counts. Drogoul, who had earlier expressed a desire to fully explain his actions, suddenly agrees to silence. "(He) decided not to provide a statement until sentencing, after debriefing over a two months' period by the government," wrote a troubled Judge Shoob to Congressmember Jack Brooks, chair of the House Judiciary Committee. "In view of the substantial public and media interest in this case, I felt that it was important and necessary that a full disclosure, under oath, be made by Mr. Drogoul, as was promised, at the time of the plea. I was not satisfied with the government's explanation . . . as to why the government would initiate a plea agreement with Mr. Drogoul the weekend before the plea, while the lead prosecutor was out of town, whereby he would plead to 60 counts rather than 347, the government would recommend a downward departure on sentencing if satisfied with the defendant's cooperation, and Mr. Drogoul would not make the lengthy statement at the time of the plea which his attorney had insisted he have the opportunity to do." After initially agreeing to name the U.S. officials involved, Drogoul changed his mind the following day. "You see, part of the problem is that I can't remember some of the names of the officials. I remember what they looked like, I remember the conversations that we may have had, but I don't remember exact names . . . " he told the court. The judge recommended bringing in a special prosecutor and wondered whether the Atlanta U.S. Attorney's office had "the resources or the capacity" to evaluate what Drogoul could tell them. He expressed concern that exactly what Drogoul had feared might happen, did happen: crucial parts of the BNL story were "suppressed." Drogoul now faces a maximum penalty of 390 years in prison, $18 million in fines, and $1.8 million in restitution. (Hennelly, 31.)

JUNE 4

At a press conference, Bush is asked about congressional charges that he actually strengthened Hussein's army through favorable trade agreements. Bush responds, "That's not right. As I said at my last press conference, we tried, not through strengthening his nuclear or biological or chemical weapons, as has been alleged, not by giving him part of Kuwait, as has been alleged. But we tried to work with him on grain credits and things of this nature to avoid aggressive actions. And it failed." (Hennelly, 31.)

JUNE 18

The White House refuses to let White House counsel C. Boyden Gray or Nicholas Rostow of the NSC testify before the House Judiciary Committee. That old canard, "executive privilege," is trotted out. Several congressional committees are investigating the Administration's pre-Gulf War policy on Iraq: the export of sensitive U.S. technology with military and nuclear uses to Iraq, the Justice Department's halfhearted pursuit of the BNL scandal, and subsequent attempts to alter the official record. The White House selectively provides documents covering its prewar policies. (Hennelly, 31.)

JULY 1

Bush appears on CBS' *This Morning*, and host Harry Smith asks why the Bush Administration continued to support Hussein while aware of the man's quest for nuclear arms. Bush responds, "We didn't know that. And I don't know where you got that, Harry. The State Department didn't know it . . . If we had known it, it wouldn't have happened." (Hennelly, 31.)

JULY 7

A Federal grand jury in Denver indicts a former U.S. ambassador and two high-profile conservative ideologues for taking almost $8 million from the Kuwaiti government to hype U.S. military intervention in the Gulf during the summer of 1990. The trio allegedly spent $2 million on the cause and pocketed the proceeds without reporting any of it as income and without registering as foreign agents. Those so charged are former U.S. ambassador to Bahrain, Sam Zakhem, who served from 1986 to 1989; William Kennedy, Jr., owner of the now defunct *Conservative Digest*; and Scott Stanley, Jr., former managing editor of the magazine. Zakhem, who insists he's innocent, was a busy Gulf War cheerleader who has been charged with hiding the fact that he was a paid mouthpiece for Kuwait's royal family, the Al Sabahs. During the war, while he was allegedly on the Kuwaiti payroll, the former ambassador was a much sought-after "expert" on the TV and talk show circuits. In his zeal to push the Kuwaiti cause, Zakhem is alleged to have met with members of Congress and top people in the executive branch including Bush's deputy assistant Edward M. Rogers (who later left the White House for BCCI.) (Hennelly, 31.)

July 9

The House Committee on the Judiciary formally requests the appointment of a special independent counsel to investigate whether officials at the highest level of the executive branch broke the law by aiding Saddam Hussein in the months and years before the war. The document cites continued refusal by President Bush to let key officials testify before Congress, the executive branch's suppression of voluminous documents, and the Justice Department's questionable handling of the multibillion-dollar BNL caper. (Hennelly, 31.)

July 24

CIA Director Robert Gates writes Congressmember Gonzalez, saying that the CIA has cooperated fully with prosecutors in the BNL case, and criticizes him for disclosing that intelligence agencies were aware of Iraq's military development program. (Boynton and Tough, 66.)

Also in July

Gonzalez announces that hundreds of millions of dollars of BNL loans helped finance Gerald Bull's supergun project for Iraq, the Condor II long-range missile project, and Iraq's chemical weapons program. The chairman also reveals that U.S. intelligence routinely shared information with British, Israeli, and Italian intelligence services on Iraq's arms procurement efforts in Britain and the U.S., raising doubts that high-level government officials of both countries had not known that technology exports to Iraq were being used to manufacture armaments. Information shared between the intelligence communities included knowledge of British tool manufacturers' involvement in two Iraqi military projects: the putting together of an artillery project code-named ABA; and K-1000, a project for the production of gas centrifuges for uranium enrichment. The investigation further revealed that U.S. and British intelligence services had been aware of Matrix-Churchill's supplying of Iraq with machinery which had allowed it to produce 500,000 155mm artillery shells per year during its war with Iran.

Drawings of the shells had been provided to British authorities by Mark Gutteridge, the Matrix-Churchill export sales manager that had been recruited by Britain's other intelligence service, MI5.[9]

August 10

U.S. Attorney General Barr rejects the House Judiciary Committee's request for an independent counsel.

September 14

U.S. District Court Judge Marvin Shoob opens Drogoul's sentencing hearing in Atlanta. (Boynton and Tough, 66.)

SEPTEMBER 30

The CIA provides Shoob with previously undisclosed cables which indicate that BNL-Rome knew about Drogoul's illegal conduct.

NOVEMBER 9

The three British directors of Matrix-Churchill, Paul Henderson, Trevor Abraham, and Peter Allen, are cleared of charges of illegally selling arms-making equipment to Iraq. The three men are cleared of the charges because evidence is given which reveals sanctioning of their activities by high-level government ministers.

British agents of MI5 and MI6 testify that Matrix-Churchill was allowed to sell machinery to Iraq by government officials. In exchange, Matrix-Churchill employees Paul Henderson and Mark Gutteridge provide information on Iraq's procurement network and plans for nuclear weaponry development. The Ministry of Trade and Industry, Ministry of Defense, and the Foreign Office had worked in tandem in allowing machine exports to Iraq after 1988, breaching guidelines against such exports as put forth by Foreign Minister Sir Geoffrey Howe to the House of Commons in 1985.

Alan Clark, the former minister of trade and industry, also testifies in the Matrix-Churchill trial that he had known that machinery exported to Iraq was to be used in making armaments.

The Matrix-Churchill court case also uncovers the involvement of four government ministers who had signed public interest immunity certificates, which had kept some 500 pages of government papers from being used in public court proceedings on the grounds that national security issues were pre-eminent. The four ministers were: Kenneth Clark, Home Secretary; Malcolm Rifkind, Secretary of State for Defense; Michael Heseltine, President of the Board of Trade; and Tristan Garel-Jones, Foreign Office Minister. Suppression of the government papers allowed the arrest of one of the Matrix-Churchill directors, Paul Henderson, by Customs officers in October 1990 to go unchallenged despite the fact that he had voluntarily assisted MI6 by providing information on the Iraqi arms procurement network and nuclear program.[10]

NOVEMBER 10

Responsibility for the investigation of the Iraqgate allegations in Britain is delegated to Lord Justice Scott, who, as a Court of Appeals judge, has had not had prior experience as a criminal lawyer. The case takes on added significance as critics of government policy charge that British soldiers had been vulnerable to attack from Iraqis armed with weapons manufactured with the help of British company exports.[11]

NOVEMBER 11

One of Britain's daily newspapers, *The Independent,* reports that opposition leaders in Parliament complain that the Iraqgate investigation headed by Lord Justice Scott is "the weakest form of inquiry." Lord Denning, who had presided over a similar government inquiry into the Profumo Affair in 1966, warns that relying on this form of inquiry compromises justice, because the inquiry will be held behind closed doors and will have no power to summon witnesses to give evidence under oath.

The format of the inquiry and the role of Lord Justice Scott parallels that of the Iran-Contra investigation in the U.S., with the appointment of Justice Walsh as an independent prosecutor in an inquiry closed to the public.[12]

NOVEMBER 16

Prime Minister John Major officially announces an independent inquiry into Iraqgate headed by Lord Justice Scott. Opposition leaders John Smith and Paddy Ashdown object to the terms of the inquiry because it will be held in private and will not be able to subpoena government ministers such as Margaret Thatcher or former Minister of Trade and Industry Alan Clark, contrary to the 1921 Tribunals of Inquiry Act.

A Right-to-Know Bill is sponsored by Member of Parliament Mark Fisher, which would give the public more access to official government documents and would apply to the current Iraqgate investigation.

Labor Party spokesman Robin Cook charges that Prime Minister John Major misled Parliament about Britain's aid in arming Iraq. He provides evidence that when Major was foreign secretary he had received a letter dated June 20, 1990, from Nicholas Ridley, former trade secretary, that warned about Matrix-Churchill's exports of arms-making machinery to Iraq. John Major had previously claimed that he had first learned about Matrix-Churchill's involvement in supplying Iraq with machinery from a *Sunday Times* newspaper report, six months after the dated letter.[13]

NOVEMBER 23

The British daily *The Guardian* writes that a CIA report dated April, 1990, shows that U.S. oil imports from Iraq rose from approximately 30 million barrels a year from 1985 to 1987 to about 250 million barrels in 1990. Multinational purchasers of the increased amounts of Iraqi oil in 1990, after the Iran-Iraq War had ended, included the Exxon Corporation, which trades as Esso in Britain.

The article also points out that the newly appointed Secretary of State in the Bush Administration, James Baker, had certified the Matrix-Churchill branch company in Solo, Ohio, as a valid U.S. company. James Baker, like George Bush, was a former Texas oilman, and Baker had personal holdings in U.S. oil companies, including Exxon Corporation, Amoco, and Texaco.

According to the same November 23rd issue of *The Guardian,* Britain's import of Iraqi oil also climbed dramatically: from 0 in 1987 and 1988 to 253,000 tons in 1989, and 1,000,000 tons, or 8.2 million barrels, in 1990.

The upsurge in oil imports from Iraq to Britain and the U.S. coincides with the time period when technology from both countries was being sent to Iraq.[14]

DECEMBER

Britain's Gulf War costs are approximately 1.5 billion pounds, while contributions from foreign governments to Britain total 2.15 billion pounds, leaving a controversial excess of just under one billion pounds.

The breakdown of financial contributions to Britain for its costs are as follows (in millions of pounds):[15]

Saudi Arabia	£ 690[16]
Kuwait	660
United Arab Emirates	278
Germany	274
Japan	192
South Korea	18
Hong Kong	16
Belgium	15
Other countries	14

ALSO IN DECEMBER

BNL headquarters in Rome sues the U.S. government in U.S. Federal Claims Court for $370 million. The amount of the suit represents Iraq's default on commodity loans that BNL had extended to Iraq, and which had been insured by the U.S. Department of Agriculture's Commodity Credit Corporation (CCC). Iraq had repaid all of its $1.7 billion debt to BNL except for the $370 million.[17] Even though the U.S. Agriculture Department had backed the BNL loans, it refuses to cover BNL's loss. Ultimately, if the Agriculture Department is forced to cover the loss, U.S. taxpayers are liable because a government agency secured the loan.

1993

JANUARY 21

Gonzalez announces that he will request all BNL and Iraq-related documents from the newly inaugurated Clinton Administration.[18]

FEBRUARY 25

According to Congressmember Gonzalez, BNL's efforts to persuade the Bush Administration not to indict the bank are revealed in the diary of Paulo DiVito, a senior official with BNL. The diary points out that several meetings had been arranged between the Italian ambassador to the U.S. and then-U.S. Attorney General Dick Thornburgh. Also, in order to influence Washington not to pursue judicial prosecution of its headquarters, BNL had hired former Secretary of State William P. Rogers (Nixon Administration) and former Attorney General Griffin B. Bell (Carter Administration) to represent it.[19]

MARCH

The Federal Reserve Board, as part of a second attempt at investigating whether BNL violated U.S. banking laws, issues a detailed subpoena for BNL documents related to loans to Iraq.[20]

MARCH 4

The *London Times* reports that Alan Clark, former British Trade Minister, will not be prosecuted for any role he may have played in allowing British arms-related exports to Iraq. Police are unable to establish "with sufficient certainty" that any of Clark's "inconsistent statements" are not true.

The Labour Party's trade and industry spokesman, Robin Cook, claims that the British government's export policies regarding Iraq are now open to legal scrutiny, since blame can no longer be placed on Alan Clark alone.[21]

MARCH 17

The three Matrix-Churchill directors, Paul Henderson, Trevor Abraham, and Peter Allen, who had been cleared earlier of violating British export laws because of government sanctioning of their activities, will give evidence at Lord Justice Scott's inquiry into government involvement in Iraqgate. However, Mark Gutteridge, another Matrix-Churchill employee and twenty-year agent of MI5 and MI6, refuses to give evidence. He tells the jury that he fears his past activities would endanger himself and his family if made public.

Some 30 witnesses, including past and present ministers, government civil servants, and intelligence agents will be called to give evidence.[22]

MARCH 31

Alan Clark, former Trade and Defense Minister, and Former Prime Minister Margaret Thatcher both affirm they will attend Lord Justice Scott's inquiry if invited.[23]

Lord Justice Scott announces that Prime Minister John Major will be asked to give evidence. All ministers and civil servants have been given blanket immunity from criminal prosecution related to charges of export violations.[24] Contrary to earlier assertions that court proceedings would be held behind closed doors, Lord Justice Scott's inquiry will be held in public unless national security reasons oblige some closed-door sessions.[25]

MAY

The U.S. Justice Department asks that a decision on whether to pay BNL $370 million be deferred pending the outcome of Christopher Drogoul's trial, scheduled for the fall of 1993. However, the Justice Department's request places the Clinton Administration in a Catch-22 situation: if Drogoul is convicted in Atlanta of bank fraud, and BNL headquarters are found innocent of having any knowledge of billions of dollars of funds being diverted to Iraq, then the U.S. government (vis-a-vis the taxpayer) must pay $370 million to BNL. On the other hand, if BNL headquarters is found guilty of complicity in the diversion of funds to Iraq, then past and present officials of the U.S. government will have to explain why the diversion of funds was tolerated, and why there was a cover-up of BNL headquarters activities.[26] (A court hearing in Atlanta in September 1992 had revealed that the CIA knew that BNL headquarter senior members had been aware of their bank's diversion of funds to Iraq. See entry for September 24, 1992.)

MAY 1

According to the *London Times*, some government ministers have complained about the earlier release of 500 pages of documents that show Britain's involvement in rearming Iraq. The release of the documents proved government complicity in export violations, and saved the three Matrix-Churchill directors from serving prison terms. Nevertheless, the ministers claim that release of the documents jeopardize national security. They feel that "immunity certificates," which when granted to ministers block the release of such documents, should be safeguarded from judicial review.

The *Times* also reports that the government of Jordan is prepared to give evidence at Scott's inquiry that the British government approved arms transfers to Iraq through Jordan.[27]

MAY 4

Lord Justice Scott's inquiry opens with evidence from Sir Richard Luce, a former Foreign Office minister.[28]

JULY 13

Former President George Bush is served with a subpoena to appear at Drogoul's trial to testify about Washington's policy toward Iraq in the 1980's and 1990's.[29]

JULY 28

Mr. Ian Blackley, the assistant head of the British Foreign Office's Middle East Department for two years up to October 1988, gives evidence at Lord Justice Scott's inquiry. He confirms that in December 1988 Sir Geoffrey Howe had relaxed export guidelines to Iraq. Howe, according to Blackley, had not wanted a public outcry about export policies to Iraq, especially at a time when Iraqis were gassing the Kurds.[30]

AUGUST

U.S. District Judge Ernest Tidwell, who is to preside at the trial of Christopher Drogoul in September, rules that at the coming trial Drogoul's defense lawyer may neither present evidence concerning Washington's policy tilt towards Iraq in the 1980s, nor evidence that senior officials of the Italian government have pleaded with the Bush Administration to limit its inquiry into the loans.[31]

SEPTEMBER 2

Drogoul, only a week away from trial, pleads guilty to one count of wire fraud and two counts of making false statements to bank regulators. His decision to plead guilty is thought to be linked to Judge Tidwell's August ruling.[32]

NOTES:

1. "How Minister Helped British Firms to Arm Saddam's Soldiers," *London Sunday Times,* December 2, 1990.
2. "How Minister Helped British Firms."
3. "How Minister Helped British Firms."
4. "How Minister Helped British Firms."
5. "Violations of the Geneva Protocols on the Environment by the U.S.," ARC/Arms Control Research Center, 1991.
6. R.D. Small, *Environmental Impact of Damage to Kuwaiti Oil Facilities,* Report (for U.S. Defense Nuclear Agency,) Pacific-Sierra Research Corporation, Santa Monica, January 1991.
7. *The Guardian,* October 28, 1992.
8. Martin Bailey, John McGhie and Peter Beaumont, "Britain Aided Saddam's A-bomb Plot," *The Observer,* November 29, 1992.

9. Andrew Alderson, "Saddam's Curse," *Sunday Times,* November 15, 1992. "Spy Says British Knew of Iraqi Deals," Eugene Robinson, November 9, 1992. "Profits Lured Britain to Accept Iraqi Deal," Eugene Robinson and Jeffrey Smith, *Washington Post,* November 24, 1992.

10. William Tuohy and Douglas Frantz, "Three Britons Cleared in Iraq Arms Sales Case," *Los Angeles Times,* November 10, 1992. Nick Cohen, "Ministers' Explanations of 'Coverup' Dismissed," *The Independent,* November 11, 1992. Eugene Robinson, "Britain to Probe Cabinet Role in Iraqi Sales," *Washington Post,* November 11, 1992.

11. Nick Cohen, "Appointment of 'Resolute and Tough' Judge Praised," *The Independent,* November 11, 1992.

12. Colin Brown and Nick Cohen, "Judicial Inquiry Condemned as Weak," *The Independent,* November 11, 1992.

13. Martin Linton, "Freedom of Information Bill Gives Campaigners New Hope," *The Guardian,* November 17, 1992. See also Patrick Wintour and Michael White, "Fowler Claims Cook Lacks 'Even A Smoking Pop-Gun,'" *The Guardian,* November 19, 1992.

14. Simon Tisdall, Richard Norton-Taylor and Simon Beavis, "Iraq Used Oil to Beat Arms Ban," and Simon Tisdall, "Need for Cheap Energy Greased Wheels for Saddam Deal," *The Guardian,* November 23, 1992.

15. David Hencke, "Gulf War Left U.K. 650 Million Pounds in Profit," *The Guardian,* December 2, 1992.

16. Of this figure, 108 million pounds were contributed in the form of free petrol, ammunition and loaned equipment.

17. Phone conversation with Joe Reilly, staff member to Henry Gonzalez's Congressional Banking Committee.

18. Douglas Frantz, "Gonzalez Vows to Pursue Full-Scale Probe of Bank Fraud Case," *Los Angeles Times,* January 22, 1993.

19. Neil A. Lewis, "Diary Said to Reveal Bank's Tactics in Iraq Case," *New York Times,* February 26, 1993.

20. John F. Fialka, "Fed, Taking Second Look at BNL Case, Issues Detailed Subpoena for Documents," *Wall Street Journal,* March 11, 1993.

21. Michael Dynes, "No Prosecution for Clark in Matrix Affair," *London Times,* March 4, 1993.

22. Christopher Elliott, "Matrix-Churchill Men Want Legal Backup In Enquiry," *London Times,* March 17, 1993.

23. Michael Dynes and Christopher Elliott, "Arms-to-Iraq Judge Explains Guidelines for Enquiry," *London Times,* March 31, 1993.

24. Michael Dynes and Christopher Elliott, "Iraq Arms Enquiry to Invite Thatcher," *London Times,* April 1, 1993.

25. Michael Dynes and Christopher Elliott, "Iraq Arms Enquiry to Invite Thatcher."

26. William Safire, "Iraqgate Giveaway," *New York Times,* May 20, 1993.

27. Michael Dynes and Christopher Elliott, "Court Gag 'Could Halt Another Matrix'," *London Times,* May 1, 1993.

28. Michael Dynes, "Civil Servants Fear Iraq Arms Evidence Will Wreck Careers," *London Times,* May 4, 1993.

29. Neil A. Lewis, "Bush Gets Served With A Subpoena," *New York Times,* July 14, 1993.

30. Chris Elliott, "Iraq Sale Wrong, Says Foreign Office Man," *London Times,* July 28, 1993.

31. Neil A. Lewis, "Plea in Bank Fraud Forecloses Questions on Iraqi Arms Sales," *New York Times,* September 3, 1993.

32. Neil A. Lewis, "Plea in Bank Fraud Forecloses Questions."

Iraq Business Forum

Set up in May 1985 by Marshall Wiley, former U.S. ambassador to Oman, the Iraq Business Forum was for any United States company interested in doing business with Iraq, and acted as a pro-Iraq lobby. The following list was excerpted from *The Death Lobby* by Kenneth R. Timmerman. Reprinted by permission of Houghton Mifflin Co. All rights reserved.

A.M.E. International, Inc.
American Cast Iron Pipe Co.
American Iraqi Finance & Trade
American Rice, Inc.
AMOCO Corporation
Anodyne, Inc.
Arabian National Shipping Corporation
Arthur Andersen & Company
AT&T
Baker Hughes Production Tools, Inc.
The Bank of New York
Bankers Trust Company
Bechtel Group, Inc.
Bell Helicopter-Textron
BMY
British Gas, Exploration & Production Division
British Petroleum
Brown & Root, Inc.
Caltex Petroleum Corporation
Caterpillar, Inc.
Charles Percy & Associates
Chevron Corporation
Comet Rice, Inc.
Conoco, Inc.
Continental Grain Company
Crescent Construction Company
Crescent International Petroleum U.S.A
Dantzler Lumber & Export Co., Inc.
Dearborn Financial, Inc.
Dresser Industries, Inc., Dresser Pump Division
Entrade International Limited
Exxon Company, International
Fairbanks Management Corporation
Fentex International Corporation
First City Bancorporation of Texas, Inc.
Fisher Scientific
General Motors Corporation
The Groney Company, Ltd.
Gulf Interstate Engineering Co.

Hunt Oil Company
International Resources Trading Corporation
Ionics, Incorporated
J.A. Jones Construction Co.
Jas. A. Miller Tobacco Co.
Lincoln-Kaltek Joint Venture
Lindner and Company
Lockheed Corporation
Luxor California Exports Corp.
Mathey International, Ltd.
Midgulf Industrial Consultants, Inc.
Mobil Oil Corporation
Morrison Knudsen Corporation
M.W. Kellog Company
Niedermeyer-Martin Company
Norwich Eaton Pharmaceuticals, Inc.
Obelisk Corporation
Occidental International Exploration & Production Co.
Ohra Corporation
Pepsicola International
Petrolite Corporation
Philip Morris International
Power Marketing Group, Inc.
Riedel International, Inc.
Servaas, Inc.
SMI/Sneed-McBride International, Inc.
Smith Meter, Inc.
Tabikh Interests, Inc.
Teletec Corporation
Telwaw International, Inc.
Texaco, Inc.
United Technologies Corporation
Unocal Corporation
Valmont Industries, Inc.
Westinghouse Electric Corporation
Woodhouse, Drake & Carey (Trading)
Xerox

The Asian Connection

Background Information

In contrast to China, which sold armaments to Iraq on the open market, Japan and India chose the alternative route of doing business by supplying Iraq with dual-use chemicals, which can be used for legitimate industrial purposes or as precursors in the final production of lethal chemical weapons. Much less is currently known about the role of Asian nations in arming Iraq than is known about the role of the West. The following is an overview of the information that has so far come to light.

In 1980, at the beginning of the Iran-Iraq War, China sold $3.3 billion worth of armaments to Iraq, according to the Stockholm International Peace Research Institute (SIPRI) 1990 report. The arms package included 1,300 T-59 and T-69 tanks and 650 troop carriers. Even though China sold weapons to both Iran and Iraq during the war, Iraq was China's principal arms client between 1979 and 1983.[1]

In 1986, China developed missile guidance systems and new cryogenic liquid-fuel mixtures for missiles being built at Brazil's CTA complex. Soon afterwards, China's breakthrough in creating new cryogenic fuel mixtures was used in Iraq's long-range missile program, Project 395, located at the SAAD 16 complex.[2]

In 1989, in a more indirect business arrangement with Iraq, the Nissho Shoji company of Tokyo sold chemicals with weapons precursor potential to the Indian company Srinivas for subsequent sale to Iraq, according to the *Far Eastern Economic Review*. A chemical company in Gujarat, India, supplied equipment to a chemical plant in Iraq that was producing fluorine, a precursor ingredient used in the production of chemical gas.[3]

Exomet Chemicals of Bombay financed shipments to Iraq, arranged by an Iraqi business-man of German nationality, Kamal Saudi. Credit for the transferred shipments to Iraq was established through another company, Kim Khaleej, which was registered in Baghdad and Singapore. Shipment documents revealed that at least 5,400 tons (10,800,000 pounds) of toxic chemicals had been sent to Iraq. The list of chemicals included phosphorus trichloride, oxychloride, thionyl chloride, phosphorus sulfide, and sodium cyanide. They were sold to Iraq by Indian firms that included United Phosphorus of Baroda and Bombay. Once again, all letters of credit were linked to the Kim Khaleej company in Singapore, according to the *Far Eastern Economic Review*.[4]

West German companies, which had been arranging chemical shipments to Iraq throughout the 1980s, had also established linkups with Indian firms such as Transpek and Exomet. Exomet's manager, Krishan Lal Khanna, admitted that he had made periodic trips to Iraq as a consultant to the Al Qaim phosphorus mine project. The mine, first constructed by the Belgian firm Sybetra in 1976, extracted phosphate deposits, which are critical for the production of the nerve agents tabun and sarin.[5]

—*Daniel Robicheau*

NOTES:

1. Stockholm International Peace Research Institute, *SIPRI Yearbook of 1990,* Report. See also Natalie J. Goldring, *Arms Transfers to the Middle East,* Report, Defense Budget Project, Washington DC, April 1991.
2. Kenneth R. Timmerman, *The Death Lobby: How the West Armed Iraq* (New York: Houghton Mifflin Co.), 1991, 256.
3. James Clad, "Chemical Reaction," *Far Eastern Economic Review,* September 6, 1990.
4. James Clad, "Chemical Reaction."
5. Kenneth R. Timmerman, *The Death Lobby,* 50-51.

Recommendations

18 POINTS ON THE GULF WAR

Many of the individuals and agencies who participated in this investigation recommended immediate actions to deal with the effects of the Gulf War. They also had suggestions for long-term reform to prevent, or mitigate the effects of, all wars. The following 18 points are an amalgam of their comments, pre-existing published recommendations, and the analysis of the Arms Control Research Center.

We present these recommendations with an important caveat. The editors feel it is important to remind the reader that these recommendations are fundamentally signposts. Each point could be the subject of an entire chapter, if not a separate volume. And while the editors have worked hard to ensure that discussions of the root causes of the conflict were incorporated into *Hidden Casualties, Volume II*, it is clear to us that at its most basic level the Gulf War is symptomatic of the conflict over resources, economics, culture and the right to self-determination between the developed world and developing countries. Without a long-term process to resolve these issues, wars in the Gulf and elsewhere will continue to plague the international community.

IMMEDIATE INITIATIVES

THE GLOBAL COMMUNITY MUST HAVE ACCESS TO INFORMATION
1) All available data on the environmental and health impacts of the Gulf War, whatever their source or political implications, should be made available to all interested parties. International information programs should be adequately funded.

A THOROUGH INVESTIGATION IS NEEDED
2) International organizations should be adequately funded in their efforts to assess the damage to the environment and public health, to monitor the effects of the war, and to clean up the Gulf region.
3) Environmental investigations should look at the impacts of the Gulf War on all nations in the Gulf region, including Iran and Iraq, where the damage caused by the war has not been adequately studied. Wider effects, including potential effects on the monsoons and global impacts, should be investigated further with a view to modeling the extra-regional impacts of future conflicts.

HUMANITARIAN RELIEF MUST BE A PRIORITY
4) Nonmilitary sanctions against Iraq should be lifted immediately to prevent further punishment of the Iraqi people.

CONFLICT RESOLUTION NEEDS TO BEGIN IMMEDIATELY

5) A regional peace conference of the Gulf states should be sponsored by the appropriate agency in the UN to begin the process of resolving longstanding conflicts and to develop a mechanism for crisis management. Regional organizations, such as the League of Arab States, should consider an early-warning system and an early conflict resolution program to initiate preventive diplomacy. The UN should have similar early conflict resolution programs.

6) Regional agreements among all the relevant governments to manage and monitor war-related and other environmental problems in the Gulf should be established. A regional agreement on environmental cooperation might include long-term environmental monitoring, management of water supplies, development of regional fisheries and the establishment of a cross-border Peace Park. The World Conservation Monitoring Centre recommends that such a park include environmentally sensitive areas (wetlands, marshes, coral islands, seagrass, mangrove and mud flats) bordering the Gulf in Iran, Iraq, Saudi Arabia, and Kuwait.

LONGER TERM PROGRAMS

THE REGIONAL ARMS RACE MUST BE STOPPED

7) Efforts to ban sales and weapons of mass destruction in the region (and globally) should be initiated without being selectively applied. Current efforts to keep additional countries from going nuclear should be supplemented by regional arms control and disarmament efforts, and talks aimed at nonaggression pacts.

INTERNATIONAL DISARMAMENT SHOULD BE AN IMPORTANT PART OF THE REGIONAL PEACE PROCESS

8) The International Atomic Energy Agency (IAEA) should get out of the business of promoting nuclear power and focus on halting proliferation. It is fundamentally impossible for the agency to both promote nuclear power and prevent its abuse as a means of creating nuclear weapons. Stricter safeguards and more aggressive inspections should be implemented and loopholes should be eliminated to ensure that nuclear materials are not being used for military purposes. Funding of the IAEA safeguards budget should be increased. There should be stricter controls on the export of nuclear or dual-capable technologies. The current moratorium on nuclear weapons testing should be formalized under a Comprehensive Nuclear Test Ban Treaty. Additional international commitments should be made to ban attacks against nuclear reactors, and the production of new fissile material including materials for reactors.

9) The United Nations should immediately move to ban the use and production of land and sea mines. Millions of these indiscriminate weapons deployed around the world remain unrecovered even though the conflicts that prompted their use have been resolved. As a result, casualties from these weapons continue to mount, with children being the hardest hit.

10) A protocol should be added to the Geneva Convention to explicitly ban the use of the environment as a weapon of war and severely curtail incidental environmental damage during war. An independent international body should automatically evaluate the behavior of all sides, including the use and abuse of the environment, in light of international law. The U.S. should sign the 1977 Protocols to the Geneva Convention.

THE UNITED NATIONS SHOULD FURTHER DEFINE ITS ROLE IN INTERNATIONAL PEACEKEEPING

11) If the United Nations is going to involve itself in using military force to safeguard national sovereignty or human rights, then it should sponsor for this purpose a multilateral force, modeled on NATO, with a rotating leadership and an open membership.

12) The United Nations should set the international standard by undertaking environmental impact assessments prior to initiating peacekeeping and police actions. Permanent independent bodies, both within the United Nations and outside it, should compile assessments, similar to the environmental impact statement in the U.S., to evaluate the likely environmental and health impacts of armed conflicts. Prewar statements should be prepared and publicized and the appropriate international relief, humanitarian, environmental and refugee organizations—United Nations Children's Fund (UNICEF), United Nations Development Programme (UNDP), United Nations Environment Programme (UNEP), and the International Committee of the Red Cross—should be consulted before any decisions are made to go to war. Assessments should be made, and updated at regular intervals, of the damage inflicted by the wars being waged around the world.[1] All assessments should be used to publicize the impacts of the damage caused by war and to ascertain where preventive diplomacy and aid are needed.

A UNITED NATIONS ENVIRONMENTAL CRISIS CENTER SHOULD BE CREATED TO COORDINATE THE RESPONSE TO REGIONAL AND INTERNATIONAL ECOLOGICAL HAZARDS

13) Permanent environmental and health crisis centers to coordinate international responses to ecological disasters should be established. Baseline studies and monitoring should begin directly after an emergency and monitoring should continue for as long as judged appropriate. A pool of funds should be available deal with the crucial first stages of an emergency. Specifically, the 1990 General Assembly Resolution 44/224 should be augmented to include the creation of an emergency environmental crisis center.

14) More comprehensive health and environmental baseline studies should be conducted around the world to more accurately assess the impacts of extraordinary events, such as wars and natural disasters.

AN INTERNATIONAL STANDARD FOR RESOURCE CONSERVATION SHOULD BE ESTABLISHED AS A MEANS OF REDUCING CONFLICTS

15) An energy conservation policy should be made an international priority to encour-

age the efficient use of energy resources and alternatives to oil, nuclear power and other hazardous energy resources.

THE UNITED NATIONS SHOULD BE REFORMED

16) Reform of the United Nations should be initiated to strengthen the role and functions of the International Court of Justice, the General Assembly, UN-affiliated regional organizations, and UN-affiliated nongovernmental organizations.

17) As it is currently configured, the Security Council can be too easily swayed or stymied by the actions of a single member. Security Council members should comply with Article 27 of the UN Charter, which curtails the power of the veto. The United Nations should establish a special commission to explore expanding the membership of the Security Council and the development of a bi-cameral decision-making process more in line with the congressional and parliamentary standard now in place in the world's democratic governments.

INTERNATIONAL LAW MUST BE APPLIED IMPARTIALLY

18) International law must be applied without bias and without double standards. All the human rights conventions should be signed, ratified and implemented, to ensure the economic, political, social, cultural and religious rights of all peoples.

NOTES:

1. Neither the UN Disarmament Agency, the U.S. State Department, the U.S. Arms Control and Disarmament Agency nor the Pentagon compile statistics on ongoing wars. The Stockholm International Peace Research Institute has tried to fill the gap, reporting that "in 1992, major armed conflicts were waged in 30 locations around the world." *SIPRI Yearbook 1993: World Armaments and Disarmaments*, Oxford University Press, 1993. For another nongovernmental estimate, see Micheael Kidron and Dan Smith, *The New State of War and Peace* (New York: Simon & Schuster Inc.), New York, 1991. Richard Griggs, Ph.D., a political geographer with the University of California, believes there is a danger of misreading the number of wars, because many are categorized as rebel attacks, or as ethnic conflicts. He counts 122 ongoing wars, most of them armed conflicts between state governments and peoples living in a historical homeland. Interview with Richard Griggs, September 28, 1993.

Appendix 1: International Law

United Nations General Assembly Resolution 44/224

International co-operation in the monitoring, assessment and anticipation of environmental threats and in assistance in cases of environmental emergencies.

22 December 1989

Adopted without a vote

The General Assembly

Convinced that one of the main global problems facing the world today is the deterioration of the environment,

Aware that increasing environmental degradation caused by human activities has led in some cases to irreversible changes in the environment, which threaten life-sustaining ecosystems and undermine the health, well-being, development prospects and the very survival of life on the planet,

Also aware that potential environmental disasters, whether natural, accidental or caused by human beings, as well as accidents could pose serious and immediate dangers to populations and to the economic development and the environment of the affected countries and regions,

Convinced that through monitoring, assessment, anticipation and prompt multilateral response, if requested—in particular, on the part of the United Nations system—environmental threats could be minimized or even prevented,

Also convinced that early warning of emerging environmental threats and degradation would help Governments to take preventive action,

Noting with appreciation that work undertaken by the United Nations Environment Programme to develop criteria for the identification of environmental threats at the national, regional, and global levels,

Stressing the need for close co-operation between all countries—in particular, through a broad exchange of information, scientific knowledge and experience as well as transfer of technology—in monitoring, assessing and anticipating environmental threats, dealing with environmental emergencies, and rendering timely assistance, at the request of Governments, in accordance with respective national laws, regulations and policies and taking into account the particular needs and requirements of the developing countries,

Affirming the need in this context for closer co-operation between the United Nations Environment Programme, the Office of the United Nations Disaster Relief Co-ordinator, the World Health Organization and the World Meteorological Organization and other competent organs, programmes and agencies of the United Nations system, bearing in mind the co-ordinating role of the United Nations Environment Programme on environmental matters in the United Nations system,

Taking note of the fact that other proposals have been made on strengthening and improving the effectiveness within the United Nations system of international co-operation in monitoring, assessing and anticipating environmental threats and the rendering of timely assistance in cases of environmental emergencies,

1. Recognizes the need to strengthen international co-operation in monitoring, assessing and anticipating environmental threats and rendering assistance in cases of environmental emergencies;

2. Reaffirms that the United Nations system, through the United Nations General Assembly, owing to its universal character, is the appropriate forum for concerted political action on global environmental problems;

3. Underlines the importance of broader participation in Earthwatch, established by the United Nations Conference on the Human Environment and operated by the United Nations Environment Programme, in order to strengthen its capacity to make authoritative assessments, anticipate environmental degradation and issue early warnings to the international community;

4. Reaffirms that States have, in accordance with the Charter of the United Nations and the principles of international law, the sovereign right to exploit their own resources pursuant to their environmental policies and also reaffirms their responsibility to ensure that activities within their jurisdiction or control do not cause damage to the environment of other States or of areas beyond the limits of national jurisdiction and the need to play their due role in preserving and protecting the global and regional environment in accordance with their capacities and specific responsibilities;

5. Requests the Secretary-General, assisted by the Executive Director of the United Nations Environment Programme, to prepare a report, on the basis of the views of Member States and existing national and international legislation in this field, containing proposals and recommendations on possible ways and means to strengthen the capacity of the United Nations:

(a) To monitor, assess and anticipate those threats;

(b) To define criteria for determining when environmental degradation undermines health, well-being, development prospects and the very survival of life on the planet to an extent that international co-operation may be required, if requested;

(c) To issue early warnings to the international community when such degradation becomes imminent;

(d) To facilitate intergovernmental co-operation in monitoring, assessing and anticipating environmental threats;

(e) To assist Governments facing environmental emergencies, at their request;

(f) To mobilize financial resources and technical co-operation to fulfill the above tasks, taking into account the needs of the countries concerned, particularly the developing countries;

6. Also requests the Secretary-General to submit the report mentioned above for consideration during the preparatory process for the United Nations Conference on Environment and Development;

7. Invites the Governing Council of the United Nations Environment Programme to consider the report referred to in paragraph 5 above and to present its views thereon to the General Assembly at its forty-sixth session, through the Economic and Social Council.

Excerpts From International Agreements on War and the Environment

Below are relevant sections of the Protocol I Additional to the Geneva Conventions of 1949, done at Berne, June 10, 1977. Both Iraq and the U.S. are signatories.

ARTICLE 35.3

It is prohibited to employ methods or means of warfare which are intended, or may be expected, to cause widespread, long-term and severe damage to the natural environment.

ARTICLE 54.2

It is prohibited to attack, destroy, remove or render useless objects indispensable to the survival of the civilian population, such as foodstuffs, agricultural areas for the production of foodstuffs, crops, livestock, drinking water installations and supplies and irrigation works, for the specific purpose of denying them for their sustenance value to the civilian population or to the adverse Party, whatever the motive, whether in order to starve out civilians, to cause them to move away, or for any other motive.

ARTICLE 55

Section 1: Care shall be taken in warfare to protect the natural environment against widespread, long-term and severe damage. This protection includes a prohibition of the use of methods of warfare which are intended or may be expected to cause such damage to the natural environment and thereby to prejudice the health and survival of the population.

Section 2: Attacks against the natural environment by way of reprisals are prohibited.

ARTICLE 56

(Prohibits attacks against) works or installations containing dangerous forces, namely dams, dikes and nuclear electrical generating stations.

Below are the relevant sections of the Convention on the Prohibition of Military or Any Other Hostile Use of Environmental Modification Techniques (ENMOD), done at Geneva, May 18, 1977.

ARTICLE 1

Section 1: (Asks that) each state party to the Convention undertake not to engage in military or any other hostile use of environmental modification techniques having widespread, long-lasting or severe effects as the means of destruction, damage or injury to any other State Party.

Article 2: (Explains "environmental modification techniques" as referring to) any technique for changing—through the deliberate manipulation of natural processes—the dynamics, composition or structure of the Earth, including its biota, lithosphere, hydrosphere and atmosphere, or of outer space.

A New Geneva Convention?

A number of organizations, including *ARC/Arms Control Research Center, Beyond War, the Sierra Club, Earth Island Institute, Greenpeace, The National Audubon Society and the Natural Resources Defense Council are calling for a new Geneva Convention based on the following principles:*

I. The environment may not be used as a weapon.

II. Weapons aimed at the environment must be banned.

III. Indirect or unintended damage to the environment (such as river pollution resulting from bombing of sanitation facilities) must be forbidden.

III. A. The attacking of targets of marginal military value, but large-scale ecological and human health consequences, such as sanitation and water treatment plants, must also be forbidden.

IV. Destruction of or damage to installations which may release dangerous radioactive or poisonous substances into the environment must be forbidden.

V. Nuclear, chemical and biological weapons must be banned.

VI. Nature parks and reserves of special ecological importance must be strictly demilitarized zones.

VII. Nuclear-powered military vessels, whose destruction in war could cause widespread environmental contamination, must be eliminated.

United Nations Security Council Resolutions

Reprinted below are the relevant resolutions passed by the United Nations Security Council following Iraq's invasion of Kuwait.

RESOLUTION 660

2 AUGUST 1990

Relating, inter alia, to the Council's condemnation of the Iraqi invasion of Kuwait.

Adopted by a vote of 14 in favor and 0 against. One member, Yemen, did not participate in the vote.

Sponsors: Canada, Colombia, Cote d'Ivoire, Ethiopia, Finland, France, Malaysia, United Kingdom, United States.

The Security Council,

Alarmed by the invasion of Kuwait on 2 August 1990 by the military forces of Iraq,

Determining that there exists a breach of international peace and security as regards the Iraqi invasion of Kuwait,

Acting under Articles 39 and 40 of the Charter of the United Nations,

1. Condemns the Iraqi invasion of Kuwait;
2. Demands that Iraq withdraw immediately and unconditionally all its forces to the positions in which they were located on 1 August 1990;
3. Calls upon Iraq and Kuwait to begin immediately intensive negotiations for the resolution of their differences and supports all efforts in this regard, and especially those of the League of Arab States;
4. Decides to meet again as necessary to consider further steps to ensure compliance with the present resolution.

The following are excerpts from the UN Charter, with reference to Resolution 660.

ARTICLE 39

The Security Council shall determine the existence of any threat to the peace, breach of the peace, or act of aggression and shall make recommendations, or decide what measures shall be taken in accordance with Articles 41 and 42, to maintain or restore international peace and security.

ARTICLE 40

In order to prevent an aggravation of the situation, the Security Council may, before making the recommendations or deciding upon the measures provided for in Article 39, call upon the parties concerned to comply with such provisional measures as it deems necessary or desirable. Such provisional measures shall be without prejudice to the rights, claims, or position of the parties concerned. The Security Council shall duly take account of failure to comply with such provisional measures.

ARTICLE 41

The Security Council may decide what measures not involving the use of armed force are to be employed to give effect to its decisions, and it may call upon Members of the United Nations to apply such measures. These may include complete or partial interruption of economic relations and of rail, sea, air, postal, telegraphic, radio and other means of communication, and the severance of diplomatic relations.

RESOLUTION 661

6 AUGUST 1990

Adopted by a vote of 13 in favor, 0 against and 2 abstentions (Cuba and Yemen).
Sponsors: Canada, Colombia, Cote d'Ivoire, Ethiopia, Finland, France, Malaysia, United Kingdom, United States, Zaire.

The Security Council,

Reaffirming its resolution 660 (1990) of 2 August 1990,

Deeply concerned that that resolution has not been implemented and that the invasion by Iraq of Kuwait continues with further loss of human life and material destruction,

Determined to bring the invasion and occupation of Kuwait by Iraq to an end and to restore the sovereignty, independence and territorial integrity of Kuwait,

Noting that the legitimate Government of Kuwait has expressed its readiness to comply with resolution 660 (1990),

Mindful of its responsibilities under the Charter of the United Nations for the maintenance of international peace and security,

Affirming the inherent right of individual or collective self-defense, in response to the armed attack by Iraq against Kuwait, in accordance with Article 51 of the Charter,

Acting under Chapter VII of the Charter of the United Nations,

1. Determines that Iraq so far has failed to comply with paragraph 2 of resolution 660 (1990) and has usurped the authority of the legitimate Government of Kuwait;
2. Decides, as a consequence, to take the following measures to secure compliance of Iraq with paragraph 2 of resolution 660 (1990) and to restore the authority of the legitimate Government of Kuwait;
3. Decides that all States shall prevent:
   a) The import into their territories of all commodities and products originating in Iraq or Kuwait exported therefrom after the date of the present resolution;

b) Any activities by their nationals or in their territories which would promote or are calculated to promote the export or transshipment of any commodities or products from Iraq or Kuwait; and any dealings by their nationals or their flag vessels or in their territories in any commodities or products originating in Iraq or Kuwait and exported therefrom after the date of the present resolution, including in particular any transfer of funds to Iraq or Kuwait for the purposes of such activities or dealings;

c) The sale or supply by their nationals or from their territories or using their flag vessels of any commodities or products, including weapons or any other military equipment, whether or not originating in their territories but not including supplies intended strictly for medical purposes, and, in humanitarian circumstances, foodstuffs, to any person or body in Iraq or Kuwait or to any person or body for the purposes of any business carried on in or operated from Iraq or Kuwait, and any activities by their nationals or in their territories which promote or are calculated to promote such sale or supply of such commodities or products;

4. Decides that all States shall not make available to the Government of Iraq or to any commercial, industrial or public utility undertaking in Iraq or Kuwait, any funds or any other financial or economic resources and shall prevent their nationals and any persons within their territories from removing from their territories or otherwise making available to that Government or to any such undertaking any such funds or resources and from remitting any other funds to persons or bodies within Iraq or Kuwait, except payments exclusively for strictly medical or humanitarian purposes and, in humanitarian circumstances, foodstuffs;

5. Calls upon all States, including States nonmembers of the United Nations, to act strictly in accordance with the provisions of the present resolution notwithstanding any contract entered into or license granted before the date of the present resolution;

6. Decides to establish, in accordance with rule 28 of the provisional rules of procedure of the Security Council, a Committee of the Security Council consisting of all the members of the Council, to undertake the following tasks and to report on its work to the Council with its observations and recommendations:

a) To examine the reports on the progress of the implementation of the present resolution which will be submitted by the Secretary-General;

b) To seek from all States further information regarding the action taken by them concerning the effective implementation of the provisions laid down in the present resolution;

7. Calls upon all States to co-operate fully with the Committee in the fulfillment of its task, including supplying such information as may be sought by the Committee in pursuance of the present resolution;

8. Requests the Secretary-General to provide all necessary assistance to the Committee and to make the necessary arrangements in the Secretariat for the purpose;

9. Decides that, notwithstanding paragraphs 4 through 8 above, nothing in the present resolution shall prohibit assistance to the legitimate Government of Kuwait, and calls

upon all States:

a) To take appropriate measures to protect assets of the legitimate Government of Kuwait and its agencies;

b) Not to recognize any regime set up by the occupying Power;

10. Requests the Secretary-General to report to the Council on the progress of the implementation of the present resolution, the first report to be submitted within thirty days;

11. Decides to keep this item on its agenda and to continue its efforts to put an early end to the invasion by Iraq.

RESOLUTION 678

29 NOVEMBER 1990

Adopted by a vote of 12 in favor, 2 against (Cuba and Yemen) and 1 abstention (China).
Sponsors: Canada, France, Romania, Soviet Union, United Kingdom, United States.

The Security Council,

Recalling and reaffirming its resolutions 660 (1990) of 2 August 1990, 661 (1990) of 6 August 1990, 662 (1990) of 9 August 1990, 664 (1990) of 18 August 1990, 665 (1990) of 25 August 1990, 666 (1990) of 13 September 1990, 667 (1990) of 16 September 1990, 669 (1990) of 24 September 1990, 674 (1990) of 29 October 1990 and 677 (1990) of 28 November 1990,

Noting that, despite all efforts by the United Nations, Iraq refuses to comply with its obligations to implement resolution 660 (1990) and the above-mentioned subsequent relevant resolutions, in flagrant contempt of the Security Council,

Mindful of its duties and responsibilities under the Charter of the United Nations for the maintenance and preservation of international peace and security,

Determined to secure full compliance with its decisions,

Acting under Chapter VII of the Charter,

1. Demands that Iraq comply fully with resolution 660 (1990) and all subsequent relevant resolutions, and decides, while maintaining all its decisions, to allow Iraq one final opportunity, as a pause of goodwill, to do so;

2. Authorizes Member States cooperating with the Government of Kuwait, unless Iraq on or before 15 January 1991 fully implements, as set forth in paragraph 1 above, the foregoing resolutions, to use all necessary means to uphold and implement resolution 660 (1990) and all subsequent relevant resolutions and to restore international peace and security in the area;

3. Requests all States to provide appropriate support for the actions undertaken in pursuance of paragraph 2 of the present resolution;

4. Requests the States concerned to keep the Security Council regularly informed on the progress of actions undertaken pursuant to paragraphs 2 and 3 of the present resolution;

5. Decides to remain seized of the matter.

RESOLUTION 686

2 MARCH 1991

Adopted by a vote of 11 in favor, 1 against (Cuba) and 3 abstentions (China, India, Yemen).
Sponsors: Belgium, France, Romania, Soviet Union, United Kingdom, United States, Zaire.

The Security Council,

Recalling and reaffirming its resolutions 660 (1990), 661 (1990), 662 (1990), 664 (1990), 665 (1990), 666 (1990), 667 (1990), 669 (1990, 670 (1990), 669 (1990), 670 (1990), 674 (1990), 677 (1990) and 678 (1990),

Recalling the obligations of Member States under Article 25 of the Charter,

Recalling paragraph 9 of resolution 661 (1990) regarding assistance to the Government of Kuwait and paragraph 3(c) of that resolution regarding supplies strictly for medical purposes and, in humanitarian circumstances, foodstuffs,

Taking note of the letters of the Foreign Minister of Iraq confirming Iraq's agreement to comply fully with all the resolutions noted above (S/22275), and stating its intention to release prisoners of war immediately (S/22273),

Taking note of the suspension of offensive combat operations by the forces of Kuwait and the Member States cooperating with Kuwait pursuant to resolution 678 (1990),

Bearing in mind the need to be assured of Iraq's peaceful intentions, and the objective in resolution 678 (1990) of restoring international peace and security in the region,

Underlining the importance of Iraq taking the necessary measures which would permit a definitive end to the hostilities;

Affirming the commitment of all Member States to the independence, sovereignty and territorial integrity of Iraq and Kuwait, and noting the intention expressed by the Member States co-operating under paragraph 2 of Security Council resolution 678 (1990) to bring their military presence in Iraq to an end as soon as possible consistent with achieving the objectives of the resolution,

Acting under Chapter VII of the Charter,

1. Affirms that all twelve resolutions noted above continue to have full force and effect;
2. Demands that Iraq implement its acceptance of all twelve resolutions noted above and in particular that Iraq;
   a) Rescind immediately its actions purporting to annex Kuwait;
   b) Accept in principle its liability under international law for any loss, damage or injury arising in regard to Kuwaitis and third States, and their nationals and corporations, as a result of the invasion and illegal occupation of Kuwait by Iraq;
   c) Immediately release under the auspices of the International Committee of the Red Cross, Red Cross Societies, or Red Crescent Societies, all Kuwaiti and third country nationals detained by Iraq and return the remains of any deceased Kuwaiti and third country nationals so detained; and

    d) Immediately begin to return all Kuwaiti property seized by Iraq, to be completed in the shortest possible period;

3. Further demands that Iraq:

    a) Cease hostile or provocative actions by its forces against all Member States, including missile attacks and flights of combat aircraft;

    b) Designate military commanders to meet with counterparts from the forces of Kuwait and the Member States co-operating with Kuwait pursuant to resolution 678 (1990) to arrange for the military aspects of a cessation of hostilities at the earliest possible time;

    c) Arrange for immediate access to and release of all prisoners of war under the auspices of the International Committee of the Red Cross and return the remains of any deceased personnel of the forces of Kuwait and the Member States co-operating with Kuwait pursuant to resolution 678 (1990); and

    d) Provide all information and assistance in identifying Iraqi mines, booby traps and other explosives as well as any chemical and biological weapons and material in Kuwait, in areas of Iraq where forces of Member States co-operating with Kuwait pursuant to resolution 678 (1990) are present temporarily, and in the adjacent waters;

4. Recognizes that during the period required for Iraq to comply with paragraphs 2 and 3 above, the provisions of paragraph 2 of resolution 678 (1990) remain valid;

5. Welcomes the decision of Kuwait and Member States co-operating with Kuwait pursuant to resolution 678 (1990) to provide access and to commence immediately the release of Iraqi prisoners of war as required by the terms of the Third Geneva Convention of 1949, under the auspices of the International Committee of the Red Cross;

6. Requests all Member States, as well as the United Nations, the specialized agencies and other international organizations in the United Nations system, to take all appropriate action to co-operate with the Government and people of Kuwait in the reconstruction of their country;

7. Decides that Iraq shall notify the Secretary-General and the Security Council when it has taken the actions set out above;

8. Decides that in order to secure the rapid establishment of a definitive end to the hostilities, the Security Council remains actively seized of the matter.

RESOLUTION 687

3 APRIL 1991

Adopted by a vote of 12 in favor, 1 against (Cuba) and 2 abstentions (Ecuador, Yemen).
Sponsors: Belgium, France, Romania, United Kingdom, United States, Zaire.
The Security Council,
Recalling its resolutions 660 (1990), 661 (1990), 662 (1990), 664 (1990), 665 (1990), 666

(1990), 667 (1990), 669 (1990), 670 (1990), 674 (1990), 677 (1990), 669 (1990), 670 (1990, 674 (1990), 677 (1990, 677 (1990), 678 (1990) and 686 (1991),

Welcoming the restoration to Kuwait of its sovereignty, independence, and territorial integrity and the return of its legitimate government,

Affirming the commitment of all Member States to the sovereignty, territorial integrity and political independence of Kuwait and Iraq, and noting the intention expressed by the Member States co-operating with Kuwait under paragraph 2 of resolution 678 (1990) to bring their military presence in Iraq to an end as soon as possible consistent with paragraph 8 of resolution 686 (1991),

Reaffirming the need to be assured of Iraq's peaceful intentions in light of its unlawful invasion and occupation of Kuwait,

Taking note of the letter sent by the Foreign Minister of Iraq on 27 February 1991 (S/22275) and those sent pursuant to resolution 686 (1991) (S/22273, S/22276, S/22320, S/22321 and S/22330),

Noting that Iraq and Kuwait, as independent sovereign States, signed at Baghdad on 4 October 1963 "Agreed Minutes Regarding the Restoration of Friendly Relations, Recognition and Related Matters," thereby recognizing formally the boundary between Iraq and Kuwait and the allocation of islands, which were registered with the United Nations in accordance with Article 102 of the Charter and in which Iraq recognized the independence and complete sovereignty of the State of Kuwait within its borders as specified and accepted in the letter of the Prime Minister of Iraq dated 21 June 1932, and as accepted by the Ruler of Kuwait in his letter dated 10 August 1932,

Conscious of the need for demarcation of the said boundary,

Conscious also of the statements by Iraq threatening to use weapons in violation of its obligations under the Geneva Protocol for the Prohibition of the Use in War of Asphyxiating, Poisonous or Other Gases, and of Bacteriological Methods of Warfare, signed at Geneva on 17 June 1925, and of its prior use of chemical weapons and affirming that grave consequences would follow any further use by Iraq of such weapons,

Recalling that Iraq has subscribed to the Declaration adopted by all States participating in the Conference of States Parties to the 1925 Geneva Protocol and Other Interested States, held at Paris from 7 to 11 January 1989, establishing the objective of universal elimination of chemical and biological weapons,

Recalling further that Iraq has signed the Convention on the Prohibition of the Development, Production and Stockpiling of Bacteriological (Biological) and Toxin Weapons and on Their Destruction, of 10 April 1972,

Noting the importance of Iraq ratifying this Convention,

Noting moreover the importance of all States adhering to this Convention and encouraging its forthcoming Review Conference to reinforce the authority, efficiency and universal scope of the Convention,

Stressing the importance of an early conclusion by the Conference on Disarmament of its work on a Convention on the Universal Prohibition of Chemical Weapons and of universal adherence thereto,

Aware of the use by Iraq of ballistic missiles in unprovoked attacks and therefore of the need to take specific measures in regard to such missiles located in Iraq,

Concerned by the reports in the hands of Member States that Iraq has attempted to acquire materials for a nuclear-weapons program contrary to its obligations under the Treaty on the Non-Proliferation of Nuclear Weapons of 1 July 1968,

Recalling the objective of the establishment of a nuclear-weapon-free zone in the region of the Middle East,

Conscious of the threat which all weapons of mass destruction pose to peace and security in the area and of the need to work towards the establishment in the Middle East of a zone free of such weapons,

Conscious also of the objective of achieving balanced and comprehensive control of armaments in the region,

Conscious further of the importance of achieving the objectives noted above using all available means, including a dialogue among the States of the region,

Noting that resolution 686 (1991) marked the lifting of the measures imposed by resolution 661 (1990) in so far as they applied to Kuwait,

Noting that the progress being made in fulfilling the obligations of resolution 686 (1991), many Kuwaiti and third country nationals are still not accounted for and property remains unreturned,

Recalling the International Convention against the Taking of Hostages, opened for signature at New York on 18 December 1979, which categorizes all acts of taking hostages as manifestations of international terrorism,

Deploring threats made by Iraq during the recent conflict to make use of terrorism against targets outside Iraq and the taking of hostages by Iraq,

Taking note with grave concern of the reports of the Secretary-General of 20 March 1991 (S/22366) and 28 March 1991 (S/22409), and conscious of the necessity to meet urgently the humanitarian needs in Kuwait and Iraq,

Bearing in mind its objective of restoring international peace and security in the area as set out in recent Council resolutions,

Conscious of the need to take the following measures under Chapter VII of the Charter,

1. Affirms all thirteen resolutions noted above, except as expressly changed below to achieve the goals of this resolution, including a formal cease-fire;

A

2. Demands that Iraq and Kuwait respect the inviolability of the international boundary and the allocation of islands set out in the "Agreed Minutes Between the State of Kuwait and the Republic of Iraq Regarding the Restoration of Friendly Relations, Recognition and Related Matters", signed by them in the exercise of their sovereignty at Baghdad on 4 October 1963 and registered with the United Nations and published by the United Nations in document 7063, United Nations Treaty Series, 1964;

3. Calls on the Secretary-General to lend his assistance to make arrangements with Iraq and Kuwait to demarcate the boundary between Iraq and Kuwait, drawing on appro-

priate material including the map transmitted by Security Council document S/22412 and to report back to the Security Council within one month;

4. Decides to guarantee the inviolability of the above-mentioned international boundary and to take as appropriate all necessary measures to that end in accordance with the Charter;

B

5. Requests the Secretary-General, after consulting with Iraq and Kuwait, to submit within three days to the Security Council for its approval a plan for the immediate deployment of a United Nations observer unit to monitor the Khawr Abdullah and a demilitarized zone, which is hereby established, extending 10 kilometers into Iraq and 5 kilometers into Kuwait from the boundary referred to in the "Agreed Minutes Between the State of Kuwait and the Republic of Iraq Regarding the Restoration of Friendly Relations, Recognition and Related Matters" of 4 October 1963; to deter violations of the boundary through its presence in and surveillance of the demilitarized zone; to observe any hostile or potentially hostile action mounted from the territory of one State to the other; and for the Secretary-General to report regularly to the Council on the operations of the unit, and immediately if there are serious violations of the zone or potential threats to peace;

6. Notes that as soon as the Secretary-General notifies the Council of the completion of the deployment of the United Nations observer unit, the conditions will be established for the Member States cooperating with Kuwait in accordance with resolution 678 (1990) to bring their military presence in Iraq to an end consistent with resolution 686 (1991);

C

7. Invites Iraq to reaffirm unconditionally its obligations under the Geneva Protocol for the Prohibition of the Use in War of Asphyxiating, Poisonous or Other Gases, and of Bacteriological Methods of Warfare [of] June 1925, and to ratify the Convention on the Prohibition of the Development, Production and Stockpiling of Bacteriological (Biological) and Toxin Weapons and on Their Destruction, of 10 April 1972;

8. Decides that Iraq shall unconditionally accept the destruction, removal or rendering harmless, under international supervision, of:
   a) all chemical and biological weapons and all stocks of agents and all related subsystems and components and all research, development, support and manufacturing facilities;
   b) all ballistic missiles with a range greater than 150 kilometers and related major parts, and repair and production facilities;

9. Decides, for the implementation of paragraph 8 above, the following:
   a) Iraq shall submit to the Secretary-General, within fifteen days of the adoption of this resolution, a declaration of the locations, amounts and types of all items specified in paragraph 8 and agree to urgent, on-site inspection as specified below;
   b) the Secretary-General, in consultation with the appropriate Governments and, where appropriate, with the Director-General of the World Health Organization

(WHO),within 45 days of the passage of this resolution, shall develop, and submit to the Council for approval, a plan calling for the completion of the following acts within 45 days of such approval:

   i) the forming of a Special Commission, which shall carry out immediate on-site inspection of Iraq's biological, chemical and missile capabilities, based on Iraq's declarations and the designation of any additional locations by the Special Commission itself;

   ii) the yielding by Iraq of possession to the Special Commission for destruction, removal or rendering harmless, taking into account the requirements of public safety, of all items specified under paragraph 8(a) above including items at the additional locations designated by the Special Commission under paragraph 9 (b) (i) above and the destruction by Iraq, under supervision of the Special Commission, of all its missile capabilities including launchers as specified under paragraph 8(b) above;

   iii) the provision by the Special Commission of the assistance and co-operation to the Director-General of the International Atomic Energy Agency (IAEA) required in paragraphs 12 and 13 below;

10. Decides that Iraq shall unconditionally undertake not to use, develop, construct or acquire any of the items specified in paragraphs 8 and 9 above and requests the Secretary-General, in consultation with the Special Commission, to develop a plan for the future ongoing monitoring and verification of Iraq's compliance with this paragraph, to be submitted to the Council for approval within 120 days of the passage of this resolution;

11. Invites Iraq to reaffirm unconditionally its obligations under the Treaty on the Non-Proliferation of Nuclear Weapons, of 1 July 1968;

12. Decides that Iraq shall unconditionally agree not to acquire or develop nuclear weapons or nuclear-weapons-usable material or any subsystems or components or any research, development, support or manufacturing facilities related to the above; to submit to the Secretary-General and the Director-General of the International Atomic Energy Agency (IAEA) within 15 days of the adoption of this resolution a declaration of the locations, amounts, and types of all items specified above; to place all of its nuclear-weapons-usable materials under the exclusive control, for custody and removal, of the IAEA, with the assistance and co-operation of the Special Commission as provided for in the plan of the Secretary-General discussed in paragraph 9 (b) above; to accept, in accordance with the arrangements provided for in paragraph 13 below, urgent on-site inspection and the destruction, removal, or rendering harmless as appropriate of all items specified above; and to accept the plan discussed in paragraph 13 below for the future ongoing monitoring and verification of its compliance with these undertakings;

13. Requests the Director-General of the International Atomic Energy Agency (IAEA) through the Secretary-General, with the assistance and co-operation of the Special Commission as provided for in the plan of the Secretary-General in paragraph 9(b)

above, to carry out immediate on-site inspection of Iraq's nuclear capabilities based on Iraq's declarations and the designation of any additional locations by the Special Commission; to develop a plan for submission to the Security Council within 45 days calling for the destruction, removal, or rendering harmless as appropriate of all items listed in paragraph 12 above; to carry out the plan within 45 days following approval by the Security Council; and to develop a plan, taking into account the rights and obligations of Iraq under the Treaty on the Non-Proliferation of Nuclear Weapons, of 1 July 1968, for the future ongoing monitoring and verification of Iraq's compliance with paragraph 12 above, including an inventory of all nuclear material in Iraq subject to the Agency's verification and inspections to confirm that IAEA safeguards cover all relevant nuclear activities in Iraq, to be submitted to the Council for approval within 120 days of the passage of this resolution;

14. Takes note that the actions to be taken by Iraq in paragraphs 8, 9, 10, 11, 12 and 13 of this resolution represent steps towards the goal of establishing in the Middle East a zone free from weapons of mass destruction and all missiles for their delivery and the objective of a global ban on chemical weapons;

D

15. Requests the Secretary-General to report to the Security Council on the steps taken to facilitate the return of all Kuwaiti property seized by Iraq, including a list of any property which Kuwait claims has not been returned or which has not been returned intact;

E

16. Reaffirms that Iraq, without prejudice to the debts and obligations of Iraq arising prior to 2 August 1990, which will be addressed through the normal mechanisms, is liable under international law for any direct loss, damage, including environmental damage and the depletion of natural resources, or injury to foreign Governments, nationals and corporations, as a result of Iraq's unlawful invasion and occupation of Kuwait;

17. Decides that all Iraqi statements made since 2 August 1990, repudiating its foreign debt, are null and void, and demands that Iraq scrupulously adhere to all of its obligations concerning servicing and repayment of its foreign debt;

18. Decides to create a Fund to pay compensation for claims that fall within paragraph 16 above and to establish a Commission that will administer the Fund;

19. Directs the Secretary-General to develop and present to the Council for decision, no later then 30 days following the adoption of this resolution, recommendations for the Fund to meet the requirement for the payment of claims established in accordance with paragraph 18 above and for a programme to implement the decisions in paragraphs 16, 17, and 18 above, including: mechanisms for determining the appropriate level of Iraq's contribution to the Fund based on a percentage of the value of the exports of petroleum and petroleum products from Iraq not to exceed a figure to be suggested to the Council by the Secretary-General, taking into account the requirements

of the people of Iraq, Iraq's payment capacity as assessed in conjunction with the international financial institutions, taking into consideration external debt service and the needs of the Iraqi economy; arrangements for ensuring that payments are made to the Fund; the process by which funds will be allocated and claims paid; appropriate procedures for evaluating losses, listing claims and verifying their validity and resolving disputed claims in respect of Iraq's liability as specified in paragraph 16 above; and the composition of the Commission designated above;

F

20. Decides, effective immediately, that the prohibitions against the sale or supply to Iraq of commodities or products other than medicine and health supplies, and prohibitions against financial transactions related thereto, contained in resolution 661 (1990) shall not apply to foodstuffs notified to the Committee established by resolution 661 (1990) or, with the approval of that Committee, under the simplified and accelerated "no-objection" procedure, to materials and supplies for essential civilian needs as identified in the report of the Secretary-General dated 20 March 1991 (S/22366), and in any further findings of humanitarian need by the Committee;

21. Decides that the Council shall review the provisions of paragraph 20 above every sixty days in light of the policies and practices of the Government of Iraq, including the implementation of all relevant resolutions of the Security Council, for the purpose of determining whether to reduce or lift the prohibitions referred to therein;

22. Decides that upon the approval by the Council of the programme called for in paragraph 19 above and upon Council agreement that Iraq has completed all actions contemplated in paragraphs 8, 9, 10, 11, 12, and 13 above, the prohibitions against the import of commodities and products originating in Iraq and the prohibitions against financial transactions related thereto contained in resolution 661 (1990) shall have no further force or effect;

23. Decides that, pending action by the Council under paragraph 22 above, the Committee established under resolution 661 (1990) shall be empowered to approve, when required to assure adequate financial resources on the part of Iraq to carry out the activities under paragraph 20 above, exceptions to the prohibition against the import of commodities and products originating in Iraq;

24. Decides that, in accordance with resolution 661 (1990) and subsequent related resolutions and until a further decision is taken by the Council, all States shall continue to prevent the sale or supply, or promotion or facilitation of such sale or supply, to Iraq by their nationals or from their territories or using their flag vessels or aircraft, of:

a) arms and related *materiel* of all types, specifically including the sale or transfer through other means of all forms of conventional military equipment, including for paramilitary forces, and spare parts and components and their means of production, for such equipment;

b) items specified and defined in paragraph 8 and 12 above not otherwise covered above;

    c) technology under licensing or other transfer arrangements used in the production, utilization or stockpiling of items specified in sub-paragraphs (a) and (b) above;

    d) personnel or materials for training or technical support services relating to the design, development, manufacture, use, maintenance of support of items specified in subparagraphs (a) and (b) above;

25. Calls upon all States and international organizations to act strictly in accordance with paragraph 24 above, notwithstanding the existence of any contracts, agreements, licenses, or any other arrangements;

26. Requests the Secretary-General, in consultation with appropriate Governments, to develop within 60 days, for approval of the Council, guidelines to facilitate full international implementation of paragraphs 24 and 25 above and paragraph 27 below, and to make them available to all States and to establish a procedure for updating these guidelines periodically;

27. Calls upon all States to maintain such national controls and procedures and to take such other actions consistent with the guidelines to be established by the Security Council under paragraph 26 above as may be necessary to ensure compliance with the terms of paragraph 24 above, and calls upon international organizations to take all appropriate steps to assist in ensuring such full compliance;

28. Agrees to review its decisions in paragraphs 22, 23, 24, and 25 above, except for the items specified and defined in paragraphs 8 and 12 above, on a regular basis and in any case 120 days following passage of this resolution, taking into account Iraq's compliance with this resolution and general progress towards the control of armaments in the region;

29. Decides that all States, including Iraq, shall take the necessary measures to ensure that no claim shall lie at the instance of the Government of Iraq, or of any person or body in Iraq, or of any person claiming through or for the benefit of any such person or body, in connection with any contract or other transaction where its performance was affected by reason of the measures taken by the Security Council in resolution 661 (1990) and related resolutions;

G

30. Decides that, in furtherance of its commitment to facilitate the repatriation of all Kuwaiti and third country nationals, Iraq shall extend all necessary cooperation to the International Committee of the Red Cross, providing lists of such persons, facilitating the access of the International Committee of the Red Cross to all such persons wherever located or detained and facilitating the search by the International Red Cross for those Kuwaiti and third country nationals still unaccounted for;

31. Invites the International Committee of the Red Cross to keep the Secretary-General appraised as appropriate of all activities undertaken in connection with facilitating the repatriation or return of all Kuwaiti and third nationals or their remains present in Iraq on or after 2 August 1990;

H

32. Requires Iraq to inform the Council that it will not commit or support any act of international terrorism or allow any organization directed towards commission of such acts to operate within its territory and to condemn unequivocally and renounce all acts, methods, and practices of terrorism;

I

33. Declares that, upon official notification by Iraq to the Secretary-General and to the Security Council of its acceptance of the provisions above, a formal cease-fire is effective between Iraq and Kuwait and the Member States cooperating with Kuwait in accordance with resolution 678 (1990);

34. Decides to remain seized of the matter and to take such further steps as may be required for the implementation of this resolution and to secure peace and security in the area.

RESOLUTION 688

5 APRIL 1991

Adopted by a vote of 10 in favor, 3 against (Cuba, Yemen and Zimbabwe), and 2 abstentions (China and India.)

Sponsors: Belgium, France, United Kingdom, United States.

The Security Council,

Mindful of its duties and its responsibilities under the Charter of the United Nations for the maintenance of international peace and security,

Recalling Article 2, paragraph 7, of the Charter of the United Nations,

Gravely concerned by the repression of the Iraqi civilian population in many parts of Iraq, including most recently in Kurdish populated areas which led to a massive flow of refugees towards and across international frontiers and to cross border incursions, which threaten international peace and security in the region,

Deeply disturbed by the magnitude of the human suffering involved,

Taking note of the letters sent by the representatives of Turkey and France to the United Nations dated 2 April 1991 and 4 April 1991, respectively (S/22435 and S/22447),

Reaffirming the commitment of all Member States to the sovereignty, territorial integrity and political independence of Iraq and of all States in the area,

Bearing in mind the Secretary-General's report of 20 March 1991 (S/22366),

1. Condemns the repression of the Iraqi civilian population in many parts of Iraq, including most recently in Kurdish populated areas, the consequences of which threaten international peace and security in the region;

2. Demands that Iraq, as a contribution to removing the threat to international peace and security in the region, immediately end this repression and expresses the hope in

the same context that an open dialogue will take place to ensure that the human and political rights of all Iraqi citizens are respected;

3. Insists that Iraq allow immediate access by international humanitarian organizations to all those in need of assistance in all parts of Iraq and to make available all necessary facilities for their operations;

4. Requests the Secretary-General to pursue his humanitarian efforts in Iraq and to report forthwith, if appropriate on the basis of a further mission to the region, on the plight of the Iraqi civilian population, and in particular the Kurdish population, suffering from the repression in all its forms inflicted by the Iraqi authorities;

5. Requests further the Secretary-General to use all the resources at his disposal, including those of the relevant United Nations agencies, to address urgently the critical needs of the refugees and displaced Iraqi population;

6. Appeals to all Member States and to all humanitarian organizations to contribute to these humanitarian relief efforts;

7. Demands that Iraq co-operate with the Secretary-General to these ends;

8. Decides to remain seized of the matter.

RESOLUTION 706

15 AUGUST 1991

Adopted by a vote of 13 in favor, 1 against (Cuba) and 1 abstention (Yemen).
Sponsors: Belgium, France, Soviet Union, United Kingdom, United States.
The Security Council,

Recalling its previous relevant resolutions and in particular resolutions 661 (1990), 686 (1991), 687 (1991), 688 (1991), 692 (1991), and 705 (1991),

Taking note of the report (S/22799) dated 15 July 1991 of the inter-agency mission headed by the executive delegate of the Secretary-General for the United Nations inter-agency humanitarian programme for Iraq, Kuwait and the Iraq/Turkey and Iraq/Iran border areas,

Concerned by the serious nutritional and health situation of the Iraqi civilian population as described in this report, and by the risk of a further deterioration of this situation,

Concerned also that the repatriation or return of all Kuwaitis and third country nationals or their remains present in Iraq on or after 2 August 1990, pursuant to paragraph 2(c) of resolution 686 (1991) and paragraphs 30 and 31 of resolution 687 (1991) has not yet been fully carried out,

Taking note of the conclusions of the above-mentioned report, and in particular of the proposal for oil sales by Iraq to finance the purchase of foodstuffs, medicines and materials and supplies for essential civilian needs for the purpose of providing humanitarian relief,

Taking note also of the letters dated 14 April 1991, 31 May 1991, 6 June 1991, 9 July 1991 and 22 July 1991 from the Minister of Foreign Affairs of Iraq and the Permanent Representative of Iraq to the Chairman of the Committee established by resolution 661 (1990) concerning the export from Iraq of petroleum and petroleum products,

Convinced of the need for equitable distribution of humanitarian relief to all segments of the Iraqi civilian population through effective monitoring and transparency,

Recalling and reaffirming in this regard its resolution 688 (1991) and in particular the importance which the Council attaches to Iraq allowing unhindered access by international humanitarian organizations to all those in need of assistance in all parts of Iraq and making available all necessary facilities for their operation, and in this connection stressing the important and continuing role played by the Memorandum of Understanding between the United Nations and the Government of Iraq of 18 April 1991 (S/22663),

Recalling that, pursuant to resolutions 687 (1991), 692 (1991) and 699 (1991), Iraq is required to pay the full costs of the Special Commission and the IAEA in carrying out the tasks authorized by section C of resolution 687 (1991), and that the Secretary-General in his report to the Security Council of 15 July 1991 (S/22792), submitted pursuant to paragraph 4 of resolution 699 (1991), expressed the view that the most obvious way of obtaining financial resources from Iraq to meet the costs of the Special Commission and the IAEA would be to authorize the sale of some Iraqi petroleum and petroleum products; recalling further that Iraq is required to pay its contributions to the Compensation Fund and half the costs of the Iraq-Kuwait Boundary Demarcation Commission, and recalling further that in its resolutions 686 (1991) and 687 (1991) the Security Council demanded that Iraq return in the shortest possible time all Kuwaiti property seized by it and requested the Secretary-General to take steps to facilitate this,

Acting under Chapter VII of the Charter,

1. Authorizes all States, subject to the decision to be taken by the Security Council pursuant to paragraph 5 below and notwithstanding the provisions of paragraphs 3 (a), 3 (b) and 4 of resolution 661 (1990), to permit the import, during a period of six months from the date of the passage of the resolution pursuant to paragraph 5 below, of petroleum and petroleum products originating in Iraq sufficient to produce a sum to be determined by the Council following receipt of the report of the Secretary-General requested in paragraph 5 of this resolution but not to exceed 1.6 billion United States dollars for the purposes set out in this resolution and subject to the following conditions:

   a) Approval of each purchase of Iraqi petroleum and petroleum products by the Security Council Committee established by resolution 661 (1990) following notification to the Committee by the State concerned;

   b) Payment of the full amount of each purchase of Iraqi petroleum and petroleum products directly by the purchaser in the State concerned into an escrow account to be established by the United Nations and to be administered by the Secretary-General, exclusively to meet the purposes of this resolution;

   c) Approval by the Council, following the report of the Secretary-General requested in paragraph 5 of this resolution, of a scheme for the purchase of foodstuffs, medicines and materials and supplies for essential civilian needs as referred to in paragraph 20 of resolution 687 (1991), in particular health-related materials, all of which to be labelled to the extent possible as being supplied under this scheme, and for all feasible and appropriate United Nations monitoring and supervision for the purpose of assuring their equitable distribution to meet humanitarian needs in all regions of Iraq and to all categories of the Iraqi civilian population, as well as all feasible and appropriate management relevant to this purpose, such as a United Nations role to be available if desired for humanitarian assistance from other sources;

d) The sum authorized in this paragraph to be released by successive decisions of the Committee established by resolution 661 (1990) in three equal portions after the Council has taken the decision provided for in paragraph 5 below on the implementation of this resolution, and notwithstanding any other provision of this paragraph, the sum to be subject to review concurrently by the Council on the basis of its ongoing assessments of the needs and requirements;

2. Decides that a part of the sum in the account to be established by the Secretary-General shall be made available by him to finance the purchase of foodstuffs, medicines and materials and supplies for essential civilian needs, as referred to in paragraph 20 of resolution 687, and the cost to the United Nations of its roles under this resolution and of other necessary humanitarian activities in Iraq;

3. Decides further that a part of the sum in the account to be established by the Secretary-General shall be used by him for appropriate payments to the United Nations Compensation Fund, the full costs incurred by the United Nations in facilitating the return of all Kuwaiti property seized by Iraq, and half the costs of the Boundary Commission;

4. Decides that the percentage of the value of exports of petroleum and petroleum products from Iraq, authorized under this resolution to be paid to the United Nations Compensation Fund, as called for in paragraph 19 of resolution 687 (1991), and as defined in paragraph 6 of resolution 692 (1991), shall be the same as the percentage decided by the Security Council in paragraph 2 of resolution 705 (1991) for payments to the Compensation Fund, until such time as the Governing Council of the Fund decides otherwise;

5. Requests the Secretary-General to submit within 20 days of the date of adoption of this resolution a report to the Security Council for decision on measures to be taken in order to implement paragraphs 1(a), (b) and (c), estimates of the humanitarian requirements of Iraq set out in paragraph 2 above and of the amount of Iraq's financial obligations set out in paragraph 3 above up to the end of the period of the authorization in paragraph 1 above, as well as the method for taking the necessary legal measures to ensure that the purposes of this resolution are carried out and the method for taking account of the costs of transportation of such Iraqi petroleum and petroleum products;

6. Further requests the Secretary-General in consultation with the International Committee of the Red Cross to submit within 20 days of the date of this resolution a report to the Security Council on activities undertaken in accordance with paragraph 31 of resolution 687 (1991) in connection with facilitating the repatriation or return of all Kuwaiti and third country nationals or their remains present in Iraq on or after 2 August 1990;

7. Requires the Government of Iraq to provide to the Secretary-General and appropriate international organizations on the first day of the month immediately following the adoption of the present resolution and on the first day of each month thereafter until further notice, a statement of the gold and foreign currency reserves it holds whether in Iraq or elsewhere;

8. Calls upon all States to co-operate fully in the implementation of this resolution;

9. Decides to remain seized of the matter.

RESOLUTION 712

19 SEPTEMBER 1991

Adopted by a vote of 13 in favor, 1 against (Cuba), 1 abstention (Yemen.)

The Security Council,

Recalling its previous relevant resolutions and in particular resolutions 661 (1990) of 6 August 1990, 686 (1991) of 2 March 1991, 687 (1991) of 3 April 1991, 688 (1991) of 5 April 1991, 692 (1991) of 20 May 1991, 699 (1991) of 17 June 1991, and 705 (1991) and 706 (1991) of 15 August 1991,

Expressing its appreciation for the report dated 4 September 1991 submitted by the Secretary-General pursuant to paragraph 5 of resolution 706 (1991),

Reaffirming its concern about the nutritional and health situation of the Iraqi civilian population and the risk of a further deterioration of this situation, and underlining the need in this context for fully up-to-date assessments of the situation in all parts of Iraq as a basis for the equitable distribution of humanitarian relief to all segments of the Iraqi civilian population,

Recalling that the activities to be carried out by or on behalf of the Secretary-General to meet the purposes referred to in resolution 706 (1991) and the present resolution enjoy the privileges and immunities of the United Nations,

Acting under Chapter VII of the United Nations,

1. Confirms the figure mentioned in paragraph 1 of resolution 706 (1991) as the sum authorized for the purpose of that paragraph, and reaffirms its intention to review this sum on the basis of its ongoing assessment of the needs and requirements, in accordance with paragraph 1 (d) of resolution 706 (1991);

2. Invites the Security Council Committee established by resolution 661 (1990) to authorize immediately, pursuant to paragraph 1 (d) of resolution 706 (1991), the release by the Secretary-General from the escrow account of the first one-third of the sum referred to in paragraph 1 above, such release to take place as required subject to the availability of funds in the account and, in the case of payments, to finance the purchase of foodstuffs, medicines and supplies for essential civilian needs that have been notified or approved in accordance with existing procedures, subject to compliance with the procedures laid down in the report of the Secretary-General as approved in paragraph 3 below;

3. Approves the recommendations in the Secretary-General's report as contained in its paragraphs 57(d) and 58

4. Encourages the Secretary-General and the Security Council Committee established by resolution 661 (1990) to cooperate, in close consultation with the government of Iraq, on a continuing basis to ensure the most effective implementation of the scheme approved in the present resolution;

5. Decides that petroleum and petroleum products subject to resolution 706 (1991) shall while under Iraqi title be immune from legal proceedings and not be subject to any form of attachment, garnishment or execution, and that all States shall take any steps that may be necessary under their respective domestic legal systems to assure this protection, and to ensure that the proceeds of sale are not diverted from the purposes laid down in resolution 706 (1991);

6. Reaffirms that the escrow account to be established by the United Nations and administered by the Secretary-General to meet the purposes of resolution 706 (1991) and the present resolution, like the Compensation Fund established by resolution 692 (1991), enjoys the privileges and immunities of the United Nations;

7. Reaffirms that the inspectors and other experts on mission for the United Nations, appointed for the purposes of the present resolution, enjoy privileges and immunities in accordance with the Convention of Privileges and Immunities of the United Nations, and demands that Iraq allow them full freedom of movement and all necessary facilities;

8. Confirms that funds contributed from other sources may, if desired, in accordance with paragraph 1 (c) of resolution 706 (1991), be deposited into the escrow account as a sub-account and be immediately available to meet Iraq's humanitarian needs as referred to in paragraph 20 of resolution 687 (1991) without any of the obligatory deductions and administrative costs specified in paragraphs 2 and 3 of resolution 706 (1991);

9. Urges that any provision to Iraq of foodstuffs, medicines or other items of a humanitarian character, in addition to those purchased with the funds referred to in paragraph 1 of the present resolution, be undertaken through arrangements that assure their equitable distribution to meet humanitarian needs;

10. Requests the Secretary-General to take the actions necessary to implement the above decisions, and authorizes him to enter into any arrangements or agreements necessary to accomplish this;

11. Calls upon States to co-operate fully in the implementation of resolution 706 (1991) and the present resolution, in particular with respect to any measures regarding the import of petroleum and petroleum products and the export of foodstuffs, medicines and materials and supplies for essential civilian needs as referred to in paragraph 20 of resolution 687 (1991), and also with respect to the privileges of immunity of the United Nations and its personnel implementing the present resolution, and to ensure that there are no diversions from the purposes laid down in these resolutions;

12. Decides to remain seized of the matter.

RESOLUTION 778

2 OCTOBER 1992

Adopted by a vote of 14 in favor, none against, 1 abstention (China.)

The Security Council,

Recalling its present resolutions and in particular resolutions 706 (1991) and 712 (1991),

Taking note of the letter of 15 July 1992 from the Secretary-General to the President of the Security Council on Iraq's compliance with the obligations placed on it by resolution 687 (1991) and subsequent resolutions,

Condemning Iraq's continued failure to comply with its obligations under relevant resolutions,

Reaffirming its concern about the nutritional and health situation of the Iraqi civilian population, and the risk of a further deterioration of this situation and recalling in this regard its resolution 706 (1991) and 712 (1991), which provide a mechanism for providing humanitarian relief to the Iraqi population, and resolution 688 (1991), which provides a basis for humanitarian relief efforts in Iraq,

Having regard to the fact that the period of six months referred to in resolutions 706 (1991) and 712 (1991) expired on 18 March 1992,

Deploring Iraq's refusal to cooperate in the implementation of resolutions 706 (1991) and 712 (1991) which puts its civilian population at risk, and which results in the failure by Iraq to meet its obligations under relevant Security Council resolutions,

Recalling that the escrow account provided for in resolutions 706 (1991) and 712 (1991) will consist of Iraqi funds administered by the Secretary-General which will be used to pay contributions to the Compensation Fund, the full costs of carrying out the tasks authorized by section C of resolution 687 (1991), the full costs incurred by the United Nations in facilitating the return of all Kuwaiti property seized by Iraq, half the costs of the Boundary Commission, and the cost to the United Nations of implementing resolution 706 (1991) and of other necessary humanitarian activities in Iraq,

Recalling that Iraq, as stated in paragraph 16 of resolution 687 (1991), is liable for all direct damage resulting from its invasion and occupation of Kuwait, without prejudice to its debts and obligations arising prior to 2 August 1990, which will be addressed through the normal mechanisms,

Recalling its decision in resolution 692 (1991) that the requirement for Iraqi contributions to the Compensation Fund applies to certain Iraqi petroleum and petroleum products exported from Iraq after 2 April 1991,

Acting under Chapter VII of the Charter of the United Nations,

1. Decides that all States in which there are funds of the government of Iraq, or its State bodies, corporations, or agencies, that represent the proceeds of sale of Iraqi petroleum or petroleum products, paid for by or on behalf of the purchaser on or after 6 August 1990, shall cause the transfer of those funds (or equivalent amounts) as soon as possible to the escrow account provided for in resolutions 706 (1991) and 712

(1991); provided that this paragraph shall not require any State to cause the transfer of such funds in excess of 200 million dollars or to cause the transfer of more than fifty percent of the total funds transferred or contributed pursuant to paragraphs 1, 2 and 3 of this resolution; and further provided that States may exclude from the operation of this paragraph any funds which have already been released to a claimant or supplier prior to the adoption of this resolution, or any funds subject to or required to satisfy the rights of third parties, at the time of the adoption of this resolution;

2. Decides that all States in which there are petroleum or petroleum products owned by the Government of Iraq, or its State bodies, corporations, or agencies, shall take all feasible steps to purchase or arrange for the sale of such petroleum or petroleum products at fair market value, and thereupon to transfer the proceeds as soon as possible to the escrow account provided for in resolution 706 (1991) and 712 (1991);

3. Urges all States to contribute funds from other sources to the escrow account as soon as possible;

4. Decides that all States shall provide the Secretary-General with any information needed for the effective implementation of this resolution and that they shall take the necessary measures to ensure that banks and other bodies and persons provide all relevant information necessary to identify the funds referred to in paragraphs 1 and 2 above and details of any transactions relating thereto, or the said petroleum or petroleum products, with a view to such information being utilized by all States and by the Secretary-General in the effective implementation of this resolution;

5. Requests the Secretary-General:
   a) To ascertain the whereabouts and amounts of the said petroleum and petroleum products and the proceeds of sale referred to in paragraphs 1 and 2 of this resolution, drawing on the work already done under the auspices of the Compensation Commission, and report the results to the Security Council as soon as possible;
   b) To ascertain the costs of United Nations activities concerning the elimination of weapons of mass destruction, the provision of humanitarian relief in Iraq, and the other United Nations operations specified in paragraphs 2 and 3 of resolution 706 (1991); and
   c) to take the following actions:
      i) transfer to the Compensation Fund, from the funds referred to in paragraphs 1 and 2 of this resolution, the percentage referred to in paragraph 10 of this resolution; and
      ii) use of the remainder of funds referred to in paragraphs 1, 2 and 3 of this resolution for the costs of United Nations activities concerning the elimination of weapons of mass destruction, the provision of humanitarian relief in Iraq, and the other United Nations operations specified in paragraphs 2 and 3 of resolution 706 (1991), taking into account any preference expressed by States transferring or contributing funds as to the allocation of such funds among these purposes;

6. Decides that for so long as oil exports take place pursuant to the system provided in resolutions 706 (1991) and 712 (1991) or to the eventual lifting of sanctions pursuant to paragraph 22 of resolution 687 (1991), implementation of paragraphs 1 to 5 of this resolution shall be suspended and all proceeds of those oil exports shall immediately be transferred by the Secretary-General in the currency in which the transfer to the escrow account had been made, to the accounts or States from which funds had been provided under paragraphs 1, 2 and 3 of this resolution, to the extent required to replace in full the amounts so provided (together with applicable interest); and that, if necessary for this purpose, any other funds remaining in the escrow account shall similarly be transferred to those accounts or States; provided, however, that the Secretary-General may retain and use any funds urgently needed for the purposes specified in paragraph 5 (c) (ii) of this resolution;

7. Decides that the operation of this resolution shall have no effect on rights, debts and claims existing with respect to funds prior to their transfer to the escrow account; and that the accounts from which such funds were transferred shall be kept open for re-transfer of the funds in question;

8. Reaffirms that the escrow account referred to in this resolution, like the Compensation Fund, enjoys the privileges and immunities of the United Nations, including immunity from legal proceedings, or any forms of attachment, garnishment or execution; and that no claim shall lie at the instance of any person or body in connection with or implementation of this resolution;

9. Requests the Secretary-General to repay, from any available funds in the escrow account, any sum transferred under this resolution to the account or State from which it was transferred, if the transfer is found at any time by him not to have been of funds subject to this resolution; a request for such a finding could be made by the State from which the funds were transferred;

10. Confirms that the percentage of the value of exports of petroleum and petroleum products from Iraq for payment to the Compensation Fund shall, for the purpose of this resolution and exports of petroleum and petroleum products subject to paragraph 6 of resolution 692 (1991), be the same as the percentage decided by the Security Council in paragraph 2 of resolution 705 (1991), until such time as the Governing Council of the Compensation Fund may decide otherwise;

11. Decides that no further Iraqi assets shall be released for purposes set forth in paragraph 20 of resolution 687 (1991) except to the sub-account of the escrow account, established pursuant to paragraph 8 of resolution 712 (1991), or directly to the United Nations for humanitarian activities in Iraq;

12. Decides that, for the purposes of this resolution and other relevant resolutions, the term "petroleum products" does not include petrochemical derivatives;

13. Calls upon all States to co-operate fully in the implementation of this resolution;

14. Decides to remain seized of this matter.

Appendix 2: Additional Resources

AUDIO CASSETTES

Crisis in the Persian Gulf (1990) 30 minutes.
How the U.S. Media Covers the Crisis in Saudi Arabia (1990) 30 minutes.
American Dialogues, 8033 Sunset Boulevard, Room 967, Los Angeles, CA 90046
Terrorism: The Sacred Rage (1986) 30 minutes.
Johnson Foundation, P.O. Box 547, Racine, WI 53401-0547

VISUAL RESOURCES

FROM THE VIDEO PROJECT

5332 College Avenue, Suite 101, Oakland, CA 94618
Nowhere to Hide (1991) 28 minutes.
Produced by Jon Alpert.
Long-time contributor to NBC News, Jon Alpert shot the only footage of the war's impact not censored by either Iraq or the U.S. No U.S. network was prepared to air the footage, and NBC ended its long affiliation with Alpert, a seven-time Emmy winner.
Report from Iraq (1991) 22 minutes.
Produced by John Knoop.
This is a video document of the journey and findings of the team of Harvard University doctors, lawyers and students who traveled without government restrictions. Their report raises serious questions about President Bush's repeated claims that the Coalition was not intent on destroying the infrastructure of Iraqi society.
Treating the Casualties of the Gulf War (1991) 29 minutes.
Produced by Sanford Gottlieb, Center for Defense Information.
From the television series *America's Defense Monitor,* this video documents how nearly 80,000 tons of bombs were dropped on Iraq, of which only seven percent were "smart" bombs. Includes interviews with Doug Waller of *Newsweek,* Francois Zen Ruffinen, International Red Cross UN delegate, and Holly Burkhalter of Human Rights Watch.
Sandstorm in the Gulf: Digging Out (1991) 30 minutes.
Produced by Sanford Gottlieb, Center for Defense Information.
Described by the *Catholic News Service* as a "non-triumphal view of the Allied high-tech military victory over Iraq," this episode of *America's Defense Monitor* looks back at the role the U.S. government played in the Gulf conflict and ahead at the problems that remain.

Behind the Flag (1991) 20 minutes.

Produced by Arden Buck, Educational Media Associates.

Featuring interviews with Ronald V. Dellums, member of Congress and Chair of the House Armed Services Committee, James Akins, former U.S. Ambassador to Saudi Arabia, and others, this video examines evidence that suggests the U.S. government deliberately exaggerated the Iraqi threat to Saudi Arabia.

The Aftermath of the Gulf War (1991) 29 minutes.

Produced by Sanford Gottlieb, Center for Defense Information.

This program looks at the underlying political and military goals of the Gulf War, with a wide-ranging mix of experts including the Kuwaiti Ambassador to the U.S. and the Israeli Military Attache in Washington.

More Videos:

Lines in the Sand (1991) 12 minutes.

Griffin-Wirth Associates, 168 Parkway Drive, Syracuse, NY 13207

Footage shot in Baghdad by producer/writer Ed Griffin-Nolan shows the faces of the victims not seen on the nightly news and explores how information was controlled and news managed during the Gulf War to keep the disturbing realities of war from affecting the conscience of the U.S. public.

Iraq: War Against the People (1991) 30 minutes.

Revolution Books, 2425C Channing Way, Berkeley, CA 94703, (510) 848-1196

Traveling through Iraq, Larry Everest interviewed Iraqis in hospitals, refugee camps and bombed cities in the summer of 1991.

Alternatives to War in the Middle East (1991) 28 minutes; and

Oil, Arms and the Gulf (1990) 28 minutes.

Center for Defense Information, 1500 Massachusetts Avenue, NW, Washington, DC 20005

Perspectives on the Gulf Crisis (1990) 28 minutes.

Institute for Policy Studies, 1601 Connecticut Avenue, NW, Washington, DC 20005

The Oil Kingdoms (1986) Series, 52 minutes each

Films Incorporated, 5547 N. Ravenswood Avenue, Chicago, IL 60640

Islam: An Introduction (1981) 22 minutes; color slideshow with cassette.

Middle East Institute, Islamic Affairs Programs, 1761 N Street, NW, Washington, DC 20036

Purchase or borrow from Mennonite Central Committee, P.O. Box 500, Akron, PA 17501-0500

Government Offices

Atmosphere and Geophysical Sciences Division, Lawrence Livermore National Laboratory, P.O. Box 808, Livermore, CA 94550

Atmospheric Sciences Division, NASA-Langley Research Center, Hampton, VA 23665

British Meteorological Office, London Road, Bracknell, Berkshire RG122SZ, UK

Congress of the U.S. Office of Technology Assessment, Washington, DC 20548

Congressional Budget Office, 2nd and D Streets, SW, Washington, DC 20515

Congressional Record Clippings, 1868 Columbia Road, NW, Suite 402, Washington, DC 20009

Congressional Record Index, Room B104, U.S. Government Printing Office, North Capitol and H Streets, NW, Washington, DC 20402

Congressional Research Service, 10 1st Street, SW, Washington, DC 20515

Gulf Interagency Task Force, U.S. Environmental Protection Agency, Mail Stop A-150, Room NEMLC 013, 401 M Street, SW, Washington, DC 20460

Infoterra/USA, U.S. Environmental Protection Agency, Room 2904; PM-211A, 401 M Street, SW, Washington, DC 20460

Norwegian Institute for Air Research, Postboks 64, N-2001 Lillestrom, Norway

U.S. General Accounting Office, Washington, DC 20548

MAPS

U.S. Geological Survey, Department of the Interior, Information Office, National Center, Reston, VA 22092

Library of Congress, Geography and Map Division, 10 First Street, SE (LM B-01), Washington, DC 20540

Central Intelligence Agency, Public Affairs, Washington, DC 20505

National Geographic Society, P.O. Box 2895, Washington, DC

CLIPPING FILES

The DataCenter, 464 19th Street, Oakland, CA 94612

Appendix 3: Further Reading

Selected further reading on the impacts of the 1991 Gulf War

ENVIRONMENT/GENERAL

Arkin, William M.; Durrant, Damian; and Cherni, Marianne. *On Impact: Modern Warfare and the Environment: Case Study of the Gulf War.* Washington: Greenpeace, 1991.

Barnaby, Frank, 'The Environmental Impact of the Gulf War.' *The Ecologist,* July–August 1991.

Browne, Malcom W.; Kaku, Michio; Fallows, James M.; and Fischer, Eric A., 'War and the Environment.' *Audubon,* September–October 1991, 89–99.

Canby, Thomas Y. 'After the War,' *National Geographic,* August 1991, 9–32.

Friends of the Earth. *Summary Report from Friends of the Earth International's Team of Scientific Experts on the Urgent Need for Extinguishing the Kuwaiti Oil Fires and Cleaning Up the Gulf,* FOE, 1991.

Greenpeace International. *The Environmental Legacy of the Gulf War,* Greenpeace, 1992.

Hawley, T.M. *Against the Fires of Hell: The Environmental Disaster of the Gulf War.* New York, San Diego: Harcourt Brace Jovanovich, 1992.

Plant, Glen. *Environmental Protection and the Law of War.* London, New York: Belhaven Press, 1992.

Pope, Carl. 'War on Earth.' *Sierra Magazine,* May/June 1991, 54–58.

Price, A.R.G. *Environmental Aspects of the Gulf War: Report on a Mission to Saudi Arabia. Draft Report, Joint IUCN/WWF Task Force Team.* Gland, Switzerland: World Wildlife Fund, 1991.

Ramachandran, K.S., ed. *Gulf War and Environmental Problems.* New Delhi: Ashish, 1991.

Renner, Michael. 'Military Victory, Ecological Defeat.' *World Watch,* July–August 1991, 27–33.

Rosenberger, Jack. 'War on the Environment: Environmental Consequences of Biochemical Weapons Could Be Catastrophic.' *E Magazine,* May/June 1991.

Smith, Gar. 'Cradle to Grave: Attacking Iraq Could Wreak Environmental Havoc.' *Earth Island Journal,* Winter 1991.

United Nations, Environment Programme, *Statement on the Results of the Consultation,* (OCA)/WG9/2, February 11, 1991, 3.

United Nations, Environment Programme, *An Interagency Action Plan in ROPME Region,* (OCA)/WG10/3, March 18, 1991.

U.S., Congress, Senate, Environment and Public Works Committee, *The Environmental Aftermath of the Gulf War: A Report,* 102nd Cong., 2nd sess., March 1992.

U.S., Congress, Senate, Environment and Public Works Committee, *Statement of Director of Arabian Gulf Program Office, National Oceanic and Atmospheric Administration (NOAA), U.S. Department of Commerce, before the Gulf Pollution Task Force,* prepared by John H. Robinson, October 16, 1991, 14.

U.S., Congress, Senate, Environment and Public Works Committee, *Statement of Director of Gulf Task Force, U.S. EPA, before the Gulf Pollution Task Force,* prepared by Timothy Titus, October 16, 1991.

U.S., Environmental Protection Agency. *United States Environmental Technical Assistance from January 27–July 31, 1991.* Washington: Government Printing Office, or The Gulf Task Force, c/o EPA, Mail Stop A-150/Room NEMLC 013, 401 M St., SW, Washington DC, 20406, 1991.

World Conservation Monitoring Centre, *Gulf War Information Service: Postwar Environmental Reconstruction.* Cambridge, U.K.: WCMC, February 28, 1991.

World Conservation Monitoring Centre, *Gulf War Information Service: Impact on the Land and the Atmosphere.* Cambridge, U.K.: WCMC, February, 1991.

Environment/Oil Spills

Ackland, Len. 'The War Metaphor.' *Bulletin of Atomic Scientists,* April 1991.

Church, H.W., et al. *Potential Impacts of Iraqi Use of Oil as a Defensive Weapon.* Albuquerque, New Mexico: Sandia National Laboratories, 1991.

Horgan, John. 'The Muddled Cleanup in the Persian Gulf.' *Scientific American,* October 1991, 106–108.

Oil and Gas Journal, 'Survey to Assess Spill Effects.' February 11, 1991.

Pearce, Fred. 'Wildlife Choked by World's Worst Oil Slick.' *New Scientist,* February 2, 1991, 24–25.

Price, A.R.G. 'Possible Environmental Threats from the Current Gulf War.' Photocopied. Washington: Greenpeace, February 2, 1991.

Saudi Arabia, Meteorology & Environmental Protection Administration, *Shoreline Assessment and Cleanup Report,* June 2, 1991.

Sheppard, C., and Price, A. 'Will Marine Life Survive the Gulf War?' *New Scientist,* March 9, 1991, 36–40.

Spaulding, M.L.; Anderson, E.L.; Isaji, T; and Howlett, E. *Simulation of the Oil Trajectory and Fate in the Arabian Gulf from the Mina Al Ahmadi Spill.* Narragansett, RI: Applied Sciences Associates, Inc., n.d., 61.

United Nations, Intergovernmental Oceanographic Commission of UNESCO, *Report of IOC Mission to the ROPME Sea Area (Bahrain, Kuwait and Saudi Arabia) April-May 1991,* by Olof Linden, and Arne Jernelow. (IOC/UNESCO), June 4, 1991, 12 .

U.S., Congress, Senate, Environment and Public Works Committee, Gulf Pollution Task Force, Statement by Richard S. Golob, 102nd Cong., 1st sess., April 11, 1991.

U.S., Congress, Senate, Environment and Public Works Committee, Gulf Pollution Task Force, *Testimony: American Oceans Campaign,* prepared by Andrew Palmer and Dawn Martin, 102nd Cong., 1st sess. (Washington: A.O.C.), July 11, 1991, 12.

World Conservation Monitoring Centre, *Gulf War Environmental Information Service: Impact on the Marine Environment,* Cambridge, U.K.: WCMC. January 31, 1991, 37.

World Society for the Protection of Animals, *Animal Expert Provides Eyewitness Account of Damage to Gulf Wildlife,* Press Release, Boston: WSPA, February 22, 1991, 4.

ENVIRONMENT/OIL FIRES

Horgan, John. 'Up in Flames: Kuwait's Burning Oil Wells Are a Sad Test of Theories.' *Scientific American,* May 1991, 17.

Hunay, Evlija. 'Black Rain in Turkey.' *Environmental Science and Technology,* vol. 26, no. 5, May 1992.

Hussein, King of Jordan. 'Chernobyl in the Oil Fields' (excerpts from a speech before the second World Climate Conference, Geneva, November 6, 1990). *Earth Island Journal,* Winter 1991, 32–33.

Janota, P.; Chase, Robert P.; Koplik, Charles M.; and Medler, Charles L. *Computer Model Assesses the Environmental Impact of Kuwait Oil Fires,* Reading, Mass.: The Analytic Sciences Program, n.d., 3.

Lameloise, P., and Thibaut, G. *Final Report: Measurement Campaign of the Regional Mobile Laboratory for Measurement of Air Quality in Kuwait,* March 27 to April 4, 1991. Paris, France: Surveillance de la Qualite de L´Air en Ile-de-France (AIRPARIF), May 27, 1991.

Lieberman, Senator Joseph, 'Statement of Senator Joseph Lieberman on the Kuwait Oil Fires,' News Release, November 6, 1991, 2.

Limaye, S.S.; Suomi, V.E.; Veldon, C.; and Tripoli, G. 'Satellite Observations of Smoke from the Oil Fires in Kuwait.' *Science,* June 14, 1991, 4.

Norway, Institutt for Luftforskning, *Air Quality Monitoring in Kuwait, First NILU Mission, June 5–12, 1991,* by B. Silversteen and T. C. Berg, Ref: 0-010402, July 1991.

Pearce, Fred. 'Desert Fires Cast a Shadow over Asia.' *New Scientist,* January 12, 1991.

Recer, Paul. 'Gulf Fires,' Associated Press, May 28, 1991.

Sandia National Laboratories, *Potential Impacts of Iraqi Use of Oil as a Defensive Weapon,* January 1991.

Saudi Arabian Meteorology & Environmental Protection Administration (MEPA), *Environmental Impact of Oil Burning in the Kuwaiti Oilfields: A Preliminary Evaluation, Prepared for Presentation at the Expert Meeting on the Atmospheric Part of the Emergency Response to the Kuwait Oilfield Fires,* (WMO, Geneva), April 27_30, 1991, 104.

Small, Richard D. *Environmental Impact of Damage to Kuwaiti Oil Facilities.* Los Angeles: Pacific-Sierra Research Corporation, January 11, 1991.

Small, Richard D. 'Environmental Impact of Fires in Kuwait.' *Nature,* March 7, 1991, 11–12.

UMWELT-DATA Gmbh (on behalf of the German Ministry of Environmental Protection). 'Aircraft Measurements to Investigate the Smoke Plume of the Burning Oil Wells in Kuwait: Preliminary Report,' July 1991, 11.

U.S., Congress, Senate Environment and Public Works Committee, Gulf Pollution Task Force, *Kuwait Oil Field Recovery,* testimony by G.M. Anderson (Santa Fe International Group of Companies), 102nd Congress, 1st sess., October 16, 1991.

U.S., Congress, Senate Environment and Public Works Committee, Gulf Pollution Task Force, *Testimony* by Peter V. Hobbs, 102nd Cong., 1st sess., July 11, 1991.

U.S., Congress, Senate Environment and Public Works Committee, *Summary of Preliminary Findings by U.S. Interagency Team on the Atmospheric Effects of the Smoke from the Kuwait Oil Fires,* prepared by Peter V. Hobbs, 102nd Cong., 1st sess., July 7, 1991, 8.

U.S., Congress, Senate, Environment and Public Works Committee, Gulf Pollution Task Force, *Controlling Damaged Oil Wells in Kuwait,* testimony by Henry W. Kendall, 102nd Cong., 1st sess., June 11, 1991, 11.

U.S., Department of Commerce, National Institute of Standards and Technology, *Report of Test FR 3985: Analysis of Smoke Samples from Oil Well Fires in Kuwait,* by G. Mulholland et al., Gaithersburg, June 20, 1991, 15.

U.S., Department of Energy, Atmospheric Chemistry Program, 'ACP Scheduled to Participate in Kuwait Oil-Fire Analysis', *Pacific Northwest Laboratory Monthly Updates,* April 1991, 1.

U.S., Department of Energy, Atmospheric Chemistry Program, 'Arabian Gulf Team Returns After Successful Mission', *Pacific Northwest Laboratory Monthly Updates,* August 1991.

U.S., Department of Energy, Atmospheric Chemistry Program 'Kuwait Oil-Fire Measurements and Analysis in Progress', *Pacific Northwest Laboratory Monthly Updates,* May 1991, 1–3.

U.S., Department of Energy, Pacific Northwest Laboratory, *Written Statement: Summary of DOE Research Aircraft Activities in Kuwait Oil-Fire Plume,* prepared by Jeremy M. Hales, October 7, 1991, 3.

U.S., Environmental Protection Agency, *Kuwait Oil Fires: Interagency Report* (Washington: EPA), April 3, 1991, 3.

U.S., Lawrence Livermore National Laboratory, Atmosphere and Geophysical Sciences Division, *Global Model Simulations of the Long Range Transport of Soot and Sulfur from the Kuwait Oil Fires,* by Joyce E. Penner (Livermore, CA: A.G.S.D.), June 1991, 16.

U.S., National Aeronautic and Space Administration, Atmospheric Sciences Division, *NASA/EPA Helicopter Operations: Kuwait Oil Fires* (Hampton, VA: NASA-Langley Research), n.d., 8

U.S., National Oceanic and Atmospheric Administration, 'Report of June 4 Scientific Meeting in Bahrain,' *U.S. Dept. of Commerce News,* May 1, 1991.

U.S., NOAA, ibid. 'Soot Over Hawaii May Be From Kuwait.'

Wines, Michael. 'Health Threat from Oil Fires May Rise in Summer.' *New York Times,* April 5, 1991, A10.

World Meteorological Organization, *Report of the WMO Meeting of Experts on the Atmospheric Part of the Joint UN Response to the Kuwait Oilfield Fires.* April 27–30, 1991.

ENVIRONMENT/DESERT IMPACTS

Aoyama, Teiichi. 'The Gulf War Environmental Destruction.' In *No More Gulf!* Tokyo: Greenpeace-Japan, March 23, 1991, 37_47.

Bakan, et al. 'Climate Responses to Smoke from Burning Oil Wells in Kuwait.' *Nature,* May 30, 1991, 367–371.

Baumgardener, Darrel. *Facilities for the Archival and Analysis of Measurements Related to the Kuwait Oil Fires.* Boulder, Co.: National Center for Atmospheric Research, 1991, 11.

Bellamy, Christopher. 'Arrow That Can Stop a Tank.' *The Independent,* November 10, 1991.

Belluardo, John. 'Controlled Burn.' *Harpers Magazine,* June 1991, 24.

Browning, et al. 'Environmental Effects from Burning Oil Wells in Kuwait,' *Nature,* May 30, 1991, 363–367.

Cohen, Nick. 'Radioactive Waste Left in Gulf by Allies.' *The Independent,* November 10, 1991.

Cohen, Nick; and Wilkie. 'Workers Did Not Get Report on Uranium.' *The Independent,* November 10, 1991.

David, Ellis. 'A Hidden Danger in the Shells.' *Time Magazine,* March 18, 1991.

Elsworth, Steve. 'A Report on the Environmental Consequences of Gulf Oil Fires.' *Greenpeace International,* February 20, 1991, 6.

Harvard University School of Public Health, *The Kuwait Oil Fires, Presentation Abstracts & Speaker Biographies,* presented at conference, Cambridge, (Boston: Harvard School of Public Health), August 12–14.

Holden, Constance. 'Kuwait's Unjust Deserts: Damage to Its Desert.' *Science,* March 8, 1991, 1175.

Miller, John M., *Hidden Casualties: the Environmental Consequences of the Persian Gulf Conflict,* Vol. I. San Francisco: ARC/Arms Control Research Center, 1991.

HUMAN CASUALTIES

Church Women United. *Women and the Gulf War.* New York: CWU, March 1991.

Clifton, Tony. 'Burying the Babies.' *Newsweek,* April 22, 1991.

Hoogland, Eric. 'The Other Face of War.' *Middle East Report,* July–August 1991.

Immigration and Refuge Board Documentation Center. *The Persian Gulf: The Situation of Foreign Workers.* Ottawa, Canada: IRBDC, May 1991.

International Development & Refugee Foundation. *Gulf Crisis.* Scarborough, Canada: IDFR, June 1991.

McCutchenson, R. 'Letter from the West Bank.' *BriarPatch,* Fall 1991, 37.

Medical Educational Trust *Continuing Health Costs of the Gulf War.* London, England: MET Report, October 1992.

Medical Educational Trust. *Counting the Human Cost of the Gulf War.* London, England: MET Report, June 1991.

Rothberg, P. 'The Invisible Dead.' *Lies of Our Times,* March 1992, 7.

United Nations, *Report to the Secretary-General on Humanitarian Needs in Kuwait and Iraq in the Immediate Post-Crisis Environment by a Mission in the Area,* by Martti Ahtirsaari, March 20, 1991.

U.S., Congress, Senate, Committee on the Judiciary, Subcommittee on Immigration and Refugee Affairs, *Refugee Crisis in the Persian Gulf,* 102nd Cong., 1991.

HUMAN CASUALTIES IN IRAQ

American Friends Service Committee. *The Starvation of a Nation: The Myth and Reality of Sanctions.* AFSC, June 1991.

Arab-American Medical Association. *Medical Conditions in Iraq, A Report by AAMA Delegation to Iraq,* July 1991.

Bloem, Martin; Farooq, Shamsul; and Kuttub, Atallah. *Vitamin A Deficiency and Malnutrition in Southern Iraq, May 14-26, 1991.* New York/Bangladesh: Helen Keller International, UNICEF, n.d.

Boyle, Francis A. 'Indictment, Complaint and Petition by the 4.5 Million Children of Iraq for Relief from Genocide by President George Bush and the United States of America.' Photocopied. University of Illinois, 1991.

Cainkar, Louise. 'Desert Sin: A Post-War Journey Through Iraq.' In *Beyond the Storm: A Gulf Crisis Reader.* Bennis, Phyllis, and Moushabeck, Michael, eds. New York: Olive Branch Press, 1991, 335_355.

Clark, Ramsay. *The Fire This Time: U.S. War Crimes in the Gulf.* New York: Thunder's Mouth Press, 1992.

Dreze, Jean, and Gazdar, Haris. *Hunger and Poverty In Iraq.* London: London School of Economics, The Development Economics Research Programme and WIDER, D.E.P. No. 23, 1991.

'Eyewitness Iraq.' *Middle East Report,* July–August 1991, 8.

Gulf Peace Team. *Interim Health Assessment Report, April 10–18, 1991.* Putney, Vermont: GPT, 1991.

Gulf Peace Team. *Report on Fourth Convoy to Iraq, March 25–29 1991.* Putney, Vermont: GPT, 1991.

Harvard Study Team. *Public Health in Iraq After the Gulf War.* Cambridge, Mass.: Harvard Study Team, May 1991.

Hattori, Manbu. 'Gulf War and Nuclear Reactor Destruction.' In *No More Gulf!* Tokyo: Greenpeace Japan, 1991, 31–36.

Hitlerman, Joost R. 'Bomb Now, Die Later.' *Mother Jones,* July–August 1991, 46–47.

Hoskins, Eric. 'Starved to Death.' *New Statesman,* May 31, 1991.

Hoskins, Eric, and Bauman, Calvin. *Gulf Peace Team Special Mission to Iraq; Health Assessment Team.* Putney, Vermont: GPT, 1991.

Human Rights Watch. *Deaths in the Gulf War: Civilian Casualties during the Air Campaign and Violations of the Laws of War.* New York: HRW, 1991.

International Study Team. *Infant and Child Mortality and Nutritional Status of Iraqi Children After the Gulf Conflict.* Re-evaluation of preliminary analysis presented in October 1991 by IST in 'Health and Welfare in Iraq After the Gulf Crisis, an In-Depth Assessment.' Cambridge, Mass.: IST, April, 1992. Request for reprints: Sarah Zaidi, Center for Population and Development Studies, Harvard University.

International Study Team. *Health and Welfare in Iraq After the Gulf Crisis.* Cambridge, Mass.: IST, October 1991.

Khanum, Saeeda. 'Inside Iraq.' *New Statesman,* May 31, 1991.

Middle East Watch. *Middle East Watch Condemns Iraq's Practices Toward Foreigners Under Its Control and Reminds Embargo Participants of their Humanitarian Obligations.* New York: MEW, August 29, 1990.

Medicins sans Frontieres. *After Its Exploratory Mission, Medecins Sans Frontieres Is Starting on Intervention in Iraq.* Amman: MSV, March 15, 1991.

Miller, John M. 'Bomb Now, Die Later: Health Impacts of the Gulf War.' *Health/PAC Bulletin,* Fall 1991, 22–26.

Mission, April 3–10, 1991, 'Press Statement,' Somerville, Mass.: PHR, April 15, 1991.

Nongovernmental Organizations Conference, Baghdad, April 28-30 1992, *Save the Children in Iraq,* Conference Papers. Amman: Arab Emergency Health Committee, 1992.

Permanent Mission of Iraq, 'Note Verbale de 1 June 1993 from the Permanent Mission of Iraq to the United Nations Office at Geneva addressed to the Secretary-General of the World Conference on Human Rights,' A/ Conf. 157/4, June 11, 1993.

Sciolino, Elaine, 'Envoy's [April Glaspie's] Testimony on Iraq Is Assailed; Includes Minutes,' *New York Times,* vol. 140, July 13, 1991.

United Nations, World Health Organization/UNICEF. *Special Mission to Iraq, February 16–21.* Geneva: WHO, February 1991.

Human Casualties in Kuwait

ABC News Nightline, 'Charge Kuwaiti Ruling Family Has Political Hit Lists,' New York: American Broadcasting Companies, March 4, 1991.

Amnesty International. 'Kuwait: Amnesty International Calls on Emir to Intervene Over Continuing Torture and Killings,' News Release, New York, April 18, 1991.

'Phoenix: Rising from Kuwait's Ashes.' *The Economist,* May 25, 1991.

Hooper, Rick. *Kuwait: Recent Human Rights Challenges Face the Returning Kuwaiti Government.* New York: LCHR, 1991.

Kuwait, Kuwaiti Ministry of Public Health. 'Untitled letter on behalf of Palestinians and Jordanian doctors in Kuwait outlining human rights violations,' National Committee for Defending Palestinian Human Rights, 1991.

Lesch, Ann M. 'Palestinians in Kuwait.' Institute for Palestine Studies and Kuwait University. Berkeley: University of California Press, Summer 1991.

Middle East Report. 'Kuwait Diary: A Scarred Society.' September–October 1991.

Middle East Watch. *A Victory Turned Sour: Human Rights in Kuwait Since the Liberation.* New York: MEW, September 1991.

Middle East Watch. *Kuwait: Deteriorating Human Rights Conditions Since the Early Occupation.* New York: MEW, November 16, 1990.

Middle East Watch. *Kuwait's Stolen Incubators.* New York: MEW, 1992.

Middle East Watch. 'Letter to U.S. Secretary of Defense Richard Cheney from Andrew Whitley, Executive Director, about Human Rights Violations in Kuwait,' March 7, 1991.

Middle East Watch. 'Middle East Watch Condemns Continuing Abuses in Kuwait,' Press Release, New York, September 11, 1991.

Middle East Watch. *Nowhere To Go: The Tragedy of the Remaining Palestinian Families in Kuwait.* New York: MEW, 1991.

Middle East Watch. *Widespread Arrests in Kuwait*. New York: MEW, May 10, 1990.

Middle East Watch. *Widespread Torture of Palestinians in Kuwait*. Scottsdale, AZ: MEW, 1991.

Physicians for Human Rights. *Medical Action Alert 33: Kuwait*. New York: PHR, October 11, 1991.

Sherry, Virginia N. 'Palestinians in Kuwait.' *The Nation*, March 18, 1991.

United Nations. *Report to the Secretary-General by a United Nations Mission, Led by Mr. Abdulrahim A. Farah, Former Under-Secretary General, Assessing the Scope and Nature of Damage Inflicted on Kuwait's Infrastructure During the Iraqi Occupation of the Country from August 2, 1990 to February 27, 1991* (s/22535), April 29, 1991.

U.S., Congress, House of Representatives, 'Human Rights in Kuwait,' Testimony of Michael Posner, Executive Director, Lawyers Committee for Human Rights, 102nd Cong., 1st sess., June 11, 1991.

U.S., Department of State, 'U.S. Emergency and Reconstruction Assistance to the State of Kuwait.' Signed by Secretary of State James Baker, December 15, 1990.

LAW AND POLICY

Albert, M. 'Conspiracy? . . . Not!' *Z Magazine*, January 1991, 17.

Amnesty International. *Iraq/Occupied Kuwait: Human Rights Violations Since August 2, 1990*. New York: A.I., December 1990.

'The Arab World and the Gulf War.' *Arab Studies Quarterly*, Special Double Issue, Vol. 13, Nos. 1 & 2, Winter/Spring 1991.

BBC World Service. *Gulf Crisis: A Chronology*. Detroit: Longman Current Affairs, 1991.

Bennis, Phyllis, and Moushabeck, Michael, eds. *Beyond the Storm: A Gulf Crisis Reader*. New York: Olive Branch Press, 1991.

Browne, Marjorie Ann. *UN Security Resolutions on Iraq*. Washington: GPO, 1992.

Carlisle, Jon. 'Brave New World Order.' *Propaganda Review*, Fall 1991.

Castro, Fidel, and Alarcon, Ricardo. *U.S. Hands Off The Mideast! Cuba Speaks Out at the United Nations*. New York, London, Montreal, Sydney: Pathfinder, February 1991.

Chomsky, Noam. *The Gulf Crisis*. Cambridge, Mass.: Noam Chomsky, 1991.

Chomsky, Noam. *New World Order: A Postwar Analysis*. Cambridge, Mass.: Noam Chomsky, 1991.

Clark, Ramsey, et al. *War Crimes: A Report on United States War Crimes Against Iraq*. Washington: Maisonneuve Press, 1992.

Colhoun, J. 'Probe: Bush Pushed Pro-Iraq Credit Policy.' *The Guardian*, March 18, 1992, 4.

Graff, James A. *Just War or Just Butchery?* Toronto: Near East Cultural and Educational Foundation, 1991.

Halliday, Fred. 'Looking Back Without Anger (the Left and the Persian Gulf Crisis.)' *In These Times*, January 15, 1992, 16.

Institute of Policy Studies. *Crisis in the Gulf*. Washington: IPS, October 1990.

'The Real Legacy of the War with Hussein.' *In These Times*, January 15, 1992, 14.

'The Betrayal of the Kurdish Rebellion,' *International Viewpoint*. [Montreuil, France], February 17, 1992, 4.

Kahlidid, Walid. *Empty Reforms: Saudi Arabia_s New Basic Laws*. New York: Middle East Watch, 1992.

Middle East Watch. *Middle East Watch Urges All Parties to Obey Rules of War Protecting Civilians*. New York: MEW, January 18, 1991.

Mohr, C. 'The Gulf War and the Technologists.' *Lies of Our Times*, March 1992, 20.

Salinger, Pierre, and Laurent, Eric. *Secret Dossier: The Hidden Agenda Behind the Gulf War*. New York: Penguin Books, 1991.

Smith, Jean Edward. *George Bush's War*. New York: Henry Holt and Company, Inc., 1991.

U.S., Congress, Gulf Pollution Task Force Committee on Environment, and Senate, Committee for Environment and Public Works, *International Legal Deterrence to Environmental Damage During Warfare*, testimony by John Ballach, 102nd Cong., July 11, 1991.

Yant, Martin. *Desert Mirage: The True Story of the Gulf War*. Buffalo, New York: Prometheus Books, 1991.

Zunes, S. 'Is U.S. Overstaying Its Gulf Welcome?' *In These Times*, February 26, 1992, 2.

THE MEDIA AND THE GULF WAR

Benjamin, E. 'The Silent War in Iraq.' *The Guardian*, January 15, 1992, 10.

Cockburn, Alexander. 'When the U.S. Press Fled Baghdad.' *The Nation*, January 27, 1992.

Cox, R. 'Too Little, Too Late/Gannet Foundation.' *Propaganda Review*, Fall 1991, 35.

Emmons, G. 'Did PR Firms Invent Gulf War Stories?' *In These Times*, January 22, 1992.

Gannet Foundation Media Center. *The Media at War*. New York: GFMC, 1991.

Gerteis, C.K. *The Gulf War: Alternative International News Reports Compiled from Computer Net Sources*. Santa Cruz, 1991.

Jhally, S., et al. 'The Gulf War: Study of Media, Public Opinion.' *Propaganda Review*. Fall 1991, 3.

Lakoff, G. 'The Arab Viewpoint' [propaganda and the Gulf War]. *Propaganda Review*, Fall 1991.

Leiper, S. 'Myths, Lies and Videotape (Gulf War lies).' *Propaganda Review*, Fall 1992, 12.

Leiper, et al. 'Propaganda Watch/Operation Desert Smarm,' *Propaganda Review*, Fall 1991, 3.

Schechter, D. 'The Gulf War and the Death of TV News.' *The Independent*. New York: Foundation for Independent Video and Film, January, 1992, 28.

Smith, R. 'Media Watch/The TV War As a Game Show.' *Propaganda Review*, Fall 1991, 32.

Taylor, Phillip M. *War and the Media: Propaganda and Persuasion in the Gulf War*. St. Martin's Press, 1992.

U.S., Congress, House/Senate, Joint Committee on Government Affairs, *Pentagon Rules on Media Access to Persian Gulf War*, 102nd Cong., 1st sess., February 20, 1991.

'Gulf War' [military restrictions on the media], *Z Magazine*. Fall 1992, 7.

MILITARY

Close, Sandy, and Bernstein, Dennis. 'Pentagon Planners Outline Key U.S. Military Role in Kuwait Recovery.' *Pacific News Service*, February 25–March 1, 1991.

Kaku, M. 'Operation Desert Lie: Pentagon Confesses.' *The Guardian,* March 11, 1992, 4.

Ringle, Ken. 'After the Battles, Defusing the Debris.' *Washington Post,* March 1, 1991, B1.

Tapp, Mara. 'Computerized War Games,' transcript of interview with Joshua M. Epstein of the Brookings Institute (Chicago: WBEZ, 'By the Hour'), January 17, 1991.

U.S. Army, 352nd Civil Affairs Command, 'Annex G (Civil Affairs) to Operation Plan Service' [for Kuwait], n.d.

U.S., Congress, *Conduct of the Persian Gulf Conflict: An Interim Report to Congress,* Department of Defense, July 1991.

PROTESTING THE WAR AND SANCTIONS

Newton, Eric, and Rapoport, Roger, eds. *The Bay Area at War: How We Reacted to the Persian Gulf Crisis.* Oakland: Heyday Books, 1991.

Sumberg, C. 'Reconciling Jewish Left.' *Nuclear Times,* Winter 1991, 43.

U.S. National Network to Lift Economic Sanctions Against Iraq (NNLESAI). *Iraq: the Impact of Sanctions. Materials for Educating and Organizing.* Nyack, New Jersey, 1992.

Appendix 4: Biographies

THE EDITORS

Saul Bloom has been an activist for over twenty years. Between 1978 and 1983 Saul served as a United States National and Pacific Southwest Regional Campaign Coordinator for Greenpeace. Campaigns conducted by Mr. Bloom at Greenpeace focused on radioactive waste transportation, nuclear weapons testing and disarmament. Mr. Bloom coordinated Nuclear California (GP/CIR 1981), a joint project between Greenpeace and the Center for Investigative Reporting which produced the first investigative anthology on the impacts of nuclear technology on California. Saul has been the Director of ARC/Arms Control Research Center since 1983 and has authored research papers on disarmament and reviewed numerous environmental impact statements and toxic waste cleanup and redevelopment planning documents. Mr. Bloom is a member of the California Environmental Protection Agency's Base Closures Environmental Advisory Committee, the Presidio Army Base Technical Review Committee, the San Francisco Hunters Point Naval Shipyard Citizen Advisory Committee on Toxic Contamination and the East Bay Conversion and Reinvestment Commission's Environmental Committee. Saul's articles and editorials have appeared in the *San Francisco Examiner, San Francisco Chronicle, Bay Guardian, Christian Science Monitor, Los Angeles Herald* and other newspapers. He is executive editor of *Hidden Casualties, Volume II.*

John M. Miller conducted most of the interviews for *Hidden Casualties, Volume I* and many of those for *Volume II.* He is the coordinator of ARC/Arms Control Research Center's International Clearinghouse on the Military and the Environment. He also serves on the coordinating committees of the National Nuclear Weapons Facilities Network and the Campaign Against U.S. Military Bases in the Philippines. In addition to being the editor of the *Mobilizer*, the quarterly magazine of National Mobilization for Survival, John is a widely published author. His printed works include *Bases and Battleships: An Introduction to Foreign Military Presence; Banning the Bombmakers: Challenging Nuclear Weapons Production;* and *No Safe Harbor: The Consequences of a Nuclear Weapons Accident in New York Harbor.* John has also given talks on related issues in England, Greece, Iceland, India, Japan, Norway, Scotland, Sweden and the Philippines.

James Warner has a B.A. in philosophy and experimental psychology from Oxford University, and a diploma in environmental management from Stirling University in Scotland. He is currently ARC's international research associate.

Philippa Winkler studied history at the London School of Economics and Political Science. Her articles on U.S. foreign policy, naval bases and naval strategy have been published in the *Oakland Tribune.* As a reporter, she revealed the existence of underseas nuclear dump sites up and down the Pacific Coast. Her story about nuclear waste leaking into San Francisco Bay spurred the reopening of congressional hearings. As a human rights advocate Philippa helped raise concerns about U.S.

human rights violations at bilateral negotiations, and recently she served as nongovernmental delegate to the UN Human Rights Commission in Geneva. She is a senior research analyst at ARC/Arms Control Research Center and the director of the Hidden Casualties project.

Contributing Editors

Ross Mirkarimi, M.A. in economics and international relations, served as Persian Gulf campaign coordinator for ARC/Arms Control Research Center. Prior to joining ARC, he was director of the San Francisco Nuclear Freeze Zone Coalition. Ross accompanied the International Study Team (IST) to Iraq in the Fall of 1991, and returned for a visit in May 1992. His articles describing what he saw on these visits have appeared in the national media, including the *Christian Science Monitor,* the *Denver Post, Buzzworm* and *Ms.* magazine. Ross is involved in an international coalition for the lifting of nonmilitary sanctions against Iraq and currently sits on the Commission on the Environment for San Francisco.

Daniel Robicheau is a freelance writer, researcher and teacher who has a special interest in U.S. foreign policy toward Third World countries.

Contributors

Bryan Barrass is a former employee of the Porton-Down Chemical Biological Defense Establishment in the United Kingdom.

Bela Bhatia, M.A. in social work, B.Sc. and M.S. in child psychology, is a lawyer and freelance writer. She has worked for five years as a human rights activist in rural Gujarat, India, organizing women's action groups. Her most recent works include "Official Drought Relief Measures: A Case Study of Gujarat" (*Social Action,* 1988) and "Lush Fields and Parched Throats: The Political Economy of Groundwater in Gujarat" (forthcoming in the *Working Paper Series of the World Institute for Development Economics Research,* Helsinki). She was a member of the International Study Team.

Francis Boyle is Professor of International Law at the University of Illinois, Champaign, Illinois. He served as an advisor to Congressmember Henry Gonzalez on an impeachment resolution against President Bush, as well as to the International War Crimes Tribunal.

Tony Burgess, Ph.D., is a desert ecologist who worked with the United States Geological Survey in Tucson, Arizona, and serves as a consultant to numerous public and private organizations. He is currently doing research at the Geosciences Department at the University of Arizona.

Hugh W. Church has an M.A. in physics and meteorology from the University of New Mexico and an M.A. in Meteorology from the University of California at Los Angeles. He has worked for Sandia National Laboratories for 36 years.

John Cox, Ph.D., C.Eng., M.B.C.S., FI.Chem.E., M.Cons.E., F.R.S.A., is a consultant chemical and oil industry engineer in Talywaun, Gwent, Wales, with experience in the Gulf region. He is the vice-president of the British Campaign for Nuclear Disarmament.

Beth Osborne Daponte has a B.A. from Boston University in mathematics and sociology (double major), and an M.A. in sociology/demography from the University of Chicago, where she is currently a doctoral candidate. She is a demographer at the Center for International Research in the U.S. Census Bureau, currently on leave of absence. Since August, 1992, she has been a visiting faculty member at the Heinz School of Public Policy and Management at Carnegie Mellon University. Daponte's recent focus examines the demographic effects of wars and violence on populations. This work involves using demographic techniques to estimate casualties from the Gulf War. She is also currently working on an examination of the domestic food distribution system to the poor.

Jay C. Davis, Ph.D., is the director of the Center for Accelerator Mass Spectrometry, a group applying ion beam and isotopic tools to research in biomedical dosimetry, geochemistry and climate change, materials research, combustion research and arms control at the Lawrence Livermore National Laboratory in California. He is a nuclear physicist by training, and has concentrated primarily on the application of nuclear and accelerator technologies.

Sam Diener is a public draft registration resister and a military and draft counselor for CCCO-Western Region, a nonprofit agency for military and draft counseling founded in 1948. He majored in peace studies and history at Washington University at St. Louis.

Atle Dyregrov, Ph.D., is the director of the Center for Crisis Psychology in Bergen, Norway. He is a clinical and research psychologist and teaches at the Faculty of Medicine and Faculty of Psychology at Bergen University. His former positions include five years of clinical and research work at the Children's Hospital in Bergen, and four years at the University of Bergen. His clinical work has covered areas such as grief reactions in parents following the loss of a child, grief in children, organizing psychosocial disaster assistance, work with disaster workers and work with children in war situations.

Sylvia Earle, Ph.D., is a marine scientist who is currently Director of Deep Ocean Technology, Inc., and Deep Ocean Engineering, Inc., who design, manufacture and operate equipment in the ocean and other remote environments. She accepted a presidential appointment as chief scientist of the National Oceanic and Atmospheric Administration (NOAA) in 1990. In 1992 she became an advisor to NOAA. She led the first team of women aquanauts during the Tektite Project in 1970; holds a depth record for solo deep diving (3,000 feet) and has written more than 70 publications concerning marine science and technology. Dr. Earle has been the subject of articles in the *New York Times* and *Scientific American,* and has been featured in a segment on ABC-TV's *20/20.*

Jorge Emmanuel, Ph.D., is president of an environmental and engineering consulting firm in California. He is a licensed professional engineer and a registered environmental professional. During his sixteen years of industrial and academic experience, he has published and presented technical papers and reports in engineering, chemistry and environmental science.

Mike Evans is coordinator of the Important Bird Areas in the Middle East Project of the International Council for Bird Preservation (ICBP) based in the U.K. He has previously worked for the National Commission for Wildlife Conservation and Development (NCWCD) in Saudi Arabia and has lived in Yemen investigating that country's natural history. His other extended nature conservation fieldwork has been in Britain, Ethiopia, Madagascar and Uganda.

Lydia Gans, Ph.D., is a professor emerita who taught mathematics and statistics at California State University, with degrees in mathematics and applied statistics. She currently works as a consultant in public policy as applied to issues of health and disability.

James Garbarino, Ph.D., is president of the Erikson Institute for Advanced Study in Child Development, and has lectured and written extensively on topics related to child care, education and abuse/neglect. Dr. Garbarino received the American Psychological Association's Award for Distinguished Professional Contributions to Public Service in 1989. For the last three years he has been at work on a book exploring the impact of war on children and has traveled to war zones in Cambodia, Mozambique, Nicaragua and the Middle East, as well as to inner-city Chicago neighborhoods.

Burr Heneman is an environmental consultant and the California director of the Center for Marine Conservation. His clients have included the U.S. Marine Mammal Commission, the National Ocean Pollution Program Office (Department of Commerce), and the International Council for Bird Preservation. Assignments have included assessing the effects of the Exxon *Valdez* spill, and the effects of marine debris in the North Sea and along the northwest Atlantic coast.

Lara Hilder is an aerosol chemist and soot specialist employed by Lawrence Berkeley Laboratory. She is a member of the Sierra Club Committee on Military Impacts on the Environment, and coeditor of *Impacts*, its newsletter.

Peter V. Hobbs is a professor with the Department of Atmospheric Sciences, University of Washington, Seattle.

Tahan Jones joined the military at age seventeen and served four years. He was a regular corporal at the time of his unauthorized absence from the Gulf War. Now aged twenty-three, he works part-time for the American Friends Services Committee's Peace and Justice Outreach Project, working with young people on issues of militarism and police brutality and on economic issues. He is studying part-time at Laney Community College.

Mahmoud Al Khoshman, B.Sc. in chemical engineering (environmental) has also completed advanced courses in computer applications, and his area of expertise is industrial pollution.

Mary Kawar, M.Sc., is a Ph.D. student in gender studies at the London School of Economics. She has conducted research on "Women and Traditional Medicine in Southern Jordan" and "Population Policy and Gender Needs in Jordan," and has worked as a research officer for the International Labor Organization project on "Employment Promotion and Manpower Planning" at the Ministry of Planning in Amman, Jordan. She is a founding member of the Women Studies Center in Amman. Her Ph.D. thesis deals with the expansion of female employment in Jordan.

Lora Lumpe is a senior research analyst at the Federation of American Scientists in Washington, D.C., where she directs the Arms Monitoring Project and codirects the Zero Ballistic Missiles Project. She compiles and edits the monthly *Arms Sales Monitor*, which reports on and analyzes U.S. arms sales and arms sales policies.

Clovis Maksoud, LL.B, J.D., is the director of the Center for the Study of the Global South at the School of International Services at The American University. From 1979 to 1990, he was Ambassador and Permanent Observer of the League of Arab States at the United Nations and its Chief Representative in the United States. Dr. Maksoud is the author of several books on the Middle East and the Third World, among them: *The Meaning of Nonalignment, The Crisis of the Arab Left, Reflections on Afro-Asianism,* and *The Arab League.*

Carol Melnick is a self-taught artist, political cartoonist and illustrator who graduated from Mills College, Oakland, California, where she studied film history and video production. Carol Melnick may be contacted through ARC/Arms Control Research Center.

Matthew Stanley Meselson, Ph.D., is a professor of biochemistry and molecular biology at Harvard University. He is known internationally for his demonstration of how DNA replicates in dividing cells and for his invention of an important ultracentrifugal method for analyzing the densities of giant molecules. He has served as a consultant on chemical and biological weapons to various government agencies, has received numerous awards, and is currently a member of the Council of the Smithsonian Institution.

Halûk Özkaynak, Ph.D., is currently a research associate in the Department of Environmental Health at the Harvard School of Public Health. He has a Ph.D. in mathematical physics from Harvard University and an M.S. in air pollution control from the Harvard School of Public Health. He is principal investigator of various Superfund exposure and risk assessment projects that involve developing probabilistic exposure assessment models to characterize the distribution of population exposures, and cancer and noncancerous risks, from exposures to a large number of chemical and radioactive pollutants.

Karen Parker is an attorney specializing in international human rights and humanitarian (armed conflict) law. Ms. Parker represented the victims of a hospital for mentally ill and retarded persons bombed during the United States military action against Grenada. In this landmark case, the Commission found a prima facie case against the United States for violations of the right to life and other human rights. Some of the humanitarian law issues publicly raised by Ms. Parker regarding United States violations against Nicaragua were favorably addressed by the International Court of Justice in its decision of June 27, 1986 (Military and Paramilitary Activities In and Against Nicaragua, 1986 I.C.J. 14), in which the Court found the United States in violation.

Farn Parungo has a Ph.D. in chemistry from the University of Colorado and a B.S. in chemistry from Taiwan University. She has worked for the U.S. National Oceanic and Atmospheric Administration (NOAA) since 1970.

Alfred P. Picardi is a private environmental consultant to financial institutions, private industry and public interest groups. He has worked with the Environmental Protection Agency Office of Toxic Substance, the Virginia State Water Control Board and private consulting firms. He has written over 120 articles and technical reports. Mr. Picardi is a certified hazardous materials manager and a registered environmental assessor in California.

Bennett Ramburg, Ph.D, is the author of *Nuclear Power Plants as Weapons of the Enemy: An Unrecognized Military Peril,* published in 1985. He is senior research associate at the Center for International Relations at the University of California, Los Angeles, and director of research for the Committee to Bridge the Gap.

Magne Raundalen is the director of the Research for Children Program, Center for Crisis Psychology, Bergen, Norway. He has published more than ten books on topics related to child psychology with a special focus on children under threat: children with cancer, children's fear of nuclear weapons, and children and war.

James Perran Ross is a biologist and a specialist in sea turtle conservation at the Florida Museum of Natural History, Gainesville, Florida.

Cyrus Salam is a software developer who has traveled to Kurdistan, most recently since the end of the Gulf War. He is a member of the Kurdish National Congress, a North American organization working to publicize the situation in Kurdistan.

Mariam Shahin is a staff reporter with the *Jordanian Times*, as well as freelancer with the *Independent* in London. She was a researcher at the Royal Scientific Society in Amman, Jordan. She has also worked as coproducer on two documentaries, *Women in Jordan* (1991) and *Portraits of Women in Iraq in the Postwar Period*.

Richard D. Small, Ph.D., M. Phil., is Director of Thermal Sciences at Pacific-Sierra Research Corporation, where he manages and conducts basic and applied research in topics related to atmospheric physics, nuclear weapons effect, and systems analysis. His broad-based research on smoke production from global nuclear exchanges was a focal point in the nuclear winter debate. Dr. Small has previously taught at the Technion-Israel Institute of Technology and the University of California, Los Angeles, has presented numerous conference lectures and seminars, and is an active reviewer for a wide range of technical journals.

Thomas J. Sullivan, Ph.D., is a computer modeler at the Lawrence Livermore National Laboratories, operated by the Department of Energy in Livermore, California. The U.S. government uses his model of the atmosphere to predict where radioactivity from nuclear accidents is headed. His model tracked the paths of particles and gases released from Three Mile Island in March 1979 and Chernobyl in April 1986.

Boyce Thorne-Miller is a marine biologist and director of science with Ocean Advocates, a national environmental advocacy group focusing on the ocean environment. Her range of environmental work has included a book on the protection of marine biological diversity, the international regulation of the disposal of wastes in marine waters, the national regulation of the disposal of contaminated dredge materials and sewage sludge in coastal waters, the effects of oil spills on marine ecosystems, identifying biological indicators of marine pollution, and the designation of marine sanctuaries. She previously worked as senior scientist at Friends of the Earth U.S., and continues to represent Friends of the Earth International in meetings on various international treaties where the organization has observer status.

Abdullah Toukan, Ph.D., is chief scientific advisor to King Hussein of Jordan and secretary-general of the High Council for Science and Technology.

Adam D. Trombly is a physicist and co-founder/director of Project Earth for the Aspen Institute for Advanced Studies. Mr. Trombly was a research physicist for the Acyclic Closed Magnetic Experiment, eventually known as ACME Energy Research, from 1980 to 1983. In 1984 he received the Reynolds Endowment Award, which enabled him to study the dynamics of large-scale self-growing atmospheric inversions, specifically concentrating on the "Sahara outbreak" phenomenon, which sends out streams of suspended dust across the Atlantic. An advisor to UNEP, Mr. Trombly has appeared numerous times on national and international television.

Sarah Zaidi, M.Sc., is currently a doctoral student at the Harvard School of Public Health in the Department of Population and International Health. Her work is concentrated on the reproductive health of women and their reproductive outcome. Her research also focuses on issues of health and hunger and the demography of Islamic countries. She is a recipient of the MacArthur Fellowship on Population and Development at Harvard University.

The following International Study Team members, along with Sarah Zaidi, helped compile *Infant and Child Mortality and Nutritional Status of Iraqi Children after the Gulf Conflict*, (April 1992):

Albert Ascherio, M.D., M.P.H., Department of Epidemiology, Harvard School of Public Health, Boston, MA, U.S.A

Robert Chase, M.D., C.C.F.P., Department of Clinical Epidemiology and Biostatistics, McMasters University, Toronto, ONT, Canada

Tim Cote, M.D., M.P.H., National Institutes of Health, Bethesda, MD, U.S.A.

Godelieve Dehaes, M.D., and **Jilali Laaouej**, M.D., both of Medical Aid for the Third World, Brussels, Belgium

Saleh Al Qaderi, M.B.B.S., Department of Community Health, Jordan University of Science and Technology, Irbid, Jordan

Saher Shuqaidef, M.B.B.S., Dr.P.H., Department of International Health, Johns Hopkins University, Baltimore, MD, U.S.A.

Mary Catherine Smith, M.Sc., Department of Epidemiology, Harvard School of Public Health, Boston, MA, U.S.A.

Appendix 5: Abbreviations and Glossary

Abbreviations

AEA	U.K. Atomic Energy Authority
AGU	U.S. American Geophysical Union
ARAC	Atmospheric Release Advisory Capability at LLNL
ARAMCO	Arab American Oil Company
BCCI	Bank of Credit and Commerce International
BNL	Italian Banca Nazionale del Lavoro
CBUs	cluster bomb units
CBWs	chemical and biological weapons
CCC	Commodity Credit Corporation
CCN	cloud condensation nuclei
CEA	French Atomic Energy Commission
CEC	Commission of the European Communities
CIA	U.S. Central Intelligence Agency
CIR	U.S. Department of Commerce Bureau of the Census Center for Investigative Research
C.I.S.	Commonwealth of Independent States (the former U.S.S.R.)
CND	U.K. Campaign for Nuclear Disarmament
CNN	U.S. Cable News Network
CTA	Brazilian Centro Technico Aeronautico
CWC	Chemical Weapons Convention
DNA	U.S. Defense Nuclear Agency
DOD	U.S. Department of Defense
DOE	U.S. Department of Energy
DSAA	U.S. Defense Security Assistance Agency
DTI	British Department of Trade and Industry
ECGD	Export Credit Guarantee Development
EMIS	electromagnetic isotope separation
ENMOD	Convention on the Prohibition of Military or Any Other Hostile Use of Environmental Modification Techniques, United Nations, 1977
EPA	U.S. Environmental Protection Agency
FAE	fuel-air explosives
FAO	UN Food and Agriculture Organization
FBI	U.S. Federal Bureau of Investigation
FDA	U.S. Food and Drug Administration

FOE	Friends of the Earth
GAO	U.S. General Accounting Office
GCC	Gulf Cooperation Council
IAEA	UN International Atomic Energy Agency
IAPGTF	U.S. Interagency Persian Gulf Task Force
ICBP	International Council for Bird Preservation
ICJ	International Court of Justice
ICRC	International Committee of the Red Crescent
ILO	UN International Labor Organization
IMO	UN International Maritime Organization
INC	Iraqi National Congress
IOC	International Oceanographic Commission
IPPNW	International Physicians for the Preservation of Nuclear War
IST	International Study Team
IUCN	International Union for the Conservation of Nature and Natural Resources
LLNL	U.S. Lawrence Livermore National Laboratory
MARPOL	International Marine Convention on the Prevention of Pollution from Ships
MEPA	Saudi Arabian Meteorological and Environmental Protection Agency
MTCR	Missile Technology Control Regime
NAC	U.S. National Advisory Council
NASA	U.S. National Aeronautics and Space Administration
NCAR	U.S. National Center for Atmospheric Research
NCWCD	Saudi Arabian National Commission on Wildlife Conservation and Development
NEPA	U.S. National Environmental Policy Act
NGOs	nongovernmental organizations
NOAA	U.S. National Oceanic and Atmospheric Administration
NPT	Nuclear Non-Proliferation Treaty
NRC	U.S. Nuclear Regulatory Commission
NSC	U.S. National Security Council
NSF	U.S. National Science Foundation
OECD	Organization for Economic Cooperation and Development
OPEC	Organization of Petroleum Exporting Countries
OTA	U.S. Office of Technology Assessment
PAHs	polynuclear aromatic hydrocarbons
PICs	products of incomplete combustion
PHS	U.S. Public Health Service
PIO	U.S. Public Information Office
PLO	Palestine Liberation Organization
RCC	Iraqi Revolutionary Command Council

ROPME	Regional Organization for the Protection of the Marine Environment
SEPP	Iraqi State Enterprise for Pesticide Production
SIPRI	Stockholm International Peace Research Institute
SLAR	side-looking aerial radar
SOTI	Iraqi State Organization for Technical Industry
U.A.E.	United Arab Emirates
UN	United Nations
UNDP	UN Development Programme
UNDRO	Office of the UN Disaster Relief Co-ordinator
UNEP	UN Environment Programme
UNESCO	UN Educational, Scientific and Cultural Organization
UNHCR	UN High Commission for Refugees
UNICEF	UN Children's Fund (formerly the UN International Children's Emergency Fund)
UNIKOM	UN Iraq-Kuwait Observation Mission
UNSCOM	UN Special Commission (for the destruction of Iraq's biological and chemical warfare and missile capabilities)
URENCO	European Uranium Enrichment Consortium
USDA	U.S. Department of Agriculture
WCMC	World Conservation Monitoring Centre
WHO	World Health Organization
WMO	World Meteorological Organization
WWF	World Wide Fund for Nature

Glossary

ACID RAIN	Rain with a pH below 5.6, often due to presence of sulfuric and nitric acids.
ACUTE	Severe but of short duration, as opposed to chronic.
AEROSOL	Particulate and liquid droplets suspended in the atmosphere.
ALBEDO	Fraction of the radiation striking a surface that is reflected—corresponds to color within the visible spectrum.
AMPHISBAENIANS	Tropical lizards of the genus *Amphisbaena*.
ANFAL	The Iraqi government's name for its military program against 4,000 Kurdish towns and villages in late 1980s.
ANTHRAX	Disease of animals and humans caused by the spore-forming bacterium *Bacillus anthracis*.

ARTESIAN WELL	A well tapping groundwater that lies in an aquifer or permeable bed of rock between zones of impermeable rock. Hydrostatic pressure causes the water to rise to ground level.
ARTHROPODS	Class of jointed invertebrates that includes crustaceans and insects.
AUTONOMY ACCORDS	1970 law passed by the Iraqi government granting a small level of autonomy to the three Iraqi governorates with a mainly Kurdish population.
BAATHISM	Political philosophy of the Arab Baath Socialist Party, units of which are in power in Iraq and Syria. A pan-Arabist movement opposed to imperialism, Zionism and Marxism.
BALLISTIC MISSILES	Long-range missiles guided for part of their flight, but becoming free-falling objects as they approach their targets.
BARRAGE	An artificial obstruction in a water course to increase the depth of the water and facilitate irrigation.
BENIGN	Not threatening to health.
BENTHIC	Sea-bottom dwelling (used to describe plants and animals.)
BERM	A long low mound or dike, either human-made or the result of wave action on a beach.
BIOASSAY	Evaluation of the effects of a substance by use of experimental animals.
BIODEGRADE	To decompose under microbial action.
BIOMASS	Mass of biological material.
BIOREMEDIATION	Restoring the environment through the addition of bacteria.
BIOTYPE	A group of organisms sharing a specified part of their genetic make-up.
BLISTERING AGENTS	Chemicals such as mustard gas that attack tissue cells.
BLOOD GASES	Gases such as hydrogen cyanide that interrupt cellular respiration.
BLOOM	Sudden increase in population density.
BOTULISM	Food poisoning caused by the botulinum toxin, causing intestinal and nervous disorders.
CALUTRON	California University magnetron, a machine for magnetically separating U-235 from U-238 isotopes of uranium.
CARCINOGENIC	Cancer-causing.
CATALYST	A substance that influences the speed of a chemical reaction and can be recovered unchanged at the end of the reaction.
CENTRIFUGE	Machine that uses centrifugal force to separate particles of different density.

CHELONIANS	Animals belonging to the order *Chelonia,* comprising the turtles.
CHOLERA	Intestinal diseases caused by *vibrio cholerae,* characterized by violent diarrhea, vomiting and muscular cramps.
CHRONIC	Lasting a long time or recurring often, as opposed to acute.
CLIMATOLOGY	The science dealing with climatic phenomena.
CLOSTRIDIUM	Any of a large genus of spore-forming bacteria, including those causing tetanus and botulism.
CLOUD CONDENSATION NUCLEI	Tiny solid and liquid particles on which water vapor condenses.
COAGULANT	Chemical that turns a liquid into a soft, semisolid mass.
COCCIDIOIDOMYCOSIS	An infectious disease caused by breathing in spores of *Coccidioides immutis.* Early symptoms resemble those of the common cold or influenza—later problems are fever, appetite and weight loss, bluish skin, breathing difficulty and arthritic pain.
COLIFORM BACTERIA	Aerobic bacteria usually found in the human colon.
COMPUTER-NUMERICALLY-CONTROLLED MACHINES	General term for automated manufacturing equipment reliant on computer techniques.
CONVECTION	Atmospheric circulation due to rising of warmer air and sinking of cooler air.
CORAL	Colonies of marine polyps of the class *Anthozoa* that deposit a hard skeleton, forming reefs, usually in tropical seas.
CYCLONE	Weather system characterized by relatively low air pressure compared with surrounding air, violent winds and torrential rain.
DEMOGRAPHY	The statistical science dealing with the distribution, density and other characteristics of human populations.
DENGUE	An infectious fever characterized by severe pains in the joints and muscles.
DEPLETED URANIUM	U-238, the less radioactive isotope separated from U-235 during the process of enriching uranium for nuclear weapons and reactors.
DESALINIZATION	The making of fresh water from salt water.
DESERTIFICATION	The destruction or degradation of vegetation in arid and semi-arid areas.
DILMUN	Sumerian name of an ancient independent kingdom that flourished around Bahrain around 2000 B.C., trading with Sumeria and Babylon.

ENDANGERED SPECIES	According to the *IUCN Red Data Book,* applies to a species unable to reproduce in numbers sufficient to ensure survival, and therefore likely to become extinct if present trends continue.
ENDEMIC	Restricted to a given locality.
EPIDEMIOLOGY	The study of the spread of disease.
ESCARPMENT	Steep slope or cliff.
ESTUARY	The area where a river's current meets the sea's tide.
EUTROPHIC	Ecological condition of a lake characterized by an over-abundant accumulation of nutrients.
FALLOUT	The raining out of particles lifted into the atmosphere after an explosion or fire.
FISSIONABLE	Consisting of atoms that can be split to release large amounts of energy.
GANGRENE	The local death of soft tissues due to lack of blood supply.
GASTROENTERITIS	Inflammation of the stomach and intestine, usually of toxic origin.
GASTROINTESTINAL	Pertaining to stomach and intestine.
GENOTOXIC	Capable of damaging genetic material.
GLOBAL WARMING	Climate change in the form of increasing average temperatures due to human-caused input of carbon dioxide, ozone, methane, chlorofluorocarbons and other gases that enhance the greenhouse effect.
GREENHOUSE EFFECT	The process by which solar radiation is trapped by gases and particles in the atmosphere and warms the planet.
GROUNDWATER	Underground water that saturates the upper portions of the Earth's crust.
GULF	Area of water reaching inland larger than a bay.
GYPSUM	Widely distributed mineral containing hydrous calcium sulfate ($CaSO_4.2H_2O$).
HADLEY CELL	Air circulation in tropical and subtropical latitudes whereby air rises over the equator and sinks around 30° N and 30° S.
HAGUE CONVENTIONS	A series of international treaties on the conduct of war passed between 1899 and 1907.
HEPATITIS	Generic name for diseases that affect the liver—Hepatitis A is caused by a virus, while other forms of hepatitis are caused by parasitical infections and drug abuse. Symptoms may include vomiting, fever and joint pain.
HYDROGEOLOGY	The branch of geology concerned with the occurrence of surface water and groundwater and the function of water in erosion and deposition.

HYDROPHILIC	Attracting water.
HYDROPHOBIC	Repelling water.
HYGROSCOPIC	Attracting moisture from the air.
HYPOTHERMIA	Abnormal lowering of body temperature generally caused by exposure.
INFLUENZA	An acute, contagious epidemic disease, caused by a virus, mainly affecting the upper respiratory tract.
INVERSION	A weather anomaly where the temperature increases with altitude, trapping the air below.
JET STREAMS	Any of several long, narrow high-speed winds floating in a generally horizontal zone in the stratosphere, tropopause and upper troposphere.
KARST	An area of limestone formations characterized by sinks, ravines and underground streams.
KELLOGG-BRIAND PACT	A multilateral agreement attempting to outlaw war and agreeing to peaceful means of settling international disputes, originally signed by 15 nations in 1928, later joined by 49 others.
LANDSAT	U.S. satellite gathering and transmitting data about Earth's natural resources and topography.
LEISHMANIASIS	Infection with protozoa of the genus *Leishmania*, affecting either the inner organs or skin tissues. Symptoms include chronic fatigue, joint pain, diarrhea, gastrointestinal complaints, coughs and fevers.
MAGNETRON	Machine that generates high frequencies and short bursts of very high power by use of electric and magnetic fields.
MANGROVES	Shrubs and trees that grow in thickets and low forests along tidal estuaries, salt marshes and coastal mud flats throughout the tropics, forming diverse local ecosystems.
MARAGING STEEL	Very strong nickel-iron alloys.
MICROPARTICLES	Microscopic particles.
MONSOON	Any wind showing a seasonal reversal in direction—and, in particular, a wind in various latitudes in the Indian Ocean and southern Asia which blows from the southwest from late April to mid-October and from the northeast for the rest of the year. On the Indian subcontinent, the season of the southwest monsoon, a season of heavy rainfall, is called the monsoon season.
MOUSSE	Frothy mixture of oil and water that may eventually weather into tar balls.

MUD FLAT	Muddy land flooded at high tide and uncovered at low tide.
MUTAGENIC	Capable of inducing random genetic change.
NAPHTHA	A product of the fractional distillation of petroleum, the fraction that boils between gasoline and kerosene.
NECROSIS	The sum total of irreversible structural alterations leading to the loss of vitality of a cellular group in a living organism.
NERVE AGENTS	A group of chemicals which induce body spasms and death by asphyxiation, by inhibiting the production of the enzyme acetylcholinesterase, which allows the muscles to relax after contraction.
NUCLEAR WINTER	Hypothetical scenario following nuclear war, in which dust and smoke obscure sunlight and there are abnormally low temperatures and strong winds.
NUCLEATION	The process of forming into or around a nucleus, as when water droplets form around particulate.
OCEANOGRAPHY	Study of the oceanic environment.
OROGRAPHIC LIFTING	The lofting of an air current caused by its passage up and over mountains.
PALEOLITHIC	The period from 2,000,000–10,000 B.C., when humans were hunter-gatherers and used primitive tools including flints for fire.
PANDEMIC	Epidemic over a large region.
PELAGIC	Applies to living things that feed near the sea surface.
PERENNIAL	Producing flowers and seed from the same root structure each year.
PETROCHEMICALS	Chemicals derived from crude oil.
PHYTOPLANKTON	Plankton consisting of plants, such as algae.
PLANKTON	Microscopic organisms found on the sea surface.
PLAYA	Barren depression or low portion of desert region that collects sediments during intermittent cloudbursts.
PNEUMONIA	Disease of the lungs, mostly caused by microorganisms but sometimes having a chemical or physical source.
POLYCHAETES	The largest and only non-hermaphrodite group of the phylum of annelid worms. It consists almost exclusively of sea-dwelling species—polychaete species can be found in almost every ocean habitat.
POLYNUCLEAR AROMATIC HYDROCARBONS	Naturally occurring compounds composed of condensed benzene (C_6H_6) rings, many of them carcinogenic.
PRESSURE	Force per unit area.

Q FEVER	Infection of cattle, sheep and goats which affects mainly the lungs. Symptoms are headache, chills, fever, muscle pain, and malaise.
RADIOLOGICAL WEAPONS	Bombs, such as neutron bombs, that disperse radioactive materials or ionizing radiation with the objective of killing humans and animals and/or contaminating the environment.
RADIONUCLIDE	Radioactive nuclide, a nuclide being a specific kind of atom characterized by the constitution of the nucleus.
RAMSAR SITE	Wetland site protected under the Ramsar Convention signed in Iran in 1971. Signatories to the treaty agree to designate at least one wetland which they will protect or replace with one of equal value if the listed site is destroyed.
RARE	According to the *IUCN Red Data Book,* applicable to a species at risk because of a small total world population.
REM	Unit of ionizing radiation that will produce a biological effect equal to one roentgen of gamma ray radiation.
RICKETS	Disease of the skeletal system, chiefly of children, caused by vitamin D deficiency.
RIFT VALLEY FEVER	Disease transmitted to humans from goats, sheep and cattle. Characterized by fever, muscle pain and headaches, sometimes gastrointestinal hemorrhage and loss of central vision.
RUNOFF	Outflow of rainwater toward rivers along ground surface and underground.
SALT MARSH	Grassland over which salt water flows at intervals.
SAVANNA	Plain or grassland with scattered trees.
SEPTICEMIA	Generalized infection with pus-forming microorganisms.
SHEEN	A thin, shiny coating of oil.
SHIITE ISLAM	The branch of Islam that asserts the legitimacy of the authority of the descendants of Ali, the fourth caliph and Muhammad's son-in-law.
SHOREBIRDS	Birds of the order *Charadriiformes*, including dunlins, plovers, snipes and sandpipers, that are especially adapted to coastal and marsh habitats.
SLANT DRILLING	Drilling for oil diagonally.
SOLVENTS	Chemicals used to dissolve other chemicals.
SPAWNING	Reproduction and the bringing forth of young in fish.
SPECTROSCOPY	A set of techniques for the analysis and interpretation of the electromagnetic radiations emitted and absorbed by matter.

STRATOSPHERE	Layer of the atmosphere extending upward from the tropopause in which the temperature generally increases with altitude, also the primary site of ozone formation.
SUBTROPICAL	Between 15° N and 35° N or between 15° S and 35° S.
SUBTROPICAL JET STREAM	A zone of unusually strong winds situated between the tropical tropopause and the midlatitude tropopause.
SUNNI ISLAM	The majority branch of Islam recognizing the first four caliphs and their successors-in-office as Muhammad's legitimate successors.
SYNERGISTIC	Pertaining to the simultaneous action of separate agencies which have greater total effect than the sum of their individual effects.
SYNOPTIC-SCALE WEATHER	Weather phenomena operating at the continental or oceanic spatial scale, including migrating high pressure systems, air masses and fronts.
SYSTEMIC	Pertaining to a system or to the body as a whole.
TAXA	Biological categories such as species or family.
TEAR GAS	Volatile gas causing eye irritation and temporary blindness.
TIME SERIES ANALYSIS	Extrapolation from a frequency distribution in which time is the independent variable.
TOXEMIA	Pathological condition characterized by toxins present in the blood.
TOXIN	Any biological substance containing or producing poison.
TRAUMA	Any injury caused by the application of external violence, applying to both physical and psychological injuries.
TROPOPAUSE	Boundary zone between the troposphere and the stratosphere.
TROPOSPHERE	Lowermost zone of the earth's atmosphere in which temperature decreases fairly regularly with altitude. The height of the troposphere varies over the polar, mid-latitude and tropical regions from about nine to sixteen kilometers above sea level.
TULAREMIA	Infectious disease of man and animals caused by *Pasteurella tularensis*, marked by conventional signs of toxemia.
TYPHOID	Acute infectious disease caused by the bacillus *Salmonella typhi*, characterized by fever, diarrhea, physical exhaustion and apathy.
VASCULAR PLANTS	Plants containing the specialized food and water conducting cells xylem and phloem. These include all flowering plants, conifers and ferns.
WADI	The channel for a stream that is dry except during periods of rain.

YELLOWCAKE

A uranium concentrate obtained by the extraction of uranium from ores.

ZONATION

Distribution of kinds of organisms in biogeographic zones.

Index

Amnesty International: 205, 206, 239, 312, 318, 347

Anfal operation: 25, 152-4, 225, 228, 248, 334, 335, 358

Arab American Oil Company (ARAMCO): 56, 58

Arab nationalism: 21-23

Argentina: 42, 248, 263, 329

Arms sales, British: to Iraq, 330, 331, 333, 336, 351, 354; to Iraq, of machine-tools, 330, 333; to Middle East, 294

Arms sales, U.S.: and the citizen, 298; congressional investigations, 296, 343, 348, 352, 353; and economic conversion, 297; and interoperability, 296; lobbying by U.S. arms industry, 295; to Egypt, 294; to Gulf Cooperation Council, 297; to Iraq, 250, 325-326, 327; to Iraq, and agricultural credits, 25, 327, 331, 335, 337-340, 341, 343, 348-349, 351, 352, 356; to Iraq, of dual use components, 251, 261, 325, 330, 332, 343, 347, 352; to Iraq, and export licenses, 330, 343, 347-348; to Israel, 294; to Middle East, 292, 294, 323; procedure for, 294; to Saudi Arabia, 294; and U.S. law, 295, 296, 297, 336

Atomic Energy Authority, U.K.: 134, 135

Austria: 307, 329, 336

Aziz, Tariq: 309, 327, 337, 339

Bahrain: 26, 42, 50, 62, 68, 75, 91, 294

Baker, James: 39, 297, 337-338, 339, 342, 355

Banca Nazionale del Lavoro (BNL): and Bank of Credit and Commerce International (BCCI), 349, 350; links to U.S. government officials, 345, 347-349, 352, 353, 356; raided by FBI, 336-337; unauthorized loans to Iraq, 329, 331, 333, 335, 339, 341; and U.S. Iraqgate case, 350, 357

Basoft, Farzad: 31, 340

Bechtel: 60, 328, 334, 360

Belgium: 42, 161, 324, 327, 361

Bell Helicopter Textron: 329, 360

Biological weapons: dispersal of, 275; historical use of, 246; types of, 268-270

Biological weapons program, Iraqi: and baby milk formula factory, 272; and Kurds, 247, 248; procurement of components, 336, 338; state of development, 251, 274-275, 284

Bioremediation: 59

Birds in Gulf region: bee eaters, 54; cormorants, 6, 12, 16, 60, 65, 67; flamingoes, 17, 66, 68; grebes: 60, 65, 67; gulls: 6, 60; habitats, 8, 12, 16, 17-18, 65; Houbara bustard, 12, 18; mortality from Gulf War oil spill, 64; swallows, 54, 66; terns, 60, 61, 64-65; waterfowl, 8, 16-18, 66-68

Bombing, of Iraq: and acid rain, 147, 165; and agriculture, 146, 147-148, 151, 154, 158, 162, 170, 175; and air pollution, 166, 169, 170, 172; of Al Ameriyah shelter, 146, 200, 221; of Al Qaim fertilizer plant, 156, 159; of animals, 11; Arab perceptions of, 32; of baby milk formula factory, 167-168, 181, 272, 279; chemicals released, 162, 164, 166, 167, 169, 247, 251; of chemical weapons sites, 246-247, 251, 272-273, 276, 279-280, 281, 287; by Clinton Administration, 35; of dams, 146; deaths caused, 180, 182, 183; of electrical network, 40, 145, 146, 148, 151, 156, 158, 163-164, 170, 171; and fiberglass, 164, 168; and groundwater pollution, 172; of infrastucture, 144-148, 218, 301, 308, 345; of irrigation system, 147, 158-159, 170; legal aspects, 301, 303; of livestock, 151, 154; of Muthanna, 279, 281, 287; of nuclear sites, 246-247, 250, 251-252, 263-265, 266; of oil refineries, 82, 151, 166-167, 169-170, 171-172; quantity of ordnance dropped, 40, 42-43, 138; and river pollution, 11, 165, 167; and sewage problem, 147, 156-7, 171, 174, 175, 176; strategic importance of, 40, 246, 295, 303; and stratospheric ozone depletion, 168; and water purification, 174; and wetland pollution, 11, 17

Bombing, of Kuwait: animals, 16; parks, 14; and unexploded ordnance, 138

Brazil: and Iraqi military program, 325, 332, 361; forest fires, 123; nuclear program, 258, 263, 325

Bush Administration: censorship of effects of Gulf War, 80, 93-93, 95-96, 97-99, 187-188; and conscientious objectors, 311-312, 313, 318; environmental assessments of possible impacts of Gulf War, 40, 46, 49-51, 85-86, 298-299; and Gulf crisis of 1991, 27, 28, 30-32, 39, 302, 342-344; members' conflicts of interest, 336, 342, 345-346, 347-348, 350; opposition to sanctions against Iraq, prewar, 336, 337, 341-342, 347; policy to Iraq, postwar, 34-35, 255, 298; support for Saddam Hussein, prewar, 337, 339, 340-342; and United Nations Security Council, 27, 31-32, 39, 302

Cardoen, Carlos: 330, 333, 339, 347, 349-350, 351

Carter Administration, Middle Eastern policy of: 24-25, 296, 322, 325

Censorship, U.S.: at conferences on meteorology, 93-94, 95, 97-99; of computer-stored information, 99, 112; of desert pollution, 133; Department of Energy "gag order", 80, 93-94, 95-96; of Interagency Persian Gulf Task Force findings, 97; of NOAA Mauna Loa soot findings, 93-94, 95, 99; of NOAA satellite photographs, 93, 95, 103; of numbers of Iraqi war deaths, 187-188; of performance of Patriot missile, 350; and the scientific community, 96, 102

Central Intelligence Agency (CIA), U.S.: reports on Iraq, 255, 288, 336, 355; reports on Iraqgate, 338, 354; role in arming of Iraq, 347, 349, 351, 353

Chemical weapons: blister agents, 152, 268, 273; blood agents, 152, 268; countries possessing, 248; defined, 246, 267-268; disabling agents, 267, 271; history of, 246; mustard gas, 273; nerve agents, 152, 154, 268; in U.S., 273, 275-276, 285; and wetland pollution, 18

Chemical weapons program, Iraqi: CS gas, 271, 272, 276; dual-use technology, 295; environmental and health safety, 251, 271; and Gulf War Syndrome, 41, 287-289; hydrogen cyanide, 152, 334; and Israel, 340; mustard gas, 271, 272, 286, 287, 288, 327-328, 334; nerve agents, 271-272, 277, 286, 287, 324, 326, 327-328, 362; procurement of components, 161, 272, 279, 324, 326, 327, 328, 334, 335, 338, 361; size of stockpile, 278, 336; sodium cyanide, 361; state of development, 278, 327, 331; used against Kurds of Iraq, 25, 152-154, 334; used against Iran, 327-328, 330

Cheney, Richard: 28-29, 342, 344, 347

Chernobyl: 264

China: arms sales to Iran, 295; arms sales to Iraq, 336, 361; arms sales to Middle East, 294; and Gulf War, 30-31, 304; floods during 1991, 100-101, 108, 112, 116, 119, 121, 123

Clark, Alan: 331, 333, 336, 354, 356-357

Cleanup of oil spill: administration of, 60; of beaches, 46, 58, 65, 74; of floating oil, 46, 50, 56; by nutrient augmentation, 59; of intertidal areas, 46; of oil lakes, 67, 68, 73

Clinton Administration, policy of toward Iraq: 35, 255, 298

Colchester Lathes: 339, 349

Commodity Credit Corporation: 327, 331, 335, 337-340, 341, 343, 348-349, 351, 352, 356

Conscientious objectors, U.S.: approval rate for applications, 312; court-martial described, 317-319; and death penalty, 318; legal issues, 311-312, 313, 314-315, 317-319; motivations of, 313, 316; numbers AWOL or UA, 312, 315, 319; numbers of registered COs, 312, 319; and racism, 312, 313, 319; treatment of, 312, 319

Conventional weapons program, Iraqi: and Brazil, 332; Condor Project, 329, 353; cluster bombs, 330, 333, 347, 350; fuel-air explosives, 330; Hilla explosion, 337; and Iran-Iraq War, 331, 333-334; procurements of components, 332, 336, 350; propellants, 281; Scuds, 288, 332, 333; size of stockpile, 278; state of development, 229, 251, 339; supergun project, 340, 341, 353

Coral: habitat importance, 3, 6; observed effects of oil, 58, 74-75; predicted effects of oil, 52, 57; sensitivity to temperature, 4-5, 75

Cormorants: 6, 12, 16, 60, 65, 67

Czech chemical warfare unit, 42, 287

de Cuellar, Javier Perez: 32, 328

Department of Agriculture, U.S.: 331, 335, 337-340, 341, 356 (see also Commodity Credit Corporation)

Department of Defense, U.S.: 133, 184, 266, 273, 285, 296, 297, 332, 348

Department of Energy, U.S.: "gag order," 80, 93-94, 95-96

Department of Veterans' Affairs, U.S.: 242-243, 289

Depleted uranium; cleanup prospects, 136; described, 134-5; health effects, 128, 135-137; quantity left in desert, 134, 134; use by military, 128, 135

Desert plain: dunes, 9, 19, 132; erosion, 114, 132, 140; heavy metal contamination, 132, 147; impact of grazing, 8, 131; impact of hunting, 11, 12; impact of troop maneuvers, 11, 16, 131-132, 133, 140-141, 147; mammals, 11-12, 140; and oil lakes, 91, 129-130, 141; playas, 9; prewar condition, 8-10, 131; restoration, 18, 131, 136; vegetation, 9-11, 18; wetlands, 8

Diving birds: cormorants, 6, 12, 16, 60, 65, 67; grebes: 60, 65, 67; numbers killed, 67; vulnerability to oil, 60, 67

Drogoul, Christopher: and loans to Iraq, 329, 331, 350; trial of, 346, 351-352, 353-354, 357, 358

Dugongs: 4, 5, 51, 55, 62, 76

Eagleburger, Lawrence: 264, 328, 345, 347-348

Egypt: and Arab League, 21, 33; arms industry, 248, 294-295, 329; and Coalition, 32, 33, 42; and

Iraq, 28, 34; and Israel, 33; military camps, 133; public sector, 37; treatment of Yemenis, 206; and U.S., 25, 28, 32, 294-295

Environmental Protection Agency (EPA): 71; measurements of toxics in Kuwait, limitations of, 87-89; statements on health effects of fires in Kuwait, 82, 94

Export-Import Bank, U.S.: 328, 330, 332

Exxon: 355, 360

Fisheries in the Gulf: economic importance, 6-7, 52-3; effects of oil spill, 52-53, 76; intensification of fishing before war, 62, 78; problems assessing impacts of oil spill, 62, 76; shrimp, 5, 6-7, 50, 58, 62, 76

Flamingoes: 17, 66, 68

Food and Drug Administration, U.S.: 135, 238-239

Foreign policy, U.S.: and arms sales, 295-298; and CS gas, 275-276; and human rights, 25; toward Angola, 35; toward Bosnia, 36; toward Gulf region, 25, 26, 31, 35, 297; Iran-Contra scandal, 331-332; and Iran-Iraq War, 26, 331-333, 334-335; toward Iraq, 34, 35, 255, 296, 325, 328-329, 330, 337, 340-342, 355; toward Middle East, 24, 295-298; toward Saudi Arabia, 26; toward Somalia, 36; and terrorism, 275

France: and arming of Iraq, 165, 260, 265, 272, 294, 296-297, 322, 324-327, 329-331, 332, 333; and colonies in Middle East, 21, 24-25; and Gulf War, 31-32, 39-40, 42, 303

Friendly fire, U.S. casualties from: 41, 134

Gates, Robert: 255, 342, 349, 353

Gazelles: 11, 12, 19

General Accounting Office, U.S.: 134

General Electric: 325, 326

Geneva Convention and Protocols: 105, 300, 307

Germany: arms to Iraq, 165, 259, 260, 266, 297, 322, 328, 329, 342; and Gulf War Coalition, 32, 43, 356; and United Nations, 105, 262, 305

Glaspie, April: 340, 341-342

Gonzalez, Henry: 298, 338, 340, 342, 343, 347-348, 350, 351, 353, 356

Grebes: 60, 65, 67

Greenpeace, U.S.: 186-187, 285

Gulf Cooperation Council (GCC): 26, 294, 297

Gulf crisis of 1991: Arab reaction to U.S. troop deployment, 29; attempts to resolve, 27-32; and Bush Administration, 28, 30-32, 342-344; hostage taking, 29, 32; Iraqi debts to Kuwait, 27; Iraq-Kuwait border dispute, 22, 27, 28, 38; League of Arab States, role of, 20, 28, 33; and National Environmental Policy Act in U.S., 343; protests against U.S. deployment of troops, 39; Rumalia oilfield, 27, 28, 29; Saddam Hussein's peace proposals, 29; threat of Iraqi invasion of Saudi Arabia, 29, 38; United States congressional debate on war, 30, 39

Gulf region: arms sales to, 23, 36, 136, 294, 295, 297; environmental consciousness, 37, 62, 79; importance of oil, 23, 38; importance to birds, 13; and MARPOL, 62; possible new protected areas, 68, 364; possibility of regional peace conference, 36, 364

Gulf, the Persian: and land reclamation, 58, 62, 66, 78; environment, 68; extremes of temperature and salinity, 3, 4-5, 53, 75; fisheries, 6-7, 50, 52-53, 58, 62, 76; habitats, 5-6, 57-58; intertidal areas, 5, 46, 51-52, 55-57, 61, 63, 66, 72, 74, 78, 80; and oil spill, 50, 78; physical environment, 3; species diversity, 4

Gulf War: British war costs, 355-356; chemical attacks, 287-288; Coalition deaths, 180; economic benefits to U.S., 347; Highway of Death, 41, 180; Iraqi conscript troops, 41, 43, 180; Iraqi military and civilian deaths during, 180, 183-185, 186-187, 190-192; Iraqi perceptions of, 201; legal issues, 32, 292, 293; live burials, 41, 180, 346; and the media, 183, 346, 352-353; military history, 40-42, 46, 145; Patriot missiles in, 229, 350; possible consequences of hypothetical Iraqi victory, 29; and Security Council *Resolution 660*, 303; and Security Council *Resolution 678*, 307; size of Iraqi army, 344, 346

Gulf War Coalition: deaths, 180; and Egypt, 32; formation of, 31; and France, 31-32; and Germany, 32; and Japan, 32; membership of, 42; and Soviet Union, 31; and Syria, 32; and United Kingdom, 31; and United States, 42, 303-304

"Gulf War Syndrome": and chemical weapons, 41, 287-289; and depleted uranium, 134; and drugs to counteract chemical warfare agents, 238-239; and Feres Doctrine, 243, 244; government response to, 242-243; and infectious diseases, 240-241; medical evaluation of veterans, 134; possible causes, 137; stress, 241; symptoms, 238, 241-242

Gulls: 6, 60

Health crisis, in postwar Iraq: diarrhea, 166, 171, 172, 176, 195, 197, 217, 218; eye infections, 154, 164, 223; hepatitis, 177, 195-196; hospital conditions, 172-

173, 176-177, 217-218; hypothermia, 195; infant mortality, 177, 195-196; malnutrition, 153, 174-175, 195-197, 217, 227; measles, 176; meningitis, 177; respiratory diseases, 176; skin problems, 223; waterborne diseases, 153, 156-157, 173, 176, 196, 217, 347; waterborne diseases in animals, 161

Hewlett Packard: 332, 349

Hill and Knowlton: 335, 342

Holland: 42, 259, 327, 328

Howe, Sir Geoffrey: 354, 358

Hussein, Saddam: as perceived in Arab world, 34; political history, 38, 324, 332; and terrorism, 329; war crimes of, 292

Incineration of chemical weapons: 272-274, 279-280

India: 39, 99, 235, 248, 361

Interagency Persian Gulf Task Force study of Kuwait oil fires, U.S.: 82, 90-91, 95-96, 107, 112, 114, 116; limitations of, 96-97, 110-111

International Atomic Energy Agency (IAEA): budget, 262, 364; intelligence-sharing, 261, 266; recommended reforms, 364; safeguards, 257, 261-262, 265-266, 364; unaccountability, 266 (see also United Nations Special Commission (UNSCOM)/ International Atomic Energy Agency disarming of Iraq)

International Committee of the Red Crescent (ICRC): 105, 153, 219, 230, 232, 233, 234, 236, 306-307

International Council for Bird Preservation (ICBP): 63, 64, 66; banding project, 61, 65

International law: and attacks on retreating forces, 303; and bombing of Baghdad in 1993, 35; and bombing of nuclear reactors, 266; Biological Weapons Convention, 267, 268; Chemical Weapons Convention, 267, 275-276, 277, 283; Comprehensive Nuclear Test Ban Treaty, proposed, 364; and CS gas, 275-276, 277-278; ENMOD, 105, 292, 300; and conscientious objectors, 313, 315, 318; Geneva Convention and Protocols, 105, 300, 307; International Marine Convention on the Prevention of Pollution from Ships (MARPOL): 7, 62; and environmental effects of Gulf War, 298-302; Iraqi violations of, 292, 293; Missile Technology Control Regime, 330; Nuclear Non-Proliferation Treaty, 253, 263, 266, 349; and U.K. arms sales, 349; and U.S. arms sales, 295; on war and the environment, 306-308

International Study Team: 144, 149, 187, 193, 207

International War Crimes Tribunal: 146, 298, 299-301

Intertidal areas, of Gulf coast: cleanup potentially damaging, 73-4; environmental restoration, 73-4; impacted by oil, 46, 51-52, 55-57, 61, 66, 72, 74, 80; invertebrates, 5, 63, 66, 72, 78; marshes, 73, 74

Inversions, atmospheric: 110

Iran: black rains in, 107; fisheries, 6; and Gulf region 34, 41, 295, 331-333; population, 297; protected areas in, 17-18; and refugees from Iraq, 231

Iran-Iraq War: and ICRC, 236; and Iraqi chemical weapons, 276, 327-328, 330; environmental damage caused by, 4, 8-9, 18, 50, 51-52, 68, 152, 174; not considered an invasion, 26; lives lost, 326; and Iraqi missiles, 331, 333-334, 353; and Saddam Hussein, 34; social impacts of, 209, 218; and United States, 24, 28, 332, 331-333

Iraqgate, British: 322, 354-358

Iraqgate, U.S.: 322, 346-354, 356-358

Iraqi civil uprising of 1991: 41-42, 149-151, 152, 153, 171, 174, 180, 227, 347; deaths from, 187

Iraq, pre-Gulf War: agriculture, 10; areas of conservation importance, 16-17; contraception, 209; crops, 160; demographics, 183, 185, 189-192; fish production, 8, 161; freshwater fish, 13, 18; gross national product, 194, 310; food imports, 174, 194; infant mortality, 194, 195; life expectancy, 190; marriage, 220; physical geography, 9-10; reptiles, 13; public sector, 24, 37, 194, 210; social welfare programs, 24; and Soviet Union, 38, 39; standard of living, 174, 175, 193-194, 210; vegetation, 9-10, 11

Iraq, post-Gulf War: abortions, 218; agriculture, 146, 151, 154, 158-161, 162, 170, 175; army, 42, 210; black market, 214; child mortality, 177, 195-196; children, 175, 177, 181, 195-197, 198-202, 211, 217, 223; civil uprising, 41-42, 149-151, 152, 153, 171, 174, 180, 187, 227, 347; contraception, 218; economic crisis, 174-175, 197, 210-211, 214-215, 310; electricity, 145, 146, 148, 151, 156, 158, 163-164, 170, 171, 194, 197; family structure, 209; fish production, 151, 161, 171; food prices, 174, 197, 209-210, 215; government food rations, 175, 214, 215, 216; humanitarian aid, 176, 194, 236, 310; inflation, 174-175, 197, 214, 227; irrigation, 147, 158-159, 170; livestock, 154, 161; malnourishment, 181; marriage, 214, 220, 223; miscarriages, 217-218; new border with Kuwait, 310; nutrition, 211-212, 216, 219, 223; oil sales, 309; pensions, 211, 223; population projections, 192; prostitution, 213, 222; public distribution system, 215, 216, 219; reaction to

1992 U.S. election result, 35; reparations, 309, 310; river pollution, 165, 167, 170; sewage problem, 147, 156-7, 171, 174, 175, 176, 194; social impacts of war, 214, 219-221, 222-224; stress, 198-202, 217-218, 221-222, 223; survival guilt, 201; trade, 310; unemployment, 175, 209, 210, 220, 223; water purification, 174, 211; water supply, 19, 156-7, 219; women's issues, 175, 177, 207, 209-211, 213-214, 216-221, 223; women, personal stories of, 211-213

Islam: 21, 35, 37

Israel: 25, 33; Iraqi Scud attacks on, 40, 228-229, 345; nuclear weapons capability, 36

Italy: 325-326, 329, 333

Jal Al Zhor national park: 9, 13, 14, 133

Japan: 42, 250, 361

Jordan: aid to postwar Iraq, 35, 177; attempts to resolve Iraq-Kuwait dispute, 28; and international law on war and the environment, 105, 306; and Iraqgate case, 346, 358; and refugees, 19, 233, 235

Kennemetal: 348-350

Kissinger Associates: 327, 336, 345-346, 347-348, 350

Kissinger, Henry: 327, 345

Kurds: and *Anfal* operation 25, 152-4, 225, 228 248, 334, 335, 358; continuing persecution in Iraq, 227, 309, 310; and humanitarian aid to Iraq, 310; in Iraqi army, 43; Kurdish Regional Government in Iraq, 149, 151-154, 227-228; obstacles to self-determination, 22, 33-34, 225; refugees, 191, 216, 217, 221, 222, 225, 230-232, 235; and "safe haven", 42, 226-227; and the Western media, 194, 225_226

Kuwait: Bedouins in, 232, 233; censorship of effects of oil fires, 94, 104; children's experiences under Iraqi occupation, 203-204; damage done by Iraqi occupation, 14, 133; demographics, 92; freshwater fish, 13; human rights, 347; Iraqi atrocities, 204, 293; Iraqi kidnappings, 204, 234; Iraqi refugees in, 232; migrant workers in, 235; oil production, 85; Palestinians in, 205, 206, 232, 233, 235; physical geography, 3, 9; protected areas, 14-16; reaction to 1992 U.S. election result, 32; stress, 203-205; vegetation, 9, 11, 14

Lawrence Livermore National Laboratory: 93, 105, 248, 260

League of Arab States: history, 20-21, 25, 27, 33; possible reforms, 35, 364; role in Gulf crisis, 20, 28, 33

Leahy, Senator Patrick: 339, 351

Lebanon: 25, 27, 30, 37, 331

Major, John: 355, 357

Mangroves: 5, 57, 58, 66, 75, 78

Marsh Arabs: 8, 17, 19

Matrix-Churchill: 259, 333, 336, 337, 339, 343, 346, 349-350, 353, 354-355

MBB: 329, 335

Mesopotamian Marshes: 8, 10, 17

Meteorological and Environmental Protection Agency (MEPA), of Saudi Arabia: role in oil spill cleanup, 56; survey in response to Nowruz oil spill, 68; oil spill cleanup estimates, 46, 56

Middle East peace process: 35, 297, 298

Mines: banning of, recommended, 364; in the Gulf, 146; in Kurdistan, 139; in Kuwait, 40, 138; along Iraq-Kuwait border, 138

Mobil: 331, 360

Mount Mitchell 100-day cruise: 46, 48, 56, 57, 58, 70, 74-5, 76-7

National Commission on Wildlife Conservation and Development (NCWCD) of Saudi Arabia: 63, 68; bird rescue center, 65; list of nature conservation areas in Saudi Arabia, 18-19

National Oceanic and Atmospheric Administration (NOAA): 70; briefings and press releases on oil spill, 53-4; detection of soot at Mauna Loa, 93-94, 101, 103; *Mount Mitchell* 100-day cruise and findings, 46, 48, 56, 57, 58, 70, 74-5, 76-7

National Security Council (NSC), U.S.: 340, 348, 352

No-fly zones: 42, 152, 226; legal basis of, 34, 40

Nongovernmental organizations: and Arab world, 37, 236; estimates of Iraqi deaths, 180-181; International Committee of the Red Crescent (ICRC): 105, 153, 219, 230, 232, 233, 234, 236, 306-307; response to Gulf War and sanctions, 35, 146, 176; response to refugee crisis, 235-236

Nuclear reactors, risks of bombing: 264-266

Nuclear weapons: Argentina, 248, 263; Brazil, 258, 263, 325; countries possessing, 248; Israel, 36; history of, 246; North Korea, 262; Pakistan, 258; proliferation, legal issues, 253, 263, 266, 349; radiological weapons, 266; Romania, 262

Nuclear weapons program, Iraqi: calutrons, 256-258, 342; centrifuges, 258-259, 342, 349, 353; and classified information, 260; cooperation treaty with Brazil, 325; dual-use technology, 254, 295, 311; environmental safety practices, 251-252; how far from completion, 251, 254, 255, 257,

258, 260, 344; and IAEA intelligence-sharing, 261, 266; and IAEA safeguards, 257, 261-262, 265-266; Israeli actions against, 253, 325, 326; and Krytons, 343; nuclear proliferation issues raised by, 136, 253, 254, 260-262, 266; numbers employed, 250; procurement of components, 250-251, 255, 258-259, 261, 265, 324, 330, 336, 337, 338, 342, 354; weaknesses of program, 259

Oil fires in Iraq: 151, 165-167, 169-170, 171-172

Oil fires in Kuwait: altitude reached by soot, 85, 91, 110-111, 114, 116, 117, 118, 122, 124; extent, 90; extinguishing of, 122, 138; origin of, 82, 93-94; seen from space, 122; size estimate, 73, 82

Oil fires in Kuwait, global impacts of: Bangladesh storm, 107-108, 114, 116, 117, 119, 121, 123; carbon dioxide, 85, 125; carbon monoxide, 123; Chinese floods, 100-101, 108, 112, 116, 119, 121, 123; chlorine, 122; climatic impacts, 79-80, 83, 85-86, 111, 118, 129, 122-124; and cloud seeding, 107, 112, 117, 118; compared to anthropogenic sources, 118, 121; compared to volcanic eruption, 90, 118, 119, 124; computer simulations, 85-86, 106-108, 109, 113-114, 124, 298-299; constraints on research, 99, 101, 102; distance traveled by soot, 83, 109, 110, 124; and global warming, 123, 125; legal implications, 299, 307; long-term impacts, 102, 116, 118-119, 121; and Mount Pinatubo eruption, 110, 111-112, 124; and nuclear winter scenario, 85, 91, 108, 109, 117; prewar predictions, 83, 85-86, 103, 113, 125; and subtropical jet stream, 114, 116, 117, 118-119, 120, 122; and sulfur dioxide, 118, 125; and turbulence, 110, 123

Oil fires in Kuwait, local impacts of: air pollution, 16, 50; bird impacts, 61, 65; carbon dioxide, 50, 90; carcinogens, 82, 89; damage to parks, 14, 133; environmental illness, 87-89, 92; eye irritations, 87; heavy metals, 50; and marine environment, 46, 73; mutagens, 82, 89; oil lost to Kuwait Oil Company, 82; and rain locally, 125, 129; reduced temperatures, 76, 91, 109-110, 111-112, 114, 125; regional fallout, 107; respiratory problems, 87, 88, 92, 240; sulfur dioxide, 50, 86, 90, 92, 240; water pollution, 50-51; and vegetation, 16, 192

Oil lakes in Kuwait: cleanup prospects, 67, 68, 73, 128, 141; and desert ecosystem, 91, 130, 132, 140-141; estimates of bird mortality, 67; evaporation of, 82; formation of, 82, 129, 139; size estimate, 67, 73, 82, 128, 139-140; trap for birds and

animals, 54, 66-7, 72, 130, 140; and vegetation, 49, 51, 140; and water pollution, 51

Oil spill, Gulf War: beaches impacted, 55-59, 69-70, 130; biodegrading of oil, 50, 77; and birds, 63-6, 67-8, 72, 80; bird mortality estimate, 64; blocked by Abu Ali island, 46, 55-6; cleanup priorities, 73; cleanup problems, 50; compared to Exxon *Valdez* spill, 46, 50, 55, 57, 71, 73; estimates of amount cleaned up, 56; evaporation of volatile component, 52-3; and fish, 50, 52, 76; and intertidal invertebrates 5, 63, 66, 72, 78; long-term effects, 50, 52-3, 77; marine ecosystem effects, 50, 52-3; natural recovery potential, 53, 55-6, 58, 72, 78; oil remaining liquid, 66; origin, 40, 46, 345; predicted by Sandia National Laboratories, 40, 46, 49-51; size estimates, 46, 50, 53-4, 56; submerged oil, 74; toxic effects of dissolved hydrocarbons, 52

Oil spill, Nowruz, 50, 51-2, 68; effects of, 50, 51-2; MEPA survey of, 68; size estimates, 4

Oil spills in Gulf: lack of historical cleanup response, 61; natural seepage, 3, 6; operational spills, 4, 7, 63, 77, 78; operational spills size estimates, 62

Oman: 26, 42, 62, 294, 360

Ordnance, in Gulf region: source of, 138; toxic content of, 132, 147; unexploded ordnance, 41, 137-138, 146, 151, 174

Palestinian question: 27, 30, 36

Protected Areas: in Gulf region, 14-16, 17-18; minimum size constraints, 78; proposed for Gulf Region, 8, 68, 79, 364

Qassem, Karim: 24, 38

Reagan Administration, Middle Eastern policy of: 25-26, 27, 296, 326-329, 330-332, 333-335

Refugees from Iraq and Kuwait: to Iran, 231; to Jordan, 19, 233, 235; numbers of refugees, 180, 185-186, 190-191, 197, 230, 234; to other countries, 234; Palestinians, 232, 233, 235; to Saudi Arabia, 232; to Syria, 232; to Turkey, 230-231

Regional Organization for the Protection of the Marine Environment (ROPME): 48, 58, 71

Reservists, U.S., in Gulf War: 311, 315

Rogers, William P.: 344, 356

Rose, Charles D.: 331, 335, 348-349

Saddam River: 19, 175

Sanctions against Iraq: and chemicals, 166, 169; conditions for removal of, 255, 309-310; and contraception, 209; and cross-border trade, 227; effectiveness of, prewar, 237, 261; estimated deaths due to, 177, 181, 182; and fertilizers, 158, 159; and impounding of Iraqi assets, 310; Iraqi perceptions of, 202, 210, 223, 236; and medicine, 172-3, 177, 194, 196, 217, 218; opposed by U.S. government, prewar military, 335, 336, 337, 341-342, 347; and nuclear program, 261; and oil sales, 309; and pesticides, 158, 159; and spare parts, 169, 175; and United Nations Security Council, 194, 309; and seed, 158, 159; and vaccines, 176; and veterinary medicine, 155; and water purification, 165

Saudi Arabia: and arms sales, 294; attempts to resolve Iraq-Kuwait dispute, 28; bird rescue center, 65; freshwater fish, 13; and Gulf crisis, 28; and Gulf War, 25, 42, 356; and Iraq, 34; and Iraqi refugees, 191, 232; and Iraqi Shiites, 41; Iraqi Scud attacks on, 40, 228; nature conservation areas, 18-19, 68; oil fire pollution in, 88-89; and oil industry, 24; and oil spill cleanup, 46, 56, 59, 60, 68; population, 297; reptiles, 14; and Rio summit, 37; threat of Iraqi invasion, 29, 38; vegetation, 10-11; Yemenis in, 206

Schwarzkopf, General H. Norman: 27, 40, 251

Scowcroft, Brent: 327, 340, 342, 344, 347-348, 350

Sea turtles: 69-70, 76, 130

Shatt Al Arab waterway: 3, 27, 326

Shiites, in Iraq: 19, 43, 227, 233, 311

Shorebirds: habitat, 5, 16-17, 55, 62, 66; mortality estimates, 60, 64, 66, 67; vulnerability to oil, 58, 63, 67

Shultz, George: 328, 329, 330, 332

Sierra Club: 94, 97

Soviet Union: and arming of Iraq, 325; and Gulf region, 26, 38, 39, 297; and Middle East, 26-7, 294

Spain: 42, 322, 328

Swallows: 54, 66

Sybetra: 161, 324, 361

Syria: 22, 27, 33, 34, 37, 232

Terns: 60, 61, 64-65

Texaco: 355, 360

Thornburgh, Dick: 342, 343, 348-349, 356

Trefgarne, Lord: 336, 346

Turkey: and arms to Iraq, 261; and Coalition, 42; and the Kurds, 33-34, 225-227, 230-231

Unexploded ordnance: and animals, 130; cleanup prospects in Kuwait, 130, 138, 140; cluster bombs, 138; estimates of casualties from, 128, 138; possible benefits to desert ecology, 12, 130, 131; quantity left by Gulf War, 138

United Nations: recommended reforms, 364-366; response to environmental crisis, 79, 104; response to refugee crisis, 216

United Nations Charter: 305-306

United Nations Children's Fund (UNICEF): 144, 174, 176, 237

United Nations Environment Programme (UNEP): 8, 71, 79

United Nations General Assembly: 301, 306-308

United Nations High Commission for Refugees (UNHCR): 231-233, 236, 311

United Nations Security Council: and arms sales, 294; and disarming of Iraq, 252; double standard, 30; and Iran-Iraq War, 26, 335; manipulated by U.S., 27, 31-32, 39, 302; and prosecution of Gulf War, 27, 32, 303-304, 365; *Resolution 660*, 303-304; *Resolution 678*, 303, 307; *Resolution 687*, 194, 236, 309, 310; *Resolution 688*, 236, 237; *Resolutions 706* and *712*, 309; *Resolution 778*, 310; and veto of permanent members, 304-305, 366; and war crimes, 300-301

United Nations Special Commission (UNSCOM)/ International Atomic Energy Agency (IAEA) disarming of Iraq: and air pollution, 280; caustic hydrolysis of nerve agents, 280; confrontations, 252, 254-255, 282, 283; dual-use technology, 309; environmental consequences, 252, 280-281; human factors, 282-283; incineration, 272-274, 279-280, 281, 285-286; information handling, 282; long-term monitoring, 255-256, 309, 310; nuclear reactor fuel, returning of, 252; organization, 250, 253; procurement, 309; proliferation, lessons concerning; and United Nations Security Council *Resolution 687*, 256, 277; and United Nations Security Council *Resolution 715*, 256, 278; and water pollution, 281

United States Congress: attempts to impose prewar military sanctions on Iraq, 335, 336, 337, 341-342, 347; debate on war in Gulf, 30, 39; investigations of Reagan and Bush Administrations, 296, 298, 335, 342, 343, 347-348, 350, 351, 352-353

Veterans of Gulf War, U.S.: financial aid to, 314; and "Gulf War Syndrome", 238-243; and unemployment, 314

Vietnam War: and accountability, 301; and Agent Orange, 243, 246; and fuel-air explosives, 330; and reservists, 315

Waterborne diseases: 153, 156-157, 161, 173, 176, 196, 217, 347

Waterfowl: 8, 16-18, 66-68

Wetlands in Gulf region: and Gulf War oil spill, 73; in desert, 8; importance to birds, 8, 12, 16, 17-18, 65; in Iran, 17-18; in Iraq, 10, 11, 16-17; in Jordan, 19; threatened by irrigation in Iraq, 9; vegetation, 10, 17; and war against Iraqi Shiites, 19, 233

World Food Programme: 236, 237, 310

World Health Organization (WHO): 171, 236

World Meteorological Organization: meetings on oil fires, 98, 107, 113, 120

Yemen: 22, 26, 27, 39, 235, 294, 297

Yugoslavia: 251, 264, 348

I t's time for peace

There has never been a better time for peace. With the Cold War ended, the world community has a chance to try new methods for resolving its disputes. Nevertheless, there are currently 122 wars, civil wars and counter-insurgency campaigns going on around the world. Each day brings new reports of violence in Bosnia, Somalia and elsewhere.

We believe that one of the most important tasks before the peace and environmental community is to investigate and illustrate the impacts of military activities and wars. If war is distant, the public need not confront its brutality. *Hidden Casualties* documents that brutality and exposes the political infrastructure that enables it to continue. It confronts the public and policymakers with the real effects of their choices, and builds a constituency for change.

We invite you to become a part of this important work. Please fill out the form below and send it in. You'll receive discounts on future *Hidden Casualties* reports and other ARC/Arms Control Research Center publications. You'll also be making an important decision to halt the spread of hidden casualties around the world, and advance the cause of peace.

NAME _____

ADDRESS _____

City, State, ZIP Code _____

PHONES _____

CONTRIBUTION LEVEL   ☐ $25   ☐ $35

_____ ☐ OTHER   ☐ $50   ☐ $100

Total for publications order from reverse side (page 436): $_____

ARC/Arms Control Research Center
833 Market Street Suite 1107
San Francisco, CA 94103

Telephone (415) 397-1452
FAX (415) 397-1462

ARC/Arms Control Research Center Publication Order Form

Please send me the publication(s) checked below:

☐ *Hidden Casualties, Volume I.* January 1991. Editor: John M. Miller. A series of interviews with leading environmental scientists on the possible effects of the war in the Persian Gulf. Volume I was released prior to the start of combat on January 16. $10.00

❧

☐ Military Toxics Roundup, *ARC Actionline* newsletter. September 1990. Principle analysts: Saul Bloom and Robert Gough. A comprehensive overview of the status of the Defense Department's environmental restoration program and related issues. $2.00

❧

☐ *California Military Toxics.* July 1990. Author: Jennifer Harris. An analysis of available public information regarding the status of the Defense Environmental Restoration Program in California, interagency agreements, and avenues for public participation. $10.00

❧

☐ *Environmental Destruction Caused by U.S. Military Bases and the Serious Implications for the Philippines.* May 1990. Author: Jorge Emmanuel, Ph.D. An analysis of the potential environmental effects of US military bases on the environment of the Philippines. This first independent analysis of the subject influenced lease contract negotiations. $10.00

❧

☐ *Navy Base Closures in San Francisco Bay Could Significantly Benefit the Bay Area's Economy and Housing Availability.* April 1990. Author: Brian McElroy, M.A. $5.00

❧

☐ *Fate of the Presidio Guidebook.* March 1990. Authors: Public Affairs Fellows of the Coro Foundation: Earl Lui, Esq., Lisa Lyon, M.A., and Ron Martinez. A comprehensive, programmatic analysis of the six-year process and issues surrounding the transfer of the Presidio Army Base from the Department of Defense to the National Park Service. $15.00

Please fill out the form on the other side of this page with your name and address, and send in with payment to: ARC/Arms Control Research Center, 833 Market St. Suite 1107, San Francisco, CA 94103. Fax (415) 397-1462.